LITIGATION
FOR THE
LAW SOCIETY FINALS

AUSTRALIA
The Law Book Company
Sydney

CANADA AND U.S.A.
The Carswell Company
Toronto, Ontario

INDIA
N. M. Tripathi (Private) Ltd.
Bombay
and
Eastern Law House (Private) Ltd.
Calcutta
M.P.P. House
Bangalore
Universal Book Traders
Delhi

ISRAEL
Steimatzky's Agency Ltd.
Tel Aviv

PAKISTAN
Pakistan Law House
Karachi

LITIGATION FOR THE LAW SOCIETY FINALS

Second Edition

by

CRAIG OSBORNE, B.A., M.A. (Econ), Solicitor
*Senior Lecturer in Law,
Manchester Polytechnic*

LONDON
SWEET & MAXWELL
1991

Published in 1991 by
Sweet & Maxwell
South Quay Plaza,
183 Marsh Wall, London, E14 9FT
Computerset by
MFK Typesetting Ltd., Hitchin, Herts.
Printed by
Richard Clay Ltd., Bungay, Suffolk

A CIP catalogue record
for this book is available
from The British Library

ISBN 0 421 44000 7

Preface

At the time when the first edition of this book was published in 1987 Litigation was widely regarded as the most difficult of the Finals subjects. In fact, in view of the length and breadth of the syllabus this is probably still the case although in recent years it has not, on the statistics, proved the subject that has had the lowest pass rate. Indeed the pass rate for the whole diet of examinations represented by the Finals has risen markedly over the recent past. The Head of one Polytechnic Law School has claimed that this is due to an improvement in the quality of Law students; more cynical observers have claimed that it is due to the Law Society dropping its standards to help cope with perceived undermanning in the legal profession. The first of these opinions seems most unlikely to be the case in the writer's experience and the second is, of course, utterly unworthy of credit. The true reason for the improvement in the pass rate is likely to be that it has become easier to spot the almost unavoidable formulae according to which most Finals papers are framed given the constraints of syllabus and possible plot. The switch in emphasis from delivering a professional course to cramming for an examination has been in no small measure assisted by internal pressures for perceived success from within institutions and the helpful stimulus of the Law Society itself publishing league tables of pass rates institution by institution.

The previous edition even after two years was badly showing its age. The present edition was largely re-written in January 1991 but with the infinite indulgence of the publishers it has been possible to incorporate very substantial updating at proof reading stage to take into account the very important High Court and County Courts Jurisdiction Order 1991 the effect of which is to transfer a great deal of civil business from the High Court to the county court. The text is therefore believed to be up to date as at July 1991 and thus should fulfil the twin purposes of contributing infinitesimally to the sum of human knowledge and killing the second hand market in the previous edition.

I have largely followed the organisation and format of the previous edition but following a number of helpful suggestions received in correspondence and reviews I have taken out that chapter from the first edition which provided illustrations and precedents of pleadings on the grounds that these are any way supplied with the core material distributed to each finals student, and replaced that chapter with two sets of past examination papers together with my own suggested answers to these. I would like to thank the Law Society and the Litigation Examiner Monica Peto for their kindness in permitting me to reproduce the previous papers.

July 1991
Craig Osborne.

Contents

Preface   v
Table of Cases   ix
Table of Statutes   xi

Introduction   1

Civil Procedure

 1 Damages   9
 2 The Financing of Civil Litigation   24
 3 Pre-Action Considerations   39
 4 Miscellaneous Matters Concerning Proceedings in the
   High Court   58
 5 Commencing Action by Writ   71
 6 Pleadings. R.S.C., Ord. 18 ____   81
 7 Discovery and Inspection   97
 8 Directions. R.S.C., Ord. 25   103
 9 Expert Evidence. R.S.C., Ord. 38   110
10 Preparing for Trial   115
11 Termination Without Trial   123
12 Payment into Court. R.S.C., Ord. 22   134
13 Interim Payments. R.S.C., Ord. 29, rr. 9–11   143
14 Third Party Proceedings. R.S.C., Ord. 16   149
15 Persons under a Disability. R.S.C., Ord. 80   156
16 The Trial   160
17 The County Court   163
18 Choice of Court   183
19 Enforcement of Money Judgments   188
20 Costs   200
21 Appeals in Civil Proceedings   211

Evidence

22 Introduction to Evidence   215
23 The Function of the Law of Evidence   217
24 Burden and Standard of Proof   220
25 Methods of Proof   225
26 Competence and Compellability of Witnesses   229
27 The Course of Testimony   233
28 Corroboration   244
29 Hearsay Evidence   250
30 Admissions and Confessions   267

31 Hearsay in Civil Proceedings and the Civil Evidence Act
    1968   280
32 Evidence of Opinion   299
33 Evidence of the Accused's Character   303
34 Improperly Obtained Evidence   314
35 Privilege   317
36 Evidence other than by Testimony: Miscellaneous   321

Criminal Procedure

37 An Outline of Criminal Procedure   325
38 Professional Ethics   327
39 Financing Criminal Litigation   330
40 Preliminary Considerations   339
41 Police Powers   345
42 The Commencement of Proceedings   359
43 Bail   362
44 Summary Trial   374
45 Classification of Offences and Choice of Courts   380
46 Committal Proceedings   389
47 Sentencing and Procedures after Conviction   399
48 Appeals in Criminal Cases   426

49 How to Pass the Examination   430

Examination Questions and Answers   444

Index   523

Selvey v. D.P.P. [1970] A.C. 304 .... 33.18, 33.19
Smith v. Manchester Corporation (1974) 17 K.I.R. 1 .... 1.17
Subramanian v. Public Prosecutor of Malaya [1956] 1 W.L.R. 965 .... 29.01

T. (H.) v. T. (E.) [1971] 1 W.L.R. 429 .... 24.01
Tito v. Waddell (No. 2) [1977] Ch. 106 .... 36.01

Wanchope v. Mordecai [1970] 1 W.L.R. 317 .... 24.01
Woolmington v. D.P.P. [1935] A.C. 462 .... 24.03
Wright v. British Railways Board [1983] 2 A.C. 773 .... 1.21
—— v. Nicholson [1970] 1 W.L.R. 142 .... 44.04

Table of Statutes

1838 Judgments Act (1 & 2 Vict. c. 110)—
    s. 17 .... 1.24
1865 Criminal Procedure Act (28 & 29 Vict. c. 18)—
    s. 3 .... 27.18, 27.26
    ss. 4, 5 .... 27.26
    s. 6 .... 27.27
1898 Criminal Evidence Act (61 & 62 Vict. c. 36) 33.02, 33.07
    s. 1 (b) 26.08
        (e) 35.08
        (f) 33.09, 49.12
        (i) 33.10, 33.22
        (ii) 33.11, 33.14, 33.17, 33.19, 33.21, 33.22, 45.15, 49.12
        (iii) 33.20, 33.21, 33.22, 49.12
1925 Criminal Justice Act (15 & 16 Geo. 5, c. 86)—
    s. 13 (3) 29.02, 29.28
1933 Children and Young Persons Act (23 & 24 Geo. 5, c. 12)—
    s. 38 .... 27.03
        (1) 26.04
1948 Law Reform (Personal Injuries) Act (11 & 12 Geo. 6, c. 41)—
    s. 2 (1) 1.16
        (4) 1.11
1952 Magistrates' Court Act (15 & 16 Geo. 6 & 1 Eliz. 2, c. 55)—
    s. 81 .... 24.05
1959 County Courts Act (c. 22)—
    s. 69 .... 6.12
1963 Children and Young Persons Act (c. 37)—
    s. 16 (2) 33.23
1965 Criminal Procedure (Attendance of Witnesses) Act (c. 69) 40.11
    Criminal Evidence Act (c. 20) 29.10
1967 Criminal Law Act (c. 58)—
    s. 2 .... 41.03
    Criminal Justice Act (c. 80)—
    s. 9 .... 29.02, 29.03 et seq., 30.01, 44.10, 40.11, 46.09, 49.12
    s. 10 .... 25.08
    s. 11 .... 30.22, 46.12
1968 Theft Act (c. 60) 47.39

1968 Theft Act—cont.
    s. 12 .... 41.03, 41.06, 45.02, 46.15
    s. 15 .... 41.06
    s. 27 (3) 33.06, 33.10
    Civil Evidence Act (c. 64) ...... 10.07, 22.01, 22.02, 27.12, 27.14, 29.01, 31.01 et seq., 31.07, 31.13, 31.22, 31.33, 31.34, 49.07
    ss. 1–9 .... 31.22
    s. 1 .... 9.11, 31.01, 31.23, 48.03, 49.07
    s. 2 .... 27.12, 31.02, 31.03 et seq., 31.08, 31.09, 31.10, 31.14, 31.15, 31.17 et seq., 31.21, 31.22, 31.24, 31.25, 31.33, 31.34, 49.07
        (2) (b) 31.04
    s. 3 .... 31.12, 31.20, 31.21, 31.26
        (1) (a) 27.19
        (b) 27.14
    s. 4 .... 31.01, 31.02, 31.12 et seq., 31.13, 31.14, 31.15, 31.16, 31.17 et seq., 31.18, 31.19, 31.25, 31.33, 49.07
        (3) 31.13
    s. 5 .... 31.19
    s. 6 (3) 31.10, 31.16, 31.24, 31.25, 49.07
    s. 7 .... 31.11, 31.16, 31.25, 49.07
    s. 8 .... 31.01, 31.02, 31.09, 31.11, 31.15, 31.24, 31.25, 31.34, 49.07
    s. 9 .... 31.21 et seq., 31.22, 31.27, 49.07
    s. 11 .... 6.16, 31.28, 31.32, 49.07
    s. 14 (1) 35.08
    s. 33 .... 48.06
1971 Attachment of Earnings Act (c. 32) 19.29
1972 Road Traffic Act (c. 20)—
    s. 152 .... 49.04
    Civil Evidence Act (c. 30) 22.01, 22.02, 31.33
    s. 3 (1) 32.05
        (2) 32.02
1973 Powers of Criminal Courts Act (c. 62)—
    s. 1 .... 47.58
    ss. 6–8 .... 47.20
    s. 7 .... 47.22 et seq.
    s. 21 (1) 47.14
    s. 22 .... 47.15 et seq.
    s. 35 .... 47.39
    s. 43 .... 47.40
1974 Consumer Credit Act (c. 39) 17.02

1974 Rehabilitation of Offenders
Act (c. 53) 32.23, 47.03
1976 Bail Act (c. 63) 41.16, 43.01,
43.02, 43.03, 43.05, 43.09, 47.01,
47.06, 49.02, 49.10
s. 3 (5) 43.17
(6) 43.15
s. 4 .... 43.02 et seq., 43.03, 43.22,
47.07
s. 7 .... 41.04
(3) 43.19
s. 8 .... 43.16
Sched. 1 .... 43.03
Pt. I, para. 9 .... 43.06, 43.09
Pt. II 43.04
Pt. IIA 43.22
1977 Criminal Law Act (c. 45)—
s. 47 .... 47.16
Sched. 9 .... 47.20
1978 Oaths Act (c. 19)—
s. 5 .... 27.02
Civil Liability (Contribution)
Act (c. 47) 14.17
1979 Criminal Evidence Act (c.
16) 33.20
1980 Magistrates' Courts Act (c.
43)—
s. 1 (4) 41.02
s. 2 (2) 42.03
(6) 42.03
s. 3 .... 42.03
s. 6 (1) 46.05
(2) 29.04, 40.08, 45.07,
45.11, 46.05, 46.17 et seq.,
46.19
s. 8 .... 46.07
s. 11 .... 44.05
s. 12 .... 44.06
s. 19 .... 45.07
s. 25 .... 45.11
s. 38 .... 48.03
s. 97 .... 40.11
s. 101 .... 24.05
s. 102 .... 29.02, 29.03 et seq.,
30.01, 40.11, 46.09, 46.17, 46.18,
46.21
s. 105 .... 29.02, 29.27
s. 111 .... 48.04
s. 123 .... 44.04
1981 Supreme Court Act (c. 54)—
s. 35A 1.20, 1.24, 6.10,
6.12, 6.14, 6.21
(5) 1.24
s. 48 .... 48.03
s. 81 .... 43.23
1982 Administration of Justice Act
(c. 53)—
s. 5 .... 1.16
s. 6 .... 1.26
Criminal Justice Act (c. 48)—
s. 1A 47.26
s. 60 .... 43.23

1983 Mental Health Act (c. 20)—
s. 35 .... 47.07
1984 County Courts Act (c. 28) 17.02
ss. 19, 20 .... 18.01, 18.05, 18.06
s. 69 .... 1.20, 1.24, 17.13
Road Traffic Regulation Act
(c. 27)—
s. 89 .... 28.04
Police and Criminal Evidence
Act (c. 60) 22.01, 30.15,
30.20, 33.14, 40.08,
41.01, 41.22, 41.23,
49.12
s. 1 .... 41.06
s. 17 .... 41.08
s. 24 .... 41.03
(6) 41.04
(7) 41.04
s. 25 .... 41.04
(3) 41.04
s. 28 .... 41.05
s. 32 .... 41.08, 41.09
s. 37 .... 41.17
s. 54 .... 41.10
s. 56 .... 30.15, 34.04, 41.20, 41.23
s. 58 .... 30.15, 34.04, 41.20, 41.23
s. 61 .... 41.11
s. 66 .... 30.02, 30.14, 41.01, 41.20,
41.25
s. 67 (11) **30.14**
s. 68 .... 29.10, 29.25, 31.01, 31.02
s. 76 .... 30.02 et seq., **30.03**, 30.04,
30.06, 30.20, 34.04, 41.14
(2) 30.07, 30.25
(3) 30.07
(4) 30.08, 30.09, 34.03
(b) 30.09
(5) 30.08, 30.09, 34.03
(8) 30.04, 30.05, 30.21
s. 78 .... 29.23, 30.02, 30.12, 30.15,
30.20 et seq., 30.21, 34.04, 34.05,
41.14
s. 80 .... 26.09, 26.10
(8) 26.08
s. 81 .... 32.06, 38.03
s. 82 .... 30.01
(3) 29.23, 34.04
s. 116 .... 41.18
(7) 41.18
Sched. 2 .... 41.03
Pt. IV 41.15
1985 Companies Act (c. 6)—
s. 725 .... 5.15
Prosecution of Offences Act (c.
23)—
ss. 16–21 .... 39.25
s. 17 .... 46.16
1988 Criminal Justice Act (c.
33) 22.01, 29.07, 29.08, 29.09,
29.10, 31.11, 31.13
ss. 23–26 .... 29.09, 29.18, 31.11
ss. 23–30 .... 29.02, 29.08 et seq.
s. 23 ...... 29.10, 29.11, 29.12, 29.14,
29.15, 29.16, 29.20, 29.23, 29.24

1988 Criminal Justice Act—*cont.*
   s. 23—*cont.*
     (2) 29.11
     (3) 29.12
   s. 24 ...... 29.10, 29.12, 29.13, 29.14,
     29.15, 29.16, 29.20, 29.22, 29.23,
     29.24, 29.25, 31.09, 31.13, 49.07
     (4)(*b*)(iii) **29.16**
   s. 25 ...... 29.14, 29.15, 29.17, 29.19,
      29.23
     (2) **29.15**
   s. 26 .... 29.17, 29.23, 29.28
   s. 28 .... 29.23
   s. 30 .... 29.11, 29.24, 32.06
     (3) 29.24, 32.06
   s. 40 .... 46.15
   s. 41 .... 46.15
   s. 71 .... 47.41
   s. 104 .... 47.39
   Sched. 2, para. 1 .... 29.20

1988 Criminal Justice Act—*cont.*
   para. 3 .... 29.19
  Legal Aid Act (c. 34) 2.06, 39.08
   s. 16 .... 2.23
   s. 17 .... 2.25, 2.26, 12.10, 20.34,
      49.05
   s. 18 .... 2.26, 49.05
   s. 21 .... 39.09, 39.16, 39.18
   s. 22 .... 39.11
  Road Traffic Act (c. 52)—
   s. 3 .... 45.02, 47.11
   s. 143 .... 3.21, 3.28, 3.30
   s. 145 .... 3.21, 3.28, 3.30
   s. 151 .... 3.28
   s. 152 .... 3.28, 3.30, 3.41,
      6.41, 14.16
  Road Traffic Offenders Act (c.
     53) **47.29, 47.37**
   s. 1 .... 42.02
   Pt. II 47.32, 47.37

Introduction

Until summer 1980 the Law Society's Final Examination consisted of seven papers in subjects all of which, except the Accounts paper, would usually have been offered as options on most law degree courses. Law graduates usually took the Finals course, which then involved only about four months of actual tuition time, straight after their degree whilst the study habit and some recollection of the substantive subjects might have been fresh. There was no Finals paper touching on any of the elements, civil or criminal procedure, or evidence, of the present Litigation examination. Thus except perhaps for a study of the bare outline of procedure usually undertaken as part of an English Legal System course in the first year of a law degree most would-be solicitors would start articles with no knowledge whatsoever of litigation.

It is my own impression that this early bad start was compounded in many cases because most principals tended to provide more haphazard tuition to their trainees in litigation than in non contentious work. Certainly this was my own experience and that of friends and acquaintances who were qualifying at the same time. Whilst I received an excellent grounding in non contentious work I was to an extent left to my own devices in litigation. This is probably partly inevitable given the nature of litigation practice. Litigation lawyers are simply more pressed for time because they are out of the office considerably more than their non-contentious colleagues. Therefore whilst there is always time to have someone qualified check an attempt at a draft contract or lease, it is in the nature ot things more difficult for a principal who is trying to give his trainee some degree of responsibility to supervise the latter, *e.g.* when conducting a meeting to negotiate settlement with an insurance company representative. It is obviously impossible to supervise advocacy as such, *e.g.* the hearing of a summons before a district judge in chambers—something a trainee might undertake very soon after starting his articles. The uncomfortable truth is therefore that litigation lawyers, more than any other category, learn their trade at the expense of their early clients. Nor is this confined to trainees. When newly qualified and undertaking criminal advocacy for the first time I certainly represented clients who were respectively convicted, refused bail, or sent to prison, in cases where with more experience I am sure I could have secured an acquittal, or bail, or a non custodial sentence. I expect that most litigation lawyers would admit the same.

As a trainee however my early experience of litigation was confined to civil matters. When in doubt about what to do next I usually obtained help by:

1. telephoning the court to ask for advice (usually very helpful except where I had recently imposed on their patience too long)

2. telephoning slightly more experienced friends for advice (results extremely erratic) or

1

3.   telephoning my opponent for advice (a disarming and surprisingly effective technique—most lawyers simply cannot resist the opportunity of showing off their knowledge).

My early experience of advocacy was of being sent scampering down to the district registry with a file at short notice having been told what orders to seek from the district judge. My apprehensiveness at this would in part be dispelled by finding that my opponent was not usually some forensic lion but a trainee in a similar state of ignorance to myself. Wordlessly we would prowl around each other in the district judge's waiting room like gun fighters in a spaghetti western until the bell summoned us. The hearing would then usually become little more than an unseemly scramble between us to be the first to bleat out the magic words "It's not my file sir." Amongst trainees the uttering of these words was considered to have a mystic talismanic quality deflecting from the utterer the putative wrath of the district judge. And indeed usually it would have this hoped-for effect. Faced with the incompetence of the "advocates" before him the district judge would usually, patiently and with infinite forebearance, explain the defects in the summons, comment sorrowfully on the lack of affidavit, suggest how the summons ought to have been framed, cogently summarise the case in favour of the application, equally cogently suggest objections, arrive at a considered synthesis of these opposing views, and then give his ruling, finally explaining to his mystified audience how the order should be drafted.

Occasionally things would go less satisfactorily. An individual district judge might feel that he was entitled to have the case before him competently presented and might make his displeasure at ineptitude or lack of preparation felt. Some district judges would indeed treat the previously hallowed words "It's not my file sir" as a positively aggravating feature. The tendency of individual district judges to take this unreasonable attitude became a matter of folk lore amongst trainees who might be seen to begin trembling on arrival at the district judge's waiting room and finding that the summons was to be heard before the demanding district judge X rather than the avuncular and tolerant Y.

With the introducton of the Finals course in Litigation and the requirement that law graduates anyway, now by far the most numerous entrants to the profession, take the Finals course before articles, the standard of competence of trainees in litigation has risen dramatically. Trainees should on their first day of articles be relative paragons of litigation knowledge. Indeed in some cases trainees clearly know more than their principals. More than one former student has expressed to me his amazement and horror that his principal, in the late 1980s, had never heard of automatic directions in personal injury cases or of the availability of interim payments. Whatever the improvements that might be suggested either in teaching method or syllabus content, the new Finals course in Litigation anyway must be accounted an unequivocal success.

Why, however, write a book for the course? One common comment is that with the core material and a year's lecture notes text books are unnecessary. To this objection there is a number of possible responses.

1.   The simple answer is that books written for the Law Society Finals course clearly do answer a need which students feel. There are already several text books written for other subjects in the Finals course which

have been welcomed by students. There is however no other book which covers the whole of the Litigation course and students who seek help from text books for this Head of the examination would need to buy at least two, and possibly three separate text books. Moreover none of the text books which are available in Litigation are expressly written for the course and those text books generally incorporate much material not relevant for Finals purposes.

2. The stresses of this very demanding course and the dire consequences of failure are such that students are typically very nervous about the examination and seem to need all the reassurance that they can get in the form of extra and alternative sources of information.

3. The core material in Litigation is very clearly only an outline requiring substantial expansion in lectures. The amount of detail given in lectures varies very greatly between the institutions offering the course. This is not to suggest that the lecturing is anywhere incompetent. It is simply that opinions may legitimately differ between teachers over what amount of detail the students need to know for the examination, and, more importantly, how much more background detail is required to make the essential detail comprehensible. Some institutions are particularly conscious of the fear of "over teaching" that is, of swamping the students in detail. This may lead in some cases to students having relatively brief notes which tends to make them nervous.

4. Often students only find a subject comprehensible if they have access to more background information than they strictly need for the examination. This is moreover true of students of very varying levels of ability. Very good students find it frustrating to be given only outline information without background detail. They may find it helps the learning process to have more detail, especially of a practical nature. Weaker students also, who have difficulty with basic ideas, may find things more comprehensible if they have access to background material so long as they appreciate that the detail is excessive for actual revision and examination requirements. Such students find that more detail tends to help the comprehension process.

5. Lecturers, especially those with practical experience, often unwittingly use technical phrases without explanation as if the words were ordinary English. Sometimes they hardly appreciate the mystification that this can induce in the uninitiated. I recall myself after finishing lecturing civil litigation being approached by an able but somewhat diffident student who came to deliver to me in a most apologetic manner a list of questions. The first question was "what exactly do you mean by 'a return day'?" Each of the questions which followed were of a similar kind, and, clearly, the student was well justified in asking them. This text aims to explain all such technical terms.

The text therefore is written for the Law Society Finals Course. If it is of any use to students on other courses, such as Bar Finals or Part II of the Institute of Legal Executives Examinations, or even to practitioners, so much the better. That however is entirely incidental. The text aims to collect in one place the necessary material on all aspects of the Litigation course. Only material relevant to the syllabus of the Law Society Finals Course appears here. Thus the civil litigation section discusses practical procedural and tactical steps relevant only to a road traffic accident and a consumer type contract dispute. So for instance the particular practical features of a factory accident or medical negligence case are not dealt with where these may differ from the above. Similarly as the criminal litigation syllabus only concerns driving offences or theft there is nothing on the text on for example the special evidential rules relevant to sexual offences.

The organisation of the book needs a little explanation. The civil litigation material comes first because it is most lengthy. There is nothing on substantive law (in which I include limitation of actions). These topics do not arise in the examination itself and I have nothing to add to the brief treatment of them contained in the present core material.

The civil litigation material commences with a discussion of the financing of civil litigation. I had at one time considered incorporating into this or following it immediately with the section on costs since costs are a vital consideration throughout the litigation process. In the event however I decided to put the section on costs almost at the end of the civil litigation material but suggest a cursory reference to it immediately after the earlier section on financing civil proceedings. The same is true of a brief section on choice of court as between county court and High Court which also appears almost at the end although reference to it might be made as part of the pre-action considerations.

Thereafter the progress of the civil action is described throughout its various stages. There is always difficulty in arranging topics in books on procedure. To follow a straightforward action through from beginning to end necessitates leaving aside all manner of alternative courses of action at each stage. The moment one does introduce alternatives and fully describe them (*e.g.* early termination, infant settlement, third party proceedings), the thread of the narrative is lost and the picture may become unclear. For this reason the main steps in the action are considered in (approximately) the right order and separate sections appear slightly later on alternatives such as early termination. There is only passing reference in the civil procedure material to matters of evidence which are all dealt with separately in the Evidence section. The text concludes with a very few precedents as illustrations of points referred to in the text.

The second section is Evidence. It is notoriously difficult to write briefly on Evidence. Brevity usually entails not merely a loss of accuracy but also of clarity and comprehensibility. The material on evidence here is in my opinion sufficient to cover the topic for the Finals Examination. It is a considerably expanded version of a handout used in lectures for some years at Manchester Polytechnic which has been very well received by students. The material on civil evidence is integrated into the general context of evidence.

The text on Criminal Procedure concentrates entirely on matters of practical significance for the examination. An example of this is the relative brevity of the procedure on police powers of entry, search and seizure. Although misconduct by the police or breach of the requirements of the Police and Criminal Evidence Act 1984 and the codes issued under it may be of great importance in such areas as excluding a confession, in the context of misconduct in the course of entry and search there is likely to be little effect on the outcome of the criminal process. These matters are therefore dealt with somewhat cursorily. There is more detailed material however on matters of practical use such as bail, legal aid, choice of court, sentencing and mitigation.

Finally there is a chapter containing advice on how to approach the course and pass the examination.

As an aid to revision technique there is incorporated in this new edition a chapter comprising two recent papers together with suggested forms of answer. The suggested forms of answer are meant to represent something that one could conceivably get down in the time available and are not a complete and comprehensive discussion of every conceivable tactical option.

The text was written in Spring 1991 and seeks to state the law and practice as at June 1, 1991. Some slight updating has been possible at proof stage.

Civil Procedure

1. Damages

In this section we shall consider damages. We shall consider in turn:

1. personal injury damages;
2. damages in contract cases;
3. interest on damages;
4. provisional damages.

Damages in personal injury cases

Establishing *liability* is not enough. It is vital at all stages of a personal injury **1.01**
case to have some idea of what amount might be awarded by the court at
trial. This can be essential both to achieve an early satisfactory settlement by
negotiation or when considering tactical steps open to the defendant, in
particular payment into court, that is a formalised offer by the defendant,
refusal of which may well put the plaintiff at risk as to costs (see para. 12.02).
Accordingly the pre-action considerations which we shall shortly consider
involve beginning to collect information at a very early stage not merely to
help prove liability against the defendant but also to establish the amount of
compensation which the plaintiff is likely to recover from the judge if the
case goes all the way to trial.

The basic principle of damages is that they should put the plaintiff in the
position in which he would have been but for the tort or breach of contract.
Where the wrong-doing by the defendant can be translated into simple
financial terms as in the non-payment of a debt or in an accident which
causes only damage to the vehicle of the plaintiff then it is easy enough to
compute the sums involved. In the one case the court will award judgment
for the amount of the debt and in the other for the cost of repairing the
vehicle. In personal injury cases however there are commonly two elements
of damages, there is firstly the question of actual provable specific financial
loss and secondly an attempt by the court to compensate the plaintiff for his
personal injuries by awarding him a sum of money.

It is important for this purpose to divide damages in a personal injuries
case into two parts namely *general damages* and *special damages*. *General
damages* are the compensatory amounts which have to be assessed by the
court of trial; *special damages* are the specific amounts which represent
actual financial loss to the plaintiff. In the plaintiff's pleading, that is in his
statement of claim, he need only claim general damages by adding the words
"and the plaintiff claims damages" at the end of the pleading. Whilst it is
proper to give particulars of the injuries suffered and any special factors
which apply, for example the loss of career prospects, it is not necessary (or
possible) to give in the pleading an exhaustive list of the aspects of the
plaintiff's life which have been affected by the injury he has suffered nor to
suggest in the pleading figures which are appropriate for each. Thus for
example a plaintiff will not in his statement of claim plead, *e.g.* that having
broken his leg his life is affected in so far as his mobility is concerned and his

favourite hobbies of tennis and football are now impossible and that he claims a specific sum for this. These are matters of evidence which a court will hear at trial and will be taken into account by the judge when awarding damages.

Special damages however *do* have to be pleaded in the plaintiff's statement of claim. Moreover as precise as possible a computation has to be provided of the exact amounts which the plaintiff is claiming. If accurate figures are given it may be that the plaintiff and defendant, however strenuously the action is contested on liability, may be able to agree the basis of the computation so that there is no dispute as to the amount of these damages subject to liability being established.

SPECIAL DAMAGES

1.02   Special damages cover actual loss incurred between the accident and the trial. Items of expense which are to be incurred after trial (even if the amount is known) are not as such special damages though a claim to them will be made at the trial and amounts allowed for them. Special damages include such basic things as:

1. Loss of earnings until trial.

2. Damage to clothing, repairs to vehicles.

3. Extra travel costs occasioned by the accident, *e.g.* by the plaintiff having frequently to visit hospital as an out-patient or by relatives having to visit him in hospital.

4. Private medical or nursing treatment.

   We shall now consider these individually.

Loss of earnings

1.03   Loss of earnings in the period between the accident and the trial forms part of the special damages. It is not of course possible to plead these fully in the statement of claim which is likely to be served quite soon after the accident and thus many months if not years before the trial. However it is necessary to compute the loss of earnings up to the date of service of the statement of claim and these figures must then be updated and worked out again at a time just before trial. Loss of earnings after the trial is part of the claim for general damages and we shall come to this in due course.

The plaintiff may only claim what he has actually lost, that is his *net* loss. Accordingly his tax and national insurance contributions must be deducted from his gross earnings. The method of computing loss of earnings is to obtain details from his employer of his actual gross and net earnings over a recent typical period, *e.g.* the 26 weeks up to the date of the accident (choosing such a long period to allow seasonal fluctuations or overtime variations to even themselves out to a true average); to then take the figure for one week's average net loss of earnings and use that as a basis for computing his continuing loss of earnings. It is important to find out when writing to the employer whether there have been any increases in pay since the accident for which the plaintiff would have been eligible or indeed whether any promotion opportunities have arisen for which the plaintiff would have been a likely candidate. So to take a simple example suppose:

The plaintiff is injured on January 1, 1991 and one wishes to compute his loss of earnings on May 20, 1991—a period of 20 weeks. His employers provide information which tells you that his pre-accident weekly average net pay was £100 but on March 11, 1991 (*i.e.* after he had been absent for 10 weeks) employees in his category received a pay rise giving a further £10 net per week. It is therefore very simple to work out the 20 weeks loss of earnings namely:

```
10 weeks @ £100 = £1,000
10 weeks @ £110 = £1,100
Total                £2,100
```

Clearly this is a simple example and to work out the loss of earnings can be complex where one is dealing with a long period. It is this item in particular which needs to be updated if the plaintiff has not returned to work before trial.

The plaintiff's contract of employment. It is necessary to carefully consider the plaintiff's contract of employment. It may be that his employer pays him for certain periods whilst he is off sick and thus the defendant benefits from this since it is only actual loss for which he is liable to compensate the plaintiff. Suppose that in the previous example the employer had a private scheme negotiated with the plaintiff's trade union whereby he paid all employees who were off work regardless of whether the cause was accident or sickness for a period of say 20 weeks and the plaintiff returned to work after 20 weeks. The plaintiff would have no claim for loss of earnings in that time. In this situation only the plaintiff's employer loses because he has paid for 20 weeks work which he has not received. He has of course no cause of action against the defendant. **1.04**

Some employers have a provision in the contract of employment which is no less generous to their employees but does provide a sensible means of ensuring that they are reimbursed by the defendant. The contract provides that the employer will make the employee an interest free loan equivalent to the amount of his net earnings whilst he is off work for a certain specified period. If the cause of absence is merely sickness or is some accident in respect of which the plaintiff is not able to recover any damages from some other person (*e.g.* an accident caused by the employee's own negligence) then he will usually not be asked to repay this loan. If however the employee is able to recover damages from some third party he is expected to include in his action a claim for loss of earnings and is then obliged to reimburse his employer.

Tax rebates. Because it is only *net* earnings for loss of which one can sue, one is obliged to give credit for any tax rebates received. This is because tax allowances are worked out over a whole year and the allowance is given in the form of a weekly allowance set against weekly salary. A person is however entitled to the whole tax allowance even if he does not work for the whole year. Suppose therefore that an individual has tax allowances equivalent to say £40 per week when spread over the whole year. He works for three months or so into the tax year and is injured in July. He does not work thereafter. Taking into account the £40 per week which has hitherto been credited to him as his allowance he is credited now with the balance of the **1.05**

whole of his tax allowance for the year and when offset against his salary received for only three months he will then clearly be entitled to a substantial tax rebate. This must be brought into account and deducted from his claim for loss of earnings.

1.06 **Benefits received.** The way in which compensation is affected by taking into account benefits received has been radically changed with effect from September 3, 1990. The need for special provisions about this is obvious. For example, where a plaintiff is injured and thus not able to work and earn his usual salary he will generally receive benefits of various kinds. If at the end of the case the plaintiff recovered in full for his loss of earnings but without having the benefits which he has received taken into account then there will be two losers, the defendant, who will have had to compensate the plaintiff for a loss which he has not in fact had (since he will have received the benefits which ought partially to offset his loss of earnings) and the state who will have paid out benefits to the plaintiff which will be irrecoverable. The new provisions attempt to rectify this apparent injustice.

Briefly, the new provisions provide that except in the case of certain exempt payments, in any case where a defendant (the *compensator*) is to pay damages for personal injury to a plaintiff (the *claimant*) whether in consequence of a judgment at the end of a trial, settlement or compromise during a case, or the procedure known as payment into court, described more fully at para. 12.02 or otherwise that benefits received by the claimant must be taken into account. At present the following provisions apply wherever the amount which the claimant is to receive under the judgment or compromise is more than £2,500.

When the solicitor for a plaintiff writes to the defendant notifying him of the claim which is to be made, the solicitor for the plaintiff should inform the defendant of the plaintiff's date of birth, national insurance number, address and the name and address of the plaintiff's employer. Thereupon the defendant must notify a body called the Compensation Recovery Unit (C.R.U.) by forwarding to them a certain form. This form will be acknowledged and thereupon the C.R.U. will maintain records of all relevant benefits claimed and paid in respect of the injury in question.

When the compensator is then ready to make an offer of payment to the claimant, he should apply to the C.R.U. for what is called a Certificate of Total Benefit. This certificate will then be issued by the C.R.U. and will show the amount of total benefits paid to the claimant in respect of that injury since it occurred. Moreover details will be given of future payments over the next eight weeks after the date of the certificate thus enabling the compensator to know with precision what amount of benefits will have been paid on any given date during that period.

Thereafter when the payment is made to the plaintiff, whether by way of court order or agreed compromise of the action, the appropriate amount of benefit must be deducted from it by the compensator and this amount must then be remitted to the C.R.U. By this procedure the Government is reimbursed for the benefits paid out, and the plaintiff has no element of double compensation.

The following points are also worthy of note:

(a) The types of benefit which are relevant for these purposes include the following:

- (i) Family credit.
- (ii) Disablement benefit.
- (iii) Income support.
- (iv) Invalidity benefit.
- (v) Mobility allowance.
- (vi) Severe disablement allowance.
- (vii) Sickness benefit.
- (viii) Statutory sick pay.
- (ix) Unemployment benefit.

(b) When negotiating settlements of claims, or advising a plaintiff about likely future compensation it is accordingly vital that a plaintiff's solicitor remembers to take into account the repayment of benefit element so that a plaintiff is not left under the mistaken belief that these things will not be brought into account by way of deduction from his total compensation.

(c) More detail will be given at individual points later in the text as to the precise practical steps which need to be taken in respect of these provisions at various stages in the action. See in particular the topics of payment into court and interim payments.

(d) The above provisions apply wherever the amount of compensation exceeds £2,500. If the amount is less than £2,500 then the former law governs the position. This law has a certain logic of its own but was latterly considered anomalous. Put briefly it provides that in cases involving compensation of less than £2,500 the plaintiff has to give the defendant credit for one half of certain kinds of benefit, and the whole of other benefits which are deducted from compensation. However, although offset from the compensation, the amounts in question are not passed on by the defendant to the state, but retained by the defendant. The rules in relation to these provisions were fairly complex caused in part by the application of section 2(1) of the Law Reform (Personal Injuries) Act 1948 and in part by a wealth of case law. In short the benefits of which one half had to be deducted from a claim include sickness benefit, invalidity benefit, non-contributory invalidity pension, severe disablement allowance, injury benefit and disablement benefit. The kind of benefits which were deductable in full included statutory sick pay, and unemployment benefit. A full explanation of these provisions is most unlikely to be required for examination purposes and is thus beyond the scope of the present text.

(e) It is important to note that if anything is received in respect of the following the amounts are *not deductible*. That is to say that the defendant does not obtain the benefit of these things:

- (i) The results of private accident insurance. Even if this comes about factually because of an accident the legal cause is the plaintiff's own prudence in arranging to have personal accident insurance. It is therefore wrong for the defendant to get the benefit of this by having it offset against his liability.
- (ii) The results of public benevolence, *e.g.* collections. Likewise it would be wrong for the defendant to gain the benefit of this by having his liability to pay damages reduced.

(iii) The result of private benevolence, *e.g.* gifts from friends or relatives.
(iv) Redundancy payments. If for example whilst a person is away from work because of disablement he and others are made redundant then unless the cause of the redundancy relates to his incapacity resulting from the accident (which is unlikely) no credit should accrue to the defendant.

(f) **Other earnings.** It should be noted that one must give credit for earnings obtained whilst off work due to incapacity if they would not otherwise have been earned.

Example:
The plaintiff is a games teacher who is injured and unable to work. His claim includes loss of earnings. Suppose however that his second subject is French and he is able to give some tuition in the day time to private students. The amount of income earned from this must be offset against his claim for loss of earnings since he would not have earned it had he been at work. If however it had always been his practice to offer private tuition in his own time, (*i.e.* in the evening) to obtain extra income then since he would have earned the sums in any event he would not be obliged to give credit for them.

1.07 **Maintenance at public expense.** Section 5 of the Administration of Justice Act 1982 provides that any saving to an injured person which is attributable to his maintenance wholly or partly at public expense (*i.e.* in a National Health Service hospital) must be calculated and set off against any income lost as a result of the injuries. This is to be set off in fact against both loss of earnings incurred up to trial and loss thereafter which forms part of *general damages* as we shall shortly see. In other words where a plaintiff is fed and saves rent, rates, lighting and heating, etc., by being in hospital rather than at home the amount should be calculated and brought into account. The circumstances in which this will be applied vary very greatly from case to case. Suppose for example that the plaintiff is a single man living in a bed sitter. Whilst he will still have to pay rent on his bed sitter he is entirely relieved of the cost of heating, lighting and food whilst in hospital. The amount saved may be reasonably substantial and of the order of say £20 or £30 per week. If however the plaintiff is a family man living in a three-bedroomed house with his wife and children then the amount saved in terms of rent and rates will be nil since the house will still be needed as a family home and also the amount saved in regard to heating and lighting will likewise be nil since the family will require as much heating and lighting whether their father is with them or not. The amount saved in regard to food likewise may not be substantial, the difference in cost between food for six people and food for five people not being nearly as great as the cost of food for one person alone.

This provision was designed to give the defendant some compensation where a plaintiff is in hospital for a lengthy period. Even in the case of the single man given above, if his stay in hospital were only a few weeks it is most unlikely that the defendants would bother to argue for or compute the amount saved. If the period of hospitalisation is more extensive then it may be that in individual cases it will be worth agreeing figures which will usually be done in round terms. There appears to be no need to refer to this item in the statement of claim. The defendant should be left to claim and argue for this if he is so minded.

Other expenses

Repairs to vehicle. One can naturally claim for the cost of repairs to a motor vehicle damaged in the accident; and for the cost of a hired car of a similar type for the period when the vehicle is off the road awaiting repair. Defendants' insurance companies often attempt to argue that this is only appropriate where the car is needed for business use but there is no reason whatsoever in law for such a restriction. Alternatively if a plaintiff chose not to hire a car for the intervening period he would be entitled to general damages for inconvenience caused by the necessity to use public transport. **1.08**

Damage to clothes, and property, etc., damaged in the accident. A certain amount of haggling here may well be necessary since there is no ready market for second hand clothes, wrist watch, etc., from which the value of such items can be computed. Generally it is possible to compromise on a sensible figure. **1.09**

Other expenses. Other more unusual expenses might involve, *e.g.* adapting a car for disabled driving or even adapting one's house by installing a lift; or perhaps the expenses of moving from a house to a bungalow for a disabled plaintiff including estate agent's commission, solicitors' fees and removal expenses. **1.10**

Medical expenses. By section 2(4) of the Law Reform (Personal Injuries Act) 1948 it is provided that a plaintiff is entitled to claim the cost of private medical treatment. This is so even if National Health Service treatment is readily available. In other words the plaintiff has the right to his choice of specialist and hospital and even if the plaintiff is not someone who would ever otherwise have had private medical treatment he will be entitled to do so here. "Medical treatment" includes not merely surgery but after care, including nursing and convalescence. **1.11**

Expenses incurred by other persons. By convention even though the expenses were actually incurred by other people rather than the plaintiff personally, if travelling expenses are incurred for the purpose of visiting the plaintiff or nursing him these are allowable in the claim as against the defendant as if they were incurred by the plaintiff. There will clearly be some element of reasonableness here. Whilst it might well be for example that if the plaintiff were badly injured and his mother lived on the other side of the world her cost of flying to visit him might be allowable, the same would not be true of a second cousin who had never seen the plaintiff before but suddenly evinced an insuperable desire to be with him in his hour of need. **1.12**

GENERAL DAMAGES

General damages may be subdivided into the following items. None of these are capable of exact calculation by the court and in some cases are entirely compensatory there being no *financial* loss at all. These amounts are assessed by the court at trial. **1.13**

Pain and suffering

1.14 An amount here is awarded to compensate the plaintiff for the pain and suffering which has been suffered not only in the past, *i.e.* at the very time of the accident and the immediate aftermath but also in consequence of any surgical treatment. Compensation includes mental suffering and takes into account personal matters which may increase the suffering. In addition if the plaintiff's life expectancy has been reduced the award for pain and suffering should take into account the plaintiff's knowledge of this.

Loss of amenity

1.15 Loss of amenity compensates the plaintiff for the loss of quality of his life. A plaintiff who has lost a leg will clearly have the quality of his life considerably impaired in relation to his ordinary every day activities. He will find it more uncomfortable and inconvenient to do many normal things that any individual would want to do. However if for any plaintiff there are special personal factors which increase the degree of loss of quality of life these must also be brought into account, for example, if he was an extremely enthusiastic sports player. In this situation he would be entitled to a greater sum than a person who had a relatively sedentary life. It is fair to say that the amount allowed by judges for these subjective factors may not be great over and above the so called "tariff" for the particular type of injury. If however a plaintiff is bona fide able to demonstrate extreme enthusiasm for, say, sport this can legitimately be used to increase his claim. Age is a subjective factor although it may cut both ways. An elderly man who is suddenly severely disabled may well be thought to have lost more in terms of quality of life for the few years remaining than a child, whereas the child, even though he may adjust better to disability has the disability to cope with over a longer period.

These two sums are assessed together by the trial judge. They are estimated on the basis of relatively conventional awards for different parts of the body. A useful text book is *Kemp and Kemp* "Quantum of Damages." This is a loose leaf and includes amounts of awards for various parts of the body. *Current Law* also has a useful section on quantum of damages in every issue reporting cases by reference to parts of the body. Most useful of all for the relatively few firms of solicitors or barristers chambers who have it is the computer data base LEXIS which now has a separate file for personal injuries from which one can obtain details of awards made up to 10 days previously in cases which often would not otherwise be reported. It is fair to say however, that the attitude of judges to having cases cited which are reported only on LEXIS is variable.

Loss of future earnings

1.16 This is the most difficult head of damages of all. From the base of loss of present net earnings previously explained one may have to launch off into a number of speculative areas. The court works on the basis of two figures known as *multiplier* and *multiplicand*. *Multiplicand* is the net annual loss that the plaintiff has suffered. If the plaintiff is likely to be able to return to work in the same job in a year or two then no great problem is involved but what if the plaintiff will never work again? Here one has great difficulty in picking the appropriate multiplicand. Suppose that the plaintiff is relatively young.

Is it fair to take as his net loss of earnings the sum he is presently earning when he might have had a glowing career before him with eventual promotion to very highly paid positions? How should one choose a figure between what he earns at say 23 and what he might earn at 60? Even in the case of a highly structured and stratified profession with an annual increment pay system such as, say, the Civil Service, assessing this figure can be an enormously difficult task. If one picks more volatile professions such as entertainment or sport the difficulties are virtually insuperable. The same to a lesser extent may be said to apply to the learned professions. How does one compensate a barrister of 24 who has suffered brain damage such that he will never work again? To take his present annual earnings which may be very small would clearly be unfair but is he to be compensated on the basis that he would inevitably have become a Queen's Counsel or High Court judge? In deciding these questions one needs to call all available evidence about the plaintiff's future career. This may still be very unsatisfactory. There may be very little information available which can guide the court especially in the case of young plaintiffs with a career where income can vary greatly. All one can say is that in fixing on this multiplicand judges use their experience and common sense. In straightforward cases the plaintiff's present net income may be chosen.

As well as the multiplicand the judge needs to select the *multiplier*. Suppose one has a plaintiff aged 25 who was earning £10,000 net per year. In principle if he is never to work again he has lost at least 40 working years until 65 (possibly longer if he was self employed). One cannot however simply multiply £10,000 by 40 because this would result in considerable over compensation. It would be received as one lump sum now whereas the real salary, whilst it may have grown over the years, would also have been received in small amounts. The sum of £400,000 received now, if invested sensibly might well yield an annual income of several times the £10,000 which has been lost. Accordingly a multiplier to take into account accelerated receipt and other contingencies such as early death, unemployment or other injury is adopted and the maximum multiplier even for a very young plaintiff tends to be 18. It should not be forgotten that from loss of future earnings credit must be given for benefits to be received within five years under section 2(1) of the 1948 Act and also for maintenance at public expense under section 5 of the Administration of Justice Act 1982.

Risk on the labour market or loss of earning capacity

This has long been recognised as a head of compensation but was re-emphasised in the leading modern case of *Smith* v. *Manchester Corporation* (1974) 17 K.I.R. 1. The facts of the case provide a good example of the principle. Mrs. Smith was a cleaner employed by the defendants who due to their negligence suffered injury to her shoulder. This made her a considerably less efficient cleaner but the defendants did undertake to keep her on and thus she had no future loss of earnings. She did however receive a separate sum of money under this head. This was because should she ever lose or give up her job (*e.g.* because she might wish to move to another part of the country or find her present job uncongenial) she would be at risk on the labour market because she would be competing with fully fit cleaners. She had thus lost her freedom of mobility of labour in that as she was now no longer such an efficient cleaner she would be considerably more wary of

1.17

moving jobs. The basis of this award tends to be relatively conventional and it is suggested that depending on degree of disability and age of the plaintiff an award of between one and one-and-a-half years' gross salary is usually appropriate. However a recent case has stressed that each case must be considered on its own facts and that earlier cases cannot be considered as precedents.

Future expenses

1.18   Where a plaintiff is likely to need to spend specified future amounts, *e.g.* for future medical treatment, adapting a car for disabled driving, moving house in consequence of the injury suffered, but has not spent these sums by the time of trial they cannot strictly be described as special damages but because they are precisely quantifiable they may resemble that. They are part of general damages and can be claimed at trial. If the claim is for future medical expenses credit must be given for any maintenance element within those expenses, *i.e.* the saving to the plaintiff of being fed and cared for in hospital.

Damages in contract cases

1.19   Where an action is brought for damages for breach of contract then the principle is *restitution* that is to put the aggrieved party in the situation in which he would have been but for breach of contract. This may involve payment of a debt in full, repayment of the whole of the purchase price to a disgruntled consumer or payment for diminution in value, *e.g.* where a disgruntled consumer has had to spend a sum of money to put right a purchased item. These amounts are precisely quantifiable. It may well be however that a claim for breach of contract may involve general damages which have to be assessed by the court, *e.g.* for distress and inconvenience.

Example:
   Suppose a newly purchased television set suddenly explodes causing a fire which causes damage to the plaintiff's house which in consequence needs to be re-decorated. Not only can the cost of the redecoration, etc., be recovered as special damages but a sum for distress and inconvenience can likewise be recovered.
   It should not be overlooked also that personal injuries are possible in a contract claim as in the example just given if the television had actually exploded injuring the plaintiff.

Interest on damages

1.20   By virtue of section 35A Supreme Court Act 1981 or section 69 County Courts Act 1984 the High Court and county court respectively have a discretion in every case to award interest on damages from the date when the cause of action arose to the date when judgment is given or earlier payment.

PERSONAL INJURY CASES

1.21   In a personal injury case these two sections respectively provide that in an action for damages for personal injuries or death where judgment is given for a sum which exceeds £200 the court *shall* award such damages unless the court is satisfied that there are special reasons to the contrary. This provides a rule for personal injury cases that there is a presumption *in favour* of awarding interest on damages. It is difficult to envisage circumstances in which payment of interest would *not* be awarded unless perhaps there had been wilful delay in the conduct of the case by the plaintiff. The rate of damages in personal injuries cases is not specified in the statute. However guidelines are provided in case law in the case of *Wright* v. *British Railways Board* [1983] 2 A.C. 773. This case provides the following simple rules:

1. Interest is to be awarded on damages for pain and suffering and loss of amenity at the rate of 2 per cent. per annum from the date of service of the writ to the date of trial. This somewhat artificially low rate is said to reflect the fact that the amounts of tariff awards for any particular type of personal injury are any way revised from time to time so that a plaintiff who say lost an eye in an accident in 1990 would have been awarded substantially more than one whose action came to trial say in 1983. The 2 per cent. is said to be appropriate in an era of relatively low inflation.

2. Damages for future loss carry no interest because the plaintiff has not yet expended the money.

3. Special damages carry interest which will be awarded at half the court's own special account rate from the date of accident to the date of trial. The court's special account rate is the rate of interest payable on funds held in court, *e.g.* funds held on behalf of an infant until it attains its majority. The rate is prescribed by statutory instrument and changes fairly frequently. At the time of writing it is 12 per cent. per annum. The reason for awarding interest at half the appropriate rate is that the majority of such claims will be for loss of earnings. Accordingly the loss will have been incurred gradually over the whole period from accident to trial but clearly it would be unfair on the defendant to award interest at a high rate on this whole amount for the whole period. Thus by awarding it at half the rate rough and ready justice is done and a great deal of very difficult calculation is avoided because the rate will in effect be equivalent to the award of interest at the full rate on the figure due at the halfway point between the accident and judgment.
    The justification for that is easy to see. What is less easy to see and indeed is quite arbitrary is the fact that usually interest is only payable at half the special account rate on other items which have been paid out in full perhaps quite early in the period and in respect of which the plaintiff is out of pocket for some considerable time (*e.g.* medical bills). The court does have discretion to depart from the guidelines however and in exceptional cases interest at the full rate may be allowed on the item in question *from the date it was incurred*, see *Dexter* v. *Courtaulds* [1984] 1 W.L.R. 372 and *Prokop* v. *Department of Health and Social Security* (1985) 10 C.L. 70.

INTEREST IN CONTRACT CASES

In cases where a claim is made in respect of a debt or breach of contract the question of interest arises in two situations. **1.22**

Where interest is payable as of right

A contract may for example provide that unless the amount due is paid in full **1.23** within, say, seven days, interest on the whole amount begins to run at a rate of say 20 per cent. per annum. In this case interest arises as of right as part of the contract and damages for the breach of contract will include interest at the contractually agreed rate. Such cases therefore provide no difficulty.

Interest payable under the court's discretion

1.24 It will be recalled that under section 35A of the Supreme Court Act 1981 and section 69 of the County Courts Act 1984 the court has a discretion to award interest on the amount for which judgment is given in any debt or damages claim. In the case of personal injuries there is a presumption in favour of the award of interest but in the case of contract actions there is merely a provision that the court *may* award interest. However the court ought usually to award interest since justice will require it. The court will have decided by its judgment that the plaintiff ought to be put in the same position he would have been but for the breach of contract and accordingly as he will have been kept out of money which should have been his since the cause of action arose he ought to receive compensation in the form of an award of interest. The rate which the court will choose is not specified as such though section 35A(5) provides that "without prejudice to the generality . . . rules of court may provide for a rate of interest by reference to the rate specified in section 17 of the Judgments Act 1838 as that section has effect from time to time or by reference to a rate for which any other enactment provides." The reference is to the Act which provides for a rate of interest on *judgment debts*. This is a different matter from interest on the *claim* itself. In the High Court where judgment is given interest continues to run until the sum is paid at a specified rate (currently 15 per cent. per annum) and this is known as the *judgment debt rate*. The section merely makes reference to this rate as a convenient one for the court to adopt and the court will usually do so unless there are special circumstances. It will not do so in the case of personal injuries because of the case law previously mentioned. Interest at 15 per cent. would seem to be reasonable in most cases given the prevailing rate of bank minimum lending rates at the time of writing but it may be that in any given case the plaintiff may wish to argue for a higher rate (or the defendant for a lower rate). It might be for example that the sum involved is a very large one which if placed on the money market might have procured for the person who has been wrongfully deprived of it over the period a considerably higher rate than 15 per cent. In the case of large sums it may be worth the party's while to argue the matter fully before the court.

PLEADING INTEREST

1.25 It is prescribed by the Rules of the Supreme Court that a party who claims interest must plead it. If no claim for interest is pleaded then unless leave to amend is given at the trial no interest can be awarded. The way in which interest should be pleaded is more particularly described in the section on pleadings (para. 6.10). In a personal injuries case it is sufficient to plead the claim to interest generally since it is not capable of exact calculation in view of the fact that unliquidated damages are being claimed. In a debt case the claim must be pleaded precisely where the right to interest arises under contract giving details of the amount accrued due at the contractual rate up to the date of issue of the writ together with a daily rate thereafter. Similarly in cases where there is no contractual provision for interest but the plaintiff is willing to accept the judgment debt rate of 15 per cent. it is both convenient and tactically wise for interest to be claimed at that rate in the pleadings and for the computations to be made in the same way as previously. This will enable the plaintiff to obtain interest should the case terminate before trial in one of the ways described below (para. 11.01).

Provisional damages in personal injury cases

In essence the award of damages in personal injury cases (and other cases) **1.26** has always been considered a "once and for all" award. That is to say that if an injured plaintiff who has settled the case or received judgment on the basis that his condition had a certain prognosis finds to his dismay that his condition rapidly deteriorates thereafter he cannot in principle go back to the court and seek further awards of damages. Nor is there any provision for the court to award damages in the form of amounts to be assessed period- ically which can be adjusted in view of changes in the plaintiff's condition. Such awards it might be pointed out would not necessarily only favour the plaintiff. It is by no means unknown for a plaintiff to receive a large award of damages on the basis of a very pessimistic prognosis for his future only to achieve considerable improvement and to be able to do what it was not expected he would ever do such as return to work. Usually there is no possibility in such a case for the defendants to receive reimbursement of any amount of the damages unless exceptionally the defendants were permitted leave to appeal out of time.

When settling a case on behalf of a plaintiff, or arguing for him at trial it was important therefore to have as clear a view as possible of his medical prognosis, and it would generally be considered negligent to attempt to settle a case before it was clear that the plaintiff's medical condition had stabilised. Where there is a great measure of uncertainty there are three options opened to the plaintiff's solicitor. These are respectively:

    (i) structured settlements;
   (ii) split trials;
  (iii) provisional damages.

(i) *Structured settlements*

Structured settlements are a very recent invention. It must be stressed that the court itself has no power whatsoever to order a structured settlement and if a case goes to trial then the judge must in essence make a "once and for all" award. In large complex cases however where plaintiffs' and defendants' legal advisers have been able to reach agreement, in the recent past settle- ments have been arrived at particularly in cases where plaintiffs will need a great deal of expensive medical and nursing care over the years to come, which provide for payment of compensation in the form of periodical payments. The exact drafting of these settlements is a matter of considerable complexity involving careful and specialist tax, pensions and insurance advice and is certainly beyond the scope of the present text. Carefully drafted settlements however have considerable advantages over "once and for all" payments and may be more just to both sides.

(ii) *Split trials*

There has for many years been a provision enabling a plaintiff to issue a summons asking the court for an order for split trials that is, separate trials of the issue of liability and quantum. If this order was made the case could proceed swiftly to a trial of liability whilst the memories of the witnesses of fact were fresh and without the added expense of calling expert evidence to court on matters relevant to quantum, particularly medical prognosis. Having won on liability it would then be possible for the plaintiff to obtain a substantial interim payment on account of eventual damages (see para. 13.01). If on the other hand the plaintiff should lose on liability then a great deal of legal expense in obtaining medical and other evidence relevant only to quantum of damages and a part of the trial that would have been devoted to assessment of such damages would be totally avoided. Applications for split trials were not particularly common and in a number of cases the reluctance of plaintiff's advisers to take advantage of this useful procedural possibility was criticised in the higher courts. It should be noted that there is now a specific provision requiring the court of its own motion to consider the possibility of split trials in personal injury cases and moreover, that this is one of the matters to which the court should devote its attention at the stage in the action known as Summons for Directions (see para. 8.01) in any kind of case. It is to be hoped therefore that this useful procedural provision will be more greatly used in the future.

(iii) *Provisional damages*

There are many kinds of cases where the plaintiff's prognosis is reasonably certain in every respect but one. The way in which it is not certain however is likely to cause a great deal of worry to a plaintiff and his legal advisers.

Common examples are that after a bone or joint injury most plaintiffs may anticipate a full recovery. A small proportion of plaintiffs however may, often in the distant future, contract osteo-arthritis in the joint affected. This is painful and indeed crippling. It is however impossible to predict with certainty whether any given plaintiff will sustain this deterioration. Similarly in accidents which have involved a bad concussion, statistically a small minority of plaintiffs develop epilepsy, again often in the distant future. The precise medical causes of this are unknown. Epilepsy, apart from the physical effects will have a number of disastrous social and professional consequences in many cases. For example if the plaintiff is a lorry driver who has apparently recovered completely from relatively modest injuries and has gone back to work as a driver, and should, in 10 years, develop epilepsy, one of the consequences of this will be that he will be forced to give up his driving licence with a very substantial consequent claim for loss of future earnings. If settlement is accepted on a "once and for all" basis nothing more can be done for such plaintiff. The way round that problem however is to apply for *provisional* damages.

This procedure was created by section 6 of the Administration of Justice Act 1982. The rules relevant to this, put simply, provide that a plaintiff may:

1. Obtain judgment as to liability at trial and then go on to obtain an award of damages which will be made on the assumption that his medical prognosis in relation to determined matters will *not* deteriorate.

2. The court must specify the type of disease or deterioration which it has been assumed will *not* occur for the purpose of the foregoing and application may be made to the court if the disease or deterioration *does* later occur. Further damages will then be assessed at the later hearing.

It is important to note that the court will not act on this matter of its own initiative. A claim for provisional damages must be pleaded so that the defendant is clearly aware of where he stands.

COUNSEL'S ADVICE ON QUANTUM

As indicated previously it is vital in any kind of litigation to keep the issue of quantum constantly under review for the purpose of realistic negotiations and for considering offers whether made in the course of negotiations or in the form of a payment into court (see later para. 12.01) whenever they are made. In a case of some complexity a solicitor is likely to ask counsel's advice on quantum of damages. The way in which counsel's advice should be obtained and the drafting of the necessary instructions is dealt with later.
1.27

2. The Financing of Civil Litigation

2.01   If a client goes in to see a solicitor in connection with some non-contentious matter such as conveyancing or probate then usually he has no illusions that any one will pay the solicitor's fees except himself. Clients who consult a solicitor about litigation however, or at least potential *plaintiffs* may well suffer from misconceptions about the question of the solicitor's fees. Three common misconceptions of litigation clients are, first that the solicitor will be prepared to wait till the very end of the case and that if the client wins he pays the solicitor's fees but that if he loses the solicitor is so disappointed that he makes no charge. Secondly, and equally optimistically that the solicitor will be prepared to wait to the end of the case to be paid and that if the client wins the solicitor's fees are paid direct by the losing opponent and the client has no obligation in relation to costs whatsoever; and thirdly that financial assistance is available almost automatically from the State for the purposes of litigation and that this is provided absolutely free of charge to the client.

It is therefore obvious that one has the essential job of disabusing one's client of these or other misconceptions and making perfectly clear the basis of one's professional relationship at the very outset. For the businesslike conduct of litigation it is usually essential to obtain substantial payments in advance from the client and to ensure that payments in advance from the client continue to be made throughout the course of the litigation so that the solicitor is always so to speak "ahead" of his own bills in terms of the money he is holding. The money when received should be paid into the firm's client account. Fees for work in litigation matters are worked out on the basis of actual time spent in the conduct of the client's case whether this represents interviews in the office, collecting evidence, attending court for the trial or preliminary hearings. Efficient firms prepare accounts for the client on a quarterly basis and send to the client every three months an account of the work they have done in the preceding quarter. Once having delivered this bill they are in principle entitled to transfer the money which they hold from the firm's client account to the firm's office account (*i.e.* this money now becomes the solicitor's firm's own money). If this exhausts the money being held then the letter sending the bill to the client should include a request for a further substantial payment on account. It ought to be said here that a vital part of running a successful litigation practice is to ensure that one's clients are satisfied. This involves giving one's clients a full account of the progress of the case and in particular trying to give an honest idea of how long a case will last. Nothing is more unsettling for a client than to have the impression that his case will last a matter of weeks only to find that it is strung out over some years by procedural developments which his solicitor may mention to him but of whose real nature he has not the remotest conception. It is thus vital to keep one's clients happy by telling them what is happening and explaining the meaning of technical terms used such as discovery or third party proceedings. This is particularly important for plaintiff clients in personal injuries actions who may be particularly vulnerable to the effect of

24

lengthy delays especially if, as is not uncommon, they are suffering financial hardship as a result of loss of income due to their disabilities.

There are three cogent reasons why it is important for solicitors to ensure **2.02** that they are paid in advance in civil proceedings in the manner previously described.

1. Litigation is often very long drawn out—a minimum of two years and something like three years on average in the case of personal injury actions which go all the way to trial. If no money was received until the end of the case then too much of the firm's assets would be represented by "work in progress" and serious cash flow problems could be caused to the practice.

2. To conduct litigation at all the solicitor will in any case have to pay out large disbursements and unless advances are received from the client these will inevitably have to be paid by the solicitor from his office account, that is from the practice's own money. For example the fee on a High Court writ is now £70; medical reports rarely cost less than £50; police accident reports cost of the order of £40 and so on. If therefore a solicitor has a substantial personal injury practice with say several hundred files current at any one time and acts mainly for plaintiffs it is easy to see that very large sums will be outstanding on his office account and the practice will have little alternative but to run on an overdraft.

3. The last and perhaps most conclusive reason is that if a solicitor should lose a case for a client it is an unfortunate but notoriously true fact that the unsuccessful client in litigation tends to blame his solicitor. Despite the fact that the reason for losing may well be that the client himself has been exposed in the witness box as untruthful even such a client tends to feel that a better lawyer might have protected him from the consequences of his untruthfulness being exposed and the case would still have been won. Unsuccessful clients in litigation place the payment of their own solicitor's costs as a relatively low priority. Accordingly there may be considerable difficulty in obtaining payment of costs at all and indeed one may in the end be forced to the unpleasant step of suing one's former client for the costs. It should also be borne in mind that if the litigation has been lost the client may well have been ordered to pay his successful opponent's costs and indeed if the client is the defendant and has lost he may have been ordered to pay damages to the plaintiff as well. Such clients may therefore have more calls upon their funds than they are able to meet.

Quite apart from the wasteful use of time represented by having to sue one's own client it is any way generally undesirable for this to occur. A client who has lost a case even if he is disgruntled in the immediate aftermath may very well still continue to come back to his own solicitor however inept he personally may feel the solicitor is on the basis of "better the devil you know than the devil you don't." If, as is more probable his solicitor has not been inept but the client's own case has been lost because of some legal point or conflict of evidence resolved in the opposing party's favour then the client, when he has overcome his disappointment, will generally have the good grace to recognise this and continue to use the services of the same solicitor.

If however litigation to obtain payment of the solicitor's costs has been necessary it is most unlikely that the client will return to the same solicitor. If the client has paid in advance then even unsuccessful litigation will prove to be less painful and the client is likely to come back.

2.03 To summarise therefore, in the case of the privately paying client one should first explain that he will have to pay your costs whatever the outcome of the case but that if he wins he may generally obtain an order that the loser pays a very substantial proportion of his costs and provided this can be enforced against the loser he may in the end have very little liability for costs. He should also be made aware that if he loses the case he may have to pay a substantial proportion of the opponent's costs as well.

Secondly, one should then obtain a substantial sum of money in advance giving him an outline of the early course of litigation and the reasons why a good deal of time will have to be expended on getting the case off the ground to say nothing of the disbursements which will be necessary. He should also be made aware that he will be required to pay further regular sums as the litigation progresses. The advance should be paid into clients account in the client's name. Interim bills, probably every quarter, should be delivered to the client and funds transferred to meet those bills to the office account thus ensuring a regular flow of cash for the practice.

Thirdly at the end of the case if the client has won one then will attempt to recover as much as possible towards the costs from the losing opponent and if one is successful in this one will naturally use that money to reimburse the client for the sums which he has already paid on account of costs.

2.04 That would represent the standard practice. There may however be very substantial variations and indeed often this will occur in those cases where firms do have substantial personal injury practices or debt collecting practices. What has been described might be considered as the best practice in the case of an individual fee paying client. However, much personal injury litigation for plaintiffs is undertaken on behalf of trade unions who use part of their income to provide benefits of various kinds for their members one of which is to support them in personal injury litigation in respect of accidents occurring in the course of employment. In such cases neither the individual trade union member nor the trade union generally pay money in advance to their solicitors. In such cases in exchange for a constant supply of good quality litigation clients the solicitors are prepared to waive any requirement to be paid money on account and to await the end of the case before delivering the bill to the trade union client. Even in such cases however the trade unions are now likely to be asked to pay disbursements as the cases go along to cover fees for the writ, medical reports and so on which will mount up to a substantial sum even in a routine case, by the time the matter come to court.

Further it is important to remember that almost all defendants in personal injury cases are covered by insurance. As we shall subsequently see it will inevitably be a term of the insurance policy that an insurance company is entitled to its own choice of solicitors to represent the insured person rather than permitting the latter to go to his own solicitor. The insurance company will naturally choose a firm in each locality who is known to be expert in the field of defendant's personal injury litigation. The arrangements which such firms come to with their insurance company clients vary considerably and may involve the payment of substantial retainers or may merely involve the insurance company paying the disbursements as the case proceeds and only paying the solicitor's costs at the end. Similarly finance companies or others who have substantial debt collecting litigation will employ the same firm and have some arrangement with the firm about the way in which they are to pay bills. And even where none of these matters apply a firm of solicitors might decide in the case of any individual client that the client is a sufficiently old client or sufficiently trustworthy for the firm to conduct the litigation without demanding payment in advance. It would still generally be financially prudent to deliver interim bills.

The final and most important exception to the principle of obtaining pay-   **2.05** ment in advance is in the case of a legally aided client. In legal aid cases one cannot generally obtain payment either in advance or on account as the litigation progresses though to this principle there are two exceptions. Firstly, where a client is legally aided payment of *disbursements* as one goes along can be made. As we shall see one simply applies to the Area Director indicating what the disbursement was, (*e.g.* writ fee, medical report, etc.) and requesting reimbursement of the amount which is then made direct from the Legal Aid Board who administer the legal aid fund. Secondly a relatively recent practice has been to make interim payments from the legal aid fund to solicitors at a standard rate per case for each legal aid case which the firm is currently conducting. This is a welcome step forward in assisting the liquidity of many firms which have large numbers of cases for legally aided clients.

Legal advice and assistance and legal aid

It is important to note that it is both unprofessional and negligent for a   **2.06** solicitor to fail to advise a client of the existence of the legal aid schemes. Even if the solicitor himself does not do legal aid work he is still obliged to inform potential clients of the existence of such schemes.

Legal aid is administered by the Legal Aid Board under the provisions of the Legal Aid Act 1988. Under the scheme England and Wales is divided into a number of areas and each has an Area Director who is in charge of legal aid locally. There is also a substantial supporting clerical and administrative staff to process the enormous number of legal aid applications which are received. Each area also has an area committee. This consists of solicitors and barristers in private practice who are paid a small fee for attending the area office on a rota basis to decide various matters concerning legal aid. Legal aid applications may be submitted to any area office but as a matter of convenience such applications are submitted to the office of the area in which the solicitor practises. We shall describe legal aid proper shortly but first it is appropriate to describe the legal advice and assistance scheme known generally as "The Green Form Scheme" from the colour of the form on which application for legal advice and assistance is made.

THE SCOPE OF THE GREEN FORM SCHEME

The Green Form Scheme permits a solicitor to give a client who qualifies   **2.07** under the scheme advice and assistance. Any person may obtain advice from a solicitor about any matter to which English law applies with some few exceptions. In general the matter may be either contentious or non-contentious and it may cover any work a solicitor may properly do for a client except taking a step in proceedings. The exceptions provide that advice and assistance in the making of a will are excluded in most cases unless the client is aged 70 or over or in some other restrictive categories; similarly advice and assistance in conveyancing services is in general excluded from the scheme.

With these exceptions however the advice and assistance given could cover such matters as advice in connection with deeds, (*e.g.* the interpretation of a restrictive covenant); conducting correspondence on behalf of a client; entering into negotiations on behalf of a client; drafting documents; interviewing witnesses; giving a client advice relating to future proceedings whether as a potential plaintiff or defendant or even, when proceedings have already commenced giving a client advice on how he, the client, may best continue with the proceedings. Thus for example for a litigant in person who requires assistance under the Green Form Scheme a solicitor could properly draft a pleading or give advice on procedure or tactics.

2.08 The solicitor may not however under the Green Form take any step in the proceedings on behalf of the client. That is to say the solicitor may not *represent* the client in the proceedings as such. There is one exception to this known as "assistance by way of representation." This is limited in civil proceedings (other than matrimonial proceedings) to cases where the court itself authorises any solicitor within the precincts of the court to represent a person who is appearing in the court. For example suppose that a solicitor was attending an appointment for a client before a district judge in chambers in the county court; suppose also that another litigant in person was to appear in an earlier case and some difficult point arose on which the registrar considered it desirable that the litigant in person should receive immediate legal advice. If the client qualified on means the district judge could authorise the solicitor who was present in court on his own client's business to assist the unrepresented person at the hearing before him. This would be entirely as a matter of speed and convenience and would always be an alternative to adjourning the proceedings so that the unrepresented person might apply for legal aid proper.

As far as we are concerned however the use of the Green Form will be for the preliminaries of litigation and particularly for preparing a case so that an application for legal aid proper can be made.

ELIGIBILITY UNDER THE GREEN FORM SCHEME

2.09 The test for eligibility under the Green Form scheme is purely financial. There is no need for the solicitor to investigate the merits of the client's case so the solicitor need not feel that the client has in any sense a winning case. For example the Green Form could be used to assist a client who admitted liability for a debt to negotiate payments by instalments or, if proceedings had already been commenced, to give the client advice as to how he himself could make application to the court to be allowed to pay by instalments. The assessment of financial eligibility is carried out immediately the client sees the solicitor. In every case the solicitor ought to ask the client (unless he already knows him from some previous occasion and is aware of his means) whether he requires assistance under the Green Form scheme and if the client has not heard of the latter some very brief general questions about the client's means ought to be asked there and then. On the assumption that the client is not obviously disqualified on the grounds of means there will then be an exact assessment of financial eligibility. The solicitor uses a "key card" which enables him to take financial details from the client and to assess quickly whether the client qualifies. The key card is used to compute the client's net disposable income after deducting from his gross income, tax, national insurance contributions and certain fixed allowances for dependants. No allowances are made for such outgoings as rent, or mortgage repayments because the allowances for these are inbuilt into the other allowances. If the client's income and capital are then below a certain net disposable figure he qualifies for legal assistance without any contribution on his part. If the client however has disposable income above the minimum figure but is still below a certain higher limit then he may obtain legal advice but will need to pay a contribution towards it assessed by reference to a scale.

Under the scheme a solicitor is entitled to work for a client for a total of up to two hours in an ordinary case. Solicitors are paid for their work on a fixed hourly rate which is adjusted from time to time. As a matter of interest the hourly rate at the time of writing is £42 per hour, except in London where the rate is £44.50. Thus the limit of the work which a solicitor can do outside London at the moment is £84.

If the client has a contribution to pay then it is important to note that the solicitor should collect the contribution at the outset and must exhaust it first.

Example:
Suppose that a client had a net disposable income such that he would have to pay a contribution of £12. Having assessed the contribution the solicitor should immediately collect it from the client. The solicitor would then commence giving advice. Suppose that the client had a very straightforward legal problem and could be comprehensively advised about it in let us say just over a quarter of an hour. Under the Green Form scheme, as we have seen, solicitors charge at fixed hourly rates and in fact £12 would just about cover the cost of a little less than 20 minutes legal advice. If therefore in the present case the solicitor had given precisely that amount of legal advice he would simply keep the £12 as his costs and that would be the end of the matter. The solicitor would not then need to make any claim from the Legal Aid Board for a further fee, the money received from the client by way of contribution representing the fee.

Suppose however in the same example the client's case necessitated longer advice so that the solicitor in fact did £50 of work under the Green Form scheme. In that case having collected the £12 from the client he would in due course make a claim to the Legal Aid Board for the balance of £38 to represent a total of £50 (together with V.A.T. on the whole).

If at the first interview the client does not have the £12 with him then it is within the solicitor's discretion whether or not to demand the money as a pre-condition of giving any assistance at all. He may trust the client and go on to give the necessary advice hoping that the client will return with the money. If the client does not return with the £12 the solicitor would still only be able to claim the balance expended over that figure, e.g. if he did a total of £50 worth of work he would then only recover the £38 from the Legal Aid Board.

29

2.10   The basic limit of two hours work may be exceeded in an appropriate case with the prior authority of the Legal Aid Board which is obtained by applying on a prescribed form to the Area Office. In an appropriate case where full legal aid is not available (let us say a difficult matter involving advice about how a client should represent himself before an Immigration Appeal Tribunal) substantial extensions may be obtained, perhaps up to several hundred pounds where the Area Office considers that the case merits it. However if full legal aid is available (*i.e.* for ordinary proceedings in the county court or High Court) it is unusual to have an extension granted because the Area Director is likely to insist that the client applies for full legal aid to cover further steps in the proceedings so that, as we shall see below, a full assessment of the merits of the client's case as well as of financial eligibility can be made.

2.11   For what can the two hours' amount of fees be spent?
      It can cover the solicitor's time as previously described whether engaged in advice, correspondence or drafting. It can however also cover disbursements. Thus for example if the matter is particularly complex the solicitor may obtain counsel's advice on behalf of the client. Equally it may be used to finance other kinds of disbursements, *e.g.* to write off to obtain a police report of an accident if this can be obtained within the total figure.

2.12   When the solicitor has completed his work under a Green Form and wishes to claim costs he simply fills in the back of the form indicating the time expended on the matter together with details of any other specific elements, *e.g.* the number of letters written or telephone calls made and any disbursements incurred and makes a claim by sending this form into the Area Office of the Legal Aid Board. In fact the practice is to wait until a solicitor has a number of such forms to send in and send them in batches of a dozen or so at a time. Payment will then be made by the Legal Aid Board. So far as we are concerned the most important use of the Green Form will be for the preliminaries of litigation and particularly for completing an application form for full legal aid. As will be seen this involves considerably more than a mere statement of means and we shall now consider the nature of an application for full legal aid.

THE NATURE OF LEGAL AID

2.13   The effect of legal aid is simply that a solicitor who acts for a legally aided person who is known as "an assisted person" is guaranteed that he will be paid whatever the outcome of the case. The Legal Aid scheme covers actions including inter alia actions in tort and contract in the High Court and county court (with the exception of defamation proceedings).

PROCEDURE FOR APPLYING FOR LEGAL AID

2.14   Application is made by completing an appropriate form. This form is in two parts and contains a statement of means which is considerably more detailed than the statement required for the Green Form, and a statement of the client's case. In the case of full legal aid, legal aid is granted on two tests: financial eligibility, and on the ground that the applicant can show that he has reasonable grounds for taking or defending or being a party to proceedings. Unlike in the case of the Green Form therefore the client must show that he has some prospect of winning the case. Legal aid would not generally be available for example where a defendant admitted liability but merely wished to be represented on an application to the court for time to pay. It is generally essential that a client should show that he is likely to win. Despite this requirement it is by no means unusual for both parties to a case to receive legal aid for the same matter. This is because in essence one is only obliged to submit one's own version of the facts in one's legal aid application (although correspondence received from the opposing party is required to be sent with it). Thus each party may produce just a version of the facts which favours himself. For this reason it is important to send any documents which assist in showing that the applicant has a good case (*e.g.* police accident report).

Legal aid is not generally available to those who are entitled to obtain representation from some other source. Thus legal aid would not be applied for by an insured defendant in a personal injury case since he would be entitled anyway to legal representation under the terms of his insurance policy. Likewise applicants who are entitled to financial assistance for the purpose of bringing proceedings from their trade union or other source are required to indicate this on the legal aid application form.

When the application form is received in the Area Office the part relating to **2.15** means is detached and sent to the Department of Social Security. They make a calculation of the applicant's disposable income and capital. This is a considerably more sophisticated process than the computation of eligibility under the Green Form scheme and involves consideration not only of gross and net income and dependants but also certain other allowances, *e.g.* for mortgage, rent, rates. The D.S.S. may call the person for interview and in this case he will be asked to bring with him documentary proof of his means. It should be noted that where a solicitor ascertains financial eligibility under the Green Form scheme, no evidence of means is required to be produced. A solicitor is entitled to act on the basis that the client is telling him the truth about his means without demanding to see recent wage slips or bank statements. Where the D.S.S. interview for full legal aid they will require full documentary evidence to be brought.

Financial eligibility will then be determined. As in the case of Green Form Assistance a party may either qualify without paying a contribution; he may be disqualified entirely because his means exceed the upper limits for legal aid; or he may fall between the two and be required to make a contribution. The contribution may be ordered in one lump sum or in instalments. The applicant will be notified of the maximum contribution required. A client who is offered legal aid with a maximum contribution of say £500 should be clearly advised about the meaning of this. It by no means follows that he will need to pay this whole sum if he wins the case. It may be that the costs recoverable from the opposing party will cover the whole of his costs in which case his contribution will be returned to him. If however a party did lose a case then it is likely that the whole of the contribution would be lost.

Where the D.S.S. conclude that a person is financially eligible for legal aid the application then needs to be considered on its merits. The Area Office will decide on the apparent merits of the case on the information supplied. It is fair to say that applications are decided in a fairly liberal way unless it is quite clear even on the applicant's own version that he has little chance.

Apart from the merits as such (*i.e.* probability of winning) a further matter is to consider whether it is *reasonable* for the applicant to have public money expended on legal representation. For example if the matter concerns something that is relatively trivial then even though the applicant may be able to establish a prima facie right, legal aid may be refused.

2.16 If legal aid is granted it is not granted in general terms. A legal aid certificate does not say for example "X is granted legal aid to take proceedings to obtain damages for personal injury." It will name the person against whom proceedings are to be taken. One consequence of this is that if at a later stage it becomes apparent that there should be some additional or different defendant application will need to be made to the Area Office to amend the legal aid certificate. The certificate must be filed with the court when proceedings are commenced. Notice of the issue of the certificate must be given to all other parties in the case because the grant of legal aid has certain important tactical and practical consequences. Civil legal aid is not retrospective and does not cover work done before the issue of the certificate and therefore one should always apply for legal aid as soon as possible. A legal aid application currently takes (with some local variation) some six to eight weeks to be considered.

2.17 If legal aid is refused on the ground of *means* then there is no appeal. If however it is refused on the question of *merits* or as to whether it is *reasonable* to expend public money then an appeal may be made to the Area Committee who will reconsider the matter. It is possible to have oral representation before the Area Committee but the Green Form scheme will not cover this and therefore the client would have to pay a solicitor to represent him.

CONDITIONAL AND UNCONDITIONAL CERTIFICATES; THE SCOPE OF THE CERTIFICATE

2.18 It ought to be remarked that once the Legal Aid certificate is granted it may be granted for the whole proceedings that is it may be *unconditional*. As an alternative it may be *conditional*. A conditional certificate will authorise the solicitor to act for the client only up to a certain stage in proceedings after which the solicitor must report back to the Area Office to confirm that the solicitor is still optimistic about the prospect of success in the case.

Example:
Suppose that there is a dispute where it is reasonably apparent that the outcome can be more successfully predicted after the stage of *discovery of documents* (*i.e.* where each side is entitled to see the documents relevant to the case held by the other side). In such a case it may well be that the legal aid certificate when issued will be limited "to all matters up to and including the discovery of documents." After this stage therefore the solicitor will be obliged to report back to the Area Committee to confirm that in the light of the documents of which discovery has been obtained he still regards the case as one which ought to be won. Other examples of limitations would be a limitation that legal aid is granted only to obtain counsel's opinion as to the likely outcome of the case or up to the close of pleadings.

A solicitor must act within the scope of the legal aid certificate when granted. This does not however mean that he is limited to just carrying out the bare procedure necessary to get the client's action to trial. In the course of acting for the client he may take all proper tactical steps. Legal aid may for example thus cover correspondence and negotiations between the parties, attempts to trace witnesses, the interviewing of witnesses and so on. It does not merely cover the actual drafting of procedural documents or hearings before the court.

Even if legal aid is unconditional it does not imply that the solicitor has carte blanche to spend any amount of money. The prior authority of the Area Office must be obtained for various steps, for instance instructing a Queen's Counsel in a case. It is advisable anyway to seek prior authority for taking any unusual steps or steps which involve the incurring of large expenditure, *e.g.* obtaining a report from a particularly expensive expert witness. In such cases it is also vital to obtain the client's approval to the proposed step after giving a clear explanation of what is involved. This is because as we shall see subsequently although the client may have obtained legal aid this ought for some purposes merely to be viewed as a loan. It may be that despite the receipt of legal aid even a winning client will be called upon to pay a part of his own costs and to reimburse the legal aid fund for such costs. Accordingly even a legally aided client may well have an interest in the cost of the conduct of the case.

AMENDMENT, REVOCATION AND DISCHARGE OF LEGAL AID
CERTIFICATES

Amendment

A legal aid certificate can be amended in the course of proceedings. Applica- **2.19**
tion to amend is made by a letter to the Area Office setting out the reason why amendment is required and any supporting documentation (*e.g.* counsel's advice about the matter). A typical amendment has already been mentioned and that would be to add a second defendant where the need to do so emerged only after obtaining the first legal aid certificate and in the course of proceedings. The amended certificate when received should be filed at court and notice of the nature of the amendment given to all other parties. Clients are financially re-assessed from time to time as the limits for legal aid change or indeed as their own income and outgoings change. Amendments may also therefore relate to the client's contribution. In this case however although the amended legal aid certificate must be filed with the court no notice of the nature of the amendment need be given to the other parties. The other parties are not in any event made aware of the size of the client's contribution or whether he has to pay a contribution at all.

Revocation

A certificate may be revoked. This implies that a client has in some way **2.20**
misled the legal aid authorities into granting legal aid. For example if a client was subsequently discovered to have told a highly material lie about the merits of the case or to have lied about his means. Where a certificate is revoked the effect is as if there had never been a grant of legal aid. The legally aided client's solicitor will be entitled to be paid by the legal aid fund

for all work done up until the date of revocation, however the fact that the client is now deemed never to have had legal aid may be important in relation to his *opponent's costs* as we shall see hereafter.

Discharge

2.21 The discharge of a certificate may occur on the conclusion of all steps in the proceedings (which may include steps for enforcement of judgments in addition to the steps taken to obtain judgment). Certificates may also be discharged earlier. For example a client whose means have risen above the legal aid limit may have his certificate discharged as may a client who requires proceedings to be conducted in an unreasonable manner. The effect is that the client has the protection of legal aid for tactical purposes (see below) whilst the certificate lasted and of course his solicitor is entitled to be paid for the work done so far but after discharge the client is no longer legally aided. This does not itself bring about the end of the case because the client is perfectly entitled to continue as a litigant in person or indeed to pay another solicitor (or the same solicitor if the solicitor is willing to continue to act). This might be the case, *e.g.* where the certificate was discharged on the ground of the client's means having risen above the legal aid limit.

THE EFFECT OF LEGAL AID ON THE SOLICITOR/CLIENT RELATIONSHIP

2.22 In principle a legally aided client is in the same position as any other client with the single exception of the payment of costs. Thus the solicitor owes the same duties of confidentiality to the client, has the same fiduciary duty in regard to any funds which come into his hands on the client's behalf (*e.g.* the damages when received) and the duties implied by the law of contract and tort still exist. The solicitor is likewise bound by the rules of professional practice. There is however one important difference. This is caused by the fact that the solicitor owes duties to the legal aid fund in addition to those which he owes the client and for this purpose the solicitor may be required to breach the basic principle of confidentiality about a client's affairs.

A common situation is the case where the solicitor comes to the view that a client no longer has reasonable grounds for continuing the litigation or the client asks him to conduct the proceedings in an unreasonable way. Two examples are as follows;

Example 1:
Suppose that as the litigation progresses and more evidence comes into the solicitor's hands it becomes apparent that the client now only has, say, a 20 per cent. chance of success in the action. The solicitor advises the client of this. However, the client, who has obtained legal aid with a nil contribution, stands to win a considerable amount of money if he is successful in the litigation. He may feel that since the ligitation is costing him nothing litigation with a 20 per cent. chance of success is perfectly reasonable. He may instruct the solicitor therefore to press on. At this stage the solicitor would have a duty to notify the Legal Aid Board of what had arisen. Whilst a client who stands to lose nothing and has a one-in-five chance of winning may feel it worth going on, the solicitor is obliged to advise the client as if he were "a privately paying client of moderate means." Accordingly when the reasonable advice to discontinue the action in view of the slight chance of success is

neglected the matter should be reported to the Legal Aid Board who will in such a case inevitably discharge the legal aid certificate.

Example 2:

Suppose in county court litigation concerning personal injuries counsel has advised that there is a serious risk that the plaintiff will lose outright and that the case on full liability is worth about £2,000 to £2,500. The defendants make an offer of £2,000 plus costs. The solicitor is of the very clear opinion that this must be accepted in view of the risk of losing outright and of the fact that it is anyway within the bracket which counsel has advised. The client however refuses to accept the advice. If the client were privately paying then the solicitor would naturally continue and follow the client's instructions, the risk of the litigation being the client's. In our example however, the risks are partly the legal aid fund's since if the client loses outright the legal aid fund will have a substantial deficit for the solicitor's costs. Accordingly the solicitor would be obliged, if he felt the client was unreasonable, to report the matter to the Legal Aid Board. This would again inevitably lead to the discharge of the legal aid certificate if the client maintained his refusal of the reasonable offer.

This aspect of acting for legally aided clients is an extremely difficult one in practice. Although on the examples previously given matters are fairly clear all practising solicitors could relate more borderline examples. For example difficult clients who insist on interviews every week (or more frequently) despite the fact that the case has not progressed in the interim and there is really nothing to discuss and thus that the time is merely wasted possibly at the legal aid fund's eventual expense; and indeed cases where the solicitor becomes aware that the client has misled the legal aid authorities in relation to his means.

In such cases reporting of suspicious circumstances or the client's unreasonable behaviour is a duty which one owes to the legal aid fund and will represent a breach of the usual rule of confidentiality in relation to a client's affairs.

We turn now to the question of the cost consequences of legal aid in civil proceedings.

THE COSTS CONSEQUENCES SO FAR AS THE CLIENT HIMSELF IS
CONCERNED

Where a client is legally aided the solicitor may not obtain money from that **2.23** client in relation to that matter. This is not to say that a solicitor may not also have an ordinary fee paying relationship with the client in regard to *some other* matter, *e.g.* a client who wishes to have a will prepared at the same time as receiving legal aid for litigation. Consequently it is wrong for a solicitor to deliver a bill to a client in respect of the legally aided matter. The solicitor will have his bill of costs assessed by the court by a procedure known as *taxation* which we shall consider subsequently. The solicitor will then be paid out of the legal aid fund the full amount of his costs and in this context the word costs means both his own fees, his "profit costs" and his disbursements being those sums he had paid out on the client's behalf for the conduct of the litigation.

The consequences therefore are that where a legally aided plaintiff has won, his solicitor will be paid his costs from the legal aid fund. However as we shall see shortly there will also usually be an order that the defendant will be ordered to pay the plaintiff's costs. Where the defendant is solvent and is able to pay this amount and does so (and in personal injuries litigation since the defendant will inevitably be insured recovery of these costs ought to be guaranteed), there will thus be, as it were a refund, made to the assisted person's solicitor, of a large proportion of, and perhaps all the costs incurred. The solicitor is then required to pass on these costs recovered from the losing party to reimburse the legal aid fund. In some cases therefore the legal aid fund may have no net outlay in connection with the case. If this happens so that the legal aid fund is wholly reimbursed for the costs it has had to pay out to the assisted person's solicitor then any contribution which the assisted person has had to make for the grant of legal aid will be refunded to him.

If however the defendant is not ordered to pay the costs in full or does not pay any order that is made so that the legal aid fund is thereby put to some loss then it has under section 16 of the Legal Aid Act 1988 a statutory charge over any money or property which the plaintiff has recovered or preserved in the action.

Let us take two examples to demonstrate the operation of the charge.

Example 1:
An assisted person who is a plaintiff in a debt case obtains judgment for £5,000. The legal aid fund have to pay his solicitors a sum of £1,000 for costs. The order made against the defendant is not that he pay all the costs but (because of various matters we shall consider subsequently) he is only ordered to pay approximately two thirds of them, let us say £650. In this case the Legal Aid Board have suffered a net outlay of £350. They therefore have a charge on the £5,000 recovered and the plaintiff's solicitors must retain this sum until such time as all questions of costs are dealt with or at least such proportion of the sum as will cover any question of costs. Accordingly the plaintiff suffers a deduction from the damages he has received of £350, the amount which is the difference between what the defendant has paid and what the Legal Aid Board have had to pay out to his solicitors.

Example 2:
Suppose a legally aided plaintiff succeeds in an action for possession of land. Here no money changes hands and in this situation, (using the same figures), the Legal Aid Board's charge for the balance of the costs not recovered from the losing party attaches to the land itself as an equitable mortgage and will be registered as such. Accordingly, the successful party will have to redeem the charge as and when he is able, by payment of the £350.

2.24   It should be noted that the Legal Aid Board has no discretion to waive the charge even though its operation causes hardship. The examples given are relatively straightforward. As we shall see, however, when we come to consider one particular procedural tactic known as "payment into court" it may well be possible for a plaintiff to recover a substantial sum of money but not in the end to receive an order for costs against a defendant in respect of the whole case. Reference to the section on payment into court (para. 12.01) hereafter ought to be made for a full explanation of the costs consequences. It might well be therefore that a plaintiff recovers say £10,000 but is firstly ordered to pay part of his opponent's costs and second has to bear his own costs for a substantial part of the proceedings. The net effect of all this may well be that in such a case the Legal Aid Board's charge together with the opponent's order for costs eat up much of the amount in question. The inter-relation of costs orders on payment into court and the operation of the Legal Aid Board's charge ought carefully to be explained to the client on any occasion where a payment into court is made. A more comprehensive example will be given later in the text at para. 12.10.

THE COSTS OF OPPONENTS OF LEGALLY AIDED PARTIES

Where a legally aided party is unsuccessful then it will not affect the amount   **2.25**
which his solicitor receives as remuneration. His solicitor will be paid on the basis previously described out of the legal aid fund.

In principle an unsuccesfully legally aided party could be ordered to pay his opponent's costs. However one must have regard to section 17 of the Legal Aid Act 1988. This section provides that where an assisted person is granted legal aid and loses then the court shall only make an order that he pay "such part of his opponent's costs as is reasonable in all the circumstances for him to have to pay having regard to the means of the parties and their conduct in relation to the case." As will be observed this is a very potent tactical advantage for an impecunious legally aided party. It means that in certain kinds of litigation it may well be uneconomic for his opponents to contest the case at all because they are unlikely to recover their legal costs even if they win, and this may be more than the amount claimed. For example consider county court litigation in respect of some fairly trivial personal injury, let us say a broken finger and two weeks' loss of earnings totalling say £800 in value. Where the plaintiff is legally aided the effect of section 17 will be such that it is likely to cost the defendants more to defend the case even successfully than to make a reasonable offer to settle the claim.

Where under section 17 the court does assess what amount it is reasonable for a legally aided party to pay very often the court decides that it is not reasonable to require him to pay anything at all. Sometimes quite artificially (for there is no justification for this whatsoever under section 17) the court will limit his liability to a sum equal to the amount that he has been ordered to pay by way of contribution to the legal aid fund. Alternatively the court may specify some relatively low round sum figure, *e.g.* £100.

Whilst tactically highly advantageous to the legally aided person the effect of   **2.26**
section 17 is obviously capable of causing great hardship. A person of modest means who is not entitled to legal aid might well be put to great legal expense in defending proceedings brought by a legally aided plaintiff and have those proceedings determined entirely in his own favour only to have to bear his own costs. There is therefore a provision which mitigates the full effect of section 17. This is contained in section 18 of the Legal Aid Act 1988 and it provides that where proceedings are brought by a legally aided party against a person who does not have legal aid the court can order payment of the defendant's costs out of the legal aid fund directly. It is important to note however that there is a number of conditions:

1.   The legally aided party must have been the plaintiff and the successful party the defendant.

2. The defendant must not himself have been in receipt of legal aid.

3. The court must first consider the *personal liability* of the legally aided party to pay any costs under section 17 of the Act.

4. The court must be satisfied that it is *just and equitable* to make the order under section 18 in favour of the winning unassisted party.

5. The court must (in proceedings at first instance) be satisfied that the defendant will suffer *severe financial hardship* unless the order is made.

This latter requirement of severe financial hardship has been construed so as to exclude from the operation of the section only large companies and really wealthy people. It has been suggested that it does not exclude even a prosperous professional man who may well have a substantial income on the face of it but one which is already devoted to commitments consistent with his lifestyle.

Where a defendant has been successful against a legally aided party an application under section 18 is usually made at the conclusion of the trial. However at that stage there will be nobody present to represent the Legal Aid Board who are the guardians of the legal aid fund. There are two possible courses of procedure here. Firstly the court may adjourn the application to give the Legal Aid Board an opportunity to be represented. Where this happens naturally the cost will be considerably increased and the non-legally aided defendant will be facing a further fee for his advocate to attend the adjourned hearing to present the argument for the application of section 18.

It will nonetheless usually be in his interests to do so. Alternatively it is possible for the court to make a provisional order which will give the Legal Aid Board an opportunity to make representations at a later stage if it objects to the order. If it does not object, or is unsuccessful in its objection then the order takes effect and the successful defendant will be paid his costs from the legal aid fund.

This provision only applies to proceedings at first instance. In appeals the court has a wider discretion to make appropriate orders for costs to be paid either between the parties or out of the legal aid fund.

COSTS

2.27 So far we have considered how a party may finance his own litigation. In addition to the matters previously dealt with it is important to note that usually a winning party will obtain an order that his losing opponent pay all, or a proportion of his costs. A solicitor may not accept remuneration by a contingency fee, that is a fee which depends on success in litigation or on the amount recovered. However when advising clients about their position in regard to litigation it is essential to advise them of the effect of likely costs orders against a losing opponent, which may be such as to mean that where success seems probable a client may have no eventual call on him for costs at all. Although costs must be borne in mind at all stages of litigation, it is most appropriate to deal with the subject of costs fully and separately at the end of the text. A cursory preliminary reference to the section on costs may be appropriate at this stage however. The section is at para. 20.01.

3. Pre-Action Considerations

In this section we shall consider the matters with which it is appropriate to deal before issuing a writ. We shall first consider matters relevant in a personal injuries action where one is acting for a plaintiff and then subsequently (and considerably more briefly) the matters which one might need to consider in relation to an action in a consumer-type contract case.

PERSONAL INJURIES LITIGATION

In the next few pages an account will be given of the steps which a prudent **3.01** solicitor might take before issuing a writ. That is not to say that some of these steps cannot be postponed until after issuing a writ. However, it is as well to remember that one will need to serve a statement of claim within a matter of at the most a month after the writ has been served. Whilst a writ can be issued on the basis of relatively little information a statement of claim is a full pleading of the plaintiff's case and contains all the factual allegations which he proposes to make against the defendant and in addition in a personal injury case some details of his medical state. There is really little point in appearing dynamic and aggressive by issuing and serving a writ immediately one gets instructions if one subsequently has to go to the defendants to ask for an extension of time in which to serve the statement of claim. The better practice is to have the statement of claim ready in draft at the time of serving the writ or at least to ensure, if counsel is drafting the statement of claim, that it will be available within a week or so.

To suggest that one should take all the steps referred to hereafter, even in a **3.02** case in which they could all be applicable, is no doubt a counsel of perfection. Few solicitors would be inclined to deal with matters so thoroughly if for no other reason than because running a litigation practice is (compared to other forms of legal work) generally considered relatively unprofitable and practitioners tend to keep what one might describe as a "high volume" approach to litigation.

Thus even a thoroughly competent solicitor might not carry out all of the steps hereafter referred to, or at least not carry them out at the pre-action stage. For example whilst it is almost always rash to tell a client that he has an "open and shut case" on liability there are no doubt cases where a solicitor can make that judgment for himself. Thus for example if your client is a passenger in a vehicle which has been involved in a collision then unless some defence in the nature of so called "inevitable accident" is advanced (*e.g.* that a tyre burst unexpectedly with no negligence on anyone's part) one can be reasonably certain that the client is going to succeed against one or other of the drivers involved in the accident. Likewise a client who is knocked down on a zebra crossing or by a vehicle which is manifestly on the wrong side of the road at the time of the accident would also have a sufficiently clear cut case that a solicitor might well omit some of the following stages.

We shall now go on to consider the most important steps in turn. The matters can best be considered under the following headings:

1. Seeing the client for the first time.

2. Collecting information relative to liability.

3. Collecting information relevant to quantum.

4. Applications to the court before issuing a writ.

5. Motor insurance.

6. Negotiations.

The first meeting with the client

3.03 The eagerness of clients to obtain compensation in respect of a motor accident varies greatly. Some solicitors receive calls from anxious relatives asking them to visit an accident victim in hospital within a few days of the incident. Yet others, even very seriously injured persons, apparently *never* approach lawyers or attempt to obtain compensation for themselves at any stage. Another group and perhaps the largest, is content to wait until after the discharge from hospital to make an appointment with a solicitor. At this meeting it is obviously appropriate to give the client some very basic information about his legal position, that is to tell him simply that if fault on the part of some other person involved in the incident can be established he ought to receive damages and to give him an idea of the main heads of damages although preferably without mentioning figures in other than the vaguest way. The question of costs should be thoroughly discussed and the legal aid scheme briefly explained. It is unprofessional conduct not to explain the legal aid scheme even if the solicitor himself does not take legal aid cases, so that the client at least has the option of going elsewhere. It may be that costs do not need to be discussed at all as where the client is referred to a solicitor by his Trade Union under some kind of retainer system. On the assumption that those matters have been dealt with a statement should be taken from the client.

3.04 Techniques of taking this statement vary very considerably even between highly experienced litigation solicitors. Clients are notoriously poor at deciding what is relevant and what is irrelevant to their case. Even to describe how an accident happened or the position of vehicles on the road, can be very difficult indeed for a layperson. It is sometimes a good idea to get the client to draw an approximate plan of a road junction and even to use toy vehicles to enable him to show who did what, how and when. As well as matters of liability, it is probably a good idea to get the client to mention matters material to the main heads of damages so that questions pertinent to these can be raised when correspondence with his employers is begun. Thus for example, one should get a client to describe the nature of his earnings, whether they are seasonal, what bonuses, overtime, promotion opportunities, pension arrangements and perks he has and so on. He should be told to keep receipts now for all expenditure incurred as a result of the accident and to keep a careful note of future outgoings of the kind for which it is difficult to obtain receipts (*e.g.* taxi fares to hospital).

Some solicitors prefer to take jottings of the client's statement and then after the client has gone to dictate a fuller statement based on their jottings which can be typed. The typed statement is then sent to the client with a request for him to alter or amend it as appropriate. This does have certain advantages, in particular that of speed, over taking down longhand dictation from the client and if matters subsequently turn sour between the client and solicitor it avoids the client making an allegation that he was stampeded into taking the statement or that the solicitor took it down wrongly and the client just signed what was put before him. An important aspect of taking statements at this stage is to ensure that the client's version is fully recorded so far as possible in his own words and not in the solicitor's interpretation of those words. It is vital in any case to get such a statement signed and dated by the client either in the office or later by sending it to him under the procedure previously described. This is not so that the statement may be admissible if the client should later die, because the statement would be admissible any way whether or not signed and dated. It is to protect the solicitor himself. For example if at trial matters come out in a very different way from the client's version and the client is put in difficulties in cross-examination he may well allege that his own solicitor got his version of what occurred wrong. Whilst one would naturally not introduce the client's proof of evidence to discredit one's own client one can at least use it should any subsequent allegations of negligence in the taking of this statement be made.

At the end of taking the statement the client should be told a rough time scale for future action which should be realistic. That is to say that even if one is proceeding immediately to the preliminaries for the issue and service of the writ it is highly unlikely, except in the simplest and most minor of cases that any settlement of a client's claim will be achieved within the first six months. One should of course keep the client fully informed about the progress of his case through the various stages hereafter described.

Taking steps relevant to liability

THE POLICE ACCIDENT REPORT

3.05 One should generally send off for the police accident report book if the police were involved at the scene of the accident. The police accident report currently costs about £40 and therefore if one is sending off for this under the Green Form one can see that there is relatively little money left for covering the preliminary stages for interview and advice.

A letter is written addressed to the Chief Constable of the force in whose area the accident occurred and in due course an extract from the police accident report book will be sent. In some parts of the country police forces are very slow to deal with this request, but in any event the accident report will not be sent until any criminal proceedings and appeals arising from them have been concluded.

Whilst driving offences do come to court fairly swiftly as compared to the civil litigation process it may still be some months, especially if there have been adjournments, before the police accident report book is available. Of course it may not be until some months after the accident that the client has consulted a solicitor in which case it may be immediately available.

The police accident report is an extremely useful source of information about a number of matters. It comprises at the very least names and addresses of the people involved; the insurance particulars of any vehicles involved; witnesses' names and addresses and often statements; details of

41

vehicle damage; quite a good plan and scale drawing prepared by a policeman at the scene of the accident showing the layout of any junctions and the position of vehicles involved together with comments on road and weather conditions and details of whether there has been a prosecution or not and with what result.

If this can be obtained at a relatively early stage of one's investigation it saves a tremendous amount of leg work for the solicitor. For example although the statements from witnesses will have been obtained rather with view to a magistrates court prosecution than a High Court hearing these statements may well be sufficient at this stage. If witnesses are mentioned from whom statements haven't been taken (for instance because there are already sufficient eye witnesses who have given statements and taking further statements seemed superfluous to police at the scene) then one can interview those witnesses. The degree of detail one needs from witnesses obviously varies depending on the apparent complexity of the accident.

INTERVIEWING WITNESSES

3.06 If there has for some reason been no police accident report one would need to interview the witnesses. It may well be wise to interview witnesses even if there is already a brief statement in the police accident report in view of what was said earlier. Whilst some solicitors are inclined to leave interviewing witnesses until it is clear whether liability is disputed (because if liability is not disputed there is obviously no need to collect evidence about it) it is undoubtedly the better practice to interview them as soon as possible. Witnesses' memories fade remarkably quickly and even if they have seen a dramatic and memorable incident their recollection of it will be substantially worse if taking the statement is left for some months. It is increasingly common for firms of solicitors themselves to employ staff solely for the purpose of taking statements. Even those firms who do not employ their own staff for this purpose often use outside firms of enquiry agents. In either case the person is likely to be an ex-policeman with good experience of taking statements. Policemen who attended the accident, or witnessed it, may be interviewed and a fee is payable for this.

INSPECTING THE SCENE OF THE ACCIDENT

3.07 If the accident occurred fairly locally it can be a good idea for the solicitor himself to go to it to see the layout of the road and attempt to visualise how things must have occurred. It can be a good idea to make a sketch of the road or junction unless there is a good one in the police accident report and even to take photographs of it. Photographs may well be essential if there is any indication that the lay out of a junction might at some stage before trial be changed, *e.g.* by the introducton of a mini roundabout or the demolition or changing of a building which may have obscured the view from the junction. It may be advisable to arrange with a client to meet at the scene of the accident so he can point out just where the vehicles were on the road. Sight of the scene of the accident may also jog the client's memory about some vital detail which he forgot to mention whilst seeing the solicitor in his office.

EXAMINING THE DAMAGED VEHICLE

3.08 If one receives instructions early enough so that the vehicle is still in the state in which it was after the accident then it may be an idea to attempt to examine it. It may of course be that it is hard to discover its whereabouts unless the police are able to let you know this. For example the initial letter to the insurance company often takes some weeks to receive attention. It is by no means unknown for solicitors simply to telephone the defendant directly at home and ask where the vehicle is and whether they may come round and inspect it! Although there is probably no direct rule of etiquette which prohibits this since the defendant will not yet have his own solicitor involved it may seem something like sharp practice to do so. A certain amount of speed is almost certainly going to be required however, since unless the vehicle is a total write-off the defendant will want to have it repaired as swiftly as possible. If one can obtain facilities to inspect it, or if it has been towed to a garage forecourt or a scrap yard, then at the very least a layman's inspection (*i.e.* by the solicitor personally) can show whether the tyres were in good condition and the nature of any body work damage. It is worth taking photographs of body work damage at this stage if possible. For example suppose the plaintiff is a pedestrian knocked down by the defendant who may subsequently contend that his vehicle was hardly moving at the time of impact and therefore the plaintiff's case is something of a "try on." If one has been in time to inspect the vehicle and finds that in fact there is a substantial dent in the wing this will be a vital piece of evidence in rebutting the defendant's allegation. If there is any suspicion that the condition of the vehicle in some way contributed to the happening of the accident (*e.g.* that it was old and inadequately maintained) then it may be desirable to take an expert witness to the inspection. A consultant mechanical engineer should be instructed for this purpose. If the police suspected that the condition of the vehicle contributed to the accident there may well be a police vehicle examiner's report in the police accident report. Although the police vehicle examiner is not of the same status as a consultant engineer his report may be sufficient for some purposes and will anyway give a useful pointer to the nature of the defects in the vehicle. As indicated earlier however being able to inspect the damaged vehicle even if it is considered material to do so depends to a certain extent on luck, in particular on whether one receives instructions early enough before the damaged vehicle has been repaired or scrapped.

ATTENDING CRIMINAL PROCEEDINGS OR INQUESTS

If one is acting for a potential plaintiff in civil proceedings arising out of a **3.09** road traffic accident there will usually be some consideration of criminal prosecution. In the nature of things criminal cases come to court very much more swiftly than civil cases, perhaps within a matter of weeks of the incident concerned. Provided one has dealt with the question of costs so that one is either in funds to cover work for the time involved or has obtained legal aid in which case the time spent will be considered legitimate expenditure, it is as well to attend, or have a member of one's office attend, any criminal proceedings. If, as is not uncommon, both drivers involved in an incident are charged with careless driving then naturally one will be representing the client in the proceedings. It will obviously be highly important for subsequent civil proceedings (although not absolutely conclusive) that the client should be acquitted. On the assumption however that one's own client is a mere innocent victim, then it can equally be important to see what happens in relation to one's potential opponent. Naturally one is merely an observer at these proceedings and has no right of audience. The reason for needing to attend is not to obtain details of the eventual outcome, which could be obtained by writing to the clerk to the magistrates, but to obtain some notes of the evidence since the practice of magistrates courts clerks is often not to take very much in the way of notes of evidence, particularly in driving cases. Useful admissions may be made by the defendant in the course of the hearing and can be noted for future use. It may also be possible to approach witnesses who attend the hearing on behalf of the prosecution and to save time by taking statements from them then and there.

If one's clients are the personal representatives or dependants of a person killed, it can equally be important to attend an inquest. Although the nature of an inquest is inquisitorial, so that one will not as of right be entitled to cross examine witnesses about how an incident occurred, the Coroner will have the discretion to permit one to cross-examine although he will not generally permit cross-examination in quite the same style which one would adopt in a criminal or ordinary civil court. It will none the less often be possible to obtain useful information by attending an inquest.

Obtaining information relevant to quantum

3.10 Some information relevant to quantum is going to be needed at a very early stage. If realistic negotiations with an insurance company can be opened soon then one would need to have some ideas of relevant figures to hand in case settlement can be achieved even before issue of a writ. This is by no means out of the question even in cases of serious injury if for example there is not necessarily any suggestion of future loss of earnings and an immediate and accurate prognosis is obtainable. The most important steps in obtaining information relative to quantum are as follows:

OBTAINING MEDICAL EVIDENCE

3.11 Writing to one's client's G.P. is useless in all save the most minor accidents. Likewise obtaining a report from the casualty officer at the hospital where the client was admitted is not of much use. What one should do in every case is to instruct a consultant of one's own choice whose reputation will be known to the judge. In other words, a consultant who has a substantial medico-legal practice already. If it happens that the consultant who has actually treated your client is within this category then some consider it as well to instruct him. An alleged disadvantage of this is that if there is some element of continuing pain and/or loss of earnings, the consultant actually concerned with treating the client may be over optimistic in his prognosis in order allegedly to indicate how excellent his own treatment of the client has been. A converse advantage however of instructing the consultant who is actually treating the client is that if there is any potential dispute about the client's injuries it will be difficult for the defendants to produce evidence which will be preferred by the judge to that of the specialist actually concerned with the care of the client. If the client's injuries are very serious so that a final prognosis is clearly out of the question, one should still not delay getting a first medical report (so long as the client is actually out of plaster of course!). Some outline of the nature of the client's injuries in medical terms must be inserted in the statement of claim and indeed, in principle a copy of a medical report should be served with it. Even if one hopes to negotiate with the defendant's insurance company to a successful conclusion it is always as well to have the statement of claim ready drafted for immediate action should negotiations break down. The client may need to be sent to more than one specialist. If he has suffered say a broken leg, facial lacerations and an eye injury then three different specialists may need to be instructed. When writing to instruct the specialist one should ask any specific questions about the client's future which are relevant. For example although specialists will undoubtedly ask the client a few personal details at the examination it might not occur to the client to explain that he has some favourite sport or hobby which he is at present prevented from pursuing by the nature of his injuries. This is a matter which might be of some effect on quantum of damages and therefore one could ask the specialist directly, *e.g.* "at what stage will the client be able to resume his hobby of ...?"

WRITING TO EMPLOYERS

When one writes to employers the nature and complexity of the information **3.12** required will obviously depend upon the type of job. At the very least it is usual to send the employer a schedule of the previous 26 weeks before the accident for the employer to fill in giving details of the client's gross and net earnings. Such a long period is necessary in the case of any job which involves bonuses, overtime or seasonal fluctuations so that a true average for weekly or monthly net average earnings can be obtained by the solicitor. In the letter one should also ask as many other questions as seem necessary at this stage. It may be that sufficient questions can be asked now to avoid the need to approach the employers again for information. This is always a goal which one should strive to achieve. Specific questions should be asked about the nature of any bonuses or overtime payments; the client's prospects within the firm; if the client is never going to work again then as much information must be obtained as possible concerning the client's prospects in his chosen career, and about earning levels that he might have achieved at say five yearly intervals for the rest of his working life, and for an assessment by the personnel department as to his future prospects; if he is going to return to work then questions must be asked about whether his absence has affected his status in the firm, whether he has lost promotion opportunities; whether he is viewed as a less valuable employee because of the nature of his disability (*e.g.* has he been facially disfigured in a job where appearances are important, has he been disabled from some kind of physical activity which is an ingredient of the job and so on). It is often as well to ask for a copy of the client's contract of employment when writing to the employers, although the actual contract supplied at the outset of the employment is often not of much help because it will have been affected by numerous variations between the parties subsequently in the way of changes in pay and other conditions.

In the light of whatever information is obtained from the employers about earnings levels, in a case of any complexity, (*e.g.* a claim involving substantial loss of future earnings) it may be appropriate at this stage to instruct an accountant to work out the tax implications of loss of earnings. This could however be left until a time closer to the actual negotiations of settlement or the trial itself.

WRITING TO THE INLAND REVENUE

Information will need to be obtained from the Inland Revenue regarding the **3.13** amount of tax rebate (although this latter information can often be obtained from the client direct). This is so that computations of special damages can be made.

Applications to the court

3.14   Both the High Court and the County Court have the power to make orders permitting a potential plaintiff (or any other party to a potential action although clearly it will be rare for a defendant to avail himself of these provisions) to obtain certain preliminary information concerning a proposed action. The two quite separate procedures are:

1.   Application for pre-action discovery of a document and

2.   Application for pre-action inspection, etc., of things.

We shall now consider these separately.

APPLICATION FOR PRE-ACTION DISCOVERY, UNDER R.S.C., ORD. 24 AND R.7A

3.15   Under this rule a person who appears likely to be a party to a subsequent action *in respect of personal injuries or death only* can apply to the court for an order for discovery against any other person who is likely to be a party to that action.

Where a potential plaintiff therefore thinks that a potential defendant has some document in his possession and it is vitally important to him to see the content of that document before the action starts then he may apply to the court for an order granting him sight of the document. The application is made by *originating summons* (called an originating *application* in the county court). An originating summons is merely a method of commencing proceedings in a case in which no writ has yet been issued. The form of the originating summons is prescribed by the White book (volume 2, part 2, Appendix A, form 10). The originating summons is drafted so as to refer to the potential plaintiff as the applicant and the potential defendant as defendant. It must be supported by an affidavit which must be sworn by the potential plaintiff (or his solicitor) and contain the following details:

1.   The grounds on which it is alleged that the applicant and the party against whom the order is sought are likely to be parties to subsequent proceedings in a claim for personal injuries. In other words the affidavit must briefly explain the background to the case and why it is alleged that the parties to the originating summons are likely to be parties to a future action for personal injuries.

2.   It must specify the documents in respect of which the order is sought and show why they are relevant to an issue arising in the potential claim for personal injuries and that the potential defendant has the documents.

3.16   At the hearing of the application the district judge will mainly direct himself to one criterion and that is whether sight of the document at this stage is so vital to the potential plaintiff that it will help him to decide whether or not to bring an action at all against the potential defendant. If, whilst interesting or relevant it is not a document of this crucial importance then the district judge may very well decide that the plaintiff, if he has a prima facie case, should issue proceedings against the defendant and seek discovery and inspection of this document in the normal course of things at a later stage. A good example of a case where sight of the document may be essential to enable a potential plaintiff to decide whether or not to sue is perhaps a medical negligence case where he would like to see the hospital notes concerning his treatment. It is difficult to think of an instance arising out of a road traffic case where sight of the document at such an early stage would in fact be so crucial. Perhaps one example might be where the plaintiff suspects that the defendant's vehicle had been inadequately maintained over a long period and that this directly caused the accident. If the vehicle was a commercial vehicle in respect of which there ought to be maintenance records kept then he might conceivably ask for pre-action discovery under this provision. In the case of this as in the case of almost every other application it is as well to ask the proposed defendant whether voluntary discovery and inspection will be given without the need to apply to the court.

PRE-ACTION INSPECTION, ETC., OF A THING

This should be contrasted with the previous provision which relates to **3.17** discovery and inspection of a *document*. Under Order 29, r.7A of the Rules of the Supreme Court the court has power to make an order providing for:

> "The inspection, photographing, preservation, custody and detention of property which appears to the court to be property which may become the subject matter of subsequent proceedings in the court or as to which any question may arise in such proceedings and the taking of samples of any such property and the carrying out of any experiment on or with any such property."

This provision applies to *all types* of action and unlike the previous one not just to personal injury cases. The procedure is identical to that under Ord. 24, r.7A, that is application must be made by originating summons in the same form supported by an affidavit which as before sets out the background to the case explaining why the application is made and specifying the property in respect of which the order is sought and the nature of the order sought.

Under this provision and its county court equivalent, the High Court may make an order in relation to property which is the subject matter of the potential action. It might for example order that a certain thing whose title was in dispute be kept at a certain place pending the outcome of the action. The provision also however applies to property "as to which any question may arise" and thus may apply to some object which is a mere matter of evidence rather than the subject matter of the action. So for example, in a road traffic accident if the condition of a vehicle is alleged to have substantially contributed to the accident and the defendant's insurance company refuse to permit inspection of the vehicle before the writ is issued, then an application can be made under this provision. Likewise if an action concerns say alleged lack of merchantable quality of perishable goods application can be made under this provision for samples of the goods to be taken so that they can be inspected with a view to obtaining an expert report on whether or not they were of appropriate quality.

3.18   It is probably appropriate at this stage before leaving the provisions of Order 24, r.7A and Order 29, r.7A to mention that *after* an action has been commenced each provision can be used, in personal injury cases only, to obtain discovery of a document or inspection, etc., of a thing which is in the possession of a person who is *not a party* to the action. For example, suppose an employer who was not the defendant was dilatory or unhelpful about supplying details of earnings records for a plaintiff or suppose the vehicle which caused an accident and which one wished to inspect was in the possession of a scrap yard. In either case one can use the provisions of Order 24, r.7A and Order 29, r.7A once an action has commenced to obtain discovery of documents in the one case, and inspection of the object in the latter case against persons who are not parties to the main action.

Motor insurance

3.19   A plaintiff who suffers personal injuries in a road traffic accident can sue the defendant in the tort of negligence. The existence or absence of motor insurance makes no difference whatsoever to the actual procedure of an action under the Rules of the Supreme Court. It does however have enormous practical significance particularly on the vital question of whether the plaintiff is going to receive any damages which he is awarded by the court.

Plaintiffs are often very confused about their rights and or liabilities in relation to motor insurance. The position is actually considerably more simple than it may appear.

3.20   In the first case, if one has a plaintiff who was a pedestrian at the time then matters are considerably simplified. His own insurance position is irrelevant and even if he had a personal accident insurance policy which paid him an enormous sum it would not be taken into account in computing the damages due from the defendant. If the plaintiff was himself a driver at the time of the incident then however clear cut liability seems he must be advised to notify his own insurers at once if he has not already done so since there will inevitably be a term under the policy requiring him to do this within some fairly brief period. If some claim *is* subsequently brought against him then the insurers will exercise the rights which they will have reserved under the policy to appoint their own choice of solicitors to represent the defendant in the matter. It must be clearly understood that insurers are never themselves joined into the action as parties save in exceptional circumstances. The action is always brought against the motorist who is allegedly liable. It is of course, however, the insurers who will be paying any judgment awarded and this is why they reserve the right to insist upon their own choice of solicitors in conducting the action. Insurance companies always employ one or two firms of solicitors in any given area who handle all their personal injury litigation and whom they know to be competent and experienced in this field.

Assuming that for the moment no apparent question of one's client's own liability in the accident arises one needs to consider certain technical matters to do with motor insurance. These are as follows:

Types of insurance policies

"Road Traffic Act insurance"

3.21   Road Traffic Act insurance is the most basic insurance that one can have in

48

respect of a motor vehicle. Such policies are actually quite rare and are often issued only (at correspondingly high premiums) to those drivers who are a very bad risk, *e.g.* drivers with recent drink driving convictions. Such a policy implies that the person insured is covered only in respect of those risks for which insurance is compulsory under sections 143 and 145 of the Road Traffic Act 1988. Under these sections it is an offence to use or permit the use of a vehicle on the road unless the driver is ensured in respect of legal liability for the following three matters namely:

(1) Personal injury or death to any other person.
(2) The cost of emergency hospital treatment.
(3) Damage to property (other than the insured vehicle itself and goods in it carried for hire or reward) up to a value of £250,000 in each claim.

Consequently where the defendant has this kind of insurance a plaintiff will be covered for damages for personal injuries and loss of earnings and for damage to his own property caused in the accident, *e.g.* his motor car and its contents.

"Third party fire and theft"

This is a wider type of liability than the last in which the person who has this **3.22** kind of insurance cover will be covered not only for personal injury and damage to some other person's property. In addition this kind of cover will protect the insured person himself against theft of or fire damage to his own vehicle so that if the vehicle is stolen and never recovered he will be paid the market value.

"Comprehensive insurance"

Under this type of cover an insured driver will be indemnified in respect of **3.23** personal injury damage or property damage to any other person and in addition will be covered in respect of damage to or loss of his own vehicle. This is so whether or not he was himself to blame for any incident in which his vehicle was damaged or destroyed. The premiums for this sort of cover are naturally considerably higher than for "third party fire and theft" liability. It must be clearly understood that the nature of the liability insured against is the negligence of the driver. Accordingly the passengers in the vehicle of someone comprehensively insured who is to blame for an accident will of course be covered but he himself will not be. Therefore a comprehensively insured motorist who is to blame for an accident and suffers personal injuries will have no claim against any insurance policy (unless he has a quite separate personal accident insurance policy) in respect of his personal injuries.
    The following terms also need to be explained:

Subrogation

An insurance company which has paid a claim by the person insured (*e.g.* **3.24** someone comprehensively insured who has had his vehicle damage paid for by his own insurance company) may exercise its rights of subrogation by using the insured person's name to bring proceedings against anyone else involved who is alleged to be negligent in the action. This right will be expressly reserved in the insurance policy.

No claims bonus

3.25 A no claims bonus is a discretionary bonus awarded by way of a discount on future premiums for years in which no claim has been brought under a policy of motor insurance. The bonus increases year by year usually up to a maximum of about 65 per cent. After several years therefore this may be a very substantial benefit typically reducing the annual premium for a policy from say £500 to, say, £200. If any claim at all is brought against the policy the bonus is lost even though the insured motorist was not himself to blame for the incident (for example if his car was rammed by a hit and run driver who has left the scene of the incident before he can be identified). It is possible to take out, for an additional premium, a type of policy where the no claims bonus is "protected" that is that the bonus is retained provided there is no more than say one claim within any two-year period.

Excess in comprehensive insurance

3.26 This involves the motorist agreeing to bear a so-called "excess" that is the first part of any claim. This may be a small figure such as £25 or £50 and will avoid the insurance company having to be bothered with very trivial claims, *e.g.* for scratches to paintwork, loss of a wing mirror, etc. It may be that an insured can obtain a reduction on premium if he is willing to have an excess of a rather larger figure, *e.g.* £250. In many cases he would be well advised to agree to this especially if his no claims bonus is anyway worth more to him than £250 a year. In that event he would not trouble the insurance company at all with a claim for minor accident damage up to this figure and his no claims bonus would be preserved. Should a claim be made involving a higher figure than this he would bear the first £250 of it which is the nature of the "excess."

"Knock for knock" agreement

3.27 If two vehicles which are both comprehensively insured are damaged in an accident the insurance companies involved may well decide to each settle their own insured motorist's claim. They will do this if they have a pre-existing "knock for knock" agreement as insurance companies increasingly have. It saves them a good deal of time and trouble and possibly litigation costs in establishing the exact cause of an accident, and motor insurance companies doubtless consider that the matter is rather one of "swings and roundabouts" that is that taking into account the saving on investigation and litigation costs over any given year they will lose nothing by the arrangement and may well gain. The problem for a motorist who finds himself involved in this arrangement is that liability may seem perfectly clear. He would normally have expected his insurance company to have attempted to negotiate full settlement of his claim by the other insurance company but may now find matters settled to his disadvantage because he will immediately lose the amount of his excess and indeed his no claims bonus. In such a situation it will usually be worthwhile for the motorist who considers he was the innocent party in the incident to bring an action against the other motorist for his uninsured losses, *i.e.* the loss of his no claims bonus and excess. Since it is actually somewhat difficult to establish the amount of a no claims bonus which may be cumulative over some years it is probably better in such a case if the client takes legal advice in time, to advise him not to claim on his own insurance policy but to try and pay for the accident damage himself and meanwhile to bring proceedings against the other driver for the whole amount involved. Alternatively if his own insurers have already paid there is no reason why he should still not sue for the whole amount involved provided that if he is successful he then reimburses his own insurers with the amount which they have already paid him in settlement of the claim. They will then reinstate his no claims bonus. A knock for knock agreement between insurers naturally does not bind the insured person himself not to proceed in the way previously described.

So far we have been concerned with one's own insurance policy. It is now vital to consider problems to do with the opponents' insurance, or lack of it.

THE OPPONENTS MOTOR INSURANCE POLICY. ROAD TRAFFIC ACT 1988 SS.151 AND 152

If a plaintiff obtains judgment against a defendant for personal injuries and **3.28** consequential loss the plaintiff may enforce that part of the judgment against the defendant's insurers even though the insurers themselves may have been entitled to avoid or cancel the defendant's policy or indeed may already have done so. This is by virtue of sections 151 and 152 of the Road Traffic Act 1988.

It will be remembered that insurance contracts are contracts *uberrimae fidei, i.e.* of utmost good faith. A vital ingredient of this is that a person taking out an insurance policy must disclose all material matters to the insurer. Suppose that a person obtained a policy of motor insurance without disclosing to the insurers that he had previous accident claims against him, or driving convictions. Under the basic law of insurance the insurers, if they discovered these matters would be entitled to repudiate the policy and thus not to pay any claims on it. The effect of sections 151 and 152 of the Road Traffic Act will generally be to stop the insurers repudiating at least to the extent that they are obliged to compensate some *other party* for compulsorily insurable damages, *i.e.* the damages which must be insured under sections 143 and 145 of the Road Traffic Act 1988.

A plaintiff however can only use section 152 to ensure this payment if *before or within seven days after* the commencement of proceedings (*i.e.* the issue of the writ) he gave written notice of his intention to commence proceedings to the insurers.

It is therefore important to remember in every case to give a potential defendant's insurers notice of intention to commence proceedings. In fact this can be done with one's original letter before action providing the letter uses the words "intend to commence proceedings." That would apparently suffice to comply with section 152 and there is no need then for proceedings to be issued immediately or within any particular period. One should ideally write the section 152 letter as soon as one has obtained the insurance details from the police after an accident. One is then covered and can safely forget the matter. There is no need to refer to section 152 in the letter and no particular form of letter is prescribed. One must always remember also that if having commenced proceedings the need to add further defendants becomes apparent it is prudent to write a section 152 letter in respect of each of them before the writ is amended to add the new defendants.

We will now consider the position if one's opponent is not insured at all.

THE MOTOR INSURERS BUREAU

3.29   The Motor Insurers Bureau is a body set up and financed by motor insurance companies. There are two distinct agreements made between the motor insurance bureau and the former Minister of Transport (now the Department of the Environment). We must consider each of these separately.

Uninsured drivers

3.30   Where it is apparent that a driver is uninsured, *i.e.* that there is no policy *at all* in force in relation to the motor vehicle in question (as compared to the position above described in relation to section 152 of the Road Traffic Act where there is such a policy but the insurance company had the right to repudiate it) then one might expect a plaintiff to be without a remedy, that is to say that whilst he could sue the uninsured motorist he might have considerable difficulty in enforcing any judgment obtained. The effect of the Motor Insurers Bureau agreement is to mitigate this problem. Where one finds out that one's potential opponent is uninsured one writes to the Motor Insurers Bureau drawing their attention to the situation. They will then appoint a local insurance company to act as their agent for the purpose of negotiating the claim. Of course one must prove that the uninsured driver was negligent. The mere fact that he was *uninsured* is not in itself grounds for bringing a claim. The insurance company appointed to negotiate on behalf of the M.I.B. will have the power to settle matters without a writ being issued. However if one cannot agree on liability and compensation then a writ must be issued against the uninsured driver. Notice of intention to commence proceedings against the uninsured driver must be given to the M.I.B. before the writ is issued or notice that the writ has been issued must be given to them no later than seven days thereafter if they are to be bound by the terms of the agreement. The action then proceeds normally except that the Motor Insurers Bureau have the right to be added as a party. More probably they will merely treat themselves as if they were the insurance company of the uninsured driver and arrange for representation on his behalf. Naturally they can take any defences open to the uninsured person, *e.g.* make allegations of contributory negligence just as in the case of any other defendant. When judgment is obtained if it remains unpaid by the defendant for seven days (as it presumably will be) the Motor Insurers Bureau will pay it and will also pay the normal taxed costs. The judgment must then be assigned to or to the order of the M.I.B. so that they are subrogated to the rights of the plaintiff and may attempt to recoup money they have paid out from the uninsured motorist. In fact it is rarely worth their while attempting to do this. In the nature of things a person who did not have the means or inclination to insure his vehicle is unlikely to have substantial assets. It must be noted that the agreement applies *only* to those claims in respect of which insurance was compulsory under section 143 and 145 of the 1988 Act.

Untraced drivers

A separate agreement applies in the case of untraced drivers (*i.e.* hit and run **3.31** drivers). However the agreement only applies in the case of personal injury and death claims. Here of course a writ cannot be issued against an unknown defendant. Accordingly there is no need to make application to the court at all, but what one does is notify the M.I.B. within the usual limitation period, *i.e.* three years of the accident, by letter. They will then arrange for the case to be investigated and must be satisfied that the untraced driver was negligent and that the death or injury was not caused deliberately by him (*i.e.* that he did not use the motor vehicle as a weapon). The M.I.B. then makes an award on a voluntary basis assessed in the same way as that in which a court would have assessed damages at common law, *i.e.* will include the usual items of pain, suffering, loss of amenity, loss of future earnings. However damage to property is not recoverable, and thus one cannot recover from the M.I.B. if a hit and run driver collides with one's parked car and makes off.

If the amount of the award is not agreed or the refusal to make any award is not accepted there is an appeals procedure by way of arbitration by one of a panel of Queens Counsel.

There is also an accelerated procedure in the case of claims up to a total of £20,000 which allows the parties to settle the application without a full investigation. In this case there is no right of appeal.

Finally it should be noted that in the case of *untraced* drivers the Motor Insurers Bureau is under no obligation to pay legal costs. In fact the M.I.B. pays a standard fee together with certain acceptable disbursements in particular the cost of a police accident report and medical reports.

Negotiations

In the case of road traffic accidents a plaintiff's solicitor is very soon going to **3.32** be in touch with the defendant's insurance company. Insurance companies employ specialist claims staff who attempt to negotiate settlement of claims made against their insured. These staff are not legally qualified but do develop considerable expertise in negotiating settlement of the types of claims that arise out of road traffic accidents, that is claims relating to personal injuries and vehicle damage. A solicitor who has a considerable volume of personal injury work is likely to meet the same claims representative time and again and may develop a reasonable working relationship with him. Insurance companies and their individual representatives vary greatly in their attitudes to claim negotiations. The more satisfactory consider that the insurance company's commercial interests are best served by making realistic offers at an early stage to settle litigation with the hope of thus saving considerable sums in legal costs. Others have a quite different approach believing that the more the negotiations and indeed subsequent litigation can be dragged out the greater pressure will be put on the plaintiff who may in the end be prepared to accept considerably less than the proper value of his claim because of the psychological pressures that can be put on him. An application for interim payments which will be described later is one way of ensuring that this kind of pressure may be less effective than the insurance company hopes. Whatever the attitude of the insurance company as a whole or of the individual with whom one is in negotiations one must always remember that insurance companies are not charitable organisations and in the end will not be terribly concerned about the plaintiff's actual state of health. They are interested in getting out of litigation as cheaply as possible. If one finds a particular insurance company or its local representative's attitude generally unhelpful there is no need to negotiate with them at all. One can issue a writ, serve it on the defendant and the case will then pass from the insurance company's own claims staff to the solicitors whom the insurance company appoint. Whilst sometimes the solicitor's attitude may mirror that of the insurance company who instruct him, generally there will be normal professional courtesy between the solicitors involved. Usually however insurance company's claims staff like to hope that they will themselves be able to negotiate claims settlements. They tend to view it as something of a failure on their own part if negotiations do break down and their own solicitors have to be involved. There is always some incentive on them therefore to behave reasonably. Although claims representatives will not attempt to deal with an action once it has commenced, if all one wishes to do is issue and serve the writ, for example, to start interest running and to be sure of not missing the limitation period, one can sometimes agree with the insurance company that one will do this but take no further steps and will continue negotiations with the insurance company until they break down or one wishes to make progress in the action.

3.33 It is not possible adequately here to summarise or explain proper negotiating techniques. There are as many different approaches as there are individuals. Many consider that it is best to acquire a reputation as a difficult and aggressive negotiator, reasoning that since one seems to see the same claims staff time after time and since one naturally will have a proportion of weak cases amongst the strong ones, one may obtain better results in the weak cases by having a reputation for aggression.

Others believe that the same result is best achieved with firmness and courtesy. The only overall guidance that can be given on the matter of negotiations is to always attempt to ensure that preliminary offers come first from the insurance company. Occasionally one will receive a very pleasant surprise in that the offer put forward is actually higher than the figure for which one was minded to ask. One should also bear in mind that defendants' insurance company representatives solicitors do sometimes treat negotiation of settlement as something of a sophisticated game. The writer was once told by a senior partner of a firm of solicitors specialising in defendant's personal injury litigation that unless he knew his opponent was experienced in the field his preliminary offer would often be as little as 25 per cent. of the figure which he would have eventually been prepared to pay. More surprisingly he said that in a significant number of cases this offer was in fact accepted.

Realistic negotiations cannot be undertaken of course until the plaintiff's medical condition has stabilised. In cases of extreme simplicity it may be possible to achieve settlement within a matter of weeks of the accident but in a case of any difficulty a considerably longer period must be allowed to elapse. The following miscellaneous matters ought to be considered in the context of negotiations with insurance company and their solicitors.

THE SCOPE OF THE AUTHORITY TO NEGOTIATE

3.34 A solicitor has no authority implied by law to compromise a claim on a client's behalf before proceedings are issued. Therefore acceptance of any offer made can only be "subject to the client's approval." It is not uncommon to get a client to agree in advance to accept a certain sum if it can be achieved in negotiations and then if the insurers do come up with this figure one can safely accept it there and then. It is always prudent to obtain a client's authority to compromise in writing and to give him advice in writing as to the appropriate sort of figures which would be appropriate in his case.

After proceedings have commenced a solicitor does actually have implied authority to compromise. However it would be very rash to rely on implied authority and again one should seek the client's express approval to accept offers and ask the client to confirm it in writing.

FACILITIES FOR MEDICAL EXAMINATION

One will be obtaining medical reports on one's own client as soon as it is **3.35** fruitful to do so. An early request may come from insurance companies for sight of one's own medical reports and/or for the right to instruct their own specialist. It is suggested that if one has obtained a medical report which is totally favourable (*i.e.* one which raises no suspicion of malingering by one's own client, stresses that the injuries are serious, and that a certain prognosis cannot yet be achieved and which says that the client will need to be re-examined in several months time), there can be no harm whatsoever in sending a copy of this to the defendant's insurance company. Indeed, in principle, a copy of the report must be served on the defendant at an early stage of the proceedings (see para. 6.21). Some solicitors do this as a matter of course though others prefer to retain the medical report for exchange at some later stage or even in the hope of avoiding exchange of medical evidence at all (see later section on expert witnesses). In any event there is a possibility that the defendant's solicitor will want to have a medical examination by his own specialist. One may as well agree to this at an early stage since the defendant will in the end be entitled to it anyway. For matters to consider on this and terms which one might seek to impose for granting facilities for medical examination reference should be made to the later section on expert witnesses para. 9.07.

"WITHOUT PREJUDICE" CORRESPONDENCE

Correspondence which is written with a view to settling a case is often **3.36** expressed to be "without prejudice." The use of this phrase means that the correspondence is protected by private privilege so that it cannot be produced subsequently in court. The clearest example of its application would be where the defendants wish to write a letter in which they were prepared to admit they were principally responsible for the accident but wish to suggest that the plaintiff was say 20 per cent. to blame and to suggest a compromise based on a reasonable offer of 80 per cent. of full liability. If such a letter is written "without prejudice" then it cannot subsequently be produced at the trial. If therefore the plaintiff rejected the offer the defendant would be entitled to withdraw it and to continue defending on the basis of a full denial of liability.

Meetings and indeed telephone discussions can also be conducted on a "without prejudice" basis so that no reference afterwards to what was said at them would be permitted in court. In fact the case law shows that it is not actually necessary to use the words "without prejudice" on correspondence if written with the bona fide intent to negotiate. It would however generally be considered more prudent to expressly mark the correspondence with the words "without prejudice" and to expressly agree at the outset of meetings and discussions that they should be on that basis. It is quite common practice for insurance companies to mark every single letter "without prejudice" although in principle only those written with a view to achieving compromise do qualify for the label. A fuller discussion of this topic appears in the discussion of privilege in the Evidence section hereafter.

PRE-ACTION CONSIDERATIONS IN CONTRACT CASES

3.37 The nature of the pre-action considerations in contract cases will be largely determined by the type of dispute and the things that are in dispute. Thus it may be sometimes appropriate to collect as much factual and eye witness information in such a case as it is in a personal injury case. More commonly however the type of action will either be relatively straightforward debt collecting, that is an action brought by an unpaid supplier of goods, or the opposite, an action by a disgruntled purchaser of goods for the return of the purchase price on the basis that the goods have proved deficient in some way. It should not be overlooked that in the latter case where there is some objection to the quality of goods supplied that one is not restricted to claiming damages either for the diminution in value of the goods or for the return of the purchase price in full. Depending on the nature of the defect and how it manifested itself the action may also involve a claim for damages for inconvenience and disappointment and distress, or even for personal injuries (*e.g.* where some electrical appliance was purchased which exploded on being switched on causing injury to the consumer). In either of these cases it is unlikely that an insurance company will be involved. Therefore in addition to the straightforward factual matters which we have so far discussed one would also need to look at one extra ingredient which is not present in the usual run of personal injury cases. That is the ability of the potential defendant to pay the damages and/or debt.

3.38 The topic of enforcement of judgments will be dealt with later but at this stage all that one need note is that there are only limited means of enforcing judgments. In particular the plaintiff who has obtained judgment in a debt case is often somewhat disgruntled to find that where the defendant fails to pay he can often do this with impunity and that there is for example no realistic possibility whatsoever of getting a person committed to prison for non-payment of a civil debt. It is of paramount importance therefore to ensure that good money is not thrown after bad in pursuing litigation, even successful litigation, against people who will not have the ability to pay the judgment when obtained.

3.39 Therefore at an early stage it is appropriate to point out the risks of this to the would-be plaintiff. It is as well to point out that to spend say £50 now on an enquiry agent's report into the financial status of the potential defendant can be very worthwhile as saving considerably more than that sum in wasted costs. If the client agrees an enquiry agent should be instructed to pursue such enquiries. How enquiry agents obtain the information which they do about a person's means is not something with which we need to concern ourselves. Suffice it to say that they are often very adept at obtaining details of a person's precise salary, career prospects, state of current account and other savings and so on. Quite often they will obtain useful information by merely doing things which a solicitor might consider it beneath his own dignity to do such as going to the person's house, looking in the window, looking at the type of car in the drive, or simply knocking on the door and asking the potential defendant about his financial situation.

When the solicitor has commissioned such a report and provided a copy of it to the client it is always as well to confirm to the client in writing the potential difficulties of enforcing a judgment and the possibility that at the end of the day one may be left with nothing more than an order for payment by instalments which even if complied with by the defendant may take some years to collect.

The letter before action

After having obtained sufficient information from one's client it is normal to start matters moving by writing a letter before action. In a contract case or a debt case this can be perfectly straightforward. One would for example allude to the nature of the goods supplied and to the fact that the client's account had been unpaid for more than the specified period. There would then be a fairly brusque demand that the amount due to be paid within a very short period, say seven days, and paid direct to the solicitor. If the contract litigation relates to a disgruntled consumer seeking the return of the purchase price then some greater length of explanation is naturally required detailing the defects complained of and making a demand for what it is that the client wants, *e.g.* return of the purchase price in exchange for the goods or the cost of repairs necessary to make the goods of merchantable quality. **3.40**

In personal injury litigation styles of writing a letter before action are many and various. Some favour giving exhaustive details of the client's allegations about how the incident occurred on the suggested basis that this letter may at some stage be put before the judge and it is as well to demonstrate consistency. Others favour writing as brief a letter as possible giving no factual detail but merely stating that the plaintiff holds the defendant liable for the accident and seeks compensation. It is suggested that this latter view is preferable. The letter can be written to the defendant directly but in fact there is very little reason to involve him if the identity of his insurance company is known. In such a case a letter can be written immediately to the insurance company containing what is necessary to comply with section 152 of the Road Traffic Act 1988, *i.e.* the statement that proceedings will be issued in due course concerning the incident. It is not of course appropriate to demand any specific sum in settlement of the claim nor indeed can an immediate offer be expected. It might however become perfectly possible at a very early stage to ascertain whether liability is seriously in dispute. **3.41**

4. Miscellaneous Matters Concerning Proceedings in the High Court

4.01 There are three Divisions of the High Court; the Queen's Bench Division the Chancery Division and the Family Division. The jurisdiction of the latter two divisions is specialised and does not concern us for present purposes. The Queen's Bench Division of the High Court consists of the Central Office, that is the office of the High Court contained in the Royal Courts of Justice buildings in the Strand, London, and also the District Registries which are the offices of the High Court outside London. The personnel of the Queen's Bench Division with whom we are concerned are:

MASTERS OF THE QUEEN'S BENCH DIVISION

4.02 These are judicial officers who deal with almost all matters of an administrative or judicial nature in a High Court Action in the Central Office in London up to the stage of the trial itself. As we shall subsequently see it will be perfectly possible for a routine personal injuries case or a contract case to get to trial with neither party ever needing to actually attend any kind of judicial hearing before an officer of the court. The writ can be issued over the counter, so to speak, and the various other steps which need to be taken can very often be taken merely by sending or taking documents to the counter of the court office and leaving them there. Proceedings in the High Court to a very large extent are carried out direct between the parties right up until trial itself. On the other hand it is also perfectly possible that there may be one or several applications to the court for some kind of order. Applications in the course of the preliminary stages of litigation are known as "interlocutory" applications. The word "interlocutory" is applied to any kind of hearing apart from one dealing with the substantive final rights of the parties. Examples of interlocutory applications are; applications for leave to amend the writ; applications for further and better particulars; application for judgment on liability whilst leaving quantum of damages to be assessed later; and so on. All of these topics will be considered in detail in due course. Where such applications are to be made they will be heard by a master who has full power to deal with them whatever the importance of the case or the amount of money involved.

There are no interlocutory matters in the kinds of action which concern us with which a master does not have the power to deal. There are some types of interlocutory application in other forms of action, for instance applications for an injunction, which must be heard by a judge and not by a master. However an application for an injunction is most unlikely to occur in the kinds of action which we shall be considering.

DISTRICT JUDGES

4.03 These have virtually equivalent powers to those of the Queen's Bench

58

Division Master, in District Registries, *i.e.* outside London. In fact a district judge has powers also in relation to the work of the other two Divisions of the High Court. District judges also deal with the assessment of bills of costs which in London is dealt with by a specialist master called a Taxing Master. The nature of and procedure on taxation is described later at para. 20.32.

JUDGES

High Court judges sit on the actual trial of cases in open court. In addition **4.04** they hear some interlocutory applications as previously mentioned (*e.g.* injunctions) and appeals from orders made by a master or district judge. In the case of orders made by masters or district judges there is normally an appeal as of right to a High Court Judge in chambers. Thus for example if a party applied for leave to amend his writ and a district judge refused, the aggrieved party could appeal to the High Court Judge who would hear the appeal in chambers.

The Rules of the Supreme Court
Procedure in the High Court is governed by the Rules of the Supreme Court. **4.05** These are contained in a book known as the "White Book" which contains rules, practice directions, various precedents and explanatory notes. The way to use the White Book is to look up the subject matter of one's enquiry in the index (which is in Volume I rather than in Volume II) and thereafter one can turn to the relevant order which is usually expressed by a method of annotation showing the order and then the sub-rule of the Order, *e.g.* Ord. 29, r. 11. Having turned to Ord. 29 r. 11 R.S.C., one can then see the text of the rule. At the foot of the text of the order or rule there are set out some extremely useful explanatory notes referring to decided points of practice and principle and cases which are authorities on relevant points.

Many of the rules seem to be expressed in fairly peremptory terms, *e.g.* **4.06** appearing to instruct that the plaintiff shall at a certain stage take some particular step, usually within a given time limit. It is important to note that in fact failure to comply with the rules almost always amounts merely to an irregularity. Although the attitude of the courts was once rather different, today the court recognises that its function is to assist the parties in obtaining justice and not to discipline the parties or their solicitors for their deficiencies in conducting litigation. Generally, failure to take a step in the right way or at the right time does not nullify the action itself or even the step taken. The court will almost always allow mistakes to be corrected, although the party who has gone astray and thus caused a waste of time and costs to his opponents will inevitably be ordered to pay the costs wasted by the mistake or oversight. One could give many examples of provisions which are often overlooked or ignored. A very common example is Order 24 rule 2 which provides in essence that after the close of pleadings each party shall attend to so called "automatic discovery" within 14 days. In fact in cases other than personal injury cases there will generally be a subsequent stage called a "summons for directions" which may not come about for months after the close of pleadings. Many solicitors do not carry out automatic discovery but instead wait until the summons for directions when they obtain an order for discovery along with the other orders for which they need to apply.

4.07 Another aspect of this is the fact that time limits given within the rules may be extended either by written agreement between the parties, or if one party is not willing to agree to an extension of the given time limit an application can be made to the court, (that is to a district judge or a master in chambers) by what is called a "time summons" for an order extending the time. A very common example to which we shall return is that when the plaintiff's statement of claim is served on the defendant the latter has in principle only 14 days in which to serve his full defence to it. Many defendants are unable to do this within this time and need to ask their opponent for an extension of time and if this is refused to apply to the court for that extension.

4.08 It should not be understood however that all rules of the High Court can be waived. There are exceptions where failure to comply with the rule may well result in serious consequences. An example is the requirement that a writ be served within four months of its being issued. Although an application to extend this period can be made if good cause is shown (*e.g.* if the defendant has disappeared and cannot be traced for service) if the failure to serve has been due to mere oversight then the court is unlikely to grant a renewal of the writ and the writ then lapses. If the limitation period has also elapsed during that time the plaintiff's rights are substantially affected. In that case his remedy naturally lies against his negligent solicitor.

Drawing up orders in the Queen's Bench Division

4.09 The Queen's Bench Division, unlike the county court, remains entirely passive throughout the conduct of civil proceedings. It does nothing of its own motion to ensure that time limits are complied with, it does not call the parties before it at any stage, it does nothing to assist the parties with the service of proceedings, and indeed it does nothing to enforce its own judgments until one of the procedures for enforcement is specifically applied for by the party concerned. One particular aspect of this passivity is that the Queen's Bench Division does not draw up its own orders. Thus, where a party has succeeded on some interlocutory application, or indeed after the trial itself, it is up to that party to draw up the order of the court and to attend court with two copies of it. The forms of the order are then checked and if approved sealed and one copy handed back to the applicant who can proceed to the next stage on the basis of the order which the court has given him.

In the procedures that follow we shall be considering each only insofar as the district registry practice is concerned. There are minor differences in procedure where an action is proceeding in the Central Office of the High Court in London but these are not really material. The differences relate to such matters as how to issue a writ, how to issue a summons and so on. These differences can easily be grasped in the course of the first days in the litigation department during one's training if one happens to be working sufficiently close to the Royal Courts of Justice. The terminology hereafter therefore will in each case refer to "district judge" and "district registry."

It is appropriate to consider a number of other miscellaneous matters.

TYPES OF ORIGINATING PROCESS

4.10 Proceedings may be commenced in the Queen's Bench Division of the High Court by a document called a "writ of summons" usually referred to simply as a "writ." In addition there is a form of procedure known as "originating summons." We shall only be concerned with actions begun by writ of summons although it is appropriate to say a brief word about originating summonses for one reason. This is that originating summonses have been dealt with already insofar as they concern applications for pre-action discovery under R.S.C., Ord. 24, r. 7A and pre-action inspection, detention, preservation etc., of an object under R.S.C., Ord. 29, r. 7A. It will be remembered that in each of those cases the common feature was that no writ had yet been issued and that one simple procedural point was all that needed to be determined. The respective orders, Order 24, r. 7A and Order 29, r. 7A in fact specify that the procedure shall be by originating summons. Originating summonses have various uses and are particularly used for determining individual points as in the instances cited and others which are not within the scope of the present text. Apart from the two instances cited where an originating summons has to be used, there is only one other which will concern us and this will be dealt with in the later section concerning persons under a disability. Where one is able satisfactorily to compromise a claim on behalf of an infant before proceedings have been issued one must apply to the court for its approval of the settlement achieved for the infant. The method of application, if no writ has yet been issued, is to apply by originating summons. As will be observed this has features in common with the other two examples of originating summonses which we have already seen, namely that there is a requirement to determine one preliminary point in a case before a writ has been issued. Apart from these instances however we shall not be concerned with originating summons procedure.

METHODS OF MAKING INTERLOCUTORY APPLICATIONS

In actions commenced by writ interlocutory applications (that is as previously explained applications to the court for some preliminary or procedural matter to be determined) can be made in the following ways: **4.11**

Ex parte

This means an application made by one party without the opponent being **4.12** notified and thus enabled to attend the court to be heard on, and perhaps contest, the application. This involves an apparent breach of the principles of natural justice and there are in fact relatively few instances of things which may be done by *ex parte* application. Examples are purely administrative steps where the opponent has not himself complied with court procedures such as for instance an application for judgment in default of intention to defend under Order 13 (see later section on termination without trial para. 11.01); applications for various methods of enforcement after judgment where the losing party has failed to comply with an order of the court; and urgent matters which need to be applied for in great haste and possibly with some element of secrecy, *e.g.* an urgent injunction.

By summons

This is by far the most common method of making interlocutory applications **4.13** in the Queen's Bench Division. A summons is actually nothing more than a method of fixing an appointment before a district judge and notifying one's opponent of the requirement to attend at the appointment and of the nature of the application that is being made. A summons of this kind as distinct from an *originating summons* described above is usually called an "ordinary summons" or "summons in the action." It can only be used in a case where a writ has already been issued. To issue a summons one obtains two blank forms from a law stationers (naturally solicitors carry stocks of these in their offices) or alternatively adapts a draft precedent held on word-processor and completes them at the top with the headings in the action which can be copied from the writ. The summons is then drafted so as to let the court and one's opponent know the order of the court that is being sought. The summons when purchased from the law stationers already has printed on it the words which tell one's opponent that he must attend at the office of the court on the hearing of one's application. The person who wishes to issue the summons then fills in details of the nature of the application that he is making, *e.g.* for further and better particulars of his opponent's pleading. Having completed the summons the applicant takes two copies of it down to the High Court District Registry. There a clerk will look at the summons and ask for an estimate of the length of hearing. One has now to say how long one estimates such a summons will take to be heard so that neither too much nor too little of the district judge's time is allotted to it. Many relatively routine summonses take a quarter of an hour or less. Suppose therefore one gives an estimated length of hearing as 15 minutes, the clerk will then look at the nature of the summons. If there is something genuinely urgent about it there may be an attempt to fit it into the district judge's diary in the immediate future but otherwise the first vacant hearing time of sufficient length will be allotted. When this will be varies, depending in part on the time of year and the nature of the locality but for relatively routine summonses it would certainly be rare to obtain a hearing date within a month of the date of the issue and considerably longer delays might occur in some parts of the country. When this date is inserted the court seal is put on the two copies of the summons and one is retained in the court file. This is what is called "issuing" or "taking out" a summons and the date of hearing endorsed on the summons is called the "return day." One then simply takes the summons away, prepares a photocopy of it and serves this on one's opponent. To this matter of issuing summonses there is one further refinement. Straightforward summonses which only require some simple procedural order of the court may be issued in the way described and served and no further steps need be taken. In the case of a more substantial application however (two examples of which would be a summons seeking summary judgment under Order 14 described at para. 11.06 and summons seeking an interim payment described at para. 13.02) there is a requirement that some *evidence* be lodged at court at the time that the summons is taken out. This evidence is in the form of an affidavit.

Affidavits

4.14   An affidavit is simply a sworn statement of evidence used at a hearing. It avoids the need to call a witness at the hearing and indeed an affidavit is usually essential because the court has neither the time nor inclination at the hearing of the summons in chambers to hear oral testimony. In such cases therefore an affidavit must be prepared. The affidavit contains the heading of the action in the same form as appears in the writ and the pleadings. It must also contain at the top right the following information, namely details of who is swearing it, on whose behalf it is lodged at court, the date on which it is sworn, and how many affidavits by that person have so far been used in the action (*e.g.* if this is the person's first affidavit so far filed at court in any matter in the action it will contain the word "first").

Although certain kinds of affidavit, *e.g.* for summary judgment or for an interim payment must by the rules contain certain information and in default of doing so will be technically defective, for many kinds of application there are no specific requirements relating to the contents of the affidavit. An affidavit is, of course, expressed in the first person (unlike a pleading which is expressed in the third person) and the opening words are therefore "I Susan Smith make oath and say as follows. . . ." The contents of the affidavit then appear in numbered paragraphs in relatively formal English but there are no other technical requirements. The contents of a typical affidavit would briefly mention the background to the case, *e.g.* describe what type of action it concerned; go on to state what application the applicant was at present making and give the reasons for this and end with a request that the court should make an order in the terms sought by the applicant. The affidavit once drafted must then be sworn by the person who makes it. For this purpose it must be taken to a solicitor who is not a member of the firm acting for the person making the affidavit. An affidavit can also be sworn before certain officers of the court. The affidavit is then "filed" or "lodged" with the summons at court and a copy of it must be served with the copy summons on one's opponent so that he is aware not merely of the nature of the application being made and the time and place where it is to be heard but of the evidence adduced in support of the application. Where an affidavit from one party is required an affidavit from the opposing party is permitted in which he may set out his version. It is rare in the types of applications with which we shall be concerned for cross-examination of the persons on the contents of their affidavits to be permitted. On the other hand in matrimonial proceedings for ancillary relief (*e.g.* a maintenance application) it is usual for the affidavits merely to provide the introductory information in the case and for both parties to be cross-examined on their affidavits. **4.15**

It is not possible exhaustively to list the types of application where an affidavit is required and those where it is not. These have to be learned through practice and the relevant information will be given as we proceed. The usual way to describe a situation where an affidavit is required is to say "an affidavit in support is needed."

Exhibits

Sometimes a party may wish to bring before a court evidence which does not conveniently fit in an affidavit. For example he may wish to refer to invoices or business records of some kind which because of their form or their length cannot conveniently be set out in the text of his affidavit. In such a case it is normal to "exhibit" the document referred to in the affidavit. This involves the "exhibit" being referred to in the text and given a number. The number comprises the initials of the person swearing the affidavit (who is called a "deponent"), and the number of the exhibit, *e.g.* in an affidavit by Susan Smith which refers to two different other documents the first will be SS1 and the second SS2. The exhibit is marked by the solicitor who takes the oath of the person swearing the affidavit and is then pinned to it and kept with it. **4.16**

Before going on to discuss the commencement of proceedings in the High Court it is important to consider two other matters, namely which parties should be joined to the action and the costs consequences, and the use of counsel in litigation.

Joinder under R.S.C., Ord. 15

4.17 In a straightforward case one might be acting for, say, an unpaid supplier of goods against his customer; or a pedestrian who was knocked down by a motorist. In these cases there is no problem whatsoever. It is perfectly clear that you have one plaintiff and one defendant. Not all situations are so simple. It may be that the unpaid supplier of the goods has also on a separate occasion been libelled by his customer and it may be that the pedestrian has been knocked down not as a result of the negligence of one driver only but perhaps where two or three may have been involved in a collision. *Joinder* concerns whether parties may link together and have heard at the same time actions which would make this convenient in terms of the parties involved or which are factually connected in some way.

JOINDER OF PARTIES

Joinder by the plaintiff

4.18 Two or more persons may be joined together in one action as either plaintiffs or defendants without the leave of the court where if separate actions were brought some common question of law or fact would arise in all the actions and all rights to relief claimed in the action are in respect of or arise out of the same transaction or series of transactions. What this means is that if for example one driver should knock down two persons on a zebra crossing the plaintiffs may combine together to issue just one writ against the driver because their actions arise out of the same facts. There is of course no obligation to do so and in many cases it might be tactically or procedurally inconvenient. In that case each could, if they wished, issue a separate writ. Where there is more than one plaintiff on the same writ co-plaintiffs must use the same solicitor and counsel and may not generally make allegations of fact which are inconsistent with each other's cases. In the instance just cited therefore if the two persons knocked down on the zebra crossing happened to be husband and wife they would no doubt be intending to use the same solicitor anyway. If however they were strangers to each other each might prefer to issue a separate writ and use his own solicitor.

Joinder with leave of court

4.19 The case previously cited is where the parties may join as co-plaintiffs without the leave of the court because some common question of fact arises. Under Order 15 parties may also be joined with the leave of the court even though the above does not apply. There are very few cases where the court will think it appropriate to join plaintiffs together in this way where their actions do not arise out of some common question of fact or law. It would usually lead to delay and inconvenience to do so.

Joinder by the defendant

4.20 It is up to a plaintiff who issues a writ to choose who the parties should be. A *defendant* cannot as such join any other party in to be a co-plaintiff with the present plaintiff or a co-defendant with himself. All he can do is add another person to an action by bringing *third party proceedings* against that person. How this is done and the effect of this will be considered in the later section on third party proceedings at para. 14.01.

JOINDER OF CAUSES OF ACTION

Joinder by the plaintiff

A plaintiff can claim relief for several causes of action in the same proceed- **4.21** ings provided:—

1. the plaintiff claims and the defendant is alleged to be liable in the same capacity in respect of all the causes of action; or

2. in any other case with the leave of the court.

This means that if a plaintiff has a number of causes of action against the same defendant he may sue for them on the same writ and it does not matter that there is no factual connection between them. Thus for example if a plaintiff is owed a sum of money by the defendant and that defendant has also libelled the plaintiff, the plaintiff is able to include both causes of action on the same writ. Whether it would be tactically wise to do this is another matter, but the right to do so certainly exists. It is important to note that the parties must be claiming or liable in the same capacity in respect of all the causes of action. Thus if one wished to sue a given individual firstly for a debt which he had personally incurred and secondly for some debt for which he was only liable as the executor of an estate one could not issue one writ in respect of both causes of action but would have to commence two separate actions.

Joinder by the defendant

If a defendant has one or several claims against a plaintiff he may raise them **4.22** in the same action by way of a *counter claim*. The nature of his action need not in any way be factually related to that on the plaintiff's writ which has been issued against him. Thus, suppose a plaintiff was owed money by a defendant whom he sued for the sum involved; in the course of seeking repayment of the sum owed to him the plaintiff had at one time assaulted the defendant and at another time slandered the defendant: the defendant could raise both of these separate causes of action by way of a counter-claim against the plaintiff.

In practice joinder is not a particularly difficult topic. Although the rules permit actions to be commenced by co-plaintiffs or actions by one plaintiff concerning two causes of action it is often tactically wiser and procedurally more convenient to issue two separate writs. Such matters as compromise of one claim, acceptance of payments into court and so on are facilitated by this. For the same reason if say, six persons were injured in a road traffic accident it would probably be wiser for each to issue his own proceedings in relation to the matter. A substantial saving in costs can any way be effected in such cases by ensuring that interlocutory applications and even the trial itself proceed in such a way that all the plaintiffs are before the court at once.

If all six plaintiffs chose to be joined in the same action then the sheer bulk of the pleadings could become very cumbersome.

Costs consequences of suing two or more defendants: Bullock and Sanderson Orders

4.23 Mention has already been briefly made of the fact that a winning party in litigation may usually recover his costs from the losing party. Where a plaintiff is proceeding against two or more defendants it is apparent that he may win against only one or other of them. Where that happens one potentially has the situation where one has a winning plaintiff, a losing defendant and also a winning defendant, that is a defendant against whom say the allegation of negligence has failed. What is to happen to the costs of the winning defendant? The answer is provided by the existence of "Bullock" and "Sanderson" Orders. Where it was reasonable for the plaintiff at the outset to have sued the defendants then he may obtain an order that in effect the losing defendant pays not only the plaintiff's costs but those of the winning defendant also. There are two separate mechanisms for this, one achieved by the so called Sanderson order and one by the so called Bullock order. Each order takes its name from that of the plaintiff in a decided case. Under a Bullock order the plaintiff has to pay the costs of the winning defendant but is allowed to add these to his own costs and recover both from the losing defendant. Under a Sanderson order the losing defendant has to pay the winning defendant's costs directly. In fact although historically Bullock orders seem to have been favoured on the basis that the principal desire of the court is to protect the winning defendant, Sanderson orders are undoubtedly more common these days and considerably more convenient because in personal injury litigation a substantial proportion of plaintiffs are legally aided and almost all defendants are insured. Accordingly it is considerably simpler for the losing insurance company to pay the winning insurance company's costs direct without the awkward mechanics of arranging for payment by the plaintiff (which can only take place from his damages and then only when the question of his own solicitor's costs has been finalised).

4.24 It should be remembered that when applying for this order it is essential to show that the plaintiff was *reasonable* in joining both defendants at the outset. However reasonableness is not of course determined by the outcome of the trial. All that matters is that it should have appeared reasonable at the time when the action commenced. Thus if a number of vehicles are involved in a collision usually it would be "reasonable" for the plaintiff to consider suing all the drivers involved. Where a plaintiff commences an action against one defendant who himself issues *third party proceedings*, that is a separate action claiming some other person was liable. (See para. 14.01), it will of course always be reasonable for the plaintiff to apply to amend his writ and pleadings to add that other person as a second defendant since it is the first defendant himself who has made the allegation that that other was to blame. Thus if the second defendant is ultimately exonerated and the first defendant found wholly liable the latter can hardly contend that the plaintiff was unreasonable in suing the former.

The use of counsel in litigation

4.25 Barristers alone at present have rights of audience in open court in High

66

Court proceedings. Accordingly in any case likely to go to trial in the High Court a barrister is inevitably going to have to be briefed. Because of the sums of money involved, and because counsel are specialists in litigation whereas solicitors may have more general practices, and because of the professional negligence implications, it is common to use counsel as a sort of "long stop" to give expert advice throughout the conduct of litigation. It is a somewhat overworked analogy but a reasonably accurate one to say that counsel's position *vis-à-vis* the solicitor corresponds approximately to that in medicine of a consultant and a general practitioner. The principal uses of counsel in connection with litigation are as follows:—

TO ADVISE IN WRITING

From the early states of litigation counsel may be asked to give his opinion **4.26** about such matters as *liability*, *e.g.* does he think that on the facts the defendant is liable; *quantum of damages*, *e.g.* does he think on the facts that the offer put forward by the defendants is a reasonable one and should be accepted? *procedural tactics*, *e.g.* does he think that an application for summary judgment would be likely to succeed on the facts as known? *evidence*, *e.g.* what witnesses need to be called to prove the plaintiff's case, what documentary evidence needs to be brought to court, what procedural action needs to be taken, *e.g.* the service of notices to admit facts or Civil Evidence Act notices. To obtain counsel's advice on any of these matters one simply drafts a set of instructions to him. These are characteristically typed on "brief paper" and folded in four to provide a brief in the form which will be familiar. Within the brief one encloses all documents which could be of any assistance to counsel, *e.g.* witness statements, computation of loss of earnings, medical reports. Then in the text of the brief one sets out a commentary on these matters leading counsel through the relevant issues by reference to the documents supplied. Thereafter one concludes with ones own observations on the case and poses the question on which counsel is asked to advise. These papers are then delivered to counsel's chambers and in due course counsel will supply a written advice in which he sets out his views on the questions put.

TO ADVISE IN CONFERENCE

It may sometimes be thought that where the questions to be considered are **4.27** complex it is more satisfactory to have a so called "conference" with counsel in his chambers than to request a written advice. Instructions as previously described should still be drafted and sent to counsel if possible well in advance of the conference so that he can give them his mature consideration. The solicitor then attends counsel's chambers and in effect despite the somewhat grandiose title "conference" discusses the case informally with counsel who will then give his views which he may later supplement with a written advice. It is not uncommon particularly in the late stages of litigation to have one's client attend this conference. This assists the client to gain confidence in the barrister of the solicitor's choice (one hopes)! Conversely it makes the client disappointed if the barrister of his solicitor's choice is unavailable on the date of trial, whereas if the client had never seen the barrister then it would presumably make little difference to him which barrister did appear at the trial. At such conferences counsel may want to see

67

how the client will perform as a witness under a testing cross-examination on his version and this may well affect the advice that counsel gives. For example a barrister who has previously been optimistic about a client's prospects may on seeing the client form the view that he will make a very poor witness indeed because he has a shifty and evasive manner. He may therefore advise that an offer which was previously thought unacceptable should now be accepted because he feels that the plaintiff may lose outright at trial. It is not only one's client that one can take to such conferences. Whilst counsel may not by the rules of conduct of the Bar see witnesses of fact he may in conference meet expert witnesses. If therefore there is some particularly difficult point of medical evidence which is in dispute he may well wish to see the consultant who is going to testify for the plaintiff and ask him to resolve matters of difficulty and explain his disagreements with the defendant's medical evidence.

TO DRAFT PLEADINGS

4.28 Counsel may be employed as specialist draftsmen in a number of fields. In non-contentious work counsel may draft partnership agreements, tax settlements or wills but in connection with litigation counsel is generally used for drafting pleadings. Pleading is a specialist art. While a solicitor would probably draft a simple indorsement on a specially indorsed writ pleading a claim for a debt, usually drafting statements of claim or defences in personal injury actions will be left to counsel. Again counsel will be sent all necessary and relevant papers in the matter and asked to prepare the draft. It is this process which may take some time and may lead to the need for one or other party to ask his opponent for an extension of time for the purpose of having counsel complete and return his draft.

AS ADVOCATE

In open court

4.29 As indicated previously counsel have exclusive rights of audience in contested matters in the High Court in open court. Whilst solicitors have rights of audience in the county court it is generally considered a more profitable use of time to brief counsel at a fixed fee to conduct a trial in the county court also. We shall return to the subject of instructing counsel to advise on evidence and preparing a brief for trial at a later stage.

In interlocutory applications

4.30 In interlocutory applications before the district judge in chambers a competent litigation solicitor will usually appear himself. This is so even on matters of some complexity. If however a solicitor is less experienced, or perhaps not available for the hearing it may be appropriate to brief counsel to attend before the district judge in chambers on interlocutory matters of some substance. Examples of cases where a solicitor would probably consider employing counsel if he were not experienced would be applications for further and better particulars where there was some complexity of pleading involved; applications for summary judgment or to defend such an application; or applications for interim payments. It would be most unusual to brief counsel to appear before the district judge in chambers on matters which are purely procedural however, *e.g.* on a routine summons for directions hearing. The costs of counsel attending an interlocutory application cannot usually be claimed from the opponent even if one is wholly successful in the litigation. However a party may apply to the district judge at an interlocutory hearing to certify that a case was "fit for counsel," *i.e.* of sufficient difficulty that the employment of counsel was reasonable and then the fees will be allowed and payable by the losing party.

Counsel's clerk

Barristers are organised in sets of chambers and employ one or more clerks. **4.31** Clerks stand somewhat in the position of a theatrical agent in relation to the barristers, that is it is their function to keep their barristers fully employed, to negotiate fees for the work which they do and so on. Most solicitors use only one or two different sets of chambers and establish a good working relationship with counsel's clerk. One particular difficulty of the relationship is where a particular barrister has been involved throughout a long running case, *e.g.* to draft pleadings and advise in a person injury case and when the matter comes to trial it becomes apparent that the barrister is not going to be available because some other case on which he is already engaged is going to run for longer than anyone had estimated. This is a not uncommon hazard of all types of litigation. It is often very difficult to give an exact estimate for a length of hearing especially when neither side is willing to disclose the number of witnesses they propose calling or the nature or length of legal argument that they intend to present. Where a case does run over therefore, there is nothing a barrister's clerk can do to get the barrister freed from it. In such a case the solicitor will have to be content with a substitute, and often as late as the night before the trial. It is as well to insist on having a barrister of equal or greater seniority from the chambers or, if this is not possible to look to other chambers for such a barrister.

It can as has been noted already, be disappointing for the lay client especially **4.32** when he has seen his counsel on one or more previous occasions. To find himself faced with an unfamiliar figure whom he may suspect cannot know the case as well as his predecessor can be most disconcerting and in some cases may make the client on the morning of the hearing considerably more willing to compromise than might otherwise have been the case. Of course if the client has not as yet seen his advocate it may make little difference to him that the person who drafted the pleadings is different from the person who appears in court. There is realistically little that can be done about the problem (apart perhaps from applying for a fixed hearing date well in advance see later para. 10.05), until the methods of listing cases and organising the work of the courts is substantially rationalised.

We turn shortly to the commencement of an action in the High Court. One final preliminary consideration is the question of choice of court. In many cases actions may be commenced in either the High Court or the County Court. One important restriction on this is that a personal injuries action may only in principle be commenced in the High Court if the value of the action appears to be £50,000 or more. Some of the matters relevant to choice of court and eventual court of trial are discussed in a separate section at the end of the section of Civil Procedure at para. 18.01. The effect of changes in jurisdiction of the County Court effective in July 1991 will be to divert a great deal of business which formerly would have taken place in the High Court to the County Court. Nonetheless because High Court Rules are very similar to County Court rules, and because in particular where County Court rules are silent on a matter High Court rules are deemed to apply we shall commence by considering an action in the High Court.

5. Commencing an Action by Writ

The contents of the writ

A writ can be issued out of the central office in London or out of any district **5.01**
registry. There is no need for there to be any local connection with the cause
of action (although see below). The heading of the writ will show the place of
issue. The forms of writ are prescribed in the White Book. They are
obtained in blank from law stationers or held on word processors and are
usually in one of two forms namely:

1.   a writ claiming unliquidated damages (*e.g.* in a personal injury case) and

2.   a writ claiming a liquidated sum (*e.g.* in a claim for a debt):

The forms of a writ are completed by the plaintiff's solicitor. Each writ must **5.02**
contain upon it in addition to the parties' names and the name and address of
the solicitor issuing it one of the two following indorsements, namely:

1.   a concise statement of the nature of the claim made and the relief or
     remedy required (this is called the *general* indorsement and is used in a
     writ which claims damages); or

2.   an indorsement of the statement of claim. This form of writ is used in an
     action for a debt and the statement of claim will be brief enough to
     indorse actually on the writ thus avoiding the need for a separate
     statement of claim to be served later. This is called a *specially endorsed
     writ* although strictly speaking, the rules no longer use that term.

Where the *general* indorsement is used it is essential to state in it the remedy
required, the cause of action and a very concise description of the facts. The
general indorsement will be supplemented (if the action is defended) with a
full statement of claim served later in which the plaintiff will set out in
considerably more detail the factual allegations on which he bases his cause
of action and the nature of the relief claimed. The statement of claim can
only allege causes of action which have been already referred to in the
indorsement on the writ. Thus if for example a writ had been issued which
only alleged negligence by the defendant and the plaintiff actually wished to
allege both negligence and, say, nuisance or breach of a statutory duty, the
writ would have to be amended so as to insert these additional causes of
action before a statement of claim referring to them could be served.

Other indorsements

THE FIXED COSTS INDORSEMENT

Where the statement of claim is indorsed on the writ there will normally be a **5.03**
computation of interest due if interest is to be claimed. We shall return to
this topic in due course. In addition there is a so called "fixed costs indorsement" on the writ. This form of fixed costs indorsement is already pre-

printed on the writ when the solicitor obtains it from the law stationers and he must complete it. The appropriate figure to claim as fixed costs is found in a table contained in the White Book as an appendix to Ord. 62. The effect of the fixed costs indorsement and of the plaintiff pleading his claim for interest precisely is simply that the defendant in such a case who is minded to pay the amount claimed by the writ can extinguish all his liability by paying the claim in full together with the interest accrued to the date on which he wishes to pay and the figure for fixed costs. Provided this sum is paid within 14 days of receipt of the writ the defendant thus knows that he will not be liable for any further sums. In such a case a plaintiff will not be able to obtain an order that the defendant pay any other costs. Consequently since this is the only sum for costs which can be recovered from the defendant inevitably in such a case the plaintiff is going to have to bear some part of his solicitor's bill (unless there has been very little work indeed involved before the issue and service of the writ so that the amount of fixed costs does actually cover the whole of the solicitor's charges to his own client).

INDORSEMENT AS TO PLACE WHERE CAUSE OF ACTION AROSE

5.04   In the case of a writ issued from a district registry, whether it is a specially indorsed writ or a generally indorsed writ, the plaintiff may complete the indorsement showing that the cause of action arose wholly or in part in the district of that district registry. Completion of this indorsement prevents the defendant from applying in his acknowledgment of service to transfer the proceedings to the central office or another district registry. An example will help to explain this.

Example:
    Suppose the plaintiff lives in Newcastle and whilst crossing the street near his home he is knocked down by a vehicle driven by the defendant, who lives in Exeter. The plaintiff can indorse on his writ that the action arose wholly in Newcastle and issue his action in the Newcastle district registry of the High Court. If he did not so indorse his writ the defendant would be able to apply, when he returned his acknowledgment of service to the court, for the action to be transferred to be heard at the district registry most convenient to him in Exeter. Actually on the facts of a case like this the defendant would be most unlikely to succeed in his application because the court would conclude that the balance of convenience favoured having the action heard in Newcastle anyway where the witnesses are likely to reside. However, indorsing the writ in such a way does prevent the defendant even making that application. In the case of a contract action, especially for a debt, it would be open to the plaintiff to allege that the cause of action arose either in the place where the contract was concluded, or, if different, the place where payment under the contract was due to be received. In this latter case since the place where payment was due to be received is most likely to be the plaintiff's premises it should ensure that the plaintiff is able to issue proceedings in the district registry most convenient for him.
    None of the above is to suggest that the advantage of issuing proceedings in one's own local district registry is that one is likely to obtain "home town justice" or anything of that nature. It is simply a matter of the convenience of the plaintiff's solicitor. Naturally a solicitor prefers to attend at the court nearest his office. If one's solicitors are involved in an action which is

proceeding in a court some miles away they need to instruct a local firm of solicitors nearer the court to act as their agents in attending court on interlocutory applications and this is inevitably both more expensive for the party concerned and less satisfactory since the agents are unlikely, however thoroughly they are briefed, to be as aware of all the facets of the case as one's own solicitor.

INDORSEMENT OF PLAINTIFF'S ADDRESS FOR SERVICE

This must also be indorsed on every writ. This will either be the plaintiff's address if he is not employing a solicitor or the solicitor's office address. The plaintiff's own address must also be given. **5.05**

Issue of the writ
A writ can be issued by attending personally at the district registry or by posting the necessary documents to it. It is more common to issue a writ in person if the solicitor is within easy reach of the district registry concerned. Two copies of the writ are prepared together with one copy for each defendant in the case and therefore a minimum of three copies of the writ will be required. These are taken to the district registry office together with the legal aid certificate if one has been issued and a cheque for the writ fee. The fees on writs are increased from time to time and at the time of writing the fee for an ordinary writ is £70. The court staff check that the writ is formally in order. One of the forms must be signed by the solicitor issuing it. The signed copy is kept at court and is stamped with a note that the fee has been paid. The other two are returned to the plaintiff one of which is stamped with the word "original." The plaintiff's solicitor should retain the "original." The court staff enter the action number at the top of the writ. The action number consists of the year of issue, the initial letter of the plaintiff's name and then a number which corresponds to the number of writs issued so far that year in that district registry. **5.06**

The date of the court seal
On the front of the writ the court seal shows the date of issue of the writ and is the relevant date for the purpose of the Limitation Acts. The writ has a life of four months from the date of issue. If the writ is not served within that period a plaintiff may apply to the court for the writ to be renewed for a further period not exceeding 12 months but such application should be made before the expiry of the first four months, and good cause for the failure to serve must be shown (*e.g.* that the defendant has not yet been traced). The writ lapses after this four months' period. Accordingly if one has failed to serve the writ within time one may need to issue a second writ. This is possible although of course the solicitor will be expected personally to pay the fee wasted by his oversight in failing to serve or obtain a renewal of the original writ. If however the limitation period has meanwhile expired, whilst a writ may still be *issued* the defendant will naturally rely on the Limitation Act in his defence. **5.07**

Service of the writ
The sealed copy of the writ which has been brought away for service on the defendant must be served on him together with an acknowledgment of service form. These are obtained from law stationers and completed by the **5.08**

solicitor in his own office. In addition notice of legal aid must be served if the plaintiff is legally aided. This alerts the defendant to the practical consequences of having a legally aided opponent.

We shall now consider the various methods of service.

SERVICE ON INDIVIDUALS

Personal service

5.09 Personal service means that the writ is actually delivered into the defendant's hands. Formerly serving writs was considered within the province of articled clerks who would often spend happy hours loitering outside houses or business premises in the hope that the defendant would emerge. Increasingly however solicitors employ process servers to serve writs, and the fees of such process servers will generally be allowed on taxation of costs and thus a solicitor suffers no loss. If a person refuses to take the writ then touching him with it and the accompanying documents will suffice. Until quite recently it was generally necessary to effect personal service but now the need for personal service and the extreme indignities which can sometimes accompany it have been alleviated because of the second method which we shall consider.

Postal service

5.10 The documents may be sent by ordinary first class post to the defendant at his usual or last known address or may be put through the letter box at that address in a sealed envelope addressed to him. Service is presumed to be effected on the seventh day after the date on which the documents were posted to the defendant or inserted through the letter box.

This is now the common method of serving documents. One must be sure that one is bona fide posting them to the defendant's own address. It will not do merely to know, for example, that the defendant has some relative who lives at a certain address and post them to him there. The reason for this is that if the acknowledgment of service is not returned to the court in time the plaintiff may generally proceed to sign judgment in default (see later section on termination without trial para. 11.01). At this time the plaintiff's solicitor will need to swear an affidavit stating that the writ was validly served. One cannot in truth swear that a writ was properly served if it was sent to some address from which it was merely hoped that the person would collect it. It must be served at the defendant's own address.

5.11 Despite the provision for postal service there are some cases, particularly so called debt-collecting cases where solicitors still prefer to rely on personal service. This is because personal service is deemed to be effective at the moment of service and thus seven days are saved and also because it is notorious that defendants in debt cases often allege the documents were not received in the course of post; that they were not at home within the relevant weeks; that the dog ate the documents as soon as they came through the letter-box, etc. In debt-collecting cases where speed is often of some importance solicitors generally prefer the greater certainty of personal service despite the increased expense.

Service on nominated solicitor

A writ is deemed to be properly served on a party if it is served on his **5.12**
solicitor. For this purpose the solicitor must have been specifically
appointed to accept and agree to accept service for the particular transaction. Merely that one knew that a certain individual had used a certain
solicitor in the past (*e.g.* for a conveyancing transaction) would not entitle
one to serve documents on that person by posting them to his solicitor.
When serving documents on a nominated solicitor one serves the writ for
service together with one's own original writ and the acknowledgment of
service and send it back to the court in the usual way but he will also indorse
on the original writ that he accepts service on behalf of the defendant and
return this to the plaintiff's solicitor.

Substituted service

If it has proved impossible for the plaintiff to effect service in accordance **5.13**
with any of the above rules he may apply to the district registrar for an order
that the document be served by some other means. This is increasingly rare
in view of the provision for postal service but was of great use when personal
service was essential and the defendant was thought to be evading service. In
such cases one could apply for an order for substituted service, *e.g.* by
inserting details of the writ in the legal notices column of some newspaper or
even by announcing the content of the writ outside the defendant's premises
over a loudspeaker. This method is hardly likely to be required in a routine
case now.

Finally it should be noted that even if none of these methods have been **5.14**
properly used provided an acknowledgment of service is in fact lodged the
writ is deemed to have been properly served. Thus if one had, contrary to
proper practice in a case where the defendant's address was unknown sent
the writ to his parent's house and it had in fact been collected and he had
returned the copy of the acknowledgment of service to the court, service
would be deemed to have been properly carried out.

SERVICE ON A LIMITED COMPANY

In the case of a limited company service is effected by leaving the documents **5.15**
at, or by posting them to, the registered office of the limited company (see
section 725 Companies Act 1985).
     If they are *posted* there is a slight difference from the rules for postal
service which apply in the case of an individual. As will be recalled in the
case of an individual, service was deemed to be effected on the seventh day
after posting. In the case of companies however they are deemed to arrive
"in the ordinary course of post" and this is taken to mean that service is
presumed to be effected:

1.   if first class post is used on the second working day after posting and

2.   if second class post is used on the fourth working day after posting.

If the documents are physically taken to the registered office however
service is deemed to be effective immediately. Any proper officer of the

limited company may complete and return the acknowledgment of service, but thereafter a limited company *must* employ a solicitor in proceedings in the High Court.

SERVICE ON PARTNERSHIP

5.16 Where partners are sued in the name of their firm then the following methods of service are acceptable:

1. Personal or postal service on any partner.

2. Postal service by ordinary first class post to the principal place of business. In this case service is deemed to be effected on the seventh day after posting.

3. Personal service at the principal place of business on the person appearing to have control or management of the business (who need not be a partner as such), in which case service is deemed to be effected immediately.

4. If partners are individually named on the writ they should be served as individuals.

Proof of service

5.17 Service is proved either by a defendant returning the acknowledgment of service to the court or by the production of the original writ duly indorsed with a solicitor's signature to the effect that he accepts service on behalf of a client. If neither of these two methods is appropriate then it is necessary to provide an affidavit of service, that is an affidavit sworn by the person who effected service, whether personal service or by the actual act of posting the envelope containing the writ to the defendant.

5.18 The method of service most likely in a personal injury case is probably now service on a nominated solicitor. In such a case an insurance company or the M.I.B. is bound to be involved. Some for no good reason still insist that service be effected personally upon their insured, the defendant, but since they will immediately then instruct a solicitor to act, it would be considerably more simple if a solicitor were nominated to accept service of proceedings. As indicated earlier the service of a writ will usually mean that the matter will no longer be dealt with by the claims representatives of the insurance companies but will be passed over to be dealt with by their solicitors. Exceptionally however if it is desired to serve the writ merely to ensure that the limitation period does not expire and that the time for interest commences to run, it may be possible to agree that service of the writ will not interrupt the course of negotiations with the insurance company. Some solicitors consider that it is often possible to get a better negotiated settlement from an insurance company representative than from the insurance company's solicitors. This belief is often misplaced but may occasionally be justified.

Service of documents other than the writ

5.19 Once the action has commenced then service of other documents, for example interlocutory applications or court orders, is achieved by posting them to the solicitor on the record for one's opponent. If one's opponent is a litigant in person although such documents may be served in the ordinary course of post on the person concerned, in the case of extremely important matters, *e.g.* a summons for an early appointment for summary judgment, it may be deemed prudent for the sake of avoiding any doubt about the effectiveness of postal service to arrange for personal service.

The acknowledgment of service

When the writ is received by the defendant a form of acknowledgment of **5.20** service will be served with it. The defendant has 14 days after service of the writ in which to acknowledge service. There are in effect four things for the defendant to consider when deciding on how to complete the acknowledgment of service:

1. He must fill in his full name in the appropriate box.

2. The form invites him to say whether he intends to contest the proceedings, that is to defend them. There are two boxes and all that need be done is to tick the relevant one. If the defendant ticks the "*No*" box the plaintiff will be entitled immediately to proceed to obtain judgment under Order 13 (see later para. 11.01). If the defendant completes the "*Yes*" box by ticking it then the defendant has given notice of intention to defend. Thereafter the action will proceed as later described.

3. Stay of Execution. Suppose that a defendant who is being sued knows that he has no grounds upon which to defend but simply cannot afford to pay the amount claimed immediately. This is only appropriate in the case of claims for a debt or liquidated demand, because in the case of a personal injuries action of course there will be an insurance company (or the M.I.B.) involved. The defendant may legitimately fear that if he merely indicates that he does not propose to defend then the plaintiff will immediately obtain judgment against him and seek to enforce it by some unpleasant method, for example by execution, that is that the sheriff's officers may come to his home and remove his furniture and personal possessions (see later section on enforcement of judgments para. 19.10 for a full description of this). If the defendant does not propose to defend but merely wishes to be heard on the method of payment of the debt or liquidated demand he may tick the box indicating that he does not propose to contest the proceedings and then tick the box in paragraph number three stating that he does intend to apply for a stay of execution. He then returns the acknowledgment of service to the court. The effect of this is that whilst the plaintiff will be entitled to obtain judgment immediately he will not be entitled to enforce the judgment for a further 14 days. Within that period of 14 days the defendant must make an application by summons to the court supported by an affidavit which discloses his full income, assets and liabilities. The summons will be served on the plaintiff and there will then be a hearing before a district registrar at which the district registrar will consider what relief if any should be given to the defendant against the prospect of immediate enforcement. He may, having taken all relevant matters into account, decide to allow for payment of the total of the judgment debt by instalments or he may make provisions for payment of the

77

amount forthwith if the judgment debtor has assets readily available which would permit this.

4. Transfer of Action. If the writ was issued from a district registry as we have already seen the plaintiff had the option of indorsing on it (if it is the case) that the cause of action arose wholly or in part in the district of that registry. Where this can be truthfully stated the action will then proceed in that district registry and no application may properly be made to transfer the case to some other. Moreover, even if the cause of action did not arise in the district of that registry if the plaintiff chooses to issue the writ in the district registry for the district where the *defendant* resides or carries on business likewise the case will continue there. Obviously if the defendant resides or carries on business in the district that is potentially likely to be the most convenient to him in any event.

If however neither of these things apply, that is the cause of action did not arise in the district of that district registry nor did the defendant reside there and the only connection with the district registry is that it suits the plaintiff's convenience to have the action proceed there then it is open to the defendant to apply by completing the box in paragraph number four for the action to be transferred either to the central office in London or to a district registry chosen by him. There will need to be a subsequent hearing which will take place in the district registry where the writ was issued as to where it would be fairest to have the action proceed. The court will have to consider the balance of convenience in the case which will involve considering not just the parties' preferences but also the whereabouts of any potential witnesses and therefore their convenience in attending court when the matter comes to trial.

5.21   The defendant must then return the completed acknowledgment of service direct to the court no later than 14 days after the day of service of the writ upon him. The form must be returned so that it effectively arrives at the court within the 14-day period which *includes* the day of service. Posting it within the period will not suffice, it is the date of receipt by the court which counts. For the consequences of failing to return the document in time see later para. 11.01. Once the document has been returned the court will make a photocopy of it and send it to the plaintiff, or if there is more than one plaintiff to each of them.

The early progress of the action

5.22   We have so far seen the stages involved in issuing the writ, serving it and returning the acknowledgment of service to the court. We will now consider how the action will proceed from that point. What will happen next will depend in part upon whether the claim was one for a debt or liquidated demand or one for damages. If the case involves a debt or liquidated demand then the form of writ appropriate to that is likely to have been used, that is the statement of claim will be indorsed on the back of the writ.

If however the case involves a claim for unliquidated damages then a general indorsement of the nature of the claim will have been inserted on the writ. This necessitates the later service of a separate statement of claim.

The two most important pleadings are the respective statements of each party's case. The plaintiff's is called the statement of claim and the defendants is called the defence. In the plaintiff's statement of claim he sets out the factual allegations relied on to establish his cause of action and the remedy he seeks. The defendant's defence meets the factual allegations made.

In the case of suing for a debt or liquidated demand therefore the plaintiff **5.23** need serve no further document apart from the writ. The defendant will have to acknowledge receipt of the writ within 14 days and indicate his intention to defend; thereafter he must serve a defence to the statement of claim which was endorsed on the writ. He must serve this further document, the defence, no later than 28 days from the date on which he received the writ itself. Service is effected directly upon the plaintiff and there is no requirement to send a copy to the court. Therefore if the plaintiff has sued for non payment of a debt the defendant will have to state precisely why he contends that he is not liable to pay the debt, for example because the goods were wholly defective and not of merchantable quality. We shall return to the kind of matters which a defendant needs to raise in his defence in due course.

If however the action is one for personal injuries and the claim is for an **5.24** unliquidated demand then the writ will not itself contain the statement of claim. A separate document will need to be prepared which sets out all the factual allegations on which the plaintiff bases his claim; an indication of the type of harm he has suffered; and some indication of the relief he seeks, *i.e.* general and special damages. In this case when the defendant receives the writ and acknowledgment of service he should return the acknowledgment of service to the court within 14 days. Thereafter the plaintiff has a further 14 days in which to serve the statement of claim and it is when this is received that the defendant's 14 days for service of his defence commences. It may well be that the writ has only been served for the sake of protecting the plaintiff in regard to the limitation period or for the sake of starting interest running. The parties may in such a case agree that they will continue to negotiate and that the statement of claim need not be served for a specified time, or at all until the defendant insists that it should and puts the plaintiff on notice that he must serve it. Alternatively the plaintiff may wish to progress the action. In such a case he would normally not have served the writ until he had his statement of claim ready prepared so that he would serve it within the further brief period allowed under the rules. If his statement of claim was not ready he would have to ask the defendant to grant him an extension of time for service and if this was not given voluntarily apply to the court by way of a time summons for an order extending his time for taking this step. It is even more likely that the defendant will be hard pressed to serve his defence within 14 days of receipt of the statement of claim. One must remember that the plaintiff may take his time over the issue and service of the writ, subject only to the limitation period. The defendant may thus suddenly receive a very detailed document to which he must comprehensively respond and with only a fortnight to do so. The solicitor for the defendant may need to reinterview his client and perhaps witnesses and thereafter usually send instructions for counsel to draft the defence. Counsel rarely take less than a fortnight to draft documents. In such a case the defendant's solicitor will usually ask the plaintiff's solicitor for an extension of time for service of the defence. It is normal professional courtesy to allow at least one reasonable extension to a defendant in such circumstances, perhaps of, say, a month. The plaintiff's solicitors sometimes contend that the defendants having been rejecting liability throughout, presumably have only done so after obtaining information on the exact happening of the accident and therefore that they should be in a position to serve their defence very promptly. Nonetheless extensions are normally given if only because one would inevitably be allowed by the court if the necessity arose to apply there. If the defendant's solicitors require further extensions, which is not uncommon because of delay in getting the draft defence back from counsel's chambers, the plaintiff's solicitors may agree to a further extension or application may need to be made to the court. If an application to the court is required it is made by issuing a so-called "time summons" which will usually be given a hearing date within a couple of days. The district judge will almost inevitably allow one extension. Costs will normally be awarded against the party needing the extension.

The nature and content of pleadings will be more fully considered in the next section.

6. Pleadings. R.S.C., Ord. 18

Pleadings in civil litigation are the formal documents in which each party   **6.01**
states his case. The pleading must show all the facts which the party is relying
upon and hopes to establish to the satisfaction of the trial court. The purpose
of pleadings is to comprehensively state the nature of one's case and the
pleading defines the issue in the case so that at the subsequent trial it is not
open to a party to allege a fact which was not referred to within his pleadings.

Types of pleading
It is necessary to briefly mention the four main types of pleading which are: **6.02**

THE STATEMENT OF CLAIM

This is the plaintiff's statement of the facts and matters on which he relies in   **6.03**
establishing the cause of action in respect of which the writ was issued. As
indicated earlier, in a case of any complexity the statement of claim will be a
separate document from the writ but in an action for a liquidated demand
especially a debt the statement of claim may be indorsed upon the writ itself.
If the statement of claim is a separate pleading it will be served not later than
14 days after the giving of notice of intention to defend. If the plaintiff fails to
serve his statement of claim within this time it may lead to an application by
the defendant for the action to be dismissed. In view of this usually a
plaintiff's solicitor will already have the statement of claim prepared in draft
ready for service by the time he serves the writ itself. Indeed some solicitors
for convenience serve the statement of claim at the same time as the writ
even though it is a separate document and not indorsed upon the writ. In
such a case the defendant has 28 days in which to serve his defence.

DEFENCE

The defence is the defendant's first pleading and must be served within 14   **6.04**
days of service of the statement of claim or within 28 days after service of the
writ whichever is the later. As we have seen this may put the defendant in
some difficulties. The plaintiff can choose his own moment to draft, issue,
and serve the writ and draft and serve the statement of claim on the
defendant. The defendant may then have to reply to very detailed allegations within 14 days. As we have seen extensions are commonly granted to
allow the defendant time for drafting his defence. If an extension was not
allowed failure to serve a defence in time may lead to judgment being given
in default (see later para. 11.18).

COUNTER CLAIM

If the defendant as well as defending the statement of claim served by the   **6.05**
plaintiff has any cause of action of his own against the plaintiff he may add a
counter claim to his defence. As has been explained already this counter

claim need have no factual connection with the plaintiff's cause of action. Where a counter claim is added to the defendant's defence this operates as a statement of claim made against the plaintiff. The plaintiff must himself then serve a defence to the counter claim within a further 14 days and failure to do so will lead to the defendant being in a position to obtain judgment against the plaintiff in default of defence to counter claim.

REPLY

6.06 The plaintiff may serve a reply if he wishes to answer any factual allegations raised in the defence. It is never compulsory to serve a reply because the plaintiff is deemed to take issue with any matter raised in the defence. A reply should be served within 14 days after receipt of the defence.

Close of pleadings

6.07 Pleadings are deemed to be closed 14 days after service of the last pleading in the case. The close of pleadings has no significance in itself but it is used as the time for fixing when certain other things ought to happen in the case to which we shall come later. Pleadings should be served direct between the parties in the High Court and copies are not sent to the district registry. Accordingly the district registry has no idea whether the parties have or have not complied with time limits, which is a specific illustration of the general point made earlier that the High Court remains essentially passive in relation to the conduct of cases before it. Accordingly if the parties have agreed to grant each other mutual extensions for serving pleadings even for some years the High Court will not take any action in regard to the matter.

The contents of pleadings

6.08 Pleadings are formal documents which must contain the heading taken from the writ. That is to say each must contain the name of the court, the Division, the year and action number, the district registry where the action is proceeding, the title of the action, *i.e.* the name and address of the parties, the title of the pleading and the name and address for service of the party who is serving it together with the date on which it is served. In addition if the pleading was drafted by counsel it should have his name typed at the foot.

The pleading should be drafted in numbered paragraphs for ease of reference and within these paragraphs there must be set out in so called "summary form" the material facts on which the party pleading relies for his claim or defence. The pleading must be as brief as the nature of the claim permits and should not contain matters of evidence, *i.e.* it should not say how a party proposes to prove the facts which he is pleading, nor should law usually be pleaded. Evidence is a matter for the trial and law is something which the court will be deemed to know. It is however now appropriate to consider certain things which must appear in the pleading apart from the facts alleged.

SPECIAL DAMAGES

6.09 Until 1990 it was customary to include a full computation of special damages up to the date when the pleading was served. That computation would usually have shown in a comprehensible form the precise amounts claimed as constituent parts of special damages and not merely the total figures. Thus in a personal injury case involving loss of earnings it was customary to show the computation based on the net figure for loss of earnings over the weeks since the accident exclusive of tax and national insurance.

Now however under a recent rule change at Ord. 18 r. 12(1A), a plaintiff is specifically required to serve with his statement of claim a statement of special damages claimed. This will now be served as a separate document. The definition given in the rule to "a statement of the special damages claimed," makes it clear that it is not only special damages up to the date of service of the statement of claim that must be dealt with but also any estimate of future expenses and losses including loss of earnings and pension rights.

Where possible therefore a plaintiff will have to make these computations involving projections of future loss so that the rule may be complied with. Thus the defendant ought to be as fully informed of the exact figures involved in the case as possible.

That anyway is the purpose of the rule. In many kinds of case however it will be difficult for the plaintiff to give very much by way of worthwhile figures at least for future loss of earnings and loss of pension rights. If for example, in a large and complex case the plaintiff has got the action off to a prompt start by issue and service of writ and statement of claim then clearly any estimate of future loss of earnings, coming at a time when it is unclear when, or even whether, the plaintiff will return to work and if so in what capacity is likely to be vague. In such a situation there is provision permitting the plaintiff not to supply such documents and then either he, or the defendant, can apply to the court to give directions about the matter. It will often be convenient for the defendant to agree that it is pointless at such an early stage to attempt to provide detailed information. Much the same applies to the case of service of medical reports with the statement of claim to which reference is made below.

It should also be noted that the plaintiff shortly before trial, if the case goes that far, must serve amended computations of special damages and future loss of earnings on the defendant and that the parties are then obliged to attempt to agree the precise figures so that a great deal of judicial time is not wasted with arguments about computations.

INTEREST

The question of interest on damages has been referred to earlier. The claim for interest must be included in the statement of claim and there must be a reference to the contractual term under which interest is claimed if that is the case or if not, to the statutory provision providing for interest, *e.g.* Section 35A Supreme Court Act 1981. Moreover in the case of interest on a liquidated sum there must be a double computation of interest, as a lump sum due on the debt up to the date of service of the pleading, and as a daily rate from the day after the service of the statement of claim continuing until the date of judgment or earlier payment. In cases where the statement of claim is endorsed on the writ itself, as will commonly be the case in debt actions, then these figures must be computed as at the date of issue of the writ, it being assumed that in such a case the writ will be served forthwith.

It is appropriate to give a brief explanation with examples here:—

6.10

6.11 (i) A claim for a liquidated sum due under a contract, *e.g.* a debt, where the contract itself contains a provision for interest in the event of non-payment of sums due under the contract.

Example:
P supplies D with 700 teddy bears at an inclusive price of £7,300 on October 10, 1990 and the contract provides that payment should be made within seven days of delivery of the teddy bears and that if payment is not made that interest at the rate of 20 per cent. per annum is payable on the sums owed. Payment is not made and P wishes to issue a writ on October 17, 1991.

The writ will be in the form appropriate for a claim for a debt, *i.e.* it will have the statement of claim indorsed on the writ itself. The claim will be for the sum owed and interest due under the contract. It will show a computation of the amount of interest owed at the date of issue of the writ and also show the daily rate at which interest continues to accrue. This is for the purpose of showing the defendant how much he needs to pay on any given date to meet his liability. If he pays the correct sum together with the amount shown for fixed costs direct to the plaintiff within 14 days of service of the writ he has met his liability in full and the action is stayed.

The statement of claim will read:

"The plaintiff's claim is for the sum of £7,300 being the price of goods sold and delivered to the defendant and for interest thereon at 20 per cent. per annum pursuant to clause four of the contract for the supply of such goods entered into between the plaintiff and the defendant and dated October 1, 1990.

Particulars:
700 teddy bears delivered on October 10, 1990.   £7,300.

And the plaintiff claims:

1. The said sum of £7,300.

2. Interest pursuant to clause four of the said contract at the rate of 20 per cent. per annum equivalent to a sum of £1,460 for the period from October 17, 1990 to the date of issue hereof.

3. Interest under the said contract from the date hereof continuing at the rate of £4 daily until judgment or earlier payment."

6.12 (ii) In a claim for a liquidated sum then if the contract makes *no* provision for interest, interest may be claimed under section 35A of the Supreme Court Act 1981 (or County Courts Act 1969, s.69). We have already considered these provisions. If the plaintiff is willing to limit his claim to a rate of interest equivalent to the rate of interest awarded on judgment debts (*i.e.* currently 15 per cent. per annum) then he should show a computation of the interest due at this rate as a lump sum up to the date of issue and a daily rate thereafter. This is tactically wise because:

(a) It allows a defendant to know exactly what his liability is on any given day if he is minded to settle the action.

(b) It may allow the plaintiff, if the defendant does not give notice to

84

defend, to obtain judgment in default under Order 13 and this judgment will be final, *i.e.* the sum for which judgment is given will include interest due, so obviating the need for any hearing to assess interest (see para. 11.02).

On the same facts as before, but supposing this time there was no contractual provision for interest (and changing the date slightly to make the arithmetic easier!) the statement of claim would read as follows:

"The plaintiff's claim is for the sum of £7,300 being the price of goods sold and delivered to the defendant and for interest thereon from the date of delivery pursuant to section 35A of the Supreme Court Act 1981.

Particulars:
   700 teddy bears delivered on October 17, 1990   £7,300   **6.13**
   And the plaintiff claims:

1.   The said sum of £7,300.

2.   Interest pursuant to the said statute at the rate of 15 per cent. per annum equivalent to a sum of £1,095 for the period from October 17, 1990 to the date of issue hereof.

3.   Interest as above from the date of issue hereof continuing at the rate of £3 daily until judgment or earlier payment."

If the plaintiff seeks to argue that in such a case he should receive interest at a higher rate than that payable on judgment debts (*e.g.* because the sums involved are very large) he should not show a computation of the amounts claimed but just claim interest at large as in the following case:—

(iii) In a claim for an *unliquidated* sum, *i.e.* damages, no computation of a   **6.14** lump sum due or a daily rate can be provided because even though in a personal injury case one knows the rates of interest that the court will allow on each constituent part of the claim for damages, one does not of course know the amount which the court will award as damages. It is sufficient to claim interest in general terms referring to the statute. It is important to note that in every case a plaintiff must allege his entitlement to interest on damages in the body of the pleading *and* claim it at the end of the pleading in the so-called "prayer," *i.e.* the statement of the precise remedies which the plaintiff seeks. In a claim for damages therefore the statement of claim might end as follows:

"In respect of damages due to him the plaintiff is entitled to interest pursuant to section 35A of the Supreme Court Act 1981 for such periods and at such rates as to the court shall seem just.
   And the Plaintiff claims:

1.   Damages.

2.   Under paragraph 7 hereof interest pursuant to the said statute for such periods and at such rates as to the court shall seem just."

MATTERS OF LAW

Although as indicated above normally matters of law need not be pleaded   **6.15** there are some few cases where it is essential to do so; examples are where the defendant wishes to rely on the Limitation Acts in his defence.

MATTERS OF EVIDENCE

6.16 It has earlier been explained that matters of evidence need not be pleaded in a statement of claim or defence. It is a common error when drafting pleadings to include matters of evidence, *e.g.* to recite what one's witnesses will say or to make contentions about matters of fact rather than merely stating the facts. The only important exception to this general rule that evidence need not be pleaded is under R.S.C. Ord. 18, r. 7A which implements section 11 of the Civil Evidence Act 1968. This topic will be discussed in greater detail in the section on Civil Evidence but for the moment a brief explanation is called for. Where a previous conviction in a criminal court is to be put in evidence under Section 11 of the Civil Evidence Act it must be specifically pleaded.

Quite often the matter which constitutes the tort and thus the cause of action in the civil case will also be a crime. A clear example is the crime of driving a vehicle without due care and attention. In such a case any criminal proceedings taken by the police are likely to come to court relatively swiftly whereas a civil action arising out of the same incident will come on much later. Accordingly at the time when one is drafting a pleading in the civil action generally the criminal proceedings will be over. If the defendant has already been convicted one can refer to his conviction in the civil action. The effect of proving the conviction in the civil action is to reverse the burden of proof about the matter, that is to say that the defendant, if he has been convicted of careless driving will have the burden of showing that he was wrongly convicted and that he was not driving carelessly at the time. But for this provision of course the burden of proof would be upon the plaintiff to prove every fact in issue. This is therefore a great help to the plaintiff.

To use the conviction against the defendant a plaintiff must plead the conviction stating the precise offence for which the other party was convicted and the date of hearing; the name of the court which convicted; and the issue in the proceedings to which the conviction is relevant.

6.17 This last matter is often one that causes some difficulty. Some examples of this are given in the section on evidence later. Where the tort is the very same thing as the crime for which there has been a conviction, *e.g.* a single act of careless driving, there is no problem. The criminal conviction is clearly relevant to the tort. There are greater difficulties however in the case of crimes of strict liability which need not necessarily connote any negligence on the part of the defendant. Thus if for instance the defendant's brakes fail and an accident is caused he may be convicted of the strict liability offence of using a vehicle with defective brakes under the Construction and Use regulations but it does not follow that he has been negligent. He may for instance have had the vehicle recently serviced and the failure of the brakes may be due to some quite unforeseeable cause. On the other hand if he has not in fact had the brakes checked for a very long time arguably his failure to adequately maintain the vehicle *is* good evidence of negligence. This matter of relevance is dealt with at para. 31.29 hereafter.

6.18 A party confronted with a pleading in which reference is made to a past conviction may respond to it in one of four ways. He may either:

1. Admit the conviction and its relevance.

2. He may deny the fact of conviction, *e.g.* say that the plaintiff has got it wrong and that he was acquitted rather than convicted or that someone of a similar name was convicted. This would of course be very rare because a prudent plaintiff's solicitor would naturally have obtained a certificate of conviction from the criminal court before drafting the pleading.

3 He may allege that the conviction was erroneous, that is that he was convicted by the magistrate's court against the weight of the evidence, or perhaps even that he pleaded guilty in ignorance of some fact which would have been a good defence. To establish this may not be so difficult as one would imagine. A High Court judge trying an action for negligence will be a considerably more expert and demanding tribunal than three lay justices who are sometimes tempted to believe that if an accident occurs at all this demonstrates that it must be as a result of an error of judgment on the part of some person. It is useful to stress that a magistrates court is not concerned with trying relative degrees of negligence anyway. It may be that in many road traffic accidents both drivers have some degree of responsibility but the police prefer merely to prosecute the one who appears the more obviously blameworthy. For this reason the finding of carelessness is not in itself conclusive either of the fact that liability was 100 per cent. that of the defendant, or indeed of liability at all.

4. He may contend that the conviction is irrelevant that is to say that whilst he was properly convicted he contends that the offence is not relevant to the cause of the civil action. A good example of this would be in the case of conviction for a strict liability offence not necessarily connoting negligence as previously described.

One other matter which ought to be mentioned in connection with pleadings **6.19** is that where a document needs to be referred to or relied upon (*e.g.* the provisions of a written contract) the wording of the document should be summarised where material. If very lengthy provisions need to be referred to it is sometimes more convenient to say in the pleading that the document will be referred to for its full content at trial.

The contents of a statement of claim
(i) A claim for debt. **6.20**

As we have seen from the examples given above, a claim for a debt or liquidated sum often does no more than set out details of the sum claimed rather as in the form of an invoice. Having given particulars of the debt and goods supplied there is then a "prayer" that is a reference to the relief or remedy claimed. It is usually preceded by the words:

"And the plaintiff claims . . ." and then the nature of the relief sought (*i.e.* the claim for the debt and interest). It is not necessary to claim costs in the writ since the court always has discretion to award costs. If the fixed costs indorsement is appropriate that should however be completed.

(ii) A personal injury claim. **6.21**

The statement of claim will be drafted so as to contain the following matters:

1. A brief account of how the accident occurred.

2. An allegation that the accident was caused by the negligence of the defendant.

3. Particulars of the negligence alleged. This is usually a set of alternative or cumulative allegations detailing the deficiencies in the defendant's conduct which allegedly amount to a breach of his duty to the plaintiff, *e.g.* "The defendant was negligent in that he:

   (a) drove too fast;
   (b) failed to stop;
   (c) failed to keep a proper look out;
   (d) failed to observe a road traffic sign;
   (e) failed to observe the approach of the plaintiff;
   (f) failed to sound his horn;
   (g) failed to heed the warning given by the plaintiff;
   (h) in all the circumstances failed so to manage his vehicle as to avoid collision with the vehicle of the plaintiff.

It is usual to plead as many variants as possible of the defendant's negligence so that one is not restricted unduly at trial. It might be for example that the plaintiff has no idea whether particular (e) above is true—it might be the case that the defendant was watching the plaintiff closely throughout and just made an error of judgment in steering. The final particular, number (h) is a somewhat compendious allegation commonly inserted to cover any kind of error by the defendant.

One common error made by beginners when drafting a pleading is to meet a potential defence before it is made, *e.g.* "The plaintiff who was at all material times wearing a seat belt and driving well within the speed limit on the correct side of the road. . . ." This is never required.

4. There will then be particulars of injury. Here some brief details of the plaintiff's injury and medical condition are set out usually in language taken from the medical report. This is so even though a medical report ought in principle to be served with the statement of claim (see below); the plaintiff's date of birth should also be given.

5. Then, in the body of the claim will be Particulars of Special Damage. A computation should be shown as previously described listing and totalling the sums specifically claimed under each heading, and stating whether any are continuing and if so at what rate.

6. There should be a claim to interest made in a separate paragraph in the body of the pleading and referring to section 35A of the Supreme Court Act 1981.

7. Finally is the "prayer" where the plaintiff states the relief or remedy he seeks. In a personal injuries case that will consist of a claim in general terms to damages and interest pursuant to statute as described in the examples given previously.

Service of Medical Report with Statement of Claim.

Under a recent rule change, in every case in which a claim for personal injuries is made there is a prima facie requirement that the plaintiff should serve with his statement of claim a medical report, by which is meant a report substantiating all the personal injuries alleged in the statement of claim which the plaintiff proposes to adduce in evidence as part of his case at trial.

If the plaintiff intends to comply with this rule therefore he will need to obtain medical reports before issue of the writ to ensure that they are readily available. Normally one would have done this anyway in a substantial claim so that the necessary particulars of injury could have been inserted in the pleading. The importance of this rule however is that in principle if the plaintiff serves the medical report (and one should bear in mind that more than one report may be necessary since *all* the personal injuries should be substantiated and thus in a complex case one may have reports from more than one type of specialist) that the defendant will be put in full possession of th plaintiff's medical evidence. If the defendant then obtains his own medical report on the plaintiff (which there is no provision requiring him to disclose forthwith to the plaintiff) he will then, paradoxically, be better informed about the plaintiff's medical condition than the plaintiff is. Accordingly the defendant, especially if fully worked out computations of special damages have also been provided (see above) ought to be in the position to make a well calculated payment into court at an early stage (see para 12.03 for the significance of this).

There is a provision as to what is to happen if the plaintiff does not comply with this rule. The plaintiff may if he wishes apply to the court to direct that he need not comply with the rule but may serve his medical report later, or perhaps may withhold it until mutual exchange is possible (see para 9.10). Alternatively the defendant may apply to *stay* (that is, bring to a halt) the plaintiff's action. At the time of writing it is unclear how the courts will deal with applications under these provisions. Certainly the new requirements to serve a fully worked computation of special damages and the medical report whilst a striking development in the general direction of "cards on the table" litigation which may encourage early settlement in many cases, are also provisions which are capable of working to the plaintiff's tactical disadvantage as he has to disclose his hand whilst the defendant is entitled to keep his secret.

The defence

We have so far mainly considered drafting a statement of claim. We now   **6.22**
turn to some specific aspects of drafting a defence. A defendant in his defence must deal with every matter contained in the statement of claim and those with which he does not deal he is deemed to admit. It is usual therefore for the defendant to go through the plaintiff's statement of claim paragraph by numbered paragraph and replying to each matter raised in one of the three following ways.

ADMITTING

Where the defendant *admits* some particular matter he relieves the plaintiff   **6.23**
of the burden of proving the matter at the trial. It is taken to be established between them. Thus if for example paragraph one of the plaintiff's statement of claim merely alleged that an accident occurred on a certain road at a certain time the defendant would probably admit in his defence that this was

so (whilst going on to deny the plaintiff's subsequent paragraphs in which he contended that the cause of the action was the defendant's negligence).

NOT ADMITTING

6.24 Alternatively the defendant may *not admit* some particular allegation. Where he does not admit some allegation it means that he will not allow the plaintiff to take it as established at trial. The plaintiff must call evidence to strictly prove the matter not admitted. However it does not necessarily imply that the defendant will contest the matter in question. A good example is an allegation in the statement of claim in a personal injury case that the plaintiff has suffered certain injuries, or some loss of earnings. In either case a defendant may be inclined not to admit them. This merely means that he has no information of his own at present about the matters and he invites the plaintiff to formally prove these matters by proper evidence at the trial.

DENYING

6.25 Finally the defendant may *deny* (or *traverse*) allegations of fact made by the plaintiff. Where this happens the defendant not only denies the version given by the plaintiff but goes on to give his own version of the matter, *e.g.* to say that not only does he deny that the accident occurred due to his negligence but that in fact the accident occurred because of the plaintiff's negligence. He then goes on to list the matters he relies upon to prove this.

Further and better particulars

6.26 As has been explained a person is required in his pleading to plead all the facts and matters on which he will rely at trial. Although the purpose of pleadings is thus to convey material facts to the other party in practice it is common to plead one's case with a certain degree of brevity and/or vagueness. The reason for this is principally to leave sufficient room to manoeuvre subsequently and not to tie oneself down to too precise a version of the facts. If however one goes too far in this and the pleading is so brief or vague that one's opponent cannot clearly see from it what the exact allegations of fact are, then the party who is left in the dark may attempt to cut down the scope for manoeuvre, or sometimes genuinely seek information, by applying for further and better particulars. Where one requests further and better particulars then one drafts a document very much like the pleading itself with the full headings in the action and then asks in the body of the document for the further and better particulars required.

Suppose for example that a statement of claim merely alleged that the defendant "drove contrary to the provisions of the Highway Code." In view of the numerous provisions of the Highway Code it will be far from clear what precisely the plaintiff's case is on this matter. A defendant's request for further and better pleadings might therefore say:

"Of paragraph three the plaintiff's statement of claim and the allegation that the defendant drove contrary to the Highway Code state precisely to which provisions of the Highway Code the plaintiff refers."

6.27 The document which is drafted like, and which looks exactly like, a pleading, is then sent with a letter to the other party with a request that he should

90

provide the further and better particulars. The party of whom the request was made ought to comply with the request if it is reasonable but if he fails or positively refuses to do so an application may then be made by the person seeking the further and better particulars to the district registrar by summons. No affidavit in support is necessary. At the hearing the district registrar will consider whether the further and better particulars are required for the proper progress of the action. One matter which is *not* relevant to this decision is whether the party seeking the particulars already has the information requested. It is sometimes contended in a response to a request for further particulars that "the plaintiff already has the information" or "the facts are already known to the plaintiff who was present at the time." This however is irrelevant. It may be that this is indeed the case but the issue is *not* what the plaintiff knows. The point is that the plaintiff is entitled to know precisely what version of the facts the defendant is going to allege at trial and therefore the response that he already knows the details of how the incident arose is no answer.

The application for further and better particulars may be made by summons **6.28** at any stage or sometimes is left until the summons for directions hearing (if any). Particulars are not however normally ordered before a defence is served and a defendant faced with an ambiguous statement of claim will have to serve the defence to what there is at the moment whilst at the same time serving a request for further and better particulars of the statement of claim. When the further and better particulars are received it may be that one or both parties will need to amend their pleadings.

Where the request for further and better particulars is to be answered, either **6.29** voluntarily by the other party or pursuant to an order of the district registrar, then it must now be answered in a particular way. The original request for further and better particulars must be set out with the other party's response to each request beneath the paragraph in which it is requested. This contributes greatly to the coherence of the answers given. Previously replies to the request for further and better particulars were set out in separate documents which might lead to the need to refer to four separate documents at once, that is the statement of claim, the defence, the request for further and better particulars and the reply to that request.

It ought to be noted that although they have the appearance of pleadings **6.30** further and better particulars are not in themselves pleadings so that a request for them does not delay the time for the next pleading to be sent. However they are pleadings in the limited sense that they do set out matters which ought to have been included in the original pleadings, and thus when the documents in the case are collected for the trial judge as we shall see subsequently, the request for further and better particulars with the answers to the request will be contained in the bundle prepared for him.

Where a summons seeking an order for further and better particulars of a **6.31** pleading is issued the general order on costs that will be made is "costs in the cause" unless the pleading is so manifestly defective that it was unreasonable for the party serving it to refuse voluntarily to supply the particulars required.

6.32   A request for further and better particulars from an opponent therefore may be seen as having two possible purposes. The first is a genuine desire on the part of the person seeking particulars to obtain information, as in the case of the reference to the Highway Code above. Thus if a party simply is left in the dark as to what the alleged facts are by the original pleading a request for further and better particulars would be appropriate. The second possible purpose would be to attempt to tie the other party down to a more specific version of events with a view to limiting the opponents, scope for manoeuvre at trial. Requesting further and better particulars may often therefore be part of the tactical manoeuvring of the parties. We turn from a request for further and better particulars to what is a much more direct attack on a party's pleading.

Striking out pleadings Ord. 18, r. 19

6.33   One party can apply to the court for an order striking out all or part of an opponent's pleading on one or other of the following grounds:—

6.34   1.   "that the pleading discloses no reasonable cause of action or, as the case may be, defence."
        An example would be a statement of claim which alleged negligence by a judge in the exercise of his judicial office which it will be appreciated is not actionable in English law. It is difficult to imagine that a professionally drafted pleading would never amount to a *defence* but one could well imagine how the situation might arise where a layman drafts his own pleading. Thus for instance if in a debt claim the defendant served what purported to be a defence on the plaintiff merely saying that he was unable to pay the debt at present, since this is not of course a defence in law the plaintiff would be entitled to apply to strike it out. We shall discuss at greater length the difficulties of coping with laymen's pleadings in the context of the county court where they more frequently arise.

6.35   2.   "That the pleading is scandalous, frivolous or vexatious." It is a fact of life that some people like to use the law courts for the purpose of causing difficulty or embarrassment to persons who have upset them and have little serious aim of obtaining redress for a genuine grievance. Habitual petty litigants may be ruled by the court to be "vexatious" and a vexatious litigant generally needs the leave of the court before issuing further writs. Here we are concerned with someone who is litigating in order to fulfil some collateral purpose, probably to embarrass his opponent. If the pleading is manifestly frivolous or vexatious it will be struck out. "Scandalous" would imply some matter introduced into a pleading for a purpose that is clearly irrelevant to the cause of action. Thus it may well be the case that in defamation proceedings allegations of a highly scandalous nature are quite properly made. However in defamation that is often the essence of the case, especially where the defence is justification. If however similar allegations were made in the course of a pleading in a debt or personal injury case the court would strike out the pleading or the relevant part of the pleading.

6.36   3.   "It may prejudice, embarrass or delay the fair trial of the action."
        In this context "embarrass" has the sense of "leave the other party totally unaware of what is being alleged." Therefore where a pleading

gives no assistance in progressing the case it may be struck out on this ground.

4. "The pleading is otherwise an abuse of the process of the court." This is **6.37** something of a catch all provision and there are very few modern cases illustrating the use of this ground when none of the others was appropriate. Generally applications to the court will be made under one or other of the three previous grounds.

One applies to strike out all or part of one's opponents pleading by summons to the district judge and preferably very soon after the pleading has first been served. If the whole pleading is ordered to be struck out then if it is the statement of claim since there will now be no valid statement of claim from the moment it is struck out the defendant may apply to dismiss for want of prosecution. If it is the defence that is ordered to be struck out then judgment for the plaintiff in default of defence may be given forthwith.

Amending the writ and pleadings

One might imagine that by the time negotiations had broken down and one **6.38** was ready to serve a writ that one would have a fairly comprehensive factual picture of how the incident in question arose and of one's cause of action and the facts necessary to plead in support of it. One would also certainly imagine that one would know who one's opponents were to be. In a surprising number of cases however one finds out vital information only after, sometimes long after, a writ has been issued and served. In this section we shall now consider the steps that need to be taken where it becomes necessary to amend one's writ and subsequent pleadings.

AMENDMENTS AS TO PARTIES

It may become apparent only after proceedings have been issued that either **6.39** one has issued them against the wrong person, or more probably that there should be a second or further defendant in addition to the present one. An example of how this could arise would be if a pedestrian were knocked down by a motor vehicle which mounted the pavement. One might imagine he had a very straightforward cause of action. It might not become apparent until proceedings had been issued against the motorist that the nature of the motorist's defence would be that he was forced to swerve onto the pavement to take avoiding action because some other motorist pulled out in front of him and that in the circumstances he contends he was not negligent. In this situation the plaintiff on discovering this information would be well advised to think carefully about adding the other driver as a second defendant. It would certainly be rash to apply to amend by dropping the first driver entirely because it might be found at trial that the allegations made in his defence were entirely groundless. One has little to lose however, as we shall see, by applying to amend the writ and subsequent statement of claim to add the second defendant. In a contract case it is obviously more rare not to know whom one should be suing at the outset since it is generally fairly clear with whom one has contracted. The situation could arise however in the case of say some electrical item which was sold to the plaintiff and exploded causing injury on first being switched on. He would have an obvious cause of action against the shop owner who sold the item but let us suppose that after proceeding with the litigation for some little time doubts began to emerge about the solvency of the shop owner and his ability to satisfy a large claim for damages. It might be that on further consideration it was concluded that there might be a cause of action also against the manufacturer of the defective item and in those circumstances it might well be wise to add him as a second defendant.

6.40 If the writ has been served at the stage where the need to amend it to add a party arises, application has to be made to the court for leave to do so. Application is made by an ordinary summons to the district judge. There is no need to file an affidavit with the summons but a copy of the proposed amendment is lodged at court and served with the summons on the opposing party. It is not of course necessary at this stage to serve notice of this application on the party whom it is intended to add as a second defendant. They are not involved in the action until leave to amend is given. If the need to amend to add another party actually became apparent after the writ had been issued but before it had been served then the writ can be amended without the leave of the court.

If the writ has already been served at the time when amendment is needed it may well be that the statement of claim has also been served. Since the statement of claim will only make allegations against the original defendant there will of course be a need to amend the statement of claim to add the new party and to make specific allegations against him.

6.41 Where one adds a new defendant there are at least two other important tactical steps to consider. The first of these is that if one is adding a new defendant in a road traffic case it will be wise to serve notice of one's intention to proceed by letter on the insurance company of the proposed new defendant in advance of the hearing for leave to amend. This is to gain protection under section 152 of the Road Traffic Act 1988. For these purposes proceedings are *commenced* against the new defendant on the date when leave to amend the writ is given.

6.42 Secondly one should not overlook the possible necessity to apply to the Legal Aid Board to amend one's legal aid certificate. Legal aid certificates when granted are not granted in general terms, *e.g.* "to take all steps necessary to obtain damages for X" they are issued in very specific terms, *e.g.* "to take proceedings against Y for damages for personal injury." If therefore one wishes to add a second defendant it would be necessary to obtain amendment to the legal aid certificate. One can generally achieve this by simply writing a letter to the Area Office setting out the background circumstances and explaining why the amendment is required. When the amended certificate is received a copy should be filed at court and notice of the amendment given to the other parties involved.

6.43 It ought to be stressed here, to avoid a mistake which is very common among students, that the *defendant* cannot apply to amend the writ by adding any other parties. It is not open to him for example to apply that somebody else ought to be made a plaintiff on the same writ nor to himself join another defendant to share the blame. How the defendant achieves this latter aim will be explained in the section on third party proceedings in due course (see para. 14.01).

AMENDMENT AS TO CAUSE OF ACTION

Precisely the same rules about the necessity to apply for leave of the court **6.44** where the plaintiff wishes to alter or add a new cause of action. If for example one had issued a writ alleging negligence against a defendant and it later came to one's attention that the circumstances might amount to both nuisance and negligence then one could apply to the court to add the second alternative cause of action. One would have to obtain leave in precisely the manner previously described and if the statement of claim had been served then the statement of claim would need to be amended also.

OTHER AMENDMENTS

The two amendments just considered, that of adding a new party and of **6.45** adding a new cause of action, are clearly amendments of very considerable substance. It may well be however that as a case develops new information comes to light which makes it apparent that extra or alternative allegations of fact ought to be added to one's pleadings for completeness. It would be rare that such matters of fact need to be contained in the writ as well as the statement of claim but the rule is the same in either case.

If new or alternative allegations of fact need to be put in the writ or pleading then the writ or pleading may be amended *once* without the leave of the court so long as this happens before the close of pleading stage is reached. If however the amendment is required after this stage, or if in any case it is a second or later amendment the leave of the court is needed unless all other parties consent to the amendment. Where leave is needed it is obtained in precisely the same way as before described by issuing a summons seeking leave and lodging a copy of the proposed amendment with the summons and serving a copy thereof on the opposing party. It is not uncommon to leave amendment of this kind to the stage of the summons for directions which will be described hereafter.

It may help to give an example of how such a thing might arise and what precisely would be done. Suppose that in the case of a road traffic accident the plaintiff is alleging that the defendant was negligent in that he:

(i) failed to allow a proper distance between himself and the vehicle in front;

(ii) failed to brake in time;

(iii) failed to keep a proper look out.

Suppose subsequently an order for discovery of documents is obtained and at this time the vehicles's maintenance records are revealed and they show that the defendant had failed to have the vehicle serviced for many months. In that case the plaintiff might want to add a fourth and alternative allegation, namely that the vehicle's brakes were defective. To do so, since close of pleadings would already have occurred, he would apply to the court by summons for leave, lodging with the court a copy of the proposed amendment to his pleading.

It should be noted that pleadings may always be amended with the consent of all other parties to the action. If therefore, at whatever time the pleading needs to be amended, everyone else consents there is no need to apply to the court for leave. When considering the question of consent to amendment the matter of costs ought also to be dealt with. The usual principles are described below.

Before passing on from the topic of amendment it is important to deal with the following miscellaneous matters:

The policy of the court

6.46   The policy of the court on applications for amendment is extremely liberal. The court does not view itself as an institution for disciplining the parties and an amendment, no matter how foolish or negligent the original oversight may have been, will generally be allowed "on terms." The terms will be that the party who requires the amendment must pay the costs of any other party who incurs costs in consequence of it. Suppose therefore that the plaintiff does wish to amend his statement of claim. The defendant will be awarded the costs "in any event" covering both the expense of attending the summons before the district judge and of carrying out any consequential amendments to his own pleadings which are needed to answer the new allegations made by the plaintiff.

The method of amendment

6.47   Amendments are carried out by inserting the new words in red on a re-typed copy of the original writ or pleading. Any paragraphs which are now to be erased from the pleading must remain typed in and legible but are struck through once in red. It may be important for example at the subsequent trial to establish just what the original allegations were even though these are no longer part of the plaintiff's case. Amendment takes effect from the date on which the original writ was issued and/or the pleading served. In other words the writ is deemed always to have been in its final form no matter how many amendments have in fact been made to it. Further amendments after the first are to be made in green ink and thereafter in violet, and then in yellow.

Consequential amendments

6.48   As has already been indicated where a party is given leave to amend his pleadings the opposing party must also be given leave to amend his to cope with any new matters that are pleaded. The costs of these consequential amendments will inevitably be ordered against the party who required the original amendment unless some special factor is present. Each newly amended pleading must of course be re-served unless the court gives leave to dispense with re-service, *e.g.* because the amendment has been allowed in precisely the form of the document lodged with the summons for leave to amend and therefore the opposite parties will already have copies of the intended amendment. Where the court gives leave to amend the amended writ or pleading should have typed on it in red "Amended this ... day of ... 1991 pursuant to the order of District Judge Jones."

7. Discovery and Inspection

Discovery and inspection is the stage of an action at which one party reveals **7.01** to another what relevant documents are or have been in his possession, custody or power, and provides an opportunity for that other party to inspect and take copies of those documents which he has and in respect of which he is not entitled to refuse inspection. A party will be entitled to refuse inspection of documents only where he claims they are irrelevant or where he claims there is some privilege attaching to them.

It is important to note that the term "discovery" therefore strictly means revealing the existence of documents, and the term "inspection" means allowing the opposite party to look at those documents. However somewhat confusingly the term "discovery" is sometimes used of the whole process, *i.e.* of both discovery and inspection, and a non-technical word "disclosure" is also sometimes used in respect of either stage or both.

We have already considered briefly the nature of discovery in the context of pre-action discovery in a personal injury case. The essence of discovery proper is that it is the stage of an action at which a party is compelled honestly to reveal documents in his possession which are relevant to the case. Documents are relevant if they "relate to any matter in question in the proceedings." Thus they are relevant if they relate to either liability or quantum and, most importantly, whether they assist or are detrimental to the case of the party who has them.

At the stage when discovery is reached one is obliged to carry it out **7.02** truthfully and comprehensively. The ethics of negotiating in litigation generally permit one to argue as fiercely as one can in favour of one's client's case and attempt to obtain as advantageous a settlement of the litigation as possible. However at the time of discovery it is absolutely vital that the procedure be carried out completely honestly. Viewed ethically this leads to somewhat odd conclusions. For example if one has in one's possession a document which is harmful to one's case, indeed conclusive of the issues against one's client, and the document is not protected by privilege then one is obliged to reveal it to the other side in the process of discovery and although one may have attempted to negotiate as aggressively as possible up to that point, if the document is conclusive the case is as good as over from the time when the other side are made aware of the document. However what if the item of evidence is the kind of document which is privileged? Suppose for instance that there is a collision between vehicles driven by P and D. Acting for P you manage to trace an independent eye witness who gives a very convincing description of the incident in which he totally blames P. You also find that D is unaware of the existence of this eye witness. A witness statement is a document which is privileged. Accordingly one need not show this document to the opposite side nor reveal the name and address of the witness concerned to them, nor subsequently call that witness at trial. One can therefore go to trial hoping that P's version will be believed as against D but knowing that the only truly independent observer exonerates D from blame. This is perfectly consistent with the ethics of litigation.

Let us take an example which illustrates the converse situation. Suppose for example that there is litigation over whether or not a certain type of engine supplied to the plaintiff is or is not adequate for certain jobs and the plaintiff is suing the defendant and alleging that there is a serious design fault in the engine. There are a number of memoranda from the defendant company's design engineers going back some months before the engine was put on the market expressing grave reservations about its capacity to do certain jobs and pointing to the very defects in design for which the plaintiff contends. These documents are not privileged and when discovery and inspection takes place therefore they must be revealed to the plaintiff. At that stage clearly the defendant's case would look hopeless. Discovery must be carried out honestly despite the adverse nature of these documents.

Time for discovery

7.03   In most actions begun by writ the parties must make so called "general discovery", *i.e.* disclose to each other the documents which they have in their possession, custody or power which are relevant to the action. Under R.S.C., Ord. 24, r. 1 within 14 days after the close of the pleadings the plaintiff and defendant must exchange lists of all the relevant documents which have been or are still in their possession, custody or power. The lists of documents must in principle be in the prescribed form which will be described hereafter. In fact if there are very few documents and the nature of them is obvious one can often agree to list one's documents in some more informal way, *e.g.* by letter but it is generally best to adhere to the rules and insist on discovery in the appropriate form.

The form of the list

7.04   The list of documents contains three separate sections, Schedule I, Part I which is a list of documents which a party has in his possession and does not object to producing. Schedule I Part II lists documents which a party has and which he does object to producing together with a statement of the grounds of his objection, and Schedule II lists documents which a party once had in his possession which are relevant to the action but which he no longer has.

An example of one document of each kind would be in Schedule I, Part I correspondence between the parties forming the basis of a contract; in Schedule I, Part II a witness statement; in Schedule II the original of some letter which had been sent to some other person which was relevant to the action (the carbon copy of that letter being a document listed in Schedule I, Part I as still being in the party's possession).

Moreover at the end of the list there must be a statement of the time and place at which the documents in Schedule I, Part I will be made available for inspection which must be in principle within seven days after the exchange of the lists. It is usual for solicitors to complete this section by saying that a party will give inspection at any reasonable time on reasonable notice at the office of his solicitor. Unless the documents are very bulky inspection generally takes place, by convention, by the defendant's solicitor attending at the plaintiff's solicitor's office with his documents so that mutual inspection can be carried out at one and the same time with saving of costs. As an alternative to attending one's opponent's office to inspect the documents physically one may simply require one's opponent to supply photocopies of the documents in his list which one considers will be of relevance. Accordingly there is only very much point in attending a physical inspection if one suspects that there may be something worth seeing in the very fabric of the document which may not reproduce on photocopying, or perhaps if the documents disclosed on discovery are very voluminous indeed so that a great deal of expense would be occasioned by simply asking for photocopies of them all.

What documents are privileged?

Documents in Schedule I Part II are those which attract privilege. The subject of privilege is considered more fully in the section on Evidence hereafter. In routine litigation one will only be concerned with documents which attract *private privilege*, and that is in particular communications between a solicitor and his client about any matter at all and communications between the solicitor and any other person in connection with the litigation. Examples of the latter would be statements obtained from eye witnesses; expert witness reports; notes from, advice from, and instructions sent to, counsel and so on. Where one's documents are within this head of privilege it is common to list them in Schedule I Part II in a vague and uninformative way so that the opposite party is only aware in the most general terms of the nature of the document and in the case of witness statements is provided with no details about the date and the name and address of the maker. For example a common way of completing Schedule I Part II is to say "instructions to and advice and notes from counsel; witness statements, expert witness reports and other documents prepared solely for the purpose of the litigation."

    We have thus discussed so called *automatic* discovery. It is fair to say that this provision under Ord. 24, r. 2 is one of those most commonly ignored in practice and many solicitors wait until the summons for directions to obtain an order for directions even though such is strictly speaking superfluous and they would have been entitled to discovery automatically if completed at the correct time. We now turn to the topic of orders for discovery.

7.05

Orders for discovery

Automatic discovery is not always applicable. There are several exceptions the most important two of which are in *third party proceedings* and in the case of claims for damages for personal injuries arising out of an accident on land. Automatic discovery in the case of a personal injury action arising out of an accident on land does not have to be as full as in other cases. In such a case:

7.06

1.   The defendant does not have to make any discovery at all; and

2.   Discovery by the plaintiff is limited to documents relating to any special damages claimed (*e.g.* details of loss of earnings, tax rebates received etc.)

This apparently strange rule is simply a matter of expedience which recognises reality. In most such cases the defendant will not in fact have any documents which are relevant to the action. Nor will the plaintiff have any documents other than those relevant to special damages. This rule however merely recognises routine situations. As we shall see subsequently if it does occur to one or other party that the opponent has some document which is important and is worth seeing then an application can be made to the court to vary this prima facie rule and to ask for an order for discovery.

Where there is no automatic discovery or no full automatic discovery as in the case of a road accident as we have discussed, a party may apply to the court on summons for an order for discovery. No affidavit in support is necessary. This matter is often left until the taking out of a summons for directions which is a stage we shall in due course discuss. At the hearing of the summons a party may ask for either *general* discovery whereby the opponent must list all relevant documents or *particular* discovery whereby a party can be ordered to list documents or a class of documents in a particular category. If one is applying for particular discovery one must show at the hearing of the summons the nature of the documents which it is believed the opponent has and why they are relevant to the case.

What can one do when one suspects that one's opponent has not made full and honest discovery?

7.07   There are two possible alternatives. Whichever one is minded to adopt then it is naturally both courteous and cost efficient to write first to the opponent pointing out that you believe that he has other material documents which he has not disclosed in his list and indicating the nature of them. Only if there is a refusal need the matter be taken further by way of summons. If that happens then one applies on summons either for an order that the opponent gives particular discovery specifying the class of document or individual document which it is supposed he is withholding or one applies for him to give discovery by *affidavit*. The list of documents which is normally completed and exchanged between the parties is not of course on oath. That is not to say that a party who dishonestly completes discovery is not anyway committing a serious breach of the Rules of the Supreme Court and if it is a solicitor who is personally responsible such action amounts to grave misconduct. However one can go a stage further in bringing home the consequences of dishonesty by asking that one's opponent gives discovery on affidavit in which he must make a sworn statement that the documents revealed by him are the only relevant ones. The consequences of swearing the affidavit falsely are too obvious to need further discussion.

What if there is non compliance with automatic discovery and/or an order for discovery?

7.08   The procedure to be adopted in such cases is a good example of what should be done in the event of non-compliance by one's opponent with any procedural requirement. One first applies back to the district registrar by summons for an order that the party in default comply either with the provisions of the rules on automatic discovery or with the specific order for discovery which has been made earlier and is now ignored. The consequences will be that the party in default will inevitably be criticised by the district registrar and be required to pay the costs of the wasted hearing in any event and moreover that some sanction will be attached to the second order. This may be in the nature of an "unless" order whereby if the party continues to fail to give proper discovery the court may order that, if he is the plaintiff, his action should be dismissed or if the defendant the defence struck out which will in either case bring about the end of the case. Moreover either in addition to or in substitution for the previous remedy, there may be an application made by summons to a judge in open court to commit the party in default (and in some situations the party's solicitor) for contempt if discovery is not properly made as required. The judge will generally make a suspended order for committal which will only come into effect if the party in contempt does not purge his contempt by giving discovery properly within a very short further period. If there is failure to do so the committal becomes operative and the party in default will be taken to prison.

We have now dealt with the basic provisions for discovery and inspection but two other matters relevant to this general area ought now to be mentioned.

DISCOVERY AND INSPECTION AGAINST A NON-PARTY UNDER ORD. 24, R. 7A

It will be recalled that there was a procedure for obtaining discovery of a **7.09** vital document even before the issue of a writ under Order 24, r. 7A in a personal injury case. Although, subject to some few exceptions which are beyond the scope of this text, discovery can in general only be ordered as between opponents in an existing action, there is in a personal injury case a power to order a person who is *not a party* to the action to give discovery of some relevant document to one or other of the parties in the action. To take a very straightforward example suppose that one has an action for damages for personal injuries for a plaintiff. The plaintiff's claim to future loss of earnings depends on obtaining a good deal of information from his present employers and the employers are proving difficult about providing this information. If every avenue of reasonable approach has failed then under the second limb of Order 24, r. 7A *in a personal injury case only* either of the parties may apply as against a non party (here the employer) for discovery and inspection of a relevant class of documents (here wages records and details of career structure of the plaintiff). The method of application is by summons in the action. However, one has for the purpose of this single application only, to add the party against whom non party discovery is sought as a further defendant to the summons. (There is no need to amend one's other documents of course). The summons is then served on both the party against whom the application is made and on all other present parties to the action and the court will, if the documents are indeed relevant for the progress of the action, make the order against the non party. There is a general provision that the non party may obtain an order for his costs both in attending the application and carrying out the court order so that a person who had no actual interest in the litigation between the other parties is not prejudiced by having to perhaps spend time going through extensive employment records to obtain the necessary information.

INSPECTION OF PROPERTY UNDER R.S.C. ORD. 29, R. 7A

We have so far only dealt with documents. It may well be that one or other of **7.10** the parties has in his possession some thing which is relevant to the action either as being the subject matter of the action itself or as being some piece of evidence in it, *e.g.* either the goods whose merchantable quality is under dispute or perhaps the car whose defective condition is alleged to have caused the accident. We have already seen how under Order 29, r. 7A one or other party to an intended future action may apply to the court for an order allowing for the detention, preservation, photographing, inspection or taking of samples of any thing which is "the subject matter of the action or as to which any question may arise." It naturally follows from this that once the action has commenced the court has a general power as between the parties to order any of those remedies in respect of a thing which is the subject matter of the action or as to which a question may arise. Application is made by summons to the district judge. In the case of this as in the case of most other orders it is prudent to apply first by letter to the other party. For completeness it ought to be mentioned that just as in the case of non party discovery once an action involving personal injury has commenced discovery can be ordered of any document in the possession of a non party so one can *in a personal injury case* where some non party has a thing which is either the subject matter of the action or as to which any question may arise, apply for an order that that person allow inspection etc. of the thing in question. Thus for instance if the vehicle which is alleged to have caused an accident has now been sold to a scrap yard, a summons can be taken out asking for an order obliging the owner of the scrap yard to let one inspect the vehicle in question.

8. Directions. R.S.C., Ord. 25

As was stressed at the outset and throughout the procedures so far described **8.01** the Queen's Bench Division of the High Court remains passive throughout the course of proceedings. With the exception of the writ which is issued at court and the acknowledgment of service which must be returned to the court before a copy is sent out to the plaintiff all further proceedings pass between the parties directly. Pleadings are served directly and no copy is sent to the court; and unless one party or other required an order for something which his opponent was unwilling to give voluntarily there would be in an ordinary case no need for either party to make application to the court. The first time when the parties do come before the court and the court takes some initiative in controlling the future running of the case is the directions stage. If one simply added together the time limits for each of the preceding stages set out in the White Book one might well imagine that the directions stage would come about in approximately three months after the writ had been issued and served. This is almost never the case. Even in strenuously contested litigation the parties' solicitors remain on sufficiently good professional terms to mutually grant reasonable extensions of time, *e.g.* for serving pleadings. In personal injury cases of any substance it would invariably be prudent and in the plaintiff's own interest to have a certain amount of delay until his medical condition has stabilised. Even in contract litigation, especially debt collecting, although one of the parties at least will want matters to proceed as swiftly as possible, the need to ensure that one is ready for each subsequent stage and that one has collected all necessary evidence means that there will still usually be delays. The directions stage is therefore almost inevitably delayed until long after the point at which one might imagine in principle it was going to occur. We shall first consider the directions stage as it is relevant in a contract action and then go on to consider a personal injury case, because there are now significant differences.

The summons for directions

In principle under Order 25 of the Rules of the Supreme Court the plaintiff **8.02** should take out a summons for directions within one month after the close of pleadings. To do this one either obtains from law stationers a standard printed form of directions or, increasingly, one is prepared from a precedent held on word-processor. This lists the directions most commonly sought together with some blanks in which any extra or further directions not otherwise accommodated in the main text of the form can be inserted. One then takes two copies of the summons for directions to the court office and asks for a hearing date giving an estimated length of hearing. This is usually about 15 minutes unless there is some unusual feature in the case which will require lengthier consideration. It is customary at this stage also to lodge at the court copies of the pleadings so this is the first time in which the court have acquired these documents. The plaintiff indicates on the summons for directions which directions he is seeking by crossing out the number of the paragraph against those printed directions which he is *not* seeking and filling in the relevant details in those which he does seek.

The defendant's notice under the summons for directions

8.03   When the defendant receives his copy of the summons notifying him of the time of hearing he may consider that there are directions (*i.e.* procedural orders) required in the case for which no provision is made on the plaintiff's summons for directions. In such a case the defendant may himself make application for those which he requires by filing at court and serving on the plaintiff a so called "defendant's notice for directions." A copy of this notice must be served on the plaintiff and all other parties not later than seven days before the hearing.

The hearing of the summons

8.04   At the hearing the district judge will be considering the case for the first time. He will be attempting to give directions to assist the parties and the court with the future progress of the case in order eventually to obtain as expeditious and economical a disposal of the action as possible.

The summons for directions is intended to provide a "thorough stock-taking" of the action. The district judge will consider the writ and pleadings and then give directions for how the case should proceed from this point onwards. It must be stressed that although the district judge will generally take something of an initiative himself in this it is basically up to the two parties to apply for the orders which they require. The thoroughness of the review of the case will largely depend on how long the appointment time is (and how much behind with his appointments the district judge is at the time when the case comes before him). It is not uncommon for a summons for directions to be dealt with merely by giving the parties the orders they seek without much in the way of further enquiry and for the whole procedure to last only five minutes.

For example if a case, even if involving a large amount of money, seems relatively straightforward and the parties have only requested discovery and inspection and a direction concerning expert witnesses, then the district judge will go ahead and give those orders without extensively reviewing the pleadings or, *e.g.* making minute enquiries of the parties as to what matters might be admitted between them. It must be admitted that in the case of a directions hearing the theory of what should happen and the practice, *i.e.* what *does* happen do not always coincide. However it is in principle the district judge's duty to consider certain matters of his own initiative in particular:—

1.   What direction should be given limiting expert evidence;

2.   Whether the case should be transferred to the county court;

3.   Whether the parties have made all proper agreements and admissions;

4.   Whether an order should be made for mutual exchange of witness statements under Ord. 38 r. 2A

It is important to consider briefly these four matters.

1. Limiting expert evidence

This is a large topic and is dealt with in its own right at para. 9.03 hereafter. **8.05**

2. Transfer to the county court

As we have seen earlier, personal injuries actions, the value of which **8.06** appears to be £50,000 or more should in principle be commenced in the High Court. Personal injuries actions of less than that value should in principle be commenced in the County Court but in relation to other kinds of actions the plaintiff may in principle commence them where he wishes. However if he has commenced an action in the High Court then at the stage of the summons for directions the court will consider which is the appropriate venue for trial. The court when considering its powers to transfer the action to the County Court will in particular have regard to the following criteria:—

(a) The financial substance of the action, including the value of any counterclaim.

(b) Whether action is otherwise important and, in particular, whether it raises questions of importance to persons who are not parties or a question of general public interest,

(c) The complexity of the facts, legal issues, remedies or procedures involved, and

(d) Whether transfer is likely to result in a more speedy trial of the action (although no transfer may be made on the grounds of this reason alone).

Where the action is to be transferred to the County Court it will be transferred at the summons for direction stage and therefore further interlocutory procedures, if there are to be any, will generally take place in the County Court.

3. Whether the parties have made all proper agreements and admissions

It is in principle important for the district judge to see whether he is able to **8.07** secure any agreements or admissions between the parties and to record them or to record the parties refusal to make reasonable agreements and admissions. The purpose of this is of course with a view to saving time at the trial. Thus if the district registrar can see clearly that the case is not seriously defended as to one particular aspect he may ask that the defendant admit the facts relevant to that aspect. Naturally such admissions should only be made under the clearest of instructions from one's client. As indicated above district registrars often have little time for conducting what would be essentially an inquisitorial process and usually merely give the parties the orders they seek.

4. Order for exchange of witness statements under Ord. 38 r. 2A

Order 38 r. 2A contains a provision brought into force in the Queen's Bench **8.08** Division in October 1988. Under this provision the court has power to order the parties to exchange the evidence of their witnesses of fact (including that of the parties themselves) in statement form before trial. If universally applied this would represent the most dramatic change in English civil procedure for many decades. It would mean that the element of surprise is virtually taken out of the English civil trial and that the parties go to trial with a "cards on the table" approach not merely in relation to expert evidence (as has been the practice for some years, see para. 9.04 onwards) but in relation to their witnesses of fact. It is clear from the rules that the court has the power to order this even if both parties object; moreover the rules indicate that such an order should in fact be the norm. Despite this, the actual operation of this rule is still in its infancy and it appears to be the case at present that the order is being very differently applied in different parts of the country. In some an order in this form is becoming normal; in others an order will only be made where neither party voices any strong objection. It should be noted that one only needs, under this rule, to supply one's opponent with statements of witnesses whom one wishes to call at trial. Accordingly if one has obtained a witness statement from a witness who has given a version adverse to the interests of one's client then one is perfectly entitled to supress the existence of such a statement as previously.

8.09   We shall consider some of the more common orders made after considering shortly the so called "automatic directions." In fact although we said at the outset that this is the stage at which the parties are actually called before the court so that the court will review the conduct of the case, even this is not always so. Where the parties are agreed on straightforward routine directions between themselves it is possible to obtain a consent order for directions by leaving an order in the appropriate form endorsed with the consent of both parties at the District Registry. This is then sealed without actual consideration of the case by the district judge. Thus there may in fact never be a stage in which the court itself reviews the progress of the case and directs the future course which it should take. It should however be noted that the parties cannot evade consideration of the issue of transfer to the county court for trial by obtaining a consent order without attendance. In such cases copies of the pleadings must be lodged with the consent order and the district judge will himself review the desirability of transfer to the county court, and if minded to order it, will call the parties before him to listen to their views.

Automatic directions

8.10   We have so far considered the basic summons for directions which ought to come about in most actions begun by writ. There is however an exception which applies in personal injury actions. In personal injury cases so-called "automatic directions" apply. In personal injury cases when pleadings have closed the following directions take effect automatically:—

1.   There shall be discovery of documents within 14 days and inspection within seven days thereafter—save that where liability is admitted or the action arises out of a road accident, discovery shall be limited to disclosure by the plaintiff of any documents relating to special damages.

2.   Where any party intends to place reliance at the trial on expert evidence he shall within ten weeks disclose the substance of that evidence to the other parties in the form of a written report which shall be agreed if possible.

3.   Unless such reports are agreed, parties shall be at liberty to call as expert

witnesses those witnesses, the substance of whose evidence has been disclosed except that the number of expert witnesses shall be limited to two medical experts and one expert of any other kind.

4. Photographs, a sketch plan, and the contents of any police accident report book shall be receivable in evidence at the trial and shall be agreed if possible.

5. The action shall be tried at the trial centre for the place in which the action is proceeding or at such other trial centre as the parties may agree in writing.

6. The action shall be tried by judge alone as a case of substance or difficulty (category B) and shall be set down within six months.

7. The court shall be notified on setting down of the estimated length of trial.

It may be wondered why there is this provision in personal injury cases. The **8.11** answer is simple. The automatic directions merely represent a recognition of the kind of directions that used normally to be sought routinely in run of the mill personal injury cases. In such cases the practice of the courts showed that these were the directions most commonly required. Accordingly if the parties could be persuaded to carry out these directions automatically a good deal of district judge's time would be saved since the parties would not require appointments for the hearing of a summons for directions. In this kind of case therefore the parties may never need to come before the court until the actual trial itself. They will carry out these directions automatically between themselves. One overriding thing that must be stressed however is that these automatic directions are not peremptory in the sense that they *must* apply to every case. If one party to an action decides that he does not think that the automatic directions or any one of them is suitable for his case or indeed he wishes for further or other directions not contained within the automatic directions, then he can in effect ignore the automatic directions. In such a case he should issue a summons for directions just as if the case were not a personal injury action and both parties will then have to attend before the district judge to consider the application for the specific directions sought in the summons for directions. Sometimes the parties are in agreement about which of the automatic directions are appropriate but one or other requires in addition some further directions. In that case each party should go ahead and carry out the automatic directions in the normal way whilst issuing a separate summons for directions seeking the further specific directions that they think appropriate.

It is now appropriate to consider a number of matters contained in the automatic directions and which indeed may be appropriate in other cases. We will do so by reference to the paragraphs of automatic directions:

DISCOVERY AND INSPECTION

1. As has previously been stressed there was provision for automatic **8.12** discovery in any case began by writ under the basic provisions of R.S.C., Ord. 24, r. 2. This provision is to that extent superfluous. However, Order 24, r. 2 was often ignored in practice, the parties preferring to wait to obtain a formal order at a summons for directions. It will be

observed that the rule previously discussed in outline is contained here but where either liability is admitted (in which case discovery as to liability is clearly irrelevant) or the action arises out of a road accident, discovery is limited to disclosure by the plaintiff of documents relating to special damages and the defendant need give no discovery at all. "Road accident" is somewhat confusingly defined as "an accident on land due to a collision or apprehended collision involving a vehicle" which could equally well apply to say a rail accident or even an accident involving a taxi-ing aeroplane.

EXPERT EVIDENCE

8.13   2 and 3.   This is a rather larger topic and will be dealt with in para. 9.01 onwards.

PHOTOGRAPHS, ETC.

8.14   4.   It will be observed that photographs, sketch plans and police accident reports should be receivable in evidence at the trial (*i.e.* that although these documents are in essence hearsay they may be put in at the trial). If either party objected to this direction of course it would be open to him to contend that it should not apply in the particular case. It will be noted that the evidence should be agreed if possible, *e.g.* there should be no dispute on the accuracy of the plan. Clearly photographs and plans are an invaluable aid to the court in visualising precisely how an accident occurred.

8.15   5–7.   The remaining directions numbered paragraphs 5–7 relate to the way in which the action will actually get into a list before a judge for hearing. They require that the case should proceed at the trial centre nearest to the district registry where the case has been proceeding; that the action should be tried by a judge alone (there is no modern case in which jury trial has been thought appropriate for a personal injury case); that it should be set down within six months (we shall deal with the meaning of "setting down" in due course but essentially it is the procedure whereby the case starts to come into the judge's list for hearing) and dealt with as a "Category B" case. Cases in the High Court are categorised under three headings and most ordinary cases fall into Category B. Category A cases are cases of great substance, difficulty or public importance. Category B are cases of substance or difficulty and Category C are all other cases. Further the court is to be notified on setting down of the estimated length of trial. Reference has already been made to the difficulty of estimating length of trial accurately, and of the great problems which can be caused in arranging the work of counsel, solicitors and indeed judges where inaccurate estimates are given. The inexperienced commonly underestimate how long a trial will take, perhaps forgetting how comparatively brief the judicial day is and how long evidence may take, even of quite straightforward matters. The problems of estimating length of hearing are compounded by the fact that neither party need tell the other how many witnesses he proposes to call nor at what length he proposes to raise legal argument (although lists of authorities relied on should be exchanged). The writer can remember estimating that a certain case would last three days which subsequently lasted 13 days to the inconvenience of all concerned and the considerable displeasure of the judge.

Orders for split trials

There is one further matter to which it is worth drawing attention. As **8.16** indicated earlier in the text there are many kinds of cases in hich there will be significant savings in time and costs if the issues of liability and quantum are tried separately. In relation to non personal injury cases this is something which should always be considered at the summons for directions stage. In personal injury cases however there is a new provision which is contained in 0.33 r.4(2A). This provides that in an action for personal injuries the court may at any stage of the proceedings, and of its own motion, make an order for the issue of liability to be tried before any issue or question concerning the amount of damages. If, despite the case involving personal injuries, a summons for directions has been issued for example because the parties required other directions that those contained in the automatic directions, then that is obviously the stage at which the court will consider ordering split trials. In routine automatic directions cases however the documents will never come before the district judge before the stage of proceedings known as setting down which will be discussed more fully hereafter at para. 10.01. In such cases when the action is set down for trial the district judge will look at the papers and if he is so minded will then order that liability be tried first and separately from the issue of quantum. Having made that order each party then has 14 days in which to object. If either or both do object there will then be a hearing for the district judge to consider the objections.

It will be recalled that only cases the apparent value of which is in excess of £50,000 should be commenced in the High Court. If opinions have changed about the value of the case so that it now appears to be worth less than £50,000 then consideration ought to be given to transfer down to the County Court at this stage otherwise costs penalties may be incurred (see para. 18.05).

9. Expert Evidence. R.S.C., Ord. 38

9.01   In the case of the evidence of ordinary witnesses no restriction whatsoever is placed upon the right of the parties to call as many witnesses as they like. However in the case of expert witnesses for more than a decade there has been specific provision under Order 38 rules 35–44 which constitutes a radical departure from the previous law and practice. Firstly a party's right to call any expert evidence he chooses has been restricted by a rule that he can only do so with the leave of the court or by agreement between the parties or subject to compliance with the direction of the court that he should disclose before the trial the substance of such expert evidence to all other parties. Secondly the right of the party to withhold disclosure of his own expert evidence until trial has been modified by the provision that he may be required to make such disclosure before trial as a condition precedent to using it at the trial. These rules thus make a significant advance in the direction of a more open system of pre-trial proceeding so as to enable the parties to prepare and present their respective cases on the basis of material evidence known to them rather than to do so in the dark. The objects intended to be achieved by the rules are described in R.S.C., Ord. 38/35/2 and include the following:—

1.   To assist the parties to reach a settlement on a fairer basis in the light rather than in the dark concerning the expert evidence;

2.   To avoid surprise at the trial;

3.   To secure agreed expert reports thus obviating the need for the attendance of experts at the trial;

4.   To shorten the evidence at the trial by identifying the matters of expert opinion which are really in controversy between the parties;

5.   To enable the experts themselves to prepare their evidence on those matters more thoroughly and helpfully.

In these ways the rules are designed to improve the conduct and quality of civil trials by reducing costs, delay and vexation and the unnecessary attendance at the trial of experts who could be more usefully employed elsewhere.

We shall now consider exactly what this means.

9.02   The rules provide that except with the leave of the court or where all parties agree, no expert evidence may be adduced at the trial unless the party seeking to adduce the evidence has either applied to the court to determine whether a direction should be given and has complied with any direction given on the application or (in a personal injury case) has complied with automatic directions.

9.03   In other words a party who has expert evidence needs to consider just how he is going to approach the trial. The rules make no difference whatsoever to the substantive law of privilege. An expert's report obtained for the purpose of litigation is still a privileged document and nothing can *make* a party disclose it. Thus if one party has obtained an expert's report which is unhelpful to his *case*, (*e.g.* where a specialist to whom one first sent one's client suggested that he would very quickly recover from the accident and one has obtained a report from a second expert which is more pessimistic), nothing need make the plaintiff reveal the contents of the first report. Since he does not wish to rely on the evidence of that expert at trial but on that of the second one he may keep that first report from his opponent. However in the case of the second report the witness cannot be called to surprise the opponent at trial without full consideration being given to the effect of Order 38. As we have seen either:—

1. The court must give leave for the expert to be called at trial (which is highly unlikely since the code provided by the rest of the Order provides a framework for the conduct of ordinary litigation); *or*

2. All parties may agree that they will call their expert evidence at trial without prior disclosure. This latter, although possible in theory is extremely rare in practice. Quite simply there is very little to be gained by so doing. The rationale behind the change in rules set out above admirably expresses the reasons why prior disclosure is usually an excellent idea; *or*

3. One can obtain a direction from the court in advance of the trial, that is either at the hearing of a summons for directions or if the case is one where otherwise there would be automatic directions and one does not wish to comply with them, by issuing a summons for the matter to be determined by the district judge.

When the court will order disclosure

Automatic directions are perfectly clear. They provide for the prior dis- **9.04** closure of expert evidence. Let us assume that the parties are not complying with automatic directions but are rather issuing a summons for directions because various other orders may be needed. There will then be a hearing before the district judge. The directions which the district judge will prima facie wish to make are likely to be in similar terms to the automatic directions, that is that each party disclose to the other the substance of his expert evidence in the form of a written report within a specified time. The district judge is guided by the following principles in considering what directions to make. In all cases, personal injury or otherwise then;

"unless the court considers that there is sufficient reason for not doing so it shall direct that the substance of the evidence be disclosed in the form of a written report or reports to such other parties and within such period as the court may specify."

In other words in all cases there is a very clear onus on the person who seeks an order that there should *not* be prior disclosure of expert evidence to satisfy the court why this should be.

Let us consider as a whole the question of expert evidence in the light of **9.05** these rules.

9.06 As we have already seen the plaintiff, probably at a very early stage will commission his own expert's report, and in the case of personal injuries let us take the case of a medical report. This is not to overlook that there might well be others such as consultant engineer's reports as to mechanical defects in a vehicle or in factory systems; accountants' or actuaries' reports on computations for future loss of earnings; in an appropriate case surveyor's reports about defects in structures, or many kinds of specialist reports about various production processes in industry. However we will concentrate on the case of a medical report.

9.07 The defendant will soon want his own medical report carried out if the case is one of any substance. The plaintiff must allow him to do this and if he refuses to do so then the court will stay his action until he consents. See *Edmeades* v. *Thames Board Mills* [1969] 2 Q.B. 69. It is important when a request is received from the defendant for facilities for a medical examination to consider the question of conditions. Reasonable conditions can be imposed. Suitable conditions might be the following:—

1. That the defendants pay the expenses of the plaintiff in travelling to attend the examination and any loss of earnings.

2. That only the defendant's specialist will be present and no other person (*e.g.* a representative of the insurance company).

3. The defendant's doctor will only examine the injuries caused in the accident and will not attempt to discuss the accident with the plaintiff.

4. In the case of a child (or conceivably a very nervous adult) that some other person such as parent or relative might be present during the examination.

Conditions that the report must be sent to the plaintiff's solicitors, or that the plaintiff's own doctor be present are not usually considered reasonable.

These conditions are very important because it would not be entirely accurate to assume that medical witnesses are disinterested medical men. In fact they tend often to exercise any reasonable doubt in favour of the party paying them and may appear quite partial.

The plaintiff may give some vague account of how he was injured if he is asked and it may do him no good at all if this is then incorporated into the substance of the report and appears to be at variance with the version in his evidence and statement of claim. The plaintiff should be warned not to discuss the accident with the opponent's doctor. Plaintiffs tend to be extremely naive about these matters and imagine that in some sense this doctor is in a physician/patient relationship with them which of course he certainly is not. The writer can recollect a case from practice where the plaintiff suddenly volunteered the statement to the defendant's specialist "I suppose it was my own fault really—I saw the oil on the floor an hour before." Naturally when this information came into the defendant's solicitors' hands (they previously appeared unaware of it) the plaintiff's case was seriously impaired.

The plaintiff must of course co-operate with the defendant's doctor to a certain extent. He must do exercises if required for the purpose of observation. If the defendant's doctor wishes to carry out tests on the plaintiff then it is very difficult to generalise about whether he should be permitted to do so.

If the tests involve considerable pain or discomfort then according to case law the plaintiff is not required to undergo this merely for the purpose of litigation. Everything will depend upon the nature of the injuries and the nature of the tests.

Naturally the plaintiff's own medical evidence will be updated at frequent **9.09** intervals, perhaps as often as every six months as the case progresses. The defendants are entitled to update their medical evidence also at reasonable intervals and therefore a plaintiff may be required to re-attend for examination.

What will then happen where each party has a report in the vast majority of **9.10** cases will be the voluntary early disclosure of them. Where a report is wholly favourable there is no harm in forwarding a copy of it to the defendants at a very early stage, even before the writ was issued. In such a situation the defendants will usually disclose their own as a reciprocal courtesy.

Once proceedings have been issued of course then, as we have noted earlier (see para. 6.21) in a personal injury case, the plaintiff is prima facie required to serve with his statement of claim a medical report, or reports, substantiating all the personal injuries. To the extent that plaintiffs comply with this rule the following procedures which in the main provide for mutual simultaneous disclosure of expert evidence are varied. Perhaps oddly, the automatic directions as set out in Ord. 25 r. 8 have not been changed despite the existence of the new provisions requiring early disclosure of medical evidence with the statement of claim.

On the assumption that earlier exchange has not occurred however, the **9.11** stage for disclosure of medical evidence is specified either in automatic directions or in such orders as will be made by the court. In case of personal injuries medical reports are almost certain to be ordered to be exchanged. One should then carefully peruse the other sides report. Personal injury lawyers become familiar with most medical terminology but it may not always be clear whether or not the defendant's expert is entirely in agreement with the conclusions of one's own expert. Let us suppose therefore that there has been no disclosure of reports until a relatively late stage in the case. The appropriate procedure is almost certainly to send the plaintiff for a further medical examination and send copies of the defendant's medical reports to one's own specialist asking for his comments on them and whether his evidence could be said to tally entirely with theirs. If the experts are agreed then the reports can be put together in an agreed bundle and given to the trial judge and neither expert needs to be called. Although the reports are of course hearsay there is no need to go through the strict provisions and formalities of serving Civil Evidence Act notices in relation to them because by virtue of section 1 of the Civil Evidence Act parties may agree that hearsay evidence shall be admitted. If there continues to be a disagreement then one will need to give notice that the opponent's expert's report is not accepted and one will be calling one's own expert.

Order for meetings of experts

By Ord. 38 r. 38 it is provided that the court may in any case direct that there **9.12** be a meeting on "without prejudice" terms of such experts as the court may specify for the purpose of identifying those parts of their evidence which are in issue. After such meeting the experts may prepare a joint statement indicating those parts of their evidence on which they are in agreement or not. This useful provision allows the court to order what was in many cases carried out as a matter of good practice between the parties anyway. Thus for example if the plaintiff's, and defendant's specialists disagree about the prognosis for the plaintiff the court has the power to order a joint examination and a joint report which can identify their precise differences. This is useful because whilst experts may well exchange quite contradictory reports when preparing them for their respective solicitors, at a face to face meeting experts are likely to be considerably more conciliatory and thus the area of dispute may be considerably cut down for trial, or differences may even be resolved entirely.

Updating medical evidence

9.13   It should not be forgotten that medical evidence will need to be updated in most circumstances after the stage of automatic directions or the taking out of a summons for directions, and one's opponent must of course be sent copies of the latest medical evidence not just of that received up to the stage of mutual disclosure.

If the evidence cannot be agreed then the experts are called at trial to give oral testimony. In such cases the expert's report is put in at the start of his testimony and stands as his evidence in chief and he is then available for cross-examination upon it. If there is a serious dispute on expert evidence it is usually prudent to take one's own expert to the conference with counsel so that counsel can explore the best lines of cross-examination to employ with the opposing expert.

Lodging experts' reports in personal injury cases

9.14   By virtue of a recent practice direction in personal injury cases all experts' reports (whether they are agreed or not and whether they relate to medical matters or not) arc to be put in bundles and lodged at court well before the case starts so that they may be read by the trial judge. The purpose of this is simply to give the judge an opportunity to familiarise himself thoroughly with the issues. If the experts' reports are agreed he is then completely in the picture. In such a situation the experts are not of course called at trial. If however the experts' reports are not agreed, then it is important to note that the experts must themselves be called as witnesses at trial. It is not a proper procedure to invite the judge to make up his mind on the basis of the written reports alone.

10. Preparing for Trial

In the following section we are going to consider the procedural steps necessary to get the case before a judge in a certain court room at a certain time with everybody present and ready. Quite separately we shall consider the tactical and procedural steps that a party needs to take to ensure that he is ready for trial and that his case is prepared as well as it possibly may be. We shall start off with the simple procedural steps by which after the stage of automatic directions or a summons for directions a case is listed for hearing by a judge.

Setting down

It will be recalled that one of the automatic directions was for the time within   **10.01**
which a case would be "set down." Setting down is a technical term and means the filing at court of the necessary documents with a request that the case be listed. To set down for trial one prepares two bundles of documents. It will be remembered that the court does not keep a court file and even though if there is a summons for directions copies of pleadings will be filed with the summons for directions these will actually be handed back at the end of the directions hearing. All the court will have in its file is a copy of the writ and acknowledgment of service and legal aid certificate if any. Now bundles must be prepared which are by custom bound up in the left hand margin with green tape. The bundles contain good copies of the following documents in chronological order—

1. writ;

2. pleadings;

3. any requests for further and better particulars of pleadings and the reply to such requests;

4. order made on the summons for directions if any;

5. any other procedural order of any importance (though not orders relating to interim payments);

6. notice of issue of legal aid certificate; and

7. any third party notice and orders and pleadings in third party proceedings.

These must be taken or sent to the court by the plaintiff together with a formal request that the action may be set down for trial and a further fee must then be paid. If the plaintiff fails to set the action down the defendants may do so if he wishes.

It will be recalled that automatic directions specify that this stage should occur within six months of automatic directions and in any other case the summons for directions will specify the time within which the case is to be set down for trial. It should not be imagined that setting it down for trial means that it will be listed for hearing by a judge immediately. Setting down for trial may well by very far in advance of the actual hearing. In essence setting down for trial leads to the final stage of procedure. The summons for directions, if any, should have been long before and although one may apply for further directions after setting down this is execptional.

There is one further document that must be lodged with the bundles above in cases which are set down outside London. In such cases the party setting the action down must lodge with the pleadings a statement which is usually called a "statement as to readiness for trial." Blanks of this form of statement may be purchased from Law Stationers, or held on word processors. The form of the statement confirms whether the order made on the summons for direction has been complied with and in particular whether experts' reports have been submitted for agreement and if so whether they have been agreed; if not states how many expert witnesses will be called; confirms whether plans and photographs have been agreed; gives an up to date estimate of the length of trial; and gives the names, addresses and telephone numbers of the plaintiff's and defendant's solicitors and of the parties' intended counsel.

After setting down for trial all other parties must be notified within seven days that the case has been set down and informed of the listing number which has been allotted to the case.

10.02 At this stage it will be remembered the district judge in automatic directions cases will also look at the papers to see whether an order for split trials of liability and quantum is appropriate and also consider the question of transfer to the county court.

10.03 It will be recalled (see para. 9.14 above) that in personal injury cases a bundle of all the experts' reports should be lodged at court whether or not they are agreed so that they may be read by the trial judge well in advance of the trial. This should happen either at the setting down stage, or if the evidence is likely to be updated after that stage, then as soon as it is complete. In non-personal injury cases only *agreed* experts' reports should be lodged for use by the trial judge.

Fixed dates for hearings

10.04 Cases move up the list a little haphazardly. Partly this is a matter of the chronological order in which they were set down for trial; but also such matters as availability of judges and the length of the case will be material. Clearly it is easier to find a space in the court's time for a case estimated to last one day than one estimated to last 30 days. A particular problem with the somewhat unpredictable way in which cases will come into the list is that one may find difficulty in procuring the attendance of all witnesses, *e.g.* if the case is coming on in a popular holiday period such as June or July; or one may find the counsel of one's choice is unavailable. A way of avoiding this difficulty is to apply for a fixed date by summons to the district judge. The price of obtaining a fixed date unfortunately is likely to be that the date fixed will be substantially later than the date on which the case would have come into the lists had one been content to take one's chance on the latter. It may nonetheless be desirable to obtain a fixed date if there may be problems with securing the attendance of some particular witness or obtaining a particular counsel.

The procedure by which the case finally comes into the list has some local **10.05** variations. Usually a preliminary warned list is sent out in advance indicating that a certain case will begin to come into the list in three weeks time. At that stage it is possible to object on the basis of unavailability of witnesses or any other good reason. If one does object the case will reappear in the warned list at some subsequent date. Bona fide objections can be put forward again. If the same thing happens a third time however one may need to provide very cogent evidence of the difficulties one has in meeting the date, and mere matters of convenience will not weigh heavily with the listing officer. If not objection is taken then in the week preceding the week of the trial one may be given some indication of which date in the following week one's own case will start. One will often be surprised to see in the list that there are three or four cases listed for the same day even though one's own case might have been estimated to last for two or three days. This is a very real problem which has to be taken into account in advising a nervous client. It may very well be that even though he has mentally prepared himself for his day in court that everybody will attend only to find that it is impossible for the case to begin because the day before's case has run over or perhaps there are other cases in the day's list which the listing officer had expected to be compromised between the parties and withdrawn, but which are in fact proceeding. The disappointment which this engenders can be a powerful incentive to the client to accept a so-called "courtroom door" settlement. If one does turn up in vain for a hearing which cannot proceed then the costs mount without either party being at fault. When this has happened it by no means follows that the case will proceed on the next day. More usually the case is re-listed some weeks later. All one can hope for is that given that degree of inconvenience the court will ensure the case is first in the list for the next time it is listed. We shall consider the course of the trial briefly in a subsequent section but for the moment we now turn from the *procedural* requirements of getting a case listed for trial to the *tactical* and other matters which need to be considered.

ADVICE ON EVIDENCE

Before setting down for trial it is wise to get counsel to advise in writing on **10.06** the evidence in the case. One should carefully go through the case seeing what matters have been agreed between the parties and what matters appear to remain in contention. A full set of instructions should be drafted for counsel explaining all outstanding matters, the progress of the case so far, and seeking advice on evidence. Copies of all relevant documents should be enclosed. It is highly unsatisfactory merely to send counsel the documents and say in effect "here are the documents, write us an advice on evidence." A well drafted set of instructions requires the solicitor himself to go through the relevant matters and give his own view. It may also be necessary to indicate to counsel matters that do not appear in documentary form, *e.g.* the contents of telephone negotiations with one's opponent. Counsel will review the evidence in the whole case on both liability and quantum so it is important to enclose with the instructions all medical evidence, details of computations of special damages, predictions for continuing loss and so on.

When one receives the advice from counsel one should of course immediately implement it. In the light of counsel's advice all or any of the following matters may be relevant:

Service of notices under the Civil Evidence Act 1968

10.07 The operation of the Civil Evidence Act is explained hereafter at para.
31.03. If one has a witness whose evidence is either non-controversial or who
is unavailable for one of various reasons specified in section 8 of the Act his
evidence may be admissible in written form. A notice containing the evidence must served no later than 21 days after setting down for trial. One
should therefore ensure that this step is taken.

Notice to admit facts

10.08 If an opposing party has failed to admit facts which it is reasonable for him to
admit then the time to serve a notice to admit facts is no later than 21 days
after setting down for trial. As will be seen in the full discussion of this at
para. 25.05 a party who fails to admit a fact which he should have admitted
will bear the costs of the other party proving the fact at trial whatever the
outcome of the trial.

Witnesses

10.09 It is wise to subpoena all lay witnesses, even members of the plaintiff's family
or close friends who have assured one of their co-operation in attending
trial. Witnesses should be told that this does not represent any slight on their
reliability and that is merely a matter of precaution. If a subpoena has not
been served and the witness does not attend at trial then whilst it may be
possible to obtain an adjournment from the judge the costs of the abortive
hearing are likely to be ordered against the party seeking the adjournment.
There are two kinds of subpoena. A *subpoena ad testificandum* requires a
witness to attend court for the purpose of giving verbal testimony and a
subpoena duces tecum is issued for a witness who is required to attend court
merely to produce and prove the authenticity of some document or thing.
Accordingly if one wishes ones client's employer to attend and bring wages
and salary records one will serve a *subpoena duces tecum*; if one has an eye
witness to the accident one will serve a *subpoena ad testificandum*. One
obtains a subpoena by attending at the High Court district registry with a
praecipe which is simply a form of request for a subpoena, and the completed form of subpoena. The court will then seal the subpoenas. It must be
served within 12 weeks of issue. The form of subpoena indicates whom the
action is between and requires the witness concerned to attend the court to
testify at the action but it does not say when the action will take place. The
subpoena should be served personally with conduct money, which is a sum
sufficient to cover the witness's expenses and subsistence in attending the
hearing. The witness should also be told that he will not lose earnings by
attending court because these will be reimbursed in due course. When the
case is finally listed for trial the subpoena is "activated" by the solicitor
contacting the witness personally or by telephone and informing him that the
hearing date has now been fixed and that he should regard the subpoena as
binding on him to attend at court on the day concerned. A relatively recent
practice is that of serving a subpoena on expert witnesses. Expert witnesses
with many commitments often request a subpoena to enable them to demonstrate the need to break other appointments. In the case of an expert witness
postal service would usually suffice. One often finds for example that when

118

telephoning a specialist to confirm a hearing date the specialist's reception staff indicate that the date is out of the question because of other commitments. The service of the subpoena can magically makes these commitments evaporate.

Documentary evidence

10.10 Naturally for the avoidance of delay and expense as much as possible of the documentary evidence should be "agreed" by the parties. In this sense "agreed" has a special meaning of "agreed as authentic and relevant to the trial." It by no means indicates that the *contents of* such documents are "agreed." In this sense it has a very different meaning from the context in which it is used of medical reports, where "agreed" means "agreed as to substance." It may for example be that there has been a great deal of correspondence between the parties before solicitors were instructed, *e.g.* commercial correspondence to do with disputed terms of a contract. This correspondence might be highly relevant at trial but it by no means follows that each party agrees with the *contents* of what is asserted in the other person's half of the correspondence. In this sense therefore the correspondence is "agreed" as being relevant and should be prepared in so-called "agreed bundles" carefully indexed and paginated.

What if there is some document whose authenticity is disputed?

10.11 A party disputing authenticity of a document which has been listed by the other party at the discovery stage in his list of documents must serve a notice to that effect within 21 days after receiving the list of documents. Thereafter the party who has given notice of non admission of the document will bear the costs of proving the document if its authenticity is in fact proved.

Production of original documents

10.12 If a party is in possession of an original document then the original should be produced at the trial. If the opposing party possesses the document notice to produce the document should be given and if there is non-compliance with that notice the other party may prove the contents of the document by secondary means, *e.g.* carbon copies or photostats. If somebody other than one of the parties is in possession of an original document then a *subpoena duces tecum* should be served on that party. It will be recalled that in a personal injury case one would have had the power to inspect the document by a proper application under Ord. 24 r. 7A after proceedings had commenced. The use of Ord. 24 r. 7A merely advances the stage of seeing the document by one step since one could in any case have served a *subpoena duces tecum*. If after inspection of the document it proves to be relevant a *subpoena duces tecum* will still be required to ensure that the original is brought to court.

CONFERENCE WITH COUNSEL

With the client

10.13 One must consider whether a conference with counsel is necessary. Usually in civil litigation a client will not have seen his own barrister up to this stage. If there are facts seriously in dispute it will usually be as well to arrange a conference with the client present. The barrister will probe the contested parts of his client's story suggesting to him the way in which he will be cross-examined about it and looking for his response to likely questions. He may explain to the plaintiff why he gave written advice at earlier stages to refuse offers or payments into court and answer questions about the possible difficulties to be faced and the prospects of success. Quite often such a conference is in two parts the first with the client present and the second with the solicitor alone. After the client has left the barrister may then give the solicitor further advice about the client's prospects, if for example the client under close questioning has seemed to be evasive or clearly gaping holes or improbabilities have appeared in his story. It may be that in the light of seeing how the client has performed as a witness even in the limited context of a conference in a private room the barrister will firmly urge the solicitor to accept some offer that has been made or to see whether any other offer can be obtained before the delivery of briefs for trial.

With expert witnesses

10.14 Another form of conference which may be desirable is in a case where there is a serious dispute on expert evidence. Although barristers are not permitted to see witnesses of fact in conference they are permitted to see expert witnesses and this may well be helpful.

   The consultant in the case should normally attend the barristers chambers for the conference so that counsel can ask detailed questions about the prognosis of the plaintiff or seek clarification of matters in the consultant's (or opponent's) reports.

SPECIAL DAMAGES

10.15 It will be recalled that it was incumbent upon a plaintiff in a personal injury case to serve as full a computation as possible of special damages (and in this context that term was deemed to include items of future loss of earnings and expenses) with his statement of claim at an early stage in the action. As is observed above (para. 6.09) though the figures to be provided under that procedure may in simple cases lead to an early compromise of the action in more complex cases where the plaintiff's prognosis is uncertain so that it is unclear when, or whether he may return to work and in what capacity no settlement is likely to be achieved on the basis of those vague early figures. Where such cases are clearly going on to trial there is a further provision.

   A party claiming damages for loss of earnings, loss of future earning capacity, medical or nursing expenses or loss of pension rights must serve full particulars of his claim on his opponent shortly before trial by preparing a schedule listing the items concerned. The opponent must then indicate in a counter document precisely whether and to what extent each item is agreed or disputed. If a matter is not agreed the reason why not must be stated and any counter proposals given. For example in a case concerning future loss of earnings it may be contended that at a certain stage in the relatively near future the plaintiff would have been promoted to the level of manager. A higher rate of loss of earnings for the future may therefore be claimed from that point. The defendants may contend that there is no acceptable evidence that he would have been promoted to manager and that he was only one of a dozen employees of comparable status and seniority from whose ranks the appointment would have been made and suggesting that future loss of earnings should be based only on his present rate of pay. It will then become apparent that the evidence of the employer as to the employee's prospects needs to be called at trial. Had the defendants agreed to this item then such evidence could have been dispensed with.

The purpose of the relatively recent *Practice Note* (1984) which calls for this step is to save the judge's time where it may have been possible to agree even quite complex figures by this procedure. Because the defendants make proposals or counter-proposals as to the method of computing special damages this is naturally not to be interpreted as an admission of liability.

BRIEFING COUNSEL

One should brief the counsel who has settled the pleadings and been **10.16** involved at earlier stages. A brief should generally be delivered not so late that counsel cannot prepare the case thoroughly nor so early that the brief cannot take account of new developments, *e.g.* offers made at a late stage. When one chooses to deliver a brief is very much a matter of feel but in a High Court action one would think at least a fortnight before the date of trial would be the minimum. Counsel's clerk could be contacted earlier than this however to be told to expect the brief and he may then use his powers of persuasion with the listing officer to ensure that the case comes into the list at a time convenient for the counsel concerned. The other side should be notified that one is about to deliver one's brief because the brief fee becomes payable upon delivery of the brief even if the case is settled immediately thereafter. This is therefore a final powerful incentive on them to consider settling since a further heavy disbursement is about to be incurred on the plaintiff's behalf for which they will be liable if they lose or settle later. In fact despite this rule if the case is settled shortly after delivery of the brief it may be possible to negotiate a reduction in the brief fee with counsel's clerk.

All too often a brief is short and uninformative, trusting to the fact that a barrister will already be familiar with the case from having drafted pleadings and given advice in connection with it. A good brief should however set out in coherent chronological order a discussion of all relevant issues of fact, evidence and law and supply good copies of all necessary documents including proofs of evidence, computation of special damages, the writ, pleadings, procedural orders, accounts of negotiations with one's opponents and so on.

If the counsel of one's choice is unavailable one should insist on a counsel of comparable seniority from the same chambers or if such is unavailable one should go to other chambers. When the brief is delivered no fee will be marked on it initially but counsel's clerk will look at what he considers the "weight" of it and will suggest a fee based on a variety of factors including the apparent importance of the case, length of trial, seniority of the barrister concerned and popularity of the barrister concerned (*e.g.* will he have to turn down something even better paid to fulfil this engagement). After some negotiation it is usually possible to agree on a fee but if it is not then one must ask for the brief to be returned. The brief fee is for the work involved in preparing the case and for the first day in court. It is also necessary to agree a so-called "refresher" fee, that is the fee for the second day in court and subsequent days. This fee is typically only a fraction of the brief fee itself. In a legal aid case there is no need to agree a fee. Counsel's clerk will in due course put forward a fee note in the sum he suggests which will be considered at taxation by the district judge.

11. Termination Without Trial

One might assume from reading an account of the various stages in a High Court case that once commenced there is little alternative but for it progress to its eventual hearing in open court by a High Court judge. This is very far from being the case. Only a tiny proportion of cases ever reach trial and in some categories of cases (*e.g.* what one might describe as "debt collecting" cases) the proportion is smaller still. There is a number of ways in which an action can be brought prematurely to an end. We shall deal first with three ways in which the plaintiff can bring matters to a satisfactory early conclusion for himself where there is some deficiency either in the procedures adopted by the defendant or in the defendant's case. We shall then briefly consider some other ways in which a case may terminate without trial.

Judgment in default of notice of intention to defend under R.S.C., Ord. 13

As has been observed, when a writ is served upon a defendant he has 14 days **11.01** from the date of effective service to return his acknowledgment of service to the court. The procedure we are about to describe can be used by the plaintiff in two situations. First where the defendant fails to return his acknowledgment of service to the court *at all* and secondly where the defendant does return the acknowledgment of service to the court but has indicated upon it that he does not *intend to defend* the case. In both cases the plaintiff can bring matters to an abrupt end without the need for trial before a judge or indeed for any kind of hearing at all. As has been noted elsewhere the Queen's Bench Division of the High Court does not draw up its own orders and it is for the successful party on any trial or interlocutory application to prepare a copy of the order or judgment to which he is entitled. The plaintiff's solicitor then, on either receiving notice that the defendant has acknowledged service but does not propose to defend the action, or after the effective 14-day period for returning the acknowledgment of service has expired and the acknowledgment has not been returned at all, takes to the court two copies of the form of judgment and also produces the original writ. He will also need to prove service of the writ. If the defendant has returned the acknowledgment of service indicating that he does not propose to defend then that is obviously sufficient proof that the writ has been served. Likewise if the writ has been served on an appointed solicitor who has acknowledged it in writing that will also suffice. However, if the writ has been served and no response to it at all has been received then the plaintiff's solicitor must produce to the court an affidavit of service, that is a sworn statement by the person who personally delivered the writ to the defendant, or actually posted the writ to the defendant, to the effect that service was regularly effected by either of those methods. These are produced to the counter staff at the district registry of the High Court and judgment may be given there and then. The copies of the judgment are sealed by the court staff and one copy given back to the plaintiff's solicitor.

11.02   The form of judgment will differ depending on whether the claim was for a liquidated sum or for damages. If it was for a liquidated sum, *e.g.* a debt, then the judgment may be *final*. That is, when the solicitor drafts the judgment in his office before taking it to the court he inserts the amount of the sum claimed and the computation of interest where this has been pleaded in accordance with the method described earlier. The judgment will then state the precise amount for which it has been granted and the plaintiff can go ahead and enforce this judgment against the defendant immediately.

11.03   However, in a damages case the plaintiff will not be claiming a liquidated sum and accordingly the form of judgment he will take to the court will be an *interlocutory* judgment, *i.e.* final as to liability only. There will then need to be a subsequent hearing before the district judge at which he will assess damages. This subsequent hearing may be applied for on summons immediately, or if the plaintiff's injuries are such that it is appropriate to wait to see how his medical condition stabilises, there may be a delay of months or even years before the final assessment of damages. However, getting default judgment at this stage will at least entitle the plaintiff to make an early application for an interim payment on account of damages and thus will be tactically advantageous. However, in road accident litigation since the defendant will be insured, or the M.I.B. will be involved, solicitors will inevitably be appointed and therefore it is most unlikely that a default judgment under Order 13 will be appropriate.

11.04   In the case of an action for a liquidated sum judgment will be final provided the plaintiff is not seeking interest at some high rate for which he will need to argue before the court. If he is content with interest at the rate of interest on judgment debts previously described he can obtain final judgment for the debt and interest. If, however, the amount is such that it is worthwhile to present to the court a serious argument on the rate of interest, judgment will be entered only on liability leaving the assessment of interest to be made by the court subsequently.

Where the plaintiff has issued a writ for a liquidated sum and has completed the indorsement as to fixed costs then when signing judgment in default he may also sign judgment for the appropriate amount of costs. If the action concerns an unliquidated sum then costs will be taxed or assessed in the usual way at a later stage after damages themselves have been assessed.

SETTING JUDGMENT ASIDE R.S.C., ORD. 13, R. 9

11.05   If a judgment has been obtained under Order 13 the defendant may apply for it to be set aside. If for example the writ, although perfectly properly served by post, arrived the day after he went abroad for a month's holiday then he may well return to find judgment has already been obtained. In such circumstances he will apply to the court on summons to set the judgment aside so that he may defend the case.

The court will set judgment aside in such a case, and since no one is at fault the order for costs will be costs in the cause. If, however, the defendant were in some way at fault, *e.g.* had delayed seeking legal advice after receiving the writ, then whilst he may still apply to set the judgment aside, this will only be ordered if he files an affidavit disclosing some arguable defence on the merits. Moreover the court may impose other terms (*e.g.* the payment of some sum of money into court). The order for costs in such a case will inevitably be "costs thrown away" in the plaintiff's favour.

Summary judgment under R.S.C., Ord. 14

As we have remarked before, one might imagine from collectively adding together the time limits for the various stages of High Court procedure that an action could proceed from issue of the writ to trial in a matter of a few months. Even in the most straightforward case, however, that would be optimistic. The pressure on court time is such that even in the rare cases where both parties comply strictly with the time limits for each step and set the case down for trial as soon as possible, a trial within a year of commencement would be most unlikely. In some parts of the country the period would be considerably longer than this. In cases where either party has any reason to spin things out by seeking extensions and delaying tactics of any kind the period will inevitably be much longer. In some kinds of action, particularly in actions for debts, a defendant who was unscrupulous, or merely impecunious, could in effect obtain credit for lengthy periods by delaying payment until proceedings were issued and thereafter by putting in an entirely spurious defence and spinning things out as much as possible until trial. Pleadings are not on oath and therefore one commits no crime or contempt by putting in a spurious defence providing one abandons it as soon as the trial starts and does not attempt to substantiate it. Of course the cost of so doing will inevitably be that the person adopting these tactics will be ordered to pay costs and interest but even these may not be sufficient disincentives to an unscrupulous person to defer payment of debts. Moreover even when judgment is obtained there may be considerable difficulties in enforcing it, as will be later described. The defendant adopting these tactics need not necessarily be an unscrupulous individual. It may be that he is in business, perhaps himself saddled with many bad debts, and there is a grave cash flow crisis in his firm. Only by deferring payment of a major debt, for instance to his trade suppliers, for as long as possible, can he even hope to stay in business, hope for an upturn in trade, hope for settlement of bad debts owed to him in his turn, and so on. Even though not himself inherently dishonest such a person may well be tempted to attempt to delay matters just to keep his own business alive.

11.06

The procedure we are about to describe is what in effect prevents these tactics from succeeding.

The following procedure applies to all actions begun by writ with a few exceptions (*e.g.* defamation, malicious prosecution) not relevant for our purposes. However, its main use is in contract actions, particularly debt cases. It will not usually be appropriate in road accident cases because it will be very hard for the court to be satisfied that all the requirements described hereafter apply. A further brief note on this appears after the substance of the text.

11.07

Let us assume then that the plaintiff is a trade supplier suing a sole trader for debts. He instructs his solicitor to issue and serve the writ as soon as the letter before action has received no response and this is done. As is normal in this kind of case the statement of claim is indorsed on the back of the writ, *i.e.* the "liquidated demand" form of writ is used. No separate statement of claim is therefore required. The plaintiff is surprised and annoyed to find

11.08

that when the acknowledgment of service is returned to the court and a copy sent out to the plaintiff's solicitor the defendant has ticked the box indicating that he intends to defend the action. On the plaintiff's view there can be no proper defence to the action. The goods were supplied and no complaint has been received about their quality. He therefore wishes to know what action his solicitor can take to bring matters to a speedy conclusion. The answer is to apply for summary judgment under Order 14.

THE TIME FOR APPLICATION

11.09 The plaintiff's solicitor will make application to the court by summons for summary judgment. He will do this as soon as notice of intention to defend has been received provided he has already served the statement of claim. He does not need to await service of the defence and nor does service of the defence if the defendant has served it immediately, preclude him from applying for summary judgment. Where the plaintiff applies for summary judgment this extends the time for service of the defence until after the hearing of the summons.

THE METHOD OF APPLICATION

11.10 Application is made to the district judge by summons seeking summary judgment and supported by an affidavit. The affidavit must fulfil the following requirements.

1. It must verify the facts on which the claim is based, (this is usually done by merely repeating that the contents of the statement of claim is true).

2. It must state that in the deponent's belief there is no defence to the action.

These are the only mandatory requirements for the affidavit and if the affidavit is sworn by the plaintiff personally this is all there need be. However, there are two possible variations. Firstly if the affidavit is not by the plaintiff personally then the person swearing the affidavit must swear in it that he is duly authorised by the plaintiff to make the affidavit. This would occur for example where, as is quite common, the affidavit is sworn by the plaintiff's solicitor rather than the plaintiff or where the actual plaintiff is a limited company and the affidavit is made by a manager or director. Secondly if there is some fact in the affidavit which is not known personally to the person swearing it he must identify the source of his information or belief. Therefore if an affidavit was sworn by, say, a company's managing director he might well say that in verifying the amount of the debt still due and unpaid he had referred to the company's accounts manager who had given him this information.

11.11 The summons having been issued and the original affidavit lodged at the district registry, a copy of the summons and affidavit is served by post on the defendant. This must be served not less than 10 clear days before the hearing date of the summons. A notice at the foot of the summons warns the defendant that if he wishes to defend the application he should serve on the plaintiff a copy of any affidavit he intends to use at least three days before the return day. The idea of this is to force a defendant to put his defence on affidavit and thus to say for the first time on oath that he believes that he has a defence. The most unscrupulous defendant will usually think twice before committing perjury about the validity of his defence. If the defendant fails to serve his affidavit in time but, as is quite common, produces it at the hearing the plaintiff may either require an adjournment to enable him to consider the affidavit or press on and deal with any allegations made in it. If an affidavit is supplied by the defendant which contains allegations which the plaintiff would like to meet by serving a further affidavit he may do so but by this stage of course it may become clear that there is a genuine dispute on the facts and where that is the case then the summary judgment procedure, as we shall see shortly, is not appropriate. Accordingly if it becomes necessary to meet allegations on affidavit the application for summary judgment may already be hopeless.

THE HEARING OF THE SUMMONS

At the hearing of the plaintiff's applications the district judge will consider **11.12** the plaintiff's affidavit and any affidavit filed by the defendant and may make one of the following four orders.

Judgment for the plaintiff

The defendant must satisfy the district judge that there is an issue or **11.13** question that ought to be tried or that there ought for some other reason to be a trial of the plaintiff's claim. Unless the defendant manages to do this the district judge will give judgment for the plaintiff. It is clear that the district judge will look behind the substance of affidavits filed. If despite the defendant having committed his defence to affidavit the district judge is not satisfied as to its bona fides he may still give judgment for the plaintiff. The test is principally whether there is some *arguable issue* which ought to be tried before a judge in open court with examination in chief and cross examination on oath and after all the normal interlocutory procedures have been undertaken. If there is such an issue then summary judgment is inappropriate. The fact that the district judge does not give judgment for the plaintiff in no way pre-empts the final decision. It may be that after full trial the plaintiff still wins conclusively on the issue of liability and the defendant is totally discredited or his arguments shown to be flawed. That does not imply that the district judge "got it wrong" when refusing an application for summary judgment. The issue is not "who will win?" but "is there a triable issue?"

Where the district judge does give judgment for the plaintiff then since usually the application will be brought in relation to a contract case for a liquidated sum the district judge may give final judgment for the debt claimed and interest thereon and make an order for costs. If the application is for an unliquidated sum then the district judge will give judgment on liability only and usually (unless the assessment of damages is very straightforward) adjourn the question of assessment of damages to some future occasions so that more detailed evidence can be presented. In such a case the plaintiff may have combined his application for summary judgment with an application for an interim payment on account of damages and the district judge will go on to deal with this latter application.

Unconditional leave to defend

11.14 When the defendant does show a triable issue (*e.g.* a serious question of fact or a question of law) or satisfies the district judge that for some other reason there ought to be a trial then he must be given unconditional leave to defend. In other words the plaintiff's application for summary judgment has not succeeded and the case will proceed to trial in the usual way. Such a decision does not necessarily imply any criticism of the plaintiff's conduct of the case. It is perhaps that he has taken an over-optimistic view of the question of whether or not there appears to be some triable issue. Indeed it may not be until this stage when the defendant puts his case on affidavit that the plaintiff was fully aware of exactly what the defendant's alleged defence would be. A somewhat odd result of this is that the more grossly the defendant is prepared to perjure himself the more likely he is to obtain leave to defend. Thus in a case where a plaintiff was suing for the price of goods delivered, if the defendant merely raised some vague allegation that the goods were not of merchantable quality the district judge might well look behind this and see whether there was any seriously triable issue and perhaps give judgment to the plaintiff. However, if the defendant is prepared to say that the goods never arrived then there is clearly a substantial dispute of fact and he will be given leave to defend. This is not to suggest that the ultimate consequences for the defendant of such perjury are likely to be entirely for his long-term good!

Conditional leave to defend

11.15 Where there is some sort of defence put forward but the district judge doubts the good faith of the defendant or is almost certain that the defence raised is bound to fail then he may give leave to defend but only upon some condition. The most common condition is the payment by the defendant into court funds of the whole or part of the sum in dispute. In other words in such a case the district judge is looking to the defendant to establish his good faith or at least to show that his reason for defending is not because he cannot afford to pay the sum claimed. The normal form of the order will be that the defendant has leave to defend the action provided he pays the sum required into court funds within a certain short period but that in default of his doing so judgment will be given for the plaintiff. The payment into court of the sum due should not of course be confused with "payment into court" in the other sense (see para. 12.02). It is not open to the plaintiff to remove the sum from the court in purported acceptance. The payment into court in the present case is entirely in the nature of security.

Where either of the two previous orders are made, that is leave to defend whether conditional or unconditional, the district judge may go on to give directions for trial of the action. This is an attempt to save the parties' and the court's time by avoiding the need for a later summons for directions. Thus directions may be given for the serving of a defence (which need not of course yet have been served since the application for summary judgment extends the time for the service of the defence) for discovery or on any other interlocutory matter. It may be, however, that the application for summary judgment has come at too early a stage for the district judge to really give very full directions for how the case should proceed to trial and that there will anyway need to be a subsequent hearing of a summons for directions.

Dismissal of the summons

The district judge may dismiss the case if the case is not within Order 14 (*e.g.* **11.16** a defamation case) or if it appears that the plaintiff's application is in bad faith, *i.e.* that he knew the defendant would be entitled to leave to defend. This form of order *does* imply a criticism of the plaintiff's conduct of his case and whereas in the previous two instances the usual order will be "costs in the cause," in this case the plaintiff will usually be ordered to pay costs in any event and in some cases to pay them forthwith. Moreover no directions for trial can be given in this case.

ORDER 14 AND NEGLIGENCE ACTIONS

As was indicated earlier the most common use of summonses under Order **11.17** 14 is in contract debt cases. Quite apart from those cases where it specifically does *not* apply by the terms of Order 14 (*e.g.* defamation actions) there are other kinds of cases where it is extremely rare. Road accident cases are one such simply because if a defendant is minded to attempt to defend and wishes to make, as is common, an allegation of negligence or at least contributory negligence against the plaintiff it will be generally very difficult for the district judge to say there is no triable issue without an exhaustive investigation of the facts for which there is no time at the hearing of an Order 14 summons. Accordingly use of Order 14 is rare in all negligence actions and very rare in road accident cases.

Judgment in default of defence under R.S.C., Ord. 19

As compared to the two previous methods of obtaining early judgment this **11.18** is relatively rare. It applies where a defendant has given notice of intention to defend the case and the plaintiff has served his statement of claim but the defendant does not then serve his defence either within 14 days of receiving the statement of claim or within 28 days of receiving the writ whichever is the later or within any further period of extension granted by the plaintiff or by the court. Where this occurs the plaintiff may obtain judgment in default of defence. It is obviously rare compared to the previous kinds of case because this does imply that the defendant has been sufficiently alert to return his acknowledgment of service to the court but for some reason could not or did not get around to drafting a defence for service. In negligence cases where the defendant will almost inevitably have legal representation the most likely explanation is some oversight or perhaps delay in getting the defence settled by counsel. In contract litigation, especially debt collecting where the defendant may be a litigant in person it is more common for a defendant to have managed to tick the appropriate box in the acknowledgment of service supplied for him but perhaps to fail to get around to actually drafting his defence to the statement of claim.

In any event where the time for service of the defence has expired then the plaintiff applies for judgment in default of defence. As in the case of judgment under Order 13 no hearing of any kind is necessary. The plaintiff simply prepares two forms of judgment and takes them to court with the original writ. This time there is no need to prove on oath service of the statement of claim but there is an indorsement preprinted on the forms of judgment under Order 19 in which the plaintiff confirms that the time for service of the defence, taking into account any extension, has expired. The forms of judgment are sealed at the court counter and the plaintiff may then proceed to enforce them as in the case of an Order 13 judgment. Thus if the action is for a liquidated demand, judgment will be final on liability and quantum. If it is for an unliquidated demand there will need to be a later hearing before the district judge at which he will assess damages.

11.19 The three foregoing instances therefore are where the plaintiff is able to obtain an early resolution of the case in his favour because of some deficiency in the defendant's case or in the procedures adopted by the defendant. We will summarise the cases when each is appropriate.

1. Judgment in default of notice of intention to defend under Order *13* will be appropriate where the defendant either fails to acknowledge service of the writ at all or returns the acknowledgment of service having indicated that he does not propose to defend the action. Application is made at the counter of the court office and no hearing is necessary.

2. Summary judgment under Order 14 is appropriate where the defendant does indicate that he intends to defend, the statement of claim has already been served, and the plaintiff bona fide considers that the defendant has no triable defence. Application is made by summons and there is a hearing before the district judge on affidavit evidence.

3. Judgment in default of defence under Order 19 is appropriate where the defendant has indicated that he intends to defend the action, a statement of claim has been served, the case is not considered appropriate for Order 14, and the defendant fails to serve his defence in time. Here again there is no need for a hearing and judgment is obtained at the court counter.

In the case of any of these three methods judgment may be final on liability and quantum if the claim is for a liquidated demand but final on liability only if for an unliquidated demand, in which case there will need to be a later hearing before the district judge at which he will assess damages. One obtains a hearing for the assessment of damages in such a case by issuing a summons under R.S.C., Ord. 37. The district judge has jurisdiction to assess damages no matter how large the sum involved.

We will now go on to consider other ways in which a case may end before trial.

By compromise

11.20 A solicitor has authority to compromise a claim on behalf of a client after a writ is issued, although a solicitor would be foolish to rely on this authority without in each case getting the express authority of the client to compromise the claim. Negotiations, as has been indicated earlier, proceed throughout the litigation and an acceptable resolution may be achieved at any time. Correspondence or meetings to discuss eventual settlement will be on a "without prejudice" basis and when agreement is concluded the matter may be resolved simply by the defendant making a payment of the sum agreed to the plaintiff. There will also need to be an agreement as to costs, the usual form of agreement being that costs will be agreed or taxed in default of agreement. Where all matters are agreed there is no need to do more than notify the court of the agreement by letter. If some court order is required to implement the agreement there is provision under R.S.C., Ord. 42, r. 5A for obtaining consent orders from the court without attendance by sending in the text of the order required with the consent of both parties indicated appropriately in writing. There is then no need to attend the court.

Judgment on admission under R.S.C., Ord. 27

11.21 If the defendant makes a clear admission of liability either in his pleadings or in open correspondence then the plaintiff may apply to the court on summons for judgment to be given on liability. The advantage of this is that it brings the case to an end as far as liability is concerned and provides a ground for the plaintiff to apply immediately for an interim payment on account of damages. It should be noted that before an application can be made the admission must be clearly one of liability. A mere offer in open correspondence to compensate the plaintiff for his injuries does not amount to an admission of liability since it may be that the offer could be interpreted as being an offer of an *ex gratia* payment.

Dismissal for want of prosecution

11.22 The procedure we are about to describe is either under the inherent jurisdiction of the court or at certain stages under the provision of specific orders, (*e.g.* R.S.C., Ord. 25, r. 1 failure to issue a summons for directions at the appropriate time; or Ord. 34, r. 1 failure to set the action down at the proper time). The previous steps considered were those where a compromise has been achieved by agreement or where the *plaintiff* is taking some initiative to bring matters to a speedy conclusion. Under this procedure it is the *defendant* who is taking the initiative to end a case. There are two quite separate situations to consider where a defendant may apply to the court to strike out an action for want of prosecution. These are as follows:

11.23 1. Where the delay is:

    (i) inordinate,
    (ii) inexcusable,
    (iii) prejudicial to a fair trial; and,
    (iv) the limitation period has expired.

The case law demonstrates that for a defendant to make a successful application he must show that all four of these factors are present. Delay is only *inordinate* usually where it amounts to years rather than months and regard is had to the whole period of delay. Thus if a plaintiff did not issue a writ until say two years 11 months after the accident and then drags his heels further for periods of years during the action, the court will look to the whole period since the cause of action arose. There must be no *excuse* for the delay and here it should be noted that default by the plaintiff's solicitor or previous solicitors will *not* amount to an excuse because it is up to him to then pursue his rights against those solicitors. The vital factor is always the third one, namely will the delay be *prejudicial* to a fair trial? Thus if in a negligence case witnesses' memories have faded or witnesses have gone missing or died it would be easier to show this ground than in say a straightforward contract case where much of the evidence would be contained in written documents. Finally the *limitation period must have expired*, for the simple reason that if this writ was struck out then even though the plaintiff could be penalised in costs, under the general law he would have a right to issue a further writ and recommence proceedings. In any event in a personal injury case it is unlikely that the defendant could possibly show that the three other factors were satisfied until well over three years had elapsed.

It should be noted that acquiescence in the delay, *e.g.* by continuing correspondence and negotiations, may prevent the defendant from being able to apply successfully for dismissal for want of prosecution.

There is, however, no obligation on the defendant to keep writing to a plaintiff demanding that he take the next stage in the proceedings and a defendant is perfectly entitled to lie in wait. The usual sequence of matters is that the plaintiff will eventually get around, after a substantial delay, to taking the next step in the action, be it an attempt to set down for trial, complete discovery or whatever. By R.S.C., Ord. 3, r. 6 where more than a year has elapsed since the last step in the action any party who desires to proceed must give to every other party not less than one month's notice of his intention to proceed (that is of the step which he intends now to take). An application to strike out for want of prosecution might therefore proceed something like this:

Example:
The plaintiff is injured in a road accident in January 1985 and eventually issues and serves a writ on the defendant in June 1987. Thereafter pleadings are exchanged and there is some desultory negotiation but the plaintiff takes no further steps from March 1989 until June 1991 at which time the plaintiff's solicitors give the required one month's notice of their intention to take the next step in the procedure by setting the case down for trial. At that stage the defendant applies to the court to strike the action out for want of prosecution.

Even on relatively extreme facts such as this the case law shows that the court will be by no means eager to strike the action out for want of prosecution unless the defendant can satisfy the test of "prejudicial to a fair trial."

11.24 2. The second and quite separate ground for application for dismissal for want of prosecution is where there is something in the plaintiff's conduct which is "intentional and contumelious." Examples would be in a defamation case where the writ is used as a "gagging" device, for instance to prevent discussion of issues at a company shareholders meeting or where the plaintiff is wilfully in default of some order of the court requiring him to take the next step within a prescribed time. Where this ground applies there is no need for the limitation period to have expired.

Stay of action
11.25 This does not in itself bring an action to an end although after a stay has been put upon an action, when a substantial further period of time has elapsed a defendant can always apply then to strike out the action for want of prosecution. The court has a wide discretion to stay proceedings. The stay may be removed and the action recommenced where the person in default of some step that has been ordered is now willing to comply with the previous order of the court. The most obvious example for our purposes would be in a case where the plaintiff was unwilling to undergo medical examination by the defendant's doctor. The court has no power to order the plaintiff to undergo

such examination but it *does* have the power to stay the action until the plaintiff consents. In the circumstances if the plaintiff never consents the action will be stayed indefinitely and after a further period the defendant will then apply to strike the action out for want of prosecution.

12. Payment into Court. R.S.C., Ord. 22

In litigation the parties will generally continue negotiations throughout the course of the pre-trial correspondence and also during proceedings, even during the trial itself. The payment into court is a powerful weapon in the defendant's armoury and is used at a stage when negotiations seem to have broken down. This is not to say that this finally represents the end of any other attempts to settle the matter and indeed negotiations may be picked up long after a payment into court has been made, but payment into court represents the formalising of a certain kind of offer. The type of pressure which it brings to bear on a plaintiff will be explained below.

Under the provisions of Order 22 a defendant may make a payment into court funds. It is a way of pressurising a plaintiff by making him aware of certain drastic costs consequences that may follow upon his refusing the offer.

A payment into court is not always made by a defendant who necessarily feels that he is certain to lose. It may be made by a defendant who realises that it is uneconomic to pursue litigation, for instance in a modest personal injuries case against a legally aided plaintiff where the operation of section 17 of the Legal Aid Act 1988 makes it unlikely that the defendant will obtain costs even if he is successful.

The procedure for paying money into court

12.01 To make payment into court a defendant completes the necessary form of lodgment and takes it to the court with a bank draft or solicitor's cheque for the amount in question. This is paid into court funds and a receipt is given. The defendant's solicitor then writes to the plaintiff's solicitor giving notice of the payment into court. Under the rules the plaintiff's solicitor must acknowledge safe receipt of the notice within three days. This is so that the date upon which notice was received can be proved because this is important for the costs consequences which will be described below. Thereafter the plaintiff has 21 days to consider the defendant's payment into court. A payment into court is *not* an admission of liability. It is merely an attempt by the defendant to compromise a case on terms.

The consequences of payment into court

12.02 We shall consider a very simple factual example and then look at some of the ramifications and matters of detail which it is important to bear in mind. The payment into court puts pressure on the plaintiff in the following way, namely, that if he does not accept the payment into court and at the trial the judge (from whom the payment in must be kept secret until after he has decided all matters of liability and quantum) awards a sum only equal to or less than the payment into court there are certain costs consequences. These consequences are that the judge, on learning of the payment into court, will almost inevitably make a so called "split" order on costs, that is:—

1. the defendant pay the plaintiff's costs on the standard basis from the date of the cause of action arising until the date of the payment into court and

2. the plaintiff pay the defendant's costs on the standard basis from the date of the payment into court until the end of the trial.

One can therefore see that the earlier in the course of proceedings that a payment into court is made the more drastic will the consequences be for the plaintiff who is not awarded a sum greater than the amount paid into court. Successfully obtaining a higher award from the judge than the amount paid into court is called "beating the payment in." A plaintiff who fails to "beat" the payment in where the payment in has been made at an early stage will be penalised very heavily in costs. The higher costs in civil litigation are usually incurred at the trial itself and just before it, that is the costs in the nature of counsel's brief fees and refreshers, solicitor's fees and expert witness fees for attending trial. The consequences for a plaintiff of failing to beat a payment in are that from the relevant date he is not only having to bear his opponent's costs on the standard basis but also will have to pay his own solicitor's costs in full because no one else will be bearing them. An example of the consequences of failure to beat a payment into court is as follows:—

Example:
There is an accident on January 1, 1990. The plaintiff instructs solicitors on January 10, 1990 and from then on costs start running; a writ is issued and served and pleadings are exchanged; in February 1991 the case is set down for trial and the defendant then makes a without prejudice offer of £20,000. The plaintiff refuses this without prejudice offer and on March 20, 1991 the defendant pays £20,000 (plus interest) into court and gives the plaintiff notice of this. The plaintiff does not accept the payment into court. At trial on May 20, 1991, the judge awards the plaintiff the sum of £19,000. The effect on costs would be as follows:—

The defendant will pay the plaintiff's costs on the standard basis up to the date when the notice of payment into court was received in March 1991; (let us say for the sake of argument that this sum is £1,500); the plaintiff will have to pay the defendant's costs on the standard basis from the date of receipt of the notice of payment in until the end of the trial (for the sake of argument let us say that this sum is likely to be of the order of £4,000); moreover the plaintiff will in addition have to bear his own costs for that period—say a further £4,500. Therefore from his damages of £19,000 the plaintiff has in effect lost the figure of £4,000 that he has to pay the defendant towards his costs and the figure of £4,500 that he has had to pay in respect of his own costs from the date of notice of payment into court.

However, if on the same facts the judge at trial had awarded the plaintiff say £21,000 (or even £20,001) then the payment into court would have been of no effect at all and the plaintiff would have got his costs on the standard basis over the whole period in the normal way. The payment in is of no effect if the trial judge does award a higher figure.

When serving notice on a plaintiff of a payment into court the defendant must notify him whether or not the payment in is in respect of all the causes of action in respect of which the plaintiff is claiming. Since in most cases, and certainly in personal injury cases, there is only one cause of action on a writ this is no problem, but if for example the plaintiff had under the joinder rules sued the defendant in the same proceedings for, say, a breach of contract and defamation, the defendant's notice will have specified to which of the two causes of action the payment related.

It is now appropriate to consider some matters of detail which must be taken into account in considering the overall position.

How much should the defendant pay in?

12.03   In a straightforward contract case it would be reasonably clear how much a defendant should pay in to obtain the tactical advantages of the procedure. Thus if for instance the plaintiff is a supplier of goods who is suing a disgruntled consumer who is unwilling to pay more than a proportion of the price because of some alleged major defect, it may be a simple enough matter to quantify the amount of the value of the supposed defect (*e.g.* the repair costs necessary to put the thing into the state in which it should have been at the time of sale). In such a case a defendant will be paying in (or indeed might earlier have tendered voluntarily to the plaintiff) the exact amount which in his view represents the value of the goods. In personal injuries litigation no such precise quantification is possible. Even though all the medical evidence is agreed and all the details about the plaintiff's loss of future earnings or career prospects may be easy to obtain, opinions, even of very experienced practitioners, may well differ markedly as to the value of a claim. Although by reference to *Kemp and Kemp*, *Current Law* and *Lexis* fairly precise figures can be discovered for what, say, the loss of an eye represents in money terms, there are always matters of detail personal to the plaintiff which may be argued in favour of increasing or sometimes decreasing the prima facie figure. In serious accident cases injuries can never really be pushed entirely into one straightforward category. A plaintiff who has for instance been in an accident serious enough to cause him the loss of an eye, is unlikely to have escaped without facial scarring of some kind and/or broken bones. The scope for educated guesswork in arriving at the eventual total award of damages in such cases is therefore considerable. Even very experienced counsel may sometimes differ by many thousands of pounds in the view they take of a case. Consequently the defendant will be trying to aim to pay into court the minimum figure which he can get away with, *i.e.* the minimum figure which the plaintiff dare not refuse. Each side will have obtained advice from counsel on the eventual quantum of damages, each predicting what the final award by the judge will be within a certain bracket. This bracket may be expressed in very wide terms, for example in a band of £5,000 so that counsel may have advised that the plaintiff may recover anything between £20,000 and £25,000 for general damages depending on the view the judge takes (and indeed sometimes depending on who the judge is). In such a case if a payment into court of £20,000 is made the plaintiff will have to think long and hard about the risks of pressing on in the hope of getting a judge who will give an award nearer the top of the bracket which counsel has advised as likely. There is also of course as in most forms of negotiation an element of bluff. Thus when a defendant's counsel has advised that the plaintiff will obtain an award in the range of £20,000–£25,000 the defendant's insurance company may decide to authorise the payment into court of only say £18,000 in the hope that the plaintiff's barrister may have been more pessimistic in his predictions and that this will actually represent a figure within the plaintiff's counsel's bracket and one which the plaintiff dare not refuse. In any event this is not necessarily the last word for the defendant because if the payment into court is refused it can be increased at any time and therefore it is still open to the defendant at a later stage to put more pressure on the plaintiff by paying in say a further £2,000 or £3,000 to top it up. We shall consider the consequences of this below.

Interest on payment in

When making a payment into court in any case in which the plaintiff is likely **12.04** to be awarded interest (and therefore in contract actions and in personal injury actions of any kind) the defendant must compute the amount of interest which he thinks will be awarded and add this to the amount of the payment in. Let us take an example.

Example:
   On the defendant's figures he considers it likely that the plaintiff may be awarded a sum of £10,000. This is the figure which he wishes to pay into court to put pressure on the plaintiff. In order to do so he ought to pay into court not just the £10,000 but his computation of the interest that would be awarded on that sum *computed to the date of payment into court*. Thus let us say that the interest at the date of payment into court works out at about £970. A prudent defendant will generally round up the amount to the nearest convenient figure, say in the present case £1,000, and will thus pay into court a total of £11,000.
   At trial the judge (from whom the payment in has of course been kept secret) decides that the case is indeed worth £10,000 and gives judgment for that amount accordingly. There then needs to be an inquiry as to whether the plaintiff has beaten the payment in. The amount of £11,000 paid into court is now examined and it will be observed that allowing for interest at the proper rates the defendant actually paid into court slightly more than the judge's award. Accordingly the plaintiff has not beaten the payment in and will suffer the consequences of a split order on costs. Suppose however that the defendant had not troubled to work out and pay in the interest and had only paid in the sum of £10,000. Because a payment into court should carry interest up to the date of payment in the court would have had to inquire what the actual figure paid in represented. If the total paid in had only been £10,000 the court would have had to address its mind to what this figure was and would have come to the conclusion that it represented only just over £9,000 together with the interest on that sum. Accordingly on the same facts the plaintiff *would* have beaten the payment in because the trial judge had awarded him a final figure of £10,000 plus interest.
   Interest on damages does of course continue after the date of payment into court. However, interest for that latter period is excluded from computation when working out whether or not a plaintiff has beaten the payment into court. The trial judge will make a separate finding of how much interest will be paid from the date of payment into court to the end of the trial and award that figure to the plaintiff in any event. The notice of payment in should inform the plaintiff that interest is taken into account. However, it actually makes little difference whether the notice does contain these words

137

since the payment is deemed to include interest for the purpose of computing whether or not the plaintiff has beaten it.

Time for acceptance and method of acceptance

12.05   The plaintiff has 21 days in which to accept the money in court without the leave of the court. This means that he has three weeks to consider the position which will in most cases not be a great deal of time to receive thorough advice from his solicitor. It may well be that the solicitor will want to take counsel's opinion on the amount of the payment into court and perhaps even obtain another medical report on the plaintiff to assist him. However, if within that period the plaintiff wishes to accept, he can obtain payment out of the money by simply giving notice of acceptance to the defendant. He then sends a duly completed form to the Court Funds Office indicating acceptance and payment will be made to his solicitor within a very short time. Where he does accept the amount paid into court there are the following consequences:—

1.   All relevant causes of action are stayed, that is, no further action in respect of those causes of action can be taken. It is in other words the end of the case.

2.   The plaintiff will be entitled to his costs on the standard basis up to the date of receipt of the notice of payment in. All he need do is prepare a bill of costs for taxation and take out a taxation appointment. It will often be possible to agree costs with the defendants. Moreover even though in principle one should only obtain one's costs up to the date of the receipt of notice of payment in, in fact defendants who are eager to compromise the case may often be more generous. They may agree that it is reasonable for a plaintiff to obtain a subsequent medical report and counsel's opinion even after the date of the payment into court for the sake of deciding whether to accept it, and agree that such costs shall form part of the plaintiff's reasonable costs on the standard basis. Thus for instance, if in a case of some seriousness a payment into court is received which needs to be very carefully considered, a plaintiff's solicitor may well telephone a defendant's solicitor and indicate that he is minded to accept but ask for an extension of the 21-day period and for an agreement that the defendants will not object to paying the costs of the further medical report and/or counsel's opinion. Agreement will often be forthcoming.

Acceptance outside 21 days

12.06   If the 21 days has expired and the plaintiff later decides that he wishes to accept the money an application to the court for leave is necessary. In fact if the acceptance is within a reasonably short period thereafter one would generally seek to negotiate with the defendants as to some arrangements on costs (for instance that the plaintiff will agree to allow a modest amount, say £100, towards the defendants for their costs incurred after the payment in should have been accepted and leave it at that). If the defendants then consent to the withdrawal of money in court by letter it will be possible to obtain the leave of the court by unopposed application on summons to the district judge.

Increasing payment into court

A defendant may make a payment in quite early for the sake of seeing **12.07** whether the costs pressures imposed on the plaintiff together with any other psychological pressures on him to get the action over and done with at an early stage may have their effect to the defendant's advantage. A defendant is however entitled to increase or "top up" his payment in at any time. Where this is done then time for acceptance of the whole of the amount paid into court begins to run again from the later payment.

Example:

A writ is issued on January 10, 1990, and after negotiations break down in January 1991 the defendant pays into court £10,000 plus his computation of interest, say a further £1,000. The plaintiff declines to accept the payment into court. Three months later the defendants decide to increase the payment into court and pay in a further £2,000 together with the further interest that would have accrued in the intervening months. This time the offer is within the band that the plaintiff finds acceptable and he decides to accept the offer. He can accept the whole amount within the 21-day further period and obtain his costs on the standard basis up to the time of notification of the second payment into court. If he had refused it and the case had gone on to trial then it would have done so on the basis that the defendants had paid the whole amount, *i.e.* £12,000 plus interest, into court on the later date.

Time for payment into court

A defendant is entitled to pay the money into court at any time after the case **12.08** has started. In a case of any complexity it will generally be very difficult to make a realistic payment into court in the very early stages before the pleadings have been served. However, the earlier that a payment into court can be made the more pressure naturally is put on the plaintiff. This may particularly be so where there is some substantial allegation of contributory negligence and the plaintiff's advisers may feel that it is very uncertain whether the degree of contributory negligence which may eventually be assessed against him may be say 20 per cent. or 25 per cent. or perhaps as high as 50 per cent. A payment in at a very early stage in such a case will be a very powerful weapon. It is, however, probably more common for a payment in to be made relatively late in the case. It is a notorious fact that as the date of trial comes close an injured plaintiff becomes more vulnerable to tactical pressures knowing that after months or years of waiting he may be now confronted with an "all or nothing" outcome where he may either obtain a substantial amount which will help towards the financial security of his family, or receive nothing. For the same reason so-called "courtroom door" negotiations where offers are put forward just before the trial is due to commence are often successful. This topic was mentioned earlier in the section on negotiations. A quite separate rule is that a payment in can be made or increased during the trial itself at which time the plaintiff has a further two days in which to accept. This provision is only of very much tactical advantage in the case of trials which are expected to last some time.

Refusal of a payment into court

Where a plaintiff is not disposed to accept a payment into court he need **12.09** actually do nothing about it. It is perhaps courtesy to write to a defendant's solicitor to tell him so but some prefer to decline to refer to it at all and continue regardless, as if the payment in was so pitiful as to be beneath one's dignity to mention.

Legal aid and payment into court

12.10 It should be noted that the making of the payment into court may well be one of the occasions on which a legally aided person's solicitor has to take some action which may displease his client. If a solicitor feels that a reasonable payment in has been made but the client wishes to refuse it it may in some circumstances be appropriate to report the matter to the Area Office of the Legal Aid Board for their views. For example in a case which is of the "all or nothing" type where the plaintiff may well lose outright (*e.g.* the issue is whether it is the plaintiff or the defendant who is liable for the accident). In such a case a reasonable payment into court which the plaintiff is insistent on refusing should be reported to the Area Office because there is a real risk of public funds suffering, *e.g.* if the plaintiff does lose outright. In other cases, however, there may be very little in the nature of a risk to public funds even if the plaintiff is minded to refuse an apparently reasonable settlement.

Suppose for example that a plaintiff seems clearly likely to win on liability and his damages could be in the bracket of £20,000–£25,000. The defendants make a payment into court of £20,000 and the plaintiff is insistent on refusing this sum. So long as he is fully advised then it would be most unlikely that the Legal Aid Board would wish to interfere with his decision. The reason will be that even if he fails to beat the payment in and only recovers, say, £19,000 the amount he will recover will be quite sufficient both to discharge any liability to the defendants for their costs and for the Legal Aid Board's statutory charge to operate to ensure that public funds are not affected. In this connection it is perhaps useful to emphasise also that section 17 of the Legal Aid Act 1988 *does apply* to costs orders in the case of payment into court and to illustrate this the following examples will help.

Example 1:
The defendant in a personal injury case pays £10,000 into court. The plaintiff refuses this sum but at the trial the judge finds entirely in favour of the defendants and thus awards no damages. Clearly here the defendant has won on the issue of liability and will be reimbursed the £10,000 which he paid into court. He may now be minded to make an application for costs against the plaintiff. In this connection the payment into court is totally irrelevant. The court will look to the operation of section 17 of the Legal Aid Act 1988 and order only that he pay such part of his opponent's costs as is reasonable in all the circumstances having regard to the means of the parties and their conduct in relation to the case. In such a case, therefore, an order for costs against a legally-aided person is most unlikely. Also in such a case although the defendant has won on the eventual issue, since in personal injury litigation the defendant is invariably insured, or the equivalent, section 18 of the Legal Aid Act 1988 will not assist the defendant because he will not "suffer severe financial hardship." Let us now take another example.

Example 2:
The defendants pay into court the sum of £20,000. The plaintiff who is legally aided refuses this sum but at trial is only awarded £19,000. Here a

costs order on the normal split terms will be made. The plaintiff will recover his costs on the standard basis up to the date of payment into court and he will have to pay the defendants' costs on the standard basis from that date. The court will have considered section 17 of the Legal Aid Act but as the plaintiff is now a person who prima facie has £19,000 (the amount which he has just been awarded by the court) he will be a person who ought to have to satisfy the normal consequence of the split order and pay from his damages the defendants' costs from the date after his refusal of payment into court.

Payments into court and infants
As will be seen in the later section on infants, a payment into court in the case of an infant cannot be accepted without the leave of the court. The method of application is described in the later section at para. 15.02.

12.11

What happens to the money in court?
When the money is paid into court it is after 21 days put on an interest-bearing account. The rate of interest varies from time to time. The money remains in court continuing to earn interest until the end of the trial, and this interest belongs prima facie to the defendant. At the end of the case an order must be made dealing with the money in court. For example where a plaintiff has beaten the payment into court the order will be in simple terms that the money in court will be paid out to the plaintiff in part satisfaction of his claim. If the plaintiff has not been beaten the payment into court then any surplus is likely to be ordered to be returned to the defendant and the amount awarded by the judge to be paid out to the plaintiff. In fact there are certain refinements on this possibility depending on the sums involved. Suppose for example that it is quite clear that because of his failure to beat the payment into court the plaintiff is going to have to bear a very substantial proportion of the defendant's costs. In such a case it may be appropriate for the court to order that a sum of money be left in court funds to satisfy the defendant's costs and only the balance over this figure be paid out to the plaintiff. After taxation of the defendant's and plaintiff's costs the sum left in court is paid out as required to the defendant in respect of his costs and any residual balance paid to the plaintiff.

12.12

Secrecy
As indicated earlier the facts that there has been a payment into court must be kept secret from the trial judge until after he has given judgment on all matters of liability and quantum. This is the essential element of the legal gamble which payment into court represents. However, as we shall see shortly where an application is made to the district judge for an *interim payment* it is permissible to mention that there has been a payment into court. Similarly it is permissible to indicate to a district judge that there had been a payment into court at the hearing of an application for summary judgment under Order 14.

12.13

Payment into court by only some of the defendants
Where payment into court is made by some only of the defendants, *e.g.* where only one of two defendants makes payment in, or perhaps only two out of three defendants get together and agree on the joint payment in, then leave of the court is needed anyway to accept the payment in. This is

12.14

obtained on summons to be heard by the district judge. At the hearing of this summons the important issue will be to decide on the position of the party who did not participate in making the payment in and any question of costs and as to whether the action is to continue against that party.

13. Interim Payments. R.S.C., Ord. 29, rr. 9–11

An interim payment is a payment in advance on account of any eventual **13.01** award of damages which a plaintiff might receive. Although it is in fact available in all types of case we shall first discuss it in the context of personal injury cases since it is in those cases that its use is most vitally important. We will conclude with a few observations about its applicability to other types of cases.

As has already been mentioned, except in those cases to which the relatively **13.02** new rule about the award of provisional damages applies (see earlier) an award of damages is a once-and-for-all matter. Therefore a plaintiff's solicitor would usually not be wise to hurry a case to trial too quickly if the plaintiff has suffered personal injuries of any seriousness. It will be important to see how the plaintiff's medical condition stabilises so that a proper judgment can be made as to how the quality of his life and particularly his potential earning power have been affected. Even if it were procedurally possible therefore to get substantial personal injury cases to trial within a few months it would, generally speaking, be highly undesirable to do so. In the normal case once an award of damages has been made one cannot go back to court for more if the plaintiff's condition deteriorates or his improvement does not reach the levels expected by his medical advisers. On the assumption therefore that the plaintiff himself has some interest in a degree of delay in bringing his case to trial one must consider the psychological effect on the plaintiff of this delay. As has previously been noted the reality of personal injury litigation is that an individual is litigating against a huge insurance company. Even in those cases where the individual has no worries about his own legal expenses (*e.g.* where he is supported by a trade union or legally aided) he is aware of the importance of the success of his claim to himself and his family's financial future. The insurance company, whilst no doubt usually guided by proper commercial principles, so that they will not wish to incur large sums in wasted legal costs fighting hopeless cases, will also be aware that there are tactical advantages for them in delaying matters and thus bringing pressure upon the plaintiff to accept the smallest sum that they can escape with paying. It would be foolish to pretend that the psychological pressures imposed by litigation on an insurance company are anything like the pressure on an injured individual. The degree of anxiety that the individual may feel will of course be exacerbated if he is now so disabled as to be virtually house-bound and may have little on which to exercise his mind for much of the day apart from the prospects of his claim. Litigation in those circumstances must seem virtually interminable. It is easy to imagine how considerable pressure could be put upon any such individual by unscrupulous defendants but the pressures will be increased still further if the individual is also suffering financial hardship as a consequence of the injury. For example if he had previously been a highly-paid employee and is reduced merely to benefit levels, he will not only see the quality of his life substantially diminished but also have the worries of mortgage arrears and other debts accumulating.

In such a case the possibility of an application for an interim payment may be vitally important both to relieve immediate financial pressure upon the plaintiff and to improve morale and make him more optimistic about the evental success of his claim.

Method of application for interim payment

13.03   An application can be made to the court by summons on one of the following three grounds set out in R.S.C., Ord. 29, r. 11, namely:

1. That the respondent to the application has admitted liability; or

2. That the applicant has obtained judgment against the respondent for damages to be assessed; or

3. That if the action proceeded to trial the applicant would obtain judgment for substantial damages against the respondent or where there are two or more defendants against any of them.

There is no difficulty with the first and second of the grounds. The first ground implies that the defendant has already admitted liability either in his pleadings or in open correspondence; the second ground applies where the plaintiff has already obtained judgment against the defendant on the issue of liability (*e.g.* by summary judgment under R.S.C., Ord. 14 or a judgment on an admission). It is the third ground that naturally causes difficulty because it requires the district judge, at a time when the defendant is still prima facie defending, to arrive at some assessment of who is likely to win the case and whether or not, on the assumption that it is the plaintiff, he is likely to receive "substantial damages." The district judge will not consider himself bound by the contents of the defendant's defence but will look behind what is actually pleaded to see whether any serious issue does arise or whether the defendant is merely trying to keep the issue of liability "alive" for tactical reasons.

13.04   To apply, the plaintiff takes out a summons and files at court a copy of an affidavit sworn by himself or his solicitor. The affidavit must:—

1. Verify the amount of the damages and the grounds of the application.

2. Exhibit any documentary evidence relied on by the plaintiff in support of the application.

It is usual when drafting this affidavit to exhibit the pleadings and to give some brief resume of the facts on which the action itself is based (*e.g.* to briefly describe the road accident). The affidavit must then conform with the two requirements above, that is there must be a paragraph in which the plaintiff must swear to the truth of the special damages so far incurred and exhibit any documentary evidence (*e.g.* medical reports, letters from employers giving details of loss of earnings) relied on in support of the application.

13.05   Although there is actually no requirement in the rules for the application to be made only in a case of hardship, so that for instance it would in principle be open to a wealthy plaintiff to make an application, where the third of the grounds above is the one relied upon (*i.e.* the issue of liability has not yet been finally determined) it is usual for a plaintiff only to apply if he can show some hardship, either actual or at least likely, because of potential delay in bringing the case to trial. A plaintiff should therefore in his affidavit include details of the reason why he needs an interim payment, for example to pay off debts or mortgage arrears which have accumulated because of his being unemployed, to pay for private medical treatment, to have a lift installed in his house, etc. Although the rules do not require the plaintiff to apply for any specific figure it is open to the plaintiff to suggest the figure he would like in his summons and affidavit if he wishes.

13.06 The summons once taken out must be served with a copy of the supporting affidavit on the defendant at least 10 clear days before the hearing. There is usually no difficulty with this since in most district registries there would be little prospect of getting a hearing date for such an application within a month. If the defendant proposes seriously to dispute liability then he should himself swear an affidavit setting out his belief in the truth of his defence and his objections to making the interim payment.

13.07 The case then comes before the district judge who will decide whether he feels liability is sufficiently clear to enable him to make an interim payment award. If he concludes that the plaintiff's case is fairly clear on liability he will then have to consider how much to award. He may adopt the suggestion made by the plaintiff in his summons and affidavit or he may make some preliminary determination of the probable eventual award of damages and give a reasonable proportion of this. One guideline sometimes suggested is to award the plaintiff the whole of his special damages incurred to date, together with a reasonable proportion (say one-third) of the approximate level of general damages which the case seems to merit.

When an application may fail

13.08 The above assumes of course that the plaintiff is successful. It may be that the defendant can defeat the plaintiff's application and there are three reasons why this may occur:—

1. That the application is irregular, *e.g.* the affidavit is not in the proper form or has not been served in time. In such a case the court may anyway waive the defect or if some prejudice has been caused, *e.g.* by the period of service not being long enough, merely adjourn the application to some later date.

2. That the grounds of the application cannot be established, *e.g.* where the defendant does show that the plaintiff is unlikely to succeed in obtaining judgment against him for a substantial sum, that is that the plaintiff is not necessarily going to win the case on the merits.

3. In a personal injury action only, that the defendant is not a person falling within one of the following categories, namely:

    (a) a person insured in respect of the claim or
    (b) a public authority or
    (c) a person whose means and resources are such as to enable him to make the interim payment.

In a personal injury case therefore this last ground is very important. The respondent to the application must either be:—

13.09   **(a) Insured**. (It should be noted here that merely because the circumstances are such that the M.I.B. will pay the claim does *not* bring the defendant within this category) and if neither of the other two provisions apply one cannot obtain an interim payment against an uninsured defendant;
or

13.10   **(b) A public authority**, which is undefined but which presumably means government departments, local authorities and statutory undertakers;
or

13.11   **(c) A person who has the *means and resources* to make the interim payment.** There appears to be no case law on the meaning of this phrase. It is, at least in the context of road accidents, prima facie unlikely that a person who cannot afford to or does not bother to insure his vehicle so as to bring himself within the "insured" category would be able to pay an interim payment from his own means and resources.

Miscellaneous matters

13.12   1.   It should be noted that an interim payment is exempt from the Legal Aid Board's charge. It can thus be paid to the plaintiff directly.
    If the final award of damages does not exceed the interim payment for any reason then naturally the charge applies to all sums in the plaintiff's hands and he may then be ordered to repay any part to which the charge would normally attach.

2.   If the interim payment is obtained on behalf of a person under a disability the court may give directions for what will happen to the interim payment which may, *e.g.* be that all or part of it remain in court for investment for the person under disability.

3.   The interim payment may be ordered to be paid in one lump sum or in several instalments. It should be noted that an application for an interim payment can be made more than once and even if the first application was refused a further application can be made if circumstances change.

4.   The amount of the interim payment and the fact of its having been ordered is not disclosed to the trial judge at the hearing of the case until all matters of liability and quantum have been decided. The amount of any interim payment made is naturally deducted from the final award made by the judge.

5.   Where a subsequent payment into court is made, the notice of payment into court should state whether or not interim payment has been taken into account in making the payment into court.

6.   On any application for an interim payment the district judge may go on to give directions for the further conduct of the action and may treat the hearing as if it were the hearing of a summons for directions. There may thus be a chance to avoid a further hearing.

7.   An application for an interim payment may be made on its own which is more normal, or it may be combined with an application for summary

judgment so that a court will be asked to give summary judgment on liability and then go on to consider the application for an interim payment.

8. If a defendant has made a payment into court then it is permissible to inform the district judge of this at the hearing of an application for interim payment. Thus if the defendant is defending the interim payment application on the basis that the plaintiff is unlikely to win at trial, the fact that a payment in has been made is obviously highly material. Whilst not strictly an admission of liability in theory, the making of a payment into court is obviously some indication of how a defendant views the likely outcome of the case. The interim payment can be ordered from the money in court.

Time for applying

13.13 An application may be made to the court at any time after the writ has been served and the time limited for acknowledging service has expired. In the normal course of things one would probably not make an application (in a personal injury case) for an interim payment until the defence had been served. However, because of the availability of orders for interim payments it has become increasingly common for defendants to agree to make voluntary interim payments. Indeed it is a good rule before making any form of application to the court, save in those cases where some element of surprise is required, to write to one's opponent and ask if they will consent to one's suggestion voluntarily. Insurance companies are sometimes willing to make voluntary interim payments even before a writ has been issued where liability seems fairly clear. Indeed where a defendant is not proposing to seriously contest liability he may as well make an offer of a voluntary interim payment since it avoids the costs of an application to the court. A particular use of an interim payment may be for private medical treatment to enable an injured plaintiff to jump a waiting list for N.H.S. treatment. An application for an interim payment for this purpose may well be received favourably by the defendant's insurers if they think it may hasten the plaintiff's recovery and return to work. One should always be alert to the possibility of making application for an interim payment in every personal injury case both as a means of improving the morale of one's own client and of keeping some tactical pressure on the opponent. One should not wait for a client to point out that he is suffering severe hardship before inquiring as to whether this might be the case and whether an interim payment might be beneficial.

Cases other than personal injury cases

13.14 An application for an interim payment can be made in contract cases also. Although in a contract case there may be some element of financial hardship, the pressures on a plaintiff are unlikely to be quite as severe as they are on a personally injured plaintiff. This may be one of the reasons why applications in contract actions for interim payments are less common but another important reason may be that since it is for the plaintiff to establish that he has a fairly clear case on liability, ground three of the grounds described above is unlikely to apply very often. In other words a plaintiff in a contract action who had such a clear case on liability, would have been likely to have applied for and successfully obtained summary judgment, either for a liquidated sum or at least judgment on liability to be followed by an assessment of damages. It is suggested therefore that although theoretically available, applications for interim payment are less likely in contract actions.

14. Third Party Proceedings. R.S.C., Ord. 16

It will be remembered from the earlier discussion of joinder of parties that it is not open to a *defendant* to join any person as co-defendant. Third party proceedings are a procedure whereby a defendant may have some issue which is in some way relevant to the plaintiff's claim against him tried as between himself and some other person. In such a case it would always be open to the defendant to issue his own writ against this other person. Third party proceedings, however, have the advantages first of preventing a multiplicity of actions and enabling the court to settle disputes between all parties in one action and secondly of preventing the same question being tried twice with possibly different results. There is also a considerable saving in costs. A claim may therefore be brought by a defendant against the third party. We shall consider the kind of claims that can be made in a moment. It is important to note at this stage, however, that there is no direct connection between the plaintifff and the third party. The plaintiff has brought an action against the defendant and against him only, and what happens between defendant and third party is irrelevant to the plaintiff, so that, if it transpires that the plaintiff has sued the wrong person he cannot obtain judgment against the third party instead of the defendant unless he has previously taken certain action to which we shall come below.

A defendant may by third party notice make a claim against a person who is not already a party to the action for:— **14.01**

1. a contribution or indemnity, or

2. any relief or remedy relating to or connected with the original subject-matter of the action and substantially the same as some relief or remedy claimed by the plaintiff, or

3. may claim to have any question or issue arising out of the plaintiff's claim determined not only as between the plaintiff and the defendant but also as between either or both of them and a person not already a party to the action.

We shall now therefore consider how these might arise:—

CLAIM FOR A CONTRIBUTION

To take a straightforward case supposing that P has been knocked down by a **14.02** vehicle driven by D. D contends that he was not the only one responsible for the accident and that T contributed to the cause of it. He may therefore join T as a third party. The consequence will be that although D will remain liable for any damages awarded to the plaintiff he may, having paid those damages, be able to obtain a contribution if the court conclude that T did bear a share of responsibility for the accident. If in a negligence case D claimed that T had *wholly* caused the accident then this would provide a complete defence for D and if the court found that this was so D would be exonerated from any liability. The consequence of this would be that as there is no direct relationship between the plaintiff and T the plaintiff would recover no damages and indeed be left to pay D's costs. The action that the plaintiff should take to cope with this possibility will be discussed below.

CLAIM FOR INDEMNITY

14.03 An example of this would be a case where a consumer sues a retailer for damages in respect of the supply of an item which is not of merchantable quality. The retailer may have a contract with the manufacturer which provides the retailer with indemnity in such cases. The retailer may anyway defend the action on the merits perhaps alleging that the item was not defective when it left the shop but broke because of rough treatment by the plaintiff, or that the damages claimed do not flow naturally from the alleged defect, but the point of issuing third party proceedings will be that if he fails in these allegations he may recover an indemnity from the manufacturer. In fact in such a situation what would happen in reality would be that the retailer would more or less drop out of the proceedings. Although strictly liable in the law of Sale of Goods for the supply of the defective item, if it was indeed impossible for him to check the quality of the item before selling it (*e.g.* canned goods) any claim which the plaintiff does have against the retailer will probably lead to a full indemnity from the third party to the latter. The third party might as well negotiate directly with the plaintiff for settlement of the action. A common development is for the third party to offer to take over the conduct of the defendant's defence of the action.

OTHER RELIEF

14.04 Possibilities 2 and 3 earlier may be briefly considered together. They allow the defendant in general to introduce in the action some issue which has some connection with the situation out of which the plaintiff's claim against the defendant arose. An example of this is a case where P is knocked down by a vehicle driven by D, D's car goes on to strike a wall and D is injured. D contends that the accident may have been caused or contributed to by T. He will issue third party proceedings against T seeking a contribution towards any damages he is found liable to pay P and in addition damages for his own personal injury.

How are third party proceedings commenced?

14.05 A third party notice in the prescribed form should be issued at court at any time after notice of intention to defend has been given. Provided the notice is issued before the defence is served then no leave of the court is necessary. The defendant's solicitor takes down to the court the necessary copies of a third party notice in the prescribed form and pays a fee. The third party notice stands as if it were a writ and brief statement of claim indicating to the third party the substance of the defendant's claim against him.

14.06 It will be observed that no leave of the court is required provided this step is taken before the defence is served. It will be recalled that the defendant only has 14 days from service of the statement of claim in which to serve his defence. However, given that there will usually have been some pre-action negotiations the need to issue a third party notice should have already become apparent. It may well be possible therefore to issue the third party notice before serving the defence. If, however, is has not proved possible or the existence or name of the third party has only come to the defendant's notice at some later stage then the leave of the court should be obtained. This is done by an *ex parte* application to the district judge. The *plaintiff* is not involved at this stage. An affidavit is sworn, usually by the defendant's solicitor. The affidavit must state:—

1. the nature of the claim made by the plaintiff against the defendant in the action;

2. the stage which proceedings in the main action have reached;

3. the nature of the claim made by the defendant applying for leave to issue the third party notice and the facts on which the proposed third party notice is based; and

4. the name and address of the proposed third party.

The defendant's solicitor takes the affidavit to the district registry and leaves it with three copies of the third party notice. There is no hearing. The district judge will in due course read the affidavit and if it seems to him an appropriate case for third party proceedings he will give leave for the third party notices to be issued. The defendant then collects them from the court. One notice is sealed as the original and the other notices are sealed for retention by the court and service on the third party by the defendant. There is no need in the Queen's Bench Division to draw up the order giving leave to issue third party proceedings. If the affidavit is not wholly convincing or the case is one of some difficulty the district judge may instead of dealing with the matter *ex parte* direct that a summons be issued and both parties (*i.e.* defendant and plaintiff) be called before him.

When the third party notice has been issued it must be served on the third **14.07** party in the same way as a writ. Copies of the writ and pleadings in the main action (*i.e.* that between plaintiff and defendant) must also be served together with a form of acknowledgment of service. The form of acknowledgment of service is basically the same as that served with the writ itself with slight modifications, *e.g.* the change of "defendant" to "third party."

The third party when served must acknowledge the third party notice in the **14.08** same way in which a defendant must acknowledge a writ by returning the acknowledgment of service duly completed to the court within 14 days indicating whether he proposes to defend the third party proceedings. If he does not return this although the defendant cannot enter judgment in default against the third party, the third party is now deemed to admit any claim stated in the notice and will be bound by any judgment in the action and will not in principle be permitted to play any further part in the proceedings.

The course of third party proceedings

We will now suppose however that the acknowledgment of service has been **14.09** properly returned. It is apparent even from reading this brief account that proceedings involving third parties are becoming rather "messy" and therefore the rules of court provide that at a very early stage there should be a sort of tidying-up operation when all the parties are called before the court. The rules provide that as soon as possible after the third party's acknowledging service and giving notice of intention to defend the defendant must take out a *summons for third party directions* The summons is issued in the usual way and a hearing date obtained from the court and the summons will then be served by the defendant on both the plaintiff and the third party. It will be noted that there has not hitherto been any requirement for the service of formal pleadings between the defendant and the third party, and the third party need take no further steps after returning the acknowledgment of service until he attends the hearing of the summons for third party directions. There is a number of orders which the district judge will consider making when all the parties are before the court. The most important ones are as follows:—

1. He may dismiss the application for directions with the result of terminating the third party proceedings. He will do this where for example it does not appear to him that the case is an appropriate one for third party proceedings and where third party proceedings may cause delay and difficulty in the substantive action between the plaintiff and the defendant.

2. If the liability of the third party to the defendant is established, (*e.g.* if there is clearly a contract for indemnity of the defendant) he may order judgment to be entered for the defendant against the third party.

3. He may order any claim, question or issue to be tried in such manner as the court may direct as between plaintiff and defendant and third party.

4. He may give the *third party* liberty to defend the *plaintiff's claim* either alone or jointly with the defendant. Such a situation has already been envisaged, *e.g.* a claim against a retailer who has a contract for indemnity by the manufacturer. The manufacturer may take over the retailer's defence letting the retailer drop out (with an appropriate order for costs) and the manufacturer may then avail himself of any defences which would have been available to the defendant retailer, *e.g.* he may say that the goods were not in fact defective.

5. He may order third party pleadings, that is the service of pleadings between defendant and third party.

6. He may make an order adding the third party as a defendant where the plaintiff applies for this and wishes to raise a claim directly against the third party, *e.g.* in the case of the motor accident referred to above where it now appears that T may have been negligent either as well as, or instead of, D.

7. He may give orders for discovery between the third party and the defendant, or the third party and the plaintiff. This will be necessary because there is no automatic discovery under Order 24, r. 2 in third party proceedings.

8. He may give directions for trial of the third party issue. The common order is to direct that the third party be at liberty to appear at the trial of

the action and take such part as the judge shall direct and be bound by the result of the trial. It should be noted here that proceedings between the defendant and third party can go on even after those between plaintiff and defendant are stayed.

When giving these directions the court will have in mind the interests of all the parties and especial care will be taken to see that the plaintiff is not subject to injustice and delay by unnecessarily allowing third parties to serve defences. The usual order giving directions for the progress of the action allows the third party to attend at the trial of the plaintiff's claim against the defendant and to oppose the plaintiff's claim so far as he personally might be affected by it and for this purpose to call oral or documentary evidence and himself to cross-examine the plaintiff's witnesses. **14.10**

Let us now consider the way in which the matter will most commonly arise in a personal injury case and what steps might be taken tactically by either party.

1. Let us first suppose that the plaintiff's vehicle has been in collision with the defendant's vehicle and that both parties have suffered personal injuries. The plaintiff contends that the defendant's negligence was the cause of the accident and issues a writ against him. The defendant may not only defend but if he contends that the plaintiff was to blame counterclaim for his own vehicle damage and personal injuries. No other parties are involved. **14.11**

2. A more complicated situation would be, for instance, if a pedestrian plaintiff is injured by a vehicle driven by D. He sues D. D, however, contends that the accident was actually caused by another vehicle driven by T which suddenly swerved out in front of him causing him to take evasive action in the agony of the moment. D is therefore in the position of claiming that he is completely innocent. Here D may take one of two courses, namely:— **14.12**

(i) He may simply blame T in his defence and leave it at that. There is no need to issue third party proceedings. If at trial his defence is accepted, *i.e.* it is found that the accident was in fact caused by T then the plaintiff's claim will fail against D, T is not involved at all and the plaintiff will in principle have to pay the defendant's costs. It must be said however that merely to do this and put it in his pleading as a form of defence would be an act of very great confidence on the part of D. He would run the risk of bearing the whole of the plaintiff's damages in such a case even if he were found to be only one per cent. to blame for the accident. Putting his defence in that way without taking any further action would therefore generally be considered extremely rash. **14.13**

(ii) Consequently in addition to blaming T in his defence he will normally go on to issue third party proceedings against T. This will particularly be the case if he has himself suffered some damage in the accident for which he can hardly blame the pedestrian plaintiff, *e.g.* where having hit the pedestrian plaintiff he then hits a tree nearby. He will accordingly in such a situation issue third party proceedings claiming both the contribution towards any damages for which he is found liable to the plaintiff and for his own damages. If therefore the court found that T was in fact 90 per cent. to blame, whilst D **14.14** would initially have to pay the whole of the plaintiff's damages he could recover 90 per cent. contribution from T, and also 90 per cent. of the amount appropriate for his own damages, if any.

What action should the plaintiff take?

14.15   In the first case where the defendant merely blames T in his pleading but does not issue a third party notice it will of course be prudent for the plaintiff to apply for leave to amend the writ to add T as a second defendant. In this he can hardly lose in terms of costs because he will at the end of the trial, should he succeed against either of the defendants, receive a Bullock or Sanderson order. It can hardly be contended that he was unreasonable in adding T as a defendant where the suggestion of T's liability came from D himself.

14.16   In the second situation where D has issued third party proceedings it may again be considered prudent to join T as a third party. Although he only has to show that D was 1 per cent. to blame for the accident to recover the whole of his damages, if there is any suggestion that somebody else may have caused or contributed to the happening of the accident then it would be a safer course for him to join that person. It might be that he would fail outright at the trial against D in which case he would be paying D's costs and of course bearing his own. It might well by that stage be too late to issue separate proceedings against T because the limitation period might have expired. Moreover even if he was in time to issue separate proceedings against T it would by no means follow that he would win against T at a trial before a different court. It must be remembered that the findings of courts in civil cases are not binding in any given case unless the parties before the court subsequently are the same. Therefore the fact that the first judge considered T had caused the accident would not bind the second one to come to the same conclusion and if he concluded that D had caused the accident P might again fail outright. It is therefore greatly to P's advantage to avoid any possible risk of this and achieve a saving in costs and time by joining everybody involved at the appropriate stage. The obvious time for the plaintiff to apply for this order adding the third party as second defendant is at the stage of the summons for third party directions when all parties are conveniently before the court. It should be remembered that the plaintiff will need to apply for leave to amend his writ and pleadings and ought before the hearing to have been prudent enough to have already written a letter protecting himself under section 152 of the Road Traffic Act 1988 and to have obtained the prior authority of the Legal Aid Board to amend any legal aid certificate to add a reference to the proposed second defendant.

Can one defendant use third party proceedings against another defendant?

14.17   For completeness it ought to be said that if P had commenced proceedings against D1 and D2, D1 would not need to issue third party proceedings merely to allege D2's part in the accident. In such a situation the courts have a wide power to apportion liability under the Civil Liability (Contribution) Act 1978 for any damages found due to the *plaintiff*. However, where one defendant has a claim *of his own* against a co-defendant (*e.g.* when both P and D1 have been injured in an accident, and D1 wishes to claim against D2) he may without leave issue third party proceedings against the co-defendant. A summons for third party directions will follow and there will be a similar "tidying-up" operation to that described above.

15. Persons Under a Disability. R.S.C., Ord. 80

Mental patients and infants (or minors) are said to be *under a disability* and as is well known this affects some aspects of substantive law. Procedurally the consequence of this disability is that they cannot themselves institute or defend proceedings. In the following discussions the term "infant" will be used which is the term still used in the Rules of the Supreme Court. Each example should be understood as in principle applying also to mental patients, although there are some further refinements in the case of mental patients which are not within the scope of this text.

An infant cannot bring or defend an action in his own right. He sues through an intermediary called "a next friend" and defends an action by a "guardian ad litem." We shall first consider the position of an infant plaintiff and then go on to consider that of an infant defendant.

An infant plaintiff

15.01 Before an infant plaintiff can issue a writ a next friend needs to be appointed to act. Appointment is not by the court but generally by agreement, and by convention the next friend is a parent unless there is a possible conflict of interest with the parents. Solicitors should be alert to the prospect of this arising. For example suppose that the infant who is injured was in the back seat of a car driven by its father. Liability for the accident is not entirely clear and liability is initially repudiated by the proposed defendant on the basis that the infant's father may have caused, or at least contributed to the accident. In such a situation it would not be possible to have the infant's father as a next friend. That is a fairly obvious example but one should be alert to the possibility of conflicts arising even where they are not immediately apparent from the outset. Anybody may in fact act as next friend for an infant, *e.g.* any relative, friend, godparent or indeed the solicitor himself.

In the High Court an infant's next friend may not act in person but must employ a solicitor. An infant who wishes to issue proceedings will issue a writ in the appropriate form, that is in the same form as any other writ except that it will describe the infant as, *e.g.* "an infant suing by X his mother and next friend." Along with the writ in the appropriate form there must be two other documents filed. The first is a written consent by the next friend to act. The second is a certificate signed by the solicitor for the infant confirming that there is no conflict of interest between the infant and the next friend. It should be noted that the next friend is personally liable for costs in the action with an indemnity against the infant when it comes of age.

Thereafter there is no difference whatsoever in any of the usual procedures so far as the plaintiff infant is concerned until one comes to the stage of considering compromise or settlement. It is now important to consider this aspect thoroughly.

COMPROMISE OF AN INFANT'S CLAIM

This can arise in a number of ways. It may arise for example before an action **15.02** is commenced. The defendants may put forward an offer before a writ is issued which appears acceptable. Equally after an action has commenced they may put forward an offer in negotiation as proceedings continue or make a payment into court which is thought acceptable by the plaintiff's legal adviser. The law is that before a compromise of an action involving an infant can be concluded application should be made to the court for the court's approval. There are a number of reasons for this given in the White Book, namely:—

1. To protect infants and patients from any lack of skill or experience of their legal advisers which might lead to a settlement for an inadequate sum of money.

2. To provide means by which a defendant may obtain a valid discharge from an infant's or patient's claim since without the court's approval no contract of compromise would bind a plaintiff unless it could be proved to have been made for his benefit and no prudent defendant would wish to take such a risk.

3. To make sure that the money recovered is properly looked after and wisely invested.

We shall now describe the procedure for obtaining the court's approval. If **15.03** the settlement is achieved before a writ has been issued then an appointment before the district judge should be obtained by the issue of an *originating summons* seeking the court's approval to the settlement. It will be recalled that the term "originating summons" means a procedural summons in cases where no writ has as yet been issued. The two examples we have hitherto considered have been under R.S.C., Ord. 24, r. 7A for pre-action discovery and inspection of documents in a case involving personal injuries and under R.S.C., Ord. 29, r. 7A for pre-action inspection of a thing. An originating summons in the prescribed form is issued by taking two copies to the district registry where they are sealed and a hearing date allotted. One copy is then served upon the defendant. Alternatively if proceedings have been issued and either it is desired to accept a payment into court or an amount offered in negotiations, an ordinary summons in the action seeking the leave of the court should be issued. In neither case is it necessary to file an affidavit in support but it is always open to the parties to do so in a case of any complexity, *e.g.* where it may be useful to explain in affidavit some of the background to the case. In principle the district judge should be able to approach the question of what sum of money would be satisfactory for him to approve compromise of the infant's claim with an open mind and there-fore no reference to the sum of money actually offered should appear in the summons in either case. At the hearing both parties should attend and, although not strictly required, it is customary for the infant and next friend to attend. In any event a letter from the next friend confirming approval of acceptance of the sum offered should be produced.

At the hearing the procedure will be as follows:—

(i) If liability is in any way in question then both sides will informally indicate **15.04** to the district judge what their evidence was on liability. For example if the infant is a 16-year-old cyclist who has perhaps contributed to the cause of the accident and a compromise of the claim has been achieved on the basis that there should be a 50 per cent. reduction for contributory negligence it will be necessary to indicate to the district judge what the evidence is on this, so as to convince him that a 50 per cent. allowance for contributory negligence is reasonable. Even in a case where no allowance for contributory negligence is actually conceded it may be appropriate to indicate to the district judge that there is some dispute on liability so that he may bear in mind the risks of litigation when considering what figure would be an acceptable compromise. Counsel's opinion on liability if there is one should be put before him.

15.05 (ii) Up-to-date evidence on quantum of damages should then be introduced. This should take the form of completely up-to-date medical reports and/or agreed figures which show the computation of special damages. If the case is a complicated or particularly heavy one a good deal of such evidence may need to be considered and one should be careful when taking out the appointment for the summons to indicate a realistic length of hearing.

15.06 The question for the court is not necessarily what amount of damages should be awarded at the trial of the action but whether the settlement presently offered is a reasonable one and is for the infant's benefit having regard to all the circumstances, including the inherent risks of litigation and the desire of the parties, including the plaintiff, to settle. If counsel has advised on the reasonableness of the amount his opinion should also be placed before the district judge.

15.07 Thereafter the district judge announces what sum he would consider, on all the evidence he has heard, to be satisfactory. If this sum is the same as the amount actually agreed or is less than the amount actually agreed then the court's approval will be given to the acceptance of the offer. If however the district judge considers that a higher figure than that which has been agreed is the appropriate one to settle the infant's claim then much will depend upon the difference between the figure at which he arrives and the figure which has been offered. If it is only a matter of a fairly small sum he may ask the parties whether if they were allowed a brief adjournment there might be some possibility of an agreement to offer the higher figure. Much will depend upon whether the defendants are able to contact their insurance clients to obtain approval of such a course. It may be possible, if telephone contact can be established, for the defendant's insurance company to put forward an offer sufficient to meet the district judge's requirements. If this is not possible or if there is a greater discrepancy between the figure offered and the figure which the court would approve then the district judge will ask if the parties think that there is any purpose in adjourning the summons so that further negotiations can continue. If they do think so he will adjourn it to a hearing date in the near future. If they think there is no point in further negotiations, *e.g.* because the figure offered represents the maximum which the defendants are prepared to offer, he will dismiss the summons for approval and give directions for the future progress of the action. These will replace automatic directions or obviate the need for a summons for directions so long as all parties are in a position to know what directions they will require for trial.

If the district judge approves the figure then he needs to go on to make **15.08** supplementary orders. The first of these will be for what is to happen to the money. In a straightforward case the money will be paid into court to be invested for the infant until he or she attains majority. The court will give directions on investment. It is common practice to allow an infant a small sum of money in the immediate future for the purchase of some treat or toy or particularly for something of educational value, (*e.g.* a home computer). Otherwise the rest of the money is invested, in principle until the infant attains its majority, although sums may be released from time to time for its welfare or education. Thus for example application may be made by the parent from time to time for sums, *e.g.* to pay for a school holiday abroad.

If there has been a payment into court the order will have to deal with the **15.09** payment into court and interest accrued on it. Costs will be ordered to be paid on the standard basis of taxation. If the infant is not legally aided it is common for the infant's solicitor to agree formally to accept the amount of costs recovered on the standard basis from the defendant in full settlement, and to waive any further claims to costs, *i.e.* on the solicitor and own client basis.

Infants as defendants

Infants as defendants act by a *guardian ad litem*. The guardian ad litem is **15.10** liable for costs only if they are caused by his personal negligence or misconduct, unlike a next friend who is always personally liable. There are the following differences also:

1. A writ to be served on an infant should be served on his father or guardian or the person with whom he resides or in whose care he is. If no acknowledgment of service is returned to the court then the plaintiff must apply to the court to appoint a guardian ad litem for an infant. Naturally in the case of an infant defendant in a motor accident (*e.g.* a 17-year-old motor cyclist) the infant's insurance company will deal with the question of appointment of a guardian ad litem. No judgment in default may be obtained against an infant until a guardian ad litem has been appointed. A guardian ad litem should when returning the acknowledgment of service of the writ also enclose his written consent to act and the certificate of a solicitor that there is no conflict of interest between the infant and the guardian ad litem. As in the case of a plaintiff infant a defendant infant must appoint a solicitor.

2. The only other rule of importance relating to an infant defendant is that as we have seen in the section on pleadings a defendant is deemed to admit any claim that he does not specifically deny. In the case of an infant defendant, however, there is no such deemed admission. However, since the defence of an infant is bound to be drafted professionally on his behalf as he must employ a solicitor in the High Court, any such inadvertent omission to deny a matter is likely to be rare.

16. The Trial

16.01   In the High Court solicitors do not have a general right of audience in open court and therefore a barrister will have to be briefed. There ought usually to be a conference at court just before the trial in which any last-minute matters can be sorted out. Counsel may them meet his client for the first time unless there has been a previous conference. The difficulties of listing have previously been examined. If a plaintiff finds on turning up ready for his day in court, perhaps after years of waiting, that there are in fact four other cases listed for the same court before the same judge who is the only High Court judge available that day for Queen's Bench Division cases then he may feel an understandable sense of frustration. The frustration after years of waiting (the reasons for which may often be incomprehensible to the lay client) may be a powerful factor in making the plaintiff client susceptible to a reasonable offer at the court-room door. In any event it would be unusual if there was no coming and going between counsel to see whether any compromise at all may be offered. This happens in a surprising number of cases, even in those cases where there has not hitherto been any offer of settlement at all. This is all the more remarkable given that at this stage there is no saving of costs apart from those of the actual hearing itself. If any kind of offer could have been put forward there seems no reason why it could not have been put forward at least before counsel's briefs were delivered, with the consequent saving in costs from that stage. However, it is a fact of human nature that the parties are more susceptible to compromise in this situation and the plaintiff may be willing to accept a lower figure than he is likely to get if he is successful at the end of the trial.

On the assumption that this does not happen then the solicitor's duties are to organise the witnesses, and physically handle the real or documentary evidence to ensure that it is available for the court in the right order.

16.02   The trial commences with the plaintiff counsel's opening speech after which he calls his witnesses and puts in documents and exhibits. There is either an official shorthand writer present in the High Court or the proceedings are recorded although it is customary for the solicitor to take a note of the evidence so that he may assist counsel there and then should any matter arise, *e.g.* the need to know precisely what was said by a witness who has testified earlier in the day. Each witness is examined-in-chief, cross-examined and may be re-examined. Thereafter the defendant's counsel opens the case for the defence and calls his evidence.

Finally the closing speeches are made, with the defendant's being made first.

It should not be forgotten that if there is a third party involved at the trial he may take such part as the court allows and in particular is usually allowed to cross-examine the plaintiff's witnesses as well as introducing his own evidence relevant to the plaintiff's claim against the defendant. This is because of course if he defeats that claim there can be no further issue, about that matter anyway, between the defendant and him although the trial may still continue between defendant and third party about any other matter in respect of which the defendant claims against the third party.

Even in a case of some complexity judgment may well be given there and then. Alternatively it may be reserved to some future date. The judgment in full will consist of a review of the facts and evidence together with the judge's specific findings in relation to the matters in issue. If rulings on points of law are required it is more likely to be the case that judgment will be reserved. The judge will review the authorities, give his decision and his reasoning. **16.03**

Thereafter a number of applications may be necessary.

1. If the plaintiff has won he will ask for final judgment to be entered and make an application for interest on damages. In a case of some complexity, *e.g.* a large personal injury case with many items of special damages where differing rates of interest are due for differing periods, pocket calculators may need to be used and there may need to be an adjournment so that the parties can attempt to agree a computation of interest and save the judge's time. It will be recalled that the parties should have attempted to agree special damages, subject to liability, before the trial. If the case is not a personal injury case where there are absolutely clear guidelines and the plaintiff is, for example, seeking some rate of interest which is higher than the norm, *e.g.* interest at a true commercial rate on a large sum of money, then there may need to be argument on this matter. Thereafter the judge will make his award of interest. **16.04**

2. If there has been money paid into court then the question of whether or not the award has beaten the question of payment into court will need to be considered. This has been dealt with earlier in the section on payment into court as have the likely costs consequences. The order will also have to deal with the money in court. **16.05**

3. There will need to be an application for costs. An application will be made by the successful party that the costs are to be paid by the unsuccessful party to be taxed if not agreed. Also a legal aid taxation will be ordered in the case of any legally-aided party to ensure that his solicitor's costs are paid. **16.06**

It must be remembered that if any of the costs of interlocutory applications were not dealt with at the time, *i.e.* costs were reserved, application must now be made to the judge to deal with the matter.

4. At the end of the trial the successful party must obtain the associate's certificate. The associate is what one might describe as the clerk of the court and his certificate certifies the time actually occupied in the trial, the judgment given by the judge, and any order made by the judge as to costs. The copy bundle of pleadings lodged with the court will also be returned by the associate. **16.07**

5. Thereafter the successful party has to draw up the judgment. This is not the full text of everything the judge said, *e.g.* the kind of judgment which appears in full in the Law Reports. It is simply the finding of liability as between plaintiff and defendant and if the plaintiff has won, the amount awarded with interest. The judgment should be taken with the associate's certificate to the district registry where the action began and with the **16.08**

original writ. It is approved by the court and then sealed and becomes the judgment of the court. It should be served on the defendant even if he were present in court when it was made.

16.09 6. It should be remembered that if an order has been made for the payment of money in the High Court the normal term is that it will be payable forthwith. However, the losing party may apply for a *stay of execution* either:

>   (i) Pending appeal. Mere giving of notice of appeal does not in itself stay execution and therefore there has to be a specific application to the trial judge at the time (or subsequently to the Court of Appeal); or
> (ii) If the judgment debtor does not have the means for immediate payment.

Application can be made to the trial judge at the time or later on summons to a district judge. The summons must be supported by full affidavit of the debtor's means and must be served on the judgment creditor four clear days before the hearing date of the summons. The debtor will by this procedure hope to obtain an order which will allow him to pay the debt due by instalments. However, this will only be relevant in the context of an action where there are no insurance considerations which assist the plaintiff. Thus in road accident litigation this will not be relevant at least in so far as personal injuries and consequential loss are concerned because the defendant will either be insured or the M.I.B. will be satisfying the judgment on his behalf.

17. The County Court

The factors governing choice of court will be outlined shortly. We must now **17.01** briefly consider procedure in the county court. This will necessarily be at considerably less length than the description of High Court procedure for a number of reasons. Most important is that in many instances the procedure in the county court is virtually identical to that in the High Court although time limits for taking certain steps are often slightly different and the time at which certain steps may be taken may also be different. Often however the county court rules do not even fully describe procedures to be followed but say merely that the procedure is as described in the corresponding Rules of the Supreme Court for a High Court case. The purpose of the county court rules contained in the County Court Practice known as "The Green Book" is of course the same as that of the High Court rules, namely to facilitate a fair trial by ensuring that cases are properly prepared so as to clarify matters in dispute and avoid surprise. The principle points of difference from the corresponding High Court rules are the methods by which actions are commenced and defences served; the existence of automatic directions in almost all cases; and the mechanism by which a case comes on for trial. The important aspect of the county court which differs from the High Court is the extent of the court's direct involvement in certain of the processes particularly in the initiation of proceedings.

Quite apart from the procedural steps which are the same as or similar to those for High Court actions, the tactical considerations vary hardly at all. Thus the procedure for serving Civil Evidence Act notices, notices to admit facts, the rules relating to expert evidence, the desirability of obtaining counsel's advice on evidence, the various considerations relating to the opponent's insurance policy in a personal injury case and so on are the same.

Constitution and personnel

The County Courts Act 1984 governs the constitution of the county court. **17.02** The county court now has no upper limit to its jurisdiction in tort and contract matters. Moreover the county court has an exclusive jurisdiction in some kinds of action particularly cases involving The Consumer Credit Act 1974 and various landlord and tenant matters. There are 300 or so county courts in England and Wales. Very often the same building is both the local District Registry of the High Court of Justice and the county court registry. There are of course more than twice as many county courts as High Court district registries and in rural areas in particular, the nearest High Court district registry may be some considerable distance away whereas there should be a county court within relatively easy reach.

The equivalent of the High Court district judge is the county court district judge. Where the district registry of the High Court and the county court occupy the same building the same person is likely to be both district judge of the High Court and county court. His jurisdiction is to try any undefended case or any case where the sum involved is £1,000 or less; to conduct arbitrations or to try cases where all the parties and the county court judge consent.

The judge who will hear trials in the county court is a circuit judge whose work is likely to consist of alternately trying county court actions on his circuit, *i.e.* local group of county courts, and periods in the Crown Court sitting on criminal matters.

The county court like the High Court district registry has substantial clerical staff under a Chief Clerk to whom communications to the court should be addressed.

It should be noted that unlike the High Court which employs nobody for the purpose of service of process or enforcement of judgments the county court employ bailiffs who are responsible for personal service of summonses and for some of the steps in enforcing judgment.

In conclusion it ought finally to be remarked that the procedure, despite the apparent similarity of the rules, is often less formal than in the High Court. This perhaps reflects the inevitable fact that there is a considerably larger number of appearances by litigants in person in the county court and considerably more laxity is allowed to them by the court staff.

Types of proceedings in the county court

There are two types of originating process of relevance to us.

ORIGINATING APPLICATION

17.03 This is used in cases where no other particular method is prescribed and for our purposes will be used in precisely the same situations in which we have already seen the *originating summons* used in the High Court. That is to say it will be used in applications to obtain the approval of the court for the settlement on behalf of a minor before a summons has been issued; and in applications for pre-action discovery in a personal injury case and for pre-action inspection, preservation, etc., of a thing under the county court equivalent of Ord. 24, r. 7A and Ord. 29, r. 7A. We shall not further concern ourselves with this except to remark that the procedure is substantially the same as that in the case of the High Court and therefore if any of these matters were relevant reference should be made to the section which describes those procedures in the High Court.

SUMMONS

17.04 A summons is used in claims for damages in tort or contract or for a debt. A summons is therefore the equivalent of the High Court writ of summons. It is now appropriate to describe the two kinds of summons though thereafter we shall only be concerned with the second kind.

Fixed date summons

17.05 This is used in an action in which there is a claim for some form of relief other than a simple payment of money or where there is a claim for payment of money combined with any other form of relief. So for example in a nuisance case where the plaintiff seeks both damages and an injunction against the continuation of the nuisance a fixed date summons is appropriate.

164

However the types of action with which we are concerned require compensation in monetary form only and we shall not therefore further consider this type of summons. We turn to the second type which is:—

A default summons

This is used in all cases where the claim is simply for money relief and thus in claims for damages or a debt. **17.06**

Commencement of proceedings

Actions are commenced by lodging at the court a request for a summons and **17.07** the particulars of claim with one extra copy for the court and one for each defendant and by paying a court fee called the plaint fee which is calculated on a scale by reference to the amount claimed. The nature of these documents is as follows:—

THE REQUEST FOR A SUMMONS

It will be noted that unlike in the High Court where the plaintiff actually **17.08** prepares his own writ, generally in the county court the plaintiff does not do so but prepares a form of request for the court staff to prepare the summons on his behalf. This leads to the fact that there will inevitably be some delay in issuing the county court summons. When one takes one's documents to the court the request for summons will take its place in the typing pile and it may be a matter of some days before the summons is actually prepared and the documents ready for service upon the defendant. To obviate this difficulty under a recent practice direction plaintiffs are now entitled if they wish to prepare their own form of summons to take down to court for issuing in much the same way as a High Court writ. Although when this provision was proposed it was envisaged that it would be used mainly by those who issued summonses in bulk, *e.g.* local housing authorities or finance companies, there is nothing to stop an individual plaintiff from preparing his own summons and thus potentially saving some days in the procedure. The form of request for the summons or the summons itself may be obtained free of charge from the court.

PARTICULARS OF CLAIM

This represents a significant difference from High Court procedure. The **17.09** particulars of claim is the exact equivalent of the statement of claim which would be used in a High Court action. The essential difference here of course is that firstly one needs to prepare it and take it to the court at the very time of issuing the summons. It will be remembered that in the High Court whilst one could issue a writ with a short form statement of claim endorsed on it in a debit case, in other cases normally the statement of claim would be a lengthy document prepared for service at a later stage, *i.e.* after the return to the court of the acknowledgment of service giving notice of intention to defend. It will be immediately noticed that another significant difference is that the particulars of claim are taken *to the court*. In the High Court, whilst if the statement of claim was endorsed on the writ since the court kept a copy of the writ they would have in their file the statement of claim, in cases where it was not endorsed on the writ there would be no need for the court to see the statement of claim which would be served direct between the parties. As previously indicated there was no obligation on the plaintiff to have the statement of claim ready drafted at the time of issuing the writ. In addition to the above documents which are needed in every case, other documents may need to be produced at the time of issue of the summons. These are:—

1. The legal aid certificate if applicable and the notice of issue of legal aid for each of the defendants.

2. In a personal injury case a medical report substantiating all the personal injuries which it is intended to adduce as part of the plaintiff's case at trial (see for further discussion of this the explanation of High Court practice at para. 6.21 above).

3. In personal injury cases full particulars of special damages just as in High Court cases (see para. 6.09 above).

It will be noted that the time at which the medical report and special damage details have to be provided comes even earlier than in the High Court namely on issue of proceedings. If for any reason these documents are not available, or the plaintiff proposes to ask the court to disapply the rule in relation to supply of them then the plaintiff in general must ask for directions, *i.e.* a preliminary hearing before the district judge to explain the matter.

17.10 When these forms are taken to the county court they are presented at the counter and the court will then either draw up the form of summons if a request for issue of the summons was lodged or will see the summons itself if the summons were taken down; see all the forms of particulars of claim and also itself provide a further form to attach to the others. This form is called an "Admission, Defence and Counter Claim" and is put with the other documents which are to be served on the defendant.

The plaintiff does not get back a sealed copy of the summons, indeed he may never see the summons itself, what he gets instead is a *plaint note* which is to some extent like the original writ in the action and in particular is a receipt for the amount of the court fee which he has paid. It also shows the number of the case which will now have been inserted on all the documents.

Before going on to consider the progress of the action it is necessary now to refer to a number of preliminary matters in a brief way.

Parties

17.11 The capacity of parties to sue and be sued and the formalities necessary to do so is precisely the same as in the High Court with the following exceptions.

1. A limited company does not need to employ a solicitor in the county court whereas for all stages apart from the filing of an acknowledgment of service a solicitor is required for a limited company in litigation in the High Court.

2. In the case of infants the documents to be filed at court are slightly different. Although the terminology is the same for the adults appointed to represent their interests namely next friend for a plaintiff and guardian ad litem for a defendant, there is no need in either case in the

county court for these persons to use the services of a solicitor and they are entitled to act in person. Apart from this there is a change also in the documentation. A next friend must deliver at court when commencing the action slightly different documents to those in the High Court. It will be recalled that in the High Court a next friend had to file a simple consent to act and a certificate from the infant's solicitor certifying that there was no conflict of interest between the infant and the next friend. In the county court however the next friend simply delivers a written undertaking to pay the costs of the infant if so ordered (*i.e.* if the infant should lose the case). This must be signed either before a solicitor (and will normally be before the infant's solicitor if one is acting) or alternatively it can be signed before a properly authorised court official at the time of issuing proceedings.

3.   A guardian ad litem when delivering an admission or defence to the plaintiff's claim must also deliver a certificate stating that he is a fit and proper person to act as such and has no interest in the proceedings adverse to that of the defendant. It will be noted that this is different from the case of a next friend who in the county court does not need to provide such a certificate.

Thereafter there is very little difference between High Court and county court procedure. In particular the stage at which there is the most significant difference between proceedings for an infant and proceedings for an adult is the requirement to obtain the court's approval to settle actions on behalf of infants. The requirements here and the procedure to be followed are the same as in the High Court.

Joinder

The rule for joinder is precisely the same as in the High Court and nothing   **17.12**
more need be said about this.

Interest

Interest on damages
The county court has the power to award interest on damages under section   **17.13**
69 of the County Courts Act 1984. The rules of pleading are the same as in the High Court and therefore a plaintiff will plead his claim for interest as follows:—

1.   In the case of a claim for an unliquidated demand he will plead it by reference to section 69 of the County Courts Act 1984 and interest will be awarded on the same principles as in the High Court.

2.   In the case of a claim under a contract reference to the term of the contract and the contractually fixed rate should be made and the precise figures up to the time of issue of the proceedings together with the daily rate thereafter should be stated in the particulars of claim.

3.   If there is no contractually agreed rate but the claim is for a liquidated sum then provided the rate claimed is no higher than the rate on judgment debts in the High Court (*i.e.* 15 per cent. at the time of writing) and precise figures of the amounts due up to the date of issue of

proceedings together with the daily rate thereafter are shown in the particulars of claim the plaintiff will be able to sign judgment if the defendant does not take sufficient steps to defend (as hereafter described) in the same way as in signing judgment under Order 13 in the High Court.

Interest on judgments

17.14 Before leaving the subject of interest it is important to note that whilst *High Court Judgment Debts* do carry interest at present, county court judgments do not. There is a provision in the County Courts Act 1984 allowing for the court to award interest on county court judgments but at the time of writing it has not been brought into force (though it may shortly be). However, county court judgments of more than £2,000 may be transferred to the High Court for enforcement and upon transfer to the High Court interest runs on the judgment debt at 15 per cent. per annum. It would accordingly be very important to remember that if one had obtained judgment in a county court action for say, £4,000 that if one were to proceed to enforce it in the county court (and depending upon the method used this could take a considerable time, see para. 19.35) the client would not be obtaining interest on this substantial sum. If it is transferred to the High Court for enforcement however then interest will begin to run at 15 per cent. per annum, *i.e.* the very worthwhile sum of £600 per year if the debt should take some time to enforce.

Venue

17.15

In the High Court as has previously been remarked a writ may be issued in any district registry. There were advantages in issuing it in the district registry for the area where the defendant resided or carried on business or where the cause of action arose because in such a case the defendant could not apply for the action to be transferred to any other district registry or to the central office in London. However, the jurisdiction in the county court is more restricted both in terms of the financial limit and because the rules require that there be some definite connection with the defendant's residence or the cause of action before the proceedings can be issued in the county court concerned. A county court summons *must* be issued therefore either in the court for the district in which the defendant (or one of them if there are more than one) resides or carries on business, or in the court for the district in which the cause of action arose wholly or in part. In the form of request for a summons the plaintiff is required to indicate in effect what the connection of the action is with the court chosen. As had previously been remarked in a debt case it could arguably be said that the cause of action arose either in the place where the contract was concluded or in the place where payment was due under the debt and since this latter will usually be the plaintiff's place of business and this will usually be in the locality of the solicitors who are acting for him, it is often convenient to the plaintiff to issue proceedings there.

Service of proceedings

17.16 We now return to the conduct of the action. The documents having been taken to the county court the question of service needs to be considered. The county court will itself arrange for postal service on the defendant at the address given. In the case of a claim for personal injury damages where there is unlikely to be any great hurry postal service will no doubt be perfectly satisfactory. In the case of a summons for a debt however, greater speed and certainty are often required to avoid the delay of unfruitful postal service. Accordingly one may ask if one so wishes for the summons and particulars of claim to be served by the court bailiff. There is an additional fee payable for this. The bailiff however is often considered not very efficient in serving documents and if personal service is required many solicitors prefer to ask for the summons to be returned to them so that they can themselves arrange personal service by employment of a process server. The fees for the latter will not be greatly in excess of those of the bailiff and the success rate and speed involved is likely to be considerably higher. Where personal service is required therefore a solicitor is most likely to ask for the documents to be sent back to him so that this can be effected and having been effected an affidavit of service should be filed in the county court by the process server within three days. Most process servers on being instructed to effect service will themselves prepare and swear the form of affidavit of service which they will return to the instructing solicitor with their letter confirming successful service.

Service on a nominated solicitor is also possible and for this purpose the plaintiff's solicitor would request the documents to be returned for personal service and he would then post them on to the defence solicitor.

One point worth noting is that in the case of county court actions where the defendant is a limited company; whereas in the High Court all documents have to be served at the registered office of the company, in the county court documents may be served at any place of business of the company having a connection with the action. Thus, if for example one is suing a major supermarket chain in respect of defective goods, proceedings can be served at the local branch from which goods were purchased rather than at the company's registered office.

Where service is by the court the court must complete a certificate of service or a notice of non service. If served by the plaintiff an affidavit of service must be filed and if served on the defendant's solicitor the latter must give a certificate accepting service and stating his address for further service. In any case the default summons must be served within 4 months of issue.

The documents will therefore now have been served upon the defendant. These will consist of the summons, the particulars of claim notice of legal aid if any, and a form of admission defence and counter claim.

Particulars of claim. Ord. 6

The particulars of claim are just like the statement of claim in the High Court and the same principles of pleading must be applied. They are to be signed by the plaintiff's solicitor and must state an address for service (note that the High Court pleading whilst it must state an address for service and the date of service does not have to be signed). If drafted by counsel, counsel's name must be typed at the foot.   **17.17**

Further and better particulars

The principles on which a party might require further and better particulars are the same as in the High Court. A written request should first be made and then if this is refused application should be made to the district judge for an order. Copies of any further and better particulars sought and given must   **17.18** be filed at court since the court keeps a full file of the pleadings. The form of further and better particulars should be the same as in the High Court, that is the form of request should be followed seriatim by the further and better particulars given.

Striking out pleadings

17.19   The principles applied in an application to strike out the whole or any part of any pleading are as in the case of the High Court.

The admission defence and counter claim. C.C.R., Ord. 9

17.20   As has been noted the documents to be served on the defendant are the summons, particulars of claim and form of admission defence and counter claim prepared by the court. Service is deemed to be effective if by post on the seventh day after posting and in the case of personal service on the date of service. It has been noted that to commence proceedings one has to proceed a little futher than in the case of the High Court and have one's particulars of claim ready for filing and service at the outset. This increased speed of proceedings is further reflected in the form of admission, defence and counter claim which the court sends to the defendant with the summons. This constitutes both an acknowledgment of service and the defence. Within 14 days of service the form of admission, defence and counter claim duly completed must be returned to the court office. It ought to be said that if solicitors are acting for the defendant they will probably not use the court form of admission, defence and counterclaim. If the defendant intends to defend and has solicitors then a proper defence should be drafted just as in the High Court which replies to each paragraph of the plaintiff's particulars of claim.

On the form of admission of defence and counter claim there is very little room to set out a properly pleaded defence. The form of admission, defence and counter-claim is mainly for use by a lay person.

In a personal injury case there will inevitably be an insurance company involved and therefore solicitors who will file a proper defence. We shall now discuss the contents of the form of admission, defence and counter claim in a debt case.

17.21   It will be remembered that in the High Court the defendant wishing to defend simply had to return the form of acknowledgment of service to the court within 14 days, ticking the appropriate boxes. He would then have a further period in which to serve his defence after receipt of the plaintiff's statement of claim. In the county court these two stages are brought together and the form which he has to return to the court acknowledging service is itself the form of defence as well.

Admissions

17.22   If the defendant wants to admit the whole or part of the plaintiff's claim, whether or not he proposes to request time for payment he should do so within 14 days of service of the summons and the court will then notify the plaintiff. Let us now consider the situations which may arise.

ADMISSION OF THE WHOLE CLAIM

If the plaintiff accepts the defendant's admission as final he should notify the court within 14 days by letter and the district judge will then enter judgment. Judgment will be for the debt, interest and fixed costs if the claim was for a liquidated demand. It ought to be noted that the county court rules permit a plaintiff who is suing merely for the costs of repairs to his vehicle to treat this as a liquidated demand for the purpose of the rules if he so wishes, as a means of simplifying procedures. Thus where there is damage to a vehicle but no personal injury and the plaintiff chooses not to claim for the inconvenience caused by loss of his vehicle whilst it is being repaired then he may if he wishes issue proceedings simply for the liquidated sum which will allow him to obtain earlier final judgment. The case is therefore over in the instance given.

In the form of admission, defence and counter-claim the defendant is entitled to put forward an offer as to the method of payment, *e.g.* as to what weekly or monthly instalments he will be able to pay. If the plaintiff accepts the offer but disputes the manner of payment the court has to deal with what is called the "disposal" which means fixing the time scale for payment by instalments. Having received the details of the defendant's offer, communicated this to the plaintiff and received his written comments on it, the district judge will proceed to "dispose" of the case by fixing an amount for weekly or monthly instalments which he considers fair on all the evidence of the defendant's means. Having communicated his provisional decision to both parties then if either objects, he will fix a "disposal hearing" at which both parties will attend before him in chambers when there will be a more detailed investigation of the defendant's means and the opportunity given to the plaintiff to cross-examine the defendant about them. Thereafter the district judge will decide whether the payment at the rate which he originally fixed is reasonable or whether it should be varied in some respect.

Example 1:
The plaintiff is suing for a debt of £700. The defendant returns the form of admission and offers to pay the sum at £100 per month which is satisfactory to the plaintiff. He writes a letter to the court enclosing the plaint note and requests that judgment be entered for the sum claimed to be paid at the rate given. He will obtain an order for that sum to be paid together with interest up to the date of signing judgment (if he has claimed it) and fixed costs.

Example 2:
Suppose on the same fact the offer is only £10 per month. The plaintiff will write in objecting and stating his reasons for his belief that the defendant can afford to pay more. The district judge will consider all the evidence before him and fix a provisional figure. Let us say that he decides that £30 per month would be reasonable. Having communicated this decision to both parties, if neither objects this becomes the court order. If however within 14 days either party objects the court will fix a hearing. Let us say in the present case that the plaintiff objects. The defendant is then obliged to bring all documentary evidence of his income and outgoings to court and to be questioned about it. If it appears that in fact he has a good enough income and some savings, the district judge may then make an order, *e.g.* that he pay £200 of the debt forthwith and the balance at £50 per month. In such a case

171

the plaintiff would also be entitled to his costs of attending the disposal. If however the district judge found that his original figure was the best which the defendant could manage then he would be likely to make no order as to the costs of the disposal.

ADMISSION OF PART OF THE CLAIM

17.23 Suppose however now that the defendant admits only liability for a smaller amount than that claimed than the plaintiff. The plaintiff now has a difficult choice. He cannot accept that amount whilst continuing to litigate for the rest. He must either notify the court of his acceptance of that sum in full satisfaction of the claim or notify the court that he does not accept that amount in which case the action goes on as defended.

ADMISSION IN ACTION FOR AN UNLIQUIDATED SUM

17.24 As in the High Court where the action is for damages and the defendant admits liability but makes no offer as yet on quantum then the plaintiff may obtain interlocutory judgment with an order for damages to be assessed. Somewhat more unusually the defendant might actually offer a specific sum in which case the plaintiff may accept or refuse as in the case of offers related to liquidated demands discussed above.

Defence

17.25 Suppose however that the defendant admits nothing. He should deliver to the court the form of admission, defence and counter-claim indicating as much or a properly drafted defence with or without counter-claim within 14 days of the service of the summons. A further copy of any defence should be supplied to the court for service on the plaintiff. In most cases automatic directions take effect. This is not limited to personal injuries cases in the county court.

Where the sum outstanding does not exceed £1000 and a defence is filed the proceedings will automatically be referred for arbitration. We shall see what this means subsequently.

Judgment in default. C.C.R., Ord. 9, r. 6

17.26 It will be recalled that in the High Court under Order 13 if the defendant returned to the court no acknowledgment of service in the prescribed time or an acknowledgment of service in which he indicated that he did not intend to defend, the plaintiff could obtain judgment at the court counter for the amount of his claim and that brought the action to an end. There is an approximate equivalent in the county court. Here if the defendant does not return his form of admission, defence and counter claim to the court within 14 days after service of the summons the plaintiff may enter judgment in default.

On a claim for a liquidated sum together with interest properly pleaded judgment will be final judgment for the amount of the claim, the interest computed to the date of judgment and fixed costs. The plaintiff takes to the court a request for judgment to be entered and produces the plaint note on which the judgment is noted. He can then proceed immediately to enforce the judgment. In a claim for unliquidated damages the judgment entered, as in the High Court, will be an *interlocutory judgment* that is it will deal finally with the question of liability but leave damages and interest thereon to be assessed at a subsequent hearing. In such a case an order will be made for costs to be taxed at that subsequent hearing.

As in the case of the High Court the court has the power to set aside a default judgment. This may be either *as of right* where service was in some way imperfect or on *the merits* where the defendant, notwithstanding that he is in default, can show some reason why discretion should be exercised in his favour and has some prospect of successfully defending the action. Unlike in the High Court one cannot sign judgment in default on a *counter claim*.

Counterclaim

The principles for a counterclaim are precisely the same as in the High Court where a defendant considers that he has some claim against the plaintiff whether or not causally linked to the plaintiff's claim against him. **17.27**

Summary Judgment. C.C.R., Ord. 9, r. 14

We will now consider a case where the defendant has returned a form of defence to the court. In such a case as we shall shortly see, the parties then go on to comply with automatic directions. If however, as in the High Court, the plaintiff believes that there is no possible defence, (*e.g.* the plaintiff is the unpaid supplier of goods about which there has been no complaint and he views the defence as spurious), he may apply for summary judgment under the county court equivalent to Ord. 14. **17.28**

In the county court there is no equivalent of a form of acknowledgment of service and the defendant is actually required to return his *defence* to the court within 14 days. This might appear to preclude the possibility of taking action for summary judgment because the defendant will not merely have said that he *intends* to defend he will actually have filed his defence. However, summary judgment in the county court *is* possible. The plaintiff is required merely to word his affidavit slightly differently to dispose of the "defence" which has been filed. The same principles apply as in the case of the High Court, provided that the sum involved exceeds £500. **17.29**

Suppose therefore that a plaintiff who is an unpaid supplier of goods worth say £2,000 has issued a default summons claiming this amount and interest and is disappointed to find that the defendant has put in some spurious defence, *e.g.* saying that the goods were worthless. Instead of now having to sit by whilst the action proceeds to trial many months away the plaintiff can still do what he would anyway have been entitled to do in the High Court. He can take out an application (the equivalent of a High Court summons) and file with it an affidavit. The affidavit must contain all the matters which an affidavit must contain in the High Court, in an application for summary judgment and it is not proposed to set them out again here. It should however also dispose of what is said in the supposed defence which has been filed and therefore it may be necessary to go into matters at somewhat greater length than is normal in the case of a High Court affidavit where, it will be remembered, all the plaintiff had to do was swear to the truth of the particulars of claim and to his belief that there was no defence. It is normal to say that notwithstanding the delivery of the defence the plaintiff believes that the defendant has no real defence to the claim.

17.30 The plaintiff must issue the application at court and have it served on the defendant not less than seven clear days before the day fixed for the hearing. When the application is heard the criteria to be applied by the district judge are precisely the same as in the case of the High Court, that is to say he must decide whether or not the documents before him disclose a triable issue. If they do not he may give summary judgment for the applicant; if they do then he must dispose of the application in one of the ways previously described as relevant to High Court proceedings, *i.e.* by giving either unconditional leave to defend, conditional leave to defend, or dismissing the plaintiff's application. If the defendant is given leave to defend then the court will proceed at that stage with a pre-trial review.

Miscellaneous matters relevant to proceedings in the county court

INTERLOCUTORY APPLICATIONS GENERALLY

17.31 Interlocutory applications, *e.g.* for further and better particulars, discovery, etc., should be made on notice of application giving two clear days before the hearing. Thus if one wishes to apply for any form of interlocutory order one simply takes to court two general forms of notice of application prepared in exactly the same way as an ordinary summons in an action in the High Court setting out the nature of the order sought. At the court office one is given a hearing date which is filled in on the notice of application and this is then sealed and a copy is served in the usual way by post on the defendant's solicitor. This is the normal method of application for interlocutory orders in the county court.

EXTENSIONS OF TIME

17.32 The practice is exactly the same as in the High Court. It may be necessary for a defendant to ask for an extension of time, *e.g.* for filing his defence and as in the High Court it is the usual courtesy to grant one reasonable extension. If one is not sufficient or indeed if the plaintiff's solicitor has instructions not to grant an extension at all then application is made on notice as previously described to the court just as in the case of a time summons in the High Court.

AMENDMENT

17.33 A party who wishes to amend his summons and pleadings to add or substitute any party must make application to the court for an order permitting him to do so. The practice thereafter follows that of the High Court. In the case of any other amendments to the particulars of claim or any other pleading amendment can be made at any time until a hearing date is fixed simply by filing a copy of the amended pleading at court and serving a copy on the opposing party. If the need for amendment arises after that then either all other parties must consent to the amendment or an order of the court is necessary, which is obtained by an application made on notice. Strangely, unlike in the High Court the county court rules make no specific provision for amendment which changes the cause of action or adds a new one. It will be recalled that in the High Court it was necessary to obtain leave for such an amendment. In the county court such an amendment is treated like any other amendment and therefore if the application is made in time, *i.e.* before the pre-trial review, apparently no leave of the court is necessary, but if made thereafter then as is the case with every other amendment leave will be necessary. The county court will apply the same principles in deciding whether to grant leave as in the High Court, that is it will exercise its discretion in a liberal manner provided any apparent injustice can be cured by an appropriate order of costs.

PAYMENTS INTO COURT

It will be recalled that in the High Court if a defendant was served with a writ claiming a liquidated amount showing interest properly computed to the date of issue with a daily rate thereafter and a fixed costs endorsement a defendant who wished to settle could by payment direct to the plaintiff of the total amount of the claim, interest and fixed costs bring the action to an end. In such a situation a plaintiff generally had no right to taxed costs and the defendant thus knew that the total amount of his liability was as shown on the writ. **17.34**

There is a similar provision in the county court. The rules are as follows:—

(i) If the whole sum claimed by the plaintiff (which naturally has to be a liquidated demand so that the defendant knows the amount involved) including interest and the amount of fixed costs shown on the face of the summons is paid to the plaintiff within 14 days of the service of the summons on the defendant the action is stayed. **17.35**

(ii) If in the case of a debt or liquidated demand the defendant pays the sum in full at any later stage (*e.g.* after delivery of defence) he should pay the full amount together with his computation of the interest but should *not* pay fixed costs because fixed costs are no longer appropriate and payment after 14 days entitles the plaintiff to taxed costs. **17.36**

(iii) If in a case where an unliquidated sum is claimed the defendant wishes to compromise a case he should pay into the court the amount he wishes to offer including a provision for interest but should not pay in any sum in respect of costs. This is then treated precisely like a payment in the High Court, that is, an offer to compromise the case on terms. If the plaintiff wishes to accept the offer he may withdraw the money within 21 days without the leave of the court and will then be entitled to an order for taxed costs up to the date when he accepted the payment in. It should be noted that in the county court where a payment into court is made the court notify the plaintiff directly although it is wise for the defendant to do so in any case in order to save costs. **17.37**

The rules applicable in the High Court in relation to payments in are applicable in the county court. That is to say that if the plaintiff declines to accept the money it remains on deposit in the county court, is kept secret from the trial judge until all questions of liability and quantum have been determined, and thereafter orders for costs will follow in the same way as in the High Court. It should be noted that the payment in in the county court is not made in precisely the same way as in the High Court. There must be a notice with it stating that it is made in satisfaction of the plaintiff's cause of action. If notice were not given by any chance the payment would merely be treated as being made on account of any sums due and would be remitted to the plaintiff. If a plaintiff wishes to accept any money paid into court outside the 21 day period he may do so but he will need to apply for leave of the court and an appropriate order dealing with costs since the date of the payment in will have to be made.

Automatic directions in the county court

17.38 It will be recalled that in personal injury cases in the High Court there are automatic directions. In the county court there are automatic directions in all cases (subject to some exceptions) and this means that in the kind of routine tort or contract actions with which we are concerned automatic directions apply. Automatic directions take effect upon the close of pleadings which, as in the High Court, is deemed to be 14 days after delivery of the defence, or if a counterclaim is served with the defence, 28 days after the delivery of the defence. The following are the automatic directions in the county court which are set out for convenience since they are slightly different from those in the High Court:—

(i) There should be discovery of documents within 28 days and inspection within 7 days thereafter except where liability is admitted or in an action for personal injuries arising out of a road accident where discovery should be limited to disclosure of any documents relating to the amount of damages. Discovery shall be made by serving lists of documents in the prescribed form.

(ii) Except with the leave of the court or where all parties agree:—
    i) No expert evidence may be adduced at the trial unless the substance of that evidence has been disclosed to the other parties in the form of a written report within 10 weeks; and
    ii) the number of expert witnesses of any kind shall be limited to two save that in a personal injuries action the number of expert witnesses shall be limited in any case to two medical experts and one expert of any other kind.

(iii) Photographs and sketch plans and, in an action for personal injuries, the contents of any Police Accident Report Book shall be receivable in evidence at the trial and shall be agreed if possible;

(iv) Unless a day has already been fixed the plaintiff shall within 6 months request the Chief Clerk of the county court to fix a day for the hearing.

(v) Where the plaintiff makes such request for a hearing he shall file a note which shall if possible be agreed by all the parties giving:—
    i) An estimate of the length of the trial and
    ii) The number of witnesses to be called.

(vi) If no request is made to fix a date of hearing within 15 months of the day on which pleadings are deemed to be closed the action shall be automatically struck out.

(vii) Nothing in the above shall prevent the court from giving of its own motion or on the application of any party such further or different directions or orders as may in the circumstances be appropriate or prevent the making of an order for the transfer of the proceedings to the High Court or another county court.

It will be observed that most of the above automatic directions correspond **17.39** fairly closely with those in the High Court. Thus the directions with regard to expert evidence, photographs and sketch plans etc. are the same. There is an extra requirement for discovery because otherwise there is no automatic discovery in a county court action. It will be observed that another important difference is that there is a prescribed penalty for the plaintiff failing to set the action down relatively expeditiously namely that the court itself will, without any application by the defendant, strike the action out if no application for a trial date has been made within 15 months of close of pleadings. With the advance in computerisation of court records it will in the near future be easy for the court to see which actions appear to have become stagnant.

APPLICATION FOR DIRECTIONS

It will be observed that, as in the case of the High Court, if either of the **17.40** parties does not wish to comply with automatic directions but wants further or different directions, he may apply to the court for those directions. Until a recent rule change there were no automatic directions at all in the county court and in every case, immediately a defence was filed, the court would itself fix a date for what was called a "pre trial review," which was the county court equivalent to the High Court summons for directions. The term "pre-trial review" is still used in relation to those few classes of action where automatic directions do not apply and probably it will continue to be used for cases where one or other party does not wish to comply with automatic directions but wishes for the court to give directions. A party should therefore apply on notice listing the directions which he requires and a date will then be fixed for a court to consider the application. One obvious example of a case which will be diverted from the usual automatic directions procedure is one where the plaintiff wishes to apply for summary judgment. At the end of that application, if the plaintiff does not succeed and leave to defend is in fact given, the district judge will no doubt go on to ask the parties whether they require any specific directions for trial.

Other interlocutory matters

DISCOVERY

Discovery means precisely the same thing in the High Court. As we have **17.41** seen, the requirement for discovery now forms part of the automatic directions. Discovery is by a list which is in the same form to that as a High Court list. If there is some dispute over discovery the matter will be determined by the court in the same way as in the High Court so that the court can make orders for particular discovery, can determine disputes as to the existence or otherwise of privilege, etc. Failure to comply with the requirements for discovery will lead to the same consequences as in the High Court so that where there has been a failure to complete discovery application will be made to the court by the other party for an "unless" order requiring that the party in default comply with the original order with the sanction that his pleading be struck out if he does not.

NON PARTY DISCOVERY AND INSPECTION. C.C.R., ORD. 13, R. 7

17.42 This is obtainable as in the High Court. That is to say that in an action for damages for death or personal injuries a person who is a party to such an action may apply for discovery of documents held by a non party in the same way as in the High Court.

PRE-ACTION DISCOVERY AND INSPECTION. C.C.R., ORD. 13, R. 7

17.43 This also is precisely the same as in the High Court in an action for damages for personal injuries or death. Application can be made by an originating application before the issue of a summons. Precisely the same contents should appear in the affidavit and an order will only be made in the same circumstances as in the High Court, that is where it is absolutely fundamental to the decision whether or not to sue for the prospective plaintiff to see the document in advance of issuing proceedings.

INSPECTION ETC. OF PROPERTY. C.C.R., ORD. 13, R. 7

17.44 Pre-action inspection, etc., of property in the possession of an opponent is obtainable in precisely the same way as in the High Court as is inspection, etc., of property in the possession of a non-party after issue of proceedings.

INTERIM PAYMENTS. C.C.R. ORD. 13, R. 12

17.45 Interim payments may be claimed in the county court in any case which the sum claimed or amount involved exceeds £500 and the procedure is the same as in the High Court. An appropriate time for application would no doubt be at the stage of the pre-trial review. No less than seven days notice must be given before the hearing of the application. Otherwise the provisions and the criteria relevant to an application for interim payment are the same as in the case of the High Court. It will be remembered that the third and potentially most difficult ground for an application for an interim payment was that that "if the action proceeded to trial the applicant would obtain judgment for substantial damages against the respondent." In this context the phrase "substantial damages" has been given a somewhat artificial application. Since the rule expressly permits application to be made in any case where the sum involved is more than £500 it would seem that the requirement for substantial damages is satisfied by any sum in excess of that amount.

THIRD PARTY PROCEEDINGS IN THE COUNTY COURT. C.C.R., ORD. 12

17.46 The situations in which one would use third party proceedings are the same as in the High Court namely where a defendant wishes to claim against someone who is not a party in the action for any contribution, indemnity or other relief or remedy relating to or connected with the original subject matter of the action.

The procedure is however very slightly different. It will be recalled that in the High Court a defendant (who had in principle not less than 28 days for serving his defence from the date when the writ was received) could issue and serve a third party notice without the leave of the court provided he did so before serving his defence. In the county court the requirement to serve the defence arises at a rather earlier stage. Consequently the provisions are a little different. The rules are that no leave to issue the third party notice is required provided this is done before *a date has been fixed* for a pre-trial review or after the pleadings are deemed to be closed. When a third party notice is issued by the defendant the court will itself give a date for a pre-trial review in the third party proceedings and this will be endorsed on the third party notice itself. This is thus unlike the case in the High Court where it is up to the third party to file an acknowledgment of service (to which there is no county court equivalent) and only then would the defendant need to issue a summons for third party directions.

The third party notice must be served on the third party together with a copy **17.47** of the summons and particulars of claim and the defence filed. A copy of the third party notice must also be served on the plaintiff. Where a third party notice is issued it prevents the plaintiff entering judgment in default and there must then be a pre-trial review. The third party should however file his defence in court within 14 days of the service of the third party notice. If he defaults the court will order him to do so at the pre-trial review.

Where leave to commence the third party proceedings is necessary an **17.48** application will be made for leave by the defendant at which naturally the intended third party will not be present. Directions will then normally include some provision for a pre-trial review to take place in the third party proceedings if leave is given. When the third party pre-trial review stage is reached in either case all the parties will be before the court and a similar kind of tidying up operation will take place as previously described in the case of a summons for third party directions in the High Court, that is the registrar will consider whether *inter alia* the third party should file further pleadings, be added as an additional defendant, or indeed take over the conduct of the defendant's case as in examples previously given in the section on High Court procedure. If the third party fails to attend the trial (whether or not he has filed a defence) he is deemed to admit the third party claim made against him.

Setting down for trial

Setting down for trial in the county court is considerably less formal than in **17.49** the High Court. There is no need to lodge bundles of pleadings because the court already has a full file, nor is there any requirement for a statement as to readiness for trial. The automatic directions simply prescribe that the plaintiff should apply to the court (and a letter is usually acceptable) giving an estimate of the length of trial and the number of witnesses to be called). It is usually considered courteous to check with the defendant that he has no great objection to the application being made because of justifiable unreadiness on his part. When the Chief Clerk fixes a day for the hearing he must give not less than 21 days notice to every party.

Preparation for trial in the county court

There is nothing to add to the discussion of the appropriate preparations for **17.50** trial in the High Court. All the same tactical considerations apply. One difference of terminology is that what was called a subpoena in the High Court is called a *witness summons* in the county court and the party requiring the witness summons files a request for the issue of a summons and may state that he wishes the summons to be served by the court bailiff in which case he should leave at court the amount of conduct money which has to be given to the witness when the summons is served. In the county court the precise date of trial is usually known in advance and therefore the summons may state where and when the witness is to attend unlike the case of the subpoena which will it will be recalled be issued and served usually before a date of trial is known. The witness summons may specify that the witness is to give evidence verbally or that he is required to bring some document with him or both.

The trial

17.51 Trial in the county court is the same in terms of order of speeches etc. as previously described in the case of the High Court. Unlike in the High Court however, the atmosphere may be relatively informal and in particular there will be no shorthand writer present and therefore it is important for the solicitor to get a full note of the evidence.

In the county court payment of any sums awarded by the judge is usually to be made within 14 days from the date of judgment although the order may specify a different time. It is not uncommon however for the judge to be called upon to make an order for payment by instalments at the end of the case on application by the defendant. The defendant will usually be required to go into the witness box and give details of his means on oath. Whether or not an application is made for payment by instalments a subsequent application may be made by the judgment debtor applying either to the judge again or more probably to the registrar of the court requesting an order varying the method of payment, *i.e.* asking for payment by instalments or payment by lesser instalments than that previously ordered. Equally the judgment creditor, if he obtains information about an increase in the judgment debtor's means, may re-apply to the court for an order increasing the rate of instalments.

Arbitration. C.C.R., Ord. 19

17.52 If an action is commenced for a sum involving less than £1,000 the action is commenced by a default summons as in every other case. If the defendant should fail to file a defence at court within the prescribed 14 days then judgment in default of defence will be given as previously described. However if the defendant files a defence then under C.C.R., Ord. 19 the case is automatically referred to arbitration.

17.53 In most county courts the inevitable preliminary is that a date is fixed for what is often called a pre-trial review but is strictly speaking what should be described as a "preliminary consideration." The preliminary consideration will continue in exactly the same way as a pre-trial review and will provide the registrar with an opportunity for a general stock taking of the case so that the issues to go on to arbitration can be clearly defined. The registrar will in particular consider whether, notwithstanding that the case is going to arbitration normal interlocutory orders such as for discovery or for further and better particulars of the pleadings are required. In particular the registrar may consider an application that the case should *not* be referred to arbitration, *i.e.* that the reference to arbitration which arises automatically is rescinded. The registrar should do so where he is satisfied that:—

1. A difficult question of law or a question of fact of exceptional complexity is involved; or

2. That a charge of fraud is in issue; or

3. That the parties are agreed that the dispute should be tried in court; or

4. That it would be unreasonable for the claim to proceed to arbitration having regard to its subject matter, the circumstances of the parties, or the interests of any other persons likely to be affected by the award.

At the arbitration hearing procedure is informal and the strict rules of **17.54** evidence do not apply. Any method of procedure may be adopted which is considered convenient and fair to the parties and this often means, particularly where the parties are both litigants in person, that the atmosphere of an arbitration lacks the structure of speech, evidence and argument which is common in other contested hearings. Another feature is that the arbitrator (*i.e.* usually the registrar personally) may with the consent of the parties consult any expert or call for an expert report on any matter in dispute or invite an expert to attend a hearing as an assessor in his own place. Thus for example suppose that an expensive coat has been ruined in the process of dry cleaning. The action concerning compensation for the coat, if the claim is less than £1,000, will be referred to arbitration. The matter may be a simple one of deciding whether on the evidence of what happened to the coat the dry cleaning process was or was not reasonably carried out. In this the registrar may call for a report, with the consent of the parties, from an expert in the subject of the effect of dry cleaning on coats.

An important feature of the arbitration procedure is that no solicitors' **17.55** charges are allowed except the costs stated on the summons or which would have been stated on the summons if the eventual award had been a claim for a liquidated sum together with such further costs as may be directed where there has been unreasonable conduct on the part of the losing party.

Accordingly it will be rare that a solicitor is instructed to act for a party in **17.56** arbitration because even if wholly successful he is unlikely to obtain any award of costs and thus the costs of taking the proceedings are likely to exceed any net benefit. There will of course always be exceptions. Some companies and in particular some statutory undertakings defend claims brought against them by disgruntled consumers and others almost as a matter of principle. The costs are not a direct consideration to them since they employ whole time salaried solicitors. Equally if the action is something of the nature of a test case and is of importance to other people then first, it should be borne in mind that the criteria for the rescission of the reference to arbitration may anyway be satisfied so that even quite a small claim may be tried in court, or even if it is not a plaintiff may find it worthwhile having legal representation particularly if the action is supported by a trade union or association or pressure group.

    In run of the mill cases however when a solicitor is consulted about a small amount the inevitable reaction will be to tell the client that he will have to bear his own costs which may exceed the benefit of the litigation. In personal injury cases which appear to involve less than a sum of £1,000, on the basis of decided cases it is usually possible to rescind the reference to arbitration by arguing that the nature of a personal injury claim might anyway be said to raise a difficult question of law since there will inevitably be matters of quantum of damages to argue. In the leading case of *Pepper* v. *Healey* (1982) 126 Sol.Jo. 497 the action concerned a road traffic accident although personal injuries were not involved. The defendant was to be legally represented through her insurers. The plaintiff also wished for legal representation but in view of the likely award of costs it would clearly have been a fruitless exercise. An application was made for the reference to arbitration to be rescinded and this was rescinded on the fourth of the grounds referred to above in that contest would have been unequal if this order were not made thus permitting the plaintiff to be legally represented with some prospect of having her costs paid should she be successful. Thus inequality between parties in the matter of legal representation may well be treated as one reason for rescinding a reference to arbitration.

17.57 In practice because of the rule on costs legal aid is not usually granted for claims involving less than £1,000. However if one could satisfy the legal aid area office that there was a prospect of a successful application for the case to be heard in open court rather than by arbitration there is no reason in principle why an application for legal aid in that kind of case ought not to be granted.

18. Choice of Court

As we have previously noted the geographical jurisdiction of the High Court **18.01**
is unlimited, that is one can issue a writ in any district registry of the High
Court no matter where the action arose. However, if there is in fact no local
connection with the action, then the defendant may well be able to apply
subsequently for the transfer of the action to a district registry which does
have such connection, *e.g.* where the cause of action arose so that witnesses
will live locally, or the defendant resides or where the contract was due to be
performed or payment to be made. The High Court's financial jurisdiction is
also unlimited so that one may sue in the High Court for either £1 or millions
of pounds. In the county court the jurisdiction is local so there must be some
connection between the cause of action or the defendant's address and the
case. In tort and contract actions however, there is no financial limit on the
county court's jurisdiction. An action may therefore be commenced in
principle in either High Court or county court in cases of tort and contract.
The following should however be noted:—

Personal injury cases
In personal injury cases an action may only be commenced in the High Court **18.02**
if the apparent value of the action is £50,000 or more. In this connection
"value of the action" means the amount which the plaintiff reasonably
expects to recover. In deciding on this value interest and costs which may be
payable to the plaintiff are left out of account but so is contributory negligence unless such negligence is admitted. In other words if a plaintiff's claim
in principle appears to be worth £55,000 the subsequent finding of say 25 per
cent. contributory negligence against him which would reduce that sum
below £50,000 does not matter. In addition the question of future awards of
damages after a preliminary award of provisions damages are left out of
account. If there is more than one plaintiff regard may be had to the
aggregate of their expectations or interests so that if say there were three
plaintiffs injured as passengers in a motor vehicle and the claim of each
appeared to be worth about £20,000 it will be perfectly proper to commence
the action for all three in the High Court in view of the likely aggregate
award.

At the time of writing there is no rule prescribing how a solicitor is to
certify the likely award in an action when commencing it in the High Court
but presumably in the near future a rule will be made requiring the plaintiff's
solicitor to lodge a certificate of value of the claim which will have clearly to
be an honest estimate.

Non-personal injury cases
These may be commenced in either High Court or county court. In non- **18.03**
personal injury actions in the High Court there will of course be a summons
for directions at which time the question of transfer to the county court will
be considered. The new rules on this provide that in deciding on which

183

should be the eventual court of trial the court should have regard to the following:—

    i) An action of which the value is less than £25,000 shall be tried in a county court unless:—

        a) A county court having regard to the criteria set out below considers that it ought to transfer the action to the High Court for trial and the High Court considers that it ought to try the action or;

        b) It is commenced in the High Court and the High Court, having regard to the said criteria, considers that it ought to try the action.

    ii) An action of which the value is £50,000 or more shall be tried in the High Court unless:—

        a) It is commenced in a county court and the County Court does not, having regard to the criteria set out below, consider that the action ought to be transferred to the High Court for trial; or

        b) The High Court, having regard to the said criteria, considers that it ought to transfer the case to the county court for trial.

    iii) The relevant criteria for consideration of which court shall try the action are:—

        a) The financial substance of the action including the value of any counterclaim.

        b) Whether the action is otherwise important and in particular whether it raises questions of importance to persons who are not parties or questions of general public interest.

        c) The complexity of the facts, legal issues, remedies or procedures involved and

        d) Whether transfer is likely to result in a more speedy trial of the action (save that no transfer shall be made on the grounds of this sub-paragraph alone).

18.04 Thus where an action is commenced in the county court it is likely to stay there, both parties complying with automatic directions and going on naturally to trial unless having regard to the criteria mentioned one of the parties considers the action should be transferred to the High Court. Where the action is commenced in the High Court then in a personal injury case where there are automatic directions it will stay there unless it becomes apparent on an honest view to either party that there are grounds for thinking that the value of the claim has fallen below £50,000 and that an application for transfer down should be made. In a non-personal injury case commenced in the High Court the court at the summons for directions will have regard to the relevant criteria and on the application of either party, or on its own motion, transfer the case down. Once the case is transferred to the county court it becomes a county court case for all purposes up to trial though the eventual judgment can be transferred back to the High Court for enforcement.

Costs penalties
18.05 If a case is wrongly commenced in the High Court, or the case continues in the High Court when the eventual court of trial finds that there were no reasonable grounds for it to have been brought there then a costs penalty can

be imposed on the successful party. Normally this will be the plaintiff who either has commenced proceedings in the High Court which should have been brought in the county court from the outset, or who perhaps, having honestly commenced proceedings in the High Court, has failed to apply to transfer them to the county court even though information has come into his possession which would have made it apparent that the value of the claim had fallen below the figure at which the case should have been heard in the county court. The penalty that may be imposed in costs is prescribed by ss.4(8) and (9) of the Courts and Legal Services Act 1990 which states:—

(8) "Where:—
    (a) A person has commenced proceedings in the High Court but
    (b) Those proceedings should in the opinion of the court have been commenced in a county court in accordance with any provision made under s.1 of the Courts and Legal Services Act 1990 or by or under any other enactment, the person responsible for determining the amount which is to be awarded to that person by way of costs shall have regard to those circumstances.
(9)   Where in complying with subsection (8) the responsible person reduces the amount which would otherwise be awarded to the person in question.
    (a) The amount of that reduction shall not exceed 25 per cent. and
    (b) on any taxation of the costs payable by that person to his legal representative regard shall be had to the amount of the reduction."

In other words the penalty which will be imposed, if the court is minded to impose any penalty, and it is clearly not mandatory to do so, will be limited to no more than 25 per cent. of the eventual gross bill. Moreover the provision in subsection (9) clearly indicates that the court would not approve of the reduction being passed on to the successful party by his solicitor so that the solicitor claimed the full amount of his own costs notwithstanding that a reduced amount had been recovered from the losing party.

Other factors in choice of court

18.06 One would appear to have little choice in a personal injury case other than to commence the action in the county court unless the value appears to be greater than £50,000. If despite an apparently low value in the action some special feature arose which made the action one of great importance for example because it was a test case, or there was a novel point of law, or great difficulties of expert evidence, then one might be able to apply to the district judge for a direction for transfer to the High Court. One would anticipate that such powers to transfer would be very sparingly used. In non-personal injury cases however one can in principle commence in whichever court one likes bearing in mind that if one commences in the High Court the matter is likely to be reviewed anyway and transferred down where appropriate at the summons for direction stage. What then are the advantages of commencing a case worth, say £15,000, in the High Court? In favour of the High Court the following features are often said to apply:—

18.07 1. The plaintiff has considerably greater control over the conduct of proceedings especially the issue and service of the writ. This might be very relevant in a debt case. The solicitor might receive instructions to proceed as swiftly as possible. He could if he wished issue and serve the writ on the same day. In the county court generally one merely prepares a request for a summons and the court itself eventually issues the summons perhaps several days later and deals with service of it. It is however now possible for plaintiffs to prepare their own form of summons for issue in the county court and therefore this factor is less important.

18.08　2. The High Court process tends to be more intimidating to a debtor, especially a litigant in person. The documents are simply considerably more impressive in appearance. A county court summons looks rather like a rate demand by comparison. Moreover the form of admission, defence and counter claim sent out with the county court summons is considered by some to be a virtual incitement to the debtor to think up some reason for prolonging matters. He is given in effect a questionnaire which he can complete quite easily and if he does so successfully this will have the effect of bringing about a pre-trial review in several weeks time and thereafter of prolonging the case to trial. In the High Court the defendant must both complete the form of acknowledgment of service and follow this up with a defence. There is no form of admission defence and counter-claim to tell him how to do it or for him to fill in.

18.09　3. In favour of the High Court also is that enforcement by the High Court sheriff is considerably more efficient than that by the county court bailiff. However it should be noted that a county court judgment in excess of £2,000 may now be enforced in the High Court.

18.10　4. If it is hoped that the action will end short of trial then it may actually be faster to take proceedings in the High Court. Thus if one hopes to obtain judgment in default or summary judgment it will make very little difference in terms of time and one then has the advantages of High Court procedure for enforcement.

18.11　5. In marginal cases issuing in the High Court may simply persuade the opponent that you view the case more seriously than he had thought. It may make him think in High Court terms and put forward better offers of settlement. Moreover High Court judges tend to be more generous than county court judges perhaps because they are used to thinking in terms of thousands of pounds rather than hundreds of pounds.

18.12　6. If it becomes apparent that the case is to be seriously defended, contrary to the solicitor's initial expectations, one can anyway apply to transfer a case which one has commenced in the High Court to the county court.

In favour of the county court

18.13　1. In favour of the county court there may be the simple matter of geographical convenience. There are approximately 300 county courts, almost three times the number of district registries of the High Court and therefore in rural areas there may simply be a more convenient local county court. Some less busy county courts however are in a group and it by no means follows that there will be a registrar in attendance every day or a judge available more often than once a week or a fortnight. The court office at least will be open every day however.

2. Some clients may prefer the lesser degree of formality in the county court **18.14** though this is not a reason which ought to persuade a lawyer.

19. Enforcement of Money Judgments

19.01   Neither in the High Court nor in the county court is a civil judgment for payment of money enforced automatically by the court. Until the successful party (the judgment creditor) puts into operation one or other of the court procedures for enforcement of the judgment against the losing party (the judgment debtor) nothing will happen. It is very important to discuss with a judgment creditor the possible problems and to seek to ensure that the method of enforcing the judgment chosen will not prove abortive because as a general principle the costs incurred in attempting to enforce judgments in a way which proves abortive are not recoverable even though by some later alternative method one does obtain payment of the judgment debt and costs. In any kind of case where the defendant is uninsured one should explain to the client that although there are a variety of procedures for enforcing judgments one cannot get money where there is none and that money spent at an early stage on a status enquiry about the defendant will be well spent if it reveals that to litigate against him at all will be throwing good money after bad. We are therefore not now concerned with enforcing judgment in a personal injury case where the defendant's insurance company will pay the damages within the time stipulated by the court. We are concerned with a contract type case.

It usually comes as a considerable shock to clients to be told that in reality there is almost no prospect of having a person who owes a civil debt committed to prison for non-payment. Nor is failure to pay or even downright refusal to pay construed as a civil contempt.

We shall now go on to consider the various alternative methods of enforcing judgment against the debtor and of seizing different types of assets. For ease and convenience since there are great similarities in the procedures, at this stage we shall consider both High Court procedures and county court procedures together.

Obtaining information about the judgment debtor's means

19.02   Suppose that despite the advice previously given the client has instructed you to proceed to obtain judgment in the certainty that the defendant is a wealthy man. Perhaps he had been a frequent previous customer of your client who had in the past purchased expensive consumer durable or luxuries and always paid cash so that your client assures you there will be no trouble in enforcing judgment and instructs you not to waste money and time in making status enquiries before the issue of proceedings. Judgment is obtained but it is not paid in the due time. You only have the vaguest of information about your opponent's means, *e.g.* his address and what your client believes to be his occupation. In such a situation one can adopt one of two methods of proceedings:—

188

STATUS REPORT

One can now instruct an enquiry agent to obtain a status report. As previ- **19.03**
ously explained the enquiry agent is likely to go round to the debtor's
premises and ask him about his means (there is no obligation on the debtor
to reply of course!), look in the windows, observe the year and model of any
motor vehicles parked at or near the property, make an approximate val-
uation of the house by reference to similar houses nearby which may be up
for sale and perhaps pursue enquiries at the debtor's place of work. One may
now obtain a body of information on which one can choose which of the
methods of enforcement later described will be most effective. This is an
informal procedure which of course does not involve the court. As an
alternative to this where there is no information one can opt for an oral
examination of the judgment debtor.

ORAL EXAMINATION. R.S.C., ORD. 48; C.C.R., ORD. 25, R. 3

It must be stressed that this should not be undertaken automatically in every **19.04**
case. If one already had sufficient information to point in the direction of
one particular method of enforcement then oral examination is not to be
lightly undertaken. At the very least it is likely to take an hour or more of a
solicitor's time to attend and conduct an oral examination quite apart from
the preliminary work in making application for it and serving notice of the
appointment date. It should not therefore be an automatic reaction to opt
for it in every case. In any event on the assumption that one is to proceed
with an oral examination this is what occurs:—

In the High Court

An affidavit is prepared by the judgment creditor's solicitor which refers to **19.05**
the fact that the judgment creditor is entitled to enforce the judgment in
question, identifies the judgment obtained by giving its date and serial
number and stating the amount remaining unpaid under it and the address of
the debtor and of the nearest county court to his home; together with this
two copies of the order required are prepared. These documents are taken
to the court and left there where they are read by the district judge who if
satisfied, (as he undoubtedly will be if the affidavit is in proper form) will
make the order for oral examination of the judgment debtor. The practice is
to have the oral examination of the judgment debtor not at the district
registry of the High Court where the action has been continuing but at the
office of the county court in the area where the judgment debtor resides. It is
for this reason that the information has to be given in the judgment creditor's
affidavit. This is an extra inconvenience to the judgment creditor which
ought to be borne in mind if the relevant county court is some way away. The
order will appoint a time and place for the judgment debtor to attend for oral
examination. Having obtained the order it is necessary to serve it personally
on the judgment debtor and thus a process server must be used for this
purpose. It is also good practice to tender conduct money, *i.e.* travelling
costs to and from the court.

A date has therefore been fixed for the oral examination of the judgment **19.06**
debtor. It may be that if the judgment debtor has played no part at all in the

proceedings so far, *e.g.* where he failed to give notice of intention to defend, so the judgment was obtained under R.S.C., Ord. 13; or failed to attend an application for hearing for summary judgment under R.S.C., Ord. 14 after he had given notice of intention to defend, that he will not have had any experience of the court process as yet. In that case he may imagine, as laymen do, that he is to be orally examined by a judge in full regalia and that amongst the judge's powers will be the one of committing him to prison for non-payment. If this is the case then the obtaining of an order for oral examination may well provoke immediate payment. Unfortunately for the judgment creditor most laymen are not as naive as this and even those who do not fall within the class of so-called "professional debtors" may well know that this is not the case. In fact the oral examination is almost invariably before an officer of the court appointed by the district judge for that purpose and the examination takes place not in open court nor even in the district judge's chambers but all too often in some non-descript room at the top of the court building which resembles nothing more than a railway station waiting room. The officer asks questions usually by reference to a *pro forma* questionnaire and copies down the answers which are on oath. The judgment creditor's solicitor then has the right to cross-examine and attempts to follow up with relevant questions. The debtor must answer all questions "fairly pertinent and properly asked and give all necessary particulars to enable the plaintiff to recover."

19.07 What if the judgment debtor in unco-operative? If the judgment debtor having attended refuses to answer a proper question then the matter must be referred to the district judge who will give such direction as he thinks fit. This may of course lead to an adjournment for that purpose. If he fails to attend at all or having been given a direction to answer the question fails to do so he may be committed to prison for contempt, however this entails a quite separate application to a judge in open court. Whilst it might be morally satisfying to the unpaid judgment creditor to have his opponent committed to prison, first it is no help whatsoever in obtaining payment of the money due and indeed it may be actually counter productive if committal to prison involved the judgment debtor losing his job, and secondly orders for committal are very rare indeed. In addition there is the costs aspects. One has already presumably had an abortive attempt to hold an oral examination with the solicitor attending with a good deal of wasted time; now to apply to have the judgment debtor committed to prison involves yet further costs in an application in open court to the judge; this may well take another half-day of the solicitor's time by the time his application is heard in the judge's list and in the High Court one will need to brief counsel. By the time that the committal stage is reached, unless one is dealing with someone whom one suspects to be well off but deliberately evasive one is generally very conscious that one is throwing good money after bad.

In any event it must be remembered that an order for oral examination is not a method of enforcement in itself but merely a method of obtaining information.

19.08 If anything useful is obtained from the oral examination then an order for costs will usually be made and these for convenience will be assessed there and then by the district judge. Usually only a relatively modest sum is likely to be awarded which will not generally cover the full costs to the client of the solicitor's work in attending the oral examination.

In the county court

The function and purpose of an oral examination is identical in the county **19.09** court. The method of application does not require an affidavit but merely the filing of a written request in the appropriate form for an oral examination. Postal service of the order for oral examination is possible provided a certificate to the effect that postal service will be effective is completed. Probably personal service is to be preferred. Conduct money must be tendered. If the judgment debtor does not appear on the first occasion it is even more likely than in the case of a High Court examination that the application will be adjourned to some other convenient day with the consequent waste of time and costs. In all other respects procedure is similar.

At the end of an oral examination in either case it is customary to ask the person being examined whether he makes any offer as to payment of the debt. He is then asked to sign a note of his evidence.

Execution. Writ of Fieri Facias and Warrant of Execution

HIGH COURT. WRIT OF FIERI FACIAS. R.S.C., ORD. 45 AND ORD. 46

This process enables the goods of the judgment debtor to be seized and sold **19.10** at auction to satisfy the judgment debt, legal costs and the costs of enforcement. We shall now describe what happens. The judgment creditor's solicitor takes to the district registry where the judgment was obtained:—

1. two copies of a writ of Fieri Facias (usually referred to as Fi Fa);

2. a praecipe (that is a request for the issue of the writ of Fi Fa);

3. the judgment obtained together with, if the costs have already been taxed by the court, a copy of the taxing officer's certificate;

4. the court fee.

These are taken to the court counter at the district registry. There is no need for any formal application to the district judge it is simply a matter of producing them to the clerk at the counter. The fee is taken and one form of the writ is sealed and returned to the judgment creditor.

The judgment creditor then sends the writ to the sheriff of the county **19.11** concerned. This county will be where the judgment debtor resides or where he has assets which it is hoped to seize. When forwarding the writ to the sheriff it is the practice to give the sheriff any information one has about what kind of assets the judgment debtor might have or where they are situated. It may be for example that although the matter has been proceeding in, say, the district registry at Nottingham that it is known that the judgment debtor has some valuable antiques which he keeps at a country cottage in Dorset. In that case one will instruct the sheriff of Dorset not of Nottinghamshire.

19.12   The sheriff's officers can seize any of the debtor's goods in the county which are sufficient to realise the judgment debt, costs and expenses. Usually the sheriff's officers are in private practice as auctioneers and thus are well used to valuing items for their second-hand value. The sheriff's officers may seize anything belonging to the debtor in his premises with the exception of wearing apparel, bedding and the debtor's tools of his trade to certain values. They may also take cash or securities found on the premises. In fact items most commonly seized are movables such as furniture and motor cars. In principle the sheriff's officers should go round and seize the items removing them immediately.. In practice however it is often the case that they will allow a further few days for payment. The practice is that they will make an inventory of the items in the house which they propose to seize which they require the judgment debtor to sign to confirm the items in the list. This is known as taking "walking possession" and the debtor must not dispose of them or permit them to be moved after that time. The sheriff's officers will then appoint a day to return to take the goods and this often has the effect of forcing the judgment debtor to find the money. If he does not they return and take the goods away where they keep them for public auction. Again a further few days are allowed before the auction takes place to give the judgment debtor a last chance to find the money. At the public auction the goods are sold and any surplus after payment of the judgment debt, interest, costs and sheriff's costs of enforcement is returned to the judgment debtor. Judgment debtors, if they have any hope whatsoever of finding the money even by taking on highly disadvantageous loan arrangements would usually be well advised to do so. At public auctions of this kind, furniture, even very new and expensive furniture, often only fetches a fraction of its value as new and therefore the value to the defendant of paying up and keeping his goods is considerably more than the value of goods at auction.

Although reference has been made above to enforcement of the judgment and order for costs by this method, since the taxation of costs will inevitably take some time, perhaps months, and the judgment creditor may not be willing to wait that long before attempting all possible methods of enforcement there is of course no need to wait until costs have been taxed. Execution can be issued in respect of the judgment debt leaving further execution to be issued in due course in respect of costs.

WARRANT OF EXECUTION IN THE COUNTY COURT. C.C.R., ORD. 26

19.13   In the county court the plaint note and a request for warrant of execution are filed together with a fee. The sheriff's officer, as has been indicated is an individual who is not an employee of the court, usually an auctioneer in private practice. The warrant of execution in the county court however is executed by the bailiff of the court. The court bailiff is an officer who has a number of functions including the service of court proceedings and the enforcement of judgments. When the warrant of execution is sent to the bailiff he in principle does much the same as the sheriff's officers in the High Court, that is, attend the debtor's premises and levy execution in the same way. In neither case can the sheriff or bailiff force entry although the sheriff's officers are usually successful in obtaining some kind of consent to enter.

192

ENFORCEMENT OF COUNTY COURT JUDGMENTS IN THE HIGH COURT

Any High Court judgment of less than £5,000 can be enforced in the county **19.14** court therefore if one was so minded one could instruct the county court bailiff by warrant of execution rather than the High Court sheriff. A county court judgment can also be enforced in the High Court where the sum involved exceeds £2,000. Why should one wish to do this? The main reason is effectiveness of enforcement. Sheriff's officers are paid by commission whereas bailiffs are employed on a salaried basis only. Accordingly the former are considered to have considerably more enthusiasm for the pursuit of the recalcitrant debtor's chattels. Many practitioners agree that bailiffs are too easily dissuaded from pursuing execution by minor difficulties and are more willing to accept transparently feeble excuses, *e.g.* "all the property in the house belongs to my mother." Consequently it would be rare for one to wish to enforce High Court judgment in the county court but ought to be common for a county court judgment worth more than £2,000 to be enforced through the High Court. Apparently however the right to transfer for enforcement is not as widely used as one would have thought. If the county court judgment is for more than £5,000, enforcement by execution must be in the High Court.

It ought to be noted that no leave is required to apply to the court for a writ of **19.15** Fi Fa save in certain exceptional circumstances of which only one matters to us now and that is that whilst a county court attachment of earnings order is in force the leave of the court to issue execution is necessary. The interrelationship between various methods of enforcement will be discussed below.

It ought also to be mentioned that on those occasions where we have **19.16** discussed the defendant wishing to apply for a stay of execution, this is the kind of execution he is seeking to avoid. Thus for example a defendant in the High Court who does not wish to defend but wishes to obtain an order for instalment payments seeks to avoid execution by completing his acknowledgment of service appropriately. If it were not for this a writ of Fi Fa could be issued on the same day as judgment in default was obtained. There is no need to serve copy of the judgment in default before applying immediately for execution.

Garnishee proceedings

19.17

This is a particularly neat method of enforcement since it requires no co-operation from the judgment debtor and indeed the crucial stage is brought about without him being informed, or having any opportunity to defeat the processes of enforcement. This method is appropriate where the judgment debtor is himself owed money by another person. Examples would be where the judgment debtor is in business and is owed trade debts by some other person or where someone has money in any kind of bank or building society account. Garnishee proceedings are a method of seizing such sums and by-passing the judgment debtor.

HIGH COURT PRACTICE. R.S.C., ORD. 49

In the High Court to obtain a garnishee order the judgment creditor's **19.18** solicitor swears an affidavit in which he identifies the judgment or order that he is seeking to enforce and states the amount remaining unpaid under it at the time of application; states the name and last known address of the judgment debtor; and states that to the best of his information the *garnishee* (that is the person who owes money to the judgment debtor) is indebted to the judgment debtor and states the sources of that belief and (if he knows it) the amount owed by the garnishee to the judgment debtor and if the garnishee is a bank, building society or similar states the branch address where the account is held and the account number if known.

19.19   Together with this two copies of an order called a *"garnishee order nisi"* or sometimes from the crucial opening words "An order to show cause" are prepared. These are taken together to the district registry where they are left to be put before by the district judge. No hearing is necessary and, crucially, the judgment debtor is not informed about what is happening at this stage. The affidavit is read by the district judge and if it is formally in order he will make the order which can later be collected from the office of the district registry, often the same day. The form of the order is an order directed to the person who owes money to the judgment debtor (*i.e.* the garnishee) and tells the garnishee to do two things:

1.   To attend court at the time and place specified in the order to show cause why he should not pay the money which he owes to the judgment debtor directly over to the judgment creditor.

2.   Meanwhile to retain the amount owed. This will have the effect of freezing a bank account or stopping the garnishee paying debts straight over to the judgment debtor.

19.20   This order must be served on the garnishee and the practice in the case of a bank is to serve both the head office and the bank local branch where the account is kept. Once this has been safely done so that the amount is frozen a copy should also be served on the judgment debtor who only now becomes aware of what has happened. He will now, therefore if he has a balance on a current account at a bank no longer be able to cash cheques on that account. The time fixed for the hearing date is at least 15 days later than service of the garnishee order nisi on the garnishee and at least seven days after service on the judgment debtor.

19.21   Most garnishees will have no interest at all in attending the hearing. It is after all irrelevant to a bank whether money held in the account of X should be paid over by court order to Y. After all X could have withdrawn all the money at any time. The usual practice for the garnishee is simply not to participate at all or perhaps to write to the court stating he will abide by any order made. If the garnishee disputes his liability to pay anything to the *judgment debtor* there will need to be a determination of that matter at the hearing.

19.22   The *judgment debtor* will however attend the hearing at which the judgment creditor will be seeking to persuade the district judge to make the order nisi into a final order, *i.e.* one directing the payment of the money due to the judgment creditor. The making of a final order is discretionary but in principle it ought to be made unless there are other unsecured creditors of the judgment debtor so that making the order would represent an unjust preferment of one creditor over another. If the judgment debtor can show no reason why the order should not be made it will be made and the order is addressed to the garnishee telling him to pay the money over within a certain short time direct to the judgment creditor. Naturally this absolves the garnishee from debts up to the relevant amount owed by him to the judgment debtor. If the garnishee fails to pay enforcement proceedings can be taken agaist him directly. Indeed any payment of money by him direct to the judgment debtor in defiance of the order would amount to conversion.

GARNISHEE IN THE COUNTY COURT. C.C.R., ORD. 30

In the county court application is also made on affidavit to the court which **19.23** will then issue the garnishee order to show cause which is served on the garnishee (usually by the court) in the same manner as if it were a fixed date summons. It is then served on the judgment debtor. Again it has the effect of instructing the garnishee to attend court on the hearing and meanwhile to retain the amount owed to the judgment debtor. The garnishee is given the option of paying the sum into court rather than attending the hearing. If the garnishee disputes that he does owe money to the judgment debtor there is provision for him to require the case to be transferred to the county court where he resides or carries on business for the issue to be decided.

Charging orders

IN THE HIGH COURT. R.S.C., ORD. 50

Where the judgment debtor owns land (even if he owns it jointly with some **19.24** other person) a charging order can be obtained on the land. The method of application is almost the same as in the case of a garnishee proceedings. An affidavit must be prepared to be sworn by the judgment creditor or his solicitor which:

1. Identifies the judgment and states the amount unpaid at the date of application;

2. States the name of the judgment debtor;

3. Gives full particulars of the subject-matter of the intended charge, *i.e.* the land concerned;

4. Verifies that the interest to be charged is owned beneficially and not as trustee by the judgment debtor;

5. States honestly whether he knows of any other creditors of the judgment debtor. This is a matter to be taken into account by the district judge in deciding whether to grant the charging order absolute (*i.e.* that it might not constitute unjust preferment of one creditor over another).

Two copies of the order to show cause (also sometimes called a charging **19.25** order nisi) are prepared and these are all taken together to the district registry. Again there is no hearing and no obligation to notify the judgment debtor. The affidavit is read by a district judge who will make the charging order nisi. This has the effect of creating a charge on the land owned by the judgment debtor. It is prudent to register this charge which takes effect as an equitable charge under hand. It is therefore registered at the Land Charges Registry in the case of unregistered land or protected by notice or caution at the District Land Registry in the case of registered land. A hearing date is fixed by the charging order nisi and this order must now be served upon the judgment debtor. It invites him to attend the hearing to show cause why the order should not be made absolute. At the hearing the district judge has full discretion as to whether or not to make the charging order absolute though the burden of showing cause why it should not be made absolute is on the judgment debtor. The charging order may be made absolute in relation to land which is wholly owned by the judgment debtor or to land which he owns jointly with some other person but in the latter case the charging order takes effect only on his interest in the proceeds of sale. If the charging order is made absolute it should again be registered at the District Land Registry in the case of registered land or the Land Charges Registry in the case of unregistered land to preserve priority over subsequently created encumbrances. The following points ought also to be noted in relation to charging orders:

1. It can only be used in the High Court in the case of a sum exceeding £5,000 (*i.e.* if the High Court was used for a claim of say £4,000 a charging order would only be obtainable subsequently in the county court if charging order were the chosen method of enforcement).

2. A charging order is not as such a method of enforcing the debt immediately; it is merely a matter of obtaining security for it. Accordingly it might be classified as a "slow but sure" method of obtaining the monies.

3. It should be noted that if the land in question is registered land then one can apply to the District Land Registrar for office copies of the proprietorship register to show whether the judgment debtor does indeed have a beneficial interest in the land.

19.26 However the judgment credit does now stand in the position of mortgagee of the land and may, if no payments are made under the debt, apply by making application in separate proceedings in the Chancery Division to enforce the charging order by application for possession and sale of the land charged in order that the judgment can be paid out of the proceeds of sale. However it should be noted that in these proceedings to enforce the sale of the land the court does have a wide discretion to take into account the interest of any other party residing on the premises. It is therefore not prima facie very likely that the court will in fact order the sale of what is a family home to procure immediate payment of a civil debt. However, interest does run on judgment debts in the High Court and this is another important matter to be considered by the court in exercising its discretion. If no attempts have been made to pay any sums due under the judgment and the amount of the judgment debt with interest now appears to exceed the equity in the property after prior mortgages have been discharged this may be a reason why the court would use its discretion in favour of authorising sale.

IN THE COUNTY COURT. C.C.R., ORD. 31

19.27 In the county court the procedure is identical to that in the case of application for a garnishee order.

It ought also to be noted that the charging order in either court is a method of enforcing judgment in relation to securities as well as land and a charging order may be made in relation to any government stock or other stocks and shares. The order may extend to any interest or dividends payable on the stocks and shares and thus payment of these dividends direct to the judgment creditor may ensure that he does at least receive part payment of the judgment debt pending sale of the securities.

Attachment of earnings. C.C.R., Ord. 27

Attachment of earnings provides a method of ensuring that money is paid direct from a person's salary before he receives it, by his employer into the county court. It is only available as a method of enforcement in the county court at present (except for Family Division cases). It is however possible to enforce a High Court judgment for a sum of less than £5,000 in the county court. To obtain an order one completes a form of application to the county court and if the judgment was obtained in the High Court the proceedings must be transferred to the county court for that purpose which is done by sending a copy of the High Court judgment and an affidavit identifying the judgment and stating that it is still outstanding.

19.28

The court then serves notice of application for attachment of earnings order on the judgment debtor together with a form of questionnaire which the debtor must complete giving details of his employment, income and financial liabilities. It is also open to the county court to send a notice to the debtor's employer requiring him to supply details of the debtor's earnings. The forms also invite the debtor to make proposals for payment. The application is made to the county court for the district in which the debtor resides. Where the district judge then feels that he has sufficient information he may make a provisional order and give notice of it to the creditor and debtor and if neither party objects the provisional order becomes final. However if either party objects in writing within five days of receiving the notice there will then be a hearing. Alternatively it may be that the district judge does not have sufficient information even to make a provisional order. In that case a hearing date is fixed.

19.29

If a judgment debtor does not return his questionnaire and does not attend then an application can be made to a judge for him to be committed to prison. Subsequent failure to give details of earnings and particulars are in any event criminal offences under the Attachment of Earnings Act 1971. Likewise it is an offence for the employer to fail to supply particulars of the debtor's earnings.

The hearing is very much like a disposal or an oral examination. There is actually no need for the judgment creditor to attend although it is probably better for him to do so. If the debtor is deemed to have sufficient means then an order will be made specifying two things the "normal deduction rate" (NDR) and "protected earnings rate" (PER). The latter is deemed to be the minimum which the debtor needs to earn to achieve subsistence level for himself and his family, if any. It can best be explained by reference to a case where the debtor's work is perhaps seasonal or dependent on fluctuating overtime or bonuses. Enforcement of a judgment of over £5,000 by execution *must* be in the High Court.

19.30

Example:

Suppose that the debtor has seasonal work and his earnings fluctuate so that his lowest net earnings can be £70 and his highest £150. The district judge may fix a protected earning rate of say £100 a week in view of the debtor's means, obligations and dependants. He may also fix a normal deduction rate of £20 per week. Thus in any week in which the debtor earns £100 or less he will suffer no deductions from his earnings; if he earns £120 or more he will suffer a £20 deduction from his earnings; if he earns between £100 and £120 he will suffer a deduction of the excess over £100.

19.31 When the order is made it is directed to the employer on whom it is served by post together with an explanatory leaflet giving details as to how to operate the attachment of earnings order. The employer is entitled to deduct a small sum from the debtor's earnings for administration expenses. The amount must now be deducted weekly or monthly depending on the method of payment and sent direct to the court until the debt is satisfied.

The choice of method of enforcement

19.32 Let us now consider these types of enforcement proceedings. First one must stress the importance of discovering details of the debtor's assets. It really is pointless starting out with a writ of Fi Fa if you do not know anything about the debtor at all. He may well live in a relative's house and none of the furniture may be his in which case a good deal of money may be wasted in abortive costs. Likewise it is hardly possible to start an application for a garnishee order or for a charging order if one has no information whatsoever about the assets of the debtor. In any event assuming that one has obtained sufficient information to give some indication as to the most appropriate method of enforcement let us consider what types of assets would be most appropriate for each.

EXECUTION

19.33 This is effective against movables of any kind. It may have a somewhat drastic effect upon the judgment debtor since the intrusion into one's home of large men intent on bearing out most of the contents is naturally unwelcome as is the eventual sale by auction of one's furniture and motor car at prices substantially less than their value to the judgment debtor personally.

GARNISHEE ORDER

19.34 This is the most satisfactory of all if one has the details of debts due on which it can attach. It is virtually immediate in its effect.

CHARGING ORDER ON LAND

This is a slow but fairly sure method of payment. If the judgment debtor chooses not to move house for some years then one may be waiting a very considerable time. If the judgment debt is a High Court debt then interest will be accruing and this may be quite satisfactory for the judgment creditor. In the case of a county court debt interest will not be accruing and thus the value of the sum secured will diminish over the years. Further enforcement may be undertaken by application for an order for sale but in these proceedings the court enjoys a wide discretion to take into account the interests of anyone residing in the property (although the judgment creditor's interests must also be given due weight).

ATTACHMENT OF EARNINGS

This is the last hope. It is a method to be used where the judgment debtor has **19.35** no seizable or chargeable assets of any kind but appears to have fairly regular employment. If the order is for a large enough amount each week it may prove satisfactory to the judgment creditor but it is very much a case of getting one's debts paid little by little, and in the case of a county court judgment which does not at the time of writing bear interest (as opposed to a High Court judgment which is being enforced in the county court) it may be highly unsatisfactory.

In the case of a High Court judgment being enforced in the county court then the figures may be such that one would find that the money recovered by attachment of earnings hardly covers the interest. However personal circumstances change and having an attachment of earnings order does not preclude one from making application for other methods of enforcement, *e.g.* if the judgment debtor is discovered to subsequently acquire a house or car. However it must be noted that leave of the court will be necessary to issue a writ of Fi Fa during the currency of an attachment of earnings order.

BANKRUPTCY

Finally *bankruptcy* ought to be mentioned. This may be the most successful **19.36** method of all against persons whose occupation makes it very difficult for them if they are bankrupt, *e.g.* solicitors and other professionals who are not permitted to retain their status if bankrupt. However as a method of enforcement it has serious defects. First it can only be used in the case of debts of over £750. Secondly whereas with all the other methods the costs of enforcement in terms of court fees, etc., are minimal, in the case of bankruptcy proceedings the costs are high because a deposit must be left with the Official Receiver in respect of his accountancy fees. The initial costs of commencing bankruptcy proceedings are currently over £200 and this may often be seen as throwing good money after bad. Moreover the nature of bankruptcy proceedings is that all creditors of the judgment debtor come forward and one may find that there are so many that there is really little prospect then of obtaining anything at all. If the judgment debtor can be made to pay anything by any of the other methods these are often seen as the best. However there is no doubt that in certain cases, bankruptcy or the threat of it, may be the most effective method of enforcement.

Finally it ought to be remembered that:

1. High court judgments of less than £5,000 may always be enforced in the **19.37** county court if one wishes. In fact attachment of earnings order is the only method one is likely to use since this is not available in the High Court.
2. County court judgments over £2,000 may be enforced in the High Court. Again the method where this is most relevant is the case of enforcement by execution where the sheriff is usually considered more efficient than the county court bailiff.

20. Costs

20.01 The word costs generally means both "profit costs" that is to say the solicitor's own fees for the work he has done and in addition any disbursements he has paid out on the client's behalf in the conduct of the litigation, *e.g.* fees to counsel, court fees, expert witness fees.

20.02 It is perhaps appropriate to say a preliminary word about the way in which a solicitor computes his bills in litigious business. From the moment when the instructions are received a solicitor should keep a note of all time expended on the client's business. This will involve not merely time in the office such as interviews with the client and his witnesses, direct negotiations and meetings with the other side, telephone calls in relation to the client's business (clients often try to circumvent the fact that they know a solicitor charges for his time by telephoning him for lengthy consultations rather than attending in person. They are often then dismayed to find that the solicitor actually charges for telephone conversations). In addition when attending court the client will be charged for all the time spent there. Suppose for instance that one has to attend court on a summons for a client and the district registry where the hearing is to take place is situated some miles from the solicitor's office. The client will be paying for the solicitor's time from the moment he leaves his office until he returns to it (unless the solicitor was able to combine the need to visit the court with some other business so that the travelling time could be shared between two clients). As the district registrar's day is divided into small sections for interlocutory appointments it may be that cases overrun their allotted time and he gets considerably behind the clock in which case one may find oneself waiting some time for one's appointment. This time unfortunately has to be charged to the client. The hourly *rate* which a solicitor is entitled to charge the client takes into account a number of specific matters. A full examination of the basis of this is not necessary here but suffice it to say that regard must be had to the complexity of the case, the skill, specialised knowledge and responsibility involved in the conduct of the case, the importance of the cause or matter to the client, the amount involved and in addition other things such as the urgency of the matter. Thus if a solicitor is required to obtain an urgent injunction for a client which will involve the solicitor in dropping all other matters with which he had intended to deal that day, including cancelling appointments, the client who requires the business to be conducted urgently must expect to pay a higher hourly rate for it. This then is the basis on which a solicitor will charge his own client. The client's liability to pay the solicitor's fees arises out of the contractual relationship between them.

20.03 As we have seen the position is however affected by the grant of legal aid. Where a client has legal aid the client has no obligation to pay the solicitor any sum in respect of the matter. If the client is assessed to pay a contribution that contribution is paid directly to and retained by the Legal Aid Board itself and not by the solicitor and the solicitor's costs are eventually then paid from the legal aid fund.

One must therefore emphasise the difference between the two situations. If **20.04** one is acting for a privately paying client then it is as well to adopt the procedure previously described, advising him that considerable sums in advance will be required as the litigation proceeds, and of the delivery of interim bills. If one is acting for a legally aided client then it is a matter between him and the Legal Aid Board for him to pay his contribution and to keep up regular payments if instalment contributions have been ordered. The client then should be thoroughly advised that costs recoverable from his opponent will not necessarily cover all the outgoings but that should the client lose his liability for his own costs is limited to the amount of his contribution. Should the client win however the nature of the Legal Aid Board's charge should be explained to him and this has previously been described.

The privately paying client therefore will have to be advised that he must pay his solicitor's costs whatever the outcome of the case. The legally aided client need not worry about his own solicitor's costs. We will now go on to consider a matter which must always be explained carefully to the client in addition to the foregoing and that is the extent to which he may hope to have part of his costs met by the opponents if he is successful.

The English theory of damages in tort and contract is compensatory. That is **20.05** to say it aims to put the aggrieved party in exactly the same position as he would have been put but for the tort or breach of contract. Where this is a purely financial matter as in the collection of a debt the law can do precisely that. Where something not directly expressable in money terms happens such as the infliction of personal injuries, then the law ensures the payment of financial compensation. A difficult problem however is the question of legal costs. In strict principle a losing party should be required to pay the whole of the winning party's legal costs because otherwise the winning party is not in fact put in precisely the same position in which he would have been but for the tort or breach of contract, in that he has had to expend some money of his own on legal costs to enforce what was his right. In some European countries it is actually the case that the loser pays the whole of the winner's legal costs. In other jurisdictions, for example the United States, there is usually no order for costs between the parties and the lawyer for the winning party will recover his costs direct from the winning party, often by a contingency fee arrangement. One aspect making this more palatable in the United States is the fact that damages there, particularly in personal injury cases, are many times higher for the same type of injury than they are in England.

In England and Wales the provision for the loser to pay the winner's costs is **20.06** something of a compromise between these two extreme positions, although since April 1986 when new provisions were introduced it is fair to say that the loser may now be required to pay costs which will be assessed in such a way that often the whole of the winner's legal costs will in fact be paid provided the litigation has been conducted in a reasonable and efficient manner. Consequently although in the case of a privately paying client one ought to deliver one's bill to the client either at the end of the litigation or as one goes along, one will then, if the client has been successful, have the duty of trying to collect from the losing party as large a sum as possible towards those costs and if the costs have already been paid in full this sum when recovered must naturally be used to reimburse the client. If the solicitor has actually not charged in advance but has been content to wait till the end of the litigation then he will attempt to recover as much as possible from the losing party and then only deliver to his own client a bill for any extra work not covered by that payment from the losing party.

20.07 We therefore now go on to consider costs between the parties. In litigation there is no right to costs. Costs are always in the discretion of the court but certain conventions have been well established. The conventions are that costs "follow the event," *i.e.* that the winner is usually entitled to an order that the loser should pay his costs. This will be the case where the matter has been litigated as far as trial. However if the parties reach a negotiated settlement at an earlier stage it is usual for the party who is putting forward the offer of compromise to agree to pay the other party's costs. Litigation may be terminated with no requirement for either party to pay costs to his opponent, for example where a plaintiff sues a defendant who raises a counter claim of an approximately equivalent amount and after a certain stage they realise that the costs of litigating outweigh the possible advantages, they might well both agree to withdraw their claim and counter claim on the basis that each pays his own costs.

Taxation of costs

20.08 As we shall see shortly, at the end of a case where the loser has been ordered to pay the winner's costs it will often be the position that the parties will try to agree what this figure should be. In the majority of cases, this is possible. If however the parties cannot agree and the loser thinks that the winner's claim for costs is excessive, there is a further hearing in court where an officer of the court (in London a taxing master and in the provinces a district registrar) assesses the bill of the winner and determines how much of it the loser should be required to pay. This process is known as "taxation" though it has nothing to do with the Inland Revenue. Where this process has to take place the person who assesses the bill will be trying to determine the amount which it is proper for the loser to have to pay the winner. In the High Court this depends mainly on the *basis of taxation* that will be used. In the county court it depends on the *basis of taxation* to be used *and* the *scale* of costs fixed in the county court rules for the case. We shall first discuss the basis of taxation.

There are now two bases of taxation.

THE STANDARD BASIS

20.09 Where a taxation of costs is to take place on the *standard* basis then by Order 62 "there shall be allowed a reasonable amount in respect of all costs reasonably incurred and any doubts which the taxing officer may have as to whether the costs were reasonably incurred or were reasonable in amount should be resolved in favour of the paying party."

20.10 The court will therefore have to determine whether the sums claimed are for *reasonable items* (*i.e.* should those items have been incurred at all) and whether the amounts claimed are reasonable for those items. Thus consider a case where a party has required his solicitor to conduct the litigation in an unreasonable way. As indicated before in essence a bill is computed on the basis of time spent. It is a notorious fact that plaintiffs vary greatly in their degree of patience. Suppose that a plaintiff in a personal injuries case calls into his solicitor's office for an hour's chat about the case every week even though nothing happened on the case to require the client's attendance for months at a time? The solicitor would have charged that amount of time to the client. Is it reasonable to require the loser to pay this sum? If the district judge determines that the number of hours spent in attendance upon the plaintiff is excessive and served no real purpose he is likely to disallow the claim for such hours. The outcome of course will be that any items disallowed as against the paying party, the loser, will have to be charged by the solicitor to his own client, the winner. It is therefore always important to remind the client at the stage where one thinks he may be requiring his solicitor to conduct the litigation unreasonably that he himself may have to pay for excessive time spent on his affairs.

Secondly the items must be *reasonable in amount.* This is a simple matter of local practice. For example if for routine High Court litigation in the area in question solicitors are being permitted to charge say £50 per hour and the current case is a routine one, if the solicitor wished to charge £75 per hour his bill would be disallowed or "taxed down" by a corresponding amount so that for instance if he claimed that he had spent 20 hours on the client's case in respect of which he was claiming £75 per hour, *i.e.* £1,500, the district judge would reduce this claim to the going rate of £50 per hour, *i.e.* £1,000.   **20.11**

The standard basis is applied in two routine situations.

1.   It is the basis on which the loser is required to pay the winner in ordinary litigation.

2.   It is the basis on which the legal aid fund pays an assisted person's solicitor.

It is therefore easy enough to see that in a routine case where a client has legal aid the legal aid fund's charge ought not to take effect. This is because since the standard basis of taxation is to be applied the losing party would be required to pay the winner's costs on exactly the same basis as the legal aid fund is required to pay the winner's solicitors costs. If there is no difference between the two therefore there is no need for the charge to come into operation and thus not only will the client get his damages untouched but also any contribution that he has to pay will be returned to him.   **20.12**

This is not however inevitably the case. It may be for example that the costs of some particular part of the proceedings were not awarded against the other party (see note on costs on interlocutory applications hereafter) or it may be that a payment into court was rejected and the plaintiff failed to beat the payment into court (see para. 12.02) so that a considerable proportion of the costs is eventually borne by the legally aided party.

However in routine litigation it will commonly be the case now that the winning legally aided person's solicitor will recover the costs in full from the loser.

20.13   The *indemnity* basis is a more generous basis and provides that where any doubts about the propriety of charging some item arise in a case the benefit of the doubt is to be given not to the *paying party* as in taxation on the standard basis but to the *party who is to receive* the amount. This basis is only likely to be awarded where the loser's conduct has in some way been disapproved of by the court. In negotiations between parties for settlement it may be possible sometimes to ask for payment of costs on this basis. It might for example be thought particularly appropriate in the case of settling an action for defamation.

20.14   Those are the *bases* of taxation *between the parties*. It is now appropriate to mention the "solicitor and own client basis."
   Here we are not concerned with an application made against some other person. A solicitor will draw up his own bill deliver it to the client and expect it to be paid. A client however does have the right to challenge his own solicitor's bill, in which case again it must be taxed by the court. As one would expect however since it is the client himself who is to pay the bill a considerably more generous basis is applied and the basis is the so-called solicitor and own client basis. This is the same as the indemnity basis but there are three modifications to it:—

1.   In so far as reasonableness is concerned it is deemed reasonable to incur expenditure on items which the client has expressly or impliedly approved.

2.   Amounts incurred are reasonable if the client also approved these amounts (*i.e.* in advance).

3.   It is however unreasonable to incur expenditure on unusual items unless the client was specifically warned in advance that those items might not be allowed on a taxation *inter partes*.

20.15   In the High Court there is only one scale of costs. There are no fixed amounts, the amounts to be allowed being within the discretion of the taxing officer. The scale merely dictates how the bill should be drawn up.
   It is now appropriate to consider costs in the county court. The same bases of taxation apply but there is a further restriction and it is one which is important to draw to the client's attention.

20.16   The county court scales, of which there are four, show certain maximum sums for items in litigation which are fixed by reference to the amount recovered if the plaintiff wins, or that claimed by the plaintiff if the defendant wins. The following are the scales.

1.   *Lower scale* for a sum of money claimed or recovered exceeding £25 but not exceeding £100.

2.   *Scale 1* for a sum of money exceeding £100 but not exceeding £500.

3.   *Scale 2* for a sum of money exceeding £500 but not exceeding £3,000.

4.   *Scale 3* for a sum of money over £3,000.

Accordingly in county court litigation the scales give certain maxima for individual items and when the bill is drawn up the amount claimed for any given item must not exceed the appropriate maximum allowed on the scale. However the district judge may exceed the scale maxima when the judge orders otherwise. Thus at the end of a case of considerable complexity if one wished to ask for authority to claim higher amounts than the maxima allowed one should make application to the judge at the end of the trial.

It should be noted that following the case of *Forey* v. *London Buses Limited*, *The Times*, January 30, 1991 it is established that the county court does have the power to order costs to be paid on the High Court scale. It is anticipated that this is likely to be an important power in the early future given the uplift in the jurisdiction of the county court so that cases for relatively substantial amounts will be brought there. At the time of writing it is anticipated that early changes will be made to the system and levels of the county court scales possibly by removal of the maxima at least for scales which correspond to the higher ranges of awards. Thus county court scales will be brought into line with the present High Court scale on which there is no maximum.

It is now appropriate to discuss a number of miscellaneous matters before returning to the procedure for taxation for costs.

RESTRICTION ON COUNSEL'S FEES

It is provided that no costs are allowed on taxation in respect of counsel **20.17** attending an interlocutory application before master or district judge unless the master or district judge has certified the attendance as proper in the circumstances. It should not be understood from this that it is impossible to get this certificate. If the matter is a difficult one which requires argument, for example an application for summary judgment or an interim payment, or sometimes on a matter relating to the propriety of discovery or further and better particulars it may be highly appropriate to brief counsel in the High Court. At the end of the hearing one should ask the district judge dealing with the matter to certify that the application was proper for counsel in which case counsel's fees, if one is successful, can be claimed from the opponent. It would however not be appropriate to brief counsel on some mundane and purely procedural matter. If one did so then the fees would inevitably be disallowed on taxation.

INTERLOCUTORY COSTS

There may be a number of interlocutory hearings as the case proceeds to **20.18** trial. At the end of each interlocutory hearing it is important to ensure that some order for costs is made. Examples of the orders that are possible would be:

Costs in the cause

This is the most common form of order. It means in effect that whoever wins **20.19** the eventual trial will also recover from his opponent the costs of the interlocutory application. It is appropriate in purely routine interlocutory applications which have done nothing but procedurally progress the case.

Plaintiff's (or defendant's) costs in any event

20.20   This is different from costs in the cause. It means that regardless of who succeeds at the trial the named person will nevertheless recover the costs of this application. It implies some criticism of the conduct of the other party. It might for example be appropriate where the other party has refused to give further and better particulars of his pleading even though it was manifestly obvious that such ought to be given.

Costs thrown away

20.21   An order for costs in this form covers costs which have been wasted in some way due to the default of a party. An example is where a default judgment has been obtained by the plaintiff after the defendant by some oversight failed to return his acknowledgment of service to the court in time. If the defendant can show some merit in defending the case he may be able to get the judgment set aside but will inevitably then be ordered to pay the costs thrown away.

Costs of the day

20.22   This order involves costs which have been wasted by the necessity for an adjournment. They will be ordered to be paid by the party who has been responsible for the necessity for the adjournment.

Costs reserved

20.23   In essence this means the same as costs in the cause, so that the winner of the eventual trial receives the costs of the interlocutory stage also. The difference from costs in the cause is that the matter may be reopened before the trial judge if the circumstances require it. If however the matter is not reopened, or no different order is made then it means precisely the same as costs in the cause.

COSTS ON A COUNTER CLAIM

20.24   It must be remembered that a counter claim need not have any relationship to the plaintiff's cause of action. Examples have been given previously. Thus a plaintiff who sues for defamation may have a counter claim for a debt made against him. If both parties succeed in the action, *i.e.* the plaintiff succeeds in his claim and the defendant in the counter claim then the usual form of order is that the plaintiff obtains costs on his claim and the defendant costs on his counter claim.

It should be carefully noted that the defendant can only recover the costs of his counter claim and not the costs of unsuccessfully defending the plaintiff's claim. If the claim and counter claim do have no relationship to each other it is easy enough to see what aspect of the work relates to which but it may well be that if they arise out of the same incident (*e.g.* an accident for which each blames the other) that the costs of claim and counter claim are considerably intermingled. For example suppose the plaintiff who has suffered moderate injuries sues the defendant for damages arising out of a road traffic accident. The defendant has suffered very serious injuries and counter claims contending that it was the plaintiff who caused the accident. At the trial the judge finds for the plaintiff but with a 25 per cent. degree of contributory negligence on the plaintiff's part. In other words the defendant has succeeded on his counter claim also although with a finding of 75 per cent. contributory negligence on *his* part. Suppose now that the extent of the plaintiff's injuries means that in principle he would be awarded £10,000, he will now be awarded £7,500. Suppose however that the defendant who is very seriously injured would have been awarded £100,000. The finding of 75 per cent. contributory negligence means he will actually get £25,000. Who then has won for the purpose of the issue of costs? The answer is that the court has the power to make a special judgment on the balance between the claim and counter claim and make an appropriate order for costs at the time.

TWO OR MORE DEFENDANTS

As we have already seen where the plaintiff succeeds against only one of several defendants the court has to protect the successful defendant. This is done as we have seen by an order that the losing defendant in effect pays everybody's costs either by the mechanism of a Bullock Order whereby the plaintiff pays the winning defendant but then recovers these costs from the unsuccessful defendant or a Sanderson Order where the losing defendant pays the successful defendant's costs direct. It is suggested that, in personal injuries litigation anyway, a Sanderson Order will be more appropriate as it is in any event a much tidier way of bringing matters to an end and since all defendants will in effect be insured the successful defendant is at no risk as to costs. **20.25**

AGREEING COSTS

At the end of a case, however bitterly litigated, it is common practice for the loser to offer to agree costs. In such a case the winner's solicitor will prepare a list of the items for which he is claiming and the rates at which he proposes to claim for them and give some overall indication of the hours spent on the case. These are submitted by letter. There will then be some negotiation and in the majority of cases a mutually agreeable outcome will be achieved. It should be noted that even where one is acting for a legally aided party it is possible to agree costs with one's opponent provided one is willing to accept the sum achieved in full settlement for costs and no further claim will be made to the Legal Aid Board. In such cases one has to submit details of the costs agreed to the Legal Aid Board so that they may confirm that they have no objection, but in a routine case there is no reason why they should have any such objection given that no claim is being made for costs on the fund. If the client has paid a contribution this will in due course be returned to him as well. **20.26**

The reasons for agreeing costs are as follows:—

(i) The process of taxation is lengthy and time consuming and one may well wait some months for a taxation hearing. **20.27**

(ii) Drawing up High Court bills (despite recent rules to simplify them) is not work which solicitors themselves now tend to do. For many years a specialist sub-profession of costs draftsmen has existed. Larger firms employ their **20.28** own costs draftsmen who will prepare all bills. Medium sized and smaller firms however are likely to go to freelance costs draftsmen who charge on a straight commission basis for drawing up bills of costs. The commission basis varies around the country but may be between five per cent. and 7½ per cent. of the bill. Consequently if one has a bill of say £10,000 drawn up and the costs draftsman is charging 6 per cent. for drawing it up one can immediately see that £600 of the solicitor's profit costs have been lost. Moreover no charge can be made on taxation for drawing up a bill of costs unless there are special circumstances. Therefore this money is simply lost to the solicitor and provides a powerful incentive for him to save the cost of having the bill formally prepared and to agree costs.

20.29 (iii) There is a court fee on taxation to be paid by the losing party and the fee is currently five per cent. of the bill. Again therefore if one has a £10,000 bill the losing party may be facing a court fee of £500 for the taxation process. Again this is money lost to the client and provides a powerful incentive to avoid it by agreeing costs.

20.30 (iv) There is the psychological factor that after lengthy litigation when the judge pronounces his final judgment (subject to any decision to appeal) both sides' solicitors are usually glad to get that particular matter over and turn their mind to others. To prolong the matter by continuing to argue about costs and to wait for what might be a very lengthy taxation involving perhaps some hours in the case of a substantial bill, is unwelcome and there is a powerful incentive to finalise matters.

20.31 (v) Finality is also in the client's interest. It may be that the client's own liability for costs cannot be assessed until the process of trying to agree the bill with the other side has taken place.

20.32 If agreement is not possible however, there will have to be a taxation hearing. The bill must be prepared in proper itemised form in the prescribed way and an appointment taken out. This ought to be within three months of the end of the case although considerably longer is often allowed within the court's discretion after an attempt to agree costs has failed. Taxation is by a taxing master in London and a district judge elsewhere and in the county court. The bill must be lodged at court together with all necessary papers and vouchers including instructions to counsel, brief to counsel, copies of the pleadings, etc. A copy of the bill must be served on every other party with the notice of the appointment endorsed on it. In the county court the court serve this.

A date for taxation is fixed in the High Court. In the county court a date will be fixed in a case of any complexity though a district judge may issue a provisional certificate stating the amount of costs he proposes to allow which gives either party a chance to accept this without a formal hearing. However if either party objects within 14 days a hearing is fixed.

At the taxation the taxing officer will go through the bill item by item and listen to objections either to items in principle or to the amount claimed for individual items. If he accedes to the objection he will then *tax off* or disallow the item, *i.e.* he will say that the item is not within the standard basis of taxation and will therefore be borne by the winner personally. At the end of the taxation the amounts disallowed or taxed off will be totalled up, deducted from the preliminary total of the bill and the final amount is then payable by the losing party.

Any party dissatisfied with the decisions made on taxation may request a reconsideration by stating his objections by letter. The taxing officer will then reconsider his decision and notify the parties of his decision made on the reconsideration. Thereafter there is a further review of taxation possible by a judge, usually assisted by assessors. Again application is made by letter.

We have now considered the procedure on taxation. It must not be forgotten however that taxation is not appropriate in every case. We have already remarked on instances where some different procedure is appropriate and we shall now briefly review these.

FIXED COSTS

It will be recalled that in both High Court and county court a plaintiff is only   **20.33**
allowed to claim fixed costs if the case terminates in early judgment or payment. Thus:—

1. In the High Court the fixed costs endorsement must be completed on any writ claiming a liquidated sum. If the defendant then pays the amount claimed together with interest as claimed (remembering that interest should be specified and computed) and the amount allowed for fixed costs direct to the plaintiff within 14 days of service of the writ then those are the only costs which the plaintiff may claim as against the defendant. The plaintiff will inevitably therefore in such a case have to bear some solicitor and client costs.

2. If the plaintiff obtains judgment in default of notice of intention to defend or of defence in the High Court again there is a specified allowance for fixed costs.

3. In the county court there is similar provision for fixed costs where the action ends by a payment of the full amount within 14 days of in default of defence or in some circumstances on summary judgment. In those cases the plaintiff will only be able to claim a fixed amount stated in the rules.

Finally it will be remembered that in cases where a claim is made for an unliquidated amount, *e.g.* damages in a personal injuries case, costs are taxed and not fixed.

ASSESSED COSTS

A party may apply at trial for assessed costs rather than taxed costs. This is   **20.34**
usually done either where the matter has come to trial swiftly with no great complexity and is particularly appropriate in certain kinds of cases, *e.g.* especially cases where there is a claim for arrears of rent or for possession by a mortgagee. As has previously been remarked the actual procedure on taxation is time consuming and long drawn out and yet with a difficult defendant there is really little prospect of agreeing costs. Accordingly one can ask at trial for costs to be assessed and can suggest figures to the judge. The figure to be allowed on assessment tends to be rather less than a party would be likely to receive on taxation but it does avoid the cost and delay of

taxation and if it is thought probable that it will be difficult to recover costs from the opponent it is advantageous for a successful plaintiff.

In addition the Area Office can assess the costs of a legally aided party in two cases:—

(i) Where the total amount payable to solicitor and counsel will not exceed £1,000.

Example:

After discovery of documents in a very straightforward case in the county court it becomes obvious to the legally aided plaintiff's solicitor that the case is hopeless. The plaintiff accepts the advice to discontinue the case and the defendants agree not to ask for costs (bearing in mind that because of s.17 of the Legal Aid Act 1988 they would have been unlikely to get an order for costs anyway). Instead of going through a taxation the plaintiff's solicitor may apply by letter for his costs to be assessed by the Area Office if the sum claimed is less than £1,000.

(ii) Where in a case where a legally aided plaintiff has won or achieved a negotiated settlement and his opponent is to pay costs, if the solicitor and counsel are willing to accept the amount offered by the opponent in full settlement the Area Director may assess the reasonableness of the costs offered.

Example:

A legally aided plaintiff wins and obtains an order for costs payable on the standard basis by the defendant and a legal aid taxation. The plaintiff's solicitor agrees costs with the defendant to avoid a taxation. He notifies the Area Office that he does not wish to claim any costs from the legal aid fund and is satisfied with those obtainable from the defendant. The Area Office assess the reasonableness of the costs and, since there is no call on the legal aid fund will authorise the return of any contribution made to the legally aided plaintiff and discharge his certificate.

21. Appeals in Civil Proceedings

INTERLOCUTORY ORDERS

21.01 Where a district registrar makes an interlocutory order there is generally an appeal as of right. It is not necessary to show any specific error or misuse of discretion by the district registrar and one is entitled to a re-hearing. The appeal is to a judge sitting in chambers and must be issued within seven days or in the case of an appeal from a master within five days of the order appealed from. Solicitors have rights of audience before a judge in chambers. The only important case where there is a different line of appeal is in the case of an assessment of damages under R.S.C., Ord. 37 where appeal lies direct to the Court of Appeal against the amount of damages awarded by the district registrar.

ORDERS MADE BY COUNTY COURT REGISTRAR

21.02 Appeal lies as of right to a judge in chambers which must be made by notice of appeal, filed and served on the opposite party within five days.

ARBITRATION

21.03 There is in principle no appeal from a registrar sitting as arbitrator. However an application can be made to the judge for the arbitrator's award to be set aside on the grounds of:

1. lack of jurisdiction; or
2. misconduct; or
3. material error of law on the face of the record.

APPEAL AGAINST INTERLOCUTORY ORDERS MADE BY A HIGH COURT JUDGE

21.04 Leave is usually required in the case of an interlocutory order. However the definition of "interlocutory order" is vague and there is a great deal of case law. The distinction between interlocutory orders and final orders is often far from clear. Reference should be made to Order 59/1/16 of the White Book.

APPEAL FROM FINAL ORDERS BY HIGH COURT JUDGE

21.05 Appeal lies to the Court of Appeal and generally no leave is required. Appeal is made by serving notice of appeal within four weeks on all opposite parties and thereafter setting the notice of appeal down within seven days from the date on which it was served.

FINAL ORDERS MADE BY COUNTY COURT JUDGE

21.06 Appeal lies to the Court of Appeal without leave where the amount involved is in excess of *i.e.* £2,500 in tort or contract. If money is not in issue (*e.g.* an application for an injunction) no leave is required. Leave is required below that financial limit.

Evidence

22. Introduction to Evidence

The law of evidence is a difficult and technical subject. It is based mainly on **22.01** case law, much of it stemming from over a century ago, with a few piecemeal statutory reforms culminating in the Police and Criminal Evidence Act 1984, and the Criminal Justice Act 1988. Unfortunately even in the case of this later statute no attempt was made to provide a comprehensive code for the admissibility of evidence in criminal cases and a number of opportunities to reform the law, *e.g.* on corroboration were missed. In a much quoted phrase it has justifiably been said that the law of evidence is:—

"Less a structure than a pile of builder's debris."

The law of evidence is often said to be the same for civil as for criminal cases "subject to exceptions." However the number of these exceptions is so large that the idea is now unrealistic, in particular:—

1. the Civil Evidence Acts 1968 and 1972 have made many changes in the law for civil cases only;

2. in civil cases the parties may, and often do, by consent waive the strict rules of evidence. This is not possible in criminal cases;

3. the rules of evidence tend to take on less importance where, as in the ordinary civil case, the person ruling on the law is the same as the person trying the facts, *i.e.* a judge sitting alone. The rules of evidence are therefore at their most vital where these two functions are separate as in a Crown Court criminal trial before a judge and jury, and almost all modern case law of importance deals with criminal appeals after jury trial.

The law of evidence presents unqualified problems of coherent and sensible arrangement of topic. With one or two exceptions there is no immediately obvious order of topics which logic demands should be followed and many of the topics interrelate so that it is hard to follow one fully until another later topic has been studied. The following order is one which it is suggested makes the subject most comprehensible at this level.

It should be remembered particularly that in a text of this length it is only possible to discuss the mainstream of the law. There is no space for material which might go some way to helping explain the background to the law and making it more comprehensible namely an introduction to the history of evidence and criminal procedure; a discussion of academic criticism; minority or dissenting opinion; or Commonwealth or American authorities.

Whilst what follows is generally accurate, it is impossible to simplify this particular subject without losing something in the way of total accuracy. Thus to avoid starting almost every section with the saving phrase "subject to minor exceptions" there is no reference at all to matters of no practical importance. Thus for example, in the section on interrogation of suspects, there is a reference to the fact that a person has a right to remain silent and not reply to police questions. In fact there are a number of statutes which specifically *do* require a person to reply to police questions in certain circumstances, especially under the Road Traffic Acts. There are other cases apart from that in this text where total accuracy has had to be sacrificed in the interests of concision. This should always be borne in mind. Where cases arc cited and sometimes the facts given this is not with a view to necessarily having the name of the case or it facts remembered. It is simply that some students prefer to have a case name on which to mentally "hang" a principle. The facts are only given because they provide a striking illustration of the principle. The cases mentioned in the text have been chosen with this in mind and are often by no means the leading case on the point which they illustrate.

22.02 It has been remarked above that there is now a considerable separation between the rules of evidence applicable in civil trials and those applicable in criminal trials. It is important not to confuse the two areas. The law of evidence applicable in civil trials has now been considerably simplified because of the Civil Evidence Acts 1968 and 1972. Therefore it should not be forgotten when considering a civil case that much of the law contained in the following text is of no relevance. In particular:—

1. all witnesses in a civil case are competent and compellable to testify provided they are able to take the oath;

2. in a civil case there is no requirement of corroboration;

3. in a civil case the character of the parties is generally irrelevant;

4. none of the wealth of peculiar rules applicable as exceptions to the hearsay rules in criminal cases now apply in civil cases because the 1968 and 1972 Civil Evidence Acts provide a comprehensive code for the admission of hearsay evidence in civil proceedings.

Most of the text that follows therefore is relevant only to the consideration of criminal trials. Where there are separate rules applicable in civil proceedings this is clearly indicated.

23. The Function of the Law of Evidence

The essence of the law of evidence it that it regulates what material may or may not be put before the person who is trying the facts, (*i.e.* the jury in the Crown Court) and the manner in which those facts may be proved. In so far as the law of evidence is concerned the judge has two very important functions and these are:—

(i) to hear argument on items of evidence whose admissibility is disputed in the absence of the jury. If the judge then rules an item inadmissible then when the jury are recalled to court the item of evidence may not be put before them, indeed they are not told of its existence or even why they were sent out of court. **23.01**

(ii) to control the jury in summing up. In the course of the judge's summing up as well as directing them carefully on the law he will review the facts for them, reminding them of the salient points given in evidence by the witnesses and then direct them on the rules of evidence. This direction must be considerably more than a mere direction for the jury to look carefully at whether they think a certain witness was a truthful sort of person and act accordingly. As the law of evidence has developed detailed and sometimes highly technical forms of direction, often in particular words, have to be given to the jury in relation to certain types of evidence. The meaning of this will become clear after the whole text has been studied but in particular the judge must give clear directions to the jury on the burden and standard of proof applicable, the question of corroboration for the evidence of certain types of witnesses, and many other instances. Failure to give proper directions at this stage will often lead to any subsequent conviction being quashed on appeal. The judge's direction to the jury is taken down verbatim by a shorthand writer and, if a question of appeal arises, a transcript is subsequently prepared. Failure to direct properly, or even one single loose phrase in summing up, may be fatal to a conviction. **23.02**

From what has been said so far we can pass to one of the greatest problems of the law of evidence in criminal cases. That is that the law of evidence is virtually the same for all criminal cases, that is whether the accused is tried before a judge and jury or before magistrates. Yet for many of the concepts which are important in the Crown Court trial there is no equivalent in magistrates court proceedings because the same magistrates deal with matters of law (including admissibility of evidence) and with matters of fact. Thus if one wishes to object to the admissibility of an item of evidence in the magistrates court the item of evidence in question is actually put before the magistrates so that its admissibility can be considered. It is suggested that even if they do subsequently rule it inadmissible they will often be unable to **23.03** put out of their minds the fact that they have seen it and what is contained in it. It may be helpful to give an example of this:—

> The defendant is said to have made a confession under interrogation in the police station. He contends that he made the confession because he was frightened, tired and did not think the police would allow him to go home unless he made a statement saying what he thought the police wanted to hear. In the Crown Court the admissibility of this confession would be tried by the judge in the absence of the jury and if he concluded that the confession was indeed unreliable because of the matters contended for by the defendant then the jury would never get to hear of the confession. In the magistrates court however the same magistrates will inevitably see the confession and even if they do consider it inadmissible may be swayed by what is contained in it.

23.04 Thus there is a problem about ruling on admissibility. Likewise there is no proper equivalent to the vital stage in a Crown Court trial at which the judge directs the jury about matters of evidence. In a magistrates court the theory is that the magistrates direct themselves about evidence. They do of course have a legally qualified clerk who may be asked to retire with them when they consider their decision and may remind them of the rules of evidence. There is however no way of knowing whether this did or did not occur and in what terms if at all the clerk did remind them of the matters on which they should direct themselves. In the magistrates court the best that a defending advocate can do is to draw the magistrates' attention to the relevant rules of evidence and explain the rationale of them; and to suggest that the magistrates ought to direct themselves very carefully. Again it may be helpful to give an example:—

> In the Crown Court where there is an accomplice of the accused who has pleaded guilty to the offence and is now testifying for the Crown the judge must direct the jury that they should view the accomplice's evidence with caution and even if they are inclined to believe it they should look for corroboration of that evidence because it may be dangerous to convict without it. In the magistrates court the defence advocate simply reminds the magistrates that the prosecution witness falls within the category of accomplices and that if it were a Crown Court trial the judge would have to direct the jury very carefully on the matter of corroboration and suggests that the magistrates ought to act similarly and to look to see if there is corroboration in the case and to refuse to convict unless there is such corroboration. The advocate then hopes that when the magistrates retire, if they seek advice from their clerk that his advice reflects what has just been said and that the magistrates have taken careful note of it.

> In such a situation therefore if one is required to discuss what needs to be said about an accomplice witness in the magistrates court it is quite pointless talking about "the judge warning the jury." One should discuss the matter in the terms suggested, that is to point out that the defence advocate ought to indicate to the magistrates the dangers of acting on the uncorroborated testimony of the accomplice and that the magistrates ought accordingly to direct themselves appropriately when they retire.

A question which arises both in theory and in practice then is whether one **23.05** should bother taking objections to the admissibility of evidence in the magistrates court. Since the magistrates will almost inevitably have to hear the evidence in dispute before they can decide whether or not it falls foul of some rule which would lead to its exclusion it is sometimes suggested that this is pointless. In most cases where the accused has a choice as to whether he should be tried by the magistrates court or the Crown Court if they are difficult points of evidence involved this may well on its own be the conclusive factor in favour of the Crown Court namely that the procedure for determining objections to items of evidence is so much more satisfactory there. Nonetheless even in the magistrates court it is suggested that technical objections to matters of evidence should, in the appropriate circumstances, be taken. Whilst cynical advocates often contend that it is impossible to underestimate the mental capacities of magistrates and no doubt every advocate can cite a horror story of some case in which this has been demonstrated by some foolish interjection or irrelevant question from the bench, it is suggested that one ought always to act on the basis that the magistrates are capable of following arguments concerning the technicalities of evidence and that they will be fair minded enough, having ruled that a certain item is inadmissible, to put it out of their minds and if the totality of what is left is not sufficient evidence against the defendant, thereafter to acquit him.

Accordingly in the text that follows, except where specifically indicated, one should take it that in a criminal trial the rules of evidence are the same for the magistrates court as for the Crown Court though there must be a considerable adaptation in the terminology used to indicate how the courts will deal with problems of evidence.

24. Burden and Standard of Proof

The burden of proof in civil cases

24.01 The party who asserts a fact must prove it. Therefore in the normal case, it is for the party who is responsible for bringing the action to court to prove his case. So in a civil case, the plaintiff must prove all the ingredients of the tort, *e.g.* duty, breach and damage; or the existence of a contract and its breach by the defendant. It is thus said that the plaintiff bears the burden of proof; this means that if at the end of the trial the trier of *fact* (*i.e.* almost invariably a judge sitting alone in a civil case, unless the issue concerns malicious prosecution, defamation or fraud when a jury may be involved) is undecided between the truth of the plaintiff's version and that of the defendant, he must enter judgment for the defendant, for the plaintiff has failed to persuade him and it was the plaintiff who had the burden. One might think that at the conclusion of the trial in the High Court or county court the judge would be reluctant to admit that he was unable to make his mind up between the truth of the versions of the opposing parties. In fact, however, there are a surprising number of cases where a judge has been willing to admit just that (see for example *T.(H)* v. *T(E)* [1971] 1 W.L.R. 429 and *Wauchope* v. *Mordecai* [1970] 1 W.L.R. 317). In both cases the judge, admitting that he could not decide between the truth of the respective versions allowed matters to be decided by reference to the burden of proof, so that in each case the party who bore the burden of proof lost.

The standard of proof in civil cases

24.02 The plaintiff is required to prove matters, not so that the judge is 100 per cent. convinced, nor so that the judge is satisfied beyond reasonable doubt, but simply on a "preponderance of probabilities" which means that the judge must consider that it is more likely that the plaintiff's version is true than that of the defendant.

The burden of proof in a criminal case

24.03 The prosecution bear the burden of proving every fact in issue. So that, for example, in the case of a murder by stabbing, the prosecution will bear the burden of proving that the act was carried out by the accused and that he had the necessary intent to kill, or do grievous bodily harm. This rule, that the prosecution have the burden of proving all facts in issue, is exemplified in the leading case of *Woolmington* v. *D.P.P.* [1935] A.C. 462.

> The accused had visited his estranged wife in an effort to persuade her to return to him. He had taken with him a loaded shotgun, and on his version, this was to be used to threaten suicide if his wife should refuse to return. In fact, he shot his wife dead, and his defence was that this had happened accidentally as he was showing her how he meant to kill himself with the shotgun. At his trial for murder, the trial judge directed the jury that once the fact of the killing had been proved, it was for Woolmington to satisfy the jury of the truth of his defence of accident. The accused

THE BURDEN OF PROOF IN A CRIMINAL CASE

appealed unsuccessfully to the Court of Criminal Appeal and thereafter appealed to the House of Lords. The House of Lords held that the judge had misdirected the jury. In a criminal case (subject to certain well-defined exceptions) the prosecution have the burden of proving every fact in issue which includes the mental state of the accused. Once, therefore, he had raised the defence of accident, it was for the prosecution to disprove that defence.

There are, however, some exceptional cases where the accused does have to prove his defence. This is the case where the accused raised the defences of insanity or diminished responsibility and in these cases, the accused has to prove the truth of his defence to the satisfaction of the jury, although only on the civil standard of proof.   **24.04**

There are many other exceptions to the general rule contained in a variety of statutes, but we are now only concerned with one further exception. Under this exception, where an accused is charged with doing some act which would be unlawful unless he were in possession of some form of licence or qualification, then it is for him to positively prove that he does have the licence or qualification and not for the prosecution to prove the negative (which in the nature of things it would often be very difficult for them to do).   **24.05**

This exception is contained in the Magistrates' Court Act 1980 Section 101 (which repeats verbatim the terms of Section 81 of the Magistrates' Courts Act 1952). This section reads:—

> "Where the defendant to an information or complaint relies for his defence on any exception, exemption, proviso, excuse or qualification, whether or not it accompanies the description of the offence or matter of complaint in the enactment creating the offence or on which the complaint is founded, the burden of proving the exception, exemption, proviso, excuse or qualification shall be on him; and this notwithstanding that the offence or complaint contains an allegation negativing the exception, exemption, proviso, excuse or qualification."

As is apparent from the title of the enactment, this provision (like its predecessor) applies only in the magistrates courts. One would, therefore, have had different rules of evidence in a situation covered by the provision depending on whether the trial were in the magistrates court or the Crown Court. Until 1974, this was indeed believed to be the case. However, in 1974, a case held that the previous Section 81 of the 1952 Act was merely declaratory of the common law and thus that the same rule applied in the Crown Court. The case, the facts of which provide a clear illustration of how the rule works whichever court is involved, is *R.* v. *Edwards* [1975] Q.B. 27.

> The accused was charged with selling intoxicating liquor without a license. He contended that it was for the prosecution to satisfy the court beyond reasonable doubt that he did not have the license to sell intoxicating liquor. The Court of Appeal held that where a person contends that he is entitled to do some act which is otherwise prohibited, it is for him to prove his entitlement. This ruling is clearly one of simple commonsense and may perhaps in part be prompted by a certain sense of frustration with the conduct of the accused in Edwards' case, since prima facie, it would seem

221

extremely simple for a person who contends that he has a license to do some act, to actually produce the piece of paper which constitutes the license.

24.06 Where none of the exceptions mentioned above apply, however, the rule is that by the end of their own case, the prosecution must have laid a clear basis in evidence to establish the accused's guilt of the crime charged. If they fail to do so, they run the risk of the defence successfully submitting that there is

"no case to answer," *i.e.* that the case should be dismissed there and then without calling upon the defence to put forward their evidence. The factors to be taken into account by a court in considering such a submission, are set out in a *Practice Direction* at [1962] 1 All E.R. 448. According to this Practice Direction, a judge should rule in favour of the submission of no case to answer where:—

1. there is no evidence to prove an essential ingredient in the alleged offence; or

2. where the evidence adduced by the prosecution has been so discredited in cross-examination or is so manifestly unreliable that no reasonable tribunal could safely convict on it.

24.07 The fact that the prosecution has in the normal case the burden of proving every fact in issue, does not, however, mean that the prosecution must, by the end of its case, anticipate and negative every possible defence, remembering that the accused (with the single exception of an alibi defence in a trial in the Crown Court) is not obliged to give the prosecution any advance notice of the defence on which he intends to rely at trial. The accused wishing to raise a general defence in a criminal trial, has to discharge what is called an *evidential burden*. This does not mean that he has to satisfy anyone of the truth of his defence, but he does have to satisfy the judge that there is sufficient evidence of his defence (and very little will do) to make his defence a fit and proper issue to be left to the jury, and one which the prosecution must be called upon to negative or disprove. This evidential burden on the accused is sometimes also called "the burden of adducing evidence" or "the burden of passing the judge." It should not be confused with the burden which the prosecution always have of satisfying the jury at the end of the case, their burden being known as the "legal burden."

To illustrate the difference between the two burdens, let us consider an accused in a criminal trial who wished to put forward any one of what one might describe as general or partial defences, *e.g.* accident, duress, alibi, self defence, etc. In such a case, the accused must adduce *some* evidence at least of the nature of his defence. It does not follow that he must give this evidence himself, or even call his own witnesses. He may extract the necessary evidence by the cross-examination of prosecution witnesses. Unless, however, *some* evidence has been given about the nature of his defence, at the end of the trial, when the judge sums up all outstanding issues for the jury, he will be entitled to disregard any defence which is entirely speculative, or for which no foundation at all in evidence has been laid. If, however, the accused has adduced some evidence of his defence, then it will be for the prosecution to positively disprove it beyond reasonable doubt and the judge will explain this carefully to the jury. Another illustration of a defence on which the accused would have an evidential burden, would be, for instance, mechanical defect on a charge of reckless driving. See for example the case of *R.* v. *Spurge* [1961] 2 Q.B. 205. In this case, the accused contended that an accident in which he had been involved and in respect of which he was being prosecuted for dangerous driving had in fact been caused by mechanical defect in the steering of the motor car. The court held that all that Spurge had to do was to satisfy the evidential burden, that is to raise some positive facts in evidence, which would allow the court to consider mechanical defect as a "live" issue and that having done so, the prosecution would then be called upon to disprove this defence. On the facts of the case, the court held that Spurge's allegation of mechanical defect was mere speculation, and that he had not in fact raised any evidence at all sufficient to leave it as a live issue.

The standard of proof in criminal cases

The prosecution must prove the accused's guilt to a very high standard of certainty. The phrase "beyond a reasonable doubt" is the most universally approved formula, but other forms of words have from time to time been approved for a judge's direction to the jury, *e.g.* "so that you are really sure of the accused's guilt." When the jury consider the accused's defence, they do not have to decide whether it is true as such, but only whether they are left with a reasonable doubt that it might be true. If they decide that there is such a doubt they must acquit.   **24.08**

In those few instances previously mentioned where the accused must satisfy the jury of the truth of something (*i.e.* discharge the *legal* burden) rather than merely raise a triable defence (*i.e.* discharge the *evidential* burden), he need not satisfy the jury or magistrates to so high a standard of certainty as must the prosecution on the general issue. The standard required of an accused called upon to satisfy the jury of his defence (*e.g.* insanity, applicability of an exception or excuse under *R.* v. *Edwards* [1975] Q.B. 27) is the *civil* one, *i.e.* he must satisfy them on a balance of probabilities that his defence is true.

In the vast majority of cases where the accused has only an *evidential* burden, he does not have to satisfy anyone of the truth of what he says. He only has to produce sufficient evidence to satisfy the judge that the issue is fit to be left to the jury. Very little evidence will suffice for this, for if a judge wrongly withdrew a potential defence from the jury, an appeal against conviction would be bound to succeed.

In his summing-up to the jury, the burden and standard of proof are important matters with which the judge must deal. Failure to direct them adequately on these matters will almost always be considered sufficient grounds for a successful appeal. At the stage of his summing-up, the judge must remind the jury of the defences advanced by the accused, and deal with the facts adduced in support of each of them. Although in routine cases there will generally only be one defence (*e.g.* alibi or accident), it is by no means impossible to envisage cases where two or more defences are not mutually inconsistent, so that an accused might potentially be able to argue for more than one. For example, suppose that a large bully begins assaulting a much smaller person, say in a public house. A scuffle develops, in the course of which the bully is fatally stabbed. It might well be open on the facts to the accused charged with murder in such a case to allege the general defences of   **24.09** accident and self-defence and the partial defence of provocation, without these necessarily being inconsistent with each other. In such a case, it would no doubt be proper for the judge to direct the jury that they must consider all three possibilities and look to see whether the prosecution have disproved those possibilities beyond reasonable doubt. If would, of course, generally be most inadvisable for the accused to put forward inconsistent defences, *e.g.* to say to the jury that he was not the man involved and has a defence of alibi, but that if he is disbelieved on this, he contends that his action was in self-defence. This is undermining one's own credibility in an obvious way. Where an accused is foolish enough to adduce inconsistent defences, the judge has the right to direct the jury to consider only what one might call the accused's "first choice" defence (see *R. v. Bonnick* (1977) 66 Cr.App.Rep. 266 in which the judge directed the jury only to consider alibi and to ignore the issue of self-defence).

25. Methods of Proof

Matters must normally be proved by evidence which is admissible. This **25.01** usually takes the form of a witness testifying on oath as to matters which he has himself perceived with one or more of his five senses. However, other forms of evidence may, in some circumstances, be put before the court, for example, if the case concerns a dispute over the terms of a lease or a will, the document itself may be produced as evidence, or an object may be brought to court for the jury to see, *e.g.* an item of bloodstained clothing, or a weapon.

There are four examples of situations, however, where a court may treat a matter as established without evidence having been adduced at all. We shall now go on to consider these examples, which are:—

1. facts of which *judicial notice* is taken;

2. facts which are *formally admitted* by a party;

3. facts which are the subject of a *presumption*;

4. certain cases where the court may *infer* facts.

Judicial notice

Facts which will be judicially noticed are those which are so notorious as not **25.02** to be capable of being the subject of any dispute, or are readily ascertainable by reference to a proper source. The more important examples of cases where a judge will take judicial notice of a matter, rather than requiring evidence to be called about it are:—

MATTERS OF COMMON KNOWLEDGE

e.g. That a fortnight is too short a period for human gestation *R.* v. *Luffe* (1807) 8 East, 193.

That criminals have unhappy lives *Burns* v. *Edman* [1970] 2 Q.B. 541.

That Elvis Presley was popular and performed mainly in the United States *R.C.A.* v. *Pollard* [1982] 3 W.L.R. 1007.

POLITICAL AND ADMINISTRATIVE MATTERS

After receiving an appropriate certificate from the Secretary of State, the court is obliged to judicially notice certain political matters, *e.g.* the recognition of a foreign sovereign, or as to whether a state of war exists.

LAW PROCEDURE AND CUSTOMS

Judges will take judicial notice without formal proof of what the law is, but will also sometimes judicially notice other matters, such as the existence of commercial customs, shipping customs, or the practice of conveyancers.

Formal admissions

CIVIL CASES

25.03 Facts may be formally admitted in civil cases by a party in advance of trial. The opposite party is then relieved of the obligation of proving the matter admitted, which is taken to be established. Such admissions may be made by letter between the parties, but more normally are admitted either:—

In the pleadings

Example:

25.04 The plaintiff in his statement of claim pleads the existence of an oral contract and says that a certain term is imported into the contract, because of previous dealings between the parties. In his defence, the defendant admits the existence of previous contracts containing the term (but goes on to say that the term was expressly varied here between the parties). The effect of this is thus to relieve the plaintiff of the obligation of proving the existence of previous contracts and the nature of the term that was imported into them. The dispute is now merely as to whether such term was expressly varied in the present case.

25.05 Or

In response to a "Notice to Admit Facts or to admit the authenticity of documents" served under R.S.C., Ord. 27, rr. 1–5, or C.C.R., Ord. 20, rr. 9–10

Under this rule a party who wishes to get his opponent to admit some fact without the need to call a witness to prove it at the trial may serve on his opponent a "Notice to Admit Facts" which specifies the fact required to be admitted. The party may use this procedure if for any reason he does not wish to call a witness, for instance in order to save time and costs, *e.g.* if the fact appears to be uncontroversial or the witness will be very expensive to call, or lives a long way away. The party receiving such notice may then either:

25.06 *Admit the fact.* This means that the other party is relieved from calling evidence about the fact at trial—it is taken as established, or alternatively,

25.07 *Not admit the fact.* If he does this then the first party must call the necessary evidence to properly prove the facts at trial. However, if the first party *succeeds* in proving the fact at trial, then *whoever wins the case at trial on the main issue* by virtue of R.S.C., Ord. 63, r. 3(5).

> "The costs of proving the facts shall be paid by the party who . . . refuses to admit them, unless the court otherwise orders."

Accordingly, the sanction for failing to admit a fact that one should have admitted, is a penalty in costs. Of course, if the party who served the notice fails to prove the fact at trial, the notice is of no effect whatever on costs. Let us consider two examples:—

Example 1:
Two cars driven respectively by P and D are in collision at a crossroads. On the back seat of P's car was a valuable painting, considered to be an authentic Flemish masterpiece of the 15th century. The painting is totally destroyed in the collision. There is a problem of establishing its authenticity and value. The leading expert on the work of the artist concerned charges extremely high fees for attending court as an expert witness. However, his written report says that the painting was authentic and was worth £100,000. P serves a notice asking D to admit the authenticity of the painting and its value. D does not admit this, but requires P to prove it at trial. Therefore, P calls the expert witness. The expert's evidence is accepted totally by the judge, who finds that the painting was authentic and was worth £100,000. However, he also concludes that D wins on liability, that is that the accident was actually caused by P himself. Although, therefore, P will inevitably be ordered to pay the costs of D for everything else involved in the trial, the judge, by the operation of this rule, will order that D pays P's costs of proving the authenticity and value of the painting.

Example 2:
The same facts apply as in the first example, but on this occasion P's expert witness's evidence is not accepted, the evidence of D's expert who values the painting at only £20,000 being preferred. Whoever wins here, the Notice to Admit Facts will be of no effect so the costs of calling the expert will follow the event.

FORMAL ADMISSIONS IN CRIMINAL CASES

In a criminal case a formal admission may be made by either prosecution, or **25.08** accused, and either at trial, or, more usually, before trial. If the accused makes an admission out of court, it must be made by, or be approved by, his solicitor of counsel (Section 10 Criminal Justice Act 1967). An admission may be withdrawn if good reason is shown, *e.g.* if it is shown that it was made in error.

Presumptions
Certain matters are presumed by the court to exist without proof. This **25.09** means that a person challenging the existence of a certain state of affairs, has the burden of disproving it, rather than vice versa. An example is the presumption of legitimacy, *e.g.* that a child born during the existence of marriage is legitimate, or the presumption of regularity expressed in the maxim *omnia praesumuntur rite ese acta.* Under this presumption, it is presumed, unless the contrary is proved, that public officials had been properly appointed and public acts properly carried out.

It should be noted, however, that the presumptions mentioned above are not irrebuttable. They are merely what a court will presume if there is no evidence sufficient to upset the presumption. Accordingly if, for example, a party can adduce good evidence that a public official was not properly appointed, the presumption is displaced. Therefore, if this is the issue in the proceedings, some act done by the public official concerned may be shown to be a nullity. In contrast to this type of presumption, there are some well-known *irrebuttable* presumptions, *e.g.* that a child of under 10 years cannot commit a crime, or that a boy of under 14 cannot commit rape. These are really not presumptions at all in any proper sense, but statements of substantive law.

25.10   The most important presumption for our purposes, is the presumption of negligence expressed in the maxim *res ipsa loquitur*. This presumption has the effect of shifting the burden of proof in a negligence case from the plaintiff to defendant once certain primary facts are proved. The essential primary facts are:

1.   that the thing causing the damage must be under the management or control of the defendant;

2.   that the accident must be such as does not, in the ordinary course of things, happen if proper care is used.

When these matters are proved, it is then for the defendant to show an explanation that is consistent with the absence of negligence. The facts of the leading case illustrate the presumption. The case is *Scott* v. *London and St. Katherines Docks Company* (1865) 3 H. & C. 596.

Bags of sugar fell on the plaintiff as he was near the defendant's warehouse. It appeared they had fallen from a crane which had not been properly loaded. The court held that as, in such a case, it was virtually impossible for the plaintiff to put his finger specifically on which of the defendants' employees had done which acts negligently, where he could show the essential primary facts described above, the burden of proof passed to the defendant, who then had to advance some explanation consistent with absence of negligence.

An example of a simple factual case where the presumption might operate would be if, say, a motor car mounted the pavement knocking down a pedestrian. Since, in the normal course of things, properly driven motor cars do not go on the pavement at all, this would seem a fairly clear example of the operation of the presumption and it would, in those circumstances, relieve the plaintiff of proving negligence, leaving the defendant to adduce evidence of absence of negligence if he was able (*e.g.* that a tyre burst unexpectedly, or that he swerved to avoid a child who had run into the road).

INFERENCES OF FACTS

25.11   These are merely examples of the court being prepared to draw common-sense inferences from situations without subjecting the matter to the need for formal proof. A clear example would be if, for instance, a five-year-old non-swimmer were washed overboard in shark infested waters 500 miles from land, the court would infer death. Another example of commonsense inference, is the so-called doctrine of continuance, *i.e.* that if a thing is known to exist on June 1, 1991, the court will, in the absence of any evidence at all, presume that the thing continued to exist on June 2, 1991.

26. Competence and Compellability of Witnesses

A witness is *competent* if he can be called to give evidence, and *compellable* if **26.01**
he can be made to give evidence. The general rule is that all persons are
competent and compellable. There are however notable exceptions to this
general rule.

Civil cases
All witnesses who are capable of understanding the oath are competent and **26.02**
compellable in civil cases. This means that if, for example, one finds that
one's opponent does not propose to testify, one can obtain a subpoena to
compel him to do so. Unsworn evidence is not admitted in civil cases where
the witness is in court, although paradoxically, unsworn evidence in the form
of written statements *is* admissible in certain circumstances as we shall see
later in the section on hearsay in civil cases.

Criminal cases
To the general rule of competence and compellability there are three impor- **26.03**
tant classes of exception in criminal cases, namely children, the accused, and
the accused's spouse.

CHILDREN

In a criminal case, if a child is capable of understanding the nature and **26.04**
significance of the oath he must give sworn evidence. If a child is not
competent to take the oath, he may, in a criminal case only, give unsworn
evidence:—

> "If, in the opinion of the court, he is possessed of sufficient intelligence to
> justify the reception of the evidence and understand the duty of speaking
> the truth" Children and Young Persons Act 1933, 38(1).

In either case, the state of the child's understanding or intelligence is
ascertained by the judge questioning the child in the presence of the jury, or
the magistrates or their clerk questioning the child in open court.
It is impossible to say exactly at what age a child is so close to adulthood
that one need not go through the formalities of assessing his ability to testify
on oath, or so far from adulthood that it is clearly impossible for a child to
testify at all. In one case a five year child was called as a witness although the
Court of Appeal subsequently doubted the propriety of calling such a young
child. One cannot say, however, that there is any hard and fast rule as to the
age at which a child will qualify to give evidence, sworn or unsworn. The
judge will test the state of the child's understanding by asking him questions
in a sympathetic manner about his general awareness. Thus, if the child is,
say, 11 years' old, and thus there is some prospect of him being able to give

sworn evidence, he will ask him about the nature of truth and lies; to give him some explanation of why telling the truth is a good thing and telling lies a bad thing; question him about his understanding of why he is in court today and what the purpose of the proceedings is; ask him, about his understanding of the words "promise" or "oath." Generally ask whether he understands about God and the Bible (although on the leading cases, a belief in God is not apparently necessary before a child can swear on oath) and so on. If he decides that the child is not capable of taking the oath, then the judge will already have formed a reasonable impression of the child's intelligence and state of awareness, so as to enable him to decide whether he can give unsworn evidence. He may perhaps go on to question further, even though he has already rejected the possibility of the child giving evidence on oath.

THE ACCUSED

26.05 An accused is, of course, competent to testify on his own behalf. He is not competent and compellable to testify for the prosecution thus, at his own trial, the prosecution cannot compel him to give evidence. The corollary of this is that one of two or more co-accused cannot be called *by the prosecution* to testify against his co-accused. This should not be confused with the situation where one of a number of co-accused testifies *on his own behalf*— there is nothing then at all to stop him giving evidence which is against the interests of his co-accused.

It is thus important to determine whether participation in a criminal trial are "co-accused" or not. Co-accused means "jointly charged at the time when competence comes to be decided." Once a person ceases to be a co-accused, he becomes competent and compellable as a witness for the Crown. There are a number of ways in which a person may cease to be a co-accused, even though concerned in the same crime. Two most important ways are:—

26.06 1. Where an order is made for each co-accused to be *tried separately*. This should only happen very rarely indeed, because the interests of justice almost always require that proceedings should be taken against all persons involved at the same time. There are dangers of inconsistent jury verdicts if this does not happen. It might, however, exceptionally arise if the trial of one of two or more co-accused has to be delayed, *e.g.* because he is still a fugitive from custody, or is too ill to stand trial. If the trial, meanwhile, proceeds in relation to the other co-accused, then at the time when the delayed trial commences, the former co-accused will be competent to testify against him. Whether it would be *desirable* for the prosecution to compel an unwilling former co-accused to testify, is a different matter, but they certainly have the power to do so.

26.07 2. Where one of two or more co-accused has *pleaded guilty* at the outset he may then be called by the Crown. Under the former practice, it was generally considered desirable to sentence a former co-accused before he testified so that he would have no motive to shift blame on to the other co-accused in order to receive a lighter sentence. However, there are general dicta in one important case (*R.* v. *Weekes* (1982) 74 Cr.App.R. 161) to the effect that it is better to postpone sentencing on such a person until the end of the trial of the other co-accused, so that the judge can properly assess the relative culpability of all concerned in the light of all the facts which emerge. Many consider that the former practice is preferable. Despite what was said in *R.* v. *Weekes*, a judge does have discretion in this matter, and may either sentence a former co-accused before he testifies so as to remove every apparent incentive for him to colour his evidence to minimise his own part in the crime, or he may wait until the end of the trial to sentence all the accused together.

We ought also to consider the position of an accused who merely wishes to testify on his own behalf. As indicated earlier, he has a right not to testify at his own trial, or he may give evidence on oath like any other witness. If he does this, he is then open to cross-examination, like any other witness, although unlike other witnesses, he may not be cross-examined as to his bad character, unless certain circumstances apply which will be dealt with in due course. **26.08**

If an accused does not testify, the prosecution are not permitted to comment to the jury in their closing speech on the refusal of the accused to give evidence. This is by Section 1(b) of the Criminal Evidence Act 1898 which has been repeated verbatim without being repealed in Section 80(8) of the Police and Criminal Evidence Act 1984. The judge may, however, comment within reason on the accused's failure to testify. If his comment is excessive, *e.g.* if he says things to the jury along the lines of "Don't innocent men usually want to give their own version and explanation—you should draw your own inferences from his failure to testify," any conviction will inevitably be quashed.

THE ACCUSED'S SPOUSE

Before the coming into force of Section 80 of the Police and Criminal Evidence Act 1984, a spouse was only *competent* to testify against the other spouse in certain limited classes of case and was never *compellable* by the prosecution. Under Section 80, the following is the position: **26.09**

For the prosecution

Unless the spouses are *jointly charged* with an offence, one spouse is now always *competent* to testify for the Crown against the other in respect of any crime. The spouse is *not*, however, *compellable*, save in respect of certain specified charges, namely: **26.10**

1. charged where the offence involves an assault on or injury or a threat of injury to the wife or husband of the accused or a person who was at the material time under the age of 16; or

2. the offence charged is a sexual offence alleged to have been committed in respect of a person who was at the material time under that age; or

3. the offence charged consists of attempting or conspiring to commit, or of aiding, abetting, counselling, procuring or inciting the commission of an offence falling within paragraphs (a) or (b) above.

One can therefore summarise the effect of this section so far as we are concerned, by saying that generally a spouse will be competent, but not compellable. For the spouse to be compellable by the prosecution, there would need to be either a sexual offence against a person under 16, or an assault, injury, or threat of injury to the spouse herself, or a person under 16. These latter provisions, although clearly aimed at what one might describe as "assault type" offences, need not necessarily be confined to them. Consider, for example, the situation of a person charged with reckless driving, where it is alleged that the nature of his reckless driving was such as to imperil either pedestrians under 16 or the spouse, if she was on the pavement nearby, or even the other occupants of the car which was driven recklessly, which might of course include the spouse or a person under 16. Arguably, it is not putting too forced an interpretation on section 80 to say that it could extend to "threat of injury" in such situations and thus enable the prosecution to compel the spouse to testify.

It should be noted that *former* spouses are now compellable at all times as if the parties had never been married, which is a reversal of the previous rule. Thus, if the accused and his spouse divorce before the trial, the spouse is in the same position as any other witness.

As a defence witness

26.11 **For her spouse.** A spouse is *compellable* to give evidence *on behalf of* the accused, unless she is also charged in respect of the same matter and remains liable to be convicted of that offence (*e.g.* she has not pleaded guilty or already been acquitted).

26.12 **For a co-accused.** A spouse is always *competent* to testify on behalf of any person jointly charged with her spouse but is only *compellable* if the crime charged is one of those where she would be compellable by the Crown (see above). However, she is not compellable even then if she is herself also a co-accused and remains liable to be convicted of the same offence (*e.g.* she has not already pleaded guilty or been acquitted).

Note that in those cases where a wife is only competent but not compellable for the Crown, then according to a recent case which would still seem to be good law (*R.* v. *Pitt* [1983] Q.B. 25) it is desirable for a judge to tell the spouse, before she takes the oath and in the absence of the jury, of her right not to testify, and to warn her that if she does decide to testify, she can be cross-examined like any other witness and may not refuse to answer proper questions.

27. The Course of Testimony

As a general rule, all evidence must be given on oath, and the form of the **27.01** oath must be such as the witness declares to be binding on him. The exceptions are:

AFFIRMATION

By section 5 of the Oaths Act 1978 a solemn affirmation may be adminis- **27.02** tered instead of an oath, if the witness is not a believer, or taking an oath is contrary to his religion, or it is impracticable to administer the oath in a manner appropriate to the witness's religion. This applies to criminal or civil proceedings.

CHILD WITNESSES

In criminal proceedings only, a child may give unsworn evidence if, in the **27.03** opinion of the court he is possessed of sufficient intelligence to justify the reception of the evidence and understands the duty of speaking the truth, by virtue of Children and Young Persons Act 1933, s.38. We have already met this point in the section on competence of witnesses and shall meet it again in due course in the section on corroboration.

Once a witness has sworn or affirmed, or it has been decided that a child may give unsworn testimony, the witness's evidence has three stages, namely examination in chief; cross-examination; and re-examination. We shall now consider these in turn.

Examination in chief

This is where the advocate for the party calling the witness (*i.e.* the party **27.04** who believes that the witness's evidence will help his case) tries to elicit the evidence required from the witness. There are four matters to consider in relation to evidence in chief (i) leading questions, (ii) refreshing memory, (iii) the admissibility and value of a witness's previous consistent statements, (iv) unfavourable and hostile witnesses.

LEADING QUESTIONS

These are questions which either suggest the answer desired, or assume the **27.05** existence of disputed facts. They are not permissible in examination in chief, because they either "prompt" the witness, or they may mislead the jury into thinking that because the advocate constantly reiterates the disputed fact that the disputed fact has been established. In essence, a witness should be left to tell his own story in his own words. A leading question is one which puts the evidence to him and generally only requires him to assent to it. For example, a question in the form "is it not right that you were in Trafalgar Square when you saw a large man with red hair hit the policeman on the head with a bottle without any provocation whatsoever?" This is an example of the first type of leading question which prompts the witness—in this case presumably into merely saying "Yes." An example of the second kind of question which assumes disputed facts would be to ask questions in the form "Where were you going when you saw the accused carry out this violent unprovoked assault?" Although the witness is actually being asked for some quite different matter (*i.e.* where he was going) the advocate is putting forward a version of the facts which will now be lodged in the jury's mind, even though as yet no direct evidence has been adduced to establish it.

Exceptionally, leading questions are permitted at the very start of a witness's testimony for purely formal or introductory matters, or where the evidence is non-controversial. It is in fact very hard to ask a question no element of which is leading in the sense that it suggests a fact which may not yet be established. It is one of the great difficulties of advocacy to draw an unintelligent or tongue-tied witness through his evidence without suggesting some of it to him as you go along. For example, suppose one wished to have a witness describe an assault which occurred in Trafalgar Square on May 3, 1991. Unless one were permitted to put the circumstances to the witness in outline, one would really be left with no other way of starting the cross-examination, than to say "Have you ever in your life seen anything interesting?" One can well imagine what response this might well draw from an unintelligent witness who might embark on a lengthy account of sporting occasions, war experiences and so on, before directing his mind eventually to the matter in issue. Yet even to say "Were you in Trafalgar Square on May 3, 1991 when you witnessed an incident?" is in principle a leading question. It is, however, the kind of leading question to which objection would not usually be taken unless the very place or date where the incident occurred was seriously disputed.

It should be remembered that the prohibition on leading questions only applies to the advocate calling the witness, that is it only applies in examination in chief and re-examination. In *cross-examination*, leading questions are permissible and indeed, essential, since the purpose of cross-examination is in part to try and persuade the witness to agree to the truth of an alternative version of the facts. Thus the whole cross-examination may be conducted in leading questions, a typical introduction to such questions being "Is it not the case that in fact you. . . ." It is sometimes hard for novice advocates to frame questions in a way which will satisfy some demanding judge or magistrates' clerk, that there is no element of "leading" the witness. One reasonable test is that if a question can be answered simply "Yes" or "No," it is a leading question.

REFRESHING THE MEMORY

27.06 A witness may refresh his memory of the matters as to which he will testify by referring *out of court* to any previous statement which he has made. It is perfectly proper for the police to give a witness his statement to read through outside the court, or come to that, for the defence solicitor to do likewise with his witness, or the parties in a civil case to do the same. One should, however, always inform one's opponent that this has occurred so that he may thoroughly test the witness's recollection in court. Moreover, where this has happened, one's opponent is entitled in court to insist on the out of court statement being produced for inspection (so that he can see for example if there is anything inconsistent in it with the evidence which the witness has actually given. He could then use the statement as the basis for cross-examining the witness as to the reason for the inconsistency).

In court, a witness may refresh his memory by referring to a documentary record (*e.g.* a witness statement or similar), whilst actually testifying. Before he can do this, however, the following conditions must be satisfied: **27.07**

1. The document must have been made at *substantially the same time* as the occurrence of the events about which the witness is testifying. This is a question of fact in each case—a gap of a few hours will not be fatal, for instance a policeman who writes up his notebook after coming off duty. In connection with this point, it might also be noted that there is nothing improper in a number of policemen writing up their notebooks together and agreeing their evidence. Despite ample case law which justifies this practice, policemen still often tend to deny that they have collaborated to write up their notebooks, preferring to attribute the existence of identical wording, even down to mis-spellings and punctuation to the existence of telepathic powers.

2. The document must either have been *written* by the witness, or *verified* by him at the time, even if not written by him. For example, in one case a ship's captain was allowed to refresh his memory from a ship's log. The log had been written up by the mate, not the captain, but the captain had checked each day's entries at the end of the day. Or see the facts of *R.* v. *Kelsey* (1982) 74 Cr.App.R. 213. In this case the witness to an incident involving a motor car dictated the car's registration number to a police constable who wrote it down and read it back to the witness to be verified. The actual note made by the police constable was produced in court and the witness was permitted to use it to refresh his memory in court. The reading back of the note by the policeman was sufficient verification by the original witness. Note that if the policeman had *not* read the note back, the note could *not* have been used. **27.08**

3. The document must be *handed to the opposing advocate* to inspect. The jury or magistrates may also see it. **27.09**

The principle of refreshing the memory is just that. In other words the witness is supposed, from the written account which he sees before him, to be able mentally to reconstruct the incident and testify concerning it. It must be seriously doubted whether in many cases this is in fact so. Take for example a traffic policeman who, in his day's work may be making notes of several incidents of speeding on the same stretches of road. It may be that a disputed incident of speeding may not come to trial for some months, by which time the policeman presumably may have seen scores of similar incidents. It would seem somewhat optimistic to claim that merely by reference to his notebook, he is actually able to mentally reconstruct the precise incident with which the case is now concerned. All too often in such circumstances, the policeman merely reads out his notebook and it must be doubted whether he does in fact have any actual recollection of matters outside the scope of the words he sees before him. The mental process is probably on such occasions that the policeman sees his own handwriting, knows himself to be a truthful person and therefore reads it out in the certainty that he is recounting the truth. In civil cases, where an action may not come to trial for several years, it is even more unrealistic to suppose that **27.10** a witness's recollection of the incident will be truly refreshed from seeing a note of it written at the time.

PREVIOUS CONSISTENT STATEMENTS BY A WITNESS

27.11 We need to consider two matters, *admissibility* and *value*. As a general rule, a party cannot adduce evidence of his own or his witness's prior statements to support his case at trial. The reason why this is so is clearly shown by the facts of the case of *R.* v. *Roberts* [1942] 1 All E.R. 187. In this case, the accused had been jilted by his girlfriend. Like Mr. Woolmington before him, he went to persuade her to recommence their relationship, taking with him, for insurance, a loaded shotgun with which he proposed to threaten suicide should the girl concerned disagree with his proposal. Also as in the case of Mr. Woolmington before him, the girl was shot dead and the defence was accident. Some few hours after being taken into custody, the accused was visited in his cell by his father and they had a conversation, in the course of which the accused allegedly told his father that his defence would be that the killing was accidental. At the trial, the accused wished to call his father to testify as to this conversation. The trial judge refused to let him do so, holding that for the father to testify as to what the son had told him in the cells would be of no evidential value whatsoever. It was merely a prior consistent statement and added nothing at all to the accused's own testimony as to the circumstances of accident. If it did show consistency, then the consistency might as easily be consistency in a lie, as in the truth, and it was a waste of the jury's time to hear the father recounting what the son had told him.

The principle is clear, but to it there are a number of important exceptions of which only two concern us at present namely (a) a witness's previous statement in *civil proceedings* and (b) statements introduced to *negative a suggestion of recent fabrication* of evidence.

In civil proceedings

27.12 A witness's previous statement may, with the leave of the court, be proved as evidence of any facts stated therein, of which direct oral evidence would be admissible. This is by virtue of section 2 of the Civil Evidence Act 1968. In fact, the leave required will only be given by the court in exceptional circumstances precisely because of the reasons given in the case of *R.* v. *Roberts* above, namely that it adds little to the witness's oral testimony and is therefore of little evidential value—it would therefore be pointless to waste the court's time by introducing a prior consistent statement. A fuller discussion of this and of these important sections of the 1968 Act appears in the later section on civil hearsay.

To negative a suggestion of recent fabrication

27.13 This will almost always occur in re-examination, rather than examination in chief but it is convenient to deal with the point here. If, after a witness has testified in examination in chief, the cross-examiner goes on to allege that the story has been invented recently, *e.g.* concocted after collaboration with other witnesses or with the accused, a previous statement of his evidence becomes admissible and the previous statement can then be brought in evidence, usually in re-examination. To use this procedure it is not enough that the cross-examiner has attacked the truth of the witness's evidence, however vigorously. There must have been a question in the nature of "When did you make this up?" Or "You got together with X and agreed on this version, didn't you?" A clear illustration of the proper use of the exception is provided by the facts of *R. v. Oyesiku* (1971) 56 Cr.App.R. 240.

> The accused was charged with assault on a policeman. The accused's wife, after he had been taken into custody and before she had had the oppor- tunity to see him in the cells, went immediately to the family solicitor and gave her account of the incident, which was to the effect that the assault had been by the police upon her husband. At the accused's trial, when she gave evidence to this effect, it was put to her that she had invented this version after collaboration with her husband. She wished the solicitor to be called to give evidence to the effect that she had seen him and told him her story before she had had the opportunity of speaking to her husband. The trial judge refused to permit this and on appeal the Court of Appeal quashed the conviction, holding that the trial judge had been wrong to refuse. The case was the clearest possible example of the proper use of the exception, and the solicitor should have been permitted to be called to give an account of what the wife had told him at a time when she had not had the opportunity to speak to her husband.

If such statements are allowed in, then they have different effects depending **27.14** on whether the case is criminal or civil. In a *criminal* case, such statements are not evidence of the facts stated in them, they are merely evidence of the *credit* of the witness and go to rebut the allegation of recent fabrication of the statement. In a *civil* case, however, by virtue of Section 3(1)(b) of the Civil Evidence Act 1968, such statements *are* evidence of any facts therein of which direct oral evidence by the maker would have been admissible. This is in accordance with the general provisions of the Civil Evidence Act 1968, which in brief, considerably relaxes the strict law of evidence for civil proceedings. It must be doubted any way whether in a criminal case a trial judge could make the jury sufficiently clearly aware of the meaning of the direction he was giving them, that is that they could use the previous statement to judge *the witness's credibility*, but not to judge the *truth* of what the witness was actually asserting *per se*.

UNFAVOURABLE AND HOSTILE WITNESSES

These terms relate only to certain special situations which may arise with a **27.15** party's *own* witnesses. The other side's witnesses, after all, may be expected to be unfavourable.

Parties prepare their case by having their solicitors take a statement from each witness which is written down and signed by the witness. This is called a "proof of evidence." It is, of course, a "proof" in the publishing sense, *i.e.* a draft, rather than the legal one. A witness whose evidence in court is generally in accordance with his statement, is said to be "coming up to proof." The following section deals with the situation where a witness fails to do so and does not come "up to proof."

Where a party is let down by the witness whom he is calling, there are two possibilities, namely that such a witness may be either "unfavourable," or "hostile."

27.16   An *unfavourable* witness is simply one who is not "coming up to proof" and fails to prove some necessary fact. Such witnesses cannot be attacked by the party calling them, nor can their previous statements be put to them to remind them or correct them. The best one can hope for if a witness proves to be unfavourable, is that one has other witnesses as to the same point, and that the jury will prefer the later evidence. Unfavourable witnesses may be so because they are forgetful, foolish or mistaken.

All advocates can remember their first experience of finding an unfavourable witness. One's witness had given a perfectly adequate proof of evidence some time before and there was no reason to suspect that the witness was unintelligent or forgetful. Then at the trial one attempts to take the witness through his or her evidence only to find there is no response at all on the very matters which the witness has been brought to court to prove. It is here that one's inability to use leading questions in examination in chief will be most telling. If one could just put a few important preliminary facts to the witness forcefully, perhaps the witness's mind might be jolted so that he or she would get back on the track of giving the hoped-for evidence. Unfortunately, it cannot be done, or cannot properly be done, although some advocates are skilled at getting a highly improper and very leading question out so fast that there is no opportunity for their opponent, or for the court to intervene until perhaps the harm (or good) has been done. Where one is confronted with an unfavourable witness therefore, one can only hope that one has later and better witnesses who will "come up to proof." If the witness is not giving the right evidence because he or she is forgetful, then it is as well to ask sufficient questions to demonstrate to the court that this is the case, so that the court does not draw an adverse inference from a witness's failure to say what was clearly expected. If the witness is giving some wholly different and quite mistaken version, then all one can generally do is attempt to ask further questions in an effort to demonstrate to the court that the witness is unintelligent, or foolish, but one cannot attack the evidence given as such.

27.17   *Hostile* witnesses are those "not desirous of telling the truth at the instance of the party calling them." So the clearest instance is that of a witness who has deliberately changed his evidence since his previous statement, whether from a desire not to be involved, fear, malice or some other motive. Where an advocate in examining in chief one of his own witnesses finds that he seems hostile, then in a Crown Court case, the following will occur:—

1.   he will ask the judge to send the jury out of court;

2.   in their absence he will apply to the judge for leave to treat the witness as hostile;

3.   the judge will decide whether the witness is hostile, or merely unfavourable. He will try to judge the degree of the witness's hostility from such things as the witness's demeanour (hostile witnesses often adopt a truculent or difficult attitude in court) but he may also be shown the witness's previous statement so he can judge how glaring the departure from the previous statement is;

4.   the jury are then recalled and if the judge has ruled the witness only unfavourable, there is nothing much that the advocate can do about it, except hope for better results with any other witnesses he has on the same points;

5. if the judge rules the witness hostile, however, the advocate can do a little more. He can now at least go some way towards undoing the harm to his case which the witness has done so far. He can now cross-examine the witness, using leading questions, and put to the witness his previous inconsistent statement. This should be sufficient to destroy the witness's credibility in the eyes of the jury. He cannot, however, attack the witness's credit further, for instance by cross-examining him as to his previous character and convictions.

In the magistrates' court the same thing happens in principle, but clearly there is no equivalent stage to sending the jury out of court. The application simply has to be made all at once.

The law on this matter is now contained in the Criminal Procedure Act 1865, **27.18** s.3. Despite its title, this Act applies to civil as well as criminal proceedings. The Section states:—

"A party producing a witness shall not be allowed to impeach his credit by general evidence of bad character; but he may, in case the witness shall in the opinion of the judge prove adverse, contradict him by other evidence, or, by leave of the judge, prove that he has made at other times a statement inconsistent with his present testimony; but before such last-mentioned proof can be given, the circumstances of the supposed statement, sufficient to designate the particular occasion, must be mentioned to the witness, and he must be asked whether or not he had made such statement."

This means that when the jury are recalled, if the judge has given leave to treat the witness as hostile, one cannot simply produce the statement to the jury. One must introduce the matter by asking the witness whether he recalls having on a previous occasion made another statement. Inevitably the answer must be "Yes." One then goes on to ask the witness if he proposes, in the light of that former statement, to stick to the evidence that he previously gave to the jury. This will of course bring home to the witness that he is about to have his previous statement proved. If the witness says that he does not wish to adhere to his previous verbal evidence, then the advocate's job is done. The witness has discredited himself out of his own mouth. If, however, the witness insists that he will stick to the version that he previously gave to the jury, then the advocate is now entitled to put in evidence the previous inconsistent statement and to have it shown to the jury.

The final question is "What is the value and effect of the previous inconsis-   **27.19** tent statement?" Again, there is a difference, depending on whether it is a criminal or civil case. (a) in a *criminal* case, the judge must not leave it to the jury to pick which of the witness's two conflicting versions they prefer. He must direct them that the *whole* of the witness's testimony (at least as to the extent of the inconsistency) must be totally disregarded. The two versions cancel each other out. In one exceptional recent case, there was a departure from this principle, but this is the clear general rule.

In a *civil* case, a prior inconsistent statement *is* evidence of its contents. By Section 3(1)(a) of the Civil Evidence Act 1968 "A statement is admissible as evidence of any facts stated therein of which direct oral evidence by the maker would be admissible." So the trier of fact in a civil case (judge or jury) is entitled to choose which of the two versions of a witness's evidence he prefers to believe. It will of course normally be prudent for him to take the view that the witness has clearly shown himself to be a liar about an important matter, whether out of court, or in it, and therefore not to speculate as to which of the two versions may be correct. However, if there is some clear evidence as to why the witness might have changed his version, the judge might properly speculate (if, for example, there is some demonstration that a grudge had arisen between the witness and the plaintiff since the giving of the earlier version he might speculate that that version was the correct one and that the witness was now changing his evidence because of the grudge).

Cross examination

27.20 All witnesses are liable to be cross-examined. All parties have the right to cross-examine any witness not called by them. Therefore, one accused's witness can be cross-examined by the prosecution and by counsel for any co-accused. There are two objectives in such cross-examination:—

1. to elicit information about the facts in issue favourable to the party cross-examining;

2. to test the truthfulness of, and where necessary, cast doubt upon, the evidence given in examination in chief. When conducting cross-examination, it is an advocate's duty:—
   (a) to challenge every part of a witness's evidence which is in conflict with his own case;
   (b) to put his own case to the witness insofar as the witness is able to say anything relevant about it;
   (c) to put to a witness any allegation against the witness which he may properly put.

27.21 In cross-examination, leading questions may be put as we have mentioned previously. Cross-examination is directed to either (1) the *issues in the case*, or (2) *collateral issues*. For our purposes, the only important collateral issue is the credit of the witness. It is sometimes hard to decide which are the issues in the case, and which are collateral issues. Let us take an example. Suppose A and B are involved in a fight. A alone is eventually charged with an assault and his defence is self defence, namely that B was the instigator of the fight and that he, A, did no more than was necessary to protect himself. An eye witness, W, testifies for the prosecution. W may be cross-examined about the issues in the case, namely how the fight started, who was the aggressor, etc. But W may also be cross-examined about collateral issues, namely the extent to which he is a credit-worthy witness. This cross-examination may range over matters which have nothing whatsoever to do with the assault itself, but are directed to show that W should not be believed. Thus, he may be cross-examined about whether he is a close friend of B, or has a conviction for perjury, or is a habitual drinker and might well have been drunk at the time he witnessed the incident which he is now purporting to describe so accurately, and so on.

There are rules relating to cross-examination on credit, designed to stop a **27.22** multiplicity of side issues being pursued in the interest of saving the court's time. The rules are:—

1. A witness's answers in cross-examination in relation to the *issues* in the **27.23** case may be *contradicted* by further evidence called by the cross-examiner. Thus taking the example mentioned above, the cross-examiner (A's counsel) can of course call his own witnesses as to how the fight actually started, to contradict W's version.

2. However, a witness's answers as to *credit* are *final*, and no evidence can be **27.24** called to rebut them. Thus, in the three examples of matters referred to above on which W might be cross-examined as to his credit, if, for instance, he denied being a habitual drunkard, then no evidence could be called by the cross-examiner to prove that this was indeed the case. To examine this side issue might involve calling one or more witnesses who would themselves be subject to cross-examination and evidence in rebuttal. The trial of whether or not W was a habitual drunkard could well last hours, or even days. This is the very kind of side issue which the rules are designed to prevent arising in such a lengthy form. However, with regard to the other two matters which might be alleged against W, namely that he was a close friend of B, or that he had a conviction for perjury, something else could be done. This is because to the above rule, namely that answers as to credit are final, there are three important exceptions, namely

    (i) where there is bias;
    (ii) previous inconsistent statements;
    (iii) a witness's previous convictions.

We shall now consider each of these in turn.

BIAS

Bias generally means taking a bribe or having very close relations with one **27.25** party. It can also mean the opposite, having a special grudge against one party. If such an allegation is put in cross-examination and denied, then as an exception to the general rule that answers as to credit are final, evidence in rebuttal may be called. A clear example is the one given above, so that if in fact W denied that he was a close friend of B (and therefore would have had every motive to give false evidence in exoneration of B's part in the incident), the cross-examiner would be entitled to call other witnesses to establish that W and B were close friends. The same would apply if it were alleged that W had a particular grudge against A arising out of some particular incident in the past. If this were denied, then witnesses could be called about the original incident which gave rise to the grudge, as an exception to the general rule that answers on credit are final.

THE WITNESS'S OWN PREVIOUS INCONSISTENT STATEMENTS

We have already considered the position where a party's *own* witness **27.26** departs from a previous statement in the section on unfavourable and hostile witnesses. It sometimes happens that a party knows that an *opponent's* witness has made a previous statement, written or oral, which is inconsistent with his present evidence. The most likely instance would be in a Crown Court trial, where the defendant will have copies of the prosecution witnesses' depositions at the committal hearing. Let us take an example of this. Suppose that an eye witness to an act of theft describes in his witness statement how the accused took some item from the counter of a shop, put it straight into his bag and walked out without paying. Suppose now that when giving oral evidence in court, the witness says that the accused looked round furtively for some time before taking the item, concealed it underneath his coat and pretended to look around the store for some time before running for the exit. Clearly the difference in the two versions will be such as to discredit the witness's testimony.

Where there is such inconsistency, matters are governed by the Criminal Procedure Act 1865 Sections 4 and 5. Like section 3 of the Act discussed earlier, the sections apply in both criminal and civil proceedings. Taken together, the sections say that if a witness denies or refuses to admit having made an earlier statement which is inconsistent with his present testimony, the earlier statement may be proved. Section 4 applies this to oral statements and section 5 to written statements. So under section 4, *another witness* may be called to prove that the earlier statement was made *verbally*, and under section 5, the *written statement itself* may be produced and put to the witness. Where this happens the effect of the inconsistency is precisely the same as in the case of a hostile witness, that is that the jury should be directed to ignore both statements in a criminal trial, but in a civil trial, the judge may choose which of the two he prefers to believe.

A WITNESS'S PREVIOUS CONVICTIONS

27.27 This is the difference between one's own hostile witness, and an opponent's witness. Whilst both can be cross-examined and have their prior inconsistent statements put to them in an effort to nullify their testimony, only an opposing witness can be asked about his character and convictions. The matter is governed by section 6 of the Criminal Procedure Act, 1865, again applicable to both criminal and civil proceedings. By this section:—

"A witness may be questioned as to whether he has been convicted of any offence and if he denies it ... it shall be lawful for the cross-examining party to prove the conviction."

This is so however little relevance the convictions may seem to have, *e.g.* whether the convictions are for perjury, or for driving offences. Clearly, there would, however, be little point in proving convictions for trivial matters (*e.g.* driving offence) against the witness. Thus, if in the example given earlier of the witness to the fight between A and B, W did in fact have a conviction for perjury, the matter could be put to him and if he denied it, it would be open to the cross-examiner to introduce evidence of the conviction.

Note that this provision applies to all witnesses other than the accused in a criminal trial. He cannot (usually) be asked about his character. This matter will be dealt with more fully in the later section on evidence of character of the accused.

Re-examination

Re-examination is the stage of proceedings after cross-examination. The party who originally called the witness now has an opportunity to further question the witness about matters which arose in cross-examination. It is an opportunity to attempt to re-habilitate the evidence that may have been shaken under cross-examination. The witness is asked (no doubt in a more sympathetic and kindly manner than that of the cross-examiner) to explain or clarify any ambiguities that arose in cross-examination. Re-examination must be limited to matters raised in cross-examination and no new matter can be introduced, except such as is necessary to explain answers given in cross-examination. Leading questions are not permitted in re-examination, any more than they are in the case of examination in chief.

27.28

28. Corroboration

28.01   As a general rule, the law does not give particular weight to particular types of evidence. It is open to a jury to convict of even the most serious crime on the evidence of one witness whom they find credible, or on an accumulation of circumstantial evidence. The jury, properly directed, must say whether they find that there is sufficient evidence to show the guilt of the accused beyond reasonable doubt.

28.02   However, in certain exceptional cases corroboration is required, or desirable, as the case may be, because the nature of the case, or of the witness himself, is considered to be such as to require caution before the court can be satisfied of guilt.
Corroboration is:—

"Other independent evidence which supports the evidence which requires corroboration in a material particular and which implicates the accused."

There are thus three requirements of corroborative evidence:

1.   It must be admissible in itself.

2.   It must be independent of the witness who needs to be corroborated.

3.   It must implicate the accused in a material particular.

So long as the evidence has these three qualities, it need not be a second witness it can, for instance, be fingerprint evidence, or a partial admission by the accused, or a false alibi given by the accused which may prove that the accused had a guilty mind. Corroborative evidence need not be such as in itself proves conclusively that the accused was the guilty person. If that were so, then the issue of corroboration need hardly arise. It must be some new fact which is independent of the witness with whom we are concerned, and helps to indicate that the accused committed the crime. The matters on which the judge should direct the jury in relation to corroboration are dealt with at the end of this section.

28.03   It should be noted that it is only *prosecution* evidence in a *criminal* trial which requires corroboration. Clearly the accused never needs to provide corroboration, because in the normal case he does not have to prove anything, he only has to leave the evidence in such a state that the jury could entertain a reasonable doubt.

28.04   Some statutes require corroborative evidence before a conviction is possible.
An example is Section 89 of the Road Traffic Regulation Act 1984. This provides that a defendant cannot be convicted of exceeding the speed limit on the *opinion* evidence of one witness. Thus, there has to be corroboration,

244

although this need not be a second witness. It has been held that where a witness is relying on more than opinion, *e.g.* by checking a radar reading or a speedometer, that this is sufficient for a conviction. It is important to remember that this statutory provision only relates to the offence of speeding itself. If speeding is an ingredient in some other crime, for instance, reckless driving, there is not necessarily any requirement for corroboration as such, and it would be possible for a conviction to be founded on the opinion of the witness, for instance, that the accused was driving the car at a certain speed on a winding road.

Apart from cases where corroboration is required by statute as a matter of **28.05** law, there are a number of cases where it is sometimes said that "corroboration is required as a matter of practice." In fact, this rather over-states the position. What is required is not corroboration as such, but in a Crown Court trial, a clear *warning* to the jury of the danger of convicting without it. If such a warning is not given by a judge in the appropriate case, then a conviction will be quashed on appeal, even if there was in fact ample corroboration. In the magistrates court, there is no one to give a "warning" as such. What one has to do is make one's submissions about the matter to the magistrates in the closing speech, emphasising that there is a danger of convicting on the evidence of a certain kind of witness without looking for corroboration. One would then hope that if the magistrates invited their clerk to retire with them to advise them on matters of law, that the clerk would underline this submission in his own advice. As magistrates are not, however, required to give reasons for their decision, there is actually no way of telling whether they did take seriously the suggestion that corroboration should be sought. This is merely one example of the difficulties of dealing with matters of evidence in the magistrates court, to which allusion has been made before.

There is one case relevant for our purposes where in the Crown Court it is **28.06** *essential* for the judge to warn the jury; one case where it is *desirable* although the judge has a discretion on whether or not to give a warning and a further case where a warning must be given of a *special need for caution* although corroboration, strictly speaking, is not essential. The cases are:—

(a) A warning is *essential* in the case of the evidence of an accomplice testifying for the Crown;
(b) A warning is *desirable* where the witness may have some purpose of his own to serve;
(c) *Special caution* is required in a case of disputed identity.

It should firstly be remembered that before looking for corroboration at all, **28.07** the jury must find the witness credible. The purpose of corroboration is to support credible evidence not to supplement the defects in evidence that the jury are inclined to disbelieve anyway. However in judging credibility the jury should take all the evidence into account. An example of the form of the warning might be:—

"Now you will remember the main witness for the Crown was X, an accomplice of the accused (judge then reviews X's evidence). If you find that X was a man whom you believed, the law requires you to consider one further matter. Experience has shown that the evidence of an accomplice may be unreliable for many reasons. So I am required to ask you to exercise caution before convicting on the evidence of X alone, even if you fully believe it. In such cases, it is generally desirable to look and see if there is other evidence which confirms the evidence of X. (Here the judge would explain the nature of corroboration and identify other items of evidence which are capable of amounting to corroboration). So, members of the jury, you should look for other items of evidence to corroborate that of X and it is usually considered dangerous to convict, unless you do find such other evidence, but you may convict without it if you are really sure in this case."

We will now consider the various categories.

The evidence of an accomplice

28.09 As we saw in the section on competence and compellability, to be competent in such a situation, the accomplice must be tried separately, or have pleaded guilty. Where this happens, the accomplice is competent and compellable for the prosecution, but a corroboration warning must be given. The question who is "an accomplice" is settled by the leading case of *Davies* v. *D.P.P.* [1954] A.C. 378. In the law of evidence, accomplice now has a highly technical meaning and must be a person in one of the following categories, either

1. participants in the crime alleged;

2. a handler of stolen goods at the trial of the thief of those goods; or

3. participants in other crimes, evidence of which is admissible under the *similar fact* principle. This latter principle will be explained later, and is not of any great practical importance for the moment.

28.10 The rationale of the rule here is the obvious tendency of accomplices to wish to shift blame on to each other. The categories of accomplices stated above are said to be fixed and not subject to judicial variation. There are some paradoxes in the categories so that for example whilst a handler is in law an accomplice when testifying at the trial of the thief, the converse is not necessarily the case and a thief testifying at the trial of the handler need not be treated as the handler's accomplice and the corroboration warning need not be given to the jury.

Thus, the clearest possible example of an accomplice would be someone who was formerly a co-accused and who has now pleaded guilty and is being called by the prosecution. In summing-up, the judge would direct the jury that the witness is in law an accomplice and that it is dangerous to convict on his evidence even if the jury are inclined to believe him without first looking to see whether there is anything that corroborates his evidence.

28.11 There is a special rule almost mutual corroboration, namely that two accomplices within the first category of *Davies* v. *D.P.P.* cannot corroborate each other. Thus let us suppose that an alleged theft has been carried out by A, B and C. A and B both plead guilty at the outset, but C pleads not guilty and the trial continues in relation to him alone. A and B are both called as witnesses by the Crown and give evidence implicating C. They cannot, in law, corroborate each other. However, this is a case where the jury need only be warned of the *desirability* of looking for corroboration and the *dangers* of convicting without it. Accordingly, it would be perfectly proper to direct the jury that they could convict if they were satisfied the accomplices were telling the truth.

Persons with some purpose of their own to serve

The above case is one where a warning is mandatory. There is a further case **28.12** where a warning to the jury may be desirable, though not essential. This is where a witness may have some purpose of his own to serve in getting the accused convicted. This may generally apply to two categories of persons

1. certain prosecution witnesses;

2. a co-accused who in giving evidence for himself implicates the other co-accused. Note in this case that the co-accused is not an "accomplice" a term which has a technical meaning referring to one who is testifying *for the Crown* and not *on his own behalf*.

Examples of prosecution witnesses within the first category would be any witness who has some personal motive to see the accused convicted. This could be something arising out of the crime itself, for example some other person who might themselves be suspected of the crime unless the accused is convicted. Or it might be someone who has some axe to grind from a matter totally unrelated to the present crime, *e.g.* somebody who may want to get the accused convicted in order to pay off an old grudge. The second category of case is where one of the two co-accused both of whom are continuing to plead not guilty, in testifying on his own behalf attempts to shift all the blame to the other co-accused so as to exonerate himself. In this situation the risk of acting without corroboration is perhaps not so great as in the former one of a prosecution witness with some special purpose of his own to serve. After all, by the time the trial reaches the stage of the co-accused testifying for themselves, the prosecution case will have closed and it would seem to follow that the prosecution will have already adduced sufficient evidence implicating both accused to have survived any submission of no case to answer against them. There ought therefore, generally, to be plenty of corroboration or potential corroboration. However, in either of these two cases, it may be desirable for the judge to give the jury some kind of warning in relation to the evidence of the person with the purpose of his own to serve. The case law is well settled and shows clearly that it is a matter within the discretion of the judge as to whether to give this warning in every case, and if he does decide to give it, as to the words in which he chooses to give it. Thus it has been held that it is not necessary for him to use the technical term "corroboration," nor to warn the jury of the need to look at the evidence with particular caution, nor any other particular form of words.

Finally we turn to the last category of evidence which must be treated with caution, namely identification evidence.

Identification evidence

In *R.* v. *Turnbull* [1977] Q.B. 224 the Court of Appeal laid down guidelines **28.13** for the treatment of cases which involve, wholly or substantially, the correctness of identification evidence which is in dispute. These guidelines are as follows:

1. The judge should always warn the jury of the special need for caution before convicting the accused in reliance upon the correctness of identification evidence, drawing their attention to the possibilities of error. In other words, he should particularly mention to them that in the case of identification witnesses, they must not necessarily merely decide whether the witness is telling the truth, or lying. Identification witnesses are only very rarely lying. The jury must have their minds directed to the possibility of the middle ground between truth and lies, that is a witness who is honest, but mistaken, and who is particularly convincing because of his obvious honesty.

2. The judge should ask the jury to examine closely the circumstances of the identification; for instance the length of observation; the distance of observation; lighting conditions; whether the witness had seen the suspect before; how soon afterwards the witness gave the description to the police.

3. The judge should remind the jury specifically of any weaknesses which have appeared in the identification evidence.

4. If there is any discrepancy between the witness's first description of the suspect to the police, and his actual appearance, the prosecution must inform the defence.

5. Where the quality of identification evidence is good, the jury may safely be left to assess it and may convict upon it. However, where the quality of the evidence is poor, the judge should withdraw the case from the jury and direct an acquittal, unless there is other evidence which goes to support the correctness of the identification. The judge should tell the jury what evidence there is which may support the identification. In particular, he must direct them that the fact that the defendant elects not to give evidence cannot of itself support the identification. He should also, where the defendant puts forward an alibi, (a defence obviously of crucial importance in identification cases) tell the jury that if the jury come to the conclusion that the alibi is false, this need not in itself support the correctness of the identification, because false alibis are often put forward out of stupidity or panic. However, if the jury conclude that the alibi was only put forward for the purpose of deceiving them, they may treat it as sufficient supporting evidence.

28.14 It should be noted that the supporting evidence necessary for an identification case need not be corroboration in the technical sense (for instance it need not be totally independent of the witness concerned). So to take an example from a decided case, suppose that a witness saw some fast moving incident, say a robbery, and got a glimpse of the face of the robber. If the witness then followed the robber and saw him getting away in a car whose number the witness took, and the car could subsequently be traced to the accused, then the witness's visual identification of the accused could be supported by the fact that the car seen at the scene of the crime could be shown to have belonged to him. This would not be *corroboration* in the technical sense because the witness himself would be giving both pieces of evidence and therefore the second would not be independent of the first but it would certainly suffice to support the identification evidence.

The *Turnbull* guidelines are very important and must be given virtually in **28.15** full in cases to which they apply. They should not be elided or paraphrased, otherwise there will be a risk of the conviction being upset on appeal. However, they do not apply to every case in which there is some element of identification. They only apply to cases of so called "fleeting glimpse" identification and this "fleeting glimpse" will usually involve sight of facial features. In every case to which the Turnbull guidelines apply there ought to be some suggestion of an identity parade subsequently. The rules to do with identity parades and the use of photographs will be dealt with separately in the section on criminal procedure. The suspect should always be given the opportunity of taking part in an identification parade, so that the witness's identification can be properly tested. Only if the suspect declines to participate in the identification parade, can some alternative method of pre-trial identification be arranged. Examples of this would be letting the witness look at men exercising in the remand prison yard to see if he could pick the suspect out, or confrontation in some more restricted situation, *e.g.* looking through the door of a cell in which the suspect is detained.

29. Hearsay Evidence

29.01 The rule against hearsay used to be considered the great rule underlying the whole of the law of evidence. However, due to the Civil Evidence Act 1968, the importance of the rule in civil cases has now been reduced very considerably. There are now very numerous exceptions to the rule in both civil and criminal cases. The most coherent way to approach the topic is to treat entirely separately the rules for hearsay in civil proceedings, which can only be explained by detailed reference to the Civil Evidence Act 1968 and the Rules of the Supreme Court. The section dealing with this appears later.

The definition of the rule against hearsay is, however, the same for criminal and civil proceedings and is as follows:—

"A statement, oral or written, other than one made by a person giving oral evidence in the proceedings is inadmissible to prove the truth of any fact stated in it."

The usual situation which one meets in the context of hearsay is what the layman would himself be able to call hearsay, that is a witness saying in court what some other person said out of court, but it should not be forgotten that two other circumstances may also amount to hearsay, that is:—

1. the witness saying in court what *he himself* said on another occasion; and

2. a *written statement* by any person tendered to prove the truth of facts stated in it. Thus, for example, a witness's proof of evidence which one party might attempt to put before the judge in a civil case, or the jury in a criminal case, would be inadmissible as hearsay unless one of the exceptions referred to later applied to it.

It is, however, crucial to understand that it is not in every case that when a witness wishes to repeat in court something which was said out of court that the out-of-court statement will be hearsay. The vital point is whether the words are repeated in court in order to persuade the court of the truth of what was said on the other occasion, or merely to tell the court that the words were spoken at all. The distinction can clearly be seen in the following examples, the first of which is pure hearsay and inadmissible, but the rest of which are not hearsay—they are not tendered to prove the truth of the words repeated, but just that they were said.

Example 1:
   A man is knocked down by a heavy stone thrown in the street. A passer-by says to a policeman "The man who threw the stone went into that house there," and points to a house. The policeman goes to the house and arrests the accused, but meanwhile, the passer-by has disappeared and cannot be found. At the accused's trial for the assault, the policeman would not be able to give evidence of either what the passer-by said, or of the passer-by's pointing to the house (which would also amount to hearsay). This case is a

pure instance of hearsay and if this was the only evidence against the accused, then the prosecution would know that unless the accused was inclined to admit the offence they would have no admissible evidence on which to base their case.

Example 2:
In an action concerning the competence of a testator to make a will, witnesses wish to say in court that the deceased suffered from strange delusions and believed that he was Napoleon. He had often said in their hearing "I am Napoleon." There would be no objection at all to the witnesses repeating this in court. To repeat what was said here is not for the purpose of proving the truth of the statement (*i.e.* that the deceased *was* Napoleon) but for the purpose of proving that the words were said at all—and thus indicating the deceased's mental state.

Example 3:
A man goes into a bank and says to the cashier, "I have a machine gun under my coat—give me all the money or I'll shoot." At the accused's subsequent trial for robbery, the cashier could, of course, repeat the words that were said to her. The purpose is not to prove the truth of anything stated by the accused—indeed it is quite immaterial as to whether he did or did not have a machine gun under his coat. The point is to prove the threat of violence, which is an essential ingredient of the crime of robbery.

Example 4:
P says to D, "I offer to sell you 100 tons of bananas at a price of £500 a ton." D says to P "I am interested in buying some bananas, but I only want 30 tons and I am only willing to pay £450 a ton for them and, moreover, they must be African and not West Indian bananas." P then says "I agree." In a subsequent dispute between the parties concerning the exact terms of the contract which they had concluded, this conversation could be repeated verbatim. It would not fall foul of the hearsay rule, because the point of proving it would not be to show the truth of anything said, but simply to demonstrate the precise terms of the contract eventually agreed.

Example 5:
A says to B, "C is a thief and is totally bent." Should C subsequently wish to bring an action against A for defamation and call B as a witness, B can of course be asked in court to repeat these words said to him out of court. The point is not to show that the words were true (although, of course, the truth or otherwise of the words might be explored as a separate issue in the proceedings) but merely to show that they were said at all, the fact of publication of a defamatory statement being essential to prove the tort.

Example 6:
A is charged with murder and his defence is provocation. In order to prove the provocation (which is an insult to the effect that he is not the real father of his own child) he would be entitled to prove the words of the insult to show the likely effect of them upon his mind. Again, the issue is not whether the words were true, but whether they were said at all and their effect on his mind.

Example 7:

The facts of the leading case of *Subramaniam* v. *Public Prosecutor of Malaya* [1956] 1 W.L.R. 965. In this case, the accused was charged with an offence arising under emergency regulations of unlawful possession of firearms. His defence was to the effect that he had been threatened by Chinese terrorists and was acting as a courier for them only because of duress, that is his fear of them in the light of the threats they had made. He wished to give evidence as to the terms of those threats and the trial judge refused to permit him to do so on the ground that the evidence would inevitably be hearsay. The Privy Council quashed the conviction, holding that the accused should have been allowed to give evidence of the threats, since this was clearly relevant to the state of mind under which he alleged he had acted as a courier. The terms of the threats were vital evidence to prove duress which would of course have been a defence to the charge. They were not hearsay.

29.02   To summarise, therefore, one can see from these examples that a reported statement of some kind which has been made out of court will only be hearsay and thus inadmissible if the purpose of putting it in evidence is to prove the *truth* of what was said. If, however, the purpose is to prove *that the actual words were said* at all, or to *show the state of the speaker's mind*, or the *effect that the words had on somebody else's mind*, then the statement made out of court will not be hearsay, and can be adduced in evidence.

The rule against hearsay applies throughout criminal proceedings, but to it there are now numerous exceptions, which we shall go on to consider individually as follows:—

These are:

1.   The Criminal Justice Act 1967, s.9 (which is in the same terms as section 102 of the Magistrates' Courts Act 1980);

2.   The Criminal Justice Act 1988, ss.23–30.

3.   Public documents;

4.   Depositions taken in Magistrates' Court proceedings:
     (i) under the Magistrates' Courts Act 1980, s.105 and
     (ii) under the Criminal Justice Act 1925, s.13(3) as amended;

5.   Statements admitted as part of the *res gestae*;

6.   Admissions and confessions.

We shall now deal with each of these exceptions in turn, giving examples of how they arise in practice.

1. Criminal Justice Act 1967, s.9 and Magistrates' Courts Act 1980, s.102

29.03   These two sections provide in similar terms for an exception to the hearsay rule. Section 102 of the Magistrates' Courts Act 1980 applies to committal proceedings, and section 9 of the Criminal Justice Act applies to the other stages of criminal proceedings in the magistrates' or Crown Court. The sections together provide that in criminal proceedings a written statement made out of court shall be admissible in the same way as oral evidence by the maker of the statement would be admissible, provided:—

1. the statement is signed by the person who made it;

2. the statement contains a declaration by that person to the effect that the statement is true to the best of his knowledge and belief and that he made the statement knowing that if it were tendered in evidence he would be liable to prosecution if he wilfully stated in it anything which he knew to be false, or did not believe to be true;

3. before the hearing, the statement shall have been tendered to each of the other parties to the proceedings and none of them shall within seven days from the service on them of a copy of the statement have objected to the statement being tendered in evidence.

These sections therefore provide that written statements will be admissible **29.04** in criminal proceedings at committal and trial, provided they are signed and contain a declaration in the words specified above as to their truth. The vital point to note, however, is that the statement must be served upon the opposing parties who have seven days in which to object to the use of the statement in court. The objection may be made on any grounds whatsoever, or indeed, no reasons at all need be given, and if the objection is made, the court has no power to overrule the objection and allow the statement to be put in evidence. Therefore, such statements are only used for non-controversial matter, or at "short form" committals, which are proceeding under section 6(2) of the Magistrates' Courts Act 1980—(see later, para. 46.17).

Although by far the most common use of the section is by the prosecution in **29.05** a criminal trial or at committal, there is nothing at all to stop the defendant from using the section. The police in fact take witness statements on forms on which there has already been printed the necessary declaration to comply with section 9 of the Criminal Justice Act/section 102 of the Magistrates' Courts Act. An example of how the section might work would be as follows:

There has been a burglary and theft from the house of A. A gives a statement to the police explaining how he returned home to find the window broken and a number of goods missing. X is suspected, arrested and charged. X's defence is alibi. To avoid the cost and inconvenience to A of calling him as a witness, the police would serve a copy of his statement under section 9 of the Criminal Justice Act, hoping that X would not object to it. In fact, since X's defence is to the effect that he was not the person who committed the burglary, he would presumably have very little reason for wanting A to testify, since he is unlikely to object to anything in A's evidence, he merely contends that whoever committed the burglary, it was not him. Therefore, he might well agree to section 9 procedure. In that case, A's statement can be read out at trial without him needing to be called to give evidence. If, however, the nature of X's defence had been that A had invited him into the house and told him to take whatever he fancied, then, of course, X would not have accepted A's written statement, but would have demanded that he be called as a witness at trial, so that he could be cross-examined.

The method of objecting is simply to write, or have one's solicitor write, a **29.06** letter within the seven-day period allowed under the Act to the prosecution, telling them simply that objection is taken to the statement and that the maker of the statement must be called as a witness.

29.07 It should not be imagined that one objects to a section 9 statement only because one proposes to hotly contest what the witness has said in it. It may be that one can perfectly well accept what the witness has said in the statement, but that one wishes the witness to be called anyway, so that he can be cross-examined about other matters outside the scope of his statement. Thus, for example, if a policeman who had come to the scene of an accident had made an apparently uncontroversial statement about where the vehicles had ended up and what damage appeared to have been done, even though the defendant on a charge of reckless driving might not actually object to the substance of the policeman's statement, it might well be that he would want to ask the policeman about matters outside his statement, for instance, whether or not the corner in question was known to be an accident blackspot, or the road or weather conditions at the time.

These two sections together provide by far the most common exception to the hearsay rule. They are in daily use in magistrates' courts and Crown Courts around the country, on thousands of occasions for the introduction of evidence of a formal, technical or uncontroversial nature. We pass from these well-established exceptions to a new exception introduced in the Criminal Justice Act 1988.

Documentary evidence. The Criminal Justice Act 1988, ss.23–30

THE USEFULNESS OF DOCUMENTARY EVIDENCE

29.08 It ought first to be remarked that documents have always been admissible in court as *real* evidence. That is to say where it is the very document, or some feature of it, that is an item of evidence in the case. Thus to take an obvious example, in a prosecution for forgery of a cheque the very cheque in question can of course be produced to the jury and no question of infringing the rule against hearsay arises. What we are now concerned with however is a document which *speaks as to the truth* of its contents, that is, a hearsay document. The main reason for the general prohibition against hearsay is the *unreliability* of hearsay evidence but it will be readily appreciated that that reason is not necessarily convincing in the case of documentary evidence. Indeed in many cases the *most* reliable form of evidence of a certain happening will be a document. A simple example is an entry in a ledger made many years before showing that monies were paid on a certain date. Obviously the cashier who received the money could be called to testify, but if he were to say that he remembered that individual transaction amongst many thousands of similar transactions in his working life his oral evidence would not be credible. On the other hand the ledger entry itself, unless some special consideration of fraud or forgery arises, is likely to be highly reliable. Therefore in relation to routine business and similar documents there are good grounds for saying that the document itself may be better evidence than any witness could be. Different considerations, of course, apply in relation to a different sort of document, namely *witness statements* in written form. If these witness statements were to be put in evidence rather than the maker of the statement being called grave difficulties could well arise and there might be a serious risk of injustice if such hearsay were admitted. In fact both kinds of hearsay are admissible, given certain conditions, under the

254

1988 Act and we shall now consider some of the different considerations which arise in relation to each of them.

Prosecutions for many kinds of offence depend on documentary evidence. **29.09** This is obviously so in major fraud trials, but is equally the case in charges of more mundane criminal offences, especially theft from trading concerns. In a very important case in 1965 the House of Lords eventually acknowledged the problem caused by the fact that such records were hearsay. That case is *Myers* v. *D.P.P.* (1965) A.C. 1001 and the facts are a good illustration of the problem, and also instructive in seeing how the provisions of the 1988 Act currently in force would apply. In *Myers* case the accused were charged with dishonesty offences involving passing off stolen cars as models rebuilt from wrecks. In order for the prosecution to identify the actual cars involved evidence needed to be called from the manufacturer's records of the numbers cast into the cylinder block of each new car. The manufacturer's records were microfilmed copies of record cards which had passed along the production line with each vehicle. It was held that these records were hearsay and came within no recognised exception to the rule and that the creation of new exceptions to the hearsay rule was a matter for the legislature and thus the evidence was inadmissible. This case is thus a striking example of the technical problems of documentary hearsay. It was highly unlikely that the motor manufacturer's records would be inaccurate. Had it been possible to identify each individual workman who had written up the records at the time, years before, then technically that workman could have given evidence about the numbers. However, had any individual workman been called his evidence would have been incredible had he purported to say that he specifically remembered the number of any individual car, given the repetitive nature of his job and the number of vehicles which had passed through the production line over the years. Nor could the workman realistically have used the records to refresh his memory.

Immediately after *Myers* case Parliament passed the Criminal Evidence Act **29.10** 1965 providing in certain limited circumstances for business documents to be admissible as an exception to the hearsay rule; that Act was in its turn replaced by section 68 of the Police and Criminal Evidence Act 1984 which provided various conditions and discretions for the admissibility of documentary evidence. Even in its short life section 68 of the 1984 Act gave rise to a considerable number of technical problems and in one particular case was very strangely applied. We do not now need to consider the history any further but shall go on to look at the relevant provisions of the 1988 Act. The Act deals with three different kinds of documents and we shall consider each of these in turn:—

(i)   First-hand documentary evidence under section 23.
(ii)(a) Second-hand documentary evidence in the form of documents which have come about in the ordinary course of business under section 24.
(iii)(b) Documents which have come about for the purpose of criminal investigation or proceedings under section 24.

(i) *First-hand documentary evidence under section 23*

29.11 Section 23 of the Act permits a statement made by a person in a document to be admissible as evidence of any fact of which direct oral evidence by him would have been admissible if (by section 23(2)) it is proved:—

> "(a) that person is dead or by reason of his bodily or mental condition unfit to attend as a witness;
> (b) that person is outside the United Kingdom and it is not reasonably practicable to secure his attendance; or
> (c) all reasonable steps have been taken to find the person but that he cannot be found."

These provisions therefore allow the putting in evidence of a written statement of any kind made by a person who is unavailable for one of the given reasons. It should first be noted that the section only permits evidence of any *fact* to be given and does not allow statements of *opinion*. (There is a separate provision in section 30 of the Act which governs admissibility of experts' reports). The section then allows evidence in written form no matter how casual the document in which the statement appears. We shall first consider a short example and then go on to discuss other points on section 23.

Example:
   W is on the way to the airport on holiday when he sees a robbery. He has no time to stop and carries on to the airport but whilst on holiday writes a letter to his mother describing the incident he saw. He comes back from his holiday but later dies in an accident. The prosecution appeal for witnesses to the robbery and his mother then provides a copy of the letter he wrote to her describing the incident. This letter would be prima facie admissible.

The reasons for unavailability under section 23

29.12 The reasons are straightforwardly expressed but clearly they may well give rise to considerable case law. We shall consider them in turn:—

(a) Death or unfitness to attend by reason of bodily or mental condition. This is unlikely to cause any substantial difficulty. Clearly the trial court will have to be satisfied by admissible evidence that the person is too ill to attend and equally clearly, if the illness is of a temporary nature consideration will be given to adjournment if the witness is very important. These are straightforward practical matters.

(b) The person is outside the United Kingdom and it is not reasonably practical to secure his attendance. This again must be proved by admissible evidence. Absence from the United Kingdom is probably easily proved but there is no guidance on how the courts are likely to interpret the requirement of "reasonable practicability to secure his attendance." Certainly witnesses outside the United Kingdom cannot be compelled to attend by any form of judicial process and therefore mere lack of co-operation ought to suffice for this. That very lack of co-operation, however, may not always be easy to prove without a good deal of evidence from persons who have tried to

256

contact and persuade the witness to return. What is unclear is the extent to which the court will give weight to considerations of cost and convenience in deciding on "practicability." Suppose for example that the trial relates to a fairly mundane shoplifting charge but that a key witness had emigrated to New Zealand meanwhile. Will the court accept that the disproportionate cost of getting the witness back for a relatively trivial charge makes it "impracticable?" If so then awkward considerations relevant to the seriousness of the offence, the importance of the witness and the cost and convenience of all concerned have to be weighed.

(c) All reasonable steps have been taken but the witness cannot be found. This reason also means the court will have to hear evidence about the thoroughness of the steps taken. There is no provision for any investigation of this at an interlocutory stage as such and it will have to be undertaken by the judge at trial in the absence of the jury.

(d) A further ground? There is a further somewhat curious provision tucked away in section 23(3) which gives one more ground for admitting a first-hand statement. This provides that a statement may be put in evidence if it was made to a police officer or some other person charged with the duty of investigating offences (such as a store detective or customs officer) provided that in the case of such statements the person who made the statement does not give oral evidence "through fear or because he is kept out of the way." This is curious because section 23 is primarily concerned with first-hand statements such as the letter in the example given above. This provision, which seems tacked on somewhat, relates to what in essence will be *second-hand* statements, that is statements put forward by the police officer who receives them. It will be observed that the section only apparently relates to the evidence of *prosecution* witnesses. We are going to consider separately the question of documents prepared expressly for criminal proceedings and it is more convenient to consider this provision in the context of that section a little later.

Section 23 therefore, to summarise, allows the putting in evidence of first-hand hearsay in written form. However, its scope is severely limited by the application of later sections, section 25 and section 26, which we shall consider in due course. These sections provide that even once one has jumped the "admissibility" hurdle in section 23 that the court has to consider various discretions before permitting the evidence to be used at trial. Before we go on to consider those discretions we should now consider section 24.

(ii) Second-hand hearsay contained in a document: section 24—
Introduction

29.13 A statement in a document may be admissible under section 24 of any fact of which direct oral evidence would be admissible even though it is second-hand hearsay provided that the following conditions are satisfied:—

"(i) The document was created or received by a person in the course of a trade, business, profession or other occupation, or as the holder of a paid or unpaid office; and

257

(ii) the information contained in the document was supplied by a person (whether or not the maker of the statement) who had, or may reasonably be supposed to have had, personal knowledge of the matters dealt with."

This provision therefore supposes that there will be either one or two people involved in the "document creating process." If there is any other person or persons involved in the chain of information then there is further provision that each intermediary in the chain between the person who supplies the information and the person who compiles it in a document must have received it either in the course of a trade, business, profession or other occupation or as the holder of a paid or unpaid office.

It may be helpful to give some examples of documents which would fit the provision:—

Example 1:
A, a delivery driver for a computer firm, delivers 20 computers to the premises of a retail company, X Ltd. On his return to his own firm he tells his delivery manager Z that he completed the delivery and the delivery manager makes a note of this in his records. Some time later at the premises of the retail company, X Ltd., two computers are believed to be missing from stock and an employee is charged with their theft. In order to prove the number of computers that were in fact delivered on this occasion the delivery record of the computer manufacturers would prima facie be admissible under this provision.

Example 2:
S is the unpaid social secretary of a rugby club. Part of his duties include the management and supervision of the bar of the club and the keeping of the accounts for it. The bar is managed by a part-time paid barman. S's job includes receiving deliveries and checking stocks. It is suspected that the barman is pilfering from stock and he is eventually charged with theft of some spirits found in his car. At his trial the records of deliveries and accounts kept by S would prima facie be admissible under this provision to establish the extent of the pilfering.

Example 3:
D witnesses a robbery. A policeman, P, comes to the scene and takes down a note of D's statement describing the robbery.

The first two examples mentioned above are taken from routine business situations. The third of them however is the case of an ordinary witness statement taken for criminal proceedings. In the case of documents in the third category there are markedly different factors relevant to admissibility, and different discretions which apply when the court is considering whether, despite technical admissibility, the documents should be received in evidence. Accordingly it is preferable now to go on to discuss documentary evidence under separate headings:—

(a) "NATURAL" DOCUMENTS

29.14 By the term "natural" documents (which does not appear in the Act but is

258

used here as a convenient description) we mean documents which are compiled in the course of everyday life without any regard being had at the time of the making of the document to its future usefulness in criminal proceedings. Where such documents are created (and the examples of the transport delivery book and social secretary's bar records above are good ones) then it should be noted there is no requirement that the person who made the document should be *unavailable* for the criminal trial. Thus in the examples above even though the delivery driver or the social secretary were available it would make no difference to the strict admissibility of the record. In each case the record is any way likely to be reliable, indeed more so than any oral testimony based on distant recollection.

Once the hurdle of *strict* admissibility has been jumped however, then as indicated earlier there is a discretion in the court as to whether or not the documents shall be admitted. This discretion is contained in section 25 of the Act and it is now useful to consider this section. The discretions in section 25 therefore apply in relation to "natural" documents admitted under section 24 of the Act and also in relation to first-hand documents admitted under section 23 such as the letter home from the holidaymaker in the example given before. This discretion is to be used by the criminal court at the hearing of a summary trial or Crown Court trial. It should be noted, however, that at *committal proceedings* a magistrates' court only has to consider the strict admissibility of the document within section 23 or section 24 and does not at that stage have to apply the discretions in section 25 which are to be left to the eventual court of trial.

SECTION 25 OF THE ACT

The court's discretion in relation to documentary evidence.   **29.15**

By section 25 of the Act it is provided that where the court is of the opinion that in the interests of justice a statement which is admissible by virtue of section 23 or 24 nevertheless ought *not* to be admitted the court may direct that the statement shall not be admitted.

The section goes on to provide that without prejudice to the generality of the Act, the court has the duty to have regard to the following matters:—

"(2)(a) To the nature and source of the document containing the statement and to whether or not, having regard to its nature and source and to any other circumstances that appear to the court to be relevant it is likely that the document is authentic.
(b) To the extent to which the statement appears to supply evidence which would otherwise not be readily available;
(c) To the relevance of the evidence that it appears to supply to any issue which is likely to have to be determined in the proceedings; and
(d) To any risk, having regard in particular to whether it is likely to be possible to controvert the statement if the person making it does not attend to give oral evidence in the proceedings, that its admission or exclusion will result in unfairness to the accused or, if there is more than one, to any of them."

The court then has a broad discretion to exclude evidence which would otherwise be technically admissible in the general interests of justice. This applies to documentary evidence introduced by *either* the prosecution or defence, but of course in the usual case the discretions will be exercised to protect the accused by excluding *prosecution* evidence. The first three of the discretions mentioned are neutral as between prosecution and defence. The last of them, however, clearly favours the accused, because the dominant consideration is "unfairness to the accused."

We now turn to the special situation of documents prepared expressly for criminal investigation proceedings to which special considerations and different discretions apply.

(b) DOCUMENTS WHICH COME ABOUT FOR CRIMINAL INVESTIGATIONS OR PROCEEDINGS

29.16 These documents are contrasted in important respects with what we have earlier described as "natural" documents. Such statements fit the prima facie requirements for admissibility under section 24 in that they are created or received by a person in the course of a profession, (*i.e.* defence solicitor, or policeman) and information contained in them is supplied by a person with personal knowledge.

Section 24 provides that if the document is supplied for any "pending or contemplated criminal proceedings or a criminal investigation" that it shall *not* be admissible unless there is a further factor satisfied. The further factor requires that the witness be *unavailable* for one of certain specified reasons. In this respect therefore there is a marked difference between "criminal investigation" documents and "natural" documents because it will be recalled that for natural documents to be admissible there was no requirement for unavailability of anyone concerned. The witness must therefore be unavailable for one of the following reasons:—

(a) The first set of reasons repeats those contained previously in section 23 of the Act namely:—
   (i) Death or unfitness by reason of bodily or mental condition;
   (ii) absence from the United Kingdom and impracticability of securing his return; or
   (iii) inability to find the witness.

In addition to these reasons, however, there are two others clumsily tucked away in different parts of the Act. We have already briefly mentioned the first of these which is:—

(b) "That the statement was made to a police officer or some other person charged with the duty of investigating offences or charging offenders and the person who made it does not give oral evidence through fear or because he is kept out of the way."

This reason would therefore seem to apply only to evidence by prosecution witnesses. The prosecution will have a difficult task here because they will have to convince the court by admissible evidence of the fear or reason for absence of the missing witness which will in the nature of things be difficult to do. The working of this part of the section is likely to give rise to substantial problems in practice.

(c) The final reason is tucked away in section 24(4)(*b*)(iii) of the Act and the reason is:—

"That the person who made the statement cannot reasonably be expected (having regard to the time which has elapsed since he made the statement and to all the circumstances) to have any recollection of the matters dealt with in the statement."

This is a somewhat curious reason. Superficially it might appear to cover the kind of situation which arose in *Myers* v. *D.P.P.* where workmen many years after the event were unlikely to be able to recollect things done in the course of their job. However, it does *not* cover that situation of course because it only concerns documents which come about expressly for criminal investigations. This therefore presupposes the situation where the police have a statement from a witness and he is likely to have forgotten its contents at trial. Given that the time between investigation and trial is usually relatively short in the United Kingdom and that it is perfectly proper to give a witness his statement from which to refresh his memory before trial, it would not seem that this reason is likely to be of much application in routine criminal litigation.

THE COURT'S DISCRETIONS IN RELATION TO "CRIMINAL INVESTIGATION DOCUMENTS"

Where a statement has come about expressly for the purpose of pending or **29.17** contemplated criminal proceedings or a criminal investigation (and as indicated above this applies equally whether the document is obtained by prosecution or defence) then section 25 and its discretions do not apply and instead the discretions are contained in section 26 of the Act. This section says simply that such documents "*shall not*" be given in evidence in any criminal proceedings without the leave of the court, and the court *shall not* give leave unless it is of the opinion that the statement ought to be admitted in the interests of justice."
There is therefore here a very strong presumption against the use of such documents. The phrase "the interests of justice" is one which has been used in statutes and case law before, and the usual interpretation of that phrase has been that in considering the interests of justice the interests of all concerned must be taken into account, including the interests of the prosecution, the interest in the efficient running of the courts, the interest of public funds and so on. However, here there is a specific definition of "the interests of justice" since the section goes on to say:—

"In considering whether its admission would be in the interests of justice, it shall be the duty of the court to have regard:—
   (i) to the contents of the statement;
  (ii) to any risk, having regard in particular whether it is likely to be possible to controvert the statement if the person making it does not attend to give oral evidence in the proceedings that its admission or exclusion will result in unfairness to the accused or, if there is more than one, to any of them; and
 (iii) to any other circumstances that appear to the court to be relevant."

These discretions are thus somewhat different to those contained in section 25. Those in section 25 as we have seen are more detailed and include some specific matters absent from section 26, namely that regard should be had to the nature and source of the document, its apparent authenticity, and the extent to which it supplies the evidence otherwise not readily available and the relevance of the document to the issues. No doubt the catch-all provision in section 26 relating to "any other circumstances that appear to the court to be relevant" will encompass all these.

The difference is thus the fundamental emphasis that such "criminal investigation documents" shall *not* in general be admissible without the leave of the court and there is thus a strong presumption against admissibility.

MISCELLANEOUS MATTERS

29.18   We shall now go on to consider some miscellaneous matters relevant to documents admitted under the general provisions of sections 23–26 of the Act.

1. *Matters of weight and credit*

29.19   What we have so far considered is of course the question of admissibility. It is perhaps somewhat confusing that amongst the matters to be considered when deciding on the strict test of admissibility are matters which really go to weight such as, *e.g.* under section 25 "the nature and source of the document and . . . whether it appears to be authentic." The mere fact that a document is admissible, however, does not mean that the document is to be taken as a conclusive piece of evidence. Such a document is just a piece of evidence like any other which the trier of fact can accept or reject as he or they see fit in the light of all the circumstances, inherent plausibility, other contradictory evidence and so on. There is a specific provision in Schedule 2, para. 3 to the Act which provides that:—

"In estimating the weight, if any, to be attached to such a statement, regard shall be had to all the circumstances from which any inference can reasonably be drawn as to its accuracy or otherwise."

2. *Using documents to discredit witnesses*

29.20   One can go further than merely introducing contradictory evidence in order to undermine the credibility of a document which is admitted under the Act. One can by Schedule 2, para. 1 to the Act:—

(a) introduce any evidence relevant to the credibility of the person who made the statement which would have been admissible if he had been called as a witness;
(b) with the leave of the court give evidence of any matter on which, if the person who made the statement had been called as a witness, he could have been cross-examined concerning his credibility even though no evidence of that could have been called by the cross-examining party; and
(c) prove in evidence any inconsistent statement, whether oral or written, made by the person whose evidence is admitted under section 23 or section 24 to show that he had contradicted himself at some other time.

3. *Production of the document*

If a statement in a document is admissible under the Act it may be proved **29.21** either by production of the original document or by production of a copy authenticated in such manner as the court may approve. This marks the further weakening of the so-called "best evidence" rule so that if it is for any reason inconvenient to produce the true document at court, (*e.g.* a business ledger in daily use) a reasonable photocopy will suffice. The word "document" includes films, tapes, videos, computer programmes, and in short any method of storing information.

4. *Confessions*

Even though a confession made to a policeman would technically fit section **29.22** 24 of the Act, the Act cannot be used as a way of getting round the much stricter rules with regard to the admissibility of confessions. There are specific provisions excluding the application of section 4 to confessions.

5. *Other discretions*

Quite apart from the discretions to exclude evidence provided by the Act **29.23** there is a specific provision in section 28 that any other discretions which the court might have to exclude evidence are preserved. Thus discretions under section 78 or section 82(3) of the 1984 Police and Criminal Evidence Act will still apply. Of course all these discretions are likely to overlap in any event so that since a court has a more or less unfettered discretion to exclude statements which would prima facie be admissible under section 23 or section 24 under the provisions of sections 25 and 26 of the Act that power would suffice in any event.

6. *Expert evidence*

It will be recalled that the kind of statements that were admissible under **29.24** sections 23 and 24 of the Act were statements of fact. Evidence in the form of experts' reports of course is a mixture of both fact and opinion. Apart from that however the circumstances in which an expert's report comes about would prima facie fit section 24 of the Act. Section 30 of the Act expressly makes experts' reports admissible in criminal cases whether or not the author attends to give oral evidence. If the expert does not attend leave of the court is required to admit the report. Section 30(3) gives various factors which are to be taken into account in deciding whether to admit evidence in the form of a written report from an absent expert. The section provides that for the purpose of determining whether to give leave to admit the report the court shall have regard:—

> "(a) to the contents of the report;
> (b) to the reasons why it is proposed that the person making the report shall not give oral evidence;
> (c) to any risk, having regard in particular to whether it is likely to be possible to controvert the statements in the reports if the person making it does not attend to give oral evidence in the proceedings, that its admission or exclusion will result in unfairness to the accused, or if there is more than one, to any of them; and
> (d) to any other circumstances that appear to the court to be relevant."

The topic of opinion evidence and experts' reports generally is more fully dealt with at para. 32.03.

Public documents

29.25   Public documents are admissible in evidence to prove the truth of the matters stated in them. An example is a public register, *e.g.* of births, deaths and marriage. Likewise, secondary documents prepared by public officers after referring to primary documents, (*e.g.* birth certificates and death certificates) are also admissible in evidence.

This old common law exception to the hearsay rule will now be of less importance because most of the kind of public documents which will be admissible would now come within section 24 of the 1988 Act. It may be, however, that there will be some cases where the old common law exception will still be needed. To come within the rule, the document does not have to just be concerned with a public matter, or come from some official source, but it must fulfil four distinct conditions, namely:

1. it must relate to a public matter; and

2. have been made in pursuance of the duty of a public officer; and

3. be intended to be a permanent record; and

4. be available for inspection by members of the public.

An interesting case which explains these conditions is *Lilley* v. *Pettit* [1946] K.B. 401.

A woman was prosecuted for making a false declaration in relation to the birth of her child. The facts were that the woman remained in the United Kingdom throughout the Second World War, but in 1941 her soldier husband who was serving in the Far East was captured by the Japanese. He remained interned by the Japanese until the end of the war in 1945. In 1944 the woman gave birth to a child and completed a declaration that her husband was the father. Given the normal human gestation period and the presumed unlikeliness of the Japanese having allowed her husband home for conjugal visits, the prosecution's success in the case might have seemed assured. However, the prosecution needed to prove the husband's absence abroad and they sought to do this by production of his Army regimental record showing his absence in the Far East between 1941 and 1945. The regimental records were, of course, hearsay and there was no provision such as section 68 of the 1984 Act in force then. They therefore sought to put them in evidence as a public document within this common law exception. The court held that they were not admissible. Although they did concern a public matter, were made in pursuance of the duty of a public officer and were intended to be a permanent record, they did not fulfil the fourth essential condition. Not only were the Army regimental records not available for inspection by members of the public, but indeed the Official Secrets Act applied to them. Accordingly, the prosecution were unable to use this evidence against the wife.

As indicated above, the importance of this exception viewed as a separate category is now much less in the light of section 24 of the 1988 Act which ought to cover most situations. A variety of individual statutes in any event makes provision for the admissibility of specific sorts of official documents.

Depositions taken in magistrates' court proceedings

29.26

A deposition is a sworn statement taken before a magistrate. Trial in the Crown Court is preceded by a committal hearing before a magistrates' court at which sworn depositions are taken (usually of prosecution witnesses only). Such depositions are not usually admissible at the Crown Court trial but in exceptional situations, they may be. The first of these concerns the special situation of a witness who was too ill to attend the committal proceedings and the second of a witness who, having appeared at the committal proceedings, subsequently becomes unavailable. The two relevant sections are:

DEPOSITIONS TO PERPETUATE TESTIMONY UNDER SECTION 105 OF THE MAGISTRATES' COURTS ACT 1980

29.27

Under this section, the deposition of a potential witness who is dangerously ill may be taken out of court and it will then be admissible in evidence at the trial, if the witness has by then died or is still too ill to travel and is unlikely to recover. In this situation, however, it is not simply a matter of the police taking a magistrate to the witness's bedside and getting a statement. There is a provision that the accused must have the opportunity of attending at the time when the witness gives his deposition and have the opportunity of cross-examining the ill witness. The answers to cross-examination are taken down and become part of the witness's deposition just as much as the part which he volunteers in examination in chief.

CRIMINAL JUSTICE ACT 1925, S.13(3)

29.28

The deposition of a witness who at the committal proceedings was conditionally ordered to appear at the trial, may be read at the trial, if he is proved to be dead, insane, too ill to travel, or kept away by the accused. The use of the word "may" clearly confers on the court a discretion and they have to consider the degree of prejudice to the accused caused by the absence of the witness, in much the same way in which they have to consider the same thing in the special circumstances referred to above under section 26 of the Criminal Justice Act 1988 where the nature of the record which the prosecution seek to put in is in the form of a statement prepared in contemplation of proceedings.

Statements admitted as part of the "res gestae"

29.29

Res gestae means "transaction" or "series of events." Under this old exception to the hearsay rule, statements out of court may be admitted if they are made at the very time of a particular incident (usually the commission of a crime). The rationale of the rule is that because such statements are spontaneous and made at the very time, there is no opportunity to fabricate evidence so they have a special probative value. A clear modern example is the facts of *R.* v. *Turnbull* (1984) 80 Cr.App.R. 104.

A man who had recently been in the company of the accused and his brother, staggered into a public house fatally stabbed and was heard to say that "Ronnie Tommo did it." "Ronnie Tommo" was the nickname of Turnbull and he was in due course arrested and charged on this, amongst other, evidence. The court held that the victim's dying words, spoken so close in time to the point at which he must have been stabbed, were admissible under this rule.

This case should not be confused with another well-known exception to the hearsay rule which is not material for our purposes, to do with dying declarations by the victim of a homicide. The words in Turnbull's case were obviously highly probative and, indeed, vital to the prosecution in view of the victim's death. It must be stressed that, in the normal case, the speaking of the words must be linked very closely in time to the incident. It should not be understood from the example given above of Turnbull's case that the words need necessarily be spoken by the victim. They can be spoken by anybody, including a witness, a bystander and so on. The vital point is how *spontaneously* they were spoken. If they are far in time from the incident, or there is any motive to fabricate and the delay sufficient to allow fabrication, then evidence of the words used will not be admissible. The question of *res gestae* rarely arises in the context of mundane crimes.

30. Admissions and Confessions

Admissions in civil cases will be dealt with separately in a later section on civil hearsay. We are now going to consider the subject of admissions and confessions in criminal cases, with the related topics of the accused's right of silence and the questioning of suspects.

Admissions and confessions are the most important exception to the hearsay **30.01** rule in practice. By this is meant not that they are the most commonly used exception to the hearsay rule, because, as has previously been explained the routine exceptions contained in section 9 of the Criminal Justice Act 1967 and section 102 of the Magistrates' Courts Act 1980 are in use in thousands of cases every day. They are the most important in the sense that courts spend more time investigating the admissibility of admissions and confessions, than on any other aspect of admissibility, and in the volume of case law that the topic has generated over the last century.

Admissions and confessions, whilst hearsay, are deemed to have peculiar value because of the unlikelihood of a person untruthfully stating something adverse to his case. The terms "admission" and "confession" are now used virtually interchangeably and they usually mean a statement accepting guilt of a crime. However, the terms do not only cover full acceptance of guilt, they may refer to the acceptance of any fact adverse to the maker's case. The definition of "confession" appears in section 82 of the Police and Criminal Evidence Act 1984, which says:—

> "Confession includes any statement wholly or partly adverse to the person who made it whether made to a person in authority or not and whether made in words or otherwise."

Thus we can see that it would amount to a "confession" for a person to, say, admit in the course of interrogation that he knew certain goods had been stolen if that point was not generally known, even whilst himself denying that he had been the person responsible. The fact of knowledge would clearly be adverse to his case and would, despite his denial, tend to indicate his involvement in the crime. Admissions and confessions may be either written, oral or non-verbal and in the latter cases may be, *e.g.* an answer during interrogation, or a nod of the head.

Police and Criminal Evidence Act 1984, s.76
The law on admissibility of confessions is now contained essentially in **30.02** section 76 of the Police and Criminal Evidence Act 1984. In addition to that section we need to consider certain aspects of various Codes of Practice on the treatment and questioning of suspects which have been issued under the authority of section 66 of the Act. These codes govern the way in which police must treat people in their custody. In addition, as we shall see, we need to consider another section of the Act, section 78.

30.03   Let us first consider the text of section 76.

"76.—(1) In any proceedings, a confession made by an accused person may be given in evidence against him in so far as it is relevant to any matter in issue in the proceedings and is not excluded by the court in pursuance of this section.

(2) If, in any proceedings where the prosecution proposes to give in evidence a confession made by an accused person, it is represented to the court that the confession was or may have been obtained—
(a) by oppression of the person who made it; or
(b) in consequence of anything said or done which was likely, in the circumstances existing at the time, to render unreliable any confession which might be made by him in consequence thereof, the court shall not allow the confession to be given in evidence against him except in so far as the prosecution proves to the court beyond reasonable doubt that the confession (notwithstanding that it may be true) was not obtained as aforesaid.

(3) In any proceedings where the prosecution proposes to give in evidence a confession made by an accused person, the court may of its own motion require the prosecution, as a condition of allowing it to do so, to prove that the confession was not obtained as mentioned in subsection (2) above.

(4) The fact that a confession is wholly or partly excluded in pursuance of this section shall not affect the admissibility in evidence—
(a) of any facts discovered as a result of the confession; or
(b) where the confession is relevant as showing that the accused speaks, writes or expresses himself in a particular way, of so much of the confession as is necessary to show that he does so.

(5) Evidence that a fact to which this subsection applies was discovered as a result of a statement made by an accused person shall not be admissible unless evidence of how it was discovered is given by him or on his behalf.

(6) Subsection (5) above applies—
(a) to any fact discovered as a result of a confession which is wholly excluded in pursuance of this section; and
(b) to any fact discovered as a result of a confession which is partly so excluded, if that fact is discovered as a result of the excluded part of the confession.

(7) Nothing in Part VII of this Act shall prejudice the admissibility of a confession made by an accused person.

(8) In this section "oppression" includes torture, inhuman or degrading treatment, and the use or threat of violence (whether or not amounting to torture)."

30.04   The test for admissibility of a confession is thus:—

1.   Was there *oppression* as defined by section 76(8)? If so, the confession will be inadmissible.

2.   If not, was there any other feature of the whole procedure which led up to the confession which renders the confession *unreliable*. If so, the confession must also be excluded.

268

We shall now consider the various matters arising from section 76.

OPPRESSION

This is defined by section 76(8). Oppression "includes torture, inhuman or **30.05** degrading treatment, and the use or threat of violence (whether or not amounting to torture)." The use of the word "includes" causes a little difficulty. It presumably means that the matters referred to are not exhaustive as definitions of oppression and that lesser conduct may qualify. The obvious problem is that in previous case law, the word "oppression" usually meant relatively mild conduct which sapped the free will of the suspect, (*e.g.* excessively lengthy questioning). The term, however, now seems to mean essentially the most serious forms of conduct. The reference to "torture and inhuman or degrading treatment" is borrowed from Article 3 of the European Convention on Human Rights and Fundamental Freedoms and a great deal of case law under that convention has demonstrated that quite a high level of maltreatment is required to amount to torture. It is somewhat odd that the statutory definition of "oppression" (albeit an inclusive one and not an exhaustive one) means that the word has a totally different meaning from its previous sense. However that is clearly the effect of the section. In one early case *R.* v. *Fulling* [1987] 2 Q.B. 426 the Court of Appeal strangely ignored the statutory definition of oppression in section 76(8) and relied on the dictionary definition. In a later case *R.* v. *Davidson* 1988 Cr.L.R. 442 the court concluded that oppression was present where police were guilty of wholesale breaches of the Act and Codes and thus had been oppressive in the sense of "exercising power in a harsh and wrongful manner." It is quite clear that only in rare cases will oppression be found to be present. Whether it is present ought therefore to be easy to see from the accused's description of what the police allegedly did to him. Any violence will amount to oppression, as will the threat of violence. On the assumption that in a given case the conduct by the police falls short of oppression we turn now to the second test.

UNRELIABILITY

This is the key word in section 76. The word "unreliable" clearly involves a **30.06** wide-ranging test. The use of the words "in consequence of anything said or done," "circumstances existing at the time" and "reliable" gives the court a very wide mandate to enquire thoroughly into all the circumstances surrounding the giving of the confession. It should be noted that there is no requirement that the police should have behaved improperly in any way for the confession to be held unreliable. The words clearly imply a subjective test, *i.e.* in all the circumstances, was anything said or done likely to render *this* confession by *this* accused unreliable? Thus conduct on the part of the police which might be perfectly proper if conducting the interrogation of a hardened criminal, might well be such as to render a confession unreliable if administered to someone of a more vulnerable nature, *e.g.* an older person, or an inexperienced young person, or a person with health worries. Good examples of things which would tend to render a confession unreliable but which would not amount to oppression as such, would be: promise of bail if a statement is made (remembering that many suspects will have little idea of their rights and may be particularly vulnerable if they imagine they are going to be kept in custody until a court hearing which they may be under the mistaken impression may be some weeks away); promise of a charge being dropped, or a lesser charge preferred; unduly lengthy or harsh questioning; promise to leave a friend or relative out of police enquiries; promise that favourable mention will be made to the magistrates or judge at the sentencing stage of the extent of the accused's co-operation with the police. We shall return to the topic of the conduct of the interrogation of suspects in due course after examining the rest of the text of section 76.

30.07 So far we have seen that by virtue of section 76(2) the prosecution must prove beyond reasonable doubt that any confession which they wish to put in evidence has been obtained in circumstances such that it is reliable and was not made by oppression. Section 76(3) provides that the court may of its own motion require the prosecution to prove these things, even if the accused makes no objection.

THINGS FOUND IN CONSEQUENCE OF A CONFESSION

30.08 Section 76(4) preserves the former common law. The effect of section 76(4) is that if a suspect gives an inadmissible confession, but while confessing says where stolen goods are to be found and these are found where he said they would be and are, for instance, covered in his fingerprints, the finding of the goods and the identification of the fingerprints can be referred to in evidence, although no mention of the confession itself can be made unless the accused himself refers to it (see s.76(5)). On the other hand, if when found, the stolen goods did not have the accused's fingerprints on them, or there was no other factor to directly link them to the accused apart from his confession, then the finding of the stolen goods would not be of any evidential value to the prosecution, because they would not be permitted to testify, if the confession were inadmissible, as to how the whereabouts of the goods came to their knowledge.

PROOF OF SOME PART OF THE CONFESSION TO IDENTIFY THE ACCUSED

30.09 Section 76(4)(*b*) provides that if there is something relevant in the confession to show that the accused speaks, writes or expresses himself in a particular way, then even though the confession is ruled inadmissible, the part of it which shows that the accused does speak or write in that way may be admissible for that purpose. An example would be, say a kidnapping case where the ransom note contains a strikingly mistaken spelling and the confession, in the accused's own hand, has the same mistake, thus showing that the accused is likely to be the kidnapper. In such a situation, if the confession is ruled inadmissible, then at least the phrase showing the mistaken spelling could be put in evidence, together with the evidence of the officer to whom the accused gave the confession to show that the accused uses that mis-spelling and thus to link him to the ransom note. Section 76(5) provides that evidence that a fact such as those under section 76(4) was discovered as a result of a confession may be admissible if the accused himself testifies concerning the matter. One would not expect in the normal course of things where a confession has been excluded that the accused would himself want to so testify and thus, to reveal the link between his inadmissible confession and the finding of the relevant fact, *e.g.* stolen goods, etc., as in the example previously explained.

We must now turn to five miscellaneous matters, which need to be discussed **30.10** before leaving the subject of confessions; these are:—

1. the interrogation of suspects;

2. the right of silence;

3. the procedure for determining admissibility of a confession;

4. editing;

5. the rule that the confession is only evidence against its maker.

Interrogation of suspects

Few confessions come about by the guilty person walking into a police **30.11** station and handing over a previously written statement admitting total guilt. In the normal case, confessions come about in response to police questioning. However much additional evidence the police have against a person, they still generally prefer to see if a confession is forthcoming believing, correctly, that it will be more difficult for a person to plead not guilty in the face of his own confession, than if he had not made one.

Confessions then usually come about in the course of interrogation, usually **30.12** at the police station. The police consider, certainly rightly, that a person who is not in his own premises may be somewhat more ill at ease, and may no doubt, not being entirely certain of his rights, wonder about the police's power to detain him for lengthy periods and may thus be generally more vulnerable. Interrogation may end in a full written confession signed by the suspect, or there may merely be statements made admitting some fact relevant to guilt in the course of answering questions without a subsequent written statement.

The interrogation of suspects and the effect of s.78 of the 1984 Act

Until recently these "confessions" were usually called "verbals" and were generally recorded by one of two interrogating policemen in longhand either in the course of the interrogation, or soon after it had finished. Much of the trial used to be taken up with establishing whether or not the words amounting to a confession were ever said in the common instance where the accused alleged fabrication or misunderstanding by the police who had recorded his alleged answers to questions. These problems have now been obviated to a large extent because tape recording of police interviews is about to become universal. Even here however there may still be occasions when "verbals" are alleged to have occurred at some stage before tape recording can start, *e.g.* in the police car taking the suspect to the police station, or at the suspect's own home.

The practice is that if, in the course of the "verbals," that is question and **30.13** answer by police and suspect, the suspect says anything which is in any way helpful to the prosecution case, then the whole of the record of the interrogation (subject to editing, see below) may be put in evidence. In principle this should actually only occur if the accused does end up giving a "confession" remembering that this may be less than a full acceptance of guilt as discussed above. However, it is not uncommon for the police to seek to render evidence of "verbals" in which there is very little at all to assist them, for instance the case of a suspect who has maintained a strong denial throughout but may have uttered one ambiguous phrase, *e.g.* to have asked a policeman what he thinks he will get by way of sentence. The accused may merely have meant "if things come to the worst and I am wrongly convicted, what sentence am I likely to get?," but such remarks are often used as the pretext for tendering the whole account of the interrogation in evidence perhaps as a way of impressing upon the court that the accused's denials were not particularly strenuous. In principle, however, the record of interrogation should only be put in at all when there is something in it which is adverse to the case of the suspect.

30.14   As indicated above, Codes of Practice have been issued under the authority of section 66 of the Police and Criminal Evidence Act 1984. The Codes will be referred to again in the section on criminal procedure. So far as is material to the law on confessions, however, the following matters are worthy of note:

Codes are admissible under sections 66 and by virtue of section 67(11) of the Act which states:—

"In all criminal and civil proceedings any such Code will be admissible in evidence and if any provision of such a Code appears to the court or tribunal conducting the proceedings to be relevant to any question arising in the proceedings, it shall be taken into account in determining that question."

30.15   Accordingly, breach of the Codes will be relevant to admissibility of a confession if it has some factual bearing on the reliability of the confession. Breach of the Codes is a police disciplinary offence and may in some circumstances also give the person wronged some rights in tort, but the court will not use the breach of the Code as a means of punishing the police in the criminal proceedings themselves by excluding the confession automatically. Everything will obviously depend on the nature and seriousness of the breach and the directness of its relevance to the circumstances in which the confession was made. The same would clearly apply in the case of breach of other substantive provision of the 1984 Act. So, for example, section 41 of the Act prima facie limits the police to a maximum period of 24 hours for the detention of a suspect without charge; section 58 guarantees a suspect the right to consult privately with a solicitor; section 56 guarantees the right for a person to have details of his whereabouts communicated to a friend or relative. We shall consider below the importance of breach of the codes so far as admissibility is concerned in particular in the light of case law under section 78 of the Act.

30.16   The Code provides a framework for the conduct of interrogation. It provides for reasonable comfort, rest and refreshment during interrogation and in particular, for a suspect to be cautioned by the police in the words "you do not have to say anything unless you wish to do so but what you say may be given in evidence." This question must be administered or re-administered at various times, in particular:—

When a police officer first has grounds to suspect a suspect of committing an offence; again upon arrest; when resuming questioning after an arrest; after any break in questioning; and upon charging.

The following matters should also be noted at this point.

1. After a person has been charged he should not be further questioned, **30.17** except for the purpose of minimising harm or loss, or clearing up ambiguities, (*e.g.* to help trace stolen property).

2. If after a person has been charged, a policeman wishes to bring to his **30.18** notice any written statement made by another person, he shall hand him a copy of that statement, but not invite comment on it, save to caution him. The purpose of this provision is to stop the police separately questioning two suspects, getting one to incriminate the other, and then provoking that other after he has been charged to then give them a statement confessing to the crime as a means of getting his own back on the other suspect by in his turn incriminating him. It should however be noted that so long as the police do this *before* charging, the practice is perfectly proper. However, the police may not delay charging past the stage at which they should have charged, merely as a tactical device to avoid the coming into effect of this rule.

3. Finally full details of every aspect of the custody of the accused must be **30.19** kept in a proper custody record by a policeman of sergeant rank who has no involvement in the case in question and whose duties include guaranteeing the welfare of suspects at the police station. Full details therefore of the time of the interrogation, the timing of breaks, the reasons for continuing custody and so on must be fully and faithfully recorded.

Unfairness and section 78 of the Police and Criminal Evidence Act 1984

Early case law under the 1984 Act led to a largely unexpected development. **30.20** Before the 1984 Act the law on confessions was relatively clear and was separate from a quite different body of law which related to the exclusion of other evidence (that is evidence apart from confessions) which had been obtained in some way *unfairly*, *e.g.* where police trick a suspect into revealing the whereabouts of stolen goods, or act as agents provocateurs by pretending to be members of the criminal gang and thus actually procuring the commission of the crime. We shall briefly consider this separate set of rules later in the text at para. 34.01.

There is a particular provision in the 1984 Act which was widely thought to make no difference at all to the common law. This is section 78 which confers a discretion on the court and provides:—

> "In any proceedings the court may refuse to allow evidence on which the prosecution proposes to rely to be given if it appears to the court that having regard to all the circumstances, including the circumstances in which the evidence was obtained, the admission of the evidence would have such an adverse effect on the fairness of the proceedings that the court ought not to admit it."

It was thought that this provision would be considered quite separately from the law on confessions, but surprisingly in many cases the courts have been prepared to apply both section 76 and section 78 together. An important early case was *R.* v. *Mason* [1988] 1 W.L.R. 139. In this case the accused had been tricked by the police who had falsely pretended that his finger print had been found at the scene of the crime. The police had maintained this pretence not only to him but to his solicitor. On appeal the conviction was quashed because of the deceit practised by the police on the appellant and his solicitor which the court described as "absolutely reprehensible." It is difficult to see whether this is really a correct application of section 78. Firstly it is actually quite a common police interrogation technique for them to pretend that they have more evidence in their possession than they actually do have, even if it is not usually a claim to such a damning piece of evidence as in this case. Secondly, it is doubtful whether section 78 was correctly applied given that section 78 requires the unfairness in the case to be "in the proceedings." *R.* v. *Mason* seems to give an extended definition to the phrase "in the proceedings" so that it appears to mean "at any stage of the whole criminal process" rather than just in the *trial itself.* It is suggested that, however laudable the outcome of this case on its own facts, the court was misinterpreting section 78. The court did however stress that it was *not* excluding the evidence in an attempt to discipline the police which the court insisted was no part of the function of the law of evidence. Another somewhat strange feature of the case was that if the court had been determined to exclude the confession it could surely have done so in simple reliance on section 76. It could surely have been argued that the confession was simply "unreliable" given that it would be quite possible that even an innocent accused, on hearing that the police had damning evidence (which the accused must have assumed the police had fabricated) would make a false confession in order to procure more lenient treatment. That process of reasoning could have led the court to conclude that the confession was unreliable without needing to go on to consider general unfairness under section 78.

There have been many recent cases which have continually extended the ambit of section 78. In some cases breaches of the Codes of Practice, wrongful refusal of access to a solicitor, failure to observe proper procedures on commencement of interrogation, and in particular, failure to keep a full custody record have led to confessions being excluded. The precise reasoning varies with the facts of each case but in general the courts have been prepared to find that impropriety in interrogation procedures of any substantial type fatally flaws the confession evidence obtained. In one or two cases in particular where the accused was a hardened criminal and well aware of his rights the court was able to conclude that there had been no substantial unfairness but certainly with suspects who are in any way vulnerable, or where there is some dispute as to what exactly occurred and no proper record of it the confession will be excluded.

SUMMARY OF THE PRESENT POSITION

30.21   The law's present confusion has really been caused by the eliding and overlapping of the three categories of oppression, unreliability and unfairness. It is suggested that the following is the correct approach:—

1.   It must always be borne in mind that if anyone suggests that the confession has been obtained by oppression or is unreliable that it is for the prosecution to prove beyond reasonable doubt that this is not so. This is why sometimes apparently technical breaches of the codes have led to exclusion because it is then difficult for the prosecution to demonstrate

(the burden being on them) that the breach has had no effect. For example, if no proper custody record has been kept. From that point the procedure should be as follows:—

2. Is the conduct complained of "oppression" in the sense of serious misconduct contemplated in section 76(8)? Although the definition given there is an inclusive definition, on any reasonable interpretation of the section for conduct to amount to oppression it must be equivalent to violence or inhuman treatment as the words indicate.

3. On the assumption that actual oppression is not found the court must then examine everything said or done which might tend to make the confession unreliable. The court thus has a wide mandate to enquire into all the circumstances in which the confession was obtained from the moment the suspect was first in contact with the police, or indeed with anyone else connected with the prosecution, (e.g. a store detective). Applying a subjective test and bearing in mind the burden of proving reliability is on the prosecution the court ought to examine whether there seems to be any causal link between everything that has happened and the giving of the confession.

4. Finally, having decided that the confession is reliable the court should then apply its mind to any representation made to it about fairness in the proceedings. It follows from the previous common law and from the express statements of the court in *R.* v. *Mason* that in deciding this, *fairness* is all that matters and the courts will not use section 78 as a means of disciplining the police. However it is clear that an extended meaning will be given to the phrase "in the proceedings" so as, again, to open up for consideration everything that has happened from the first moment when the suspect was in contact with the police.

We now turn to some other related matters.

The accused's right of silence

Under the general law, no one is obliged to answer police questions, nor to give evidence at his own trial. If an accused refuses to answer questions out of court, then if the question comes from a person with whom the accused is *not on even terms* the judge should tell the jury that they must not draw an inference of guilt from his silence, or his failure to answer police questioning by telling them of his defence. The phrase "not on even terms" tends to mean that if a person is being questioned by someone in authority of some kind, particularly a policeman but also, *e.g.* a store detective, perhaps an employer, etc., no inference can be drawn from the exercise of the right of silence. If, however, a person is being asked a question by an ordinary layman with whom he is on even terms, failure to reply to a question may indeed lead to an adverse inference being drawn, even to the effect that the suspect accepted the truth of the allegation made in the question. Thus, if, *e.g.* a passer-by says to a suspect "You are the man who stole that lady's handbag" and the suspect remains silent, that may amount to an acceptance of the truth of the allegation. It will of course always be open to the suspect to give his explanation of the silence. Thus, for example, he may say that he preferred to treat the accusation as so ridiculous that it was not worthy of a reply, or say that he preferred not to provoke an inflammatory situation by participating in the discussion. It will then be up to the court to decide what

30.22

inference they place upon the suspect's silence in the face of the allegation. If, however, the same accusation in the same circumstances had been made by a policeman, then *no* inference at all could be drawn from the suspect's silence. It should be remembered here that the giving of the caution is merely a reminder of a right which the suspect has in any event. It is thus immaterial whether or not the caution has been administered—no inference may be drawn either way.

One aspect of the accused's right of silence out of court is that an accused is under no obligation to give the prosecution any advance notice of his defence before trial, with the single exception of an alibi defence in the Crown Court under section 11 of the Criminal Justice Act 1967. In this case, an accused must give particulars of his alibi to the prosecution, either at the end of or within seven days after the course of committal proceedings, otherwise unless the trial judge gives leave, he will not be able to adduce evidence in support of an alibi defence.

With regard to the accused's silence *in court*, (*i.e.* refusing to testify) the prosecution may not comment at all on this, but the judge may comment within reason. As mentioned earlier, he may not invite the jury to infer guilt as such, *e.g.* by saying words to the effect that innocent men usually want to give their versions and that the jury must draw their own conclusions from the accused's failure to testify. If the judge does go too far in commenting then any conviction will be quashed.

The procedure for determining admissibility

30.23   In making its opening speech to a jury in the Crown Court, the prosecution must refrain from referring to any item of evidence, the admissibility of which will be challenged by the defence. The defence are, of course, aware of the nature of the prosecution's case because of the committal proceedings at which stage the prosecution must reveal their evidence. If objection is to be taken to a confession, then no reference to the confession must be made. If the opening speech is unintelligible without reference to the confession, (*i.e.* if it is the only real evidence against the accused in the case) the admissibility issue may be taken as a preliminary matter before the opening speech. Otherwise, the case proceeds after the opening speech with witnesses being called, examined and cross-examined, until the item of disputed evidence is reached. In the case of a confession, this will probably be quite early in that the investigating officer is usually the second prosecution witness after the victim, although there is no real rule as to this. As soon as the question of the disputed confession is reached, the jury are sent out of the court (without of course knowing why) whilst the issue of admissibility is tried by the judge alone. This hearing is known as the "voire dire" or "trial within a trial." Witnesses may be called and are cross-examined in the usual way, legal argument is then presented by both sides, and the judge then decides on the admissibility of the confession. This will usually involve him deciding a dispute of fact, (*e.g.* whose version as to what happened at the police station to believe) and then deciding admissibility as a question of law, dependent on the facts as found.

30.24   If the judge rules that the confession is *inadmissible* under the above principles, as obtained by oppression or in such circumstances as to be unreliable, the jury when recalled to the court, are never told of the existence of the "confession" and the trial proceeds. If the confession is ruled *admissible, i.e.*

reliable, the confession is put before the jury. It is still open to the defence to challenge it in any way, for instance by trying to show the jury that it is untrue because of the circumstances in which it was obtained. This may often involve them challenging the police evidence (for instance as to what happened at the police station) in exactly the same terms in which they have just challenged it before the judge on the voire dire. Indeed, often hours of cross-examination are repeated virtually word for word as the defence seek to show the jury that the confession is of no weight, the weight to be attached to it being of course entirely a question of fact for them. The judge has only ruled on the issue of "reliability" as a matter of law.

In the magistrates' court there has also to be a formal *voire dire* because **30.25** section 76(2) requires it. However whereas in the Crown Court if the judge rules the confession admissible when the jury returns all the evidence is likely to be repeated in an effort to show the jury that whilst admissible in law the confession is of little weight, in the Magistrates' Court the evidence is heard once only. If the magistrates do not exclude the confession they do not of course need to have the evidence rehearsed for them to consider separately the question of weight. Of course if the magistrates do exclude the confession then the problem remains of whether they will truly be able to put the terms of it out of their minds. This is a problem with every question of admissibility of evidence in the magistrates' court because of the absence of the separation of function of trying facts and law.

It ought finally to be stressed that the judge's function is to decide *admis-* **30.26** *sibility* of the confession. It is for the jury to decide whether it is *true*. If one has a situation, therefore, where an accused challenges the words of a confession, not as to the circumstances in which they were obtained, but as to whether they were ever said at all, then one has a problem. Suppose, for example, a policeman has been questioning an accused and the accused maintains that he was treated perfectly properly and that the questioning only lasted 20 minutes and that throughout he maintained a firm denial, but the policeman insists that the accused finally gave a verbal confession. If the accused denies that he ever said the words alleged to amount to a confession, then there should *not* be a voire dire. The question of whether the words were ever said, like all other questions of fact, is a matter for the jury alone.

Editing of confessions

Suppose that the words of a confession refer to a previous offence or some **30.27** other inadmissible matter. This will most commonly occur in the case of a confession which is in the form of "verbals," *i.e.* responses to interrogation and indeed the words of reference to previous offences may be made by the interrogating officer, rather than the accused himself. The rule is that where a confession is to be placed before the jury and it contains inadmissible matter (quite independently of any question of reliability) the confession may be "edited" to omit the offending part. If the editing is so substantial that the confession is unintelligible after it, the whole may need to be excluded. If the actual document is to be shown to the jury, it should be re-typed without blanks or erasures which might lead the jury to speculate on the reasons for them. If a witness is going to give evidence of the contents of the confession, defence counsel should indicate to prosecuting counsel that the witness ought to be warned not to say the offending words. It might be helpful to give an example:—

In the course of an interrogation the following question and answer occur:

Policeman: "We think you've been at it since you came out of Brixton in 1989. You may have got a result on that one last year, but with a habit like yours screwing is the only way you're going to get the money."

Suspect: "I'm saying nothing."

In this example, there are three quite inadmissible matters in the policeman's question. One is a reference to the suspect having been in prison before (on the assumption that "Brixton" is a fairly clear reference which will be picked up by the jury). The second is to the suspect having "got a result on" something last year, implying that he has been acquitted on a similar charge. Although in legal theory an acquittal may be a demonstration of innocence, it is something which an accused is entitled to have kept from a jury since the jury may begin suspecting that he was wrongly acquitted, or otherwise speculate about his character, and thirdly the reference to his "habit" is again a reference to an aspect of bad character (*i.e.* drugs dependency) which may adversely influence the jury against the suspect. It should be mentioned that in this example the word "screwing" means burgling and that although such words are rarely used by real criminals, most policemen learn what they suppose to be criminal *argot* from television series such as "The Sweeney" and "Minder." This is a case of life imitating art, rather than the reverse.

Accordingly in the example the question and answer would be edited out of any version put before the jury.

Confessions implicating others

30.28   It should not be forgotten that a confession is an exception to the hearsay rule based on the peculiar probative value of statements made against a person's own interests. A confession is therefore only evidence against its maker. This leads to considerable practical difficulties in the case of the trial of more than one accused. If A and B were charged with the same offence and A alone had made a confession that he and B had carried out the crime, then if they were tried separately there would be no problem. The confession would be quite inadmissible at B's trial as hearsay and of course at A's trial it would be evidence against A if proved to be reliable in the usual way. However, the much more normal procedure with co-accused is to try them together. So, in the above example, what is to happen to A's confession which is clearly not admissible as against B? The prejudicial effect as against B will *not* normally be a ground for ordering separate trials. There are thus two options. (1), the confession may be edited to exclude any reference to B. (2), if this cannot be done without rendering the whole confession quite unintelligible, then the confession may be put in evidence but the judge must give the jury a strong direction that they must not treat what A said about B in his confession as any evidence against B. The jury are sometimes helped in this exercise in mental gymnastics by the judge explaining that it is clearly unfair to hold a statement made by A in B's absence against B, when he had no chance to reply, and to point out that A may have had his own motives for implicating B. Failure to give this direction is fatal to B's conviction.

It should be very clearly noted, however, that this is a rule relating to A implicating B *in his confession.* If A actually goes into the witness box and gives evidence *on his own behalf* in the course of which he implicates B, then this is admissible evidence in the normal way, just as any other evidence at the trial itself is. It will be remembered that in such a case, a corroboration warning, whilst not essential because A is not a prosecution witness and thus not an "accomplice" within the strict technical meaning of that word, may be desirable because he may have a purpose of his own to serve in attempting to procure B's conviction.

31. Hearsay in Civil Proceedings and the Civil Evidence Act 1968

31.01   The 1968 Civil Evidence Act now governs the admissibility of hearsay evidence in civil proceedings in the county court and High Court. Hearsay means precisely the same thing as in criminal cases. By section 1 of the Act, hearsay evidence is to be admissible in civil proceedings only:—

1.   by virtue of the following sections of this Act, or

2.   by virtue of any other statute, or

3.   by agreement between the parties.

Section 1 of the Act, therefore, has the effect of abolishing all common law exceptions to the hearsay rule in civil proceedings. Hearsay can now only be admitted in civil proceedings by virtue of the 1968 Act, some other statute, or by agreement of all the parties to a case that they will, for the present case, waive the strict rules of evidence and admit hearsay. This last is merely an example of the general rule that in civil cases the parties can agree to waive any rule of evidence and (usually) any rule of procedure as well.

In this area of the law, therefore, there is now more or less complete separation between the rules for criminal and civil cases, although there are some approximate equivalents. For instance, sections 4 and 8 of the 1968 Act, which we shall examine shortly, are clearly very similar to section 68 of the Police and Criminal Evidence Act 1984 for criminal proceedings, which we have previously examined, and their general effect is the same.

31.02   The most important of the sections of the Civil Evidence Act 1968 ("the Act") are sections 2, 4 and 8. The operation of these sections in practice is governed by R.S.C., Ord. 38, rr. 20–34 and County Court Rules, Ord. 20, rr. 20–30. To explain the effect of the Act, it is best to divide hearsay into first-hand hearsay, and second-hand hearsay.

Example of first-hand hearsay:
An accident occurs at a cross-roads. Eye witness W tells X, another person who comes to the scene later, what he has seen at the accident. If X were to be permitted to narrate what W told him in court this would be first-hand hearsay. Likewise, if W's written proof of evidence were admitted at the trial, *e.g.* by being handed to the judge or read out to him, this would also be first-hand hearsay.

Example of second-hand hearsay:
Second-hand hearsay merely involves, as its name suggests, the interposition of one other person between the direct observer and the course of testimony in court. So if, to take the same facts, W, having told X what he had seen, X now tells Y and Y comes to court to narrate what X told him that

W had said. Here there are three people involved and this is second-hand hearsay. It would also be second-hand hearsay if what was brought to court was X's written statement about what W had told him.

The general effect of the Act is that the court must admit all *first-hand* hearsay, provided certain conditions are satisfied, and even if these conditions are not satisfied, the court still has an *inclusionary* discretion to admit. However, the court will *not* usually admit *second-hand hearsay*, unless it is contained in a record and certain other conditions are fulfilled, although again, the court has an *inclusionary* discretion, even if these conditions are not in fact fulfilled.

Before going on to discuss the provisions of the Act, it is important to remember that the Act, where it makes hearsay admissible, only deals with curing the hearsay defect of evidence. In this respect, it is exactly like section 68 of the Police and Criminal Evidence Act 1984, which has already been discussed. Thus, if a piece of evidence suffers from some other defect as well as being hearsay, then the Act will not make if admissible. For example, the opinion evidence of a layman is usually inadmissible. If an item of evidence were hearsay, as well as opinion, the Act could not be used to have it admitted, for despite the hearsay defect having been cured by the provisions of the Act, it would still suffer from the same other defect, that is it would still be inadmissible opinion evidence.

Civil Evidence Act 1968, s.2

The Act makes a distinction between cases where the maker of a hearsay **31.03** statement is to be called as a witness, and cases where he is not.

Section 2 of the Act provides:

> "In any civil proceedings a statement ... made whether orally or in a document or otherwise by any person, whether called as a witness in those proceedings or not, shall ... be admissible as evidence of any facts stated therein of which direct oral evidence by him would be admissible."

It is important to examine the effect of this and of R.S.C., Ord. 38, rr. 20–34 in two differing circumstances, therefore:

(a)   where the maker of a hearsay statement is to be called as a witness, and

(b)   where the maker is not to be called as a witness.

WHERE THE MAKER IS TO BE CALLED

In such a case, a party will clearly only want to prove the witness's own prior **31.04** consistent statement. There is, after all, no point in attacking your own witness's credibility! To enable this to be done, therefore, that is to use one's witness's own prior consistent statement, there are two conditions with which one must comply:

1.   the party calling the witness must have complied with Order 38, Rule 21 and given notice to all other parties within the prescribed time after setting down, of his desire to use the statement; such notice must contain the substance of the words used, if the hearsay is oral, or a copy of the statement, if written. This means, therefore, that if one is going to

use the section, one loses the advantage of surprise at trial—there would normally of course be no obligation at all to tell the other side what one's witnesses were going to say;

2. the trial judge must give leave for this statement to be used. This means that the judge must normally be convinced that the statement has some value. This will only rarely be the case—after all if the previous statement is merely consistent with the witness's present sworn testimony, what point is there in using it? It is merely the pointless repetition of evidence which has already been given. So usually a judge would refuse leave for the earlier statement to be used. Further, by section 2(2)(b) such a statement can usually only be put in evidence at the conclusion of the witness's evidence in chief. Thus it would not be possible to use the statement as a way of avoiding the witness having to give any evidence in chief at all, that is merely calling the witness, giving him a copy of his statement, asking him if it was true, and asking him to read it out as evidence.

It is useful to give two examples of how the section might work, therefore; the first is a relatively straightforward example, but in the second there is some special factor present.

Example 1:
An eye witness to an accident, W, gives the plaintiff's solicitor a proof of evidence, which is largely favourable to the plaintiff's case. Within 21 days of setting the case down for trial in the High Court, the plaintiff's solicitor complies with the provisions of *Order 38* and serves on the defendant a copy of the statement and a notice that he proposes to use the statement in evidence, as well as calling the witness. At the trial, W gives evidence which is exactly along the lines of his previous statement. The plaintiff's counsel then applies to put in evidence the witness's prior written statement. The judge will refuse leave in such a case. He has seen the witness giving his evidence verbally, and it adds nothing, and is merely a waste of time for the witness's previous written statement now to be put in evidence as well. That, therefore, is a relatively straightforward case. Consider, however, the following.

Example 2—The facts of *Morris* v. *Stratford on Avon R.D.C* [1973] 1 W.L.R. 1059:
A witness gave the defendants a statement concerning how an accident had arisen, which was generally helpful to the defendants' case. For various reasons, the plaintiff's action did not come on for trial for five years after the cause of action arose. When the defendants at trial called the witness, W, to testify, his evidence was confused and vague. The defendants therefore applied to put in evidence his earlier written statement to supplement, and in parts, correct his testimony. The trial judge permitted them to do so, because there was some sensible purpose in doing so in the present case.

31.05 It should also be noted that although in this case the defendants' solicitors had not given previous written notice, as is strictly required under Ord. 38, r. 21, the court does have the discretion to waive that procedural rule on good cause being shown. Since, in the present case, no criticism at all could be levelled at the defendants' solicitors (they were not to know, for example, that the witness was going to give confused evidence) the judge allowed the previous statement to be used, despite the failure to give notice, because no prejudice had been caused by that failure. It should be noted, however, that if a party deliberately fails to give notice in any particular case, as a tactical ploy, and hopes to take the opposition by surprise by presenting a written statement in evidence, the court will inevitably refuse leave for such statements to be used.

We can see from these examples, therefore, that where a party wishes to call a witness and thinks there is anything to gain from proving his previous statements, he ought to serve a notice on the other parties of his intention to do so, sending them a copy of the statement (if written), or indicating the words used (if oral). If the judge then gives leave the statement may then be put in evidence at the end of the witness's evidence in chief. The judge may then have regard to the totality of all the evidence that has been given by that witness and may, as happened in the case of *Morris* v. *Stratford on Avon R.D.C.* prefer the witness's earlier written version of his evidence, which was close in time to the accident he was describing, to the later confused version.

As explained above, by R.S.C., Ord. 38, r. 29, the judge has the discretion to admit the statement if it will be just to do so, even though the proper notice has not been given.

WHERE THE WITNESS IS NOT TO BE CALLED

In a case where a party wishes to prove some fact by a hearsay statement **31.06** (usually by putting in evidence a witness's proof of evidence) rather than by calling the maker of the statement, the procedure is as follows:—

1. the party wishing to use the statement (P) must serve a notice at the appropriate time in the pre-trial procedure (no later than 21 days after setting the case down for trial in the High Court, and no later than 14 days before the hearing date in the County Court). This notice must be in the form prescribed by Ord. 38, r. 22, that is, it must enclose a copy of the statement and also give certain other particulars, namely details of who made the statement; to whom; where and when; and a description of the circumstances in which the statement was made;

2. the other party (D) may within 21 days thereof, (seven in the County Court) serve a counter-notice requiring the witness to be called at the trial. If D does this, in principle the witness must be called at the trial. The witness's statement could still be used at the trial after he had testified if leave were given, but as previously explained, there will now usually be little point in proving the statement, as the witness's verbal evidence is likely to be more convincing;

3. note that again by Ord. 38, r. 29, the court has a discretion to admit the statement, even though a counter-notice has been served, and a witness has not been called, *i.e.* the counter-notice has not been complied with. However, the reason for failure to call the witness would have to be very cogent in such circumstances. One example is where the witness concerned is the employee, or spouse of the opposing party and may be expected to be unfavourable as a witness. It is always then open to the opposing party to call that witness;

4. there will, of course, be many instances of evidence which is totally uncontroversial, so that giving evidence by reading out a witness's written statement will save time and money, *e.g.* a policeman who was not an eye witness to an accident, and who gives evidence of the position of the vehicles and road conditions afterwards—if P serves a notice in relation to his evidence, D would probably not object. To summarise, therefore, where a party has any objection to a witness's statement (or even if he has no objection, but merely wishes to ask a witness further questions outside the scope of his statement) he may, by counter-notice, insist that the witness is called. We shall now consider three brief examples to illustrate the position.

31.07 Suppose that a road traffic accident is witnessed by an eye witness A, who blames the defendant for having caused the incident; a policeman, B, comes to the scene of the accident afterwards and records details of where the vehicles ended up; and the plaintiff also wishes to call evidence of C, the manager of his employers to prove his continuing loss of earnings and career prospects because he is so badly injured that it is unlikely he will be able to go back to work. In the case of each of these witnesses, the plaintiff's solicitor serves on the defendant a Civil Evidence Act notice giving the required particulars and a copy of the statement to be used.

Example 1:
    With regard to the evidence of A, the eye witness whose evidence is hotly in dispute, the defendant will serve a counter-notice within 21 days demanding that A be called at the trial. This will, in effect, prevent the putting in evidence of A's statement, and A must be called so that he can give his evidence verbally and be cross-examined, in the normal way. This demonstrates that it is usually futile to serve the evidence of controversial witnesses under the Civil Evidence Act, because they will inevitably attract a counter-notice demanding that the witnesses be called. Therefore, one has given away the substance of one's witness's evidence in advance of the trial, and lost a possible tactical advantage to no purpose.

Example 2:
    The policeman whose evidence was simply as to the position where the vehicles finished after the accident. If his evidence is served in Civil Evidence Act form, then quite possibly, the defendant would not serve a counter-notice requiring that the witness be called at the trial. If his evidence is genuinely uncontroversial there would be little point in doing so. When the 21 days has expired without the counter-notice being served, therefore, the plaintiff would know that he was entitled to put in evidence the policeman's written statement and have it read out at trial without calling the policeman.

Example 3:
    In the case of the evidence of C, whilst the defendants might not have any direct reason to doubt the truth of C's version of the plaintiff's loss of earnings and career prospects, they would normally nonetheless serve a counter-notice insisting that the witness be called. It is, for example, very hard to give a comprehensive picture in a written statement of a plaintiff's career prospects and as a large proportion of the damages might depend on

this evidence, there is no doubt that the defendant's lawyers would want to have C present in court to be cross-examined about matters outside the scope of his statement, to do with the career pattern of other employees of the plaintiff's status, and so on. Therefore, where there is a witness, even one whose evidence is relatively uncontroversial, but one wishes to ask questions outside the scope of his statement, one is likely to serve a counter-notice.

This then deals with the basic class of case, where a party does not, for reason of cost or tactics, want to call the maker of a statement. One will tender the evidence in the form of the Civil Evidence Act Notice, but one is only likely to be able to use the statement without calling the witness where the other side are co-operative and thus where the evidence is in any way likely to be disputed, there is really little point in attempting to avail oneself of section 2. There is, however, one exceptional class of case, where a party can give a hearsay statement in evidence *as of right* under section 2 and no counter-notice may insist that the maker is called. This exceptional case is created by section 8 of the Act and applies where one of five specified reasons for not calling the witness exists.   **31.08**

CIVIL EVIDENCE ACT 1968, S.8

These reasons are where the witness in question is either: **31.09**

1. dead; or
2. beyond the seas; or
3. unfit by reason of his bodily or mental condition to attend as a witness; or
4. cannot with reasonable diligence be identified or found; or
5. cannot reasonably be expected (having regard to the time which has elapsed and to all the circumstances) to have any recollection of matters relevant to the accuracy of his statement.

It will be immediately observed that these five reasons correspond fairly closely with the similar reasons which apply to make evidence of a record admissible under section 24 of the Criminal Justice Act 1988. There are, however, some slight changes of wording. For example, the somewhat archaic phrase "beyond the seas" instead of the corresponding provision in section 24 of the Criminal Justice Act which requires that the witness should be outside the United Kingdom and that it should not be practicable to call him. The effect of this difference is that where the witness is overseas, questions of practicability and so on have no part to play. If your witness is abroad, then no matter how easy or practicable it would be to call him, *e.g.* where the witness lives in Calais and the trial is proceeding in Dover, one would be entitled to rely on this reason for not calling the witness.

In any of these cases, therefore, an appropriate notice must be served on all other parties at the prescribed time and the notice must contain the particulars previously described, and include a statement as to which of the five reasons under section 8 of the Act applies in the present case.

Where a notice claims one of the section 8 reasons for not calling the witness, no counter-notice can be served requiring the witness to be called.

However, a counter-notice is possible to allege that the reason does not apply. If such a counter-notice is served, there is a preliminary hearing before the district judge to try the question of whether the section 8 reason is proved to apply. If the section 8 reason is then shown to apply, the statement becomes admissible at the trial, as of right, and there is no discretion to exclude it. However, it may be that the section 8 reason can be successfully challenged. Let us consider two examples.

Example 1:

W is an eye witness to an incident and he gives a statement to the plaintiff's solicitors. Some time later he dies. The plaintiff's solicitors could use his statement in evidence by giving notice to the defendant's solicitors within the prescribed period, (*i.e.* no later than 21 days after setting down for trial) and sending them a copy of the statement and including the other particulars required by Order 38. They would, in their notice, claim that the statement should be put in evidence because one of the section 8 reasons applies to it, namely that the witness is now dead. The defendant would not be able to challenge the truth of this reason. The defendant could not therefore serve a counter-notice and in due course the plaintiff would be entitled, as of right, to put the statement in evidence at the trial of the action.

Example 2:

Suppose, however, that a witness W has given a statement relating to a road traffic accident to the plaintiff's solicitors. The action takes some three years to be set down for trial and at this time the plaintiff's solicitors find that W appears to have moved away from his former address and they have no apparent means of tracing his whereabouts. Accordingly, they serve notice of their intention to put his statement in evidence at the trial, claiming as the section 8 reason, that he cannot "with reasonable diligence be found." W's evidence is apparently crucial and the defendant's solicitors are very unhappy that he is not to be called at the trial so that he can be challenged in cross-examination. Accordingly, they serve a counter-notice disputing the truth of the reason claimed, *i.e.* that he cannot without reasonable diligence be found. There will then be a hearing before the district judge in chambers at which it will be for the plaintiff to establish the truth of the reason. Obviously, the key phrase here is "with reasonable diligence" and therefore the plaintiff's solicitors will have to show that they have indeed exercised reasonable diligence in trying to trace the missing witness W. If it proves that they have in fact made very little effort, but have merely had correspondence returned from W's former address marked "Gone Away," then the district judge is most unlikely to be satisfied that they have used reasonable diligence. In that situation, he is likely to adjourn the hearing and suggest to the plaintiff's solicitors what further steps they ought to take to show reasonable diligence in trying to trace W. He may, for instance, suggest that an inquiry agent be employed to try to trace W, through neighbours, relations, or his last job; that advertisements for W be inserted in the local or national newspapers; and so on. The plaintiff will be given some weeks to try these steps and then when the case comes back before the district judge, he will decide on the basis of what is now known, whether the plaintiff has used reasonable diligence. If he finds that he has, then he will rule that the statement can be used at trial. If he finds that the plaintiff has not then he may adjourn matters further until he has. Of course, if the efforts made now lead to W being found, W can be called as a witness and the need to use the section 2 and section 8 procedure disappears.

THE VALUE OF STATEMENTS ADMITTED UNDER SECTION 2

This concludes the discussion of section 2 of the Act. It is important to remember that because a statement is admitted under the Act, it does not mean that the court must accept it as conclusively true. It is just a piece of evidence and the weight which the court may attach to it varies depending on the circumstances. There is a provision in section 6(3) of the Act which gives guidance on how the court should view a statement admitted under the Act. The section provides that in estimating the weight to be attached to any such statement, the court shall have regard to all the circumstances from which any inference can reasonably be drawn, and particularly to how contemporaneously with the facts stated the statement was made, and to any motive the maker may have had to conceal or misrepresent facts. **31.10**

   Therefore, if the witness whose statement is to be put in evidence under section 2 happens to have some particular motive for testifying in favour of one or other of the parties, *e.g.* a very close personal relationship with that party, or perhaps some grudge against the other party, then the court may refer to these matters in deciding how much weight to attach to the evidence contained in the statement. Likewise, the court will no doubt bear in mind that an eye witness account of the facts, if written down very shortly after the incident, is going to be considerably more exact than one given say a year after it.

One further matter to consider is section 7 of the Act. It is apparent that where a party is permitted to use a hearsay statement as of right where one of the section 8 reasons exists, or at the court's discretion, even if it does not, this may obviously disadvantage the other party who is now deprived of the opportunity to cross-examine a witness whose evidence is to be put before the court. Cross-examination and indeed the sight of the witness's demeanour by the judge, are two matters which are often crucial to helping a court to determine the credibility of a witness's evidence and these two things are now going to be denied to the party against whom the statement of the absent witness is to be used. Can anything be done about this? The answer is provided by section 7 of the Act. This section is similar to a provision in the Criminal Justice Act 1988 which we have already considered when discussing the scope of sections 23–26 of that Act. Where a party has evidence with which he could attack the credibility of the maker of a hearsay statement which is to be admitted under the Civil Evidence Act, either generally or by proof of prior inconsistent statements, then such evidence is admissible. In the case of a prior inconsistent statement by the absent witness, notice of the statement must be served on the other party, that is the party seeking to use the original hearsay statement in advance of the trial. So, by section 7 of the Act, one may attack the credibility of the absent witness. **31.11**

Civil Evidence Act 1968, s.4

We shall deal briefly with section 3 of the Act somewhat later, but to preserve continuity, it is now appropriate to consider section 4 of the Act. This provides:— **31.12**

"In any civil proceedings a statement ... contained in a document shall be admissible as evidence of any facts stated therein of which direct oral evidence would be admissible if the document is, or forms part of, a record compiled by a person acting under a duty from information which was supplied by a person (whether acting under a duty or not) who had ... personal knowledge of the matters dealt with in that information and which, if not supplied ... directly, was supplied by him to the compiler of the record indirectly through one or more intermediaries each acting under a duty."

31.13 This section renders admissible second-hand hearsay contained in a document, provided that the document is part of a record compiled by a person acting under a duty from information supplied by a person who had, or who may reasonably be supposed to have had, personal knowledge of the facts concerned. It will immediately be observed that this section is very similar to section 24 of the Criminal Justice Act 1988 which applies in Criminal Proceedings. The 1968 Act requires the existence of a "record" in a document and also an employment-type duty before the requirements of the subsection are fulfilled. In section 4 the word "record" which is not defined in the Act, means a document compiled from information supplied and the word "duty" is defined by section 4(3) of the 1968 Act as "duty includes acting in the course of any trade, business, profession or other occupation in which he is engaged or employed, or for the purpose of any paid or unpaid office held by him." Thus the draftsman of the Act, like the later draftsman of the 1988 Act, sought to acknowledge situations where the formality of the coming into existence of the document would be some guarantee of its reliability, as it was thought would be given by stipulating that it should be created under a duty in an employment-type of situation. However, one problem with the wording is that the definition uses the word "*includes* acting...." This does not therefore necessarily say that it *excludes* documents which are brought into being under other kinds of duty, such as social, public or moral duties. The position is undecided by case law even 23 years after the Act came into force. It is perhaps useful to give two examples here of how section 4 might apply.

Example 1:
An eye witness to a road traffic accident describes to a policeman who comes to the scene what he has seen and the policeman writes it down in his notebook. The policeman's notebook would, in due course, be a document which is admissible under section 4 of the Act, because it is a record compiled by a person acting under a duty from information supplied by a person with first-hand knowledge, *i.e.* the eye witness.

Example 2:
A, a delivery driver, works for PRQ Ltd. He delivers a load to the premises of his firm's customers, XYZ Ltd., and then returns to his own premises. There he calls out to his transport foreman that he delivered the load earlier that day; the transport foreman telephones the sales manager to inform him and the sales manager passes a memo to the accounts clerk, who makes a note of the delivery in the records of PRQ Ltd. If, in future litigation, the fact of delivery should be called into question, then the ledger entry will be evidence that it was delivered. The entry is made in a record

compiled by a person acting under a duty (the accounts clerk) from information supplied by a person with first-hand knowledge (the driver) and the intermediaries through whom the information passed all also have a duty, that is their normal employment duty, to pass on and collect information relevant to their employer's business.

To summarise, therefore, for section 4 to operate, there are three essential ingredients:

1.   there must be a record;

2.   the compiler of the record and all intermediaries, if any, must have been acting under a duty;

3.   the original supplier of the information must have had first-hand knowledge of the facts related, but need not have been acting under a duty. In the second example given, the delivery driver, of course, did also act under a duty, namely the same employment duty as in the case of the other employees, but this was not essential for the section to operate.

The person wishing to use a record under section 4 in evidence must comply **31.14** with a procedure substantially similar to that required in the case of section 2, that is to say:

1.   he must serve a notice on the opposing party within the time prescribed (the same as in the case of section 2) and the notice must have annexed to it a copy of the record and the other particulars previously described, namely a description of who compiled the record from information supplied by whom, where, when and in what circumstances and, in addition, a notice served under section 4 must include a description of the duty under which the compiler acted;

2.   thereafter, a counter-notice may be served by the opposite party demanding that any person named in the notice be called as a witness at trial. So let us consider how this would come about. Take the example most recently given, that is of the delivery driver who passed information which eventually arrived at an accounts clerk who entered it in a ledger. If PRQ Ltd. wish to put this ledger in evidence to prove that the load was delivered at the time and place mentioned, then they would have to serve a notice containing the particulars just described, namely, who made the record, under what duty he acted, from information supplied by whom, through which intermediaries it was passed and what duties they had to pass on the information, where, when and in what circumstances. In the present case, having received the notice, the defendants, if they were disputing that the load was ever delivered, would serve a counter-notice. They could, in the counter-notice, ask that any of the persons named in the notice be called to court to testify, but in the present case there will clearly be little point in calling the transport manager or the accounts clerk who may be presumed to have faithfully recorded whatever they were told. We will assume that the nature of the defendant's case is to allege that the delivery driver either did not deliver the load, or delivered it to the wrong premises. Accordingly, they would serve a counter-notice demanding that the delivery driver, A, be called. A would then have to be called at trial and matters would naturally then turn on his verbal evidence. The record would be

of little use, if A's evidence is to be doubted, as it entirely depends on the truthfulness of A's evidence. In such a case, if A is called and gives evidence in accordance with the record, the record can be admissible with the leave of the trial judge at the end of A's evidence in chief, but again, the trial judge is unlikely to give leave to put the record in evidence, unless the record in some way adds something to the witness's verbal evidence.

31.15 As in the case of section 2, however, if one of the reasons for not calling the witness contained in section 8 of the Act exists, and is claimed in the notice, then no counter-notice is possible, except one to dispute the truth of the section 8 reason.

Let us therefore assume the same facts, of the delivery driver reporting delivery of the load which is eventually recorded in the firm's ledgers. Suppose the delivery driver dies before trial. The firm's ledger could then be tendered in evidence under section 4 and this time the section 8 reason will be claimed as to why A cannot be called, namely that he is dead. In those circumstances, the defendants would not be able to serve any counter-notice demanding that A be called, though they may of course, if they wish, demand that the other persons named in the notice are called, *i.e.* the transport manager, sales manager, or ledger clerk—the intermediaries and ultimate compiler of the record. If the nature of the defendants' case is that the load was never delivered, then it will not really do them very much good to challenge these witnesses who have merely mechanically passed on and recorded information supplied by the absent witness. If, however, the nature of the defendants' defence is that PRQ Ltd.'s accounting and office procedures are so chaotic that quite possibly the wrong details were recorded, they may well wish to have these witnesses called for the purpose of cross-examining them about these matters.

31.16 This concludes our discussion of section 4. Section 6(3) applies to section 4 also and so the court will look at the contemporaneity of the record with the events described in it and at any possible motives of the persons involved to conceal or misrepresent the facts. Thus, for example, in the factual instance given, if it is suggested that there is some fraud being carried on by the staff of PRQ Ltd., or that they have invented details later to conceal their own incompetence in keeping proper records, the court may have regard to this evidence as throwing some doubt on the value of the record tendered under section 4. Likewise, if some absent witness is involved in the procedure, as in the example given where the delivery driver has died, section 7 of the Act can be used to attack the credibility of the absent witness, *e.g.* to demonstrate that on other occasions there have been shortages and misdelivered loads involving A and therefore it is possible that in the present case, there has been some oversight, or possible theft carried out by A.

The relationship of section 2 and section 4
31.17 There is often considerable confusion in understanding whether a piece of evidence falls within section 2 or section 4. In practical terms, it makes very little difference, since the procedure for admitting evidence under each is more or less the same and can be challenged in the same way. Let us, however, take a fairly simple factual example to demonstrate the difference. A common case which is found puzzling is that of a straightforward receipt.

It is often thought that because a receipt seems to be some kind of "record" that it must automatically be considered as a document under section 4 of the Act, rather than section 2, but this is not necessarily the case. Let us suppose that after a road traffic accident the plaintiff wishes to prove the amount of damage to his car by tendering the bill of the garage that repaired the car. Suppose first that this was a small one-man garage where the owner actually estimated the work to be done, diagnosed what was wrong with the car, himself repaired it, himself made out the bill and received the money. The plaintiff will wish to tender the receipt which will describe the work found necessary and done and give evidence that the sum described in the receipt stamped on the bill was paid for the work. Quite clearly, this document can be tendered under section 2 of the Act as first-hand hearsay. There is only one person involved, that is the owner of the garage, who himself is in effect giving a written statement in the form of his invoice, as to what work he found necessary, what work was done, the amount he charged for it, and the amount he received.

Suppose now, however, that in the same situation, the work is done by the **31.18** servicing department of a major motor dealer. In that situation, the work may well have been estimated by a service manager, given to one or several mechanics to carry out, the bill partially completed on the basis of information supplied by them, but eventually probably typed by somebody in the service reception area. The bill is then tendered to the plaintiff and paid by him and the receipt indorsed on it. This time, there is no doubt that the receipted bill is a document which can only be put in evidence under section 4 of the Act. It is not, like the former example, a statement by one single person of what was seen, done and paid for. It is, in effect, a statement prepared by typing staff in the service reception of the garage on the basis of information supplied, perhaps in note or memo form, but possibly verbally, by the mechanics and manager involved in the actual repairing of the vehicle. When the money is paid at the counter a person in the service reception staff will receive it and stamp the receipt on the bill. This then forms a record under section 4 which has been compiled by the service reception staff from information supplied by first-hand observers, that is their mechanics and manager who actually diagnosed and carried out the work in question. Therefore, since the same person who compiled the record is not the person who was the observer of the work that needed to be done, the receipted bill is second-hand hearsay and would need to be tendered under section 4. In either case, the defendant could, if he wished and thought there was anything to gain by it, refuse to accept the evidence contained in the receipted bill and insist by counter-notice that in the first case the owner of the garage and in the second case, either the mechanics involved or the service reception staff come to court to give evidence about the bill, or the vehicle.

Before leaving section 4, it is appropriate to mention section 5 of the Act **31.19** which makes evidence in the form of computer records admissible "as evidence of any facts stated therein of which direct oral evidence would be admissible." There are procedural requirements similar to the operation of section 4. The section, however, seems of little practical importance and there appear to be no recorded cases on the operation of the section.

Civil Evidence Act 1968, s.3

31.20 We will now go on to consider two other sections in the first part of the Act. First, section 3 of the Act. We have in fact already come across section 3. It provides that certain statements, when proved or tendered under other rules of evidence, (*e.g.* as prior inconsistent statements, or to rebut an allegation of recent fabrication) are evidence of *the facts stated in them* unlike such statements in criminal proceedings which are evidence only of the *inconsistency of the witness*. Thus, where one has a prior inconsistent statement of a witness which is to be tendered to counteract his evidence, first there is no notice procedure at all and the statement can simply be produced in court against the witness, and second, the effect of producing the statement is to allow the judge to choose which of the two versions he prefers to believe. It will be remembered that in a criminal context this is not possible, and the production of the inconsistent evidence merely confirms the unreliability of the witness generally. It is not necessary to say any more about the operation of section 3.

Civil Evidence Act 1968, s.9

31.21 We turn now to section 9 of the Act, which like section 3, also provides a useful way of using a prior statement without needing to give notice. Section 9 of the Act preserves the admissibility of informal admissions in civil proceedings. It will be remembered that section 1 of the Act abolished all common law exceptions to the hearsay rule and provided that hearsay in future would only be admissible under the provisions of the Act, some other statute, or by agreement between the parties. Where one has an informal admission made by the other party, it can therefore, under section 9, be used at the trial, and moreover, unlike the case with section 2, there is no notice procedure. One therefore has the tactical possibility of using such a statement at trial without warning and surprising the other side.

31.22 Let us take an example. There is an accident at a cross-roads between P and D. D gets out of his vehicle and says to a passer-by "I am so sorry—I was going much too fast and didn't see the stop sign until too late." As the litigation develops, D's insurers continue to deny liability. At the trial, it would be open to P to produce the passer-by as a witness to testify concerning this informal admission made at the time by D. (Tactically, of course, it might have been better to give the defendant's insurers notice of this anyway, so as to enable them to see that their case was hopeless on liability at a much earlier stage), but section 9 does preserve the tactical possibility that one can take them by surprise at trial. Of course, such a statement would be hearsay generally, and could have been admissible under section 2, anyway. The importance of section 9 is to allow it to be used without warning.

Before going on to the second part of the Civil Evidence Act and to the one particular provision that concerns us, let us summarise the provisions of the Act so far. The first part of the Act, sections 1–9, deals entirely with hearsay.

31.23 A. Section 1 abolishes the common law on hearsay. Accordingly, terms like *res gestae* have no meaning at all now in the context of civil hearsay. Hearsay in civil proceedings is only admissible under the code provided by the Act and the Rules of the Supreme Court.

B. Section 2 of the Act permits first-hand hearsay, that is a verbal account of **31.24** what a witness said out of court, or the witness's written statement made out of court to be produced at trial provided that:

1. notice has been given to every other party at the appropriate time and either

2. (a) no other party served a counter-notice demanding that the witness be called at trial; or
   (b) one of the reasons contained in section 8 of the Act applied so that the witness is either unavailable to testify, or of no use as a witness even if he can be called.

Such evidence, when admitted, is not conclusive, but must be viewed by the judge in the light of section 6(3) of the Act, so he must examine all the circumstances, including how contemporaneously the statement was made with the events described and any motive which the person who has made the statement may have had to conceal or misrepresent the facts.

C. Section 4 of the Act permits second-hand hearsay to be adduced in **31.25** evidence, provided it was contained in a record compiled by a person acting under a duty and from information supplied by a person with first-hand knowledge. Moreover, if the information has passed through any intermediary between the first-hand observer and the compiler of the record, each intermediary must have also acted under a duty which is inclusively defined as meaning principally employment duties.

As in the case of section 2, objection may be taken by counter-notice which will mean that the record cannot, in principle, be used. However, if no objection is taken, or one of the section 8 reasons applies to account for the absence, etc. of the witness involved, the record can be put in as of right. Again, the court will have regard to section 6(3) of the Act in deciding how much weight to attach to the record. In the case of either section 2 or section 4, where there is a witness who is absent because of the provisions of section 8, the credibility of the absent witness may be attacked by virtue of section 7 of the Act by the giving of prior notice by the person who wishes to attack that witness's credit.

D. Section 3 of the Act provides that in cases where a witness's previous **31.26** statement was to be used in evidence anyway under some other rule, *e.g.* proof of a prior consistent statement to rebut an allegation of previous fabrication, or proof of prior inconsistent statement in the case of a hostile witness, or of an opponent's witness, one can do so by simply using the statement in court without any notice procedure. In that event, the statement is evidence of the facts stated in it and the judge may, if he wishes, choose to rely entirely on the statement, rather than on the verbal evidence given by the witness.

E. Section 9 of the Act preserves the common law on the admissibility of **31.27** informal admissions. Therefore, if one party to an action makes some informal admission out of court, evidence of this may be given, without notice, at the trial.

Example:
P and D collide at a cross-roads. D gets out of his car and says to a

passer-by "I'm so sorry, I lost control." This is an informal admission and can be proved against D at trial by calling the bystander to testify. There is no notice procedure and so one can take one's opponent by surprise.

It is important to note that for this purpose an admission to be used under section 9 must be made by a party or a person with an identity of interest with that party. Thus an admission made by a partner is admissible against the partnership and admissions by a solicitor are admissible against his client but it by no means follows that, say, admissions made by a spouse bind the other spouse nor do admissions made by an employee necessarily bind his employer.

Civil Evidence Act 1968, s.11

31.28 We now turn to the second part of the Act which deals with miscellaneous matters, and particularly to section 11. We have already come across this section in the context of pleadings. The law used to be that a party's conviction for criminal offences was not admissible in civil proceedings. This was so, even where the conviction appeared directly relevant to the civil suit, *i.e.* arose out of the same facts. For example suppose that a collision occurred between vehicles driven by P and D. The police eventually prosecuted only D who was convicted of the offence of careless driving. Before the coming into force of section 11 of the Civil Evidence Act 1968, in subsequent civil proceedings between P and D, no reference at all to D's conviction for careless driving could be made, even though the issue in the trial, negligence, is almost exactly the same as the issue which has already been judged in the criminal proceedings, *i.e.* carelessness. Now, however, by section 11 of the Act:

> "In any civil proceedings the fact that a person has been convicted of an offence by a court in the United Kingdom is admissible to prove, where relevant, that he committed that offence and he shall be taken to have committed it unless the contrary is proved."

The section therefore means that if there is some *relevant* conviction, it may be proved at trial and will prove that the convicted person committed the crime concerned, unless he proves the contrary.

THE RELEVANCE OF THE CONVICTION

31.29 The clearest use of the section is where the crime and the subsequent civil action are based on the very same facts, *e.g.* an error of judgment whilst driving. An example is given above where after a collision between P and D the police prosecute only D who is in due course convicted of the offence of driving without due care and attention in the magistrates' court. In the subsequent civil proceedings between the parties, the conviction can be used by P against D and will have the effect of reversing the burden of proof on the issue. In other words, it will now be for D to prove positively, on a balance of probabilities, that he was wrongly convicted, that is, that he did not drive carelessly at the time of the incident. Here with the interchange of the words "careless" and "negligent" it can be said that the issue in the civil proceedings is precisely the same as that in the criminal proceedings, insofar as it relates to D's conduct.

There is a more difficult case where the crime is not precisely the same as the **31.30** tort, but may or may not be relevant to it. Suppose for example that there is a collision between P and D caused by D's brakes failing. D is subsequently charged with, and convicted of the offence of using a vehicle with defective brakes under the Construction and Use Regulations. There is no doubt that in factual terms, D's vehicle caused the accident, but the question is what use this conviction is to the plaintiff. Under the Construction and Use Regulations there is strict liability and therefore if the brakes were in fact defective, this is sufficient to ground a criminal conviction. In the tort of negligence, however, there is no such strict liability and what must be shown in every case is that there was a breach of the duty of care viewed in terms of the conduct of the reasonable man. Accordingly, one might envisage two different situations. In the first, D does not have his vehicle serviced for many months, even after the need for such servicing becomes apparent. He continues driving the vehicle even after it has become obvious to him that the brakes are very weak indeed and finally they fail leading to the collision. If all these facts could be proved there is no doubt that negligence is established and therefore that he will be liable in tort to P. Imagine, however, a situation in which D is scrupulous about having his vehicle properly serviced and in fact has had the vehicle serviced only an hour before the accident occurs. The braking system was thoroughly overhauled and checked but a mechanic at the servicing garage fails to fit some part properly with the effect that the brakes fail the first time they are applied at speed, leading to the accident. In this situation, D is certainly still guilty of the criminal offence, which is one of strict liability. There is, however, no element at all of lack of reasonableness in his conduct this time. Therefore under these circumstances, the conviction would be of no use in proving D's negligence. Any action by P would be better in these circumstances brought against the negligent garage.

Therefore, with offences of strict liability and which relate to the condition of the vehicle, rather than to the manner of its driving, one cannot always immediately see whether a conviction will or will not be relevant. Suppose, for instance, a vehicle is driven with windscreen wipers which do not work. The criminal offence of driving a vehicle without effective windscreen wipers is certainly established. If an accident occurs to that vehicle, however, then clearly the state of the windscreen wipers is quite irrelevant to the causation of the accident, unless it happens to be raining at the time, so that the driver's vision is substantially impaired. If the accident occurs during dry weather, then it is neither here nor there that the windscreen wipers were deficient. In each individual case, therefore, unless the tort is the *very same thing* as the crime, *e.g.* cases of reckless or careless driving, one must look closely at the circumstances to decide how relevant the conviction is.

THE EFFECT OF THE CONVICTION

It is important to note that where such a conviction is pleaded, it is not by any **31.31** means conclusive proof that the person committed the crime concerned. It merely reverses the burden of proof on the issue and makes the convicted person have to prove that his conviction was wrong. This is by no means impossible. Although in principle one would be trying to show that a conviction reached on the standard of proof appropriate in a criminal case, *i.e.* beyond reasonable doubt, was wrong, in many situations there may be a reason why this is what actually occurs. This is because most driving offences are prosecuted in the magistrates' court. Many people may actually plead guilty by post to relatively trivial driving offences, or may not choose or be able to have legal representation when answering such charges because some magistrates' courts have a policy of not granting Legal Aid for driving offences. Where one has a collision between vehicles, the same incident in criminal terms may be the relatively trivial offence of careless driving, but in the civil action in the High Court, sums of tens of thousands of pounds may be involved. The degree of legal expertise brought to bear on the civil action by the solicitors and barristers on each side and the High Court judge, may lead to a very different conclusion to that reached by three lay magistrates who have received a plea of guilty by letter, made mainly because the person concerned could not afford legal representation or the time off work to attend court, and thought that conviction was inevitable because of police evidence against him.

PROCEDURAL REQUIREMENTS FOR THE USE OF SECTION 11

31.32   Section 11 of the Civil Evidence Act is implemented by R.S.C., Ord. 18, r. 7a which provides that a party wishing to rely on a conviction must state in his pleading full particulars of it and the issue to which it is said to be relevant. When the other party receives such a pleading, then by Order 18, r. 7a(3) he may:—

1.   deny the conviction itself, (*e.g.* say that it does not in fact relate to him); or

2.   allege that the conviction was erroneous, (*e.g.* that he pleaded guilty in ignorance of some fact which could have constituted a defence or was otherwise wrongly convicted); or

3.   deny that the conviction is relevant to any issue, (*e.g.* say that although convicted of using a vehicle with a defective tyre, the state of the tyre did not contribute in any way to the accident).

The use of the section and operation of Order 18, r. 7a is illustrated in the following example:

Vehicles driven by P and D are involved in a collision. Subsequently the police prosecute D for three offences on each of which he is convicted, namely (1) driving the vehicle without due care and attention, (2) having a vehicle with two defective tyres, (3) driving a vehicle whilst uninsured.

The plaintiff's solicitors will obtain a certificate of conviction from the magistrates' court and will then insert in the plaintiff's statement of claim (not the writ itself) details of the relevant convictions. They will only plead convictions for the offence of driving without due care and attention and driving with defective tyres. Obviously whilst it may be relevant to the source from which compensation comes, lack of insurance does not in itself contribute to how an accident occurs and therefore they will not plead this third offence.

In his defence, the defendant may well meet this plea by alleging (1) that the conviction for driving without due care and attention was erroneous in that he was convicted against the weight of the evidence by the magistrates.

In that case, the burden of proving this is on him on the civil standard of proof and it will now be for him to establish at the subsequent trial, on the balance of probabilities, that he was not driving carelessly. Accordingly, if the judge is undecided about the matter, *i.e.* he cannot make his mind up which version to believe as to how the accident occurred, he must now find in favour of the plaintiff, because the defendant now bears the burden of proof on this issue. If it were not for the operation of section 11, then in that situation he would have to decide in favour of the defendant because it is normally for the plaintiff to prove every element of his claim. Therefore the effect of section 11 is simply to reverse the normal burden of proof.

With regard to the plea concerning the conviction for driving with defective tyres, the defendant may admit the conviction and that it was correct, but go on to deny that the conviction is in any way relevant to how the incident occurred, *e.g.* he may say that the conviction arose because of a head-on collision when neither party had the time to brake. Accordingly, the state of the tyres is factually quite irrelevant to how the incident came about. It will then be for the plaintiff to establish the relevance of this matter.

31.33 For completeness, it is worth pointing out that if two motorists are involved in an accident and the police prosecute only one of them who is convicted of driving without due care then that conviction can be used by the other driver; this does not, however, mean that the driver who was not prosecuted (or was acquitted) must necessarily be held totally free from any liability in tort. The police are not concerned with degrees of blame, only with assessing whether there is sufficient evidence to establish guilt to a criminal standard of proof. Motorists charged with careless driving often try to show that some other driver was partly to blame, but this is *no defence* to the criminal charge. It may, however, be very important in the civil action because of the effect of a finding of contributory negligence by the plaintiff. Thus the fact that the police chose not to charge one party is no evidence at all that he bore no proportion of responsibility and it is open to the other party to seek to show (1) that his own conviction was wrong (2) that the other party was wholly to blame for the accident, or (3) even if he cannot establish (1) or (2) that the other party was at least contributorily negligent.

This concludes the discussion of the Civil Evidence Act 1968. The Civil Evidence Act 1972 makes one important extension to the 1968 Act by extending the general provisions of sections 2 and 4 which make hearsay evidence of facts perceived admissible to include matters of opinion in certain specified circumstances. This will be considered in the later section on evidence of opinion.

Affidavit evidence

31.34 Before leaving the question of the admissibility of evidence in civil proceedings, it is appropriate to mention that there is one further basic way in which evidence can be put before the court, apart from calling the witness, or relying on the 1968 Act. That is to give evidence by affidavit, *i.e.* the sworn statement of the witness. The rules are quite straightforward and are:—

1. Evidence is not normally permitted to be given *at trial* by affidavit.

2. However, by R.S.C., Ord. 38, r. 2 a court may, at or before the trial of an action begun by writ, order that the affidavit of any witness may be

read at the trial if, in the circumstances of the case, it thinks it reasonable so to order. The use of this provision is very rare in run of the mill tort and contract actions. The judge would have to feel that there was some very convincing reason before depriving a party of his right to cross-examine a witness which is of course the effect of allowing affidavit evidence. If there was some cogent reason for the non-appearance of the witness, then the case ought normally to be able to be brought within the scope of section 2 and section 8 of the Civil Evidence Act, in which case the evidence can be given by ordinary written statement and need not be put on oath. If none of those special factors in section 8 apply, then basically the witness must be called and the evidence cannot be admitted. However:—

3. In *interlocutory* applications, affidavit evidence is quite normal. For example, in applications for summary judgment under Order 14; or in interim payment applications, or applications for leave to issue third party proceedings ex-parte. In such cases, affidavits are not confined to first-hand knowledge, but may include statements of information or belief provided the source of the information is stated. For example in an affidavit seeking summary judgment under Order 14, the managing director of the plaintiff company can say that the amount claimed is owed by the defendant. He must also go on to verify that the debt is still owing and he will probably say that this is the case and that he has found out that this is so by speaking to his firm's accounts manager who has confirmed the information. This kind of hearsay is perfectly acceptable within an affidavit.

Finally, one should note in conclusion that in some cases, rules of evidence are forgotten entirely. For example, in a summons for approval of a settlement of an action involving an infant, the infant's lawyer probably will indicate to the district judge what the evidence is on liability, quite informally.

32. Evidence of Opinion

The usual rule is that a witness may only give evidence of facts which he has **32.01** personally perceived by one or more of his five senses. A witness may not give evidence of opinion. It is of course sometimes difficult to draw the line between what is a description of a fact and what is merely opinion. This is particularly so in the case of a person describing some complicated situation or activity. Take the following examples.

Example 1:
   A witness proposes to testify that the accused drove through traffic lights while they were red, and on the wrong side of the road. This is a case of pure factual perception, with no element of opinion in it.

Example 2:
   A witness proposes to testify that the accused was driving "recklessly like an utter maniac." This is a matter of pure opinion. It is based on facts and if the witness had been able to narrate the facts (for example if they were the same facts as in example 1) then that would have been perfectly in order. It is, however, not for the witness to draw inferences from the primary facts such as he is doing in this example, but merely to relate the facts, allowing the court to draw the inferences.

Example 3:
   Naturally in real life, matters are not so straightforward and clearly categorised as the examples given above. Much more normal would be for a witness, particularly in describing some activity on the roads to give a combination of fact and opinion, *e.g.* to say "He was driving like a maniac—much too fast for the road conditions—nearly hit an old lady when she stepped into the road—went through a light on red and ended up with his wheels on the pavement. I'll bet he'd been in the 'Red Lion' all night." This contains a mixture of fact, opinion and indeed mere inadmissible speculation.

The rule is that an *ordinary witness* is not permitted to testify as to his **32.02** opinion. However, because of the problems of differentiating between fact and opinion, then in *civil proceedings only* by virtue of Section 3(2) Civil Evidence Act 1972:—

> "Where a person is called as a witness . . . a statement of opinion by him on any relevant matter on which he is *not* qualified to give expert evidence if made as a way of conveying relevant facts personally perceived by him . . . is admissible."

This, therefore, would allow an ordinary witness to recite the kind of matters referred to in example 3 above with the exception of the reference to the probability that the person had been drinking, which is a matter of pure speculation.

The problem may arise at its most acute where a witness who has no mechanical device such as a speedometer to assist, may be trying to give some account of the speed at which the vehicle is driven. Speed is something which most people can judge to some extent. For example, suppose one is in a 30 m.p.h. speed limit area and a vehicle is being driven at 70 m.p.h. Most people would be able to judge that it was being driven substantially in excess of the speed limit. The same would not be true if the vehicle were only being driven at say 40 m.p.h. The dividing line between fact and opinion is clearly somewhat thin here. A witness would certainly be entitled to say in evidence that he thought that a vehicle was substantially exceeding the speed limit although evidence from a pedestrian that a vehicle was doing any precise speed would not be of very much weight. Evidence that vehicles were being driven "very fast" or even "too fast for the road conditions" would probably be generally admissible.

The provision we have just discussed, of course is contained in the Civil Evidence Act. It is accepted by at least one modern writer on the law of evidence, that a similar rule is now tacitly applied in criminal proceedings. Thus, if the incident we are concerned with is to do with a charge of reckless driving, rather than an action in negligence concerning a motor accident, it is suggested that witnesses in the criminal proceedings might well be able to testify in the same way as indicated above for witnesses in the civil proceedings.

Despite this relaxation of the strict rule about evidence of opinion, it should not be forgotten that the rule applies in all its vigour to an ordinary witness who purports to testify about what is unequivocally a matter of opinion. To this rule forbidding evidence of pure opinion there is one major exception applicable in both civil and criminal cases which is the case of *expert witnesses*.

Who is an expert?

32.03 The rule is that an expert witness may give evidence of opinion concerning matters within the sphere of his expertise, usually matters of a scientific, technical or medical nature. Before a witness can give such opinion evidence, the judge must decide that the witness does qualify as an expert. Counsel will usually call the witness and ask him about his degrees, or other qualifications before he begins his evidence. However, degrees or paper qualifications are not always essential, it depends entirely on the nature of the thing concerning which opinion evidence is required. For example, a skilled carpenter of long experience would be acceptable as an expert opinion witness concerning the behaviour of wood when sawn, despite not having formal qualifications as such. Or as in the well known case of *R*. v. *Silverlock* [1894] 2 Q.B. 766 where a solicitor who had studied handwriting analysis as a hobby was accepted as an expert witness on the subject. In each case, it will be a matter for the court to decide as to whether a witness who is tendered as an expert is sufficiently qualified. Consider for example a police vehicle examiner. This will normally be an ordinary policeman who has received some special training in examining motor vehicles. There may be many matters within the sphere of his expertise on which he would be perfectly competent to give evidence. If, however, the evidence concerning some aspect of a car's performance became extremely technical, *e.g.* the performance of some very sophisticated device within an electronic system in a car, there is no doubt that the vehicle examiner would probably not suffice as an expert witness and a consultant motor engineer, or electronics engineer, would need to be called to give evidence. This is perhaps less a matter of actual qualification to give the evidence than of commonsense in the party who wishes to prove the fact. Naturally, a party would wish to call a properly qualified witness on whom the court would place reliance. Thus, whilst a general practitioner might be called as a medical witness about some matters, if the nature of the medical problem involved some more high level expertise it would obviously be prudent to call a consultant who is a specialist in that area.

The ambit of expert opinion evidence

CRIMINAL CASES

32.04 Opinion evidence is not admissible if the subject-matter is within the competence of the court. This means that an expert should not be asked for his opinion about the very matters which it is for the jury to decide. For example, whilst psychiatric evidence is admissible as to an accused's medical state, a psychiatrist may not give his opinion on matters of ordinary human nature and behaviour. An example is the facts of the leading case of *R.* v. *Turner* [1975] Q.B. 834.

The accused beat his girl friend to death with a hammer when she confessed her infidelity and the fact that the child she was carrying was not his. In support of his defence of provocation, he wished to tender evidence by a psychiatrist to the effect that his personality was such that because of his deep love for the girl he would have been uncontrollably provoked by her confession of infidelity. The court refused to permit the expert evidence, holding that since no medical state such as insanity or diminished responsibility was in issue, matters of ordinary human reaction and behaviour were within the province of the jury and it was for them to decide whether the accused was sufficiently provoked.

CIVIL CASES

32.05 By section 3(1) of the Civil Evidence Act 1972 an expert may give his opinion "on any relevant matter on which he is qualified to give expert evidence. In this section 'relevant matter' includes an issue in the proceedings."

Procedure for admitting expert evidence

32.06 The test as to whether a person is an expert is the same as in a criminal case. Although as a matter of law, expert evidence may be admissible in a civil case, it is vital to comply with the correct procedures. It is therefore essential either to agree the evidence with the other side, or to comply with the rules which govern expert evidence, *i.e.* to comply with the Rules of the Supreme Court requiring prior disclosure of the substance of expert evidence which is to be called at the trial and limiting the number of such witnesses, *e.g.* under Order 25 Rule 8 and Order 38 Rules 36–44. Neither should it be overlooked that in an appropriate case (which in routine personal injuries or contract litigation will be rare) one may apply to the court to give a different direction where for any particular reason the parties wish to vary the usual procedures on mutual prior disclosure.

Similar provisions now provide for pre-trial disclosure of expert evidence in criminal cases in the Crown Court under rules made pursuant to section 81 of the Police and Criminal Evidence Act 1984. It will be recalled that there are special provisions relating to admissibility of experts' reports in criminal proceedings under section 30 of the Criminal Justice Act 1988. In principle in a case where the expert evidence is likely to be contested the expert should attend court. Exceptionally however the court may admit the evidence in the form of a report having regard to the various matters contained in section 30(3) of the Act which are outlined above at para. 29.24.

32.07 Finally, it should be noted that an expert is not expected to be omniscient even in the field of his expertise. It is thus perfectly proper for an expert to draw on the work of others in this field (including professional journals, textbooks and unpublished works and scientific data) in arriving at his conclusion but he should, in the course of his testimony, refer to the sources of his information so that the opposing expert can testify concerning the cogency of the conclusions reached.

33. Evidence of the Accused's Character

Character means a person's general reputation and disposition. Evidence of **33.01** good character is always admissible on behalf of an accused. An accused will wish to lay before the jury his good character, if he has one, in an effort to show them that he is not the kind of person who would commit the offence with which he is charged. This is just one item of circumstantial evidence which the jury may take into account, and of course is in logic only of marginal relevance. "Good character" may mean merely absence of a criminal record, but defendants also tend to put before the jury details of any especially praiseworthy activity in their past, *e.g.* service record, public service, charitable acts and even good employment record. A good example of the latter would be a case concerning alleged dishonesty on the defendant's part where he was able to call a former employer to say that he had been employed for many years in a position of trust handling large sums of money and no shortages or discrepancies had occurred.

Where an accused proposes to give evidence of good character, he will usually do so himself in testimony, but may also, or in addition, call character witnesses, as in the case of the employer in the example given above.

"Bad character" tends to mean simply a criminal record. The prosecution **33.02** cannot call evidence of an accused's record or cross-examine him about it, unless one of the following circumstances applies. Such evidence is inadmissible and the accused is said to have a "shield" against its disclosure *unless*:—

1. the "*similar fact*" principle applies or

2. some *statute* permits the prosecution to adduce evidence of bad character; or

3. the accused is foolish enough to attempt to show he has a *good character* and in fact he has not; or

4. under the Criminal Evidence Act 1898 where the accused *gives evidence* and either:—
   (a) makes *imputations* against prosecution witnesses; or
   (b) attempts to assert his own *good character*; or
   (c) gives *evidence tending to undermine* the defence of a co-accused in which case the co-accused's counsel may cross-examine him as to his character.

We shall now go on to consider these in detail.

The "similar fact" principle
Evidence of past criminal acts by the accused is not normally admissible **33.03** because it is not legally relevant, that is, it does not tend to prove the accused's guilt of the present crime. However, in the very exceptional class

of case covered by this principle, there is some factor in the earlier crime which points directly to the accused's guilt of the present offence. The modern test for whether the principle applies comes from the case of *D.P.P. v. Boardman* [1975] A.C. 421. The facts of this case are not material, indeed despite it being the leading case it has sometimes been criticised as being a poor application of the principle. The test is two-fold and is as follows:—

1. "is there some *striking similarity* in the other crimes committed by the accused to the present offence such that a reasonable man would say that they must have been committed by the same person?"

2. if so, is the evidence of *more probative than prejudicial* value?

The principle, therefore, requires a highly unusual and striking feature common to previous offences and the present crime. It is for the judge to rule that this feature appears to be present and if he is satisfied that this is the case, the prosecution may prove that the accused committed previous crimes (or subsequent crimes) and the *modus operandi* of the commission of those crimes to indicate to the jury his especial disposition to that kind of behaviour.

33.04 Because of the requirement of such unusual feature, this principle is rarely relevant in the more mundane crimes such as theft, burglary and driving offences. There are, naturally, only so many ways in which one can commit these crimes and since some unusual *modus operandi* is required for the operation of the principle, these sorts of crime will only rarely fall within it. In modern times, the principle has been virtually confined to sexual crimes and murder. Merely to illustrate the principle, the following cases show the kind of unusual features required:—

Makin v. *Attorney General New South Wales* [1894] A.C. 57. Evidence was given that the accused husband and wife had adopted a child from its natural mother and had received a small sum of money to provide for the child's wants in the early weeks of the adoption. The child was shortly after found buried in the garden of the Makins' house and the cause of death could not be shown. In order to rebut any potential defence of accident or natural causes, evidence was given that the Makins had on nine other occasions adopted young children in similar circumstances, all of whose bodies were found buried in the gardens of houses occupied then or previously by them.

R. v. *Straffen* [1952] 2 Q.B. 911. Straffen was charged with the murder of two young girls by strangulation. He made a confession, but his trial did not proceed because he was found to be unfit to plead and was confined to Broadmoor. Some time later, he escaped from Broadmoor and very soon thereafter another young girl living nearby was found strangled. The *modus operandi* was identical and the following features were said to be common to the third murder and to the other two, namely:

(i)   the victims were all young girls of a similar age;
(ii) they were all killed by manual strangulation;
(iii) there was no sexual or other apparent motive;
(iv) although there were ample opportunities for concealment, their bodies were all left in public places.

At Straffen's trial the principle was held to apply and enabled the prosecution to prove Straffen's confession to the earlier crimes, even though he had not been tried for them.

R. v. *Barrington* [1981] 1 W.L.R. 419. The accused was charged with sexual assault on three young girls at his home. The following features were said to be common to all the cases and were also said to have been common to approaches made by him to three other girls whom he had not got as far as assaulting:

(i) the accused enticed the girls to his house to babysit;
(ii) the accused introduced his girlfriend who was present throughout, as a professional photographer;
(iii) the accused represented to the girls in each case that he was the scriptwriter of "Dr. Who" and a "friend of the stars";
(iv) the accused showed the girls magazines with pornographic pictures of young girls;
(v) the accused told the girls that there were prizes for a competition for pornographic pictures of young girls;
(vi) the accused attempted to persuade the girls to pose for photographs to be taken by his girlfriend.

One can see, therefore, from these cases, the degree of unusual behaviour required before the principle can be said to apply.

For completeness, although the rest of this whole section is confined to **33.05** evidence to do with the character of the accused in criminal cases, the "similar fact" principle can apply to civil cases also. Thus, where some particular form of behaviour is alleged against one or other party to a civil case and can be linked to similar behaviour on some other occasion, if the behaviour is of relevance it may be proved. The leading case is *Mood Music Publishing Co. Ltd.* v. *De Wolfe Ltd.* [1976] Ch. 119. The facts of this case are a good illustration of how the principle can apply in civil cases.

The plaintiffs and defendants were both music publishers. The plaintiffs suspected the defendants of breaching their copyright in various published musical works by slightly changing the arrangements and attempting to pass them off as original works, alleging that any similarities between their work and that of the plaintiffs was entirely coincidental. On one particular occasion, the plaintiffs believed that the defendants had "lifted" a particular tune which they had previously published and had then sold it under another title of their own as the theme music for a popular television series. The plaintiffs arranged a so called "trap" for the defendants whereby someone in their employ sent to the defendants a cassette of a piece of music and told the defendants that the tune had been recorded from the radio in the United States and that the person concerned wished to pass it off as his own original work and asked the defendants if they could manage to prepare a slightly different arrangement of the work, so that it could be passed off as original. The defendants agreed to this and charged a fee of £250 for so doing. The plaintiffs were allowed to prove the defendants' dishonest response to this trap laid for them in their subsequent action against the defendants for breach of copyright. Lord Denning observed that in civil cases the courts would be less wary of admitting similar fact evidence than in criminal cases. In a criminal case, the probative value of the evidence admitted would have to be very strong indeed to overcome the inevitable prejudice of revealing to the jury that the defendant had engaged in misconduct on other occasions. In civil cases, however, the courts will admit evidence of similar facts, if it is logically probative, that is, if it is relevant in helping to determine the matter in issue; is not unfair to the other party; and that other party has fair notice of the allegation and is able to deal with the matter.

From this one can see that similar fact evidence in a civil case will be admitted more readily than in a criminal case. However, the evidence must still be logically relevant to some fact in issue. Examples of this might be where it could be proved that the defendants habitually sold defective goods; or were habitually negligent in carrying out work of a certain kind. A more questionable application of the principle would be where a plaintiff in a personal injury case wished to prove that the defendant habitually drove very fast, or carelessly. This would almost certainly not be properly within the principle. If the similarity of the conduct was narrowed down somewhat, *e.g.* by an allegation that the defendant habitually drove very fast on a certain stretch of road, at a certain time of day, for instance because he was commonly late for work, even that would be a questionable application of the principle. There is no modern reported case in which the issue has concerned an application of the principle to the facts of a road traffic accident negligence case.

Cases where some statute permits the prosecution to prove the previous conviction

33.06   A number of statutes permit this and where one applies the prosecution may prove some previous conviction. One obvious example is in the case of a charge for the offence of driving whilst disqualified. It is obviously inevitable that in proving the offence of driving whilst disqualified the prosecution must prove that the accused was disqualified from driving and proving this inevitably shows that he had committed other driving offences. Another example is section 27(3) of the Theft Act 1968. In general terms, this permits the prosecution in the case of a charge of handling stolen goods, to give evidence of the accused's convictions for theft or handling which have occurred within the previous five years. The rationale of this statutory provision is that on such a charge there is likely to be only one real defence (assuming that the prosecution can prove that the goods were stolen) namely innocent possession. It is obviously relevant to this defence to show that the accused ought from bitter experience of dishonesty convictions, to know better, for example than to buy goods from people other than in the normal course of business. It assists the jury to presume knowledge or wilful blindness to the fact that the goods are stolen in such cases to know that the accused has previous convictions for dishonesty. It ought to be mentioned, that here, as in every other case, the judge has a discretion to prevent the prosecution using section 27(3) even though the facts are within the section.

Cases where the accused tries to show his good character

33.07   Where an accused is foolish enough to put before the jury something which he hopes may persuade them of his good character, but in fact he has a criminal record, the prosecution may call evidence of his criminal record to rebut this. This is the common law rule which still applies and is more extensive than a similar part of the 1898 Criminal Evidence Act with which it overlaps (see below). It applies *no matter how* the accused tries to get evidence of his good character before the jury, whether he says something himself, calls a character witness of his own, or even tries to get something favourable from a prosecution witness by cross-examination. As an example, suppose that an accused, who has a criminal record, has also been an active worker for charity and he hopes that the jury will so approve of this conduct on his behalf that they will perhaps be less inclined to consider him likely to have committed the present offence and more inclined to give him the benefit of any doubt that may exist. It would make no difference whether he himself gave evidence of his charitable work, called an official of the charity to testify on his behalf about it, or even had his counsel put questions directly to a police witness asking if the policeman was aware of the accused's charity work. In each case, he would have fallen foul of this rule and the prosecution would have the right at common law to call witnesses in rebuttal of his assertion of good character. That is not to say that the prosecution witnesses when called will comment unfavourably about his charitable work, but rather that the prosecution will be entitled to put the whole of his character before the jury, that is his criminal record. Moreover, at common law this will be the case whether or not the accused testifies himself.

The cases show that it will not take very much in the way of self-praise by an accused, before the judge will rule that he has "put his character in" or "lost his shield" and allow the prosecution to give evidence of his criminal record. For example, consider the following fairly mild assertions which each led to the accused losing his shield:— **33.08**

"I am a regular attender at Mass" *R.* v. *Ferguson* (1909) 2 Cr.App.R. 250.
"I'm a family man in regular work" *R.* v. *Coulman* (1927) 20 Cr.App.R. 106.

The point of these cases is that by these assertions the accused was not saying anything in any way directly relevant to the case or to his defence. He was in fact hoping to persuade the jury that because of his basic decency he was not the sort of man who would be likely to have committed the crime in question. In each of the above cases, the accused, whilst their assertions about Mass and family and regular work were true, also had criminal records for dishonesty and the prosecution were permitted to prove those records. The rule is that character is *indivisible*, so that an accused cannot try to show that he has a good reputation for one form of behaviour only, without having his whole record revealed. An example is the facts of the leading case of *R.* v. *Winfield* [1939] 4 All E.R. 164.

The accused was charged with indecent assault on a woman. He attempted to introduce evidence to the effect that he had a good reputation for being courteous in his dealings with women. Whilst this may have been true, he also had convictions for dishonesty and the prosecution were held to be entitled to prove these convictions on the basis that character is indivisible and it was not open to a defendant merely to attempt to show his good character for one aspect of his behaviour.

It must be stressed that a mere plea of not guilty on the present charge, does not of course amount to trying to show good character. The good character must relate to acts separate from the present crime to invoke the principle and thus one may argue one's innocence as vigorously as possible on the present charge, without losing one's protection against disclosure of past record.

The Criminal Evidence Act 1898

33.09   We turn now to the most important exceptions to the rule that the prosecution may not put the accused's previous character before the court namely section 1(f) of the Criminal Evidence Act 1898.

The Criminal Evidence Act 1898, s.1(f) states:

> "A person charged and called as a witness ... shall not be asked and if asked shall not be required to answer any questions tending to show that he has committed or been convicted of or been charged with any offence other than that wherewith he is then charged or is of bad character, unless:—
>
> (i) the proof that he has committed or been convicted of such other offence is admissible evidence to show that he is guilty of the offence wherewith he is then charged;
>
> (ii) he has personally or by his advocate asked questions of the witnesses for the prosecution with a view to establish his own good character, or has given evidence of his own good character, or the nature or conduct of the defence is such as to involve imputations on the character of the prosecutor or the witnesses for the prosecution; or
>
> (iii) he has given evidence against any other person charged in the same proceedings."

Until the passing of this Act, strange though it now seems, an accused in criminal proceedings was not competent to testify on his own behalf. This Act was passed to make the accused a competent witness and to give him some protection from cross-examination on his record. But for section 1(*f*) an accused would prima facie be open to questions as to his credit, like any other witness and therefore the prosecution would, in principle, have been able to put his previous bad character to him. The 1898 Act prevents this and gives the accused a shield against the disclosure of his past record, even where he testifies. It must be clearly understood that this sub-section *only* covers the situation where an accused gives evidence. If he chooses not to testify, the section has no application. We will now consider the three sub-sections of section 1(*f*).

SECTION 1(*f*)(i)

33.10   This provides that where the prosecution can adduce evidence of other crimes (*i.e.* under the similar fact principle, or where some statute, for instance section 27(3) Theft Act 1968 applies) they can go on to cross-examine the accused about those previous offences if he should give evidence. It follows on from the common law and is clearly logical. In its normal form, it will apply in the case where the prosecution have already, as part of their own case, under the exceptions previously mentioned been permitted to introduce evidence of the accused's previous character. Unlike the two following sub-sections, the operation of section 1(*f*)(i) is not dependent upon the way in which an accused chooses to conduct his case.

The two remaining sub-sub-sections only apply if the accused both *testifies* and *decides to conduct his case in a certain way*. We shall now consider the precise meaning of the sub-sub-sections.

SECTION 1(*f*)(ii)

This has two separate limbs. The first merely re-states the common law, as **33.11** discussed above. It would permit the prosecution to cross-examine an accused about previous offences if he tries to show good character. It will be remembered that the common law actually goes further than this section in that the common law would allow the prosecution to rebut evidence of good character, even if the accused does not himself testify. There is, therefore, no need to further consider this aspect of the sub-section.

The second limb is the most important in practice. It leads defence lawyers to have very carefully to consider their tactics when they are conducting the defence of a man who has a criminal record. The sub-section in effect provides that an accused may "lose his shield" by personally, or by his advocate, making imputations against prosecution witnesses. However, again, it is vital to remind oneself that the accused only does this if he testifies. If he has already decided not to give evidence, then he can, by his counsel, make all the imputations against prosecution witnesses he likes, with complete impunity.

What is an imputation?

It is for the judge to rule what amounts in any given case to an "imputation." **33.12** The cases show that judges are fairly prompt to accept that an imputation has been made. In one case where an accused called a prosecution witness "a liar" it was held that this was merely an emphatic denial of the evidence, and not an imputation. To go any further than this, however, and to make any specific allegation of perjury or fabrication of evidence, is bound to be ruled an imputation and to lose the accused his shield. It is particularly important to consider this when cross-examining police witnesses. The following miscellaneous points may assist with the interpretation of the section:—

1. if there is a disputed confession, then if the jury are out of court, one can **33.13** make the imputations one likes against policemen during the voire dire. This will not lead to the prosecution being permitted to cross-examine the accused as to his character once the jury return to court, unless of course, the accused then repeats what he said in the jury's absence. The judge himself will in any event be aware of the accused's criminal record at the outset of the trial;

2. it will not *necessarily* amount to an imputation to suggest that the police **33.14** have in some way disregarded provisions of the Police and Criminal Evidence Act, or the Codes of Practice. Everything will depend upon the seriousness of the breach alleged. Thus if it is suggested that they failed to contact his solicitor as promptly as they should, they asked him questions in an offensive manner, they exceeded by some slight amount the permitted length of periods of detention, etc., these will not in themselves amount to sufficient imputations to permit the prosecution to cross-examine the accused on his character. To go further than this, however, and particularly

309

to allege that a policeman's version is untruthful and therefore that he is committing perjury, is likely to be ruled an imputation. The cases do show, however, that the courts must address their minds to the fact that people in the witness box, perhaps because of their emotional state, do often use exaggerated language and every allowance must be made for this in deciding whether an accused is actually making an imputation sufficient to bring himself within the scope of section 1(f)(ii). For example, an accused who in the middle of searching cross-examination by prosecution counsel suddenly blurted out that one of the policemen was "a liar" would probably not have fallen foul of the sub-section, unless he went on to amplify his remark;

33.15 3. it is wrong for prosecuting counsel to "tempt" or "trap" the accused into making such imputations where he would not otherwise have made them;

33.16 4. where the accused loses his shield, it is a simple case of "tit for tat." There is no need for the conviction to have any relevance to the present charge, for example, a dishonesty conviction would be admissible under the section, even though the accused was at present charged with a sexual crime.

The judge's discretion

33.17 Where the accused has made an imputation, it does not necessarily follow that the loss of the shield will be automatic. The judge still has an overriding discretion to prevent the prosecution relying on section 1(f)(ii). He might thus prevent them cross-examining the accused on his record, or perhaps just on part of it. An example of an occasion when he might exercise this discretion would be if, for example, the imputations were relatively trivial and the present crime also relatively trivial, but there was something in the accused's criminal record which would be highly prejudicial. An example of this is as follows:—

Suppose the accused has a criminal record for a type of crime which is notoriously highly unpopular with the public. For instance, rape, sexual assault on young children, or even cruelty to animals. If the accused is at present only charged with some relatively mundane incident of theft and in the course of it he goes so far as to suggest that the policemen have fabricated evidence to incriminate him then normally he would fall foul of section 1(f)(ii) and lose his shield. One can easily see, however, in a case such as the one described, how this would be gravely prejudicial to him. The types of crime mentioned are so unpopular with the public, that not only might learning of them make the jury heartily dislike the accused, it might also make some of them think that he is the kind of person who is quite capable of committing theft and, more importantly, might make some members of the jury not care whether or not he had committed the present theft, but merely feel that it would be a good idea to punish him again for his previous crimes. This is the nature of the prejudice to the accused potentially caused by the revelation of such convictions. In such a case, therefore, the judge would very probably rule that although the accused had in principle made an imputation, he would exercise his discretion and prevent the prosecution cross-examining him about his previous offences. Naturally any discussion of whether or not an imputation has been made and whether the prosecution may exercise their rights under the section of course occurs in the absence of the jury. This is brought about by a sort of coded interchange between

310

prosecuting counsel and the judge. Where the accused has made an imputation and prosecuting counsel wishes to cross-examine him about his record, prosecuting counsel says that he wishes to make a "certain application" and the judge will then send the jury out of court without their knowing why they have gone whilst counsel makes his application for leave to cross-examine the accused on his record.

The effect of the accused's bad character

Where the accused has lost his shield, there is another point to consider. **33.18** That is that the judge must carefully direct the jury on the use they may make of their knowledge of his record. He should direct them that the accused's bad character is only relevant to the accused's credibility as a witness, and *not* to the issue of whether or not he committed the crime. Clearly, this is a distinction which is likely to be lost on many members of the average jury. The temptation for members of the jury is to assume that a person who commits crimes is likely to commit other crimes, rather than merely to view their knowledge of his previous record as an aspect of deciding on whether he makes a credible witness or not. The case which illustrates this point, and that in the preceding sections is the leading case of *Selvey* v. *D.P.P.* [1970] A.C. 304.

In this case, the accused was charged with committing a homosexual offence involving a young man. The accused had several previous convictions for homosexual offences and for offences of dishonesty. The nature of the accused's defence was that the incident had been fabricated by the alleged victim, who had made a proposition to him (Selvey) that they should indulge in homosexual activity for a certain sum of money. The refusal by Selvey of this proposition had prompted the alleged victim to fabricate the incident.

Since the nature of Selvey's defence naturally involved the suggestion both that the alleged victim, who had already testified, was a homosexual prostitute and a perjurer, an imputation had clearly been made. The judge ruled that Selvey's character could be put in issue and he could be cross-examined about his past by the prosecution.

What is a little bizarre about the judge's judgment in this case, however, is that he only permitted the prosecution to cross-examine Selvey about his homosexual convictions, and *not* about his offences of dishonesty. It is suggested that this was in fact the reverse of what should have occurred. If one's previous criminal conduct is only relevant to one's *credibility* as a witness, then naturally offences of deceit or dishonesty are much more relevant to that than convictions for sexual offences which do not necessarily involve any suggestion that an accused is an untruthful person.

In any event, the principle in *Selvey* v. *D.P.P.* after having been judicially **33.19** considered in a number of cases in recent years, has now been firmly reasserted. Where an accused who has a criminal record "loses his shield" it is a simple case of tit for tat. The judge, unless the previous offences are very prejudicial indeed, as in the case of the example previously suggested, should allow the prosecution their rights under section 1(*f*)(ii). He must, however, go on to strongly direct the jury that even if the previous offences involve some fairly similar type of crime (although not so similar that the prosecution could have availed themselves of the similar fact principle) this

311

previous bad record is only relevant to the issue of whether or not *they believe the accused as a witness*, and *not* as to whether they consider that *he is the type of person* who is likely to have committed the present crime.

33.20 We shall now go on to consider section 1(*f*)(iii) of the 1898 Act (as amended by the Criminal Evidence Act 1979). This provides that where an accused "gives evidence against" a co-accused, the co-accused's counsel may *as of right*, (*i.e.* this time the judge has *no* discretion to prevent it) cross-examine the accused about his record. The words "gives evidence against" are interpreted to mean "say anything that tends to undermine the co-accused's defence." No actual hostile intention between the two co-accused is necessary—it is the objective tendency of the evidence that matters. A good example of this is the case of *R.* v. *Davis* [1975] 1 W.L.R. 345.

The accused and X went to the house of a person who was selling some antiques. They looked round the house, but declined to buy anything. After they had left the house, the owner noticed that two valuable antiques were missing and contacted the police. Davis and X were arrested. They were jointly charged with theft and the circumstances were clearly such that either one or the other, or both, were the only people who could have stolen the items. At the trial, Davis merely maintained a vigorous denial of his own involvement in the crime. He actually went so far as to say that he was not saying that X had committed the crime. Despite this, since the facts were such that only one or the other or both could have committed the crime, it was held that Davis had "given evidence against" X and thus X's counsel was permitted to cross-examine Davis about his criminal record, as of right.

Thus, when a judge rules that there is such a tendency in co-accused's A's evidence, he must permit co-accused B's counsel to cross-examine A on his criminal record. Again, the section only applies if A testifies. If A merely calls a witness whose evidence is against B's interests but does not testify himself, nothing can then be done to prove A's record.

33.21 It is worth considering, therefore, a straightforward situation to see how sections 1(*f*)(ii) and 1(*f*)(iii) may interlock. Suppose there are three persons charged with an offence of theft, A, B and C. A pleads guilty at the outset and is called as a prosecution witness. B and C both plead not guilty. B's case, however, is that A and C alone committed the crime. In the course of putting forward this defence, he will of course wish to cross-examine A about his participation and put it to A that he was involved in the crime, as his plea of guilty admits, and is now lying, on oath, in saying that he, B, is involved. If B decides subsequently to testify, he will certainly have thrown his shield away under section 1(*f*)(ii) by making these imputations of perjury against A. If B says whilst conducting his own defence that C did commit the crime with A, then this will also involve him falling foul of section 1(*f*)(iii), since he will be giving evidence against C, and accordingly in such a case, C's counsel will be entitled to cross-examine B as of right about his criminal record, even on the assumption that prosecuting counsel had failed to do so.

To expand the example slightly for another purpose, it is as well to remember that if C also goes into the witness box and blames B for his part in the crime, then the judge would have to consider the form of the corroboration warning that would be required. A is an accomplice in the strict sense, having been a participant in the crime who is now a prosecution witness, and he will need to give a full corroboration warning to the jury about the risk of convicting on A's evidence alone. In the case of C, he is a person in the slightly vaguer category of "person with a purpose of his own to serve" and it will therefore be necessary for the judge to consider what kind of warning he thinks it desirable to give and the exact terms in which such a warning should be given, though the full corroboration warning as such is not required.

What may be proved under section 1(f)(ii) and (iii)?

Where an accused may be cross-examined on his record under the provisions **33.22**
of section 1(*f*)(ii) or 1(*f*)(iii), then he may only be asked about the type of offence of which he was convicted. He may not be asked about details of the manner by which he committed the offence. That is because to prove the manner of the offence, would tend to show that the matter was relevant to the issue of whether he was guilty of the present charge. Where the only issue is whether he is a *credible witness* and the previous record's relevance is *only* to that point, then no question of how he committed the previous crimes can be introduced. The only matters which can, therefore, be put forward are the nature of the previous crime and the question of whether or not he pleaded guilty. This is because if he had pleaded not guilty, but nonetheless had been convicted, it would be relevant to his present credibility as a witness to show that a jury had, on a previous occasion, disbelieved him also. If, however, section 1(*f*)(i) applies so that the prosecution were anyway permitted to prove some details of his previous offences and thereafter, if he testifies to cross-examine him about them, it should be remembered that section 1(*f*)(i) *unlike* (ii) and (iii) is relevant to guilt, and not to the accused's credibility as a witness.

Finally note that even where under one of these exceptions the evidence of **33.23**
bad character is, in theory, admissible, there are two other matters which may lead to its being excluded:

1. The Rehabilitation of Offenders Act 1974 provides that in a civil court, evidence of a "spent" conviction is not admissible. The conviction becomes "spent" after a certain length of time, depending on the sentence passed. The Act has no application to criminal proceedings as such. However, by a Practice Direction at [1975] 1 W.L.R. 1063, it is provided that reference should not be made to a "spent" conviction, without leave of the judge, to be granted only if the interests of justice so require. This should always be borne in mind therefore, where an accused's previous record involves relatively old and trivial offences.

2. It is provided by section 16(2) of the Children and Young Persons Act 1963, that where a person over 21 is charged with an offence, no evidence may in any circumstances be adduced of any offence of which he was found guilty while he was under the age of 14.

34. Improperly Obtained Evidence

34.01 A difficult problem exists in the case of evidence which has been obtained illegally or improperly. Such evidence has usually come within one of three categories, *i.e.*

1. evidence obtained by unlawful search, seizure or entry;

2. evidence obtained by entrapment, *e.g.* by a plain clothes policeman working with and pretending to participate enthusiastically in the activities of criminals; or

3. evidence obtained as a result of an inadmissible confession, *e.g.* a confession is obtained by threats and is thus inadmissible, however in the confession the criminal tells the police where they can find other incriminating evidence, for instance the stolen goods. Is the finding of the goods admissible?

34.02 In all three cases, English law decided that the law of evidence is not to be used as a means of disciplining the police, so that if evidence is admissible in itself and relevant, it is not made inadmissible by virtue of having been obtained illegally or unfairly. The leading case is *Kuruma* v. *R.* [1955] A.C. 187. In this case, at a time when emergency regulations applied in Kenya, it was a capital offence for natives to possess ammunition. Powers of search were conferred by the regulations on policemen of a certain rank. The accused was unlawfully searched by two policeman of a lower rank than that stipulated in the regulations, and they found ammunition upon him. At his trial, he contended that since the search was illegal it would be improper to permit the Crown to take advantage of its own misconduct. The Privy Council held that the *only* test is whether evidence in such a case is *relevant*. If it is relevant, it is admissible.

34.03 In the third of the cases mentioned above as we have already seen section 76(4) of the Police and Criminal Evidence Act 1984 expressly provides that the finding of a thing in consequence even of an inadmissible confession is admissible although we must also remember section 76(5) of the Act which provides:

> "Evidence that a fact to which this subsection applies was discovered as a result of a statement made by an accused person shall not be admissible unless evidence of how it was discovered was given by him or on his behalf."

In other words where a confession is excluded but the accused said in it, *e.g.* where something was to be found, the evidence of finding the thing is admissible but no reference back to the reason why the police looked in that place may be made *unless* the accused himself gives evidence as to how the thing came to be discovered. Therefore if the discovery of the thing in question cannot otherwise be linked to the accused, (*e.g.* by the fact that it has his fingerprints on it) there may be no point in the prosecution adducing the finding of the evidence.

In relation to the other two cases mentioned above namely evidence obtained by unlawful search, seizure or entry or by entrapment the authorities remain entirely in favour of admissibility of the evidence under the principle in *Kuruma* above.

THE DISCRETION TO EXCLUDE

In criminal cases there is a general discretion to exclude evidence if its prejudicial effect outweighs its probative value. This is a rule of general application to every item of criminal evidence and is not only applicable to illegally obtained evidence. The discretion, which existed at common law, was expressly preserved by the words of s.82(3) of the Police and Criminal Evidence Act 1984. In addition we must consider s.78 of the Police and Criminal Evidence Act 1984. This provides as we have seen previously (see para. 30.20 above) that: **34.04**

"The court may refuse to allow evidence on which the prosecution proposes to rely to be given if it appears to the court that having regard to all the circumstances, including the circumstances in which the evidence was obtained, the admission of the evidence would have such an adverse effect on the fairness of the proceedings that the court ought not to admit it."

The test remains "will it have an adverse effect on the fairness of the proceedings?" It was at first considered difficult to visualise an example of how the *method* of obtaining the evidence can affect the "proceedings" rather than merely demonstrating "unfairness" in some more general sense which would surely be irrelevant on the clear wording of the section. It was widely considered that the section added nothing to such discretion as existed under the common law and that the section would certainly *not* be used to discipline the police. However, surprisingly and with one must say a good deal of rather suspect reasoning the courts seem to have taken a robust view of the nature of their discretion under section 78. We have already considered the surprising line of cases which have treated section 78 as supplementary to section 76 so that breaches of other sections of the 1984 Act, (*e.g.* section 56, section 58) or the Codes of Practice have led to the exclusion of confessions that were not necessarily unreliable. Of these the most important case we have seen is that of *R.* v. *Mason* (above para. 30.20).

What we are now considering is whether the court would use section 78 to exclude evidence which is obtained, *e.g.* by entrapment (such as by a policeman pretending to be a member of the gang and enthusiastically participating in their enterprises even to the extent of helping to set up crimes which they would not otherwise have committed) or evidence obtained in pursuit of illegal search and seizure. **34.05**

Of course cases where Crown Court judges may have used section 78 to exclude evidence are unlikely to be fully reported since the prosecution have no general right of appeal to a higher court. There is some anecdotal evidence that Crown Court judges are using section 78 to exclude evidence obtained by impropriety quite apart from in confession cases. However there is no clear instance of a case where evidence obtained either by entrapment or by illegal search, seizure or entry has been excluded under the discretion in section 78. For the time being therefore it is suggested that the orthodox view is that the court will not use section 78 to discipline the police in such cases and therefore that the principle in *Kuruma* v. *R.* remains.

35. Privilege

Although the general principle of litigation, civil or criminal, is in favour of full disclosure of all relevant evidence to the court so that witnesses must attend court if ordered to do so, and must answer all relevant questions in court, or produce any document when ordered to do so, there is one ground upon which they may legitimately refuse to do this, namely privilege. Privilege is usually sub-divided into public privilege and private privilege.   **35.01**

Public privilege

This was at one time called "Crown privilege" although it extended beyond the Crown (*e.g.* to Local Authorities and bodies such as the N.S.P.C.C.) and more recent cases usually call it "public interest privilege" or "public interest immunity." The principle is that where it is claimed that the disclosure of evidence (documentary evidence or oral answers in cross-examination) would harm the public interest, the judge will weigh the conflicting public interests (*i.e.* that litigation should be frank and open on the one hand and that on the other hand certain activities of public bodies should have the right of confidentiality) and decide whether to allow the claim to privilege. To make his decision, the judge may demand to see any document involved and after consideration may disallow the claim for privilege and order the document to be produced or the witness to answer the questions. The leading case is usually said to be *Conway* v. *Rimmer* [1968] A.C. 910, where the court held for the first time that merely because the Minister of a Government department makes a claim that the public interest requires that documents should not be disclosed, the court need not accept such a claim as conclusive and may demand to see the documents in question and arrive at its own judgment of the public interest.   **35.02**

Two relatively recent cases illustrate how nicely balanced the decision may sometimes be. On the one hand, in *D.* v. *N.S.P.C.C.* [1978] A.C. 171 the court found in favour of confidentiality. In this case, a malicious person had complained that D's children were mistreated. The N.S.P.C.C. began investigations which caused D some distress. D commenced an action against the N.S.P.C.C. for negligence and in the course of the action sought discovery of the original report so that the malicious informant could be identified with a view to defamation proceedings being started. The House of Lords eventually upheld the N.S.P.C.C.'s claim to privilege holding that even though the unfortunate effect in the present case was to protect the interests of some wholly malicious person, the public interest demanded that informants should feel free to report suspicions of child abuse to the N.S.P.C.C. without fear of subsequent defamation proceedings should their fears be unfounded. This case also demonstrates how widely the courts are prepared to construe the principle of "the public interest" so as to protect the interests of bodies like the N.S.P.C.C. who could in no sense be said to constitute the Crown.   **35.03**

35.04   The second case in which the opposite conclusion was reached was *Campbell* v. *Tameside B.C.* [1982] Q.B. 1065. In this case, a teacher had been attacked by an unruly pupil. She contended that the pupil's disposition towards violence was well known to the Education Authority and that he should have been educated in a special unit. In the course of her action against the Local Authority, she sought discovery of the child's school records, which included child psychologists' reports. The Local Authority resisted disclosure of these reports on the ground of public interest immunity, namely that in future teachers, educational psychologists, etc. would be more wary in writing frank reports if they knew that they might subsequently be used in litigation. The Court of Appeal held that in this case the public interest was best served by openness in litigation and disallowed the claim to privilege, directing that the reports be disclosed.

Finally, one special rule of public privilege (to which *D.* v. *N.S.P.C.C.* was claimed to be analogous) is that policemen are not required to answer questions in cross-examination if the answer would tend to identify the informer of a crime. This is to protect the anonymity of informers, it being considered in the wider public interest to promote close relations of confidence between police and informers.

Private privilege

STATEMENTS MADE "WITHOUT PREJUDICE"

35.05   As was mentioned in the section on civil procedure, evidence cannot be given of the contents of "without prejudice" letters or discussions. Such letters or conversations must be made with the view to settling a dispute to attract the privilege and therefore merely marking a letter "without prejudice" will not confer privilege on it unless it was written bona fide with such intention. For example, one would gain no protection for a defamatory letter by so marking it. Provided the intention to settle exists, however, it is not essential that the words "without prejudice" appear on a letter—the privilege will still apply. It is, however, obviously prudent to mark letters "without prejudice" or to agree at the outset of meetings or telephone conversations about compromise that they shall be on a without prejudice basis.

The privilege conferred by the words is mutual, and therefore cannot be waived only by the party writing the letter without the other party's agreement. However, if the exchange of "without prejudice" correspondence results in settlement of the action, the correspondence may then be produced in court to show the terms agreed (*e.g.* if one party later reneges on the agreement). The agreement is said to "open" the correspondence.

LEGAL PROFESSIONAL PRIVILEGE

35.06   The principle that a person should be able to be totally frank with his own lawyer is paramount. Therefore there is a privilege applicable to communications between client and lawyer which has a partial extension to communications between the client or lawyer and third parties in litigation.

1.   Solicitor/client communications. The rule is that neither client nor solicitor can be compelled to produce documents or answer questions

about communications which passed between them in their capacities as solicitor and client. This applies whatever the nature of the matter on which the communication passed (provided it was bona fide concerned with legal advice), whether it was contentious or non-contentious.

2. Communications between solicitor and client to a third party when litigation is current or contemplated. There is an extension of the principle in (i) above in cases where litigation is actual or contemplated. In such cases, in addition to the usual privilege between solicitor and client, there is a further privilege for communication between the solicitor (or the client direct) and third parties. The most common example of this is a simple witness statement obtained by the solicitor where litigation is pending. The written statement is privileged and the privilege is important at two stages in the action. First at discovery and inspection, whilst the statement must be referred to in the List of Documents, (usually briefly and vaguely without identifying the witness, *e.g.* "witness statements") it will appear in Schedule 1, Part 2 with privilege being claimed and the opposing party will not be able to inspect it (nor know the identity of the witness concerned). Secondly, at trial, the opposing side cannot make one produce the statement so if, for example, it was decided not to call the witness, the other side would never know what he had to say (or even who he was).

This privilege applies to all such communications between a solicitor and   **35.07**
third parties, though if for any reason the client himself had such communications with third parties direct in connection with the action, these would also be privileged. For example, if the client himself went to see a witness to obtain a witness statement, the witness statement would attract the privilege referred to above. Thus, witness statements, letters about the action and experts' reports are all privileged. In the case of experts' reports, however, it is important to remember that the price of calling the expert at trial might be the prior disclosure of his report in the interests of fair and open litigation. This is the effect of R.S.C., Ord. 38, rr. 36–44 and the corresponding provisions of the County Court Rules in Ord. 20, rr. 33–34. It does not mean that such experts' reports are not privileged—they are, so that for example, nothing can make one disclose a report which is unhelpful and on which one does not wish to rely at trial. The principle is, however, that the overriding requirements of open litigation may require one in the usual case to waive the privilege, if one wishes to call the expert at trial. This is especially the case in respect of medical reports (see para. 9.01 earlier).

One should remember, finally, that this privilege is confined to the legal profession and does not apply to other professional relationships, *e.g.* accountant/client, doctor/patient, priest/penitent.

SELF INCRIMINATION

In any civil proceedings, a person may refuse to answer questions on the   **35.08**
ground that to answer would tend to expose that person or his or her spouse to prosecution for an offence committed in the United Kingdom. This is by virtue of section 14(1) of the Civil Evidence Act 1968.

In any criminal proceedings, a person may likewise refuse to answer questions on this ground. By section 1(*e*) of the Criminal Evidence Act 1898, it is provided that:—

"A person charged and being a witness . . . may be asked any question in cross-examination notwithstanding that it would tend to incriminate him as to the offence charged."

The effect of this is that an accused who testifies cannot refuse to answer questions on the grounds that his answers may incriminate him of the present offence, although he can if they tend to incriminate him of other offences. Also note that once a spouse testifies at the trial of the other spouse, even if the spouse was not compellable, once the oath is taken, he or she is in the position of any other witness and cannot refuse to answer proper questions.

35.09 One should finally remember that (with the exception of without prejudice communication) the fact that one party can claim privilege for a document or matter, does not prevent some other party from proving it if he is able to do so. So, for example, if a plaintiff's solicitor, in sending some documents to a defendant's solicitor inadvertently enclosed a witness statement, it would be perfectly proper for the defendant's solicitor to make use of it at the trial (for instance, as a prior statement on the basis of which to cross-examine the witness and subsequently to put it in evidence himself).

In fact there has been a flurry of recent case law on facts very similar to this in which in different cases solicitors have inadvertently sent statements or expert reports to their opponents, or in one case where a barristers clerk returned a brief to the wrong solicitors. The outcome of this case law is at present somewhat inconclusive and each case has turned on its own particular facts but it is suggested that the general proposition just referred to, *i.e.* that once a document does come into an opponent's hands the privilege is lost, is in the main accurate.

The same rule applies in a criminal case, and for a striking illustration consider the facts of *R.* v. *Tompkins* (1977) 67 Cr.App.Rep. 181.

The accused wrote a note to his counsel from the dock. The note was subsequently found on the floor of the court and handed to prosecuting counsel who was permitted to use it for the purpose of cross-examining the accused. The Court of Appeal held that although the note had originally been privileged, the privilege was lost once it fell into the hands of another party.

36. Evidence other than by Testimony: Miscellaneous

Apart from witnesses recounting to the court what they have to say relevant to a case, there are two other kinds of evidence.

Real evidence

Examples of this are; objects produced to the court (*e.g.* weapons, piece of **36.01** machinery); the appearance and demeanour of parties or witnesses (for judging their credibility); going on a "view," *e.g.* visiting the scene of an accident or some other place of importance, *e.g.* as in the well-known case of *Tito* v. *Waddell* (No. 2) [1977] Ch. 106 where the Vice-Chancellor of the Chancery Division and sundry assorted lawyers for each side felt it incumbent on them in deciding on a dispute to do with some land in Ocean Island in the South Pacific to visit Ocean Island for some days.

Documentary evidence

In civil litigation, documentary evidence is very common. Many documents **36.02** are "agreed" that is, exchanged between the parties before trial and accepted as authentic at trial. Such exchange is usually informal, for example a party who wishes to use a clearly uncontroversial witness statement at trial without calling the witness, might very well not bother with the formal Civil Evidence Act Notice but just send the statement to the opposite side with a letter requesting agreement. The same applies to experts' reports. Note that for a document to be put before the judge as "agreed" in this sense, it must be accepted as *true* by all concerned, *e.g.* it is not proper to put before the judge conflicting expert reports and leave him to make up his mind on the basis of the reports. In such a case the reports are not "agreed" and the witnesses must be called. Unfortunately, the word "agreed" is also used in a different sense. In this sense it means "documents which are agreed between the parties as being authentic, useful and relevant to the action." It may well be, for example, that where the action concerns a substantial contract dispute, there is a great deal of correspondence between the parties and subsequently between their respective solicitors, in which contentious statements are made. It may be thought worthwhile to have this correspondence produced to the judge at the trial, to help him gain an overall view of the situation. In one sense, the correspondence is not "agreed" because each party is in fact saying that their own version, as contained in their half of the correspondence, is true, and the opposing side's version is untrue. However, both parties do "agree" on the relevance of the correspondence being produced to the judge. One should be careful, therefore, not to confuse these two senses of the term.

PRIVATE DOCUMENTS OTHER THAN WITNESS STATEMENTS

Apart from documents which are merely statements as above, it is often **36.03** necessary to use other documents in litigation. The rule regarding "public documents" has already been given in the section on hearsay. Such documents are admissible as evidence of the truth of facts stated in them in civil or criminal pleadings. We are now concerned with what might be called private documents, *e.g.* contracts, leases, wills, business records, or photographs or tape recordings, to which the same rules apply. The rules are complex but may be summarised as follows:

1. A person wishing to put a document in evidence must produce the original, not a copy, and prove its authenticity unless this is accepted by the opposing party. This may involve proving the handwriting, signature, or attestation in the document.

2. So called "ancient documents" that is a document made more than 20 years ago and produced from proper custody (*i.e.* by a person who might reasonably or naturally be expected to have it in his possession, *e.g.* a land owner who produces old deeds of his title) are presumed to be authentic and properly executed unless the opposite is proved.

3. Tape recordings, video films, photographs etc. are admissible as "documents" providing their authenticity can be proved. This is usually done by calling the photographer and the person who developed the film to show that they have not been tampered with.

4. If the original document cannot be produced, then in the following circumstances, secondary evidence of its content may be adduced:
   (a) if the original is proved to be lost, *i.e.* a full search has been made in vain, a party may use secondary evidence of its contents
   (b) where a stranger lawfully has the document in his possession and is entitled to refuse to produce it, *e.g.* if it is privileged in his hands or he is out of the jurisdiction, then secondary evidence of its contents is admissible
   (c) where another party to the action has failed to produce the original after a notice to do so the contents may be proved by secondary evidence. This applies to criminal proceedings as well as civil.

Example:
   In an action concerning a lease the landlord has served on the tenant the original of a notice to quit. He wishes to prove that notice was given properly by having the tenant produce this document at trial. He serves a notice to produce it in due course, but at trial the tenant fails to produce the original notice to quit. In these circumstances the landlord would be entitled to prove the contents of the notice to quit from a carbon copy of it.

PUBLIC DOCUMENTS

36.04 Certified copies of original public documents are normally admissible, *e.g.* extracts from the Register of Births, Deaths or Marriages by duly completed certified copies, *e.g.* birth or death certificates.

Criminal Procedure

37. An Outline of Criminal Procedure

In order to show in simple form the course of criminal proceedings a very brief preliminary outline of the progress of a criminal prosecution will be given here.

After a crime has been committed it will be investigated by the police and unless the offender has been apprehended at the scene of the crime detection work of various kinds may occur until the police have a suspect. They have powers of arrest, and search and the right to interrogate. They may also, *e.g.* hold an identity parade, finger print, and so on. We will then assume that they know who it is they consider committed the offence.

They have an option to proceed against him by way of two methods:—

1. Causing a summons to be issued against him or

2. Charging him.

The first would be much more likely in the case of routine or trivial crime such as driving offences. In such situations the accused may well have been apprehended at the scene of the crime. He will usually be released there and then and told that he may later be prosecuted.

Subsequently the police will adopt a procedure known as laying an information before a magistrates court and a summons will then be issued against the suspect. The prosecution will then be taken over by the Crown Prosecution Service and will come before the courts where it may be dealt with on the first occasion or adjourned for a variety of reasons depending on what course the trial takes.

Alternatively the accused may have been arrested by the police and actually charged at the police station. In this case the charge sheet which notifies the charge will specify the date on which he is to appear before the magistrates court.

With very few exceptions not relevant for our purposes all prosecutions do **37.01** commence in the magistrates court. Offences may broadly be classified into three types for procedural purposes and these are:—

1. Those that are triable *purely summarily, i.e.* those of relative triviality where only a magistrates court has jurisdiction (*e.g.* careless driving).

2. Those triable *only on indictment* in the Crown Court before a judge and jury namely those offences too serious to be tried by magistrates (*e.g.* murder, rape) and

3. Those offences which may be more or less serious depending on a variety of circumstances including *inter alia* the degree of violence (*e.g.* assaults) or the amount involved (*e.g.* theft). These offences are known as "either way" offences.

In the case of these latter offences there needs to be a decision as to which court, magistrates or Crown Court will try the case.

37.02   (i) In the case of purely summary offences when the accused person appears before the magistrates court it is unlikely that his case will be dealt with at the first appearance if he is pleading not guilty. This is because of the expense of calling witnesses and preparing the case fully which can be avoided if the accused pleads guilty. Thus if he pleads guilty he will be dealt with then and there, if he pleads not guilty the case will be adjourned for trial at some later convenient date. In the case of some offences (mainly motoring offences) the accused may be offered the opportunity to plead guilty by post without attending court.

37.03   (ii) In the case of an offence triable either way the court has to decide on the mode of trial. It will hear representations about what factors relevant to the offence make it more suitable that he should be tried in either the magistrates court or the Crown Court, and the magistrates court will then decide. However whilst the magistrates court may themselves decide to send the case to the Crown Court for trial, if they decide that they are themselves willing to try it then in the case of "either way" offences the accused always has the power to overrule them and insist on his right to jury trial.

37.04   (iii) In the case of offences which are triable purely on indictment or those triable either way which are being taken to the Crown Court there is a preliminary stage known as a *committal hearing* in which the magistrates may make a preliminary examination of the case. Thereafter they either dismiss the case if there is not shown to be sufficient evidence on which to commit it to the Crown Court or allow the case to go to the Crown Court for trial.

At any stage of this procedure questions of bail, legal aid and adjournment may arise. The magistrates court has the power to adjourn a case at any time and when it does so it must in some circumstances consider how to deal with the accused during the adjournment. That is whether or not to allow him bail and also whether he is entitled to legal aid.

The accused will be tried in the magistrates court or committed for trial to the Crown Court. At the end of his trial in either court if he is convicted matters of sentencing and mitigation will arise.

38. Professional Ethics

Duties of the prosecutor

In principle a prosecutor has a duty to act as a Minister of Justice and to see **38.01** that all relevant facts and law are before the courts. He should not strive for a conviction at any price and should indeed even in theory present matters favourable to the defendant. Other aspects of this are that the prosecution generally play no part at the sentencing stage and do not as in other countries press for any particular sentence or for the defendant to be dealt with severely; nor do they present facts in emotive language.

The prosecution have a specific duty to make available to the defence any evidence which they have obtained which is favourable to the defence, and to inform the defence of any material inconsistency in witness statements obtained by the prosecution, *e.g.* where a witness having given one version of events on one occasion subsequently gives a significantly different version.

Duties of the defence solicitor

The defence solicitor has a basic duty to do what is best for his client but in **38.02** addition has an overriding duty not to mislead the court. Within these confines however he can act as vigorously as possible in his client's interests even if he privately believes him to be guilty.

It is appropriate here to consider a number of aspects of this.

CONFIDENTIALITY

A solicitor may not reveal anything which the client has told him while the **38.03** solicitor client relationship existed, without the client's proper authority. One aspect of this is that a solicitor is under no obligation to give the prosecution any advance warning of the nature of his client's defence to a charge. He is entitled to maintain the secrecy of this, in principle until the defence case opens, although usually it will be necessary to indicate the nature of the defence case when cross-examining prosecution witnesses. To this principle there are three exceptions where the prosecution are entitled to some notice of matters relevant to the defence case.

1. Under Section 81 of the Police and Criminal Evidence Act 1984, a person who proposes to rely on expert evidence in a criminal trial must give advance disclosure of this to the opposition.

2. In the case of an *alibi* defence. In the case of trials on indictment details of an alibi defence must be disclosed no later than seven days after the committal proceedings.

3. Matters of law. As is common throughout the criminal and civil process authorities to which a party intends to refer ought in principle to be disclosed to the opponent before hand.

Finally it will be noted that unlike in the case of civil legal aid there is no requirement as such to report to the legal aid authorities, *e.g.* if one considers one's client is behaving unreasonably. It may be a prudent step to obtain prior authority for the incurring of major items of expenditure but even where a solicitor personally feels that his client's case is hopeless if the latter persists in pleading not guilty there is no duty to report the matter and the solicitor may continue to represent him and do his best for him.

A CLIENT WHO ADMITS HIS GUILT

38.04 Where a client admits his guilt a solicitor may continue to act for him even on a not guilty plea to a limited extent. A solicitor may permit the client to plead not guilty and thereafter may do everything possible during the prosecution case, for example cross-examine their witnesses as vigorously as possible (provided this does not involve advancing any untruthful version of events) and in particular, if the prosecution case depends on a confession he may make every appropriate attempt to have the confession ruled inadmissible. Thereafter he may make a submission of no case to answer. If however the case is not dismissed at that stage then a solicitor may not permit his client to go into the witness box or call perjured evidence. Accordingly if a client does admit his guilt it is vital to point out to him that you may continue to act for him even if he pleads not guilty, but only if he agrees not to call evidence.

KNOWLEDGE OF A CLIENT'S PREVIOUS CONVICTIONS

38.05 What if a client has previous convictions and the solicitor is aware of this but the court is not? As indicated previously one would not be permitted to let the client assert in the witness box that he was a person of good character in the trial itself nor would one's own conduct of the case take that path. More commonly the problem will arise after a guilty plea or conviction. When mitigating for such a client if the prosecution has not got proper details of his criminal record or think that he has no offences recorded against him then whilst one may not positively stress his good character one can do everything possible otherwise by way of mitigation. One can so to speak therefore leave the court to conclude that he is of good character from the absence of criminal record but one must not positively state that this is so.

CLIENTS WHO GIVE INCONSISTENT INSTRUCTIONS

38.06 Clients often change their instructions. They may significantly change their version of much that has occurred. Here one is essentially in no different a position from when one is acting for a party in a civil case who gives differing versions of events. So long as one is not absolutely sure that the client is positively trying to invent some version, one can still continue to act although it may be appropriate to give the client advice with regard to his plea and the risk of conviction for perjury.

INTERVIEWING PROSECUTION WITNESSES

38.07 There is no property in a witness and it is perfectly proper to interview prosecution witnesses. In the course of interviewing them of course no attempt ought to be made to put words into their mouths nor should one misrepresent whom one is, *e.g.* leave the person with the impression that one might be a prosecution solicitor. Apart from this however no tribunal is likely to conclude that a respectable solicitor is trying to pervert the course of justice. It is sometimes thought appropriate to warn the prosecution of one's desire to interview their witnesses. It is doubtful whether there is any rule positively requiring this. Certainly in the converse cases when the police are checking on defence alibis they do not trouble to give the defence solicitor a chance to be present.

CONFLICTS OF INTEREST

It is very important when acting in a criminal case to ensure that there is no conflict of interest between co-defendants. This is particularly so because in many courts where legal aid is granted to the accused there is an attempt to assign the same solicitor to each of the accused in the interest of saving time and costs. Sometimes if there is only a slight possibility of conflict of interest in such a situation and the matter is proceeding to the Crown Court matters may be satisfactorily resolved by briefing separate counsel for each of the accused. In criminal cases however one should always be aware of the possibility of a conflict of interest suddenly arising. If, having taken on two clients a conflict of interest does arise then generally it will be impossible to continue to act for either. This is because one will have received confidential information and would have wished to use it in the conduct of client A's case against former client B. This might particularly be so where one of two clients changes his plea and pleads guilty perhaps even subsequently testifying for the prosecution. In such a situation if one would have wished to cross-examine former client B in a very vigorous manner one would be hopelessly hamstrung in the conduct of client A's defence. It should also be borne in mind that a conflict of interest may even arise at the mitigation stage although there is nothing apparent at the stage when guilt is still being contested. Thus for example if one is faced with two clients who are aged say 18 and 28 and the latter has a bad criminal record, then when mitigating for the younger should they both be convicted, it might well be appropriate to suggest that he has been corrupted and led astray. This is clearly not possible if one is also acting for the elder. Great care should always be taken therefore to beware of a conflict of interest in a criminal case and to act appropriately where such arises. If one is assigned to act on legal aid for two or more co-accused one should always interview them separately. If it is then apparent after seeing the first accused that there is a possibility of conflict arising one can decline to act for the other accused then and there. If there is no such apparent conflict then one can interview the second accused. If it transpires from *his* version of events that there is a conflict, as one will by now have obtained confidential information from both one cannot act for either. **38.08**

Finally one should not overlook the possibility that one may have acted for both of two co-accused on previous occasions. If there now seems to be any possibility of a conflict arising then everything will depend upon the nature of the confidential information which one obtained on those previous occasions. If the information could in any sense be used against B to A's benefit one cannot act for either. **38.09**

39. Financing Criminal Litigation

39.01 What was said earlier about the need to ensure that the financial basis of the relationship between litigation client and the solicitor is clearly established applies as much in criminal as in civil litigation. Thus subject to obvious individual exceptions (*e.g.* a wealthy regular client on a driving charge) it is prudent, indeed essential to obtain payment in advance for work done in criminal litigation. Whilst the criminal case will not run for as long as the average civil case, there are, for obvious reasons, even greater risks of non-payment by the clientele.

Privately paying clients are, however, considerably rarer than in civil litigation. We shall now therefore consider the question of legal aid. As we shall see there are important differences from civil legal aid in the manner of application, criteria for eligibility, and other ancillary matters.

Finally, we will briefly examine the principles for the award of costs in criminal proceedings.

Legal aid and advice

THE GREEN FORM SCHEME

39.02 The Green Form scheme has already been explained in the general context of legal aid in civil proceedings. As was stated there, legal advice and assistance on any matter of English law can be given to a person who qualifies on a financial eligibility test. Naturally, criminal matters come within the scope of this scheme. Work up to a total value of two hours fees can be done by a solicitor for a client and this would cover such things as taking the first statement, filling in application forms for legal aid proper and perhaps some preliminary collection of evidence.

ADVICE AT THE POLICE STATION

39.03 If a client is at the police station, and this applies whether he is in custody or attending voluntarily in connection with assisting the police with their enquiries into an offence, a person is entitled to free legal advice and assistance from either his own solicitor or the duty solicitor (see below) up to an initial limit of £90 worth of work. Unlike the Green Form scheme, this scheme is not means tested in any way so even the wealthy are entitled to assistance under it.

ASSISTANCE BY WAY OF REPRESENTATION (A.B.W.O.R.)

39.04 Neither the Green Form scheme nor the police station scheme referred to above cover actually taking a step in proceedings (*i.e.* representing the client in court). For this, in general, full legal aid is required. However there is an exception namely under Regulation 7 of the Legal Advice and Assistance (Scope) Regulations 1989 which provides for assistance by way of representation in the Criminal Courts in certain circumstances. This scheme is means

330

tested in a similar way to the Green Form Scheme and it is available to cover representation for a defendant who does not have full legal aid but has not been refused legal aid where the Magistrates Court:—

    (i) is satisfied that the hearing should proceed on the same day;

    (ii) is satisfied that that party would not otherwise be represented; and

    (iii) requests a solicitor who is within the precincts of the court to represent that party.

This might come about therefore if a person, newly taken into custody or otherwise, happened to be before the court without legal representation and it appeared that a solicitor was available and the matter seemed relatively straightforward and brief, (e.g. a plea in mitigation after a guilty plea). If a solicitor was present in the precinct of the court for the purpose of representing somebody else and was able to come to represent this client then the court can authorise such representation under the ABWOR scheme. In fact many courts deal with applications for legal aid proper very swiftly and in such cases there would be no advantage in granting assistance by way of ABWOR over considering a full legal aid application except such time as it takes to fill in a full legal aid application form. The use of the ABWOR scheme therefore varies considerably from court to court.

Duty Solicitor schemes

Duty Solicitor schemes were schemes originated nearly 20 years ago in some parts of the country on a voluntary basis, whereby solicitors experienced in criminal work would attend on a rota system either at a police station or magistrates court cells in the early morning before the day's sittings to give advice and assistance and to represent persons in custody (or in some cases also persons not in custody who came to court and were in need of assistance and were unrepresented) on such matters as a preliminary bail application or a plea in mitigation. The method of remuneration was sometimes by the Green Form, in others by the prompt grant of legal aid and the persons attending as duty solicitors were, if the client wished, entitled to act for the client for further stages of the proceedings. These voluntary schemes have now been replaced by a formal duty solicitor scheme under the Legal Aid Board Duty Solicitor Arrangements 1989. The duty solicitor scheme has two principle aspects:—

39.05

AT THE POLICE STATION

Under this scheme persons who are at a police station whether under arrest or voluntarily are entitled to free legal advice and assistance up to an initial limit of £90 from a duty solicitor or if they prefer from their own solicitor. The main point of duty solicitor schemes however is that they operate throughout the night and therefore there ought in principle always to be a duty solicitor available whereas one's own solicitor may well not be willing to come out, even if the client knows his home telephone number. The remuneration for duty solicitors under this scheme is by a combination of fees for various elements of the duty, e.g. for being "on duty" overnight, and a fixed fee per telephone call to persons in custody where the duty solicitor does not attend at the police station, together with various other fees on a time basis

39.06

for actual work at police stations. Duty solicitors in this scheme are volunteers in ordinary private practice with experience of criminal cases, who participate on a rota basis.

AT COURT

39.07 The duty solicitor will as before see persons before they go before the court for the first time and may represent them at that stage. Many courts now deal only with bail applications on the first occasions where the duty solicitor is present though others may deal with pleas in mitigation after a guilty plea. If the case goes past that first hearing then the defendant must apply for legal aid proper.

Legal aid proper

39.08 The 1988 Legal Aid Act allows application for legal aid at any stage in criminal proceedings. The most important and significant differences from civil legal aid are as follows:

1. Application is made not to the Legal Aid Board but to the court before whom the accused is to appear, whether it is a magistrates court or Crown Court; and

2. There is no time for an exhaustive and thorough investigation of means as occurs in civil proceedings. Often the accused is in custody and the case ought for that reason to proceed very swiftly, but in any event the delays of some weeks which are common in deciding on financial eligibility in civil legal aid applications would clearly be out of the question in criminal cases. Accordingly, the courts both assess the applicants' means and decide whether or not the person should receive legal aid in principle.

39.09 There are two criteria for the grant of legal aid in a criminal matter. By section 21 of the Legal Aid Act 1988 legal aid must be granted when:

1. it is desirable to do so in the interests of justice; and

2. it appears that the applicant's financial resources are such that he requires assistance in meeting the costs of the proceedings.

39.10 We shall consider the second first. A person applying for legal aid, as we shall see below in a moment, has to provide some evidence as to his means. This is done by filling in a legal aid application form giving details of income and capital. The court will then assess his means. This will be done very swiftly indeed, often on the same day on which the legal aid application is received by the court, or indeed, if application is made at the court in the course of proceedings, there and then. The accused's financial eligibility is worked out on a sliding scale in a somewhat similar way to the computation in civil proceedings. However, no evidence need be adduced to the court of what the accused alleges to be his income and capital, nor is he subject to cross-examination or interview about these matters. As in the case of civil legal aid, the person whose disposable income or capital are below a certain amount will receive legal aid without contribution; those above certain prescribed maxima will have legal aid refused on financial grounds; and between the two a legal aid contribution order will be made on a sliding scale requiring the person to make some contribution towards the amount of his legal aid. The contribution may either be required in one lump sum, if it is from capital, or if it is from income in instalments over a period of six months. The court is required to assess the approximate likely cost of the case also which is naturally somewhat difficult in view of the fact that the case may take several different courses, *e.g.* the costs may be multiplied many times by the defence electing a full committal hearing. Legal aid may be re-assessed throughout the course of the case should the client's means change.

We turn now to the second criterion that of "desirable in the interests of justice." This naturally confers a discretion on the court and in deciding on whether the interests of justice make it desirable for an accused to have legal aid regard must be had to section 22 of the 1988 Act. This section lays down that legal aid should be granted whenever one of the following factors applies:— **39.11**

1. The offence is such that if proved it is likely that the court would impose a sentence which would deprive the accused of his liberty, or lead to loss of his livelihood or serious damage to his reputation.

2. the charge may involve consideration of a substantial question of law; or

3. the defendant has inadequate knowledge of English, or suffers from mental illness or physical disability; or

4. the defence will involve the tracing and interviewing of witnesses or the expert cross-examination of a prosecution witness;

5. legal representation is desirable in the interests of someone other than the defendant.

It is now appropriate to consider these matters.

THE OFFENCE IS SUCH AS MIGHT LEAD TO THE DEFENDANT LOSING HIS LIBERTY, LIVELIHOOD, OR SUFFERING SERIOUS DAMAGE TO HIS REPUTATION

A client's *liberty* will obviously be at risk if the charge is serious in itself; if there are serious aggravating circumstances, *e.g.* breach of trust of some kind; if the accused already has a bad criminal record, especially if the accused is already under a suspended sentence; and possibly if the accused will be in breach of probation if convicted. Loss of *livelihood* would especially be applicable in the case of a driving offence which might lead to the loss of a driving licence in the case of someone who needs it for his job. Thus, an offence which is disqualifiable in itself, or disqualifiable under the "totting up" procedure, would be good examples and this might be so even where the actual offence charged is not a particularly serious one, *e.g.* speeding, if the points allotted for the offence might lead to the defendant being disqualified with the loss of his job. This would also be applicable in the case of other offences which are not sufficiently serious to merit a custodial sentence. For example, in the case of someone whose job requires them to handle money and of whom utter financial probity is required, *e.g.* a **39.12** bank clerk or a cashier, any conviction for an offence of dishonesty may be sufficiently serious to lead to their dismissal. Finally, viewed as a separate ground, an offence which would cause *serious damage to reputation* but which is not in itself serious enough to be likely to lead to a custodial sentence under the earlier part, would be for example where the person accused had a certain standing in the community such that a conviction would cause grave embarrassment, *e.g.* a vicar charged with shoplifting some trivial item.

Similarly the suggestion of loss of reputation can sometimes be prayed in aid even for a client who has a criminal record if the kind of offence with which he is now charged is significantly different, *e.g.* where previous convictions were for, say, trivial public order offences but the present charge involves some element of dishonesty.

THE CHARGE RAISES A SUBSTANTIAL QUESTION OF LAW

39.13 If the facts of the offence are such as to raise a difficult matter of law, *e.g.* there is a conflict of authority on some relevant matter, then this ground may apply. The defendant clearly will need the assistance of a solicitor in saying whether or not this is the case.

INADEQUATE KNOWLEDGE OF ENGLISH OR SUFFERS FROM MENTAL
ILLNESS OR PHYSICAL DISABILITY

39.14 This ground needs little explanation. If legal aid would otherwise normally be refused on the basis that the particular case was sufficiently minor or straightforward for the person to be able to represent himself, then this might be appropriate.

THE DEFENCE INVOLVES THE TRACING AND INTERVIEWING OF WITNESSES
OR EXPERT CROSS-EXAMINATION OF A PROSECUTION WITNESS

39.15 In other words, the case needs a lawyer's special skills and a layman could not do these things for himself.

LEGAL REPRESENTATION IS DESIRABLE IN THE INTERESTS OF SOMEONE
OTHER THAN THE DEFENDANT

39.16 An example commonly given is the case of a sexual offence against a young child where it is undesirable that the defendant should personally conduct the cross-examination of the child which might distress the latter. This example would, of course, be covered also by the first of the criteria.

The criteria are not in themselves exhaustive. Moreover, there is specific provision that where a doubt exists about the granting of legal aid, the doubt should be resolved in favour of the applicant.

There is one additional ground of importance where the court must grant legal aid (subject to means only) and that is where after conviction in a magistrates' court the defendant is remanded in custody for the carrying out of enquiries or reports. This is by virtue of section 21 of the Legal Aid Act 1988.

Method of application

A legal aid application is made in writing to the magistrates court on Form 1, **39.17**
together with a prescribed form of information about means and resources
(Form 5). In principle, legal aid cannot be granted until form 5 duly completed has been lodged. The application should be taken or sent to the
magistrates court as soon as possible. Generally it will be dealt with very
swiftly, perhaps even the same day, and the result telephoned through to the
solicitor's office. The solicitor will then be sent a legal aid order together
with a form of "Report on Case" on which the eventual application for fees
must be made. The application forms when received are dealt with by a
magistrates clerk, or referred to the magistrates. It will be observed that the
"interests of justice" criteria do not require as such that the accused is *likely
to win* the case, which is (roughly speaking) the criterion for the grant of civil
legal aid. Indeed, one may obtain legal aid even though the accused intends
to plead guilty. If the magistrates court refuses to grant legal aid, then a
further application can be made and this will be referred to a different
magistrate or bench of magistrates, and therefore there will in effect be fresh
minds considering the application. In principle, this can be done any number
of times. Moreover, even if previously refused, a further oral application can
be made to the magistrates at the start of the hearing to which the application
relates. It may be possible then to amplify the grounds upon which the
application is made. In fact refusal of legal aid is often because the solicitor
has not given sufficient information as to why legal aid is required in the
interests of justice. For example, in the case of a person with a bad criminal
record who might be under a suspended sentence at present, the solicitor
might merely have put "accused may receive custodial sentence" on the
application form without giving details. If the application is refused, it will
usually be accepted the second time where full details are given so as to
enable the magistrates to see that there is a real possibility of a custodial
sentence. It goes without saying that since in the application form it may
often be appropriate to disclose a client's past criminal record, that the same
magistrates who consider the written legal aid application form or hear an
oral application, will not then go on to deal with the trial of the accused if he
is pleading not guilty. Magistrates courts making a legal aid order may make
one just for the magistrates court proceedings, or in the case of an indictable
offence may make a so called "through" order which will cover the accused
for the proceedings when they reach the Crown Court. In fact, in principle, it
makes very little difference because at the end of committal proceedings, if
one has not obtained a "through" order, one simply applies to the court to
extend the legal aid to the Crown Court. Moreover, if, for any reason that
was not done or forgotten (the application could hardly be refused unless the
accused's means had changed) legal aid application may be made to the
Crown Court itself in writing on a prescribed form.

What if legal aid is refused?

First, as has previously been stated, a person who is refused legal aid can **39.18**
always make another application to the court, either in writing or at the
hearing itself. Second, under section 21 of the 1988 Legal Aid Act, a person
who has been refused legal aid in the case of an indictable offence, or an
offence triable either way (that is triable either in the magistrates court or
the Crown Court) may apply to the Legal Aid Area Committee. This

committee is a body composed of practising solicitors and barristers who sit part-time on a rota basis. Application is made on a prescribed form and may be made as follows:—

1. In the case of offences which are indictable or triable either way:

2. Where the refusal has not been on the grounds of means alone:

3. Application must be made within 14 days of receiving notification of refusal:

4. The original application for legal aid should have been made at least 21 days before the proposed hearing date of the case, whether committal or summary trial, assuming that such a date had been fixed at the relevant time (which is unlikely). The Area Committee will then review the case and may grant legal aid.

What does legal aid cover?

39.19 It covers preparation for and the conduct of proceedings in the court that grants it, whether magistrates court or Crown Court. As just explained in the magistrates court a "through" order may be made which will also cover proceedings in the Crown Court. Once legal aid is granted, then usually the conduct of the case is not reviewed in the same way as might be the case for civil legal aid. A solicitor who bona fide chooses a particular course of action which may be considerably more expensive than its alternative, will not be subject to criticism or refusal of fees. For example, one crucial stage at which a defence solicitor has a choice which may involve considerable expense is the case of the decision whether or not to insist upon a full committal where the charge is eventually going to be tried in the Crown Court. A solicitor who chooses to have a full committal will not be subject to review, criticism or disallowance of fees.

Legal aid orders in the magistrates court do not usually cover representation by counsel, unless specific approval has been given by the clerk to the justices. Legal aid may be specifically granted for representation in the magistrates court by both solicitor and counsel only where the offence is indictable and the court considers it to be unusually grave and difficult. If such an application is refused, the solicitor concerned may apply again to the court or to the Area Committee. It should not be understood that this means that in those cases where barristers are seen in the magistrates court acting for legally aided defendants that each necessarily concerns an indictable offence which is unusually grave or difficult. The individual advocacy resources of any given firm may mean that the firm is unable to cover all the criminal cases which are coming up on any given day. In such a case it is always open to the firm to instruct counsel on any particular case, but in such a case, the allocation of fees payable will be affected in that the maximum fee to be paid would be that which would be appropriate if a solicitor had conducted the case. Consequently the fees to the barrister and the solicitor will be apportioned in a way that seems reasonable. Payment for solicitors is on an hourly basis with differing rates prescribed for *e.g.* preparation; travelling time, waiting time at court and actual advocacy.

Legal aid in the Crown Court usually consists of representation by solicitor and counsel. Exceptionally if the person is before the court and unrepresented, legal aid may be ordered to be by counsel alone, *e.g.* for a plea in mitigation. Counsel will take instructions direct from the client in such a case.

There is one other vital difference also between legal aid in civil and in **39.20** criminal proceedings. Legal aid certificates are never retrospective in civil cases. Any work done for the person before legal aid is actually granted cannot be paid under the legal aid certificate. In criminal cases, practice has recognised that it is often necessary for a solicitor, not only in his client's interest, but also in the interests of the smooth running of the court itself, to take instructions and take some action before the legal aid application can be considered. For example, suppose that an accused person came into one's office the day before a charge was to be heard. One would use the Green Form to complete a legal aid application and for a preliminary interview with the client, but suppose that some further work was done in any way of contacting witnesses, etc., trying to get them to court for the next day. All this would be done in expectation of legal aid eventually being granted. In such a case, if legal aid is in fact granted, then work done in urgent circumstances can be paid for even though the work was done before the grant of legal aid.

Legal aid orders also cover preliminary advice on the giving of notice of appeal from the magistrates court to the Crown Court, but further steps in connection with the appeal will not be covered and one will be required to apply to the Crown Court itself for legal aid.

Payment of fees under legal aid
A solicitor is entitled to claim payment for work actually and reasonably **39.21** done. Application is made after magistrates court cases for payment on a form of "Report on Case" to the Legal Aid Area Office. The fees claimed will be assessed to ensure that they properly correspond to the time said to have been spent on the case, and payment will be made. In the Crown Court a bill on the prescribed form must be lodged with the Taxing Officer of the Crown Court and the costs will in that case be paid direct from the Crown Court itself. There are standard fees for most kinds of work done on Crown Court cases which do not directly relate to time. There is a discretion to allow fees in excess of the standard fee where appropriate.

What happens where a legally aided person is acquitted?
In such a case whether in magistrates court or Crown Court it is usually **39.22** inappropriate for there to be any order for costs between the parties or from central funds. The normal order is that in such a case if the legally aided person has not had to pay any contribution, that no order for costs is made, but that if he has paid a contribution, then the order will be that the contribution be returned to him and any unpaid parts of his contribution be remitted. This is the usual practice, although it is not invariably the case (*e.g.* if it appears to the court of trial that the accused has been acquitted on some unmeritorious technicality).

Legal aid for appeals by way of case stated
This is considered to be within the civil jurisdiction and consequently appli- **39.23** cation is for civil legal aid to the Legal Aid Board.

Orders for costs

39.24   1. If an accused is convicted the court has a discretion to order that he pay all or some part of the prosecution's costs in addition to any penalty it imposes.

39.25   2. If an accused who is not legally aided is acquitted then under ss.16–21 of the Prosecution of Offences Act 1985

    (i) The court may order that the acquitted person receive from central funds (*i.e.* a Government fund established *inter alia* for this purpose) an amount sufficient to compensate him for any expenses properly incurred by him in the proceedings. Alternatively it may order some lesser sum, *e.g.* if it felt that the accused's own conduct had brought suspicion on himself.

    The court may make this order in favour of an acquitted or discharged accused whether the offence was triable purely summarily, either way, or on indictment.

    (ii) Alternatively or in addition to this under regulations made by the Lord Chancellor an acquitted accused may obtain an order for costs against the prosecution where any "unnecessary or improper" conduct by the latter has put the accused to expense. This would thus only be appropriate in the case of a prosecution unreasonably brought.

40. Preliminary Considerations

In this section, we shall consider the matters which are likely to arise in the   **40.01**
course of routine criminal proceedings. In the case of civil proceedings,
there is generally no particular urgency about the issue of the writ. If the
limitation period has not yet expired, then one would generally be well
advised first to collect all the information one could relevant to liability, and
possibly to quantum. In the case of civil proceedings, it may of course be
possible to obtain a negotiated settlement at a very early stage, or even
without the issue of proceedings at all. There is nothing that corresponds to
these features in criminal practice. In criminal practice, one will usually only
be consulted after proceedings have been instituted and one has no control
over when one's client is likely to be brought before the court. The one
obvious exception to this is the case of a client who is suspected of an offence
and may already have been interrogated at a police station but has not yet
been charged. He might require advice about, say, the nature of police bail,
about whether if he returns to the police station as he has been requested to
or bailed to do in a few days time, he should consent to having his finger
prints taken or to taking part in an identity parade, and so on. More
experienced criminal clients who are well aware of their right of silence may
wish to discuss whether they should maintain silence, or whether the giving
of some carefully prepared exculpatory statement or even the giving of some
limited assistance to the police in enquiries, might result in their not being
charged at all. In this sense, therefore, one might act for a client to help
achieve the best outcome for him, (*i.e.* that he is not charged at all!) without
there needing to be any court proceedings as such. In the mainstream of
cases, however, the prosecution will already have been instituted and one's
duty is to do the best for the client as defendant. We shall therefore consider
steps to take in the conduct of a normal case, although some individual
tactical considerations, *e.g.* whether to opt for summary trial or Crown
Court trial where that choice arises, will be dealt with separately under the
relevant aspects of procedure.

There are two essential preliminary matters which are likely to need consid-   **40.02**
eration. The first will be bail. If, when the client comes into your office,
having been charged, he has already been granted police bail, then one can
generally anticipate that there will be no objection to his having continued
bail from the court. This is the reality, although one can never entirely rely
on it. The courts are given a broad mandate to enquire into the question of
bail and the absence of a prosecution objection may not always be treated as
conclusive, although cases where it is not are rare. Exceptionally even where
the police have released someone on bail, they may find, after having done
so, good reason to object to bail at the first hearing. Such a case might well
be where the alleged victim expresses terror at the continued freedom of the
accused, or the police become suspicious that the accused may have committed offences other than the one which they were initially investigating. So
bail must always be considered. However, where an accused has been

339

released on bail, then the date of the preliminary hearing might well not be for some little time. It ought to be mentioned here, that one common trait of persons charged with criminal offences is that they are not always as well organised, or systematic as they might be, and despite the fact that they may well have been charged weeks ago they may only get around to making an appointment with a solicitor the day before the first hearing. There may thus be very little time to take many preliminary steps before that hearing. This is a well known facet of criminal litigation with which all practitioners learn how to cope. It may be appropriate in cases where there seems any possible doubt to telephone the prosecution to get confirmation that no objection to bail will be raised.

40.03 The second matter that needs to be considered is legal aid. The initial interview can be given under the Green Form Scheme if the client qualifies, and a full legal aid application will need to be completed and sent, or perhaps taken round by hand to the magistrates' court if the case is to be heard in the immediate future. If the case is to be heard say the next day, then it is for the solicitor to decide whether he is prepared to risk legal aid being refused, or not dealt with in time and to continue with the case. An option might be to send the client down to court to ask for an adjournment for the purpose of obtaining legal aid but many consider it unwise to do this. Firstly, there is always the fear of the policeman involved in the case "persuading" the unrepresented accused to see sense and plead guilty for his own good, and secondly, there is always the risk that the court might insist on dealing with the case, particularly if there has already been one adjournment, and might instruct the accused to seek the assistance of the duty solicitor or some other solicitor who is within the precincts of the court and therefore one will have lost the client. Normally, if one can get the legal aid application down to the court at least a day before, that will be long enough for it to be dealt with in most urban courts.

We now turn to the other important aspects of preparing the case.

The first interview

40.04 If this takes place in a police station or in custody just before a first appearance, this will inevitably be rather hurried. All one may have time to do is to find out matters relevant to a bail application. But whatever the outcome of that first meeting, subsequently there will be an opportunity to interview the client in complete privacy and at greater length. If the bail application has been successful, or no objection to bail has ever arisen, this will be in one's own office; if the bail application has been unsuccessful, it will be in the remand centre or prison. There are a number of important matters which need to be discussed with the client. These are as follows:

40.05 1. The precise charges.

If the client has come in to see you in your office it is commonly the case that he will have forgotten, or lost, his charge sheet, in which case a duplicate will need to be obtained. In such a situation one should never rely on a client's recollection of what offence has been charged. "Theft" will all too often prove to mean "robbery" in such circumstances. The charge sheet ought also to reveal whether he has been charged with other people, which it is vital to know.

2. Personal details should be taken from the client and then he should be **40.06** invited to give his account of the incident resulting in the charge. This is as important in the case of a criminal client as it is with a client in a civil case or a witness in either case. The more fresh the events are in the mind of the accused, the better the statement will be. This is particularly so where some fast moving or interlinked series of events is what needs to be described, for example, precisely how a fight started, or the precise course of events at work which led to the accused being charged with theft of the employer's property. It may be that something will be thrown up which can be immediately investigated to good effect. Many clients in criminal cases give vague or apparently unconvincing accounts of incidents. This may be because of lack of intelligence or natural diffidence. Every attempt should be made to draw the client out about his case. In some cases, kindness and sympathy may be needed for this, in others it may perhaps be better to attempt to put the client through a sort of cross-examination about the vaguer or apparently more improbable features of his version. Everything will depend upon the circumstances and the personality of the client.

3. All the foregoing assumes that the client is intending to plead not guilty. If **40.07** he is pleading guilty, then circumstances and details relevant to a plea in mitigation need to be considered. Indeed details of these matters may also be taken from a client who denies the charge. In the case of a client pleading not guilty, however, which is what we are primarily concerned with, then once one has tested the client's own story and looked for possible leads to further avenues of enquiry, (*e.g.* other witnesses who could be contacted), this is perhaps as much as can be done at this stage. The client should be asked to give any account he can of his own criminal record, if he has one, but as we shall see below it is most unwise to rely on this.

There will inevitably need to be another full interview with the client to discuss matters in the light of what you subsequently manage to find out about the prosecution evidence, or about lines of investigation that you have yourself pursued. If the client requires advice about how to plead it may be possible to give this at this stage or it may need to be postponed until a later stage.

Writing to the prosecution

In contrast with the position in a civil case, in a criminal case one is entitled to **40.08** a certain amount of assistance from one's opponent. The prosecution is supposed not to press for conviction at any price in the full adversarial manner, but rather the Crown Prosecutor, whether solicitor or counsel is supposed to act as "a minister of justice" presenting facts and law impartially and fairly to the court. In the heat of the action it may be sometimes difficult for the accused or his advocate to discern this in the manner in which the Crown Prosecutor seems to be conducting the case and one may feel that on occasions a somewhat indecent enthusiasm for the fray for its own sake may colour the Crown Prosecutor's attitude. However, at this stage anyway the prosecution are obliged to assist the defence solicitor and a letter should be written requesting the following:

1. A copy of the client's criminal record, if any.
2. A copy of any written records required to be kept under the 1984 Police and Criminal Evidence Act, *e.g.* custody records.

3. A copy of any statement made by the client under caution.

4. The criminal record of any co-defendant.

5. The criminal record of any prosecution witnesses.

6. The names and addresses of any persons interviewed whom the prosecution do not propose to call at trial. It should be remembered that the prosecution are obliged to inform the defence of any evidence that comes into their possession which is favourable to the defence.

These are the only things which are likely to be forthcoming at this stage. If the case is proceeding to the Crown Court for trial on indictment there will inevitably be committal proceedings. Almost invariably, the prosecution, unless highly exceptionally they have themselves decided on a so-called "full" committal where most of their witnesses are brought before the court, will wish the defendants to agree to a short form committal under section 6(2) of the Magistrates Courts Act 1980, in which case written statements of their evidence are served on the defendant in advance. Furthermore, if the matter is proceeding as a summary trial and concerns an offence such as theft, (*i.e.* an "either way" offence—for definition see para. 45.04) then advance information as to the facts and matters on which the prosecution proposes to rely must be given to the accused, in accordance with the Magistrates Court (Advance Information) Rules 1985. This must include a copy of the statements of the witnesses who are going to be called by the prosecution, or a summary of the evidence in those statements.

Moreover, even in the case of summary offences, then depending upon the defending solicitors relationship with the prosecution the Crown Prosecutor may well be willing to let the solicitor look at copies of his witness statements in advance, no doubt in the hope that when seeing the overwhelming nature of the case against the accused, the accused can be persuaded to plead guilty.

Re-interviewing the client

40.09   One will thus in many cases find out the substance of the prosecution evidence. One will then need to see the client again to get his comments on this evidence. At this time, it may be appropriate, in the light of all that is known about the prosecution case, to suggest to the client lines of questions which will be put to him in cross-examination, so that he can consider how he might deal with them. This is not in any sense with a view to inviting him to think up glib answers well in advance, but genuinely to see whether he does have answers to the points that will be raised. It may be that when the full weight of the prosecution evidence is known, the case will appear overwhelming against the client. In such a situation, the client should be questioned carefully to see whether he might not wish to plead guilty. An advocate has a difficult and delicate task here. A client ought to be given the advantage of having explained to him that a plea of guilty might, in a borderline case, make the difference between going to prison and not going to prison, especially if the nature of his defence involves a frontal attack on the truthfulness or integrity of prosecution witnesses, *e.g.* policemen. Such advice, however, to a client who is at the moment maintaining a not guilty plea must be tempered with the very strongest affirmation that he should not consider pleading guilty unless he actually is. In other words, no attempt should be made to bully a person into pleading guilty but this must be combined with the realistic advice on sentence previously referred to.

It is at this stage where one is reviewing the whole of the evidence, that the client should be taken through his own previous convictions and asked to explain something of the background to each of the offences, or those which are most recent. We will return to this in the section on sentencing and mitigation later, but the point is that it may well be that something can be said to make an apparently bad criminal record look at least a little better. For example, some of the offences may have occurred at a time when the accused had a drug addiction and stole to finance the habit. This is obviously a matter which might, in the eyes of some courts, present some explanation for an apparently consistent course of criminal conduct.

Other steps

In the light of all the information obtained from the accused, and it is very much a matter of "feel" whether one does this immediately after the first interview, or somewhat later in the light of having seen some of the prosecution evidence, one will need to consider other steps. These may briefly be summarised as being: **40.10**

1.   Consider interviewing other witnesses as soon as possible. If these are prosecution witnesses already, it is normally considered courteous to inform the prosecution that one proposes to do this, although there is in fact no property in a witness and it ought not to be considered an attempt to interfere with the course of justice merely for a reputable solicitor to want to interview a witness.

2.   Consider whether expert evidence, (e.g. a psychiatrist's report on the accused) is needed. This is unlikely in a routine case.

3.   If the location where a thing happened is material, visit it so that one can gain a clear picture. It may even be desirable to take photographs or make a plan. For example if a fight broke out in the confines of a crowded public house, then a plan of the layout of the public house might assist. If one is concerned with a driving offence, just as in the case of a civil action involving a road accident, it may be appropriate to make plans, or photographs of the scene to enable the court to get a full picture of the layout of the road junction etc. In this connection also, one should ensure that the accused shows you his driving licence to ensure that actual endorsements correspond to his criminal record.

Calling witnesses

It is perhaps useful here to summarise the ways in which witnesses may be called before the magistrates and Crown Court. **40.11**

1.   In the magistrates court, one obtains a witness summons from the clerk to the justices. This is done by attending in person, or writing a letter requesting the issue of the summons. A summons can, in principle, only be issued if the clerk (or a magistrate) is satisfied that a witness at a summary trial or committal proceedings will not attend voluntarily. This requirement is contained in section 97 of the Magistrates Courts Act 1980. Individual courts and clerks vary in the enthusiasm with which they require this condition to be fulfilled. Many will issue a witness

summons anyway on request from a solicitor and his assurance that it seems in all the circumstances to be likely to be required. Others, more pedantically, require some positive assertion that the witness will not attend voluntarily. Indeed, they may require there to be a first attempt to have the witness attend voluntarily, and only if he does not, will a summons be issued. This can be highly inconvenient and is arguably very foolish in view of the difficulties in efficiently arranging the listing of criminal cases. The time of many people may be wasted if the trial cannot go ahead because a clerk has insisted that there be some evidence that the witness will not attend voluntarily before a summons can be issued. It is a fact of life that even witnesses who have given an assurance of attending voluntarily, often fail to do so because they wish to avoid the inconvenience, possible expense and loss of earnings of attending court proceedings. It is for this reason that it is prudent in every case in civil proceedings to subpoena witnesses.

2. In the Crown Court. There will be a committal before a Crown Court trial at the end of which "full" or "conditional" witness orders will be made in respect of *prosecution* witnesses. For *defence* witnesses, a witness order may be obtained on request from the Crown Court under the Criminal Procedure (Attendance of Witnesses) Act 1965. This is achieved by lodging a simple form of request and there is no need in this case to assure the court that the witness will not attend voluntarily.

3. Finally, consideration ought to be given in the case of the evidence of apparently uncontroversial witnesses to the serving of the evidence in the form of a statement prepared under section 9 of the Criminal Justice Act 1967, (or section 102 of the Magistrates Courts Act 1980 for committal proceedings). The use of these sections has been considered previously.

41. Police Powers

In this section we shall be considering the early stages of the investigation of **41.01** an offence. We shall be considering the powers of the police in relation to:

1. Arrest.

2. Search.

3. Taking fingerprints and photographs.

4. The detention of a suspect.

5. Interrogation of a suspect.

6. Identification procedures.

   In legal theory the police have no greater powers than the ordinary citizen save where such powers are expressly conferred by statute or have been deemed to exist at common law. The law has constantly striven to strike an appropriate balance between the liberty of the citizen to come and go as he pleases without being impeded by officers of the state and the realistic need to confer upon police and other investigating agencies limited powers to interfere with the freedom of citizens for good cause in the general interest of the supression of crime.

   The law at present is largely contained in the Police and Criminal Evidence Act 1984 (the "Act") and in Codes of Practice issued under section 66 of that Act. In some cases the Act merely restates the previous law with some additional refinements but in other cases express new powers are conferred. We shall now go on to consider the various stages of the investigation process and police powers in relation to it.

Arrest

ARREST WITH A WARRANT

If the police know the identity of a suspect whom they wish to arrest they will **41.02** lay an information in writing on oath before a magistrate. This is commonly done orally. The warrant of arrest then obtained may be endorsed for bail which would authorise the police to release the suspect once having arrested him and after they have made the decision whether to charge him or alternatively may not in which case the suspect must be brought before the court. Such warrants may only be issued where:

1. the offence is triable on indictment or punishable with imprisonment; or

2. the defendant's address is not sufficiently established for him to be subject to the alternative procedure of a summons being sent to him.

This is by virtue of the Magistrates' Courts Act 1980, section 1(4).

Arrest with a warrant is now somewhat unusual. As we shall see shortly the police have such wide powers to arrest without a warrant that it will only be exceptionally that a warrant is required. We turn now to the more common procedure for arrest, namely arrest without warrant.

ARREST WITHOUT WARRANT

41.03 The power to arrest without warrant is now contained in section 24 of the 1984 Act which broadly restates the law previously contained in section 2 of the Criminal Law Act 1967 with some refinements. It provides a power of summary arrest, that is immediate arrest without prior formalities, for the police in the case of arrestable offences. "Arrestable offences" means:

1. offences for which the sentence is fixed by law, (*e.g.* murder);

2. offences for which a first offender of 21 or older may receive a prison sentence of five years or more. This therefore means that certain offences are always arrestable offences. Thus theft is one such offence since it carries a maximum penalty of ten years. It is irrelevant that for the purposes of the offence with which one is concerned there is no prospect whatsoever of the arrestee receiving a prison sentence of five years. Thus for example a person suspected of shoplifting some small item may still be arrested under these powers notwithstanding that there is little prospect of them going to prison at all, still less for five years;

3. sundry other offences listed in Schedule 2 to the Act which are expressly made arrestable offences notwithstanding that they do not carry a maximum penalty of as long as five years, *e.g.* offences of indecent assault on a woman;

4. certain other offences which the statute creating the offence expressly made arrestable notwithstanding that they did not carry a penalty as long as five years, *e.g.* the offence of taking a vehicle without the owner's consent under section 12 of the Theft Act 1968.

41.04 By section 24(6) and (7) of the Act a constable has the following powers:—

1. if he has reasonable grounds for suspecting that an arrestable offence has been committed he may arrest without a warrant anyone whom he has reasonable grounds for suspecting to be guilty of the offence;

2. to arrest without a warrant anyone who is about to commit an arrestable offence or anyone whom he has reasonable grounds for suspecting is about to commit an arrestable offence;

3. to arrest without a warrant anyone who is in the act of, or whom he has reasonable grounds for suspecting to be in the act of, committing an arrestable offence.

In addition by section 25 of the Act where a constable has reasonable grounds for suspecting that any offence which is *not an* arrestable offence, (*e.g.* careless driving) has been committed or attempted or is being committed or attempted he may arrest the relevant person if it appears to him that service of a summons is impracticable or inappropriate for any of the reasons specified in section 25(3) of the Act, *e.g.*

1. that the name of the relevant person is unknown to and cannot be readily ascertained by the constable; or

2. the constable has reasonable grounds for doubting whether a name furnished by the relevant person as his name is his real name; or

3. the relevant person fails to furnish a satisfactory address.

In these latter cases therefore a policeman who stops someone whom he believes to be committing a driving offence which is not arrestable would be entitled to arrest the person concerned if he felt that he was not being given a true name and address so that criminal proceedings could be instituted through the summons procedure which as we shall see shortly does not usually involve the preliminary arrest of the suspect.

Quite apart from this, certain other statutory powers of arrest are expressly preserved, *e.g.* that in section 7 of the Bail Act 1976 for the offence of absconding.

PROCEDURE ON ARREST

On arrest a person is to be cautioned in the following words:— **41.05**
"you do not have to say anything unless you wish to do so but what you say may be given in evidence." In addition under section 28 of the Act an arrest is unlawful unless at the time or as soon as is practicable thereafter the person is informed of the ground for the arrest and this applies whether or not it is obvious what the ground for the arrest is. This does not mean that a suspect must be told in technical language what the offence is, still less must reference be made to the section of the statute under which he may eventually be charged, but the circumstances said to constitute the offence must be clearly indicated to him. Thus the kind of language used in television police dramas, *e.g.* "you're nicked for the Bermondsey Co-op blag" would no doubt suffice.

Search

STOP AND SEARCH

By section 1 of the Act a police officer has the power to detain and search any **41.06** person or vehicle for stolen or prohibited articles. "Prohibited articles" are:—

1. offensive weapons;

2. articles made or adapted for use in or intended for use in
    (a) burglary;
    (b) theft;
    (c) offences of taking away a motor vehicle under section 12 of the Theft Act 1968;
    (d) obtaining property by deception under section 15 of the Theft Act 1968.

It will be seen that this is a fairly wide power. A constable, however, must only do this if he has reasonable grounds for suspecting that he will find stolen or prohibited articles. It has been stressed that searches will not be carried out simply on the basis of the racial origin of the person or because the person is found in an area in which offences of a certain kind are relatively common. There must be a specific reason for suspecting the individual concerned. The Notes for Guidance accompanying the Code of Practice which supplements section 1 warns that the degree or level of suspicion required to establish the reasonable grounds justifying stop and search is no less than the degree of suspicion required to effect an arrest.

POWERS TO ENTER AND SEARCH PREMISES

41.07   1.   A policeman may enter and search any premises with the written permission of the occupier.

41.08   2.   A police officer may enter and search any premises (*inter alia*);
    (a) to execute a warrant of arrest or commitment to prison;
    (b) to arrest a person for an arrestable offence;
    (c) to save life or limb or prevent serious damage to property, s.17.

3.   A police officer has power to search premises where an arrest took place for evidence relating to the offence for which the person has been arrested, but only to the extent that the power to search is reasonably required for the purpose of discovering any such evidence, s.32.

4.   A police officer has power, in the case of arrestable offences only, to search premises occupied or controlled by the person arrested for evidence relating to that offence or connected or similar arrestable offences.

   Thus in this latter case a general fishing expedition is not permitted but no doubt a search will be easy enough to justify unless all the stolen property has been recovered and there can be no conceivable grounds for thinking that the individual was involved in other similar offences. A full record of any searches made under this provision must be made and entered on the individual's custody record (see below).

5.   Finally a search may be executed under a search warrant which may be issued on application to the magistrates in certain circumstances.

   In none of these cases do the police have powers to seize items subject to legal privilege. This includes the contents of a solicitor's files or solicitor/client communications unless they could be regarded as coming into existence with the intention of furthering a criminal purpose, (*e.g.* communications between a solicitor and a client constituting a conspiracy).

SEARCH OF PERSONS AFTER ARREST

Away from a police station

41.09   This is governed by section 32 of the 1984 Act.
   An arrested person may be searched upon arrest away from a police station if the constable has reasonable grounds for believing that the arrested person may present a danger to himself or others, or has reasonable grounds for believing that a person might have concealed on him anything:

1.   which he might use to assist him to escape from lawful custody; or

348

2. which might be evidence relating to an offence.

However, the search may only take place to the extent that it is reasonably required for the purpose of discovering such things and in any event the constable may not require a person to remove any of his clothing in public other than an outer coat, jacket or gloves.

At the police station

Under section 54 of the Act a custody officer may order the search of an **41.10** arrested person if he considers it necessary to ascertain or record property that that person has in his possession when he is brought to the station.

Fingerprints
Previously the police had no power to take a person's fingerprints before he **41.11** was charged with an offence unless he consented. However, now under section 61 of the Act a person who gives his consent must give it in writing but in any event if he does not consent an officer of at least superintendent rank may authorise the taking of fingerprints:—

1. before the individual has been charged where it is believed that finger-prints will tend to confirm or disprove his involvement in the commission of a particular offence; or

2. after he has been charged or informed that he will be prosecuted for any recordable offence (that is an offence conviction for which will be recorded in national police records).

Photographing
A person's consent in writing must be provided for the taking of photo- **41.12** graphs before charging, but after he has been charged with a recordable offence he may be photographed without his consent.

So far we have considered in very brief outline police powers in relation to **41.13** the preliminary conduct of an investigation. The description given is hardly adequate as a full treatment of the law and practice. There is, however, a reason for this which is that the nature of this text is essentially practical. We are only concerned with police powers and conduct in the context of the criminal process. In any of the cases previously described breach of the law or misuse of powers may be a police disciplinary offence. Moreover in many cases misconduct would also give rise to liability in tort, *e.g.* an arrest that was unlawful would be false imprisonment; entry of premises in improper circumstances would be trespass to land; and taking fingerprints forcibly in situations where it was not appropriate would be battery. We are not, however, for present purposes concerned with the consequences to the individual police officers or the police force of complaints or actions in tort. We are concerned with the effect of any abuse of the process on the criminal prosecution. What then is the effect of any such misuse of police powers? The answer is likely to be that so far as the criminal prosecution is concerned, misconduct by the police will have very little effect at all.

As we have seen in the context of criminal evidence on the basis of the case law before the Act there is no power for the court to exclude evidence merely to indicate disapproval of the way in which it was obtained. Therefore if a prosecution were commenced by an unlawful arrest and involved obtaining evidence by unlawful entry and seizure and the wrongful obtaining of fingerprints, these things would have had no effect whatsoever on the criminal process. Whatever the consequences (if any) in terms of disciplinary action against the police or action in tort, misconduct would not have given grounds for excluding the evidence thus unfairly or illegally obtained.

41.14   The law is now contained in section 78 of the Police and Criminal Evidence Act 1984 which provides:

> "in any proceedings the court may refuse to allow evidence on which the prosecution proposes to rely to be given if it appears to the court that, having regard to all the circumstances, including the circumstances in which the evidence was obtained, the admission of the evidence would have such an adverse effect on the fairness of the proceedings that the court ought not to admit it."

The effect of this is far from clear but is widely considered to make little change to the previous law. It will be noted that the trial judge has to have regard to whether or not the conduct will have an effect on the *fairness of the proceedings*. "Fairness" relates to the question of whether the jury will be adversely affected *not* by the item of evidence concerned but by the *circumstances in which it was obtained*. It is suggested that the way in which evidence is obtained will not in itself affect the fairness of the proceedings, however "unfair" in general terms police conduct has been. If evidence is relevant it will still be admissible. Accordingly it is suggested that for the sake of the criminal prosecution misconduct by the police in arrest, search, fingerprinting, etc., will not have a great effect. This is why these matters have been dealt with somewhat cursorily in the present text.

It ought to be stressed, however, that if the police are *relying on a confession* then by virtue of section 76 of the Act the court needs to investigate the circumstances in which the confession was obtained to see whether it should be admissible, that is whether it was obtained by *oppression* or whether there is anything in all the surrounding circumstances which might render it *unreliable*. Therefore it could well be that the conduct of the police generally which might include unlawful search, seizure or arrest might have had such an effect on the mind of the person confessing that it could be said to contribute to the unreliability of his confession. These matters have been discussed earlier in the section on confessions. It will also be recalled that under section 78 of the Act a confession may be excluded even if it is not unreliable if the circumstances in which it was obtained lead to the conclusion that the admission of the evidence would have an adverse effect on the fairness of the proceedings. The occasions when sections 76 and 78 together have most frequently led to the exclusion of confessions have mainly been connected with police misconduct or omission in the course of detention and interrogation, a stage of procedure at which the suspect is clearly vulnerable to improper pressures. We shall now discuss the rules in relation to detention and interrogation.

Detention

THE CUSTODY OFFICER

Part IV of the Act creates the post of custody officer who is a police officer of at least sergeant rank who has various responsibilities at "designated police stations." Designated police stations are those which have sufficient accommodation and facilities for the purpose of detaining arrested persons. The custody officer in principle takes formal charge of arrested persons on the premises and has the duty of supervising the detention and interrogation of such persons. He must also keep a "custody record" which records details of the course of a suspect's detention and interrogation.

41.15

When a person is brought to the police station after arrest he must be brought before the custody officer who will at that stage decide whether there is sufficient evidence to charge him with the offence for which he was arrested. If so then he should be charged forthwith. He may then be released on bail (with securities or surety as appropriate) unless;

41.16

1. His name or address cannot be ascertained or the custody officer has reasonable grounds for doubting whether a name or address furnished by him is his real name or address;

2. The custody officer has reasonable grounds for believing that the detention of the person arrested is necessary for his own protection or to prevent him from causing physical injury to any other person or for causing loss of or damage to property; or

3. The custody officer has reasonable grounds for believing that the person arrested will fail to appear in court to answer bail or that his detention is necessary to prevent him from interfering with the administration of justice or with the investigation of offences.

Thus where the person is charged the custody officer must consider bail. It will be noted that the matters which he has to consider correspond approximately to some of those contained in the Bail Act 1976. It ought to be stressed that the Bail Act does not apply at this stage. The Bail Act governs the grant of bail by a *court*.

If the individual is not released on bail he must be brought before a magistrates' court as soon as practical and in any event not later than the first sitting of the court after he has been charged with an offence.

What however if the custody officer decides that there is as yet insufficient evidence to charge? The suspect must then be released unless detention is necessary to secure or preserve evidence or to obtain such evidence by questioning him. This is provided by section 37 of the Act. A written record of the grounds for detention must be made in the presence of the person arrested and the grounds must be conveyed to the person.

41.17

There are further limits on detention before charging namely;

41.18

1. There is an overriding duty on the police to charge an individual as soon as there is sufficient evidence to justify a charge.

2. No person may be detained for more than 24 hours from the time at which the arrested person is brought to the police station save where the offence being investigated is a "serious arrestable offence." "Serious arrestable offences" are a special category of offences. Where a "serious arrestable offence" is concerned the police have greater powers than they have in the case of other offences. Serious arrestable offences comprise:
(a) certain offences which are always serious, *e.g.* murder;
(b) any other arrestable offence which is serious if its commission has led or is intended or likely to lead to certain serious consequences as defined in section 116 of the Act. For our purposes the relevant consequences are:
(i) serious interference with the administration of justice or the investigation of offences;
(ii) substantial financial gain or serious loss to any person.

It should be noted that there is a subjective criterion for establishing whether the offence involves "serious loss." By section 116(7) "serious" means "serious for the person who suffers it." Thus theft, *e.g.* of a person's welfare benefit Giro cheque might well qualify even though the amount is modest.

41.19 In the case of serious arrestable offences the police have the right to detain the suspect for longer than the basic 24 hours. However, even in such cases the total period may only be up to 36 hours with the authority of an officer of at least superintendent rank who has reasonable grounds for believing that it is necessary to detain that person without charge in order to secure or preserve evidence or to obtain such evidence by questioning him, and the investigation is being conducted diligently and expeditiously.

The concept of serious arrestable offence allows the police other greater powers than in the normal case. If the police do require to detain a person beyond 36 hours they must apply on oath by way of information to a magistrates' court for a warrant of further detention and the person must be present at the hearing and has the right to be legally represented. Detention may then be authorised until up to 96 hours from the "relevant time," *i.e.* from the time at which a person first came to the police station.

Reviews must be made of a person's detention (whether charged or not) not later than six hours after the detention was first authorised by the custody officer and thereafter every nine hours to ensure that the reasons justifying detention still exist. The review officer is an officer of inspector rank who must not have been directly involved in the investigation (in cases where the arrested person has not been charged) or the custody officer if he has. If the criteria for continued detention are not satisfied then the arrested person must be released.

The conduct of interrogation

41.20 Interrogation is now governed by the code issued under section 66 of the Act concerning the detention, treatment and questioning of persons by the police. We shall consider this shortly but meanwhile it is important to note two specific powers provided in the statute itself namely:

1. By section 58 of the Act a person arrested and held in custody in a police

station shall be entitled to consult a solicitor privately at any time if he so requests. Any such request must be recorded in the custody record. The consultation may be in person or by telephone either with his own solicitor, if he has one, or with a duty solicitor. A delay in compliance is permitted only where the detainee is being held for a serious arrestable offence and an officer of at least superintendent rank has authorised the delay and is in any event only permitted if the officer has reasonable grounds for believing that receiving such legal advice would;

    (a) lead to interference with evidence of an offence or to interference with or physical injury to some third person; or

    (b) lead to persons suspected of an offence being warned that the police are looking for them; or

    (c) hinder the recovery of the proceeds of an offence;

2.   Under section 56 of the Act a person has the right to not be held incommunicado. Section 56 of the Act provides that a person under arrest at a police station shall be entitled on request to have one friend, relative or other person likely to take an interest in his welfare informed of his arrest and of the station where he is being held. Delay in permitting the person to exercise this right is only permitted in the same situation where the right to legal advice may be delayed or refused.

Finally an individual held in custody has the right to read the relevant Codes of Practice. However, a person arrested is not entitled to cause unreasonable delay to the investigation while he reads the Codes.

THE CONDUCT OF INTERROGATION—CODE OF PRACTICE

The Code provides that: **41.21**

1.   There is a basic duty to inform a person arrested of certain rights.

2.   Where there are grounds to suspect a person of an offence he must be cautioned in the same terms as those of the caution upon arrest. Further, where there is any break in questioning the suspect should be recautioned when it resumes or he should be reminded that he is still under caution. Moreover, a detailed record must be made of the conduct of the interrogation; of meals and refreshment breaks; of complaints; and of any reasons for delaying a break in the interview.

A person must be charged as soon as the prosecution have sufficient evidence on which to charge him. In other words the prosecution having already obtained such evidence may not delay charging merely because they wish to collect further information from the suspect. Having charged the suspect he may not be further questioned with regard to that offence except;

1.   Where necessary for the purpose of preventing or minimising harm or loss to some other person or the public; or

2.   In order to clear up an ambiguity in a previous answer; or

3.   Where it is in the interests of justice that he should have to put him, and have an opportunity to comment on, information concerning the offence which has come to light since he was charged.

In the latter case he should be cautioned again before questioning is resumed. He should not be referred to any written statement made by another person or to the contents of any interview with such person without first being cautioned and then shown the statement or interview record without any further comment being invited by the officer who tenders the statement, etc., to him.

41.22 The temptation for the police to delay charging is therefore considerable but is in part alleviated by the provisions referred to above. As indicated at the outset breach of these provisions is likely to be considerably more relevant to the criminal process than breach of the provisions with regard to arrest and search. A suspect will now be in the confines of a police station and unless he is already well used to custody he may have little idea of his rights (and the average suspect is unlikely perhaps to obtain much benefit from reading the Act and the Codes with which he may be supplied). He may have no idea about how long the police can keep him, what their powers are whilst he is there, or what they may be doing at his home or with his family meanwhile. He is therefore in a very vulnerable situation. The new provisions requiring the keeping of exhaustive custody records are meant in part to ensure that the police thoroughly rationalise and justify each of the steps they propose to take with regard to the way in which they treat the suspect or the reasons why they are keeping him in custody or prolonging his custody. They also ensure that the police themselves keep their actions under review in the light of the fact that the custody record may come up for examination in court and they may be asked then to justify exactly why they behaved in the way in which they did. Thus for example suppose that a suspect was arrested on a Saturday night and put in a cell before questioning started some hours later. It would be easy enough at the trial for the police to say that due to the volume of activity in the police station on the Saturday night it was impossible to question the suspect immediately. In fact they may very well have left him in the cell for a few hours as part of a well-recognised softening-up process to make him more amenable to questioning later. Whilst the keeping of records does not prevent this kind of practice they will need to be very sure that they can justify it at the very time they are writing up the custody record.

Interrogation procedures now involve a careful review of the case not by the investigating officers but by the custody officer and in some cases by a review officer who is not connected with the case. In both cases it is intended that the officers concerned will be sufficiently aware of the need to preserve their personal reputations and integrity to ensure that they do their job efficiently and do not merely succumb to the enthusiasm of their colleagues involved in the investigations who may wish to conduct matters in a certain way. It will be noted that both the custody officer and the review officer may well be of inferior rank to the investigating officers whose procedures they may be charged with supervising.

41.23 The process of interrogation may be vital for the success of the eventual prosecution. As previously remarked no matter what evidence the police already have they like to try to obtain a confession from a suspect if at all possible, thinking it will then be harder for him to plead not guilty and a great deal of time and cost may well be saved. Breaches of the Codes or of the substantive sections of the Act, *e.g.* sections 56 and 58 are not in themselves matters which invalidate a confession. They are, however, things which will be seriously taken into account in considering whether in all the circumstances the confession is unreliable.

TAPE RECORDING OF INTERVIEWS

Interviews at a police station should now be tape recorded in the case of **41.24** indictable offences or those triable either way. In principle the consent of the suspect is required though the police may carry on with tape recording even in the event of objection if they think it appropriate. To do so, however, might involve them in adverse comment in court. The following are the main features of the tape-recording process:—

(a) The tape recording must be done openly and not without the knowledge of the suspect.

(b) Two tapes must be used on a twin deck machine; one of these will be the "master tape" which is sealed at the end of the interview and will not be opened until the court proceedings.

(c) A balanced summary of the relevant parts of the interview will be prepared from the "working" copy of the tape and this balanced summary will be sent to the defence. If the defence require it they may insist on listening to the whole tape.

(d) A transcript of the tape may be prepared for use in court to avoid the time needed to set up the recording and playing equipment. Naturally the tape may in some situations be played in court in order to resolve difficulties; to indicate authenticity; or so that the full picture can be conveyed to the court in terms of pauses, breaks, tone of voice, etc.

(e) Any interview which is not tape recorded must be contemporaneously recorded in note form whether or not the interview takes place at the police station or somewhere else. At the end of the interview an arrested person must be given the opportunity to read the interview record and to sign it as correct or to indicate the respects in which he considers it inaccurate.

(f) The tape or interview record must indicate where the interview took place, when it began and ended, any breaks in it, and the persons present. This will usually be done by the interrogating officer giving details at the start and end of the interview.

The criteria for determining unreliability or whether the evidence should be excluded on the general grounds of unfairness have already been described.

Identification procedures
It will be recalled that following the guidelines in *R.* v. *Turnbull* [1977] Q.B. **41.25** 224 the jury or magistrates are to exercise caution in convicting in a case depending wholly or substantially on disputed identification evidence. The normal case will be where an eye witness at the scene of some incident believes he can recognise the perpetrator who is not apprehended at that time. Subsequently a suspect is found. At one time the suspect might have been tried and the identifying witness would have seen him for the first time since the crime whilst he is actually sitting in the dock and would purport to

identify him then and there. There are clearly grave dangers in this course. The witness may feel sure that the police will have the right man and even if he entertains doubts may identify the man in the dock simply because he is there. Accordingly for a very long time now "dock identifications" have been disapproved and identity parades have been used. An identity parade is an opportunity for a witness to see the suspect as soon as possible after the crime and to test the witness's ability to pick the suspect out of a group of people of approximately similar appearance. The guidelines for the conduct of identity parades are now contained in the Identification Code issued under section 66 of the Act. Where the police have a suspect and the evidence on which they base their case is wholly or substantially that of identification they should hold an identity parade. They must give the suspect the right to refuse to take part. If, however, he does refuse there are two important points to note and these will generally mean that it is prudent for a suspect to consent. If he refuses:—

1. The refusal may be given in evidence at any subsequent trial and may be subject to comment;

2. Some less satisfactory method of identification, such as group identification or identification by video of the suspect and others, or even confrontation that is one to one with the witness, or allowing the witness to see the suspect and a few other prisoners in the cell, may be adopted. Generally speaking a properly conducted identity parade gives the suspect a better chance.

THE CONDUCT OF THE PARADE

41.26 1. Certain information must be given to a suspect in a written "notice to suspect."

2. The suspect may have a solicitor or friend present at the parade unless the parade officer reasonably considers that this cannot be arranged without causing unreasonable delay having regard to the lawful period of detention.

3 The parade must be conducted by a uniformed officer of at least inspector rank who is not personally involved in the investigation. The point of this is to ensure that the procedure is scrupulously carried out and that the officer charged with organising the parade has no personal interest in the case which might lead him to short cut any procedures.

4. The parade must consist of at least eight persons other than the suspect who are so far as possible of the same age, height, general appearance and position in life as the suspect. The suspect may choose his own position in the line and may change positions if he wishes in between identifying witnesses if there are more than one.

5. It is vital to ensure that the witnesses are segregated from the parade so that they do not see any member of the parade, and are not prompted by any photograph or description of the suspect or given any clues, or communicate with each other or with any witness who has already seen the parade.
    The procedure on the parade is then simply that the witnesses are brought into the room where the members of the parade are and they

walk past. It is important that each witness is told before the parade that the person involved may or may not be in the parade and that he has no obligation to make a positive identification. This is to avoid the risk of embarrassment leading to the witness perhaps feeling that the police are now looking to the witness for vital evidence and thus there is some pressure on him to pick *somebody*. The witness will make the identification by saying at which number in the line the person is standing. The witness may ask, if he wishes, for any member of the parade to speak, move, or adopt any posture. If this suggestion comes from the witness then the officer in charge of organising the parade is required to remind the witness that the parade has been selected on the basis of physical appearance not, *e.g.* similarity of voice and the officer must specifically ask the witness whether he is capable of identifying any person on the basis of appearance alone. However, thereafter the witness's request may be met.

THE USE OF PHOTOGRAPHS

The Identification Code likewise sets out rules for the use of photographs **41.27** and these provide:

1. Photographs should not be used where there is a suspect already available. At that stage one should go straight to an identification parade. Clearly an identification parade is preferable to photographs and moreover if photographs have been used they substantially invalidate any subsequent identity parade so far as that witness is concerned. This is because the witness who may have seen an incident for some few seconds and is able to pick out a photograph on the basis of his recollection of that incident will obviously clearly recollect the features in the *photograph* should any subsequent identity parade be held. There is thus one vital further remove between the crime and the parade and a witness who has an opportunity of studying a photograph at leisure is unlikely to fail to pick out that person at the parade.

2. A witness must be shown at least 12 photographs at a time as far as possible of a similar type and with a resemblance to the suspect.

3. If one witness makes a positive identification then there should be no further showing of photographs, and an identity parade should be held for other witnesses involved.

Exceptionally if a witness attending an identification parade has previously been shown a photograph or photofit pictures the suspect and his legal representative shall be informed of this fact before committal proceedings or summary trial.

To summarise therefore one can say that photographs should only be used **41.28** where there is *no suspect at all*. Thus if for example some offence is committed in a large city and the police have little idea who might have committed it they will first look in criminal records for persons who have a propensity to that type of crime and who live locally. They will then show photographs of such suspects to one eye witness in the hope that a lead can be obtained. If the eye witness then identifies someone an identity parade will be held with that suspect (if he is willing) for any other eye witnesses involved. As indicated above there will not usually be any point in holding such an identity parade for the same eye witness who picked out the photograph.

41.29 What if there is irregularity in the showing of photographs or conduct of identity parades? The answer depends on the degree of the irregularity:

1. The showing of photographs will render valueless any subsequent identification parade for the same witness. Where it becomes apparent to the defence that this has occurred then it is suggested that the judge ought to be asked to send out the jury and that a submission should be made that the evidence of identification obtained by the identity parade is of so little evidential value that the prosecution should not be permitted to adduce the evidence at all. Consequently in that case the identifying witness will not be called to give evidence.

2. Any deliberate leading of a witness, *e.g.* by showing only one photograph, or indicating which is the suspect in a parade, ought similarly to invalidate the whole of the identification evidence thus obtained from the witness concerned.

3. If there is some lesser breach of the rules, for example, say that a parade had two individuals in it who did not look very much like the suspect and was one short then that would be a matter within the discretion of the trial judge. He might very well rebuke the prosecution for these deficiencies but it is most unlikely that he would rule the evidence out entirely though he ought to comment that because of the defects in procedure the evidence might be less reliable.

41.30 It ought to be mentioned that if a suspect has a very unusual appearance, *e.g.* in terms of height, hairstyle, etc., it may simply be impossible to organise a proper parade. In those circumstances there may be no alternative to group identification or simple confrontation, *i.e.* letting the witness see the suspect at the police station.

41.31 Finally, it is important to note that unless exceptionally the defence wish them to do so, (*e.g.* to explore the procedure involved) the prosecution must not lead any evidence before the jury of the use of photographs. This is because the reference to police photographs is tantamount to telling the jury that the accused has a criminal record.

42. The Commencement of Proceedings

With very few exceptions not relevant for our purposes all prosecutions are   **42.01**
commenced in a magistrates' court. They may be commenced in principle by
one of two methods, namely, the laying of an information which leads to the
issue of a summons by the court, and by charging. We shall shortly consider
these two methods but before doing so it is necessary to say a few words
about some preliminary matters.

TIME LIMITS

In criminal cases there is in principle no statute of limitation comparable to   **42.02**
that which applies in civil proceedings. There is thus no time limit within
which a prosecution must be commenced. However in the case of *purely
summary* offences, that is those triable only before the magistrates' court
there is a provision that an information must in principle be laid within six
months of the date of commission of that offence. This provision is *not*
applicable to an *either way* offence, however the statute creating such an
offence may itself lay down a time limit for prosecution although this is rare.
An information is laid for these purposes when it is received by the clerk to
the justices of the magistrates' court concerned.

    Note that by section 1 of the Road Traffic Offenders Act 1988, in the case
of certain driving offences including reckless driving, careless driving and
driving in excess of the speed limit there is an additional provision. In the
case of these offences a defendant may not be prosecuted unless he was
given notice of intended prosecution either orally at the time of the alleged
offence or in writing within 14 days thereafter or been served with the
summons itself within 14 days of the offence. However where an accident
occurs at the same time or immediately after the offence, provided the
defendant was aware that the accident occurred there is no requirement to
give him notice of intended prosecution.

GEOGRAPHICAL RESTRICTIONS

Magistrates' courts have jurisdiction to try summary offences committed   **42.03**
within their respective counties. Additionally a magistrates' court has jurisdiction over offences committed outside its county:—

1. Under section 2(6) of the Magistrates' Courts Act 1980 where in addi-
    tion to an offence (either summary or triable either way) which is
    alleged to have been committed in the court's county the accused is
    charged with any other summary offence wherever committed;

2. Under section 2(2) of the 1980 Act where it is "necessary or expedient"
    that a person charged be tried "jointly or in the same place as" another
    person;

3. Under section 3 of the 1980 Act offences committed within 500 yards of the county border and continuing offences begun in one county and completed in another may be treated as having been committed in either of the relevant counties. A similar rule applies in the case of offences against persons or property committed in a moving vehicle which at the time crossed a county boundary.

These provisions are fairly commonsensical. They allow the convenient joinder of offences and offenders and save difficulty in cases where it is not entirely clear where a substantive offence occurred because of closeness to boundaries (county boundaries in any event are often notoriously hard to define).

It should be noted however that this applies only in the case of purely summary offences. In the case of an offence triable either way (*e.g.* theft) the magistrates' court does not have this limit on its jurisdiction. In effect therefore the prosecution have the choice of courts in the case of an offence triable either way and may seek to commence proceedings in the court most convenient to them.

Commencing proceedings

PROCEDURE BY INFORMATION

42.04 The laying of an information fulfils two distinct purposes:—

1. it is the charge to which the accused must plead at the commencement of a summary trial and

2. it is the procedural device which leads to the issue of a summons in those instances where the accused's first appearance before the court is secured by summons.

An information may therefore come about in three ways:

42.05 1. By the prosecutor delivering a signed written allegation against the accused to the court.
The information must describe only one offence in ordinary language and must cite any relevant statutory provision. It may however allege in the alternative different ways of committing the same offence. Reasonable particulars must be disclosed but it is not essential that every legal element of the alleged defence be described. An information may be laid against more than one person.
If it is required to bring more than one charge against an accused separate informations must be delivered to the court.

42.06 2. As an alternative to the above an applicant may appear in person before a magistrate or magistrate's clerk who then reduces an oral allegation to writing. Following the laying of an information in this manner the court decides whether or not to issue a summons requiring the accused to attend the court. Although often a relatively automatic process this procedure is nevertheless judicial in nature and case law provides that the question of whether or not to issue a summons must be properly judicially considered by the court concerned. If the summons is issued it is then served on the accused and the contents of the information is embodied in the summons. A single summons may cover more than one information, *i.e.* may contain several different charges. A summons may be served personally or by post on the accused.

3. As an alternative to the above procedure which applies where a defendant is *not* in custody at the time of laying the information, the police may proceed by arrest without warrant, and charge. In these cases the police will have arrested the defendant and charged him at the police station. They will subsequently either release him on bail until the date specified in the charge for his appearance at court or bring him before the magistrates' court in custody normally within 24 hours of charging. In these cases the charge sheet serves as the information and no separate summons is issued. **42.07**

The charge sheet will be read over to the accused and he will be given a copy, whether he is released on bail or kept in custody by the police pending his first appearance. In the case of a release on bail the charge sheet will specify when he is to surrender to his bail at court.

Cases therefore commence in one of the previous ways. The question of defects in, and amendments of a summons will shortly be described. In the case of charges these may similarly be amended however it should be noted that if the case is going to be dealt with in the Crown Court that the form of the indictment which will constitute the final charges which an accused has to face at his Crown Court trial will not be drafted until the end of the committal proceedings. This is because it is open to the magistrates to commit on different charges from those originally brought by the prosecution and on any charge disclosed by the evidence they have heard. In a case of complexity the form of the indictment itself may need to be drafted by counsel before the Crown Court trial commences.

43. Bail

43.01   Bail is the release of a person subject to a duty to surrender to custody in the future. We have already briefly considered the nature of "police bail" that is when the police make the decision whether to release from custody either in the course of their enquiries with a duty to report back to the police station at some subsequent time, or after charging. When the question of bail arises in that context, the time for the suspect or accused to surrender to custody is fixed by the police either, in the former case, telling him when to return to the police station, or in the latter, specifying on the charge sheet the date on which the case will first come before the magistrates' court. The provisions of the Bail Act 1976 which we are about to consider in detail do not apply strictly in those situations, although the matters which the police will take into account when deciding whether to release a suspect who has been charged on bail, will largely correspond to the provisions of the Act.

We will now consider bail under the Bail Act 1976 ("the Act"). On occasions when magistrates grant bail, they will specify the date of the next hearing, with the exception of the occasion on when they commit an accused for trial in the Crown Court. The date of trial in the Crown Court is not fixed by the magistrates and thus bail is, so to speak, open ended and the duty to surrender to custody comes about when the accused is notified of the date for the commencement of the Crown Court trial.

The question of bail therefore arises from time to time in the magistrates' court when they adjourn proceedings, either when the case is adjourned to be heard on some later date; or when the case is part heard and is adjourned over night or for a longer period; or even, in principle, over the lunch adjournment.

Until the coming into force of the Bail Act 1976, it was common practice to grant an accused bail "on his own recognisance." This was a fixed sum of money which the accused did not have to provide at the time of granting bail but which, should he fail subsequently to surrender to custody would be forfeited. This practice has been abolished and in its place section 6 of the Bail Act provides that "a defendant who fails without reasonable cause to surrender to custody is guilty of the offence of absconding." The burden of proving reasonable cause lies on the defendant. It is easy to imagine things which might give a defendant reasonable cause to fail to appear on the date to which he had been bailed, for instance, sudden serious illness, or being involved in an accident on the way to court. Absconding is therefore now a separate offence which may lead to punishment quite separately from the question of the charge on which the offender is due to stand trial. The penalties are on summary conviction either three months' imprisonment and/or a fine up to £2,000, or in the Crown Court the offence is punishable as a criminal contempt with an unlimited fine and/or up to 12 months' imprisonment. If a defendant fails to surrender to bail the court may (and usually will) issue a warrant for his arrest.

362

The right to bail under section 4 of the Bail Act 1976

Section 4 of the Act gives an accused person what might be described as a **43.02** prima facie right to bail. However, it must be remembered that this section does not apply at every stage of the criminal process. It does not apply in particular:—

1. where the custody officer has to consider the question of granting a person bail at a police station after he has been charged; or

2. where the magistrates, having convicted a person, commit him to the Crown Court for sentence; or

3. where a person has been convicted by the magistrates and wishes to appeal to the Crown Court against either conviction or sentence.

Although section 4 does not apply in any of these situations the custody officer or court will consider the nature of the situation and whether on the broad commonsense criteria contained in the Bail Act generally, it seems appropriate to grant bail. Thus, if there is in reality little risk of the defendant absconding, offending further, or interfering with the course of justice, and he has a fixed address, then there may be little likelihood in any of those situations that the accused would actually be refused bail. The point is, however, that he is not granted the protection of section 4 and has no prima facie *right* to it. One can summarise, therefore, and say that in essence the court has the prima facie obligation to grant bail to all accused who do not fall within any of the three categories above where the Act specifically does not apply. In other words, the court has to consider the question of bail and the prima facie right to it

1. for all defendants at all stages of the criminal process up to conviction;

2. even after conviction, where the court adjourns the case for reports or enquiries; or

3. in sundry other circumstances, in particular where an accused is brought before a magistrates' court for breach of a probation or community service order.

To the prima facie right contained in section 4 of the Act, there are naturally **43.03** exceptions. The exceptions we shall consider are those contained in Schedule 1 to the Bail Act and this provides that where an accused is charged with an offence which is *punishable with imprisonment*, he *need* not be granted bail if any of the following matters apply, namely:

1. the court is satisfied that there are *substantial grounds* for believing that if released on bail he would:
   (a) fail to surrender to custody; or
   (b) commit an offence while on bail; or
   (c) interfere with witnesses or otherwise obstruct the court of justice whether in relation to himself or some other person; or

2. the court is satisfied that he should be kept in custody for his own protection or, if he is a juvenile, for his own welfare; or

3. he is already serving a custodial sentence on some other matter; or

4. the court is satisfied that it has not been practicable to obtain sufficient information for the purpose of taking the decisions required by the Bail Act for lack of time since the commencement of proceedings against him; or

5. the defendant need not be granted bail if, having been released on bail in connection with the proceedings for the same offence he has been arrested for absconding; or

6. where the case has been adjourned for enquiries or a report, the defendant need not be granted bail if it appears to the court that it would be impracticable to complete the enquiries or make the report without keeping the defendant in custody.

43.04 Those are the exceptions which apply where an accused is charged with an offence punishable with imprisonment. Where the offence is one which is *not* punishable with imprisonment (*e.g.* careless driving) then different conditions apply and these are contained in Part 2 of Schedule 1 to the Act. These provide that a defendant need not be granted bail if:

1. it appears to the court that having been previously granted bail in criminal proceedings, he has failed to surrender to custody in accordance with his obligations under the grant of bail; and

2. the court believes in view of that failure, that the defendant if released on bail would fail to surrender to custody; or

3. the court is satisfied that he should be kept in custody for his own protection or if he is a child or young person, for his own welfare;

4. the defendant need not be granted bail if he is already in custody in pursuance of the sentence of any court;

5. the defendant need not be granted bail if, having been released on bail in connection with proceedings for the present offence, he has been arrested already for absconding.

To take first the latter cases of the refusal to grant bail in the case of a non-imprisonable offence. It is apparent that these are not of really great practical importance. They would for example apply in the case of someone charged with careless driving who persistently failed to appear before the court. We shall now consider the matter of an application to the magistrates' court for bail in the case of someone charged with an imprisonable offence.

43.05 The basic requirement is fairly self explanatory. The phrase "substantial grounds for believing that" implies that the court must satisfy itself to a reasonably high standard of proof. The three subdivisions of the first ground are likewise self explanatory. Ground 2. concerning "custody for his own protection" might apply to the alleged perpetrator of some highly unpopular kind of offence, for example a sexual attack on a young child where the alleged offender would return to live in the same locality as the victim's parents or relatives. Ground 3. is a matter of commonsense. If someone is already in custody in respect of some other offence when the fact of his alleged guilt of the present offence first comes to light so that he is actually charged while still in custody, it would obviously be ridiculous if the prima facie right to bail in the Bail Act could override the fact that he is already legitimately in custody. Ground 4. that there has not yet been time to obtain the necessary information, is one relied on very frequently by the police. It will be remembered that when producing the accused before the court, he may well have been in police hands for only a matter of a few hours. The police will often contend in such circumstances that the kind of information necessary to enable the magistrates to reach an informed conclusion about the matters they ought to take into account when considering the grant of bail, is not as yet available until further enquiries are made. Grounds 5. and 6. are likewise self explanatory. On ground 5. it is a matter of the defendant being re-arrested after already having absconded in the present proceedings in which case naturally there would be no further presumption of bail as such, though it is by no means impossible that on some proper explanation being given for the failure to surrender to custody (*e.g.* sudden illness) further bail might be granted.

The other exception concerns the case where proceedings have been adjourned for enquiries but it may be clear that it will be difficult to complete these enquiries because of the nature of the accused. For example, it might be suggested that one cannot complete a psychiatric report upon the accused because it is unlikely that he will voluntarily attend at a hospital to be psychiatrically examined. He may, therefore, be remanded in custody for the purpose of a medical report being prepared.

In considering whether or not the grounds for refusing bail above, apply, one must have regard to the following matters which are contained in paragraph 9 of Schedule 1, Part 1 to the Act. This provides that in taking decisions (*i.e.* whether or not to grant bail) under the Act, the court shall have regard to such of the following considerations as appear relevant, namely:— **43.06**

1. The nature and seriousness of the offence and the probable method of dealing with the defendant for it;

2. The character, antecedents, associations and community ties of the defendant;

3. The defendant's record in respect of the fulfilment of his obligations under previous grants of bail (if any) in criminal proceedings;

4. Except in the case of a defendant whose case is adjourned for enquiries or a report, the strength of the evidence of his having committed the offence;

5. Any other matters which appear to be relevant.

It is now appropriate to consider the procedure by which the bail application is made on first or subsequent appearance in the magistrates' court. **43.07**

Generally, the accused will already be in custody, having been arrested and will be produced from the police station. He is brought before the court and the court will first need to consider the future course of the proceedings. Local practice varies, but in some courts hardly anything other than the question of bail is dealt with on a first appearance. Sometimes however, a defendant who is pleading guilty in a straightforward case may be dealt with **43.08** on first appearance. Let us assume, however, that the defendant is proposing to plead not guilty. The question of an adjournment inevitably arises therefore since contested trials invariably do not proceed on first appearance if only for the reason that the police will not yet be prepared or have their witnesses available. Where the court adjourns a matter it will remand the defendant. "Remand" merely means "specify whether the accused is to be on bail or in custody at this stage."

43.09   The question of bail must be considered, therefore, in the light of the Act. The court is granted an inquisitorial function by the Act so that it ought really to enquire as to whether bail is appropriate in every case. However, if the police themselves do not object to bail, it is highly unlikely that the magistrates will raise objections or require to hear any more about the matter. In that case, a merely formal application for bail needs to be made. If there are objections to bail, however, the court will go on to consider them. The course of the proceedings will then be as follows:

1.   The prosecution will put forward their objections. Practice tends to vary from court to court and from case to case. Sometimes the Crown Prosecutor will put forward the nature of the objections to bail; sometimes the officer in charge of the case goes into the witness box and gives evidence concerning the question. The rules of evidence do not apply. Indeed, as the criteria to be considered when assessing the question of bail make clear, the accused's criminal record is highly relevant to the question of the grant of bail and therefore will become known to the magistrates at this stage. Quite apart from that, however, much of the police officer's evidence will amount to hearsay (*e.g.* "I was told by the victim that . . .") Moreover, much of the officer's evidence may be merely speculative. A common objection to bail is that the police are investigating other matters in which they suspect the accused might be involved. Clearly, this is highly prejudicial to the accused's prospect of obtaining bail.

2.   Although the rules of evidence do not apply, some attempt may then be made to cross-examine the officer. It is, naturally, difficult to cross-examine effectively about matters to do with other enquiries because the officer may legitimately refuse at present to answer (for instance because it may alert the defendant, and his associates to the course of those further enquiries).

3.   The accused's advocate then makes his application for bail. This ought to be in the form of a considered response to the precise objections put forward by the prosecution. There is prima facie no need to respond to potential grounds for objection which the prosecution have not relied upon although it is often as well for the sake of clarity in the minds of the magistrates, to just pass through other grounds for objection if only to dismiss them. The contents of this application will naturally mainly consist of a discussion of the objections in the light of the considerations referred to in paragraph 9 of Schedule 1 Part 1 of the Act. It is perhaps now as well to consider these points individually:

NATURE AND SERIOUSNESS OF THE OFFENCE AND THE PROBABLE
METHOD OF DEALING WITH THE DEFENDANT FOR IT

In fact, there is no rule as such that a defendant charged with very serious **43.10**
offences cannot have bail. Bail on a murder charge is far from unknown. The
criterion is simply one of commonsense. If it is inevitable that the accused, if
convicted, is going to receive a custodial sentence, perhaps a very lengthy
one, then clearly as a matter of human nature the temptation to abscond or
perhaps commit further crimes whilst at liberty with the object of providing
for his dependants during the period of custody, will be stronger than in the
case of someone charged with a relatively trivial crime. The discussion of the
probable method of dealing with the defendant may involve the defending
advocate speculating (somewhat optimistically on occasion) that despite an
apparently serious criminal record, it is by no means sure that the defendant
will receive a custodial sentence even if convicted because of mitigating
factors to do with the offender's personal circumstances;

CHARACTER, ANTECEDENTS, ASSOCIATIONS AND COMMUNITY TIES

"Character" means in this sense, criminal record. "Antecedents" means the **43.11**
accused's history and background, *e.g.* upbringing, education, job record
and so on. "Associations" naturally means the type of person with whom he
mixes. It may well be contended by the prosecution, for example, that the
accused is a member of a gang of professional criminals and habitually mixes
with them. The very address of the accused may indicate this to magistrates
with local knowledge in some cases. The method of meeting this particular
objection, with others, will be referred to below. "Community ties" means
naturally, matters which tend to cement the accused to his present place in
terms of family circumstances and location. It is self evident that a family
man with a mortgage and a regular job is considerably less likely than a
casual worker living in a bedsitter to think it is worthwhile uprooting himself
and going "on the run." Of course, even this is not conclusive and much will
depend upon the intermixing of the various criteria. For example it may be
suspected that even a family man with a mortgage and job may well
"abscond" if the offence with which he is charged is in fact serious enough;

THE ACCUSED'S RECORD IF PREVIOUSLY GRANTED BAIL

If the accused has not been charged with any offence before, this is some- **43.12**
thing which will be to his credit under other criteria but is of no help on this
one. If he has committed a number of previous criminal offences and always
received bail and always turned up, this is a reasonably powerful argument.
Again the intermix with other matters must be considered. If he has indeed
had bail on previous occasions, then clearly he is likely to have a bad criminal
record. This may, in its turn, make it more likely that he receives a substantial custodial sentence this time and thus will weaken his argument on
the objection to do with "the probable method of dealing with him for it."

THE STRENGTH OF THE EVIDENCE

This is naturally extremely hard to assess at such an early stage in the **43.13**
proceedings. The prosecution themselves will say in general terms that they

have substantial evidence, but will certainly not be called upon to name their witnesses or give the gist of what the witnesses will say. Any kind of forensic evidence will probably not be available at the stage of a first bail application, *e.g.* the results of fingerprints or blood sample tests. All one can do is respond in general terms to whatever evidence is alleged to exist by the prosecution by saying, *e.g.* that the admissibility of an alleged confession is strongly disputed.

Conditions of bail

43.14   Before going on to suggest how a bail application ought to be framed, it is appropriate to consider some other matters. Although a defendant prima facie has a right to bail, and to unconditional bail at that, the court may where it considers it appropriate, impose *conditions*. These conditions will be of one of three kinds, namely:

1.   sureties;

2.   security by the accused;

3.   miscellaneous conditions.

43.15   By section 3(6) of the Act a defendant may be required by a court to comply with such requirements as appear to the court to be necessary to secure that:

1.   he surrenders to custody;

2.   he does not commit an offence while on bail:

3.   he does not interfere with witnesses or otherwise obstruct the course of justice;

4.   he makes himself available for the purpose of enabling enquiries or a report to be made to assist the court in dealing with him for the offence.

In other words, the court may not impose conditions merely because it has some general sense of unease about the grant of bail. It must only impose conditions specifically tailored to coping with the problems it foresees in the grant of what would otherwise be unconditional bail. We shall now consider the nature of conditions:

SURETIES

43.16   A surety is a person who enters into a recognisance to ensure that the accused appears at court. Accordingly, if the accused does fail to appear, the surety is liable to have his recognisance estreated (*i.e.* forfeited). In other words, a surety is someone who guarantees the accused's appearance in court in a specified sum of money (which does not have to be provided in advance). If the person does not surrender to custody, then prima facie the amount of money is forfeited to the court. The surety, therefore has every interest in ensuring first that he does not undertake his duties lightly and secondly that he does what he can to ensure that the person does appear at court. The court does have a discretion where the accused does not appear as to whether or not to order forfeiture of the sum. The court will generally require to be satisfied that the surety has exercised extreme diligence in the matter before the sum will *not* be ordered to be forfeited. In principle, the surety might escape forfeiture by keeping a very close watch on the accused so as to assist the police by notifying them immediately should there be any hint of the accused absconding.

In considering the suitability of a surety, the court must have regard to matters contained in section 8 of the Act namely:

1. the surety's financial resources;

2. the character and previous convictions of the surety; and

3. the proximity (whether in point of kinship, place of residence or otherwise) to the person for whom he is surety.

Let us suppose, therefore, that one has a defendant whom one suspects may not be granted unconditional bail. A surety would seem to help the situation and one has come forward. The first thing the court will do is consider an appropriate amount and whether the proposed surety's resources are sufficient. In fact they will generally accept evidence from the surety that he has resources of that amount whether in the form of savings or value of goods. If documentary evidence is available, then it is of course as well for the surety to bring it to court (*e.g.* building society accounts, bank statements). The matter of suitability extends beyond resources, however, to the question of the surety's own standing. If he has a bad character or criminal record, then (while not necessarily absolutely fatal) it may make him less acceptable as a surety. Finally there is the question of proximity between the two. In principle, the surety is "keeping an eye" on the accused to ensure he fulfils his obligations. Obviously, therefore, a close relative or someone who lives very close by will be best for this purpose. However a spouse is often not considered appropriate as a surety in some courts and also on the authority of a case which is more than a century old it is considered improper to accept the solicitor of an accused as surety.

It need not in fact follow that the surety is at court although this is preferable. It is possible to obtain agreement from the magistrates to the grant of bail, subject to sureties, if the sureties come forward to a police station where their suitability can be investigated by the police, and if the police are satisfied then an accused may then be released from custody.

SECURITY

The giving of a surety does not imply payment of money in advance. **43.17** However, under section 3(5) of the Act, if "it appears that the accused is unlikely to remain in Great Britain until the time appointed for him to surrender to custody he may be required before release on bail to give security for his surrender to custody . . . the security may be given by him or on his behalf." In this situation, therefore, money must be provided in advance, either by the accused personally, or by someone else. A common example is that of a wealthy foreign person accused of a substantial shoplifting offence (*e.g.* some very valuable item of clothing) from a West End store. It would not generally be appropriate to keep a first offender in custody but equally, it is somewhat unlikely that they will wish to return to stand trial, especially if they live thousands of miles away. In these circumstances, the practice is somewhat informally to set an amount of security which would roughly correspond to the potential fine and leave it at that. An alternative might be to require surrender of the defendant's passport but this likewise may not be appropriate, *e.g.* the wealthy visitor may need to return home before the time fixed for the hearing or may wish to go to Paris to continue shoplifting.

MISCELLANEOUS CONDITIONS

43.18 The court may impose other conditions. Some of the most common are:—

1. surrender of passport;

2. the observing of a curfew, that is being at home after a certain hour at night and until a certain hour in the morning;

3. to reside at a particular place, or with a particular person;

4. not to go to a particular place, or within a particular area (*e.g.* the area where the offence occurred);

5. not to contact certain individuals.

MEETING OBJECTIONS TO BAIL

43.19 It is now appropriate to consider how one meets objections to bail, assuming that these have been put forward by the officer in the case or perhaps by the Crown Prosecutor. One must ensure that the argument, which should be soundly based on facts, deals with the specific objections. One must immediately assess the prospects of obtaining unconditional bail. Whilst no doubt it is in a sense a more clear cut "victory" on the issue to obtain unconditional bail for a client, if there is any substantial risk of it being refused, then it is more prudent to examine what conditions might be offered to meet the objections raised. For example, if the nature of the objection is that the accused, who is a habitual burglar, will continue to commit further burglary offences if allowed bail, there really is little point in offering that he will surrender his passport; in such a situation, the obvious suggestion is a curfew; if it is contended that he will abscond the appropriate conditions will be that he should report to the police station daily and that he can provide adequate sureties. If the objection is that he will interfere with witnesses then a condition that he will not go to certain places where those witnesses live or work or will not contact them would be adequate to meet the suggested objection. The interplay between the various grounds set out for refusing bail and the criteria by which the existence those grounds are to be judged is obviously capable of enormous variation in any given case.

It should finally be noted that the court may vary conditions imposed on the application of either the prosecution or the defendant subsequent to the granting of bail and that the police have power to arrest without warrant for breach of conditions under section 7(3) of the Act.

43.20 When the prosecution and defence have put forward their arguments the magistrates will give their decision. If the accused is granted unconditional bail, he is merely notified of the date upon which he is required to surrender to custody. If he is refused bail, or given bail subject to conditions, then there must be a record made of the decision in the prescribed manner and a copy ought to be given to the defendant in the appropriate form.

Where a bail application has been refused by the magistrates they will **43.21**
remand the defendant in custody. Before conviction, or committal for trial
this must be for a period which does not exceed eight clear days. In fact, the
custom is usually to remand the defendant in custody for a slightly shorter
period than this, often to the same week day of the following week. If a case
is to be adjourned many times before trial or committal a defendant must be
produced to the court on each occasion successively within the eight-day
maximum period referred to. Since (as we shall see below) he will not be
able to make a further bail application after one full application has been
refused unless there are changes in circumstances, there may seem to be
little point in him being produced to the court. Accordingly in certain
circumstances a defendant may be remanded in his absence. The court must
still deal with him (*i.e.* formally remand him for a further period not
exceeding eight days) but he does not have to be there. This can happen
where a defendant is over 16, the adjournments are before committal or
summary trial, the defendant is legally represented, and he consents. In such
cases he may be remanded in his absence on up to three successive occasions. He must therefore be produced to the court on every fourth occasion.
The defendant may withdraw his consent to this arrangement and insist on
being produced to the court on each successive remand. He might do this
because some change in circumstances makes it possible to bring a fresh bail
application before the court. Indeed if he is remanded over a very lengthy
period and the prosecution are still not ready for trial or committal this in
itself might be a new factor justifying a further application.

Further applications for bail
We shall now consider what further applications for bail may be made where **43.22**
the initial one has been refused.

Until 1981, it was not uncommon for a full length bail application to be
made for a defendant on each successive appearance before the magistrates.
It should by no means be imagined that at a defendant's second appearance
he will be substantively dealt with either by summary trial or committal
proceedings. There may be adjournments, sometimes many adjournments
in a case, especially a case of some substance, in order to enable the police to
collect their evidence and prepare. The repetition of bail applications did
have some point to it since the case would be adjourned to be heard each
time potentially before a new bench of magistrates, and arguments that did
not impress a first bench might sometimes impress a more leniently-minded
bench. However, there is now a restriction on the number of times that an
application can be made, with the object of avoiding undue repetition and
waste of court's time. By virtue of Part IIA of the 1976 Act if a court refuses
bail it is under a duty at each subsequent hearing to consider bail providing
that:—

   (i) The defendant is still in custody; and
   (ii) the right to bail under section 4 of the Act still applies.

At the first hearing after that at which the court decided not to grant bail the
defence can put forward any argument (including those advanced previously) to support an application for bail. However thereafter on each
subsequent remand the court need not hear arguments as to fact or law

which it has heard previously although the duty to at least consider bail remains.

In essence therefore a defendant is allowed two "full" oral applications for bail, that is one when he first appears in court and a second on his subsequent appearance after the defence solicitor has had longer to marshall his arguments, find sureties, discuss conditions with the defendant, investigate police objections to bail, and so on.

In particular at the end of committal proceedings, however often bail has been refused before, it is often possible to suggest new arguments in the light of the further evidence which will have been revealed by that stage. In particular the relevant criterion which requires consideration of "the strength of the prosecution evidence" may well be viewed differently.

43.23 If bail is refused by the magistrates after a full application thereafter there are two separate methods for further applications. These are sometimes described as "appeals" but they are not in truth appeals as such. The first method of application is under the Supreme Court Act 1981, s.81 as amended by the Criminal Justice Act 1982, s.60. One applies to the Crown Court on the prescribed application form and one must file with the application a so-called "full argument certificate" from the magistrates' court which certifies that the magistrates did hear full argument on the bail application. If legal aid has been granted, it will cover one such application to the Crown Court.

The hearing takes place in chambers before a Crown Court judge and solicitors have right of audience. Usually the Crown Court will list the case for hearing before a judge in chambers before he starts the day's criminal work at 9.45 am or 10.00 o'clock. The Crown Court will usually give a hearing date as soon as the form is taken down to the court and notice of this must be served on the prosecution at least 24 hours before the application is made. In fact, it is not uncommon for a Crown Court to list such applications for the following day and for the prosecution to waive the strict requirement for a full clear day's notice. At the hearing, one rehearses all the matters that were put before the magistrates, and indeed any new matters which have arisen.

One may make this application to the Crown Court either immediately bail has been refused or at any stage up to committal for trial. It should not be overlooked, however, that one can also apply to the Crown Court for bail in three other circumstances, namely:—

1. after a person has been committed in custody for trial; or

2. after a person has been committed in custody for sentence; or

3. after a person has received a custodial sentence from the magistrates and given notice of appeal to the Crown Court.

In the case of any of these applications, it is not necessary to file a "full argument certificate" although the same procedure for the application is otherwise followed.

43.24 Finally, one can apply to a judge of the High Court in Chambers. This can either be straight after refusal by the magistrates (in which case no "full argument certificate" is required) or after previous unsuccessful application to a Crown Court judge. The application is considered to be within the civil jurisdiction of the High Court and is governed by R.S.C., Ord. 79. Application is made by way of a summons with an affidavit in support. The affidavit will be sworn by the defendant's solicitor and describe the background to the case and why it is suggested that the defendant ought to have bail. The summons will be issued at the nearest district registry and a hearing date obtained by agreement with the listing officer of the nearest High Court. Again, 24 hours' notice must be given to the prosecution, but again it is common practice for this to be waived. The hearing is in chambers and a solicitor will therefore have a right of audience. Legal aid issued for the criminal proceedings will not cover such an application but a separate application may in principle be made for civil legal aid. The Legal Aid Board suggests that there is no firm policy of automatically refusing such applications, although the success rate of applications is not high. Bearing in mind, however, the criteria for the grant of legal aid in civil proceedings, very few such applications, bail having been refused by magistrates and perhaps by a Crown Court judge already, are likely to be considered meritorious.

44. Summary Trial

44.01 Where a defendant is charged with an offence which is triable purely summarily, or after a mode of trial hearing has consented to summary trial of an either way offence, then the trial will take place. As we have seen this is most unlikely to be at the first hearing. If the accused has been in custody, then the first hearing will be the day after he is charged; if he has not been in custody, it may be some time later, but even so the practice of most courts is to inform the defendant in advance that if he pleads not guilty the case will not proceed at the first hearing. Indeed, in the case of purely summary offences which have been commenced by the issue of a summons, *i.e.* so that no question of bail arises, the accused may be told that if he proposes to plead not guilty, he should notify the court in writing and then need not attend court on the first hearing because the prosecution will not have their witnesses present. Even after a mode of trial hearing there may well be two or three further hearings before the actual trial takes place. This will particularly be the case over the summer months when police witnesses and others may be away on holiday, thus rendering a number of hearing dates ineffective. Eventually, however, the date fixed for the trial will come about and the accused will be expected to be there. Before we can discuss summary trial, it is important now to consider a number of preliminary matters.

JOINT TRIALS

44.02 1. Two or more accused may always be charged in one information with having committed an offence jointly. Where this occurs then almost inevitably they will be tried together.

44.03 2. Where there are two or more informations against one accused, the magistrates may try the informations together if none of the parties object. However, even if the defendant does object, the court still has power to try two or more informations together, if it is of the opinion that it is in the interests of justice to do so because they form part of a series of offences of the same, or similar character. The interests of justice include a consideration of the convenience of the prosecution, as well as the question of minimising any risk of injustice to the accused. This arises from the case of *Re Clayton* [1983] 2 A.C. 473. This case overturned the former general rule that an accused had the right to object to being tried by the same court on different informations at the same time. In principle under the old law, an accused was entitled to insist on separate trials for each of the informations no matter how many there might be. If the accused does successfully represent to the magistrates that a number of informations against him ought to be tried by different benches and the magistrates agree, those magistrates should not then proceed to try any of them because they will of course now know of the other alleged offences. They would therefore adjourn the trials so that they could be heard successively by differently constituted benches.

DEFECT IN PROCESS

Section 123 of the Magistrates' Courts Act 1980 provides that a defendant **44.04**
cannot object to an information summons or warrant on the ground of any
defect in it in substance or form or because of any variance between it and
the prosecution evidence. However, if the accused has been misled by a
variance between the information and the prosecution evidence, he must be
granted an adjournment if he requires one.

This section is worded in such a way that in principle it would seem to
enable the court to continue with the trial, no matter how defective the
information was. However, a restricted meaning has been given to the
section by a number of cases. These establish that where the defect is trivial
so that there can be no question of the accused being misled by it, the section
applies, *e.g.* the mis-spellings of names, places or the giving of wrong dates
due to typing errors. In such a case, there is probably no need for the court
even to consider formally amending the information. If there is a more
substantial variation, then the prosecution should apply for leave to amend.
If the amendment has been such that the accused is prejudiced (*e.g.* if he has
not collected and called his evidence to meet matters which are relevant to
the amendment) he is entitled to an adjournment. An example is the leading
case of *Wright* v. *Nicholson* [1970] 1 W.L.R. 142 where an information
charged that an accused committed a certain offence on August 17. The
evidence of the alleged victim was vague as to when the incident happened
and it could have been at any time in the month of August. W had called alibi
evidence in respect of August 17 only but was convicted on the basis that he
committed the offence some time in August. It was held on appeal that W
had been misled and had been severely prejudiced since he had been unable
to consider calling alibi evidence for other days in August.

Amendment of the information can remedy almost any defect if there is
an adjournment granted to enable the accused to meet it. However, an
information laid against completely the wrong person is so fundamental a
defect that it cannot be cured by amendment. This is not to say however, that
a mere mis-spelling in the defendant's name will bring the case within that
category.

ABSENCE OF THE DEFENDANT

If the defendant is absent, then in cases begun by summons, he may be tried **44.05**
in his absence provided service of the summons has been proved to the
satisfaction of the court. This is by virtue of section 11 of the Magistrates'
Courts Acts 1980. A plea of not guilty will be entered and the prosecution
will be required to prove their case strictly.

If the defendant is represented in court by counsel or a solicitor, he is
normally deemed to be present unless he is on bail, in which case his
personal attendance to surrender to custody is required. Thus, the accused
must in principle be present at mode of trial proceedings and generally at
committal proceedings. If he has been bailed to appear and does not do so,
then the magistrates may issue a warrant for his arrest.

Where the trial proceeds in his absence and he is represented by counsel
or solicitor, his representative may conduct the case on his behalf, cross-
examine prosecution witnesses, call defence witnesses and make speeches,
just as if the accused were present.

PLEA OF GUILTY BY POST

44.06 Under section 12 of the Magistrates' Courts Act 1980 the prosecution may give the accused the opportunity of pleading guilty by post where he is called to appear to answer an information alleging a summary offence for which the maximum penalty does not exceed three months' imprisonment.

In such a case, the prosecution serves on the accused, together with the summons, a notice explaining how he can plead guilty by post and what the course of events will be if he does so. In addition, the prosecution serve a brief statement of the facts as they allege them to be. The form sent to the defendant notifies him that if he pleads guilty by post, he will only have evidence given against him to the extent of the reading out of the statement of facts in open court and no other evidence will be brought. The prosecution are usually quite happy to put the statement of facts in a fairly neutral form in the hope of persuading the accused to plead guilty and to save the court and the prosecution time.

The accused in such a situation should return the form to the court indicating that he proposes to plead guilty. There is space on the form for him to set out any mitigating circumstances and details of his means. He is informed, however, that he is not bound by his plea of guilty and may appear at court at any time up to the hearing of the summons and withdraw the plea of guilty and be tried on the basis of a not guilty plea. The procedure thereafter is as follows:—

1. The prosecution will read out the charge and the particulars of the offence as stated in the statement of facts, but may give no other information to the court about the crime.

2. The defendant's form setting out his means and any mitigating circumstances is read out by the clerk of the court.

3. The court will normally pass sentence straight away. If, however, it does propose to disqualify the offender from driving or imprison him, it must call him before the court and will adjourn the case for that purpose.

If there is something ambiguous in the plea of guilty by post, for example where the accused's statement of mitigating circumstances suggests facts which it seems would actually amount to a defence, rather than to mitigation then the magistrates may refuse to accept the plea and adjourn the case for a hearing.

If the prosecution do not offer the accused the opportunity to plead guilty by post, then there is nothing he can do to compel them to adopt this procedure. This is so even in the case of straightforward driving offences. Normally the prosecution will in fact opt for this course in the case of driving offences unless it is obvious from the circumstances that the accused is likely to be disqualified.

NON-APPEARANCE OF PROSECUTION

44.07 If the prosecution fail to appear at the time and place fixed for summary trial, the magistrates have discretion either to dismiss the information or adjourn. If the case has already begun and been adjourned as part heard, then the magistrates have the option to proceed in the absence of the prosecution, although this will only happen rarely.

Outline of procedure

We shall now consider an outline of the procedure at summary trial on a not guilty plea.

1. The charge will be read to the defendant and he will be asked whether he proposes to plead guilty or not guilty. In such a situation his plea must be unequivocal. The court has a discretion to allow a change of plea from guilty to not guilty at any time before sentence. Thus if for example as in the case of mistakenly pleading guilty by post the accused pleads guilty, say, to a charge of theft but in stating his mitigation says something along the lines of "I never knew I had it" or "I thought it was mine at the time" the magistrates ought to allow him to withdraw his guilty plea, substitute a not guilty plea and either proceed with the hearing then and there, or more probably, adjourn it so that he can receive legal advice and/or call evidence. **44.08**

2. The prosecution may make an opening speech stating the facts of the case and indicating which witnesses will be called to prove them. It is important to note that in the magistrates' court, the prosecution do not in general have a closing speech and therefore this is the only chance the prosecution have to address the court. However, it must be remembered that magistrates are likely to be considerably more experienced than jurors and thus may need less in the way of introductory matter. **44.09**

3. The prosecution then call evidence which may consist of witnesses or written evidence tendered in the form of statements under section 9 Criminal Justice Act 1967. This topic has been lengthily dealt with in the section on hearsay evidence earlier. The witnesses will give evidence and are then subject to cross-examination and may be re-examined. **44.10**

4. At the end of the prosecution evidence, the defence may make a submission of no case to answer. This submission should be upheld if:— **44.11**
   (a) there is no evidence to prove an essential element of the offence charged; or
   (b) the prosecution evidence has been so discredited as a result of cross-examination or is so manifestly unreliable that no reasonable tribunal could safely convict upon it.

   In other words, at this stage, the magistrates may simply decide whether on the basis of what they have heard so far, there is any possibility of them finding the case proved beyond reasonable doubt. The prosecution have a right of rely to this submission. If the submission is successful, the case is over. The magistrates discharge the accused and then go on to make any appropriate orders for costs or return of legal aid contribution. If the submission is not upheld the case continues and the defence may then present their case.

THE DEFENCE CASE

1. The defence may make an opening speech but in principle are limited to one address only and it is customary for the defence solicitor to make a closing speech rather than an opening one, for obvious reasons. Such a speech gives the advocate the opportunity to comment on all the evidence if made at the end, but if made at this time only gives a chance to **44.12**

comment on the prosecution evidence and to introduce the defence evidence.

2.   The defence witnesses are then called and the defendant testifies first.

3.   Exceptionally the court may grant the prosecution leave to call further evidence after the defence case for the purposes of rebutting defence evidence. Rebuttal evidence may only be called on a matter which could not reasonably have been foreseen and which arises suddenly. It will be recalled that the defence have no general obligation to give details of their case in advance of the trial. Accordingly, if for example a sudden allegation is made against a policeman and the prosecution are taken by surprise, they will now have the opportunity to call evidence to rebut it. A similar situation might arise in the case of an alibi. It will be recalled that in the magistrates' court there is no obligation to give advance notice of intention to call alibi evidence (whereas there is in the Crown Court as we have seen). Accordingly, the prosecution, if they have time to get the witnesses to court (and they may be allowed an adjournment for this purpose) may call rebutting evidence. If it is perfectly clear from the outset, however that the kind of trial is one in which evidence of a certain kind would inevitably be necessary, then the prosecution will not be permitted to call evidence in rebuttal. An example taken from a leading case is one where the case involved a charge of forgery and at the close of the defence evidence after the defendant had denied the forgery the prosecution applied for leave to call a handwriting expert to prove that the forged signature was written by the accused. It was held that it should have been obvious from the outset that in a case of alleged forgery handwriting evidence would be required and the prosecution were penalised for their lack of foresight by their application to call rebuttal evidence being refused.

4.   Finally, there is the defence closing speech, unless the defendant has already made an opening speech. The prosecution may only address the court after this with the leave of the court, but leave will always be granted where there is a matter of law on which the prosecution wish to reply. This is merely one aspect of the right either party has to raise a point of law and argue it at any stage during the proceedings. If exceptionally the prosecution were allowed to address the court on the facts or evidence, then the defence would always have the right to address the court last. The magistrates then reach their decision. They may retire for this purpose. Their verdict is by a majority. If there are only two magistrates and they disagree, they should adjourn the case for re-hearing by a different bench. The magistrates may be advised by their clerk on matters of law or evidence, but not on issues of fact. Accordingly, if no matter of law arises in the course of the hearing, it is wrong for the clerk to retire with the magistrates.

44.13   If the defendant is acquitted, he will be discharged and may be able to make an application for costs. If he is convicted, the court will proceed to sentence after dealing with mitigation and other matters. These matters are dealt with at greater length hereafter at para. 47.01 onwards.

GUILTY PLEA

If the accused has pleaded guilty at the outset, the prosecution will then read **44.14** out a statement of how the offence occurred and the court will proceed to hear mitigation, consider the obtaining of reports, and sentence.

45. Classification of Offences and Choice of Courts

45.01   For procedural purposes, criminal offences are classified into three categories, namely those triable only summarily; those triable only on indictment;
and those triable "either way."

Purely summary offences

45.02   These offences are those that can only be tried by a magistrate's court. They
include almost all motoring offences and the vast bulk of regulatory
offences. Good examples are the offence of driving a vehicle without due
care and attention under section 3 of the Road Traffic Act 1988; and taking a
conveyance under section 12 of the Theft Act 1968. Although these in
principle are triable only summarily, that is can be dealt with only in the
Magistrates Court, they can be added as extra counts to an indictment where
linked offences are being tried by the Crown Court. (See para. 46.15.)

Offences triable purely on indictment

45.03   These are the more serious offences at the opposite end of the spectrum
which can only be tried before a judge and jury. They include murder, rape
and robbery.

    In the case of either of the former two classes of offence, there is no
procedural problem concerning which court will try them. In each case, only
one court has the jurisdiction to do so, namely the magistrates' court for the
former and the Crown Court for the latter.

Either way offences

45.04   This group of offences consists of crimes which may be tried either in the
magistrates' court, or in the Crown Court. These are offences whose nature
and seriousness is not necessarily indicated merely by the name of the
offence. Thus, for example "theft" can cover a whole spectrum of behaviour
from shoplifting a tin of peaches to stealing a Leonardo da Vinci. These
offences may be tried by either a magistrates' court or Crown Court depending on a number of matters and we will now consider how the decision as to
which court shall try the case will be taken and matters relevant to the choice
of court.

45.05   If a defendant appears before a magistrates' court charged with an either
way offence, there will be a *mode of trial hearing*. The practice of the courts
varies as to when this takes place. It may sometimes happen at the very first
appearance of the accused before the court, but more commonly will happen
at an adjourned hearing. Before the mode of trial hearing, the court should
be satisfied that the defendant is aware of the requirement on the prosecution under the Magistrates' Courts (Advance Information) Rules 1985 to
disclose certain advance information about the nature of the prosecution
case. We shall return to this shortly.

380

The procedure at a mode of trial hearing

First, the charge is read to the defendant but he is not at this stage asked to plead to it. Then the prosecution and the defence each has an opportunity to make representations as to mode of trial. It will usually be the case that the prosecution in a marginal matter will for considerations of cost and speed favour the magistrates' court. Their representations will often consist of no more than saying something along the lines of "there seems nothing special about this case to warrant the time of the Crown Court and it would appear that the magistrates' sentencing powers are adequate." The defence will have already decided which mode of trial they prefer and will now present their arguments. For example if the prosecution are contending that there is something very serious about the matter so that it should be tried in the Crown Court, then the defence may need to meet this by suggesting to the magistrates that it is less serious than it may appear and that the magistrates' sentencing powers are adequate should they convict. If the defence have already decided to ask for trial by Crown Court, they will then make their representations as to why this should be so. A number of factors which might make the Crown Court preferable are suggested below.

45.06

Thereafter, the magistrates consider the matter and by section 19 of the Magistrates' Court Act 1980 have to take into account the following features:—

45.07

1. The nature of the case;

2. Whether the offence is of a serious character; and

3. Whether the punishment which a magistrate's court would have power to inflict for it would be adequate;

4. Any other circumstances which make the case more suitable for one method of trial rather than the other.

Under recent guidance given by the Lord Chief Justice it is suggested that in most cases courts should take the following matters into account also in addition to those mentioned in section 19 of the 1980 Act. The further considerations are:—

1. That the court should never make a decision on the grounds of convenience or expedition.

2. The court should assume for the purpose of deciding mode of trial that the prosecution version of the facts is correct.

3. Where cases involve complex questions of fact or difficult questions of law the court should generally consider committal to the Crown Court for trial.

4. In considering whether its sentencing powers are sufficient and whether the offence is of serious character the court should have regard to the likely sentence for the defendant on the basis that he were to be convicted eventually and that he is at present of good character. In this connection they should look at specific features of the offence charged which might make it more serious than run of the mill offences. So for example in the case of a charge of theft the fact that it was allegedly

381

committed in breach of trust, *i.e.* by a person in authority; or where it has been committed or disguised in a sophisticated manner; or where it is committed by an organised gang; or where the victim is particularly vulnerable, *e.g.* the elderly or infirm; or where the property has not been recovered and is of high value. In the case of driving offences the fact that reckless driving is alleged to have occurred involving *e.g.* grossly excessive speeds; racing on a public road; or that alcohol or drugs have contributed to it would be exacerbating features. In these kind of cases therefore magistrates should look closely at the possible eventual sentence as a factor in their decision about mode of trial.

It is important to note that at this stage the court does not have the defendant's previous convictions before it and therefore it must act on the basis that it is dealing with a person who is of good previous character. The reason for this is that in principle the magistrates may proceed from the mode of trial hearing to the trial of the offence itself and they should not of course be aware of any criminal record of the accused. In fact, more commonly, there will be an adjournment in either case in the one for summary trial and in the other for committal proceedings. The reason for this is simply the saving of time and costs. The prosecution would be foolish to call their witnesses to court in the expectation of summary trial if it might in fact be the case that the accused will elect trial on indictment, in which case he might also be willing to accept short form committal proceedings under section 6(2) of the Magistrates' Courts Act 1980 as we shall see subsequently.

45.08 The magistrates retire if necessary and return to announce their decision. If the magistrates consider that trial on indictment is more appropriate, the accused is then told of their decision and committal proceedings proceed either then, or more probably at some subsequent date. The accused has no choice in the matter. The question of bail may arise again at this stage if the accused has hitherto been refused bail or if some new matter has arisen which leads to the police now objecting to bail (*e.g.* it is suggested he has tried to intimidate a prosecution witness in the interim).

45.09 If the court decides that summary trial is more suitable, then there is an obligation on the clerk of the court to give the defendant certain information. The clerk must carefully explain to the defendant personally (even if he is legally represented) that he has a choice as to which court he may be tried in but that if he does consent to summary trial and is found guilty by the magistrates, information will be obtained about his character and antecedents and if the magistrates then consider that greater punishment should be imposed than they have power to inflict, they may commit him to the Crown Court to be sentenced. In other words, the accused is being told that if his only reason for preferring the magistrates' court is his knowledge that the maximum sentence that they can in principle inflict is six months imprisonment for any one offence that he need not think that is conclusive because if he is convicted and after hearing all the details of his character and antecedents the magistrates consider that some greater penalty should be imposed, they may still commit him to the Crown Court for sentence and there he may receive the maximum which the Crown Court is empowered to impose.

Thereafter, the accused is asked where he wants to be tried and he has a final **45.10** say. He may say that he prefers to be tried in the Crown Court or that he is content to accept magistrates' court trial.

Why bother making representations to the magistrates if the accused had already made up his mind to "overrule" the magistrates no matter what and opt for Crown Court trial? Frankly, many consider that there is little point in making detailed submissions in favour of Crown Court trial where the accused has already decided (on legal advice) to opt for Crown Court trial whatever the magistrates' preliminary decision is. However, there is one advantage in doing so. If the case does go to the Crown Court, let us say on a relatively trivial shoplifting charge and one has successfully managed to persuade the magistrates themselves to choose that as the more appropriate forum (let us say because of some alleged difficulty in a matter of evidence which can be more satisfactorily dealt with before the higher court) then if the accused is convicted in the Crown Court the record will reveal that it was the magistrates themselves who decided to send the case there. The accused will not then be subject to any criticism. Suppose, however, that one had not tried, or, having tried, had failed to persuade the magistrates themselves to send the case to the Crown Court for trial and had in fact "overruled" the magistrates' preliminary decision to try the case themselves. In those circumstances, the Crown Court judge may feel that it was wrong for the accused to overrule the magistrates' decision and spend the time of the higher court on a trivial matter. Although it is certainly wrong in principle for him to impose a greater *sentence* to take into account his disapproval of this course of action, he is perfectly entitled to make the order which he imposes in respect of costs reflect his view of the waste of time of the higher court. He will therefore probably impose a more draconian costs order than would otherwise have been the case. This is why in such cases it is still worthwhile trying to persuade the magistrates themselves to choose to send the case for trial by the Crown Court.

Section 25 of the 1980 Magistrates' Courts Act allows the court to change **45.11** from summary trial to committal proceedings and vice versa. This may either be on its own motion, or on the application of either party. What was a summary trial may become committal proceedings at any time before the close of the prosecution case. The most common example is likely to be, however, where, the accused having previously consented to summary trial perhaps on an occasion when he was unrepresented, now in the light of legal advice wishes to elect in favour of trial on indictment. In such a case the magistrates have a wide discretion as to whether or not to permit the change of election for trial. It will only very unusually arise that after hearing prosecution evidence in a summary trial the nature of the offence seems to take on a greater seriousness than it had formerly been seen to have, so as to merit the magistrates wishing of their own motion to send the case to the Crown Court. This should only happen rarely because of the opportunity which the prosecution had at the outset to stress factors which will have made it more suitable for trial on indictment.

An accused who has elected trial on indictment may also wish to change his election. The magistrates may permit this change if proper. Again, it is more likely to occur before any kind of hearing has started given that the vast majority of committal proceedings are in the form prescribed by section 6(2) of the Magistrates' Court Act 1980, *i.e.* short form committals. An example might be where an accused now wishes to change his plea to guilty and would naturally wish to stay in the magistrates' court with its prima facie lesser sentencing powers. It is important to remember that a mode of trial hearing will still be necessary in the case of an either way offence even though the defendant intends from the outset to plead guilty.

45.12 It should be noted that if there is more than one co-accused, then generally the election of any one of them for trial in the Crown Court will bind the others. In principle, co-accused ought to be tried together so that consistent verdicts and sentences may be reached and since the magistrates have no power to overrule a decision for the Crown Court the need to try all the defendants together will mean that they all have to go to the Crown Court.

Choice of court
45.13 We have so far merely described the *procedure* by which the magistrates' court makes a preliminary decision as to which court will try the case. As we have seen in cases of offences triable either way, the accused is always in a position to ensure that he has jury trial, either by persuading the magistrates to choose trial on indictment themselves, or by overruling their preliminary decision against it. We will now have to consider the factors which his solicitor will take into account in advising an accused on choice of court.

In favour of the Crown Court

ACQUITTAL RATE

45.14 Despite somewhat inconclusive statistical evidence and strong local variations there is no doubt that many lawyers feel that in certain kinds of case the accused stands a much better chance of acquittal from a jury than in the magistrate's court. The magistrates are believed to become "case hardened" in certain types of case. An example is shoplifting where the only likely defence is that the accused forgot to pay or put the object into the wrong basket. Magistrates will have heard this defence on dozens of occasions and may generally be disinclined to believe it because the frequency with which it is advanced appears to make it improbable to them in any individual case. A jury is very likely to be hearing this defence for the first time and to take the judge's direction on "proof beyond reasonable doubt" more to heart when considering the case. Juries are thus more open minded (or perhaps more naive!) and in this kind of offence, anyway, the accused would generally seem to have a better chance before a jury. It is also sometimes suggested that particularly in some locations, magistrates have a belief in the invariable truthfulness of policemen which the ordinary layman no longer has and therefore that on a jury of 12 people, one is likely to find a higher proportion of sceptics about police evidence. Allied to these points there is also the undoubted factor that "sympathy" verdicts are not impossible. This means a verdict based on the personalities involved or on the jury's regard for the personal circumstances of the accused, or on some other legally irrelevant matter. An example is generally thought to be the trial of the civil servant Clive Ponting on Official Secrets Act charges in 1986 where in the face of a clear direction from the judge on the issues, the jury chose to acquit the accused. In such cases a feeling that the accused has been oppressively treated by the State, be it the police, or even sometimes the harsh treatment an accused may have received when testifying from prosecuting counsel, may contribute to this possibility.

MATTERS OF LAW OR EVIDENCE

In a case which involves difficult legal points, many lawyers doubt whether **45.15** magistrates, even with the expert assistance of a clerk, really do grasp the legal niceties involved. There are no such problems in the Crown Court where the judge will certainly be capable of grasping them. More importantly still, there is the question of evidence. As we have seen the device of having a judge and jury with separate functions in relation to evidence proves to be a very happy one in the common law system. Thus, the fact that matters of admissibility are generally dealt with by the judge with the jury excluded from court, means that the jury never hear evidence which is excluded. In the magistrates' court, there is unfortunately no equivalent to this and one needs to make submissions about admissibility which inevitably involve discussing, describing or hearing the evidence in question, in front of the very magistrates whose minds may well be affected by it even if they do rule in favour of exclusion. There are other cases where in the magistrate's court matters of evidence have to be dealt with in what is at the best, a somewhat clumsy way. Applications to cross-examine the accused on his criminal record under Section 1(f)(ii) of the Criminal Evidence Act 1898 are necessarily somewhat difficult. In the Crown Court, the judge might, having considered the application in the absence of the jury, refuse it, or perhaps limit cross-examination to certain parts of the accused's record. In the magistrate's court, merely to make the application for leave to cross-examine under s.1(f)(ii) tells the magistrates that the accused does have a record. Nor can there be any equivalent of letting the prosecution cross-examine on only part of the record, since the magistrates themselves will need to see the record to rule on any such application. Likewise, the fact that directions about evidence are given to the jury in open court, *e.g.* on corroboration, etc., must inevitably be more favourable to the accused than the somewhat bodged counterpart in the magistrates' court where the defence advocate in effect tells the magistrates what rules of evidence they ought to apply and how, and hopes that his submission is understood and remembered and perhaps repeated by the magistrates' clerk. This therefore is likely to be the single most significant feature favouring Crown Court trial in any case where a matter of evidence arises.

KNOWING THE PROSECUTION CASE IN ADVANCE

Formerly, this was perhaps the greatest factor in favour of the Crown Court **45.16** namely that the committal proceedings meant that the prosecution had to disclose their evidence before trial. In the magistrates court, it was sometimes possible if one had a reasonable relationship with the prosecuting solicitor to persuade him to let one look at the prosecution statements in advance, but this would inevitably be only shortly before the trial and was considered much less satisfactory. Now, however, this has been resolved by the bringing into force of the 1985 Magistrates' Courts (Advance Information) Rules. Before the court considers the mode of trial, the defendant or his representative may request that the prosecution furnishes him with advance information and on receipt of such request, the prosecution shall, as soon as practicable, furnish either:

1. a copy of those parts of every written statement which contains information as to the facts and matters which the prosecution propose to adduce in evidence; or

2. a summary of such facts and matters.

In fact, since it is obviously quicker and more convenient to send a simple photostat of the statements, this will often be what the prosecution do, rather than separately preparing a summary of the relevant matters. If only a summary is provided then it can later be susceptible of leading to disputes in that it would be open to the defendant to suggest that vital matters had been omitted from the summary. It seems however, that despite the extra work involved, in many areas of the country Crown Prosecutors supply summaries, and brief ones at that, rather than copies of their witness statements. In any event, in every case of an offence triable either way, whether proceeding in the magistrates or Crown Court, there will now be a prior disclosure of the prosecution case. However, although this is now a neutral feature, it does lead on to another matter which is in favour of the Crown Court, namely:—

COMMITTAL PROCEEDINGS

45.17 Committal proceedings in essence give one two bites at the cherry in that one might get a weak prosecution case thrown out at an early stage. It will be seen in due course when we discuss committal proceedings that these can be either *short form* where the accused consents to being committed for trial, or *long form* which involves a full examination of parts (or perhaps the whole) of the prosecution evidence. In this latter case, prosecution witnesses are called and will give their evidence just as if it were a trial proper and be subject to cross-examination. To see the impression which prosecution witnesses make on the court can often be invaluable in helping one to plan one's strategy for the Crown Court trial and, secondly, there is also the possibility of getting the case dismissed at that early stage. A discussion of the tactics involved in conducting a long form committal and of the possible advantages to be gained from cross-examining prosecution witnesses fully, will be considered in the later section on committal proceedings. In an appropriate case, however, this is an important factor in favour of trial on indictment.

MARGINAL FACTORS

45.18 The one certain feature about trial on indictment is that it will take a good deal longer to happen. Accordingly, in some cases there may be some use to which the delay can be put. The best example would be where some considerable time was necessary perhaps to trace witnesses or explore some difficult avenue of evidence; it may also be easier to obtain some kinds of expert evidence if there is a lengthy delay, especially in the case of psychiatric evidence. A delay could also be useful with matters relevant to mitigation, although in that case one would be anticipating the conviction of the accused. For example, if the accused can put the delay to some use in a way which changes the pattern of his life for the better such as getting married, settling down in some way, or acquiring a job after a lengthy period of unemployment, those things would be useful at the stage of mitigation.

Factors in favour of the magistrates' court

GUILTY PLEA

If the defendant firmly intends to plead guilty then unless he can use the delay inherent in Crown Court trial to provide mitigating factors for himself, the lesser sentencing powers of magistrates would normally be a conclusive factor in favour of the latter. **45.19**

SPEED

There can be no doubt that a magistrates' court trial will come on significantly faster than a Crown Court trial. If the accused is nervous, or in custody, this may be a vital factor in favour of the former. **45.20**

STRESS

There can be no doubt that the actual trial itself is a greater ordeal in the Crown Court. Not only is it likely that there will be many more people present in court, but the atmosphere, the greater deference accorded to the Crown Court judge, the wigs and gowns, and the feeling that the accused is being constantly scrutinised by the 12 jurors, the judge and the prosecuting counsel, will all put a greater stress on the accused. This is something not lightly to be dismissed in the case of an accused who is in any way vulnerable. **45.21**

PUBLICITY

It is difficult to generalise about this. In general, the press will have more representatives at a busy Crown Court centre but all of these may be in the same court where something particularly newsworthy is happening. Whether the press will be present in the smaller courts where individuals are being tried on, say, minor theft charges, is doubtful. There is no doubt that a "tip-off" system exists whereby policemen receive money from the press for forewarning the latter that newsworthy individuals are coming up for trial in a certain court. Some local worthy may well fall into this category, *e.g.* a local councillor or clergyman. In such a case this kind of person may be lucky to escape the attention of the press wherever he is tried. It is fair to say that the press take less interest in magistrates courts; however, much will depend on the locality. If it is a small country town with the magistrates' court only sitting say two days a week, the press, if there is a local newspaper, will generally have a representative present throughout every case. It is not unusual, for example, to see in the local press headlines such as "Barchester Man's Day of Shame" and on reading the report one finds that it is concerned only with a motoring offence. In a major conurbation, however, there may well be more chance of escaping any press report at all in the magistrates' court. **45.22**

SENTENCE

Magistrates have limited sentencing powers. In principle, they can only sentence a person to a maximum of six months imprisonment for one offence and a maximum of 12 months for any number of offences. Their powers to fine are also limited to £2,000 for each offence, except those for which there is some different statutory maximum. However, it must be noted that if after trying an either way offence summarily and convicting they conclude that their sentencing powers arc inadequate in view of what they have heard about the offender's antecedents and character, they do then have the power to commit the accused for sentence to the Crown Court, who may impose any sentence authorised by law for the offence. Therefore, sentence would only make a difference where the accused concluded that he might receive a sentence which would be longer than six months in prison, but not so much longer that the magistrates would be minded to commit him to the Crown Court. In other words, he is gambling on the magistrates not doing the latter. It must be said that much will depend on one's knowledge of the bench of magistrates and local Crown Court judges. Certainly any advocate in the Crown Court can tell you of judges who are notoriously "hard" or "soft," but there is no controlling which judge will deal with one's case and there must be many cases where it would be preferable to be dealt with by a "soft" judge in the Crown Court, rather than a hard local bench of magistrates. A Crown Court judge dealing with a relatively trivial offence may anyway prove more lenient than magistrates, if only because his usual daily diet involves considerably more serious crime.

COST

45.24 Trial in the Crown Court will inevitably be more expensive, perhaps many times so, than summary trial. Even for a legally aided client this is not a negligible matter, *e.g.* if a costs order is made on conviction.

46. Committal Proceedings

As we have seen criminal offences fall into three categories:— **46.01**

1. Those triable only summarily in which case trial before the magistrates is inevitable and there is no option.
2. Those triable only on indictment in which case trial is by the Crown Court before a judge and jury.
3. Those triable either way where there will be a mode of trial hearing to determine the manner in which the case is to continue.

With very few exceptions nor relevant to this text all criminal proceedings **46.02** commence in the magistrates court. In the case of those triable only summarily or those triable either way where the magistrates opt for, and the accused is happy to accept summary trial that is precisely what happens. In those triable only on indictment and those triable either way where the magistrates themselves choose to send the case to the Crown Court or where the accused elects trial there is still a preliminary hearing before the magistrates.

Crown Court trials are expensive and time consuming. Moreover there is always a considerable waiting list for trial on indictment which means that an accused remanded in custody may be detained for a substantial period before trial and even if released on bail will be possibly subject to stress and anxiety before the trial.

In order to filter out prosecutions with little prospect of success almost all **46.03** trials on indictment are preceded by a preliminary hearing before the magistrates which is known as committal proceedings. These proceedings are not a trial as such. They simply involve the prosecution demonstrating that it has a reasonable or prima facie case which it is proper to call upon the accused to answer before a judge and jury in the Crown Court. Magistrates conducting these preliminary hearings are referred to as examining justices, and contrary to the usual rule one examining justice may sit alone for the purpose of committal proceedings.

The onus on the prosecution to show that it has a prima facie case is not a high one. The examining justices only have to be satisfied that there is sufficient evidence on which a reasonable jury *could* (not would) find the defendant guilty. In practice this means that most preliminary hearings do result in a committal for trial.

Before 1967 all committal proceedings took the form described below which **46.04** is often referred to as "full" committal proceedings or "long form" committal proceedings. However since 1967 two different types of committal proceedings have been available, those with consideration of the evidence and those without such consideration. The provision for both types of committal proceedings is now found in section 6 of the Magistrates' Courts Act 1980. We shall now consider both types of committal proceedings.

Committals with consideration of the evidence

46.05 These are provided for by Section 6(1) of the Magistrates' Courts Act. It should be noted that it is open to either the prosecution or the defence to insist on a Section 6(1) committal in any case. If the prosecution choose not to offer the defence the choice of a committal without consideration of the evidence under Section 6(2) of the Act (see below) or if the defence having been offered this choice do not accept the option, then a Section 6(1) committal, that is a *full* committal will be held.

The procedure is as follows:—

46.06 (i) The charge is read to the accused although he is not required to state his plea at this stage.

46.07 (ii) The next matter to be dealt with is the question of publicity.

Committal proceedings, even full committal proceedings, often involve only the prosecution side of the case as we shall see below. If it were open to the press to report these proceedings then a one-sided view of the case might emerge and moreover matters highly prejudicial to an accused might come out. For this reason the press are prevented by section 8 of the Magistrates' Courts Act 1980 from reporting anything more about committal proceedings than the names, address, ages and occupation of the parties and witnesses and the names of their legal representatives; the charges against the accused; and the outcome of applications for bail and legal aid. The point of this restriction is so that the persons in the area from whom the jurors will be chosen who eventually try the case in the Crown Court should not be prejudiced by hearing a one-sided version of events (or preferably any version of events) in advance but should be open-minded when they judge the case on what they hear in the Crown Court at the appropriate time. Full reporting of what happens, that is of the allegations made an the evidence given, is allowed only if reporting restrictions are specifically lifted by the court. It ought to be said that section 8 also applies to any previous hearings before the court, *e.g.* the mode of trial hearing or remands. If the accused actually *wants* publicity however, for example so that a missing witness might come forward to give evidence on his behalf, then it is open to him to apply to the examining justices to lift reporting restrictions. If he does so they must comply in which case the press (if it is sufficiently interested) may report more about the case. Where there is more than one accused and one wants reporting restrictions lifted and another or others do not then the magistrates should consider the interests of justice before deciding whether to grant the application. The burden is on the person who wishes the reporting restrictions to be lifted to show that his chance of a fair trial is prejudiced through lack of publicity.

46.08 (iii) The prosecution then opens its case.

The Crown Prosecutor makes a speech telling the examining magistrates what the case concerns and the charge or charges on which it is suggested the accused should be committed for trial and the nature of the evidence he intends to call. It must be noted that the prosecution does not have to present all its available evidence at this stage. All that it needs to present is that which it deems sufficient evidence to establish a prima facie case. Thus if there are half a dozen eye witnesses to the same thing the prosecution may be content to call only one or two of them at this stage.

(iv) The prosecution then calls its evidence. **46.09**

The evidence may be oral and if so the witness is subject to the usual process of examination-in-chief, cross examination and re-examination. During this process the clerk makes a written note of the evidence and when testimony is complete the clerk reads this to the witness and invites him to sign it. When signed and authenticated by a counter signature of one of the examining magistrates the document is known as a deposition. Depositions may be used as evidence at the trial in the Crown Court in certain exceptional circumstances, which have been previously explained at para. 29.26.

As well as verbal evidence the defence may accept at this stage the giving of some of the prosecution evidence in the form of written statements under section 102 of the Magistrates Courts Act 1980. We have already seen the effect of this section which is in identical terms to section 9 of the Criminal Justice Act 1967. It provides that hearsay evidence (*i.e.* written statements) may be tendered to the courts in committal proceedings provided that:

1. Each statement is signed by the maker;

2. It contains a declaration by the maker that it is true to the best of his knowledge and belief and that he makes it knowing that if it is tendered in evidence he could be prosecuted for wilfully stating anything in it that he knew to be false or did not believe to be true;

3. It was given in advance to each of the other parties to the committal proceedings; and

4. It was not objected to by any other party.

Accordingly if there are parts of the prosecution evidence which are at this stage uncontroversial or purely formal they may be put in evidence and read out to the court. The defence will normally only object to the use of a Section 102 statement if it wishes to cross-examine the maker at this stage, *e.g.* with a view to discrediting the witness.

At the end of the committal hearing the court will make a witness order for prosecution witnesses to attend the eventual trial at the Crown Court. Such witness orders are made in one of two forms, either *full* witness orders in which case the witness is required to attend to give oral evidence or *conditional* witness orders in which case the witness is only required to attend court if the defence subsequently notify the prosecution that they require the witness's presence there. If the defence accept conditional witness orders and do not later give the prosecution notice that they require the witness to attend Crown Court trial then the prosecution may read out the witness's statement which will be in the form required by Section 9 Criminal Justice Act 1967. In this way the defence can partly control the witnesses which the prosecution must call in the Crown Court.

(v) At the conclusion of the prosecution's evidence at the committal the **46.10** defence may make a submission of no case to answer. We have already seen the considerations which apply where such a submission is made. For the sake of completeness we will repeat them here. The submission that there is no case to answer may properly be upheld:—

1. When there has been no evidence to prove an essential element in the alleged offence; or

2. When the evidence adduced by the prosecution has been discredited as a result of cross-examination or is so manifestly unreliable that no reasonable tribunal could safely convict on it.

It must be remembered at this stage that it by no means follows that the magistrates will commit the accused for trial on the same charge which the prosecution have brought. For example the prosecution may have charged the accused with robbery. The magistrates may come to the conclusion that while the circumstances do disclose a prima facie case of theft there has been no evidence to prove the element of violence required for robbery and therefore they may decide to commit the accused on a charge of theft alone. This must be borne carefully in mind at this stage. Thus merely showing that the element of violence was lacking on a robbery charge would by no means lead to the accused's discharge.

46.11 (vi) If no submission of no case to answer is made or if one is made and not upheld by the magistrates then the charge is read over to the defendant who is cautioned in terms similar to the police caution and asked whether he has anything to say in answer to the charge. This is not as such an invitation to plead.

46.12 (vii) The alibi warning is given to the accused.

As has been explained in the section on evidence an accused has no general obligation to indicate to the prosecution what his defence will be at trial. There is one exception to this principle and that is where the accused wishes to raise an alibi defence, that is, to say that he was somewhere other than at the scene of the alleged offence at the relevant time. By section 11 of the Criminal Justice Act 1967 an accused must give to the prosecution particulars of his alibi either at or no later than seven days after the end of committal proceedings. If he fails to do so then he may only give evidence of an alibi defence where the trial judge gives him leave to do so. It is customary to give written notice of alibi to the Crown Prosecution Service after the Committal proceedings rather than at them. The particulars required are the name and address of any alibi witnesses and details of where the accused says he was at the relevant time.

46.13 (viii) The next step is for the defendant and, if he wishes, any witnesses to give evidence to the magistrates. Where the defendant or his witnesses do give evidence then it is again taken down in longhand and signed and constitutes a deposition. The giving of defence evidence is rare, most defendants preferring to reserve their position until the Crown Court trial.

46.14 (ix) If defence evidence has been given the defence may make a submission that there is not sufficient evidence taken as a whole on which to commit the accused for trial. The test is again whether there is a prima facie case but the magistrates must have regard to all the evidence that they have now heard. If they decide that there is no case they discharge the accused. This does not however constitute an acquittal. The prosecution may, so to speak, make a further attempt to "get their act together" and may recharge the accused for that offence or other offences and start the procedure again.

46.15 (x) If the magistrates decide to commit the accused to the Crown Court then they have to decide to which Crown Court they will commit him and on which charges. In relation to the first of these matters it is simply a matter of geographical convenience unless there is some special feature, such as that the incidents have provoked some local feelings which may make it better to have the accused tried out of the area. On the question of the charges on which they commit the accused, this will usually be the charges which the prosecution brought against him at the outset. Sometimes however the magistrates may decide that there is insufficient evidence of some aspect of those charges and commit him for some other offence. For example although the prosecution originally charged an accused with robbery it may be that no evidence has been brought of any element of violence and therefore that theft is the better charge on which to commit. In addition regard must sometimes be had to the relatively new powers under sections 40 and 41 of the Criminal Justice Act 1988. Under these sections magistrates who commit an accused for trial at the Crown Court may be able to commit him also in respect of linked summary offences so that all matters can conveniently be disposed of on the same occasion. The provisions are as follows:—

(a) By section 41 of the Criminal Justice Act 1988 magistrates who commit a defendant to the Crown Court for trial of an either way offence (such as theft) may also commit for trial in respect of any summary offence which is:
  (i) punishable with imprisonment or disqualification (such as careless driving or taking a conveyance) and
  (ii) arises out of circumstances which are the same as, or connected with the either way offence.
  If the defendant, on conviction of the either way offence, pleads guilty to the summary offence the Crown Court can sentence for the summary offence but its power are then limited to the maximum sentencing powers of the magistrates. If however the defendant pleads not guilty the summary offence must be remitted to the Magistrates Court for trial.

Secondly under section 40 of the 1988 Act the prosecution may add a count to an indictment in respect of a purely summary offence (such as taking a conveyance under section 12 of the Theft Act) if it is either founded on the same facts or evidence as the indictable count or is part of a series of offences of the same or similar character and the facts or evidence on which it is based were tendered at committal. Again the Crown Court only has the sentencing powers of the magistrates in respect of the summary offence.

(xi) Other matters.   **46.16**
    At the end of the decision to commit for trial, then certain other matters require to be dealt with.

Witnesses

The defence will be asked for which prosecution witnesses it requires full, and for which only conditional, witness orders.

Bail

As we have seen the mere decision to commit the defendant for trial will not constitute in itself the change of circumstances sufficient to ground the making of a third bail application if two full applications have already been made unsuccessfully. Despite the fact that the accused may after committal be in custody uninterruptedly for some weeks or months that is not in itself a sufficient new feature. It may well be however if the prosecution evidence has been thoroughly explored by cross-examination at the committal that some submission can be made that the court might take a different view of the strength of the prosecution evidence which is of course one of the relevant considerations for deciding on a bail application.

Legal aid

Unless a through order has been made for legal aid to cover the Crown Court trial then it is appropriate to apply to the magistrates for legal aid to be *extended*. In fact it is in principle a *new* legal aid order that is made but this is the terminology invariably used. If one forgets to do this at the committal proceedings one can in any event apply to the Crown Court directly by completing a straightforward application form. One usually tells the magistrates in committal proceedings that the accused's means have not changed since his earlier application for legal aid for the magistrates court.

Prosecution costs

Under section 17 of the Prosecution of Offences Act 1985 the Crown Prosecutor who will conduct the case before magistrates need make no application for costs at the end of committal proceedings. There is no point in applying for costs from central funds, as was previously the practice, where the prosecution is publicly funded. If there is a private prosecutor then it may be appropriate to make application for costs out of central funds. It would not of course be appropriate ever at this stage to claim costs from the defendant since his guilt has not been established.

Defence costs

If the defendant is discharged then defence costs may be claimed from central funds unless (subject to regulations made by the Lord Chancellor) the court concludes that the prosecution's unnecessary or improper conduct has put the defendant to expense, in which case the order may be made direct against the prosecution.

Committal without consideration of the evidence under section 6(2) of the Magistrates' Courts Act 1980

46.17 This section allows the accused to *consent* to being committed for trial and would be appropriate where:—

1. the accused intends in any event to plead guilty; or
2. where although he intends to plead not guilty he accepts that on the prosecution evidence there is a prima facie case against him.

The section permits the accused to be committed without consideration of the evidence if:

394

1. all the evidence to be tendered consists of written statements made in the proper form in compliance with Section 102 of the 1980 Act; and

2. the accused (or where there is more than one all the accused) is legally represented; and

3. none of the accused wishes to make a submission of no case to answer.

In the case of a committal under section 6(2) of the Act the accused will have been served (usually at his solicitor's office) with copies of the prosecution's statements in section 102 form sometime in advance of the hearing. It must be noted that although in the overwhelming majority of cases the prosecution themselves want a short form of committal in view of saving time and costs and because they will naturally consider that they *do* have a prima facie case, there is no obligation on them to offer this form of committal to the accused. If they do not want to do so and propose to go ahead with a full committal there is nothing that the defendant can do about it. Having received the section 102 statements with a view to committal under section 6(2) it is always open to the defence solicitor to change his mind in the light perhaps of how weak the prosecution evidence does look, and to insist on a full committal.

The defendant should attend, in principle, although (unless he is on bail) he **46.18** need not do so provided that his solicitor is present. Thereafter the following is the order of events:—

1. The charge is read out though again no plea is taken.

2. The clerk will ask the defence whether they wish for reporting restrictions to be lifted.
    The same considerations as before will apply although of course the press will not actually hear the substance of the prosecution evidence. It is open however to the defence solicitor to mention any matter to the court on which press assistance might be required (*e.g.* the tracing of a missing witness).

3. The clerk then asks the prosecution to confirm that all their evidence is in the form of section 102 statements, that copies have been given to the defendant already and that the defendants are all legally represented. The clerk then asks the defence formally to confirm that they do not object to any statement, wish to testify themselves or call witnesses or wish to submit no case to answer.

4. The section 102 statements are not read out to the court nor do the magistrates need to consider their contents. It is simply a matter of counting the number of section 102 statements presented. Thereafter the magistrates announce the committal for trial to the Crown Court on the charges which the prosecution have brought. Since they do not examine the evidence at all they will naturally not need to consider whether all the elements on some lesser charge might be appropriate.

5. Thereafter the applications to be made will be the same as those in the case of a committal with consideration of the evidence that is:
    (a) The alibi warning and defence notice of alibi either then or within seven days.

(b) Witness orders either full or conditional in respect of each witness whose evidence is contained in the section 102 statements.
(c) Bail application if necessary.
(d) Application for legal aid.

Choice of committal proceedings

We shall now consider the factors which might make either party choose one rather than the other form of committal proceedings.

46.19 1. The prosecution may decide upon a full committal where they wish to test their own witnesses. This is particularly appropriate where identification is in issue. In cases of disputed identity the Attorney-General issued guidelines in 1976 suggesting to prosecutors that the prosecution should always ask for a committal with consideration of the evidence and call their identification witnesses. Thus if the identification evidence is discredited the case will go no further. In further guidelines issued in 1979 however, the Attorney-General in effect reverted to leaving the matter to the discretion of the opposing parties. These guidelines provide that the prosecution should not usually in identification cases seek a committal under section 6(2) of the Magistrates Court Act but might do so where both parties and the examining magistrates considered the short form of committal the more appropriate procedure. With the exception of identification cases and miscellaneous cases where the prosecution may wish to see how their own witnesses perform the prosecution will almost always be willing to have the short form committal. It must be emphasised again that neither at the long nor the short form committal are they required to call or put before the court *all* the evidence which they will eventually call in the Crown Court.

46.20 2. Accordingly the tactical decision as to whether or not to insist on the long form of committal is usually that of the defence. There are two basic reasons for the defence to choose a long form committal:—
(a) The hope of having the case disposed of there and then, that is making a successful submission of no case to answer or "no case on which to commit" as it is sometimes called;
(b) Whether or not this may be successful, in any event to see the prosecution witnesses and assess their performance and to probe the prosecution's case.

We shall now consider the points in favour of and against having a full committal.

POINTS IN FAVOUR OF A FULL COMMITTAL

46.21 1. One can see how prosecution witnesses perform. This may be an invaluable aid in assessing the strength of one's own case. Moreover one may probe their version for details not given in the bare bones of their statements to the police. These will be the section 102 statements which will probably have been disclosed to the defence anyway. It will be recalled that the Advance Information Rules entitle the defendant to see the prosecution evidence (or a summary of it) in advance of the mode of trial hearing.

2. The magistrates must of course consider the evidence available on **46.22** which to commit the accused for trial. This means naturally that the rules of evidence do apply. If it is therefore suggested that a material part of the prosecution case is inadmissible, *e.g.* is based on hearsay, then it is appropriate to make submissions about this matter at the committal proceedings. The magistrates cannot properly say that there is evidence on which to commit the accused for trial if the evidence in question is not admissible.

3. One may wish to see how prosecution witnesses respond to certain lines **46.23** of speculative cross-examination. It may be for example that one wishes to consider a somewhat dangerous path which may, if unsuccessful, lead to the witness giving evidence in a way which is more harmful to the accused than appears from the basis of his statement. If this does in fact occur at the committal proceedings one can be sure to advise counsel at the Crown Court trial to avoid that approach to that particular witness.

4. One can attempt to draw prosecution witnesses out into areas beyond **46.24** the scope of their brief statement to the police. It is a fact of life that even with intelligent lay witnesses the more one can get them to say the more likely it is that apparent inconsistencies and self contradictions will arise or can be exploited. Although the depositions are not in themselves evidence to be put in at the trial in the Crown Court they can be used as a previous inconsistent statement on the basis of which to cross-examine a witness. Suppose therefore that in the course of lengthy cross-examination one can get a witness to say something in the magistrates court about how a certain event occurred. If in the Crown Court when he is testifying on the same matter there is any difference in the version he gives, even quite a minor change in terminology, one can sometimes seize upon this as the weak point in his evidence on which perhaps to discredit him. Giving evidence in the Crown Court is a considerably more stressful experience than in the magistrates court. Witnesses may tend to an exaggerated use of language under these stresses. Suppose that in describing an incident which led to a fight a witness who in the magistrates court had said that the defendant was "acting pretty stupidly" in the Crown Court could be persuaded to say that the defendant was "acting like a maniac." One can easily see the line of cross-examination about the witness's credibility that would follow. It could be put to the witness that he had changed his evidence since the magistrates court, and he was now deliberately exaggerating to try to incriminate the accused, and thus forfeited all credibility. Thus the sheer bulk of additional testimony that one can get to flesh out the sometimes skeletal statements which the police will have obtained when they took the witnesses's statement down, may be of great tactical assistance.

5. Even if one has opted for a committal with consideration of the evidence **46.25** then it does not necessarily follow that one needs at this stage to attack the evidence or cross-examine each of the prosecution witnesses. Moreover if one has been asking for a long form committal with a realistic hope of the magistrates not committing the accused for trial rather than for gaining a tactical advantage in the eventual Crown Court

trial one still has a tactical decision to make. Suppose that one's submission of no case to answer has been rejected after a thorough cross-examination of the prosecution witnesses. There is still the option as to whether or not to call one's own client. The general practice is not to give any of the defence evidence at this stage. This is because firstly one is perfectly entitled to keep one's evidence secret until the trial (with the single exception of an alibi defence) and secondly because putting the defendant or his witnesses in the box will give the prosecution that self same advantage that has just been discussed in relation to prosecution witnesses namely they will now be able to cross-examine at length on the circumstances of the incident and themselves obtain a detailed version of what the accused and his witnesses will say. One would normally therefore only consider calling the accused and his witnesses where one felt that the prosecution evidence was not strong and that there was some realistic hope that the magistrates, having heard the totality of the evidence, prosecution and defence, would decide there is no case on which to commit. An example might be where the accused had very strong alibi evidence, *e.g.* not just his own testimony but that of, say, two wholly reputable and disinterested witnesses.

POINTS AGAINST A FULL COMMITTAL

46.26   The disadvantages of having a long form committal are obvious as the converse of the advantages. One may rehearse prosecution witnesses in their evidence and give them a taste of how cross-examination feels so that they are more assured the next time. Likewise by the very manner in which one conducts one's cross-examination one may give away to the prosecution the nature of the defence and allow them to call other evidence with which to meet it. The advantages to the prosecution of giving their witnesses a "dry run" should not be underestimated. Testifying may be a nerve racking experience for a witness and there is no doubt that it is less of an ordeal where one has had an opportunity to practise.

46.27   There is additionally the matter of cost. A full committal may need several hours, or days, to achieve what the short form committal can achieve in minutes. For a privately paying client this is obviously an important factor, and even for the legally aided client cost may be of some relevance in view of possible contribution orders or orders for payment of prosecution costs if he is eventually convicted.

46.28   Finally one further point should be noted. It has been stressed throughout that the prosecution are under no obligation to call all their evidence whether in person or by statements in section 102 form at the committal hearing. All they need to call is sufficient evidence to show a prima facie case. This does not however mean that they are entitled to keep secret, and surprise the accused with, the evidence of other witnesses. In a case where there has been a committal the prosecution are obliged to give the accused notice of the evidence of *all* the witnesses whom they propose to call at the trial. This is done by subsequently serving on the accused's solicitor copies of the statements comprising the additional evidence which is to be called at trial in the Crown Court.

47. Sentencing and Procedures after Conviction

We shall now discuss sentencing and procedures after conviction. Conviction may occur either on a plea of guilty or after a plea of not guilty. In neither case need the court proceed to sentence immediately. It may adjourn the proceedings and sentence at a future date for a number of reasons. Examples would be: **47.01**

1. Where a social enquiry report, psychiatric or medical report needs to be prepared so that the court has more information available.

2. Where there is any way insufficient information to enable the court to proceed immediately to sentence.

3. Where the defendant has been convicted in his absence and the court has in mind either to disqualify him from driving or imprison him they must adjourn the case to enable the defendant to be brought before the court.

It should be noted that when the court does propose to adjourn proceedings for sentence for any reason the defendant will be remanded. In other words the court will have to consider the question of bail or custody pending sentence. It must be remembered that the prima facie presumption in favour of bail contained in the Bail Act 1976 does not apply at this stage except where the court is adjourning to obtain reports on the offender. Even here the court may well now impose conditions even if bail has previously been unconditional. The initial procedures are likely to include one or all of the following matters:

1. Outlining the facts of the case.

2. The defendant's antecedents.

3. Offences taken into consideration.

The facts of the case

If the defendant has been convicted after a not guilty plea then the court will have been made aware of all the evidence in the case. In addition to deciding the issue of guilt or innocence they will know which precise version of the facts they are minded to believe. In other words they may have already heard matters relevant to sentencing. For example if the accused is charged with an assault arising out of a fight and his defence has been self-defence. It may well be that although the court convicts him having found that his actions did not amount to self defence, it will nonetheless be apparent that there was gross provocation and this may clearly be a matter relevant to the sentence which it will impose. There is more difficulty where the defendant has pleaded guilty. In this case there will be no evidence on oath but the **47.02** prosecution will summarise the facts of the case. In a straightforward case there is no problem but what if the defendant, whilst admitting his guilt, wishes to give some entirely different version of how matters occurred? What if there is a substantial difference between how the prosecution says an incident occurred and what the defendant has to say? At this stage it must be remembered that the prosecution is supposed to be acting as a minister of justice. They should maintain a relatively neutral attitude about matters and in particular never press for any particular sentence nor explain the facts of the crime in an emotive or exaggerated way. If it appears that there is a genuine and material dispute about how an incident occurred, then the advocates for prosecution and defence should each make their submissions about the matter, but thereafter the sentencing court should either:

1. Accept the defence account or

2. Allow prosecution and defence to call evidence about the matter.

In the Crown Court where this happens after a guilty plea there is no jury, the judge himself deciding which version of the facts he prefers to believe.

The sentencing court will therefore now be aware so far as possible of the facts of the crime itself.

The defendant's antecedents

47.03   These are usually presented to the court by the Crown Prosecutor or one of the police officers involved in the case. The "antecedents" are details of the offender's age, upbringing, education, employment record and domestic circumstances. Also there is some account of his previous criminal record although this is not in substitution for the actual printout of his criminal record which will also be supplied.

The rules of evidence do not apply at this stage but the antecedents officer may be cross-examined by the defendant's advocate in an effort to elicit more favourable details about the defendant's past. It must be remembered that the Rehabilitation of Offenders Act 1974 does not apply in criminal proceedings but pursuant to the Practice Direction of 1975 details of "spent" convictions should not be read out in court unless the court gives leave to do so.

Offences taken into consideration

47.04   In the course of being questioned about the present offence the offender may well have been questioned also about other offences. Where the offender proposes to plead guilty then he may well have admitted other past crimes. There is no need necessarily for the prosecution to charge him with each of the crimes which he has admitted. One option available to the prosecution is merely to charge him with a few selected crimes and allow him to have the others "taken into consideration." This is a somewhat informal procedure although sanctioned by long usage, in which the prosecution have the advantage of clearing up unsolved crimes and the defendant has the advantage of having the slate wiped clean insofar as these other offences are concerned so that he could not be prosecuted for them after his trial for the present offences is concluded.

The offences to be taken into consideration should be prepared in a proper schedule with all relevant details by the police. They should be offences of a broadly similar nature or of a less serious nature than the present charge. The sentencing court cannot specifically impose a sentence in respect of offences which are to be taken into consideration (although it may order compensation to the victims of those offences) but such offences will be taken into account in a general way when deciding on sentence.

It may be helpful to give an example. A very common type of crime which is taken into consideration is house burglary. Suppose that the offender has made it his habitual practice to go out to one of the wealthier suburbs of the city in which he lives and break into houses at weekends. He may well have done this over a period of a year or more before he is caught. When he is caught he may admit the most recent crimes in the course of interrogation. As other incidents which have not been solved by the police are put to him he may well be prepared to admit those also. It is very important to stress when acting for a defendant that the list of offences to be taken into consideration should be gone through very carefully with the defendant to ensure that he is right in admitting those other offences. For example in the incidents just cited it is probably most unlikely if regular weekend burglaries had been carried out over a year that the defendant will any longer remember the precise locations or addresses of the houses which he has burgled or the exact goods which he took away from each. There may be a tendency on the part of the police to slip in anything conceivably likely in order to improve their detection statistics. On the assumption however that the defendant was to admit let us say 30 such burglaries the probable practice of the prosecution would be to charge him only with a selected four or five and to have the others "taken into consideration." Whilst it may appear to the layman that to admit a course of conduct of regular burglary involving say 30 houses is a very significantly different scale of crime to admitting only four or five with which one is actually charged, the sentencing practice of the court is such that very little in the way of an extra sentence will be imposed for the other offences. The maximum penalty for burglary is 14 years and therefore in relation to the five offences to which the accused specifically pleads guilty the maximum is ample and would far exceed anything the court would realistically be minded to impose. The consideration of the other offences referred to in the example would probably make very little difference.

It ought to be mentioned that "T.I.C.'s," as they are called, may also be relevant for a defendant who has been convicted after pleading not guilty. In the nature of things however such cases will be rare and the usual case of offences taken into consideration occurs where the offender is prepared to admit the crimes with which he is presently charged in advance of trial and the prosecution will thus have ample opportunity to put the other matters to him.

We shall now go on to consider remaining matters in the following order:

1. Reports.
2. Types of sentence.
3. Other orders including compensation and costs.
4. The plea in mitigation.

Reports

There may be some situations where the court, even with the offender's **47.05** criminal record and a detailed and helpful plea in mitigation made by the defence advocate feels it is unlikely to have sufficient information about the convicted person to enable it to pass sentence. In such a situation it may obtain reports on the offender from a variety of sources and we shall now consider these.

SOCIAL ENQUIRY REPORTS

47.06   Such reports are prepared, in the case of adults, by the probation service. They are not usually prepared in advance of trial unless the defendant has already indicated a guilty plea or is already on probation and thus his personal circumstances are well known to the probation service. The report is prepared after one or several interviews between probation officer and the offender, sometimes in the offender's home environment. The offence will be discussed with the offender and the report will deal with his background, education, upbringing, circumstances, financial position and any particular personal medical or social problems which he seems to have. It will often conclude with a recommendation for a particular type of sentence and may especially deal with the offender's likely response to probation or community service. If there is no report prepared before conviction then inevitably there will have to be an adjournment to enable one to be prepared and the usual term of such adjournment is three weeks. It is generally considered more satisfactory to have such a report prepared whilst the offender is at liberty though it is not conclusively the case that when adjourning for a social enquiry report the magistrates should never remand in custody. Everything will depend upon the facts of the case, remembering that the prima facie right to bail in the Bail Act *does* apply at this stage.

A social enquiry report should in principle be prepared before imposing a custodial sentence on a person who has not previously suffered a custodial sentence. In either case however, the court may, provided it states its reasons in open court proceed without such a report if it considers it unnecessary, (*i.e.* if it considers it already has all necessary facts at its disposal).

There are other occasions on which social enquiry reports are certainly desirable.

1.   Before probation itself is ordered.

2.   If a community service order is possibly appropriate.

The court is not in fact empowered to impose a community service order unless there has previously been a social enquiry report which both recommends the offender for it and states that there is available work locally. In a case where a community service order seems one of the possible options it would clearly be proper to order the obtaining of a report. Failure to do so would mean the court, in effect, losing the option of imposing a community service order.

MEDICAL AND PSYCHIATRIC REPORTS

47.07   It may be that the court will consider that the occurrence of the offence is connected with some medical condition in which case they may require the making of medical reports on the accused. A common example is where there is some suggestion of a drug habit or alcoholism which is relevant to why the offender committed the offence, *e.g.* to provide money to sustain the habit or whilst under the influence of alcohol or the drug. In such a situation the court has power to remand the offender (in custody or on bail) for the preparation of such reports. It will be remembered that here the prima facie right to bail contained in section 4 of the Bail Act *does* apply. Alternatively the offender may be remanded to a hospital for a report to be prepared under section 35 of the Mental Health Act 1983. The court is likely to do this either if the offender appears dangerous or if it seems he will not co-operate with the making of a report voluntarily.

In the case of both social enquiry reports and medical reports they are presented to the court but will be disclosed on a confidential basis in advance to the offender's legal representative.

Although reports in both the instances so far considered are made by order **47.08**
of the court it should not be forgotten that it is always open to the legal representative of an offender himself to commission suitable reports. This would pre-eminently be the case where it is already apparent that the prosecution have medical evidence to the effect that the offender should be committed to a secure hospital. It may be that the offender is meanwhile receiving treatment from his own consultant who may be prepared to make a different recommendation, *e.g.* that the offender could safely be released into the community provided he voluntarily agrees to adopt a certain course of treatment. The possibility of the defence commissioning its own reports should not be overlooked.

One important thing to consider is the stage at which a social enquiry report might be requested. Suppose that an offender has been convicted and there is no special enquiry report available (as there will not normally be in the case of an offender pleading not guilty). One can make a lengthy plea in mitigation as part of which one might suggest that the court ought to obtain more information before finally sentencing the offender.

More usually an attempt will be made to save the court's time by asking the court to form a preliminary view as to whether they would like to have a social enquiry report. This may be done quite early on. The defendant's advocate may simply say that there appear to be matters to do with the offender's upbringing or home circumstances which have contributed to the problems which led to the offence and in view of the relative scarcity of information which is available that the court should obtain social enquiry reports. One can then ask the magistrates for a preliminary indication of whether they are in sympathy with that view. If they are not then one should go ahead and make the full plea in mitigation while still indicating gaps in information which might make the attaining of a report desirable so that the magistrates might reconsider the matter having heard more. If a social enquiry report is then ordered the full plea in mitigation can be made when the report is to hand. It may be that otherwise there will be a great deal of repetition of material which is any way contained in the eventual social enquiry report.

Types of sentence
We shall now consider the types of sentence which the court has the power to **47.09**
impose. It should not be forgotten that sentencing has a number of purposes some of which are mutually contradictory. They are generally considered to be:

DETERRENCE

That by seeing that an accused is detected, convicted and punished in some disagreeable way for a crime like-minded people may be deterred from committing such offences.

RETRIBUTION

To express society's dislike or outrage at the type of conduct for which the offender has been convicted.

PREVENTION

Where the offender is a menace to society then by incarceration he is at least kept out of circulation for the period of that incarceration and society's welfare improved by his being prevented from committing further offences during that time.

REHABILITATION

The desire to reform the offender, to help him to return to ordinary social living and to mend his ways and become a useful member of the community.

In pursuance of these diverse aims sentences may very broadly be classified into two categories namely *tariff* sentences which represent so to speak the "going rate" for the type of crime involved and which look to the punishment pure and simple of the offender and "*individualised*" sentences which look in some way to treat the needs of the offender. The offender's needs will generally be treated by a rehabilitation type sentence, *e.g.* community service or probation, although it should not be overlooked that rehabilitation may on occasion be prompted by something that also appears a deterrent to future misconduct.

We shall now consider the sentences available to the particular courts.

THE CROWN COURT

47.10 The Crown Court may impose any penalty up to the maximum prescribed by law for the offence. Thus in the case of a theft which is punishable under the Theft Act by a penalty of up to ten years imprisonment the court may impose ten years or less and/or a fine of an unlimited amount or any other penalty prescribed by law which is applicable up to the maximum for that type of penalty, *e.g.* community service up to the maximum. Moreover where the Crown Court tries more than one offence in relation to the same offender, it may in principle impose consecutive prison sentences each within the maximum prescribed by statute for the offence or it may make those sentences concurrent so that they run together.

Example:
An offender is charged with theft (maximum ten years) and burglary (maximum 14 years) and is convicted of both. The Crown Court may decide to impose a sentence of two years in respect of the theft, one year in respect of the burglary and make them consecutive. The total term to be served (subject to remission etc.) will be three years. If the court makes the terms concurrent the total term to be served will be two years.

THE MAGISTRATES COURT

The magistrates court has the power to impose a penalty of up to six months   **47.11**
imprisonment and/or a fine of £2,000 for any one offence unless the statutory
maximum for the offence is less than that. An example is careless driving
under Section 3 of the Road Traffic Act 1988 where the maximum punishment is a £1,000 fine and there is no power to imprison. Where magistrates
try more than one offence against the same offender then their total powers
are as follows:

1. If all the offences are summary offences the aggregate total sentence
    imposed must not exceed six months.

2. If however there are two or more offences both triable either way then
    the magistrates may impose up to a total aggregate sentence of 12
    months.

3. If the magistrates convict of one offence triable either way and one
    purely summary offence the maximum is six months.

Which Court?

As we have seen a magistrates court may commit a person to the Crown   **47.12**
Court for trial in the case of an either way offence or an offence triable only
on indictment. In addition however it should be noted that a magistrates
court, after hearing a case triable either way and convicting the offender,
may commit him to the Crown Court for sentence if, on obtaining information about his character/or antecedents it is of the opinion that greater
punishment should be inflicted than it has power to impose. Where this
happens the Crown Court may deal with the defendant as if he had been
convicted on indictment and thus impose a sentence on him up to the
maximum provided by the statute concerned. It should be noted here that
this power, to commit for sentence is only exercisable in the light of information which comes up after conviction in relation to the offender's character
and antecedents. Thus for example if in the course of the summary trial the
magistrates found that there were *features of the offence itself* which made
them take a more serious view of the offender's conduct that would not
permit them to commit for sentence. In other words if in the course of
dealing with an offence say, of theft, it came out that the offender had
carried a loaded firearm with him at the time of the theft this extra feature
would not permit them to commit him to the Crown Court for sentence.

THE POWERS OF ONE COURT TO DEAL WITH SENTENCES IMPOSED BY
OTHERS

(a) *Suspended sentences*

It should be noted that the Crown Court may deal with a suspended or partly   **47.13**
suspended sentence of imprisonment imposed either by that or any other
Crown Court or by any magistrates court. Thus any Crown Court may
decide whether or not to activate a previously imposed suspended or part
suspended sentence on further conviction. A magistrates court however can
only deal with a suspended or part suspended sentence imposed by itself or
by some other magistrates' court.

(b) *Probation*

The Crown Court can deal with an offender who has re-offended whilst on probation no matter which court imposed the probation order. However, if a probation order was made by a magistrates court the Crown Court's sentencing powers in respect of the breach of probation and its powers of re-sentencing in respect of the original offence are limited to those of the magistrates. A magistrates court can in general only deal with probation orders imposed either by itself or by some other magistrates court, and in the case of other magistrates courts the consent of the supervising court must be obtained. This is not generally a difficult matter and consents may be obtained by relatively informal means.

Sentencing offenders over 21 years of age

Imprisonment

47.14   A person of 21 years or over may as we have seen be sentenced to imprisonment by the Crown Court up to the maximum length of the term fixed by the statute creating the offence in question or by a magistrates court within the limit of six months for any one offence or up to a maximum aggregate of 12 months when dealing with two or more offences triable either way. Time spent in custody before trial and during trial is treated as part of the term of imprisonment. One half of prison sentences of 12 months or less and one third of longer terms of imprisonment (except life imprisonment) is subject to remission for good conduct. In principle this is credited to an offender immediately he arrives at the prison thus, *e.g.* where a sentence of three years is imposed on an offender he knows that in effect he has only to serve two years if he behaves himself. Apart from remission for good conduct there is also a provision whereby the Home Secretary in the light of reports received and acting on the recommendation of the Parole Board may allow release of a prisoner on licence where the prisoner has served six months or one third of his sentence whichever is greater. A prisoner released on parole is in principle on licence for the rest of his life and may be recalled to continue serving his sentence if so required.

A person who has not previously received a custodial sentence and who is not legally represented at the time of sentence cannot be sent to prison unless the person has had the opportunity to apply for legal aid and declines to do so or his application for legal aid has been refused only on the ground of means. This is by virtue of section 21(1) Powers of Criminal Courts Act 1973.

Some general comment on what one should say in a plea of mitigation appears later. Obviously unless there is some very special consideration in the case, (*e.g.* a foreigner who above all fears a deportation order from the court) an immediately effective term of imprisonment is the worst thing that may happen to an offender. The plea in mitigation will generally be aimed above all else at avoiding this.

It will be recalled that we have previously discussed briefly the question of tariff and individualised sentences. Imprisonment for routine offences provides a fair example of tariff sentencing. So let us take the case of a very common type of crime, say house burglary, where the offender breaks a window to get in whilst the occupants are out of the house and steals whatever money he can find, credit cards and some small valuable items.

Such a crime ought in principle to attract a more or less standard "tariff" sentence. Once the court has the tariff sentence in its mind it will then apply its mind to any *aggravating* features, (*e.g.* was the defender known to be armed at the time) and then to any *mitigating* features which the offender's advocate is able to put forward, (*e.g* was it the first offence or did the offender have serious financial pressures at the time which led him to this course of conduct).

Suspended sentences under section 22 of the Powers of Criminal Courts Act 1973

A court which passes a sentence of imprisonment for a term of no more than **47.15** two years may order that it be suspended for a period of between one and two years. This latter period is called "the operational period" and if the offender does not commit an imprisonable offence during that time the suspended sentence lapses. If however he does commit an imprisonable offence during that period the sentence is brought into effect unless the sentencing court for the later offence decides that it would be unjust to do this.

This power is available to both the magistrates court and the Crown Courts although naturally in the magistrates court the period of imprisonment imposed is subject to the maximum powers of the magistrates before described.

A suspended sentence may often be seen by the layman or by the popular press as a very easy option. Headlines of the type "X walks out of court a free man" are not uncommon where somebody has received a suspended sentence. The mood of outrage which this is supposed to express is of course all the greater when the crime has been well publicised or is viewed as being in a particularly bad category. However suspended sentences ought not to be an easy option. In principle the court should approach the matter in two stages. It should first decide whether it wishes to impose a sentence of imprisonment upon the offender and only after it has decided that this is the appropriate course should it then apply its mind quite separately to the second aspect, namely whether the sentence of imprisonment imposed should be immediately effective or suspended.

In what circumstances should a suspended sentence be activated? Suppose that a person convicted of an offence of dishonesty and who has some previous convictions is sentenced to a term of imprisonment for six months suspended for one year. That sentence will be activated if during the year he reoffends unless the court considers it unjust to impose it. Circumstances which might make a court hesitate to impose the original six months term even after a further offence would be where for example the subsequent offence is of a completely different type, say an assault arising out of football hooliganism whereas previous offences have been for dishonesty, or where the second offence happened very late indeed during the operative period, *e.g.* after 11½ months of the year. In principle however a suspended sentence represents something of a "last chance" for an offender and thus ought generally to be activated, in addition of course to any further punishment imposed for the subsequent offence.

The Crown Court has a further power not open to the magistrates court which is a useful addition to the sentencing options. It has the power to impose a *suspended sentence supervision order* under which the offender receives a suspended sentence but in addition there is a condition that he should be under the supervision of a probation officer. To all intents and purposes this may be seen as something like a period of probation allied to a suspended sentence. (It is not otherwise in principle possible to combine probation with another penalty for the same offence as we shall see subsequently.)

Part suspended sentences

47.16   Under section 47 of the Criminal Law Act 1977 a further type of sentence which increases the flexibility of the options available is a part served, part suspended sentence. Under this section where a court passes a sentence of imprisonment of between three months and two years it may order that after an offender has served not less than either 28 days in prison nor more than three quarters of the whole term imposed the balance shall be held in suspense over him for the rest of the period imposed. The court which sentences must indicate the period to be served immediately.

Thereafter if an offender is subsequently convicted of an offence committed during the whole period of the original sentence the part which has been held in suspense will normally be restored in addition to any other penalty for the later offence.

This is a further option designed to give greater flexibility. It may be that a court takes the middle view as between an immediate custodial sentence and suspended sentence and thinks that perhaps a brief taste of real imprisonment together with the rest being held in suspense over the offender's head will provide the most effective combination. Suppose then that the accused is sentenced to two years imprisonment. The court may require that he serve any amount of time between 28 days and 18 months as a term of imprisonment immediately effective and have the balance held in suspense for the period from when he comes out up to the lapse of two years from the date of sentencing. So for example in the present example they might order the accused to serve six months immediately and have the balance held in suspense. In fact the accused would not serve six months but would obtain the usual one third remission for good conduct and would be released after four months. If he then reoffended in the period of the balance then in principle the rest of the sentence would be activated subject to the considerations before referred to in the case of suspended sentences generally.

THE MAGISTRATES' POWERS TO ACTIVATE A SUSPENDED SENTENCE

47.17   It ought finally to be noted that a magistrates court does not have the power to activate a suspended sentence imposed by the Crown Court although it does have the power to activate a suspended sentence imposed by itself or by any other magistrates court. Where an offender comes before the magistrates court whilst still subject to the operational period of a Crown Court suspended sentence the magistrates must either commit the offender in custody or on bail to the Crown Court in relation to that matter or notify the Crown Court in writing of the action they have taken. It is then up to the Crown Court to take action in relation to the offender, if the appropriate judge of the Crown Court so requires. The magistrates may go on to sentence for the new offence which has occurred within the operational period. By not committing the offender to the Crown Court however the

408

magistrates are impliedly indicating that they do not consider it appropriate to activate the sentence.

Fines

A magistrates court may impose an overall maximum of £2,000 per offence **47.18** unless the statute creating the offence prescribes a different figure as the maximum. If the offence is also punishable with imprisonment the statute will indicate whether the fine is alternative to imprisonment or may be imposed with it.

The Crown Court may fine an offender any amount at all unless statute prescribes a maximum. Fines can be imposed as well as or instead of imprisonment.

Fines are obviously an appropriate method of dealing with trivial offences especially motoring offences (in combination with other penalties). They may also be appropriate for offences of dishonesty or even violence where the offences are not serious and the offender has no substantial criminal record. The do however present obvious problems of fairness. For example it is in principle wrong to fine an individual who is only in receipt of welfare benefits since by definition welfare benefits are generally taken to be subsistence level living and it would be wrong to depress a person below even this. Equally however it is wrong that wealthy persons should in effect be able to "buy" their way out of a sentence of imprisonment because of their ability to pay a substantial fine. The proper approach is said to be somewhat the same as in the case of considering a tariff sentence in imprisonment. The court should first make a provisional assessment of what would be an appropriate level of fine for the offence. The court should then consider other mitigating factors than means which might have the effect of reducing this fine. They should then consider the offender's means and the effect of this on the fine which they had in mind to impose. Of course if at that stage they find that he has no means whatsoever they may have to consider an entirely different sentencing option. Regard must be had when imposing a financial penalty to the total financial liability of the offender including any order for costs, any order for compensation to the victim, and the fine.

COMBINING FINES WITH OTHER SENTENCES

A fine for one offence can be combined with most sentences other than **47.19** probation or community service orders or conditional and absolute discharges. If more than one offence is before the court then any combination is permitted, *e.g.* probation on one charge and a fine on another.

Payment of fines is usually permitted by instalments. It is enforced by the clerk of the magistrates court and a defendant may be arrested or summoned before the court and committed to prison for non payment of fines.

Probation

All the sentences so far discussed (with the possible exception of a sus- **47.20** pended sentence supervision order in the Crown Court) are in the nature of tariff sentences. They look to punishment rather than reform. Probation however may be imposed by either magistrates or the Crown Court. Either court dealing with an offender who is 17 or over may *with his consent only* place him on probation for a period of between six months and three years. The nature of probation is that a person must keep in touch with his probation officer and comply with the latter's directions. He must in principle visit the probation officer at times to be specified by the latter. The court may additionally impose conditions in the probation order. Examples of additional conditions might be that the person resides at a fixed address, *i.e.* with his family or some other relative or at a probation hostel, or that he receives treatment for some medical condition or attends a day centre, *i.e.* premises where there are facilities and advice to assist in the rehabilitation of offenders. Also negative requirements may be imposed requiring the person on probation to refrain from certain activities during the term of the probation order.

The probation officer allotted to the person on probation will be one who is attached to the magistrates court area in which the person on probation resides and may therefore be different from the court imposing the sentence. The magistrates court for that area then becomes known as the "supervising court." Failure to comply with the requirements imposed by the probation officer or the order itself may result in the probation officer bringing the offender back before the supervising court and the offender being fined and indeed being re-sentenced for the offence for which he was put on probation. In addition, where a person who is on probation commits a further offence during the subsistence of the order he may be sentenced *de novo* for the original offence as well as for the latter offence, see sections 6–8 Powers of Criminal Courts Act 1973.

Probation should not be combined with any other sentence for the same offence. Although it follows conviction it does not count as a conviction for the purpose of activating any suspended sentence to which the person now on probation is already subject. Probation may however be combined with disqualification or endorsement of a driving licence and with orders for compensation or orders for costs. Moreover if the offender is charged with more than one offence and convicted of them he may be given probation in respect of one offence and some other sentence in relation to the other. It would however clearly be wrong in principle to impose a sentence of immediate imprisonment for one offence and probation for another since this would defeat the purpose of attempting to rehabilitate the offender in the community. Probation cannot be combined with suspended or part suspended sentences by the express provisions of Schedule 9 to the Criminal Law Act 1977.

A probation order, like a suspended sentence is not meant to be an easy option. It should only come about when someone seems to be the kind of person for whom probation would be useful in the sense of assisting his reform or rehabilitation. The consent which must be obtained from the offender must be genuine and must not be obtained, for example, by the judge indicating that the offender either consents or will as an alternative receive a custodial sentence. A probation order is usually made only after some preliminary report or recommendation to the effect that probation would be helpful in the circumstances of an individual's case. It would be most obviously useful for someone who has some discernable social or family problem. It would not for example be imposed upon a mature person who is living in settled family circumstances without any apparent difficulty of adjustment to the community.

If there is a further offence committed during the period of the probation order then when the offender is brought back before the sentencing court or the supervising court the individual may as we have seen be sentenced for the original offence in addition to being sentenced for the new offence. The original probation order may be quashed and another sentence substituted for it or the probation order may be left in force with a fine being imposed for the breach or may be extended for a further term if the accused consents.

Community Service Orders

47.21

Where the court is dealing with an offender aged 16 or over and the offence is an imprisonable one a community service order may be made. This is an order that the person perform without pay work which is deemed to be of value to the community. The order must fix the precise number of hours to be worked and there is a minimum of 40 and a maximum of 240 (120 if the offender is aged only 16). If the offender fails to comply with the order he may be fined up to £400 or the order may be revoked and the offender re-sentenced.

Before such a sentence can be imposed there must be a report from a probation officer indicating that the offender is suitable for the work and that he consents and that appropriate work is available in the locality. The type of work is usually gardening, improving public spaces, decorating old people's homes etc. It must be performed under the supervision of a probation officer.

Whilst there is no prescribed maximum age this sentence is often thought to be appropriate for fairly young offenders. This is especially the case where the offender has been convicted of offences which are unpleasant but not necessarily extremely serious, for example vandalism of some kind. The work is meant to be both a temporary restriction on his liberty and to give him some sense of usefulness and social purpose. A community service order may not be combined with most other penalties for the same offence although it may be combined with disqualification from driving, endorsement of driving licence and orders for compensation and costs. It may however as in the case of probation be combined with other penalties and imposed in conjunction with penalties for another offence where these have been tried together.

Absolute and conditional discharges under section 7 of the Powers of Criminal Courts Act 1973

47.22

The court may impose these penalties in relation to relatively trivial offences. A court dealing with an offender which does not wish to punish him at all, for example because his offence was merely technical may give an absolute discharge. An example would be in the case of a driving offence of strict liability where there is no real moral blame on the defendant. Take for example a defendant who has just had his vehicle serviced by a reputable garage when the brakes suddenly fail. He would be guilty of the offence of driving a car with defective brakes for which no mens rea is required. However in all the circumstances a court would not consider his offence sufficiently blameworthy to impose any punishment and an absolute discharge would suffice.

A conditional discharge is like a somewhat watered down version of a suspended sentence in that if the offender does not offend during the period of the discharge the conditional discharge lapses. For example an individual who is conditionally discharged for a year and commits no further offence is then free of any punishment in respect of the original offence but if he does re-offend then in principle he can be dealt with again for the first offence.

Discharges are imposed where immediate punishment is deemed to be unnecessary and probation is not required by the circumstances. Discharge may be for a period of up to three years.

SENTENCING OFFENDERS AGED BETWEEN 17 AND 20

Custodial sentences

47.23 1. In the case of an offender aged between 17 and 20 a custodial sentence should not be passed on him unless it is the only appropriate method of dealing with the defendant in that:
    (a) the offender appears unlikely to respond to non custodial alternatives; or
    (b) a custodial sentence is necessary for the protection of the public; or
    (c) the offence was so serious that a non custodial sentence is not appropriate. *Moreover*:

2. the accused must be represented or have been given the opportunity to apply for legal aid and failed to do so or legal aid has been refused on the grounds of means. (It is considerably less likely that a person will be refused on the grounds of means within this age group for obvious reasons.) *Moreover*:

3. a social enquiry report should have been obtained unless the circumstances of the case render this unnecessary.

TYPES OF CUSTODIAL SENTENCE

47.24 An offender within these age ranges is sentenced to detention in a Young Offender's Institution. Under section 1A of the Criminal Justice Act 1982 a convicting court may impose such a sentence in respect of an imprisonable offence if it considers that the defendant qualifies. The maximum term is the maximum available to that court in respect of the events in question, in other words a magistrates court may impose detention for up to six months for each offence unless the statute in question prescribes some other maximum, and the Crown Court may impose up to the maximum for the offence in question. The *minimum* term which the court may impose is, however, prescribed and is 21 days.

These orders are broadly subject to the same provisions in respect of remission and release on licence as sentences of imprisonment for persons of 21 or over in adult prisons. In addition it should be noted that the court which imposes a detention order must:

(i) give reasons why the defendant qualifies for an order; and
(ii) explain to the defendant in ordinary language why it is imposing such a detention order.

It should also be noted that the courts have no powers to suspend custodial sentences in respect of persons of under 21. Thus neither suspended nor partly suspended sentences nor a suspended sentence supervision order can be imposed. Accordingly when one is presenting a plea in mitigation for someone within this age group it is worth stressing in the plea in mitigation that if the offender were 21 or over the option of a suspended sentence would be available to the court and that therefore the court might consider that this offender merits a "last chance" by virtue of some non custodial sentence since the courts do not have the option of suspending the sentence which they might otherwise impose.

Attendance Centre Orders

The court dealing with an offender under the age of 21 for an imprisonable **47.25** offence may make an attendance centre order if

1. the court has been notified that there is a suitable centre available; and

2. the offender has not previously received a custodial sentence.

The number of hours attendance must be fixed by the court. It must be at least 12 and not more than 36.

Attendance centres are generally run by police officers in their leisure time. There is a certain amount of discipline and physical exercise and perhaps, depending on availability of staff, handicraft. The aim is partly to deprive the defender of leisure time but also to encourage more sensible use of leisure. Often such centres are held on Saturday afternoons. Although not primarily intended for football hooligans it has occurred to magistrates that by making attendance centre orders for one hour at a time over successive Saturdays they do have the power to prevent an offender attending football matches for virtually an entire season. More commonly attendance centre orders in two hour sessions are imposed.

It should also be noted that an attendance centre order may be made for default in paying a fine or breach of probation or supervision order.

Non-custodial penalties for offenders aged 17 to 20

1. Such offenders may be fined up to the same maximum as an adult (an **47.26** attendance centre order may be imposed for non payment of a fine in addition to any other powers).

2. A community service order may be made in respect of an offender within this age group with his consent and subject to the same conditions as previously described.

3. Probation may be imposed with the consent of a person in the 17–20 age group.

4. Absolute and conditional discharges may be imposed upon offenders within this age group, in the same circumstances and subject to the same criteria as in the case of offenders aged 21 or more.

Other orders, including compensation and costs

DISQUALIFICATION FROM DRIVING

The Road Traffic Acts and the Road Traffic Offenders Act 1988 provide a **47.27** code for penalties in the case of criminal offences committed in connection with vehicles. In essence there are two types of offences namely:

1. Those punishable by disqualification which may be either mandatory or discretionary.

2.   Those where in addition to some other penalty imposed, (*e.g.* a fine) the offender's driving licence must be endorsed with a certain number of penalty points as prescribed in The Road Traffic Offenders Act 1988. In some cases the offence, however committed, is subject to a prescribed number of penalty points, (*e.g.* using a motor vehicle with defective brakes—three points), in others there is a band of penalty points prescribed and the court may impose any number of points within that band depending on the gravity of the offence, *e.g.* careless driving which may vary in circumstances from one isolated act of inattention to something only just short of recklessness and a band of between three and nine points is prescribed for such an offence.

In principle when within a period of three years the individual has endorsed on his licence a total of 12 penalty points or more he must be disqualified for at least six months unless there are certain circumstances which make the court think it appropriate not to disqualify him.

That is an outline of the code and we shall now consider the provisions in somewhat more detail.

Disqualification

47.28   Certain offences carry *mandatory* disqualifications, *e.g.*

1.   causing death by reckless driving;

2.   reckless driving committed within three years of a previous conviction for reckless driving or causing death by reckless driving;

3.   offences connected with driving with excessive alcohol in the blood or when unfit through drugs.

Secondly in general terms where an offence carries obligatory *endorsement, e.g.* careless driving, there is a *discretion* in the court to disqualify the defendant for that offence alone. They would normally only do so if the facts of the offence were very gross indeed. Reckless driving is perhaps the best example here since it does not carry obligatory disqualification but may be committed in circumstances varying from the merely rash to the positively homicidal.

47.29   Quite separately from the above, an offender may be disqualified under the *points system* still often called the "totting up" system, where when an offender is convicted and a penalty imposed which involves the number of points endorsed on the offender's licence within the preceding three years totalling 12 or more the court must in principle disqualify him for at least six months unless it thinks it fit not to do so.

Endorsement of driving licences

47.30   A driving licence must be *endorsed* with the appropriate number of penalty points within the limits set out in Part II of the Road Traffic Offenders Act 1988 unless there are circumstances permitting the court not to do so (to which we shall come in due course).

If the offender is disqualified for the *offence itself* (rather than under the totting up provisions) then the licence is not endorsed with further penalty points although particulars of the offence for which the offender is disqualified are recorded on the licence. In other words a person who is being disqualified for a specific offence does not receive any penalty points.

Example:

Suppose that an offender who has a clean licence is disqualified for a particularly bad act of reckless driving and the period of disqualification is one year. Reckless driving carries ten penalty points generally. However in the present case these are not endorsed on the offender's licence. Thus at the end of a year's disqualification the offender has no penalty points on his licence and if when he begins driving again he soon commits a speeding offence which carries three penalty points he is not subject to disqualification for exceeding 12 penalty points as he would otherwise have been. If the court had not punished the reckless driving by disqualification then the 10 penalty points would have been imposed and consequently when committing any subsequent endorsable offence carrying two points or more he would have been liable to disqualification within the period of three years under the points system.

It should be noted that where the defendant is convicted of two or more endorsable offences which arise out of offences committed on the same occasion then only the highest number of penalty points will be endorsed and not the cumulative total, *e.g.* suppose an offender commits the offence of taking a vehicle without the owner's consent (eight points) and speeding (three points) he only acquires eight penalty points and not 11.

For what period should the offender be disqualified?

1. If the offence carries *obligatory* disqualification then generally this is for **47.31** at *least* 12 months. Above that period then the court must weigh a number of important factors. It has been stressed in many cases that the court should be careful not to impose too long a disqualification from driving. In the case of young offenders particularly who are "car mad" the effect of over-lengthy disqualification is to make them lose all hope of recovering their driving licence and to merely invite them to commit offences of driving whilst disqualified. This is not to say however that very lengthy disqualifications may not in some situations be appropriate. Indeed disqualification for life is possible and in some cases may be rightly applied.

   It should also be noted that an offender who has been disqualified for a longer period than two years may apply to the court for the disqualification to be lifted. The prosecution must naturally be informed of the application and there is a hearing in open court at which the prosecution will describe the circumstances of the original offence and may put forward their objections.

2. Under the totting up points system a disqualification is generally for *at* **47.32** *least* six months. It may be for a longer period within the court's discretion.

It should also be noted that periods of disqualification now always run concurrently and not consecutively. Therefore if an offender is convicted of a number of offences, whether or not committed on the same occasion, and is liable to disqualification either under the totting up system and/or for the offences themselves any disqualifications imposed must run concurrently. Of course the total length of the sentences imposed will affect the court's overall view of the gravity of the situation and thus whilst sentences of say 18 months disqualification and six months disqualifications may be imposed for different offences the longer penalty will reflect the court's overall view of what is appropriate for the whole "disqualification package" so to speak.

Finally it should be remarked that an offender cannot be disqualified in his absence. Thus where an offender is given the opportunity to plead guilty by post, say to an offence of speeding he will do so while sending his licence to the court as is required. If the points to be imposed for speeding take the points on his licence to a total of more than 12 then he is prima facie liable for disqualification. It does not inevitably mean that he will be disqualified because there may be circumstances in which the court will see fit not to impose that ultimate penalty but certainly in such a case the matter will be adjourned to enable the defendant to attend court.

When may disqualification or endorsement not be imposed?

47.33 Where disqualification for the offence itself (rather than under the penalty points system) is *obligatory* or endorsement of penalty points is obligatory they must on the face of it be imposed. However in either case if the defendant can show "special reasons" for either not disqualifying or for not imposing the endorsement at all then the court may decline to do so. "Special reasons" however in this context must relate to the circumstances of the very offence *not* to the offender's personal circumstances and must not therefore be in the nature of mitigation generally. A good example of a reason which might justify non-disqualification is in the case of a drink-driving offence where the offender's orange juice was "laced" with vodka without his knowledge so that he is taken just over the legal limit (if of course he had any reason to suspect that he was drunk and his drink had been laced he could not argue this if he had continued to drive). Or that in the case of an offence of reckless driving which would be the second within three years and thus mandatorily disqualifiable that the offender was driving someone to hospital in an emergency when the act of recklessness occurred. Likewise in the case of a speeding offence where endorsement of penalty points is obligatory, if the offender admitted the offence but was able to show that he was driving a dangerously ill passenger to hospital at high-speed the magistrates, whilst finding guilt proved might well impose only an absolute discharge and no endorsement.

It must be said that the courts have not been eager to find special reasons established. Evidence on oath must be given by the offender in each case and it is not sufficient for these matters to be advanced merely in a plea in mitigation. The offender may well be subject to searching cross-examination by the prosecution. Although the prosecution do not generally concern themselves at all with sentence this is one occasion where they do have an overriding duty to see that justice is done and that any reasons put forward as justifying non endorsement or non disqualification are thoroughly examined.

In the case of discretionary disqualification, (*e.g.* for a first offence of reckless driving) then general mitigation can be advanced in relation to any proper matter, either the circumstances of the offence or the offender's personal circumstances with a view to avoiding disqualification entirely or of obtaining a reduction in the period imposed.

Disqualification under the penalty points system

If an offender is sentenced for an offence and penalty points are imposed which take his total to over 12 within the relevant period of three years he should in principle be disqualified for six months or longer. However an offender need not be disqualified if there are "grounds for mitigating the normal consequences of the conviction." This is not the same as the case previously described where there are special reasons for not imposing penalty points or an endorsement *at all*. In the former case there was a necessity for those matters to involve the circumstances of the *offence itself*. However in connection with non disqualification under the penalty point system the court may have regard to all the circumstances including the personal circumstances of the offender. **47.34**

Part II of the Road Traffic Offenders Act 1988 however provides that a court in deciding on this matter may only take into account hardship to the offender caused by loss of his licence where the hardship is "exceptional." Unfortunately there is no definition of "exceptional hardship" and little guidance in case law. Circumstances which under previous law were considered suitable for avoiding the consequences of disqualification often involved, *e.g.* loss of one's job because it depended on one's driving licence or sometimes because of the remoteness of the place of work which required a car to reach; or the need to have a vehicle for important family reasons, *e.g.* transport of a disabled relative. Such things might still be sufficient. Hardship which is less than exceptional, *e.g.* for a private individual who does not need his motor vehicle for his job and who would be merely inconvenienced by having to use public transport would seem therefore not to be an adequate reason for not imposing disqualification. In addition the court may not take into account the *triviality* of the present offence. Thus the fact that the speeding offence presently committed only involved exceeding the speed limit by say five m.p.h. would not in itself be ground for mitigating the normal consequences. If three points imposed in this case take the offender past a total of 12 then he ought still in principle to be disqualified. **47.35**

It may well be that a person appears before the court and has penalty points imposed which take his total over 12 but is able to persuade the magistrates that there is exceptional hardship and thus is not disqualified. What if a further offence is committed still within the period which would take his penalty points up by a further number? The 1988 Act provides that a person who has been excused disqualification because of mitigating circumstances on a previous occasion may not rely on any circumstances which the court took into account on that occasion. So for example one cannot avoid disqualification on two consecutive hearings merely by arguing that loss of one's licence will involve loss of one's job. In such a situation if that is the only mitigating circumstance disqualification will be imposed on the second occasion. Accordingly the court should carefully record the mitigating factors it found present when dealing with an offender so that these are available in any future case. All too often these mitigating factors are recorded in extremely short summary form and it may well therefore be the case that one can give a fuller version of the reasons on the second occasion.

417

It also leads to the somewhat strange conclusion that if one has two separate excellent grounds for avoiding the normal consequences of the totting up system it would usually only be wise to put one of them forward. Suppose for example that a person desperately needed his car because he lived in a remote place and needed to transport a disabled relative to and from hospital and that he needed his driving licence for his job. If his penalty points were taken over 12 he would be well advised to put forward only one of these cogent reasons so that in the event of him falling foul of the law on a further occasion he could then use the other.

47.36 It ought finally to be repeated that in driving offences disqualification and endorsement may be combined with most other penalties. Very commonly they are combined with fines, often of a fairly standard amount following recommendations of magisterial bodies. It should not be overlooked however that driving penalties may be imposed in addition to custodial sentences, for example in the case of offenders who take motor vehicles without their owner's consent where both an eight-point endorsement and custodial penalty would not be uncommon.

The court may also consider the following orders which may be imposed on an offender either additionally to or instead of other forms of punishment.

COMPENSATION ORDERS

47.37 Under section 35 of the Powers of Criminal Courts Act 1973 (as amended by section 104 of the Criminal Justice Act 1988) a court may order compensation for any personal injury, loss or damage, (including payment for funeral expenses or bereavement) resulting from any offence (including any offences taken into consideration) when imposing any other penalty, or instead of imposing any other penalty on an offender. However a court cannot make any order in respect of injury, loss or damage arising out of the presence of a motor vehicle on a road unless:

    (i) the offence concerned was one under the Theft Act 1968 and damage occurred to the property in question whilst it was out of the owner's possession, (*e.g.* damage to a motor vehicle which was taken away for joy riding); or

    (ii) the offender was uninsured at the time and compensation is not payable under the Motor Insurers Bureau Schemes.

The court may make an order up to any amount in the Crown Court or a maximum of £2,000 in respect of any one offence in the magistrates court but the court must have regard to the offender's means in the same way as they must have regard to those means in relation to imposing a fine.

A compensation order may be made as an alternative to dealing with the offender in any other way and thus if the offender has not got sufficient income to pay both the fine and compensation the court ought to impose a compensation order to ensure that the victim is compensated. Compensation orders are enforced by the court in the same way as a fine with the ultimate penalty of imprisonment for non payment.

FORFEITURE ORDERS

Under section 43 of the Powers of Criminal Courts Act 1973 where the court **47.38** convicts an offender of an offence which is punishable on indictment with two years imprisonment or more it may order forfeiture of any property which was in the offender's possession or control at the time of apprehension if the property was used for committing or facilitating any offence or was intended by the offender to be used for that purpose.

Thus for example the owner may be ordered to forfeit a car which has been used to transport stolen goods.

CONFISCATION ORDERS

Under section 71 of the Criminal Justice Act 1988 a Crown Court may in **47.39** addition to dealing with a defendant in any other way make a confiscation order in respect of the proceeds of the crime. In order for this provision to apply the defendant must have benefited from the relevant offence (including any offences taken into consideration) in a sum of at least £10,000. If he is convicted of more than one offence then the benefit of all the offences is taken into account. The amount that can be ordered is the benefit gained, (*i.e.* at least £10,000 must be involved for this order to be made).

COSTS

A convicted offender may be ordered to pay costs to the prosecution as **47.40** earlier described.

The Plea in Mitigation

We have now considered the total package of orders which may be made **47.41** against a convicted defendant. We have considered penalties on the defendant, the making of compensation orders and the question of costs has previously been discussed in connection with the financing of criminal litigation.

It is now appropriate to consider the plea in mitigation which will be made in an attempt to persuade the court to impose some lesser sentence than the tariff for the offence might appear to warrant. The task of an advocate making a plea in mitigation is to persuade the court to view the offender or the offence in the most favourable light possible. The ultimate purpose is so to speak to get the offender as light a penalty as possible. From this point of view an immediate custodial sentence would generally be regarded as the most drastic penalty that could be imposed and it will often be the primary concern to avoid this. However even if a custodial sentence is inevitable it may still be important to make a full plea in mitigation so that the term imposed may be as short as possible.

It is best generally to divide a plea in mitigation into four sections and to treat these separately. This avoids putting forward a mish-mash of unrelated matters which albeit that they are all favourable to a defendant may give a sometimes unstructured impression. The four categories which one should always seek to discuss are:

1.   The offence itself;
2.   The offender;

3. The offender's conduct in relation to the investigation of the crime and the proceedings; and

4. The capacity to reform

THE OFFENCE ITSELF

47.42 Here one should see what can be found in the immediate circumstances of the offence which makes it less serious than it might at first appear. A good example would be in the case of an assault where the offender had been subject to considerable provocation. One should not put forward one's mitigation so enthusiastically as to appear to indicate something which is in effect a defence, *e.g.* as in the previous example to suggest that it was self defence rather than provocation. To do this is obviously to go behind either the plea of guilty and re-open the case or to impugn the jury's verdict. An example of something which might mitigate a dishonesty offence might be drink. This has to be advanced with some care. It is not unknown for example for sentencers to have a view of drink which make them view it as an aggravating factor rather than as mitigation. It goes without saying of course that in any driving offence drink is unlikely to be a mitigating factor. It may well be that on the facts of the case the element of drink can be presented in a favourable light because as a general rule the courts view it as some mitigation that an offence was committed on impulse rather than premeditatedly. Thus for example on a charge of say stealing £100 if the sum was left lying around and taken on a rash impulse the offence would be regarded as rather less serious than for someone to procure the same amount by a cunning and premeditated plan. Since drink may well affect impulsiveness to that extent it may be a mitigating factor. It ought to be mentioned here that an advocate should be alive not only to *mitigating* factors in an offence. *Aggravating* factors may also be important and it can be particularly vital to try and dispose of apparently aggravating factors. The worst aggravating factors are breach of trust or corruption of a junior. Thus for instance a senior employee who handles his employer's money would be considered to have committed a more serious offence if he stole a sum of money than in the case of the same theft between strangers. Likewise if in the same instance the senior employee had involved another junior employee who had no previous criminal record in the crime this would be a further aggravating feature. It is important not to ignore such matters and hope that the court will not notice but to address them and do everything possible to explain them.

THE OFFENDER HIMSELF

47.43 This is the point at which the advocate has the opportunity to discuss at length and in detail the personal circumstances of the offender. It will be remembered that if there is a risk of a custodial sentence, by this stage probably the advocate will have suggested that a social enquiry report be obtained. This may in itself set out a number of matters relevant to the plea in mitigation. It may lengthily rehearse the offender's upbringing, education and background, and family circumstances and deal with personal problems. Bad advocates often merely parrot these, indeed sometimes actually reading them out despite the fact that the report is already before the magistrates. This is clearly boring and bad practice. One should seek to give the magistrates new information not already contained in the social enquiry report and if the social enquiry report is very full then one should refer the magistrates to it and stress or expand on the more favourable matters revealed. Matters which might be treated as being mitigation would be some of the following if applicable:

Previous record

The best possible mitigation is no criminal record. It always gives a court **47.44** pause for thought even in the case of a relatively serious crime that it is the offender's first offence. In addition to mere absence of criminal record however, positive features about the individual ought to be put forward such as any record of public service, service in the forces, good employment record, and settled family background. If the offence is one of dishonesty, reference to any positions of trust which the offender has had and faithfully carried out in the past, *e.g.* that he has handled a great deal of money for his employer for many years without shortages or discrepancies.

If an offender does have a criminal record then it is important to deal with this so far as possible. For example it may be possible to look back through the record and point to things which favour a particular course of action. Thus if for example there are lengthy gaps in the record and these correspond to periods of employment and the offender is presently in employment this might be a feature worth putting forward. It might tend to show that his offences are born out of frustration and financial hardship when he is unemployed. Equally if he has received some particular kind of penalty in the past and this seems to have worked for him, *e.g.* a period of probation where he kept out of trouble for some time or even, at the worst, a suspended sentence which had the desired effect this should be stressed. Another point worth making is that if the bulk of his criminal record is for one particular type of offence and the present offence is of a completely different type then arguably one can suggest that the court ought to treat him as a first offender. Suppose for example that the offender has a bad criminal record for, say, offences of violence arising out of fights whilst under the influence of drink and the present offence is one of straightforward dishonesty. Arguably the court ought not to pay too much attention to his record.

Circumstances at the time of the crime

The offender's circumstances at the time of the crime should be described to **47.45** the court if relevant. For example if the offence is one of dishonesty and occurred at a time of grave financial pressure on the defendant especially if this was caused through circumstances beyond his own control, *e.g.* having been made redundant. Health problems of himself or his loved ones may also be relevant, for example alcoholism or drug dependency, although the circumstances of this latter must be treated with caution. Anything which in any way affected him at the time and made him more vulnerable or susceptible to pressures is worth stressing such as bereavement or some personal tragedy. Perhaps connected to this is the next point.

The effect of his offence and punishment an others

The effect on others of his crime or potential punishment ought to be **47.46** stressed. It is of course a commonplace that if an offender goes to prison he will lose his job. Magistrates will hear this argument very often but it is still one worth putting forward. Another argument commonly advanced is that when considering the penalty to be imposed on the offender the court should have regard to its effect on society as a whole. Thus if he loses his job by being sent to prison it may be unlikely he will easily obtain another one, so an additional point to make is that his family will be reduced to welfare benefits whilst he is there and indeed indefinitely afterwards. The cost to society of an individual being kept in prison has been variously estimated but the sheer weekly cost of providing prison facilities alone is said to be over £300 depending on the type of institution in which he is detained. When one takes into account the additional cost to society of keeping his family the cost is a very significant one. It has indeed been pointed out by one leading criminologist that it would in purely financial terms be considerably better for the state to pay persistent offenders to take extended holidays abroad rather than to imprison them in England. A sentencing court is unlikely to take great specific notice of the financial argument when presented in these terms though it will of course always bear in mind the relative undesirability in every case of imprisoning an individual in terms of prison over-crowding and cost.

Other penalties suffered

47.47 Linked to this point of effect on his family, one should stress other penalties which the offence has occasioned of a non-judicial nature such as personal humiliation in the light of publicity, loss of job or status, perhaps break up of his family if for example his wife has left him because of the offence, loss of earnings in the future and possibly the effect of being totally unemployable in his chosen job, *e.g.* where he was employed as a cashier and dishonesty has led to his dismissal and the certainty that he will never again obtain a position of trust.

Time in custody

47.48 Finally one might stress, if one hopes to avoid a custodial sentence, any period in custody which he has already spent in consequence of the investigation of the crime or remands. For example if he has already spent some weeks in prison before conviction it might be suggested that this is in itself sufficient penalty and represents sufficient of a shock to him to amount to an effective deterrent.

CONDUCT IN RELATION TO THE INVESTIGATION OF THE CRIME AND CRIMINAL PROCEEDINGS

47.49 It is always a potent feature in favour of an offender that he has co-operated in the prompt and efficient disposal of his case. This may take two aspects:

Co-operation with the police

47.50 The earlier that this co-operation commences the better. The best case of all would obviously be relatively rare, that is a person who was not even a suspect but walked into a police station and made a full confession. Whilst this is unlikely, prompt co-operation with the police from the onset of questioning is almost as good, for example an offender who makes a full confession leading to the recovery of stolen property in early course. The fact that property is recovered for the victim of the crime is a potent consideration in favour of an offender. So is giving evidence against, or giving information leading to conviction of his associates in crime, *e.g.* a thief who names the handler or vice versa. When advising a client one should leave this matter very much up to the client himself. Obviously giving information leading to the arrest and conviction of one's criminal associates may lead to a lesser penalty from the court, but it may have certain undesirable consequences of a personal nature in relation to the behaviour of those former accomplices towards one's client as and when they are all at large again.

Proceedings in court

A guilty plea at the earliest opportunity is also a powerful mitigating factor. **47.51** It saves a great deal of the court's time, costs to the Legal Aid fund, and may also save embarrassment to the victims of the offence especially in sexual cases. In an appropriate case a guilty plea is said to lead in the case of a custodial sentence to a reduction on the apparent tariff figure of up to one third and guilty plea together with giving useful information about one's co-offenders may, in the case of serious crime anyway, lead to a reduction in sentence of more than 50 per cent. (see *R.* v. *Lowe* (1977) 66 Cr.App.R. 122, 11½ years reduced to five years on appeal because of such mitigating factors).

CAPACITY FOR REFORM

First it should be mentioned that the showing of contrition is an important **47.52** factor. This can of course hardly be combined with conviction after a not guilty plea and must realistically only be urged in the case of a guilty plea. Factors which tend to show this might be that the offender has already made voluntary restitution to the victim in an appropriate case or has made a serious offer to do so by instalments and commenced paying them. Care should be taken to ensure that this is not seen as a sign of insincerity or an attempt to "buy off" a sentence.

Other circumstances which show capacity to reform might be something in the offender's personal life which is about to change for the better to show that he is prepared to take on a more responsible role in society or in the family context. Thus factors such as finding a new job after a long period of unemployment; being about to get married; becoming pregnant in the case of a female offender; that one's wife or co-habitee is pregnant in the case of a male offender (though this latter may be something of a double-edged weapon; circuit judges are not unknown who actually hold the openly expressed view that criminals should not procreate and thus this might in the eyes of such a person tend to be an aggravating factor). Indeed an important general point to make is that when one is considering a plea in mitigation one should have regard, if one knows it, to the personality and foibles of the individual who is to pass sentence. The plea in mitigation should be structured and concise. It is better to avoid cliches especially the phrases "victim of society" and "he stands at the crossroads of his life" (unless at least two of the magistrates have beards or can otherwise be proved to be *Guardian* readers).

CHARACTER EVIDENCE

47.53 Those are the main matters which one will urge in a plea in mitigation. It is also open to the advocate to call character witnesses. The rules of evidence do not strictly apply at this stage and of course the accused's character is now known to the court. It is generally considered not of much use to call a close relative such as a mother or wife since she will inevitably say the same thing namely that the accused has always been a good responsible and loving son/husband and deserves a last chance. There may be cases however where a suitably impassioned plea can have some effect and certainly does no harm. Much better is to call as a character witness someone such as an employer who is willing to hold the accused's job for him despite his knowledge of the conviction. The best of all of course and, perhaps surprisingly, by no means unknown, is to call as a character witness the employer against whom the theft was committed to say that notwithstanding this the employer will give the accused another chance. Where an employer is prepared to make this commitment it is a very powerful argument to put to the court that the court ought also to give the accused this further chance and not impose a custodial sentence.

Three final matters ought to be mentioned.

THE USE OF THE SOCIAL ENQUIRY REPORT

47.54 As has been previously suggested the social enquiry report may often contain a great deal of useful background information. It is pointless to read this to the court and one should merely refer the court to the relevant passages. To an extent a social enquiry report does a good deal of the mitigator's work for him. Commonly social enquiry reports end with a recommendation for a particular type of sentence. There must be such a recommendation as to suitability for a *community service order* where that is to be imposed and in the case of probation also if a court had this in mind as a potential way of dealing with the offender a social enquiry report would normally have been ordered as a matter of course. Where the probation officer who will have carried out such a report does in fact make a recommendation for treatment of the offender by one or other particular type of sentence and this is acceptable to the offender then one may at the end of the plea in mitigation suggest that the court adopt the course recommended. Indeed the whole procedure of a plea in mitigation may in an appropriate case be short-circuited by an early enquiry of the court as to whether they would agree to adopt the recommendation of the probation officer. If they indicate that they will then no more need be said.

If the probation officer makes no particular recommendation for a type of sentence then in some courts this will be treated as equivalent to the probation officer saying that there appears to be no other method of dealing with the offender than custody. In such a case one needs to try even harder in a plea in mitigation to avoid the offender receiving a custodial sentence. It is fair to say that whilst most courts regard the contents of a social enquiry report with great seriousness it is a notorious fact that individual probation officers may on occasions recommend wholly unrealistic alternatives, *e.g.* in a very serious case may recommend probation where it is clearly inappropriate. If the advocate independently forms the view that the probation officer's recommendation is hopelessly optimistic then it may well not be enough simply to ask the court to adopt that recommendation but a full plea in mitigation stressing all possible factors in the defendant's favour may need to be made.

SHOULD THE ADVOCATE RECOMMEND ANY PARTICULAR TYPE OF SENTENCE?

In cases where the probation officer in a social enquiry report is not recommending any particular type of sentence there is nothing to stop the advocate from doing so or anyway from recommending one different to that recommended by the probation officer. Thus one may suggest to the court that a fine is an appropriate way of dealing with the offender and in that case details of the offender's means and outgoings should be given. Whilst one may recommend the *type* of sentence it is not generally considered appropriate to recommend a specific term or amount. One would not for example suggest to a court that a case merited say nine months imprisonment rather than some longer term or a fine of any particular amount. One merely recommends a type of sentence and asks the court to impose the minimum it sees fit. In this connection and in connection with mitigation generally it is appropriate to mention one further matter.   **47.55**

DEFERRED SENTENCE

Advocates who make pleas in mitigation often make some relatively optimistic claims on behalf of offenders concerning some change in lifestyle and capacity to reform. For example it may be suggested that a person will stay out of trouble if he is able to get a job and that he has an interview for a job in a few days time. Likewise claims may be made that an offender will pay compensation to the victim of the offence.   **47.56**

   The court has a power under section 1 of the Powers of Criminal Courts Act 1973 to defer passing any sentence for a period of up to six months. The main reason why a court might defer sentence are to enable it to take into account the offender's conduct after conviction and any change in circumstances that comes about.

   When a court defers sentence the offender is released until the date when he is instructed to reappear, which should preferably be fixed by the court there and then. Moreover in principle the offender should return to be dealt with by the same judge or magistrates who have dealt with the case hitherto. When the offender does reappear before the court he or his advocate will be expected to explain what has occurred in the meantime in particular with regard to any promises or undertakings given on the previous occasion. In principle if the offender has carried out his promise, *e.g.* to obtain a job or pay compensation and has not meanwhile reoffended he should be safe from a custodial sentence. However merely staying out of trouble on its own is not sufficient to ensure that an offender will not be sent to prison. It is also important to consider whether the offender has done the best he can to change his lifestyle in the way suggested on his behalf at the mitigation stage. If the sentencing court does impose an immediate custodial sentence it should state precisely in what respect it considers there has been a failure to comply with the underakings previously given.

48. Appeals in Criminal Cases

Appeals from the magistrates court to the crown court

AGAINST CONVICTION

48.01 A defendant who has been convicted in the magistrates court following a plea of not guilty may appeal against either conviction or sentence or both to the Crown Court. This is done by giving notice of appeal in writing to the clerk of the magistrates court concerned and to the prosecution within 21 days of sentence being passed. The notice of appeal need not go into any detail on the grounds and indeed it is usual to use a pro forma form of appeal which merely states that "the defendant proposes to appeal on the grounds that the magistrates erred in fact and in law in convicting him," or "the defendant appeals against sentence on the grounds that the sentence imposed was excessive in all the circumstances."

There is no filtering mechanism as with appeals to the Court of Appeal so there is no discretion to refuse to accept the appeal nor is any application for leave to appeal necessary. If notice of appeal is not lodged within the prescribed time there is a discretion to extend the time for giving notice of appeal by application to a Crown Court judge. Reasons for the lateness in appealing need to be supplied.

It should be remembered that if an immediate custodial sentence has been passed on a convicted person a bail application pending appeal may be made to the magistrates court although the presumption in favour of bail does not apply. Accordingly in those circumstances a verbal notice of appeal should be given immediately sentence is passed, but this must still be supplemented by a written notice within the prescribed period.

The appeal is heard by a circuit judge sitting with an even number of magistrates (usually two) but with no jury. The form of the appeal is a complete re-hearing. The parties may call the same evidence as in the court below in the hope that the higher court will take a different view of it or may call different evidence including not calling witnesses whom they did call in the court below. Matters of law may also be argued and new or different points of law may be raised.

AGAINST SENTENCE

48.02 A person who has pleaded *guilty* in the magistrates court may appeal against *sentence* to the Crown Court by the same procedure but not generally against conviction. However it may be open to a person to argue that his plea of guilty was equivocal, that is to say that although he pleaded guilty matters were put before the court then or subsequently, probably as mitigation, which actually undermined the plea. For example an accused who when charged with theft says "guilty but I only took it because I thought it was mine." In these circumstances the words which accompany the plea are such as to indicate a full defence and the plea should not have been accepted. In such a case an appeal against a conviction may be heard and the case will then be remitted by the Crown Court to the magistrates court with the direction that the matter be treated as if a plea of not guilty had been entered. There will then be a re-trial before the magistrates court. It should be noted however that this jurisdiction only applies where there is something which occurs at the time which renders the plea clearly equivocal. If it later comes to light that the defendant had an arguable defence which was unknown to him at the time he is generally bound by his plea.

POWERS OF THE CROWN COURT

The powers of the Crown Court when hearing an appeal from a magistrates **48.03** court are contained in section 48 of the Supreme Court Act 1981. The Crown Court may, having heard the appeal:—

1. confirm, reverse or vary the decision appealed against; or

2. remit the matter with the court's opinion to the magistrates (for example where it found that the plea was equivocal); or

3. make any such other order as the court considers just, and by such order exercise any power that the magistrates might have exercised (*e.g.* make appropriate orders for costs); or

4. award any sentence whether lesser or greater than that which the magistrates actually awarded provided that the sentence is one which the magistrates' court had power to award. It should be noted therefore that there is a possibility of an increase in sentence which may act as some deterrent to frivolous appeals.

Finally one should note that it is important not to confuse the procedure for appeals to a Crown Court with the powers of the Crown Court where magistrates *commit* an accused to the Crown Court *for sentence* having tried the case summarily, under section 38 of the Magistrates Courts Act 1980. Where this occurs the Crown Court has the power to impose any sentence up to the maximum sentence permitted by law for the offence in question.

Finally for the sake of clarification it ought to be noted that only the defendant has the right to appeal to the Crown Court.

Appeals from the magistrates' court of the Queen's Bench Division Divisional Court

As we have previously seen, an appeal to the Crown Court may be on any **48.04** matter of fact or law and brought by the defendant alone. There is an alternative avenue of procedure which is open to *either side* and this is provided under section 111 of the Magistrates Courts Act 1980 which provides that "any person who is a party to any proceedings before a Magistrates Court or is aggrieved by the conviction, order, determination or other proceeding of the court may question the proceeding on the ground that it is wrong in law or in excess of jurisdiction."

The appeal may therefore be made by either party, prosecution or defence as long as it concerns a matter of law or an allegation of excess of jurisdiction. The procedure commences by requiring the magistrates to "state a case" for the opinion of the High Court. The aggrieved party applies in writing to the magistrates within 21 days of the acquittal or conviction or sentencing and the application may be by letter and should identify the question of law on which the High Court's opinion should be sought. The application is sent to the magistrates' clerk.

A "statement of case" is prepared by the court which will outline the facts called in question, state the facts which the magistrates found and then state the magistrates' finding on the points of law in question, listing any authority cited and finally posing the question for the High Court. The case is drafted by the magistrates' clerk in consultation with the magistrates. Drafts of the case are sent to the parties who may suggest amendments. The final form of "case" is then sent to the appellant who must lodge it at the Crown Office of the Royal Courts of Justice in London. Notice must then be given to the respondent with a copy of the case.

The appeal is subsequently heard by the Divisional Court of the Queen's Bench Division in London in which at least two judges but more usually three sit. Evidence is not called and the appeal takes the form of legal argument for the appellant and respondent based solely upon the facts stated in the case.

The Divisional Court may reverse, affirm or amend the magistrates' decision or may remit the matter back to the magistrates with its opinion, e.g. with a direction that they continue the hearing, convict, acquit or may remit the case to a different bench of magistrates. Costs may be awarded to either party out of central funds.

It should finally be noted that where an individual has been convicted in the magistrates court and appeals to the Crown Court by the procedure previously described there is a subsequent appeal on a matter of law only by way of case stated from the Crown Court to the Divisional Court. This should not be confused with an appeal from the Crown Court after trial on indictment (i.e. before a jury) for which the procedure is as we shall subsequently describe.

Appeals from the Crown Court to the Court of Appeal (Criminal Division)

48.05 A person convicted on indictment may appeal to the Court of Appeal against his conviction by virtue of section 1 of the Criminal Appeal Act 1968.

There is an appeal as of right on a matter of law alone (e.g. that the trial judge misinterpreted a statute). However where the ground of appeal is on a question of fact or of mixed fact and law (for example points of evidence are often mixed fact and law) then appeal can only be made either:

1. with the leave of the trial judge given at the end of the case; or

2. with the leave of the Court of Appeal.

In fact the leave of the trial judge is only rarely sought and most appeals to the Court of Appeal follow leave given by the Court of Appeal itself.

A convicted person who has legal aid for his trial is covered by legal aid for initial advice on appeal and the drafting of the grounds of appeal if his counsel recommends an appeal be pursued. The procedure is a follows:

1. Within 28 days of conviction or sentence the appellant must serve on the

Registrar of Criminal Appeals a notice of application for leave to appeal accompanied by draft grounds of appeal.

2. If the appeal is against conviction then there will probably need to be a transcript provided either of the judge's summing up or perhaps of some part of the evidence at the trial. The court shorthand writer will then be asked by the Registrar of Criminal Appeals to transcribe the appropriate part of his notes.

3. The papers are then put before a single judge who may be either a Lord Justice of Appeal or a High Court Judge sitting as a member of the Court of Appeal. The papers will include the grounds of appeal, transcript and any other relevant documents.

This is a filtering stage at which the single judge considers whether leave ought to be given. If he does grant leave to appeal he will grant legal aid (if necessary) for the hearing itself. If the single judge refuses leave to appeal the appellant has 14 further days in which to service notice upon the Registrar if he wishes to continue with the case, that is to renew the application before the full court. The papers are then put before the full court. If the full court grants leave to appeal they may also grant legal aid for the hearing of the appeal proper.

If the Registrar of Criminal Appeals after a preliminary look at the grounds of appeal considers that the appeal has a prima facie chance of success he may bypass the single judge procedure, grant legal aid himself and list the application for leave to appeal for hearing by the full court. He will notify the prosecution and invite them to be represented and the court will then whilst considering the issue of leave to appeal usually treat the application for leave as the hearing of the substantive appeal.

Appeals to the House of Lords

Under section 33 of the Criminal Appeal Act 1968 either prosecution or **48.06** defence may appeal to the House of Lords from a decision of the Criminal Division of the Court of Appeal provided:

1. The Court of Appeal certifies that the decision involves a point of law of general public importance and

2. Either the Court of Appeal or the House of Lords gives leave to appeal. Such application for leave to appeal should be made immediately after the court's decision or at the latest within 14 days of the decision.

49. How to Pass the Examination

"Nur Lumpen sind bescheiden"

Johann Wolfgang von Goethe

"It's time to stop messing about—show some commitment going forward— get some bodies up there in the box and get the ball over to the far post"

Ron Atkinson

"All God's children love to party"

Little Richard

Success on the Finals course results from bearing in mind, achieving a judicious synthesis of, and putting into effect, the views of the educational thinkers quoted above.

The course: maintaining morale

49.01   The course begins in September and lasts until around the late May Bank Holiday. It is thus considerably longer than the usual degree student year. New material may well be given in lectures until well after Easter. The sheer bulk of material soon becomes depressing and intimidating. By the time the dark days of February have arrived already students will have many many hundreds of pages of notes over all subjects and the course is barely half way through. Moreover the subject-matter of the course may well be found less than enthralling. Many students will find it much less intellectually stimulating and interesting than a degree course. Indeed a student once compared the course to doing 40 GCSE or "O" levels at once.

It is nonetheless important to approach the course as enthusiastically as possible and attempt to maintain that enthusiasm. This is after all the career that you yourself have chosen and although the course does not correspond to the pressures, and indeed pleasures, of practice itself, it does at least give you a taste of them. If you dislike the taste are you sure that you will enjoy the daily diet? Maintaining enthusiasm means that one should try to achieve maximum concentration in lectures and get good legible notes and prepare thoroughly for seminars and tutorials. Moreover if a "mock" examination is provided at the end of the course it is worth approaching this as thoroughly as possible. Such a test is a useful guide which may disclose remediable faults of knowledge, approach or technique.

It would be superfluous here to suggest in any detail study or note-taking or revision methods. By the time of this examination, the last examination which most students will ever take, everyone will know what works best in his or her particular case. There are as many methods of revision, particularly, as there are individuals. We all know someone, or know of someone, who supposedly ceased all revision three weeks before Finals and then took a job on a building site/went to a Greek Island/hitch-hiked around Europe and still got a First. This is really taking to extremes the frequently given advice not to work too close to the examination. Contrary to this advice my own experience was that the best method of revision was to revise frantically until midnight before each examination, get up again at 4.30am to start revising and the most valuable revision of all was done on the 20-minute bus ride into the examination.

One is therefore stating the obvious in stressing the importance of concentration during lectures and thorough preparation for tutorial work. Constant revision throughout the course is also essential. It really will be hopeless if you leave the start of revision until Easter. Serious revision should start as soon as each separate topic within a subject is completed. This is absolutely vital. I know they told us about the need for constant revision at GCSE or "O" level, at "A" level, and on our degree and/or C.P.E. course and in each case we proved them wrong by first picking up a book in April and we still passed. But this time it really won't work! The sheer bulk of the material to be digested is too much for even the best short-term memory. The only guarantee of passing is constant work.

Nonetheless the demands of the course should not be overstated. If you can really use your time sensibly you will have ample time for leisure. In my opinion if you treat the course like a 9.00 to 5.00 job and work hard whilst at college between those hours (including attendance at lectures etc.) then evening and weekend work should not usually be necessary at least until the last few weeks before the examination. If you use the time at college profitably, (i.e. revising and working between lectures and tutorials) that ought to be enough. Of course it is in the nature of things that you will want to take breaks in the coffee bar or play sport in the day time, but if you do this you should be prepared to make up the time lost out of your 9–5 day in the evenings, preferably the same evenings on which the time has been lost.

Finally one method which is quite extraneous to formal tuition, but which I know has worked well for all students who have tried it is to use the study group system apparently popular in American law schools. By this I mean that a group of students, preferably but not essentially those who are in daily contact anyway, i.e. in the same seminar/tutorial group, get together regularly in their own time to discuss problems, go through their notes and work through past papers. The groups where this works best seem to be those of mixed ability and experience, e.g. containing in addition to the majority of law graduates and/or C.P.E. students, a Legal Executive, a mature student, a court clerk. The extent to which this kind of self help can assist all concerned cannot be overstated. Every single group who has tried this to my knowledge has done considerably better in terms of examination pass rate than their basic levels of ability might have led one to expect.

The examination

From a discussion of the course I pass to the examination. There is no **49.02** point here in discussing whether two two-hour examinations are actually the best way to test the competence of potential solicitors. In favour of the present system are its relative objectivity and the great cost of alternative methods of assessing students' knowledge and aptitude. The objections, that examinations test qualities which are quite irrelevant to competence as a solicitor such as rote learning and handwriting speed are also well known. Certainly for the foreseeable future we must accept that examinations will form part of the method of assessment. I will first make a few general points and then turn briefly to specific topics and how they occur on the examination paper.

1. Read the whole question thoroughly and all the accompanying documents and do this first. Students sometimes fail to grasp even the basic plot, (*e.g.* who we are supposed to be acting for). It will probably be necessary to read the whole question and accompanying documents up to three times and to make brief notes of the plot and salient details (*e.g.* dates and order of events). It is my own impression that if you do this first then whilst your conscious mind is working and writing the answer to the first part of the question your subconscious is mulling over the other parts and will often come up with a good line of approach or good idea.

2. Use your time in the examination sensibly. There are a number of aspects of this:
   (a) As between parts of the question. To take an example suppose part (a) of the question carried 16 marks and part (b) carried 8 marks. It ought to be obvious that the former part is going to require twice the length and depth of treatment of the latter. Unbelievably, students often write as much or more on the shorter part. This is transparently a foolish approach.
   (b) Don't let time run out to the extent that you fail to attempt any part of the question. It ought to be obvious that it is a better use of time to get a few points down on any sub-section of a question than to write more on an already well answered part in an attempt to squeeze out the last few marks. The first few marks on any question are always the easiest to obtain.

3. Stay calm. There are a number of aspects to this:
   (a) Don't panic if the paper on first reading looks very tough. On closer acquaintance it will probably prove less intimidating than you at first thought. Moreover the harder the paper is the more (relatively) generously it will be marked.
   (b) Don't let a poor performance in one examination put you off for other examinations. This is especially so as between the two parts of the Litigation examination. Put a poor morning performance behind you for the afternoon exam. Worrying about the morning exam cannot possibly do you any good. You have probably done better than you think however many obvious points you think you forgot to put down. Remember that you only need pass the two papers in aggregate.
   (c) If you have a total blank on one part of the question leave it until last. The sub-sections are not inter-linked so it should not affect your performance on other questions.

4. Style
   (a) Don't be afraid to write your answers in note form giving numbered points. There are no marks for a flowing prose style and a note form answer may actually be a better approach to some questions. Writing points in numbered form helps to impose order on your mind and may make the marking of the question easier for the marker, which is a point not to be ignored.
   (b) Do the questions in any order you think appropriate. If you really think it helps your morale to get off to a flying start by doing the part of the question you find easiest do that by all means. However it

ought to be pointed out that the order of the questions does follow the chronological order of the plot and it will usually be considerably easier in fact to follow the order of the question.

(c) Don't worry about overlap between parts of the question. This very frequently occurs. For example on a recent paper one part involved a full discussion of committal proceedings and the next part a discussion of points of evidence. Some points of evidence were very relevant to the way in which one would have conducted the committal. There is a system of transferring marks which appear in one part rather than the other. Nonetheless students might well be wise to say expressly on the paper "please refer to my earlier answer on part (c) . . ." This helps to concentrate the marker's mind on the point.

5. Content
There are a number of aspects of this:—
(a) Try to see what the examiner wants. Ask yourself what the examiner is getting at. In particular see whether the question is asking for procedure or tactics or both. This will be most clearly seen in an example. Suppose the question said "explain the circumstances in which the defendant's case can be heard summarily. Outline the procedure by which the mode of trial will be determined." This question clearly requires a description of classification of offences and mode of trial procedure but it does *not* call for a discussion of the factors in the case which might make you want to recommend one form of trial rather than the other. Alternatively the question might have said "if the defendant had a choice of courts explain the factors which are relevant as to which court he should choose and advise him." In this case the discussion of the factors in his case which are relevant to choice of mode of trial *is* called for. In the civil context a question might similarly ask "after summons for directions what steps are necessary to get the case to trial." This asks for the *procedural* steps, *i.e.* setting down and filing bundles and statement of readiness for trial. Worded differently however the question might have called for a discussion of the practical and tactical steps, *e.g.* getting counsel's opinion on evidence, serving Civil Evidence Act notices, subpoenaeing witnesses, exchanging medical reports and so on. The lesson is therefore to read the question carefully and see what the examiner requires.

(b) Treat the examination as an opportunity to display knowledge. Some candidates, inexplicably, treat the examination rather as if the examiner was some insistent inquisitive bore encountered in a public house. In other words they give curt and brief answers almost as if they grudged parting with the information. You can only get marks for what you write down. Even if you are successful in giving the impression of great learning lightly worn, you still cannot get any marks for your knowledge unless you display it. Do not be afraid of stating the obvious. For example students in writing an answer on payments into court, even where it is clear that they are very familiar with the topic, often omit to state that the payment into court is kept secret from the trial judge. Such students probably think that this point is so obvious that it is not worth putting down. It is however by no means obvious even to the intelligent lay person and since the whole nature of the legal gamble which is a payment into court depends upon this fact, it is a major omission in an answer to fail to put it down.

(c) Apply the law and procedure to the facts. This is perhaps the most important message of all. It is a common and very expensive mistake to fail to do this. Let us take an example. There is often a question on bail. The question will usually say something like "On what ground or grounds do you expect the police to object to bail and what arguments will you put forward and what steps will you take to counter these objections." Some candidates manage to recite completely the provisions of the Bail Act 1976 giving in word perfect form the relevant sections and extracts from the schedule. Such candidates do not pass. There must be an attempt to relate the law to the facts and to select only the relevant grounds and criteria to the grant of bail. A word perfect answer which made no reference to the facts of the question itself would fail to get a pass. It is vitally important to apply the law and practice to the facts given. This after all is the skill of a solicitor. In the making of an actual bail application the court would find it very strange if the solicitor merely read out the provisions of the Bail Act.

(d) Discretionary Marks

The markers of this examination are supplied with a very full model answer and mark scheme. However no-one can foresee all the possible good and arguably relevant points that candidates, especially those with practical experience, might put down. Accordingly there are always bonus or discretionary marks available for matters which are off the mainstream of the answer. Therefore if you do have a few minutes to spare it might be worth putting something else down in an answer which you think is already complete. Putting something else down cannot lose you marks and might well win you some. This must however be applied with common sense. There is no point in learning parrot-fashion a potted summary of a favoured topic (*e.g.* payment into court) and squeezing it into the answer no matter how irrelevantly, *e.g.* by saying "although the question doesn't mention it, it is always possible for a defendant to make a payment into court. If the defendant in this case did this then the plaintiff should. . . ." There must be *something* in the question which at least arguably presents the possibility of the extra material you are putting down in the hope of obtaining bonus or discretionary marks.

6. Finally, the obvious. Every year in the examination students throw away chances by:—

(a) Failing to turn up on time.

(b) Arriving for the wrong examination, *i.e.* thinking that this is the Accounts examination when actually it is the Probate examination. At the very least this is highly unnerving and as well as that it will mean that you have missed the opportunity for any desperate last hours of revision and those which you have done for the wrong paper will be virtually wasted.

(c) Ensure you know how long the examination is. Unbelievably, despite a loud announcement from the front of the examination room and the fact that the examination times are clearly printed on the examination paper every year *somebody* groans in disbelief on being told to stop writing and contends that he or she believed it to be a three-hour examination rather than of a two-hour examination.

I now turn to the individual subject areas of the examination taking civil procedure first because that is the order in which the topics appear in this book.

Civil litigation

ETHICS

Questions on professional ethics in civil litigation are likely to be on poten-   **49.03**
tial conflicts of interests either between clients or potential clients (*e.g.* an injured passenger in a car driven by someone in the same family who may have contributed to the accident) or some discussion of the difficulty caused by the conflict of interest where a legally aided client may wish to conduct the litigation in a way you think unreasonable. Another alternative is the possibility of a client who you discover has failed to give you the documents so you can complete discovery honestly. These areas should be carefully revised.

PARTIES

You will usually, though not invariably, be called upon to act for the   **49.04**
plaintiff. Make sure you do know for whom you are acting if more than one person is named as being involved in an accident. Consider the problems of joinder particularly—can all or any of the persons in the plot be co-plaintiffs or co-defendants?

If the defendant blames the accident on a third person or actually commences third party proceedings always carefully consider joining the third party as the second defendant. If the question suggests you should do this don't leave your answer as a statement of the bare minimum but go on to discuss all the consequences of this decision to involve the second defendant, *i.e.*

1. describe the procedure for amending the writ and obtaining the leave necessary.

2. explain how you will be protected as to costs by the operation of a Bullock or Sanderson order.

3. consider the other steps that may be necessary where a second defendant is joined such as getting a legal aid certificate amended and writing a letter to protect yourself under section 152 of the Road Traffic Act. Reference to the text on third party proceedings will explain these matters more fully.

LEGAL AID

The question will indicate if legal aid or green form assistance needs to be   **49.05** discussed or explained fully. The question might mention that the client is impecunious and ask what can be done and it will therefore require a full discussion of legal aid and advice. Alternatively the question may indicate that legal aid need not be discussed, *e.g.* by clearly telling you that the client is wealthy or just saying that legal aid has already been granted. If the question requires a discussion of legal aid always consider whether the form of the question requires also a brief description of the Legal Aid Board's charge, and the operation of sections 17 and 18 of the 1988 Act.

DRAFTING DOCUMENTS

49.06   If there is a drafting question then there are always marks for style and layout. These are marks which are easy to obtain yet candidates all too often forfeit them by poor technique. A drafting question might ask for one of the following:

A letter

If the question asks for a letter then put the answer in the form of a letter. Do not merely describe the contents. If the letter is to your own client write it in terms that the layman can understand. The examiner may be testing communications skills and your own comprehension of the subject-matter by asking you to demonstrate how you explain matters to a layman. If the question asks you to advise the client do so. Don't just offer him the options with no guidance. It will not matter if tactically your advice is wrong (*e.g.* to accept a payment into court) so long as you can give a good reason for it. Topics that you might particularly be asked to explain to a lay client are payment into court, interim payment or discovery.

Put the name and address of the solicitor's firm at the top. You will usually be given correspondence in the documents which will indicate the name of your firm. Ensure that you get the right firm and don't adopt the name of the opposite party's solicitors. If no name is given for you invent some neutral name such as A, B, C and Co. Do not use your own name. It is also unwise to invent humorous, or still worse, obscene names. The marker may not share your sense of humour or propriety.

Affidavits and pleadings

Set out the formal parts of these (*i.e.* the headings). There will usually be some other documents supplied with the question from which you can copy these formal parts.

An affidavit Complete the headings giving details of the deponent at the top right as explained in the text earlier. Put the affidavit in the first person "I _____ make oath and say . . ." and then put what it is that you are saying in numbered paragraphs in ordinary English. There is no need to use or seek for technical jargon or to fill the affidavit with "heretofores" and "hereins." The affidavits which will be required are most probably affidavits in support of or opposing an application for summary judgment or perhaps seeking an interim payment or pre-action discovery. Consider carefully the formal requirements of each. There is an excellent question on drafting an affidavit on the Summer 1984 paper which it is recommended should be attempted as a revision guide.

Pleadings Set out the formal parts. Put the pleading in the third person, *i.e.* "the plaintiff did ..." not the first person "I did ..." It is as well to study carefully, even to the extent of learning by heart, the wording on the form of an endorsement to the writ seeking liquidated or unliquidated sums and to study carefully the illustrations given in the text. In addition when drafting a pleading remember the following points:—

1. Plead facts not law or evidence.

2. How to plead a conviction under section 11 of the Civil Evidence Act 1968.

3. Don't meet defences in advance.

4. When to plead a claim for interest and in what form of words.

Further and better particulars

If you have to draft a request for further and better particulars or write notes on what further and better particulars you would seek see what it is in the pleading with which you are supplied which needs to be amplified. Don't ask for matters of law or evidence. *E.g.* don't ask "why is it submitted that this case comes within the principles in the Wagon Mound" or "which of your witnesses says that ..." Remember also that a request for further and better particulars need not necessarily be a genuine request for information; it may merely be an attempt to tie the opponent down to a more precise version of his allegation.

CIVIL EVIDENCE

This area should be studied particularly carefully because it is a relatively small one and one on which it is easy to obtain the good marks. Remember particularly:— **49.07**

1. Don't confuse the concepts of criminal evidence with civil evidence where they are different. For example don't discuss *res gestae*—all the common law exceptions to the hearsay rule are abolished by section 1 of the Civil Evidence Act 1968; don't discuss corroboration—this is never necessary in a civil action.

2. Ensure that you thoroughly understand sections 2, 4 and 8 of the Civil Evidence Act and don't confuse them with the very similar provisions of section 24 of the Criminal Justice Act 1988. Remember to mention section 6(3), the weight to be accorded to hearsay evidence admitted under the Act, and consider section 7—the possibility of attacking the credit of absent witnesses. Remember also section 9—admissions by a party admissible without any notice procedure and carefully study section 11 on the use and effect of previous convictions in civil proceedings.

3. Remember alternative methods of proving facts to the use of the Civil Evidence Act. Ensure that you carefully understand the use of a notice to admit facts and its effect and what amounts to "real" evidence.

4. If the question asks you how you will prove all relevant matters at trial remember to discuss quantum of damages as well as liability. This may

involve the consideration of items of expert evidence, *e.g.* the procedures necessary to introduce them, obtaining directions, and exchange
of medical reports with a view to agreement.

Remember that you will need to prove each item of special damages
which is not admitted and consider carefully how this needs to be done,
e.g. by the calling of witnesses, the use of a notice to admit facts or a
Civil Evidence Act notice etc.

ENFORCEMENT

49.08 If you are asked to describe enforcement of a judgment which you have
obtained restrict yourself only to relevant methods. There will be no marks
for describing in exhaustive detail a method which is transparently inapplic-
able, *e.g.* attachment of earnings in the case of someone who we know from
the facts is unemployed or self-employed. Consider whether an oral examination is necessary—it may well be superfluous if there are already two
options clearly indicated on the facts of the question. However if rejecting
the need for an oral examination say so expressly—this ought to obtain
marks for practical common sense.

Criminal litigation

49.09 It is important particularly in criminal litigation to ensure you know which of
the parties named is doing what and what facts are in issue, *i.e.* what defence
is put forward on the facts related. There is an excellent example of the
pitfalls of failing to do this in one past paper in which one of three persons
originally charged admitted being at the scene of the crime and acting in an
apparently suspicious manner but went on to give an innocent explanation of
his conduct. Despite these admitted facts many candidates wrote exhaustively about the problems of identification evidence. This was clearly irrelevant since the person in question admitted being at the scene of the crime. So
it is vital to see what your client and each of the persons originally suspected
is doing in relation to the criminal proceedings. A typical plot may well
involve three persons originally charged of which one is pleading guilty and
you may well be invited to act for the other two. This is a good plot because it
poses several complications of a procedural and evidential nature. In such a
case you are likely first to have to consider whether you can legitimately act
for two or more co-defendants. You should be prepared to discuss conflicts
of interest and the possibility of this arising at any stage in criminal proceedings. Bear in mind that even if your two defendants' defences are quite
dissimilar you still need to examine whether they are likely to incriminate
each other. It may well be that their defences, although dissimilar, are not
inconsistent, *e.g.* one whose defence is alibi and one whose defence is non
participation in the crime despite his presence. It is so important to ensure
that you keep the facts in issue clearly in view that it may well be worth
jotting them on some separate piece of paper and underlining them and
constantly referring to them throughout particularly at the stage of answering the evidence question. The following topics on the paper are also
particularly worthy of consideration.

BAIL

49.10 Learn the Bail Act in a systematic manner. Do mentally not mix up the grounds, the criteria for applying the grounds, and practical matters. For example the question might say "on what grounds do you anticipate that the police will object to bail and what arguments will you put forward and what steps will you take to meet those objections." A weak candidate would write a bad answer as follows.

"the police will object on the grounds that:

1. He will abscond.
2. He has no settled address.
3. He has no surety."

This is a muddled response which will obtain few marks. Had the candidate structured his answer rather better however, then from the same basic information he could have obtained a much better mark if he had written as follows:—

"The accused has a basic right to bail before conviction but the court may consider that he should not be allowed bail if there are substantial grounds for believing that inter alia he will (as the police will suggest here) abscond. In judging the relevance of this objection the court will have regard to a number of matters (in particular here to the accused's lack of community ties as demonstrated by the fact that he has no settled address in the area). Although an accused is basically entitled to unconditional bail if it is anticipated that bail may be refused it may be wise to propose conditions which could be attached to bail to meet the objections made. A condition which would be particularly appropriate here would be the offering of a surety, that is a person who is willing to offer a recognisance (*i.e.* a sum of money which will be forfeited if the accused should fail to appear on the date to which he is bailed). Unfortunately the facts of the question do not suggest anyone who could stand surety for this accused and therefore this is a major difficulty in the presentation of his case . . ."

This is a highly simplified version of the question and answer because usually there will be several factors relevant but the point is clear enough that if you put what information you have into a structured form the answer will look considerably better. On a bail question it is important to consider all the possible grounds for objection to bail and select only the relevant ones, then one should examine the criteria for judging the applicability of the grounds and consider conditions and action needed to meet those objections.

CHOICE OF COURT

The examiner will make it clear from the wording of the question whether what is demanded is a discussion of mode of trial procedure or of the factors and tactical points in favour of one court or the other. If it is the latter form of question it is important not to list these in a random way but to select only those that are suggested by the facts. One highly material factor which is always in favour of the Crown Court is that there will usually be substantial points of evidence to raise. Apart from this feature which is always likely to be present other features of the case may militate against the Crown Court. Only those that are relevant should be contained in your answer otherwise it becomes all too apparent that you have learned a list of factors in favour of

49.11

one or the other and are listing them regardless of the specific circumstances given in the question.

49.12 EVIDENCE

An understanding of evidence is of crucial importance to your prospects of success on the criminal litigation question. Often matters of evidence carry as many as half of the marks. It is the most academic area of the course and perhaps the area on which students have most difficulty. You will be given perhaps four different types of statement. Firstly you will be given your client's own statement to you. This should obviously be read first for his version. You will then be given prosecution witnesses' statements. You ought also to be given a further statement from your client in which he comments on matters contained in the prosecution statements. This further statement of your client is of crucial importance for framing cross-examination. Your client will tell you the very points in the prosecution's statements with which he disagrees and on which you may therefore have to cross-examine the prosecution witnesses. Fourthly, and more rarely, you might be supplied with witness statements in your client's favour.

The prosecution's statements will usually be in the form necessary for them to be admitted under section 9 of the Criminal Justice Act 1967. This is because the police take witness statements on forms on which the necessary paragraph to bring the statement within section 9 is pre-printed. In addition to the section 9 statements however, the prosecution must also supply you with, if there is one, a copy of statements made under caution by any other person who has been charged with your client (*i.e.* a co-accused). They are also obliged to supply you with a copy of any statement your own client made under caution. You may therefore have statements of various types to consider. It is crucially important to understand what is the nature of each and to look carefully at the wording of the question. Almost certainly the question will only be asking you to comment on matters of evidence arising from and points of cross-examination to do with the prosecution's statements.

The form of the question will probably be to ask you either to draft a brief to counsel or to make notes for such a brief if the trial is proceeding in the Crown Court, or to make notes yourself on the basis that you are to conduct the case in the magistrates' court. In either case the law and procedure is more or less the same but the terminology you must use in your answer will be very different. I will return to this below.

An important first point is to make sure you understand the plot of the question fully. If there is another person charged with your client ensure that you are clear in your own mind whether or not he is pleading guilty. If he is pleading guilty then the prosecution may call him as a witness if they wish in which case he is an *accomplice*, and this leads to three relevant matters arising:—

1. you should mention the question of his competence and compellability and the issue as to whether or not he should be sentenced before testifying for the prosecution.

2. the question of corroboration will arise—in the Crown Court a warning is mandatory.

3. if you attack him and make imputations against him you may fall foul of

section 1(*f*)(ii) of the Criminal Evidence Act 1898. (*NOT* section 1(*f*)(iii)!)

If on the other hand the other person charged is pleading not guilty and in his statement he appears to incriminate your client then the consequences are:—

4. He is a co-defendant not an accomplice and testifies on his own behalf so he is *not* competent for the prosecution.

5. If he does testify, whilst any confession he has made is strictly only admissible against him and not your client he can say the same thing when giving evidence in which case the content of what he says *is* admissible against your client.

6. A corroboration warning may be desirable in the Crown Court although not mandatory, because he may have *some purpose of his own to serve.*

7. If your client gives evidence against him then your client will fall foul of section 1(*f*)(iii) (*NOT* section 1(*f*)(ii)!)

The question will ask you to discuss the statements. Unless you accept the statements which are in section 9 form which is highly unlikely, they will not of course be put before any court. You should therefore proceed in the question as though you are discussing what the witnesses will say when they attend court. It is therefore wrong to say "this statement must be edited to omit. . . ." You should discuss it rather on the basis that the witness in court will say the same thing so the appropriate terminology is "the witness must not say . . . and so the prosecution will be warned that this evidence must not be led."

With regard to the difference between magistrates' court and Crown Court proceedings referred to above it is vital to get the terminology right to create a good impression on the marker. If you are dealing with a Crown Court case it is right to discuss evidence in terms of directions to the jury and right to say that some kinds of defects in the judge's directions will lead to a conviction being quashed on appeal. In the magistrates' court however, these terms are meaningless and must be adapted so that you say what points you will make in your closing speech by way of reminding the magistrates of the law on, *e.g.* corroboration. It is pointless to say that if the magistrates fail to take a particular course their decision can be quashed on appeal. Appeals from a magistrates' court to the Crown Court are as of right and amount to a complete re-hearing, so what the magistrates specifically did that was allegedly wrong is irrelevant in the Crown Court appeal.

You should consider the statements in the order in which they appear. It is perhaps best to bear in mind each of the following points about them although all the points will by no means arise on each statement:—

1. Consider what factual objections you have to the witness's evidence. In other words what matters you must challenge on cross-examination.

2. Consider questions of competence and compellability about each witness, *e.g.* is the witness a spouse, a child, or a co-accused?

3. Get perfectly clear in your mind whether any given witness who has been charged with the crime is an accomplice or a co-defendant, *i.e.* is he pleading guilty or not guilty. Then go on to consider the consequences as outlined above.

4. Is there any hearsay in the statement? Of course the statement itself is hearsay if it were to be adduced at trial, but we are considering the case of a witness who is going to come to court and testify verbally to the same effect of his statement. Is he nonetheless going to say something referred to in his statement which will amount to hearsay? For example does it say somewhere in his statement "X at work told me that the accused. ..." This is something which is inadmissible and so the prosecution must be warned that the evidence must not be adduced.

5. Is there any other inadmissible material within the witness's statement? Is there any speculation about the accused's guilt or reference to his previous criminal record? If so the witness must not be allowed to give the evidence.

6. Consider your client's own character. Bear in mind:
   (a) If he has no criminal record then not only can he conduct his defence in any way he likes and make imputations on prosecution witnesses or a co-accused with impunity, he may even call character witnesses as to the likelihood of his guilt (*e.g.* on a dishonesty charge an employer who will confirm that he has handled money in the course of his employment without any shortages resulting).
   (b) If he does have a criminal record then remember:—
      (i) To say that a witness is genuinely mistaken, *e.g.* a witness as to identity based on a fleeting glimpse, will not make you fall foul of section 1(*f*)(ii)
      (ii) To suggest that a policeman was guilty of a minor breach of the Police and Criminal Evidence Act or of a Code of Practice, *e.g.* failed to give a caution at the right time, will certainly not involve you falling foul of section 1(*f*)(ii)
      (iii) If you do make a frontal attack on a witness however or suggest that the police are deliberately lying then section 1(*f*)(ii) does come into play and if your client testifies he is liable to be cross-examined upon his character. Remember however that the court does have a discretion as to whether to permit this and also to stress that the jury should be reminded, or you should remind the magistrates, that the fact of your client's criminal record is relevant only to his credibility as a witness.
      (iv) If your client is going to give evidence against his co-defendant then he will fall foul of section 1(*f*)(iii).
      (v) Bear in mind that your client is entitled to keep out of the witness box in which case he cannot fall foul of section 1(*f*) at all since the section relates only to cross-examination of the accused. However it is probably tactically unwise in the kind of crimes which are on the syllabus for a client to fail to give evidence.
      Despite all the problems of having his criminal record brought out sometimes there is no alternative but to make a frontal attack on the prosecution evidence or a co-accused. Sometimes the only possible defence is to suggest that the witness or co-accused is lying in which case the problems inherent in section 1(*f*) must be faced.

Finally it goes without saying that if in your client's own statement he has put something relating to his past creditable behaviour but he also happens to have a criminal record then you ought to stress that he should not make the allusions to his worthy past because to do so will entitle the prosecution to call rebutting evidence about your client's criminal record.

SENTENCING AND MITIGATION

The sections on these topics should be studied very carefully. In a question **49.13** on sentencing and mitigation there may often be a social inquiry report supplied. Careful use should be made of this. Relevant aspects should be highlighted and developed in your draft plea in mitigation. A question on sentencing and mitigation is often, in my experience, very badly done indeed. This is strange because in theory it ought to be quite an easy question. Indeed if asked to cobble together a plea in mitigation even an intelligent layman with no legal experience ought to be able to get *some* marks on the question by simply stressing in a commonsense way the kind of factors that are likely to attract the court's sympathy. A plea in mitigation should be structured in the way suggested earlier in the text, and if you are asked to suggest the sentences which the court might consider it is important to approach the question realistically. If your client has a bad criminal record and the present crime is of some seriousness then it is pointless to suggest an absolute discharge. A plea in mitigation, perhaps more than any other question, is susceptible of a good treatment in the form of writing numbered points. This will also help you to structure the answer and not to overlook any of the categories given in the text which ought to be considered when framing your plea in mitigation.

By way of illustration it would now be worthwhile carefully to work through the two past examination papers from Summer 1989 and Summer 1990 with suggested answers which appear in the next chapter. These past papers have been chosen from all those available so as to give a wide spread of plot and subject areas. Between them these papers deal with most of the important areas of the syllabus. So as to provide a useful revision guide as well as an indication of examination technique the answers are intended to be fairly complete and are thus a little more full than it would be realistically possible to get down in the two-hour examination period and therefore candidates should not despair at the sheer length of the answers!

Summer 1989

SOLICITORS' FINAL EXAMINATION QUESTIONS

THURSDAY, 6TH JULY (10 A.M. TO 12 NOON)

Candidates should answer all questions.

LITIGATION

(CRIMINAL)

In the afternoon of 30 June 1989 you are telephoned by Mrs. Laura Williams. She asks you to act for her husband, Vincent Williams, for whom you have previously acted. She tells you that her husband was arrested on 29 June 1989 and appeared before the Exbridge Magistrates' Court on the morning of 30 June charged with theft of a diamond bracelet valued at £5,000. At the hearing at the Exbridge Magistrates' Court he had been represented by the duty solicitor who made an unsuccessful application for bail on his behalf. Mrs. Williams says that the police have also interviewed her in connection with the case but have told her that she is not being charged.

You see Vincent Williams in custody and take a statement from him (Document 1). Mr. Williams is not financially eligible for legal aid.

1. Mr. Williams asks you to apply for bail on his behalf.

   (a) When will you next have the opportunity to apply to the Magistrates' Court for bail?

   (b) On what ground or grounds do you expect the prosecution to object to bail being granted to him?

   (c) What arguments will you put forward, and what steps will you take, to counter these objections?

   (d) Are there any further steps that can be taken to obtain bail if your application is refused?

Your attempts to obtain bail for your client are unsuccessful. You subsequently receive statements from the prosecution under the Advance Information Rules (Documents 2 to 4). You obtain your client's comments on the prosecution statements which you add to his statement. (*20 marks*)

2. Explain to your client the circumstances in which the case can be tried summarily. By what procedure will the mode of trial be determined and what factors would you bear in mind when advising him which court to choose? (Do not assume that because the case proceeds in the Magistrates' Court this is necessarily on your advice.) (*16 marks*)

3. Your secretary is telephoned by Mrs. Laura Williams. She tells your secretary that the police pressurised her into giving the statement implicating her husband (Document 4) because they told her that she would be liable to be charged with theft jointly with her husband unless she co-operated. She has two young children and was worried about what would happen to them if she was kept in custody. She wants "to take back her statement and be a witness for her husband."

   (a) Could the prosecution ensure that Mrs. Williams gives evidence in court against her husband?

   (b) Would it be in order for you to interview Mrs. Williams to obtain a statement from her?

   (c) If she is not called by the prosecution, can she be called as a witness for her husband? Assuming that she can, what would be the advantages and disadvantages of doing so? (*10 marks*)

4. You obtain a report from a jewel dealer, Mr. Cyril Wheeler-Jones (Document 5). You telephone Mr. Pieter Van Trapp. Mr. Van Trapp confirms that he sold six diamonds to your client but makes it clear that he is not willing to go to court to give evidence to that effect because he does not wish to be cross-examined about his business dealings. He does, however, send you a letter enclosing a copy of the receipt (Documents 6 and 7). The case proceeds in the Exbridge Magistrates' Court. Vincent Williams pleads not guilty. By what means could you bring the following matters before the court—

   (a) Mr. Wheeler-Jones' evidence;

   (b) the information contained in the letter from Mr. Van Trapp (Document 6); and

   (c) the information contained in the receipt (Document 7). (*16 marks*)

5. Comment on Documents 2 and 3 and on how you would conduct Vincent Williams' defence. You should consider:—
   —the evidence against Vincent Williams revealed by Documents 2 and 3 making it clear whether you would challenge any of it as inadmissible and dealing with any evidential points which arise;
   —the matters (if any) on which you would cross-examine Michael Lindley or Stanley Carter;
   —any evidential or practical matters which arise from Vincent Williams' statement and which may affect your proposed conduct of his defence.

(14 marks)

6. Vincent Williams is convicted. The Exbridge Magistrates' Court commits him in custody to the Crown Court for sentence. When you see him after the hearing he admits that he is guilty of the offence. He also tells you that the police have questioned him about an unconnected offence, the theft of an emerald necklace which he believes to be worth about £500. He refused to answer any of their questions but he admits to you that he did steal the necklace in question and that it is hidden in his house. He wishes to return the necklace and to tell the police about the offence so that "he can wipe the slate clean."

   (a) Advise him how the theft of the necklace should be dealt with.

   (b) Explain to your client why the Magistrates have not sentenced him and inform him of the maximum penalties (excluding compensation) to which he is liable.

   (c) Your client wishes to be represented in the Crown Court by you (a solicitor) rather than by counsel. Would you be able to do so?

   (12 marks)

7. A Social Enquiry Report is obtained (Document 8). Outline the matters that could be raised in mitigation (bearing in mind the penalties which it is realistic to suppose the Court will consider). *(12 marks)*

Total = *100 marks*

DOCUMENT 1

Vincent Williams of 12 Harrow Road, Exbridge will say:—

I am a self-employed business man working from home. My main business is as a stamp dealer but I also deal in jewellery. My wife works as a shop assistant at a jeweller's shop, Lindley and Son, 14 Silver Street, Exbridge. I went there to pick her up from work at about 5.30 p.m. on Wednesday 28th June 1989. I parked the car outside the shop and waited for her to come out. She locked the shop and joined me. I never entered the shop. We then went home and spent the evening at home together.

The next day, Thursday 29th June, I went out to a business meeting. It was early closing day so my wife was not working in the shop. On Thursdays she picks the children up from their nursery school herself. I returned home at 3.30 p.m. to find that the house had been ransacked. I thought that the house had been burgled, but before I could discover what had been taken two police officers knocked on the door. They accused me of stealing a bracelet from the shop where my wife works. They showed me six diamonds which they had found in my desk drawer and which they seemed to think had come from the bracelet. They asked me where I had acquired the diamonds and asked several other questions. I know that if you make statements to the police without having a solicitor's advice the police twist everything you say. I have had it happen to me before. So I decided to say nothing. In any case I did not think that they were entitled to know where I got the diamonds from.

The police then arrested me on suspicion of theft. They took me to the police station where they refused to let me telephone my solicitor. I refused to answer any questions and finally they charged me with theft.

Personal background

I am aged 29. I married for the first time in 1981. In March 1986 my wife got a court injunction to force me to leave the matrimonial home. She is still living there with our daughter aged 6. She does not let me see my daughter. I met my present wife, Laura, in November 1987. We have been living together since January 1988 and married in November 1988 when my divorce came through. She has been married before and her two children live with us.

I have the following previous convictions:—

September 1985—theft of £300 (Southgate Magistrates' Court—fined £100).

April 1986—theft of a television set valued at £250 (Exbridge Magistrates' Court—two years' probation).

September 1987—burglary, goods valued at £780 (Exbridge Magistrates' Court—six months' imprisonment suspended for two years. No order was made in relation to the breach of probation.)

In 1984 I lost my job as a welder. I could not find another job and this caused tension between me and my first wife. I was desperate for money and a friend of mine persuaded me to join a gang of villains. The two charges of theft arose out of my involvement with jobs that they organised. My wife forced me to leave our council house when I was charged with the second offence. She would not let me see our daughter. I had to live in a squat with the friend who got me into trouble with the police in the first place. I became very depressed and only got involved with the burglary in 1987 because I felt I had nothing to lose. In November 1987 I met Laura and everything changed for me. I moved in with her and her two children. She had a little capital and helped me to start my business as a stamp dealer. I also deal in other items. It has been very successful.

I go abroad quite a lot in the course of my business. I have built up a number of foreign business connections. I have arranged an important business trip abroad next week. I must get out on bail so that I can fulfil my obligations.

I owe Laura a great deal. She had a bad time with her first husband and I promised her that I would make it up to her and justify her confidence in me. I would never do anything to hurt her.

COMMENTS ON PROSECUTION STATEMENTS

Document 2

I know nothing about the theft. I think I know what happened though. I have heard from my business contacts that Lindley is in financial difficulties. My wife does some of his paper work. I know from her that he recently took out a large insurance policy. I also know that he does not usually have large single items of jewellery on the premises. It is only a small shop. I reckon he took the bracelet himself so that he can claim on the insurance policy.

Lindley must have known of my criminal record when he employed Laura. I am not proud of it but it is no secret. I think he took her on so that he could make it look as if I had stolen the bracelet.

Laura is not timid and she is certainly not afraid of me.

Document 3

The police account of what happened is about right. I may have said something like "Christ I'm on a suspended sentence. This could mean prison." I was not admitting that I had done anything wrong. But I know what the police are like. I was just afraid they would pin something on me.

The diamonds found in my house did not come from the bracelet. I bought them from a Dutch business contact of mine called Pieter Van Trapp. I no longer have the receipt he gave me.

Document 4

I remember that Laura mentioned that Andrew Lindley had written the combination number of the safe in his diary. We have always thought that he is a twit and we had a good laugh about it. But it is not true that I asked her what the number is or that she told me. I do not know what the number is. I do not get angry with Laura and she has no reason to be frightened of me.

On Wednesday 28th June I arranged with Laura to pick her up from the shop at 5.30 p.m. as usual. I waited for her in the car outside the shop. I did not enter the shop.

Laura has told me that on the afternoon of Thursday 29th June the police took her to the station and made it clear to her that she would not be allowed to go home until she made a statement. The children are usually picked up by a friend of hers but on Thursdays she stops work at 1.0 p.m. and picks up the children herself. She was due to pick up the children from nursery school at 4.00 p.m. They are aged 3 and 4 and she was really worried about what would happen if she could not leave the police station in time to collect them. The eldest one, Mark, gets asthmatic attacks if he gets worried. He has been to hospital with them. Also the police told her that they would assume that she was involved with the theft unless she co-operated. The police just put words into her mouth. So she made a statement under caution. After the court hearing on 30th June the police told her that they would drop any charge against her if she gave evidence against me. This caused her to make another statement (Document 4) on the lines of the first statement.

She is now prepared to swear that I never entered the shop on 29th June and that she did not tell me the combination number of the safe.

DOCUMENT 2

BLANKSHIRE POLICE

Name: Michael Lindley

Exbridge Station

Address: The Grange, Fortune Road, Exbridge

Age/date of birth: over 21

Occupation: Jeweller

Who states:—

This statement consisting of one page signed by me is true to the best of my knowledge and belief and I make it knowing that if it is tendered in evidence I shall be liable to prosecution if I have wilfully stated in it anything which I know to be false or do not believe to be true.

Dated 29th June 1989   (signed) M. Lindley

I own a jewellery shop at 14, Silver Street, Exbridge, Blankshire. My son Andrew works in the shop with me and I employ two assistants, Miss Pamela Sharpe and Mrs. Laura Williams.

On Wednesday 28th June 1989 Miss Sharpe was off work sick. My son had gone to an auction. That afternoon I had to go to an unexpected business meeting. I left Mrs. Williams in charge of the shop. I wanted her to stay there until my son returned but she told me that she would not be able to wait after 5.30 p.m. because her husband was due to collect her then. So I instructed her to lock the shop at 5.30 p.m. if my son had not returned by that time. She does not have keys but the shop can be secured without them. I placed the most valuable single item in the shop, a gold bracelet set with six diamonds, into the wall safe and locked it. The safe has a combination lock.

On the following morning I came to the shop and unlocked the safe. I found that the diamond bracelet was missing. The shop did not appear to have been broken into. So far as I am aware the assistants do not know the combination number of the safe. But it is possible that one of them might have observed me opening it without my noticing. The safe is very sophisticated. I do not think that it would be possible to open the safe without knowing the combination or using explosives.

I acquired the bracelet in question on 26th June 1989. It is insured for £5,000. I prepared a photograph and a detailed description of the bracelet for insurance purposes, and I now produce copies of both the photograph and the description (M.L.1 and M.L.2) **[Note to candidates—the photograph and description are not provided.]**

Miss Pamela Sharpe has been working for me for fifteen years. Mrs Laura Williams has been in my employment for four months. I would not have employed her if I had known that her husband has a police record for theft and burglary. She is a timid woman who appears to be afraid of her husband. I must say that he is a tough looking individual.

                                         M. Lindley (signed)

Statement taken and signature witnessed by Detective Constable Carter at Exbridge Police Station at 9.45 a.m. on Thursday 29th June 1989.

                                         S. Carter (signed)

Further to my statement taken on 29th June 1989, I have now been shown six diamonds (marked S.C.1 to S.C.6). I confirm that these six diamonds are identical to those in the bracelet stolen from my shop.

                                         M. Lindley (signed)

Statement taken and signature witnessed by Detective Constable Carter at Exbridge Police Station at 11.0 a.m. on Friday 30th June 1989.

S. Carter (signed)

DOCUMENT 3

BLANKSHIRE POLICE

Name: Stanley Carter   Exbridge Station

Address: Exbridge Police Station

Age/date of birth: over 21

Occupation: Detective Constable

Who states:—

This statement consisting of one page signed by me is true to the best of my knowledge and belief and I make it knowing that if it is tendered in evidence I shall be liable to prosecution if I have wilfully stated in it anything which I know to be false or do not believe to be true.

Dated 29th June 1989   (signed) S. Carter

On Thursday 29th June 1989 at 1.20 p.m. acting on information received I visited 12 Harrow Road Exbridge, in company with D.C. Jessop, intending to interview Vincent Williams. There appeared to be no one at home but the back door was unlocked and we entered the premises. We then searched the premises and discovered six diamonds (S.C.1 to S.C.6) in a leather pouch in the right hand drawer of a desk in a room which appeared to be used as an office.

We waited for some time. At 2.10 p.m. a woman who identified herself as Mrs. Laura Williams came into the house. She voluntarily accompanied us to the police station where she made a statement under caution. We returned to the house at 3.40 p.m. having dropped Mrs. Williams off at St Anthony's nursery school so that she could collect her children. We knocked at the door and a man opened the door who identified himself as Vincent Williams. When he saw us he said "Get the hell out of it" and tried to shut the door in my face. I prevented him from doing so. The following exchange took place.

Williams: "What the hell do you think you're doing?"

D.C. Carter: "We're investigating a theft of jewellery and we think you can help us in our enquiries."

Williams: "What theft?"

D.C. Carter: "Do you recognise these." I showed him the six diamonds I had taken from his desk.

450

Williams (turning pale): "Christ I'm on a suspended sentence. This could mean prison."

D.C. Carter: "So you admit they are stolen?"

Williams: "Don't put words into my mouth. I'm admitting nothing. I demand to see my solicitor. I know my rights."

D.C. Carter: "Where did you get them then?"

Williams: "I told you I'm saying nothing without my solicitor. I know you'll twist everything I say."

I then arrested him on suspicion of theft of a diamond bracelet from Lindley and Son and cautioned him. I took him to the police station where he declined to make a further statement. At 4.32 p.m. I produced him to the custody officer who charged him with theft of a diamond bracelet, the property of Lindley and Son. He made no reply. He was then detained in custody pending his appearance at the Exbridge Magistrates' Court the next day.

S. Carter (signed)

DOCUMENT 4

BLANKSHIRE POLICE

Name: Laura Williams   Exbridge Station

Address: 12 Harrow Road, Exbridge

Age/date of birth: over 21

Occupation: Shop Assistant

Who states:—

This statement consisting of one page signed by me is true to the best of my knowledge and belief and I make it knowing that if it is tendered in evidence I shall be liable to prosecution if I have wilfully stated in it anything which I know to be false or do not believe to be true.

Dated 30th June 1989   (signed) L. Williams

I am employed as a shop assistant by Mr. Lindley at his shop at 14 Silver Street, Exbridge. I also do some typing for him.

Every evening Mr. Lindley locks up most of the jewellery into the wall safe. I know the combination number of the safe. So does Miss Pamela Sharpe, the other assistant. Mr. Andrew Lindley, Mr. Lindley's son who works at the shop, wrote the number down in his desk diary and we saw it there about four weeks ago. Pamela and I had a bit of a laugh about it. I told my husband, Vincent, about it as a joke that evening. He said he would guess that the number was based on Mr. Lindley's birthday and then he asked me what the number was. I did not want to tell him but I was frightened. He gets very angry if he does not get his way. So I told it to him.

451

On Wednesday 28th June 1989 I was left in charge of the shop. Pamela Sharpe was off work that day and Andrew Lindley was at an auction. Mr. Lindley had to go out. He told me he was leaving me in charge and asked me to lock up the shop at 5.30 p.m. He locked the diamond bracelet into the safe. My husband collected me from the shop. He came into the shop. I put the door on the latch and went to the Ladies on the first floor to get ready to go, leaving him alone in the shop for a few minutes. I then returned, locked up the shop and left with my husband.

Vincent must have taken the bracelet while I was in the Ladies. I am very sorry that I told him the combination number of the safe. It never occurred to me that he would use the information to steal anything. I hope Mr. Lindley does not think that I told my husband on purpose.

L. Williams (signed)

Statement taken and signature witnessed by Detective Constable Carter at Exbridge Police Station at 11.40 a.m. on Friday 30th June 1989.

S. Carter (signed)

DOCUMENT 5

This is a report prepared by Cyril Wheeler-Jones of 201, Hatton Garden, London EC1.

I am the senior partner in the firm of Wheeler-Jones, Smith and Co. I have been in business as a jewel dealer, specialising in diamonds, since 1958.

I have examined the six diamonds marked S.C.1 to S.C.6 which I understand were found in the possession of Vincent Williams. I have been supplied with a photograph and detailed description (marked M.L.1 and M.L.2) of the bracelet which is the subject of the prosecution against Mr. Williams.

In my opinion the six diamonds do not match the photograph or the description. [Note to candidates: there follow detailed reasons which have not been reproduced here.]

(signed) C. Wheeler-Jones
Dated 10th July 1989

DOCUMENT 6

31 Willem I Str.
Amsterdam
7 July 1989

Dear Sirs,

With reference to our telephone conversation today, I confirm that I am a jewellery dealer. I have on several occasions in the past done business with Vincent Williams. Last month I visited London. On 22nd June 1989 I met

452

Mr. Williams in the Metropolitan Hotel, Piccadilly, London where I sold him various jewels for which he paid me £4,525. Among the jewels were six diamonds. I understand that these were found in his possession by the police.

I keep a carbon copy of all receipts issued. I have checked my records and enclose a copy of the receipt which I gave Mr. Williams.

I understand that this letter may be produced in court and hope that it will help Mr. Williams to prove his innocence.

Yours faithfully
(signed) Pieter Van Trapp

DOCUMENT 7

[Note to candidates: this is the receipt referred to in Document 6]

31 Willem I Str.
Amsterdam

Pieter Van Trapp acknowledges that he has received the sum of £4,525 from Mr. V. Williams for the supply of precious stones.

22nd June 1989

(signed) P. Van Trapp

DOCUMENT 8

SOCIAL ENQUIRY REPORT

To the:
Crown Court at Exbridge

Name: VINCENT WILLIAMS

Date of birth: 15th April 1960 (29 years)

Address: 12 Harrow Road, Exbridge.

Offence: Theft

1. Vincent Williams was born on 15th April 1960 in Rudgate. He is an only child. His father is an insurance salesman and his mother works as a secretary. He was brought up in Rudgate and had a normal family life. He continued to live at home until his marriage in 1981.

2. He had a secondary education at Rudgate Comprehensive school leaving school at 16 with 4 "O" levels and three CSEs. After leaving school he trained as a welder.

3. In 1981 he married a local woman. They moved to Exbridge where he got employment as a welder. Their child was born in 1982. He was made

redundant in 1984 and was unable to find work. His unemployment led to matrimonial tensions. This was further aggravated by his convictions for the offences mentioned below. His behaviour towards his wife became increasingly violent. Matters came to a head when she finally obtained a court order requiring him to leave the matrimonial home. For a while he had no fixed address. Since January 1988 he has lived with his present wife, Laura, and the two children of her previous marriage. The couple married in November 1988.

4. Mr. Williams runs a business as a stamp dealer from his home with his wife's help. She keeps his books and acts as his secretary. The business was started in January 1988 and seems to be earning the family a comfortable income.

5. Mr. Williams has three previous convictions. The first two, for theft, were committed in 1985 and 1986 when he was unemployed and under considerable financial pressure. He was fined for the first offence and was placed on probation for the second offence in April 1986 for two years. I was his probation officer. Shortly before his conviction for that offence his first wife obtained a court order requiring him to leave the matrimonial home. She refused to allow him access to their child. For some time he refused to admit that the marriage was at an end. He was depressed, unemployed and in financial difficulties. Despite my advice he resumed his former association with a man who instigated the previous thefts.

6. In those circumstances I was not surprised when he came before the courts again charged with burglary. He pleaded guilty and on 17th September 1987 was sentenced to a six months term of imprisonment suspended for two years. No order was made in relation to the breach of probation. He and the man mentioned in paragraph 5 above had together broken into a wine shop and taken goods valued at £780. It appeared that his co-defendant had put considerable pressure on him to participate in the offence.

7. The present offence concerns the theft of a diamond bracelet valued at £5,000 from his wife's employer. Mr. Williams pleaded not guilty, but now frankly admits his guilt. An unexpected set of circumstances led to his wife being left in charge of the shop where she works. He tells me that he acted on impulse on finding himself alone in the shop. He seems to have been unable to resist taking advantage of an unexpected opportunity. He further admits another unconnected offence. The second offence concerns the theft of an emerald necklace valued at £500 which Mr. Williams took from the counter of an antique shop. Here again he tells me that he acted on the spur of the moment taking the necklace when the assistant's back was turned. I understand that all the stolen property has been handed to the police.

8. Mr. Williams has been in custody since he was arrested for the offence in question on 29th June 1989. His period of custody appears to have given him a salutary shock. He seems genuinely contrite for having given in to temptation on two occasions. He wishes to make a fresh start. He realises that by his behaviour he has endangered his marriage, his home-life and his business and assures me that he will make every effort to ensure that he will not come before the courts again. I have to say that I find it surprising that in his present situation with so much to lose he has not been able to resist temptation.

9. Mr. Williams is a straightforward likeable man. He went through a bad patch after his redundancy followed by the breakdown of his first marriage. But he seemed to make a fresh start when he met his second wife. Their marriage appears to be stable and happy and the success of the business is a tribute to the strength of their partnership. He is a caring father to his two step-children aged 3 and 4. The eldest child suffers from severe asthmatic attacks which started after his father deserted the family. Mr. Williams has shown a surprising degree of patience and involvement and I have no doubt that he is at least partly responsible for the improvement in the child's health in the last year. From the children's point of view it is very unfortunate that the stability of their present life is in jeopardy. However, in view of Mr. Williams's previous convictions it may be felt that there is no alternative to a custodial sentence.

17th August 1989

(signed) Hilary Ashford

Summer 1989

LITIGATION

(CRIMINAL)

SUGGESTED ANSWER

1. (a) W will have been remanded in custody. The general rule (applicable in this case) is that he cannot be remanded in custody for more than eight clear days at a time and therefore he will have to be brought back before the court within that time. At that stage a further application for bail can be made. The defendant may make a further application and in support of it put forward any argument of fact or law whether or not he has put forward that argument previously.

   (b) Under section 4 of the Bail Act 1976 a defendant has a right to bail unless (in the case of an imprisonable offence such as this) one of the exceptions contained in the Schedule to the Act applies. The refusal of bail by the court on the last occasion will have been made on one of the relevant grounds and it will be important to examine the certificate to see which ground was found to exist by the court.

   If the prosecution oppose the second bail application the relevant ground is likely to be that there are substantial grounds for believing that, if released on bail, W would fail to surrender to custody. In deciding whether that ground is applicable the court must have regard (*inter alia*) to the nature and seriousness of the offences and the probable methods of dealing with the defendant; the defendant's character antecedents, associations and community ties and the strength of the evidence against him. The prosecution are likely to argue that the offence is serious because items of substantial value are involved; that in view of his previous convictions and the fact that he is subject to a suspended sentence he is likely to receive a custodial sentence; that he has foreign business connections and therefore may have the ability to set up home and make a life abroad tempting him to abscond; and that the evidence against him seems to be strong because of his wife's statement and the identification of the diamonds.

   It might further be argued by the police that W if released might interfere with the prosecution witness (*i.e.* his wife). She has allegedly indicated her fear of her husband. It might be that if granted bail he will return to the matrimonial home and pressure her to withdraw her evidence.

(c) It will be important to put forward arguments to counter the first objection; these points will include the fact that he appears to have stable community ties living with his wife and children and running an apparently successful business; that he appears to have surrendered to bail on previous occasions since there are no offences of absconding on his record. The other objection is much more difficult to counter. It is possible to call evidence on a bail application and perhaps if his wife is now willing to say that she has been misunderstood and is not in fact afraid of him that would be worthwhile. Prima facie there is a right to unconditional bail. However the court may impose conditions so far as may be necessary to meet objections. It might therefore be prudent in the present case to offer conditions to the court so that bail may be secured. In the present case to meet the objection relating to absconding abroad it may be appropriate to either offer security from W himself, *i.e.* the deposit of a sum of money; or to suggest one or more sureties to secure his surrender. The nature of a surety is that it is someone who agrees to forfeit a sum of money if the defendant does not appear. A spouse is not an acceptable surety and therefore instructions should be taken as to whether any business acquaintances, parents, etc., might be available. The prosecution may object to sureties and the magistrates must consider a variety of factors including the sureties' own record and their proximity in point of kinship or place to the defendant. No details are given in the question of any such persons. Other conditions which may be suggested are to abide by a curfew or to report to the police station or to surrender the passport. All these may be unacceptable to W in view of his proposed business trip but perhaps it would be in his best interests to postpone that if possible in the event of strong prosecution objection and to offer these conditions.

(d) After a second refusal of bail the defendant can make a further application for bail at each subsequent hearing. Although the application must be heard the magistrates need not on subsequent hearings listen to arguments as to fact or law which they have heard previously. These matters will be known because they are recorded.

If W is remanded in custody the magistrates must issue a "full argument certificate" certifying the reason why bail has been refused. Thereupon the defendant can apply for bail to the Crown Court. Application is made on 24 hours' notice (this is often waived) to the prosecution and heard by a circuit judge in chambers.

Application may be made in any event to a High Court judge in chambers on summons with affidavit. W is not dependent on legal aid and he may well instruct us to make application in this form. (Criminal legal aid is not available for this).

2.   W has been charged with theft which is an "either way offence." In other words it can be tried either in the Magistrates' Court or the Crown Court before a judge and jury. The mode of trial hearing takes place in the Magistrates' Court. The magistrates must decide, after hearing representations from prosecution and defence whether the case is more

suitable for summary trial or Crown Court trial having regard to; the nature of the case; whether the offence is of a serious character and whether their powers of sentencing are likely to be adequate; they do not at this stage know of W's criminal record. Before the hearing commences the magistrates must be satisfied that W is aware of the requirement on the prosecution to furnish details of the case against him in advance under the Advance Information Rules 1985.

If the court decides that trial on indictment is more suitable then that is the end of the matter. However if it decides that summary trial is more suitable W will be asked if he consents to summary trial or whether he wishes for jury trial. The court must explain that if he does consent to summary trial he may, if convicted, be committed to the Crown Court for sentence if the magistrates on hearing about his character decide that their powers to sentence him are not sufficient. Only if he then agrees can the case be tried summarily.

The relevant factors to be borne in mind by W include the following:—

1. **Costs.**
Since he is paying for himself this may be an important factor. The case will be much cheaper in the magistrates' court.

2. **Stress.**
The proceedings in the magistrates' court will be quicker and less formal and therefore less personally stressful. However W may be a relatively strong character and this may not matter much to him but he may be anxious to minimise stress to his wife and stepchild.

3. **Speed.**
Proceedings in the magistrates' court will also be quicker which may be an important factor if W is in custody especially bearing in mind the damage that may occur to his business interests.

4. **Publicity.**
Local factors differ here. However generally Crown Court trial is more likely to be reported.

5. **Sentence.**
This is not a major factor because the magistrates have the power to commit for sentence and therefore the fact that generally they have lesser powers of punishment is not vital.

6. **Factors in favour of Crown Court trial.**
  (i) *Acquittal.*
  Although the statistical evidence is inconclusive it is generally thought that a jury is more likely to take such concepts as "a reasonable doubt" seriously than magistrates. This is particularly important in this case.

  (ii) *Evidence.*
  The procedure for deciding questions of admissibility is much more satisfactory in the Crown Court. The separation of function between judge and jury means that inadmissible evidence is not heard

by the jury whereas in the magistrates' court the same magistrates decide on admissibility as then decide on the facts and they may be unable to put out of their mind items of evidence even if they have ruled them inadmissible. There are a number of particular factors present in this case which will be discussed later in the evidence question. In addition concepts such as corroboration are much more realistically dealt with by direction in open court from the judge to the jury.

(iii) *Committal proceedings.*
Sometimes full committal proceedings are useful to test the strength of the prosecution evidence and in a way to give a "second bite at the cherry." A submission can be made that there is no case on which to commit thus giving a chance to have the case thrown out early.

3. (a) LW is the wife of the accused. She is therefore competent but not compellable on these facts. Therefore the prosecution cannot make her give evidence against her husband. Should she be willing to testify she should be warned before she commences to testify that she has a right not to do so but that once she has chosen to do so she must answer any proper question.

(b) As there is no property in a witness it would be perfectly proper for us to interview LW. It is sometimes said that it is prudent to give notice to the prosecution of intention to interview their witnesses so that they may be present at the interview. Views about this differ between practitioners.

(c) LW is competent and compellable for the defence. She now appears to be willing to give evidence in support of her husband's version of events. The advantage of calling her is that she can give that evidence to the effect that he did not in fact enter the shop that afternoon. However of course the disadvantage is that once she starts to testify the prosecution can cross-examine her on the facts and she is likely to be shaken in view of her previous inconsistent statement. The prosecution can then put her previous inconsistent statement to her. In the circumstances it is likely to make a bad impression on the court that she has made such a previous inconsistent statement. Whilst in a criminal case the court is not meant to speculate on which of two statements may be accurate and should discount them both, in practical terms the magistrates are quite likely to speculate about this change of mind and to prefer the earlier of the statements. It would therefore be disadvantageous to call her.

4. (a) Mr. W-J appears to be an expert witness. If the court is prepared to accept that he is an expert he can give opinion evidence on matters within the sphere of his expertise.

It would undoubtedly be better if he were called to give oral evidence and if it seems he is likely to be unwilling a witness summons may be obtained from the magistrates' clerk. Where an expert report is to be given then under section 30 of the Criminal Justice Act 1988 such a report is admissible as to any fact or opinion of which the maker

459

could have given oral evidence. It may even be admissible if the maker does not propose to give oral evidence with the leave of the court. In deciding whether to grant that leave the court is directed to have regard to all the circumstances.

(b) The receipt in itself is not very helpful unless it is supplemented by further evidence that the "precious stones" included six diamonds. Mr. V-T cannot be made to attend the court because he is outside the United Kingdom. His letter is hearsay evidence and in principle is inadmissible unless an exception to the hearsay rule applies.

By section 23 of the Criminal Justice Act 1988 a statement made by a person in a document is admissible in criminal proceedings as evidence of any fact of which direct oral evidence would be admissible provided one of the requirements of the section is satisfied. The relevant one here is that he is outside the United Kingdom and it is not reasonably practicable to secure his attendance. However since the statement has been prepared for the purpose of pending criminal proceedings it cannot be given in evidence unless the court gives leave. In deciding whether to give leave the court has to have regard to the matters in section 26 of the Criminal Justice Act namely whether it should be admitted in the interests of justice. In considering that the court should have regard to all the circumstances including the contents of the statement and the risk that its exclusion would result in unfairness to the accused. This latter criterion favours the accused and therefore might in the present case lead to the admission of the document. It will still be necessary for the accused to prove that V-T's attendance cannot practicably be secured.

Parts of the letter are not admissible even so. The last sentence of the first paragraph to the effect that the six diamonds were the same as those found in his possession is not within V-T's knowledge and therefore inadmissible.

(c) The receipt is also hearsay evidence although this is admissible under section 24 of the Criminal Justice Act 1988. It is a document created by a person in the course of business and the information contained in it was supplied by a person (V-T) who had personal knowledge of the matters dealt with. It might also be considered to fit section 23 as above.

On this occasion the receipt was *not* prepared for the purposes of criminal proceedings so it is prima facie admissible provided that the court applies the factors in section 25 of the Act. These include (*inter alia*) the extent to which the statement appears to supply evidence which would otherwise not be readily available and whether it is likely that the document is authentic. Again the main criterion is the risk of unfairness to the accused and since the receipt is in his favour it is unlikely to be ruled admissible in the present case.

5. (a) **Document 2.**
Lindley is clearly a competent witness and despite the vague suggestion of an insurance fraud it would not really seem appropriate to suggest that there is any need for corroboration in his case.
His statement is largely unobjectionable except for the last paragraph.

The reference to our client's police record, Mrs. Williams's fear of her husband and his general appearance are inadmissible as unnecessarily prejudicial. We will accordingly advise the Crown Prosecutor to ask Lindley not to say these things and ensure that no questions are asked to lead him into such statements.

The suggestion that Lindley is engaged in an insurance fraud involves imputations on the character of the witness. It would therefore cause Williams to lose his shield rendering him liable to be cross-examined under section 1(*f*)(ii) of the Criminal Evidence Act 1898. Once his criminal record was known to the magistrates then although they should in principle direct themselves that it is relevant only to his credibility they may well be prejudiced against him by their knowledge and conclude that he is back to his old ways.

In the circumstances it would be best to advise our client that it would be too dangerous to pursue this line of defence in view of his criminal record. It does not seem that there is any evidence at all to substantiate our client's suspicion of this insurance fraud. It would be much better to drop this line of defence.

(b) **Document 3.**

The worst aspect of this statement is the parts that tend to incriminate him, namely the turning pale and the statement "Christ I'm on a suspended sentence this could mean prison." These things are in principle admissible either as a reaction on being accused or as a confession within the meaning of PACE, *i.e.* an admission by a defendant wholly or partly adverse to him.

The prosecution will need to prove, if it is disputed, that the "confession" is admissible under section 76 of PACE but there is no suggestion either of oppression or that anything has been said or done to render it unreliable. The main problem with the statement is that it is highly prejudicial because of its reference to Williams's criminal record. Even if the words "I'm on a suspended sentence" were edited out it would be difficult to explain the rest of the statement without them. The court has a general discretion to exclude the prosecution evidence if it appears that in all the circumstances its admission would have an unfair effect on the trial. This is both at common law and under section 78 of PACE. It therefore ought to be argued that the court ought to exclude this statement. The procedural problem is that since the case is being heard in the magistrates' court the magistrates cannot decide to exclude it without having heard that evidence. The best that one can do therefore is to approach the Crown Prosecutor and see if he is prepared to agree that the statement ought to be excluded. The Crown Prosecutor is meant in principle to act as a "Minister of Justice" and not to strive for a conviction at all costs and it may be possible to persuade him to agree. Our client gives no explanation in this statement of how the diamonds came into his possession. In some ways this may appear strange because he has a credible innocent explanation. However he has a right of silence and therefore no adverse inference may be drawn from his exercise of that right when he was questioned by a policeman.

The entry and search of Williams's house may well have been illegal. There was no search warrant nor had Williams been arrested. Nevertheless evidence, however it is obtained, is prima facie admissible unless it would be unfair to the accused under section 78 of PACE. The finding of real evidence by illegal search is most unlikely to be excluded.

In the circumstances there seems very little upon which to cross-examine Carter since there are no disputes of fact.

6. (a) Williams can ask the Crown Court to "take into consideration" the theft of the emerald necklace. "Taking into consideration" involves a defendant admitting other offences of which he is not at that stage necessarily suspected and which should usually be of a similar, or less serious nature. The court will then take the offence into account when sentencing him for the substantive offence and in many circumstances the actual sentences given is no greater, or little greater than the sentence would have been for the substantive offence alone. It is important that Williams is seen to hand the necklace back himself and therefore it would be as well to arrange on his behalf for you to collect and return it.

   (b) The magistrates have committed Williams to the Crown Court for sentence because they have, on hearing details of his character and antecedents, formed the opinion that the punishment that should be inflicted on him is greater than they have the power to inflict.

In the Crown Court he may be dealt with as if he had been tried in the Crown Court that is, he may be sentenced to up to 10 years' imprisonment and/or an unlimited fine. In addition the Crown Court may activate the suspended sentence of six months' imprisonment since he has committed this further offence within the period of suspension. The activated sentence is usually imposed to run consecutively to any term of imprisonment imposed for the present offence.

   (c) Solicitors do not have a general right of audience in the Crown Court. However, a solicitor who has represented a client in the magistrates' court can represent that client at the stage of committal for sentence to the Crown Court.

7. Obviously Williams's main concern is to avoid a sentence of imprisonment, or a lengthy sentence of imprisonment if some custodial sentence is inevitable. The following matters should be considered:—
   (i) *The offence.*
      Since Williams now admits his guilt the best that can be said about matters is that the offence was committed on impulse rather than by a cunning premeditated plan; and that the property has been recovered without substantial loss.

   (ii) *The offender.*
      Williams's personal circumstances should be taken into account. The fact that he now has a settled and stable home life and that absence from home might well prejudice his stepson's health; the responsible way he has acted in relation to his new family; the fact that he has a successful and apparently honest business and that this is likely to collapse if he remains in custody.

It is also vital to consider his conduct generally in relation to the suspended sentence and the offence taken into consideration:—

(a) The suspended sentence.

Prima facie there is a duty for the court to activate a suspended sentence where the defendant has committed another imprisonable offence within the operational period. The court has a discretion not to activate a sentence or to activate only part of it, if the court is of the opinion that it would be unjust to do so in all the circumstances, and in particular where the second offence is committed towards the end of the operational period or is trivial. Sometimes if the second offence is of a completely different nature that fact is also relevant. Here one can argue that the period of suspension had less than three months to run at the time of the second offence. Unfortunately however this new offence is of the same type as the first offence and is far from trivial.

In reality the question of punishment for the suspended sentence is bound up with how Williams is dealt with in relation to the present offence and the "package" of punishments that is to be imposed. If the court concludes that Williams should go to prison immediately for the present offence they are likely to impose at least part of the suspended sentence. Often in these cases the court considers what global punishment it considers appropriate. In relation to the offence for which the suspended sentence was imposed one can sometimes gain some advantage by mitigating retrospectively that is to say stressing the factors which may have contributed to the last offence such as the break-up of his marriage, his being led astray by another and his awkward domestic arrangements.

Even if the magistrates do decide to impose the suspended sentence they can always be urged to make it concurrent with the sentence for the present offence.

(b) With regard to the offence taken into consideration clearly this offence is a serious one and it may well tend to show a course of deliberate criminal conduct in relation to jewellery. That Williams's business also involves jewellery may well lead the court to draw unfortunate conclusions of a general nature. In the light of the further offence the best that one can say is to stress Williams' co-operation in returning the property which may be a sign of genuine contrition and a determination to go straight in future for the sake of his new family.

Summer 1989

SOLICITORS' FINAL EXAMINATION QUESTIONS

THURSDAY, 6TH JULY (2 P.M. TO 4 P.M.)

Candidates should answer all questions

LITIGATION

(CIVIL)

In June 1989 you are consulted by John Dickens. He tells you that he was involved in a collision when riding a bicycle in which another cyclist was injured. He hands you a summons from the Exbridge County Court (not supplied) and two further documents (Documents 1 and 2). You obtain a statement from him (Document 3). Mr. Dickens instructs you to defend the case. You ascertain that he is not eligible for legal aid (on financial grounds).

1. Explain to your client the significance of Document 2 and the effect that it may have on him as the defendant in the case. (*8 marks*)

2. You wish to obtain a police accident report before preparing the defence and anticipate that you will not be able to file the Defence within the time limit shown on the Summons. How would you seek an extension of time? (*4 marks*)

3. Your client is particularly upset about the allegations in paragraph 3 of the Particulars of Claim. He asks you whether anything can be done about that paragraph. Advise him. (*8 marks*)

4. You receive the police accident report (Document 4. extract consisting of three statements marked respectively 4A, 4B and 4C) and obtain a statement from Mrs. White (Document 5).

   (a) Draft the Defence. (*18 marks*)

   (b) Having regard to the nature of the defence, what other documents would you draft, and what other steps would you take, at this stage of the proceedings? (*6 marks*)

(c) What steps would you expect the plaintiff's solicitors to take when they consider your client's defence? (*8 marks*)

5. How would you seek—

(a) to establish the extent of the plaintiff's injuries and (if possible) to agree their extent with the other side? (*6 marks*)

(b) to verify the amount of the plaintiff's special damages and (if possible) to agree this amount with the other side. (*6 marks*)

6. After some unsuccessful negotiations you advise Mr. Dickens that a payment into court of £4,000 (inclusive of interest) should be made. Explain to Mr. Dickens the purpose and effect of such a payment (on the basis that he is the only defendant). (*8 marks*)

7. Your client accepts your advice and you make a payment into court of £4,000 on 20 August 1989. It is not accepted. The date of the trial is fixed for 1 November 1989. Consider how far (if at all), and for what purposes—

(a) the oral statements made to Vera Marsh by Mr. Dickens at the time of the accident could be used by the plaintiff at the trial; and

(b) the evidence of Mrs. White could be adduced by your client at the trial.
Would any procedural steps be necessary in either case? (*14 marks*)

8. On 21st September 1989 your client comes to see you. He tells you that he has heard that Mr. Pickford exaggerated the extent of his injuries. Your client hands you a statement he has obtained from a Mr. York (Document 6). He is now anxious that Mr. Pickford will get to hear that Mr. York has been in touch and will take the opportunity to settle the case by accepting the payment in.

(a) What steps would you take to ensure that evidence of the plaintiff's participation in cricket is brought before the Court?

(b) Advise Mr. Dickens whether Mr. Pickford can still withdraw the money paid into court. (*12 marks*)

Total = *100 marks*

DOCUMENT 1

IN THE EXBRIDGE COUNTY COURT   Case No. 890120
BETWEEN

ROBERT PICKFORD   Plaintiff
– and –
JOHN DICKENS   Defendant

PARTICULARS OF CLAIM

1. On the 3rd February 1989 at about 11.30 p.m. the Plaintiff was riding his pedal bicycle in a northerly direction along Banchurch Road, Exbridge in the County of Blankshire. When the Plaintiff had reached a point about three miles South of Exbridge and approximately level with a lay-by on the East side of Banchurch Road the Defendant who was riding his pedal bicycle in a southerly direction along Banchurch Road swerved in front of the Plaintiff, colliding with the Plaintiff and his bicycle and causing the Plaintiff to fall from his bicycle to the ground.

2. The collision was caused by the negligence of the Defendant.

PARTICULARS OF NEGLIGENCE

The Defendant was negligent in that he:

(a) Swerved sharply and without warning to his right, into the path of the Plaintiff.

(b) Failed to observe or heed the Plaintiff while he was riding his bicycle.

(c) Failed to steer or to control his bicycle adequately or at all.

(d) Failed to stop, swerve, steer or otherwise take adequate action to avoid the Plaintiff.

(e) Rode his bicycle while unfit through drink.

3. By reason of the matters aforesaid the Defendant was convicted on the 28th March 1989 by the Exbridge Magistrates' Court of the offence of cycling while unfit through drink contrary to section 19 of the Road Traffic Act 1972. Further, the Defendant by his drunken driving caused a motor accident on the 2nd November 1988 and was on the 30th November 1988 convicted by the Exbridge Magistrates' Court of the offence of driving a motor vehicle with blood alcohol concentration above the prescribed limit contrary to section 6 of the Road Traffic Act 1972.

The said convictions are relevant to the issue of negligence and to the issue of the Defendant's propensity to drive or ride vehicles while unfit through drink and the Plaintiff intends to rely on them as evidence in this action.

4. As a result of the negligence of the Defendant, the Plaintiff has suffered injury, loss and damage.

PARTICULARS OF INJURY

Cuts, bruises and fracture of the right patella. The Plaintiff's right leg was in plaster for 6 weeks. He was in hospital for 3 days. He attended a fracture clinic as an out-patient once a week until the 1st June 1989. He was off work for 15 weeks after the accident. He still suffers from discomfort from the injury and is unable to participate in sport. The Plaintiff was born on 18 September 1968.

PARTICULARS OF SPECIAL DAMAGE

Loss of earnings from February 4, to May 22, 1989 (15 weeks) at the net rate of £130.03 per week.	£1,950.45	
Less statutory sick pay received (15 weeks at £52.10 per week).	£781.50	
		£1,168.95
Cost of bicycle damaged beyond repair.		£150.00
Cost of trousers damaged beyond repair.		£24.00
Travelling expenses to and from hospital at £1.50 per visit (16 visits).		£24.00
		£1,366.95

5. The Plaintiff is entitled to interest on the damages pursuant to section 69 of the County Courts Act 1984 at such rates and for such periods as seems just to the court.

And the Plaintiff claims

(1) Damages

(2) Interest pursuant to section 69 of the County Courts Act 1984.

Dated this 3rd day of June 1989.

> Hills & Co
> Plaintiff's solicitors of
> 11, High Street, Exbridge,
> who will accept service of
> all proceedings on behalf of
> the Plaintiff at such address.

To the Chief Clerk
and to the Defendant.

DOCUMENT 2

LEGAL AID ACT 1988
NOTICE OF ISSUE OF LEGAL AID CERTIFICATE

IN THE EXBRIDGE COUNTY COURT   Case No. 89/0120
BETWEEN
              ROBERT PICKFORD   Plaintiff

– and –

JOHN DICKENS   Defendant

TAKE notice that a Legal Aid Certificate No 55/89/10/2345 dated the 2nd day of May 1989 has been issued in Area No. 1 to ROBERT PICKFORD in connection with the following proceedings:—

to prosecute a claim against John Dickens for damages for negligence

TAKE further notice that, in consequence thereof, the Plaintiff in these proceedings is an assisted person.

Dated this 3rd day of June 1989.

(signed) Hills and Co
of 11, High Street, Exbridge
Solicitors for the Plaintiff

To the Chief Clerk
and to the Defendant

DOCUMENT 3

John Dickens of 13, Marlborough Court, Banchurch, Blankshire will say:—

I am a senior lecturer of ancient history at Exbridge University.

In November 1988 I was involved in a motor accident. I was breathalysed and convicted of drinking and driving. I was disqualified from driving for one year. I am using a bicycle until I get my licence back.

On Friday 3rd February 1989 I went to a college dinner in Exbridge. After the dinner I cycled home. The night was clear. I cycled in a Southerly direction down the Banchurch Road towards Banchurch. At about 11.30 p.m. I approached a lay-by on my left. A lorry was parked there. I was passing the lay-by when the lorry's lights were turned on and the lorry started to pull out into Banchurch Road in the same direction as me. I do not think the driver saw me. In order to avoid the lorry I swerved right and collided with a cyclist travelling North up the Banchurch Road towards Exbridge. We both fell to the ground. The other cyclist's leg appeared to be broken and he sustained cuts and bruises. I was very shaken but was not hurt. My bicycle was not damaged.

The lorry driver stopped and came to the scene. A woman called Mrs. White (whom I know slightly and who lives on the Banchurch Road) came running up. She said that she would telephone for an ambulance. I suppose she did because shortly afterwards both a police car and an ambulance arrived at the scene. The other cyclist was taken away to hospital but I said that I would be all right. The police came to speak to me. I am afraid that I was not very coherent, but that was because I was in a state of shock. I have been very nervous about accidents since my motor accident last year. I had consumed about two glasses of white wine, two glasses of red wine, a glass of sherry, some port and a small brandy. I was definitely not drunk and was perfectly capable of riding my bicycle.

I was charged with riding a bicycle while unfit through drink. I pleaded not guilty but was convicted by the Exbridge Magistrates' Court and fined £50. I still say I was not drunk. Even if I had had too much to drink I could not have stopped myself from colliding with the other cyclist. The accident was the fault of the driver of the lorry who would have hit me if I had not taken avoiding action. In avoiding the lorry there was really nothing that I could have done to prevent the collision with Mr. Pickford.

I received a letter from Mr. Pickford's solicitors some time ago. They advised me to pass it to my insurers. As I am not insured for cycling accidents I ignored the letter.

DOCUMENT 4

POLICE ACCIDENT REPORT: EXTRACT ONLY

4A

Exbridge Constabulary

Division: traffic   Section: Exbridge

Name: Vera Marsh

Address: Police station, Exbridge

Age/date of birth: over 21

Occupation: Police Woman

This statement (consisting of one page signed by me) is true to the best of my knowledge and belief and I make it knowing that if it is tendered in evidence I shall be liable to prosecution if I have wilfully stated in it anything which I know to be false or do not believe to be true.

(signed) V. Marsh

On 3rd February 1989 I was on duty on mobile patrol with P.C. Graham Scott. At 11.45 p.m. I received a report of an accident in Banchurch Road, Exbridge about three miles from Exbridge. I arrived at the scene of the accident at 11.55 p.m.

At the scene I found a cyclist, Robert Pickford, who had received injuries to his leg. An ambulance arrived some minutes later and he was taken to Queen Mary's Hospital, Exbridge.

It appeared that another bicycle being ridden by Mr. John Dickens had collided with Mr. Pickford's bicycle, causing both cyclists to fall. Mr. Dickens was sitting on the side of the road with his head between his hands but appeared to be unhurt. I approached Mr. Dickens and asked him how the accident had occurred. He said "I feel terrible about this. I only took up cycling because I did not want to cause another accident ever again. I don't know how this could have happened. I'm sorry." His speech was slurred and I smelt alcohol on his breath. I asked him if he had been drinking. He said "That's none of your business, I'm not driving a car only a bicycle." He then became abusive. I formed the impression that he was intoxicated. I then cautioned him and warned him that he would be reported for riding a bicycle while unfit through drink.

At the time that I attended the scene of the accident the weather was fine. The road surface was dry and in good condition.

Date: 4th February 1989 (signed) V. Marsh

4B

Exbridge Constabulary

Division: traffic   Section: Exbridge

Name: James Gower

Address: 4, Churchill Drive, Northton

Age/date of birth: over 21

Occupation: Truck driver

This statement (consisting of one page signed by me) is true to the best of my knowledge and belief and I make it knowing that if it is tendered in evidence I shall be liable to prosecution if I have wilfully stated in it anything which I know to be false or do not believe to be true.

(signed) J. Gower

I am a driver for Associated Biscuits (Northton) PLC. On Friday 3rd February 1989 I was driving a loaded truck registration number C123 YTZ from Northton to Southampton in the course of my employment. I stopped for a rest at a lay-by on the Banchurch Road about three miles to the South of Exbridge. At about 11.30 p.m. I decided to resume my journey. I switched on my engine and my head-lights. I looked in my mirror and saw a middle-aged man cycling Southwards on the Banchurch Road alongside my truck. He was cycling unsteadily. Suddenly and for no apparent reason he veered to the wrong side of the road and collided with a young man who was cycling Northwards towards Exbridge. Both cyclists fell down.

I got out of the truck and ran to their assistance. A woman said that she would call for help. I put my coat over the young man who seemed to be in some pain and waited for the ambulance to come.

(signed) J. Gower

Recorded by V. Marsh
Where taken: Banchurch Road, Exbridge
Time commenced: 12.25 a.m.

470

Time completed: 12.45 a.m.
Date: 4th February 1989

4c

Exbridge Constabulary

Division: traffic   Section: Exbridge

Name: Robert Pickford

Address: 61, London Road, Exbridge

Age/date of birth: over 21

Occupation: Fitter

This statement (consisting of one page signed by me) is true to the best of my knowledge and belief and I make it knowing that if it is tendered in evidence I shall be liable to prosecution if I have wilfully stated in it anything which I know to be false or do not believe to be true.

(signed) R. Pickford

On Friday 3rd February I spent the evening at my girl friend's house in Banchurch. At about 11.15 p.m. I set off for home on my bicycle. I saw a cyclist coming towards me. He was wobbling. I thought he might well fall off. Suddenly he swerved over to my side of the road. I tried to avoid him but he went straight into me. I fell down and the other bicycle fell on top of me and my bicycle. I realised that I had broken my leg.

(signed) R. Pickford

Recorded by V. Marsh
Where taken: Queen Mary's Hospital, Exbridge
Time commenced: 11.20 a.m.
Time completed: 11.35 a.m.
Date: 5th February 1989

DOCUMENT 5

Mary White of The Elms, 34 Banchurch Road, Exbridge will say:—

At about 11.30 p.m. on Friday 3rd February I went to the front door to put the milk bottles out. I saw a lorry parked in the lay-by opposite. The headlights were suddenly switched on and the lorry started to move out of the lay-by into Banchurch Road. He did not give way to a cyclist coming up the Banchurch Road. The cyclist swerved to avoid the lorry and collided with another cyclist going in the opposite direction. Both cyclists fell down. I went out to see if anyone was hurt. I then saw that the first cyclist was Mr. Dickens whom I know socially. He seemed very shaken. He said "It's all the lorry driver's fault." In my opinion he had been drinking. But he did not appear to be drunk. The other cyclist had injured his leg. I returned home and telephoned the emergency services.

I cannot judge whether it would have been possible for Mr. Dickens to take avoiding action without colliding with the other cyclist.

I am afraid that I cannot come to court to give evidence for Mr. Dickens because I have to stay at home to look after my mother. She is 91 years old and is confined to bed. She requires constant nursing and I can only leave her for very short periods of time.

(signed) M. White
Dated 28th June 1989

DOCUMENT 6

TO WHOM IT MAY CONCERN

I am an Australian student and have spent the last year reading for a postgraduate degree course in Chemistry at Exbridge University. I will be returning to Sydney, Australia on 20th September where I will be taking up an appointment on 1st October.

During my stay in England I have been living in a flat in East Dean, a village about 5 miles from Exbridge. The village has a cricket team which plays matches every Sunday. They are chronically short of players. So I volunteered to play for them this summer. The cricket season started on Sunday 7th May. Robert Pickford plays for the team as well. He played for the village on 7th May, and has not missed a match all summer.

When my supervisor (a colleague of Mr. Dickens) mentioned recently that Mr. Dickens is being sued by Robert Pickford I was sure that the man referred to is the Robert Pickford I know. Robert told us that he had been involved in an accident and was afraid that he would not be able to play cricket. In the first few matches of the season he could not run properly and was given fielding positions where he would not have to move around much. We all thought he was a terrific sport to play at all. But by about July he seemed to have no further difficulty in running and no longer complained about the injury. We all assumed his leg had healed up.

(signed) Bruce York
Dated 19th September 1989

Summer 1989

LITIGATION

(CIVIL)

SUGGESTED ANSWER

1. Document 2 is notice that the plaintiff has received legal aid to assist him in his action. This is unwelcome for three reasons:—

   (i) It demonstrates that P has convinced the legal aid authorities that he has a reasonable case. In practice this is not in itself of much moment because only his own version of the incident will have been put with his legal aid application and he will not have had to satisfy a very demanding test to get legal aid.

   (ii) It indicates also that he is unlikely to be deterred from continuing his action by reason of personal cost to himself.

   (iii) The main difference is on the question of costs. If P won the case it would make no difference. Our client would still have to pay his costs on the standard basis. However it is if our client wins that he will be in a worse position. Normally costs are awarded against the loser in litigation on the standard basis. But since P is legally aided then by section 17 of the Legal Aid Act 1988 the amount of costs which can be awarded against him cannot exceed the amount (if any) which it is reasonable for him to have to pay having regard to all the circumstances, including the financial resources of all the parties and their conduct in connection with the dispute. Typically the court requires a legally aided party to pay either no costs at all or a modest round sum figure. Accordingly the costs of even a successful defence of the litigation could be substantial and irrecoverable.

Since our client is the defendant he may be assisted by section 18 of the Legal Aid Act 1988. By this provision the costs of a successful unassisted defendant may be ordered to be paid by the Legal Aid Board provided that the personal liability of the assisted party has been considered under section 17; that it is just and equitable that our client should receive costs; and that he will suffer severe financial hardship unless the order is made. The words "severe financial hardship" are to be generously construed so that even reasonably prosperous persons may have an order made in their favour.

2. The parties may agree to an extension of time for filing the defence. No formalities as such are really required in the county court. Accordingly we should write to the plaintiff's solicitors asking for this extension of

time. If no agreement is reached then either a holding defence could be filed which we could later amend after we have received the report or alternatively an application could be made to the Registrar for an extension of time.

3. In general in civil cases one party may not adduce evidence of the other party's bad character or criminal record unless it is relevant. By section 11 of the Civil Evidence Act 1968 in civil proceedings the fact that a person has been convicted by a court in the United Kingdom is admissible to prove, where it is relevant, that he committed the offence in question. It raises the presumption that he committed the offence unless the contrary is shown. In paragraph 3 of the Particulars of Claim P has pleaded D's conviction of two offences and these must be separately considered.

The conviction for riding a bicycle while unfit through drink is prima facie relevant to the issue in this case since it occurred on the same occasion. The issue is the negligence of D. It raises a presumption that he was unfit to ride the bicycle through drink. Nonetheless our client may still allege that the conviction was erroneous or that, even if he were unfit through drink the collision was nevertheless not caused in fact by negligence.

On the other hand the conviction of November 30, 1988 is of no relevance to this case. The only purpose of pleading this conviction would be to show that our client is generally unsafe on the roads and a habitual drinker. Although similar fact evidence is admissible in civil cases this matter is clearly not within that rule. Accordingly our client may deny in his defence that the conviction is relevant; he may also apply to the court to strike out that part of paragraph 3 that relates to the earlier conviction on the grounds that it is irrelevant and/or scandalous and/or may prejudice the fair trial of the action.

4. (a) See separately.

(b) Our client is claiming that the accident was caused by the lorry driver. If it is found that our client was even partly to blame for the accident he will be liable to P for the full extent of damages. Our client will therefore wish to claim a contribution against the driver's employers on the assumption that he was driving within the course of his employment.

We will therefore issue a third-party notice containing a statement of the nature and ground of our client's claim. In these circumstances leave of the court is not required. When the third-party notice is issued without leave (as it will be in this case) the court fixes the date for a pre-trial review and endorses that date on the third-party notice. We then serve the third party with the third-party notice accompanied by the Summons, Particulars of Claim and Defence.

(c) The plaintiff's solicitors are likely to want to join the lorry driver's employers as second defendant. If it is shown that the driver wholly or partly caused the collision the plaintiff would have no remedy against the third party unless he had joined them. A particular consideration in the present case is that our client is uninsured and therefore the plaintiff may anticipate some difficulties in enforcing judgment against him. However if he has joined the lorry driver's employers and the accident is indeed found to be wholly or partly due to his negligence then the whole of the judgment could be enforced against the employers.

Even if the lorry driver is found not to be liable at all then the plaintiff will not be at risk as to costs because of the fact that a Sanderson order is likely to be made whereby the losing defendant (our client) will pay the winning defendant's costs.

In order for the plaintiff to join Associated Biscuits (Northton) plc he should, at the third-party pre-trial review, seek leave to amend the request for summons and Particulars of Claim to add the new defendant. Once leave is given then he will serve the amended summons and Particulars of Claim on the new defendant. It would also be prudent for the plaintiff to apply to have his legal aid certificate amended so as to cover the claim against the additional defendant. The amendment of the certificate should be filed with the court and notice of the amendment served on all defendants. It would also be prudent to serve on the insurers of Associated Biscuits (Northton) plc a notice under section 152 of the Road Traffic Act 1988 which will mean that any judgment for damages will be enforceable against those insurers even if they would have had, prima facie, the right to repudiate the insurance policy for some reason.

5. (a) The necessary procedure will involve obtaining expert medical evidence. The rules provide that in general no expert evidence may be adduced at the trial unless the party seeking to adduce it has previously applied to the court to determine whether and to what extent he should be ordered to give his opponents early disclosure of the substance of that evidence and has complied with any directions given. There is a presumption in favour of early disclosure unless there are strong reasons to the contrary. In the County Court there are now automatic directions for early disclosure of medical reports.

   Accordingly we should seek the agreement of the plaintiff to a medical examination. Such a request cannot be refused. If it is refused a stay will be imposed should we apply for such. However the plaintiff's solicitors may impose reasonable conditions such as the payment of P's costs and/or loss of earnings in attending the examination. The medical report should then be agreed if possible.

   (b) The special damages appear to consist of loss of earnings, cost of the bicycle, cost of clothing and travelling expenses. We should obtain documentary evidence from the other side verifying each of these where possible especially a letter from P's employers as to loss of wages and payment of statutory sick pay.

   Since P is claiming the cost of bicycle and trousers there may be receipts available for these. If not details must be provided of the time when they were purchased and their cost when new. If they are not of recent purchase we should argue for a deduction for wear and tear.

475

With regard to travelling expenses we should request details of the mode of transport used. It should be easy enough to agree these in view of our client's own local knowledge of distances.

6. A payment into court is not an admission of liability. It is an attempt to force a compromise on terms. It represents a legal gamble the nature of which is as follows:—

The plaintiff is allowed a period of 21 days from receipt of notice of payment in to decide whether to accept. If he does accept within that period he sends notice of acceptance to the court and to the defendant and the cause of action is then stayed. The plaintiff is entitled to his costs up to the date on which he accepted and the plaintiff can then obtain payment out of the amount in court.

If the plaintiff does not accept then the action continues. The money remains in court and after 21 days is transferred to an account where it will earn interest which belongs to the defendant. The trial judge is not told of the payment in until he has given judgment on liability and quantum. It is at that stage that the legal gamble comes into play. If the judge awards damages in excess of the paymen in the plaintiff is said to have "beaten" the payment in. Then the norma order for costs is made, that is that the defendant will pay the plaintiff's costs of the whole action. However if the plaintiff establishes liability but is awarded an amount of damages only equal to or less than the amount paid in a "split" order is made whereby the defendant will pay the plaintiff's costs up to the date of receipt of notice of payment in and the plaintiff will pay the defendant's costs thereafter. This split order will usually be made even in legal aid cases. The payment in must include a figure for interest such as the court would have awarded at the date when the payment in is made. Accordingly the actual amount tendered to the plaintiff will be somewhat less than £4,000 because this figure is to include interest.

7. (a) What the defendant said to Vera Marsh is not helpful to his case because it appears to imply that he acknowledged responsibility for the accident. P will wish to put this in before the court by calling Vera Marsh to give sworn evidence of what was said to her. What was said to her by the defendant will be hearsay evidence that is evidence of an oral statement other than by a person made on testifying in court which is adduced to prove the truth of the statement made. It is an informal admission by D and is admissible under section 9 of the Civil Evidence Act 1968.

Another unfortunate aspect is that the statement makes no mention of blaming any one else such as the lorry driver. Accordingly if our client gives evidence blaming the lorry driver then it will be damaging if he is cross-examined to the effect that he has made this matter up recently.

(b) It would be better if Mrs. White gave oral evidence at trial. If she is unwilling to come she can be served with a witness summons. She can give first-hand evidence as to the cause of the accident and about the defendant's sobriety. This is admissible opinion evidence because it is really evidence of facts perceived. By section 3(2) of the Civil

Evidence Act 1972 there is a relaxation on the general bar on evidence of opinion from laymen in such cases.

The evidence of what D said about the lorry driver is not admissible to prove the cause though it may be helpful to negative a suggestion of recent fabrication if such is put. This statement is then admissible as evidence of the truth of the statements by virtue of section 3 of the Civil Evidence Act 1968.

Mrs. White's statement could also be admitted in evidence under section 2 of the 1968 Civil Evidence Act; however, none of the section 8 grounds apply and therefore it could not be admitted as of right. We would therefore have to serve a notice complying with the rules not less than 14 days before the date fixed for the trial. However if a counter-notice was received then prima facie the statement would not be allowed and Mrs. White would have to come to court. The court exceptionally does have an inclusionary discretion to permit such evidence to be given and it might perhaps give sympathetic consideration to her problems with her invalid mother though in a matter of this importance such seems unlikely. If her evidence were admitted under section 2 then in deciding on the weight to be attached to it the court should have regard to section 6(3) of the 1968 Act under which the court must have regard to all the circumstances including the question of how contemporaneous the evidence is with the within described and any motive that the maker may have had to conceal or misrepresent the facts. The evidence is fairly neutral from this point of view.

8. (a) In view of the information given in this statement one option would certainly be to trace other members of the cricket team and get them to come to court to give oral evidence about the plaintiff's participation in cricket. Oral evidence is usually better than written evidence.

However the statement from Mr. York comprised in Document 6 will be admissible under section 2 of the Civil Evidence Act 1968. The statement could be admitted as of right because there is a section 8 ground namely that the witness is beyond the seas. It would be better to have the letter put in statement form sent out to Mr. York for agreement and then served (the procedure is described above in question 7). There could be no counter-notice in such a case demanding that York attend. One slight problem is the question of identification since it is not impossible that there is more than one Robert Pickford. This is why it is probably preferable to obtain oral evidence from another team member if such is available.

Once admitted the court must judge the weight of the evidence in accordance with section 6(3) and on the face of it this is good evidence in that York is most unlikely to be mistaken about the incident in view of any lapse of time, and appears to have no motive for fabrication.

(b) Even if more than 21 days have passed since the payment into court was made the plaintiff may still apply for leave of the court to accept the payment in out of time. There will be a hearing of that application at which we shall have the opportunity to attend and oppose the application to withdraw the money out of time on the grounds that new evidence has come to light which puts a wholly different complexion on the case.

4 (a)

IN THE EXBRIDGE COUNTY COURT   Case No. 890120
BETWEEN

ROBERT PICKFORD   Plaintiff
– and –
JOHN DICKENS   Defendant

DEFENCE

1. The Defendant admits that a collision occurred between a bicycle ridden by the Plaintiff and a bicycle ridden by the Defendant on the date and place alleged in the Particulars of Claim but denies the collision was caused by negligence either as alleged or otherwise on his part.

2. The collision was caused wholly by the negligence of one James Gower in the course of driving a lorry registration number C123 YTZ, as the servant or agent of the lorry owners Associated Biscuits (Northton) plc.

Particulars of negligence of James Gower

James Gower was negligent in that he:

(a)   Emerged from a lay-by on the Banchurch Road without warning when it was unsafe to do so causing the Defendant to swerve into the path of the bicycle ridden by the Plaintiff.

(b)   Failed to observe or heed the approach of the Defendant's bicycle and otherwise failed to keep a proper look out.

(c)   Failed to give way to the Defendant.

(d)   Failed to manage, steer or manoeuvre his said vehicle as to avoid coming into the path of the Defendant's bicycle.

3. The Defendant admits the conviction on the 28th March 1989 as alleged in the Particulars of Claim. The Defendant contends that the conviction was erroneous and in any event denies that the conviction is relevant to the issue in these proceedings. The defendant admits the conviction of 30th November 1988, but denies that the said conviction is relevant to any issue in these proceedings.

4. No admissions are made as to the alleged or any pain, injury, loss or damage referred to in paragraph 4 of the Particulars of Claim.

Dated this   day of   1989.

ABC & Co

Solicitors of the Defendant of

1 Main Road, Exbridge

who will at that address
accept service of all
proceedings on behalf of the
Defendant.

To the Chief Clerk
and to the Plaintiff.

NOTE TO READERS

The plot of the Summer 1989 Civil Question involves one important matter which has changed since then and affects Q.5 which presumes that no medical report was filed on issue of the proceedings (a procedure introduced in June 1990).

Summer 1990

SOLICITORS' FINAL EXAMINATION QUESTIONS

FRIDAY (10.00 A.M. TO 12.00 NOON)

Candidates should answer all questions.

LITIGATION

(CRIMINAL)

On Sunday 1st July 1990 at about 7.30 p.m. you are telephoned at home by Geoffrey Harris who tells you that he is on police bail and is due to appear before the Exbridge Magistrates' Court on Monday 2nd July. You agree to see him that evening. He hands you the charge sheet from which you see that he has been charged with "Theft of a motor car jointly with Brian Windsor on Friday 29th June, namely a Porsche motor car registration number 1 RMK the property of Rupert Morrison-Keys contrary to section 1 of the Theft Act 1968." You take a statement from him (**Document 1**). As it happens you are to be the Duty Solicitor at the Exbridge Magistrates' Court on 2nd July. Brian Windsor is in police custody and is not yet represented.

1. (a) What matters will be covered at the hearing on 2nd July?

    (*6 marks*)

   (b) Would it be proper for you to represent Brian Windsor in your capacity as Duty Solicitor at the hearing on 2nd July?   (*4 marks*)

2. Geoffrey Harris wishes to apply for legal aid. Assuming that he is financially eligible for legal aid, complete the enclosed extract from the legal aid application form for him. [Please include the completed form with your answer paper and ensure that you have written your Examination Number on the form.]   (*10 marks*)

3. Geoffrey Harris wishes to know the maximum penalties to which he will be liable if he is convicted. Write a letter to him explaining his position.

    (*14 marks*)

On advance disclosure you receive **Documents 2 to 6** from the Crown Prosecution Service. You satisfy yourself, by listening to the tape, that the Balanced Summary is an accurate record. You obtain comments on Documents 2 to 6 from your client which you add to his statement. You write to Queen Charlotte's Hospital with a view to obtaining evidence to confirm your client's account of his admission there. But, despite reminders, you are unable to obtain any substantive reply. Geoffrey Harris subsequently elects to be tried at the Exbridge Crown Court. He will be pleading not guilty but you understand from Brian Windsor's solicitor that Brian Windsor intends to plead guilty.

4. You advise Geoffrey Harris that committal proceedings with consideration of the evidence (under section 6(1) of the Magistrates' Courts Act 1980) should be held.

   (a) On what grounds may you have given this advice?

   (b) Briefly describe how you would conduct the section 6(1) proceedings giving reasons for your answer. Your answer should include any applications which you would make, or matters which the court would deal with, at the commencement, in the course of, or at the end of the proceedings. (*18 marks*)

5. Your client is committed for trial at Exbridge Crown Court. In relation to the trial, assess the evidence against Geoffrey Harris revealed by Documents 2 to 6, making it clear whether you consider any of it to be inadmissible and dealing with any evidential points which arise.

   (*28 marks*)

6. Before the trial, the Crown Prosecution Service receive a letter from Alex Gibson (**Document 7**).

   (a) What steps should the Crown Prosecutor now take?

   (b) If you were to learn of the letter, what steps would you take in the light of the new information it contains? (*6 marks*)

7. Before the trial, you receive a late reply to your letter to Queen Charlotte's Hospital from a Dr. Metcalfe (**Document 8**).

   (a) Would the hospital records be admissible to show the time at which Geoffrey Harris arrived at the hospital?

   (b) For what purposes would the evidence of Dr. Metcalfe be admissible at the trial?

   (c) Would it be necessary for her to appear in person? If so, how could her presence be secured? (*14 marks*)

   Total = *100 marks*

DOCUMENT 1

Geoffrey Harris of 31A Gower Road Exbridge will say:—

I have been charged with theft of a motor car and intend to plead not guilty.

Details of the charge of theft

On Friday 29th June I went to the White Horse public house, Exbridge after work. I got there at about 8.00 p.m. I was on my own. I started to drink with Brian Windsor and about 4 or 5 other young men. I know Brian because I went to school with him. I only know the others casually. I do not know their surnames.

After an hour or so we started talking about cars. Brian said that his favourite make was a Porsche. Someone mentioned that there was a Porsche in the car park. We went out and had a look at it. It was a brand new red one. We then went back. Brian said that he could do with one like it. Some of the others started to dare him to take it. I thought that Brian was starting to take the idea too seriously. I put my hand on his shoulder and told him not to be silly. He swung round and hit out at me. He swore at me and shouted that I was a fine one to talk what with my police record. I could see he was drunk. I told him to cool it and walked out of the pub.

I am rather hazy about what happened once I left the pub. I was upset and I have a vague memory of walking about town for a bit. I had intended to go out for an Indian meal but I no longer wanted to. Then I started feeling ill. The next thing I was aware of was that I was lying on the pavement and a man was leaning over me and asking me whether I was all right. I am diabetic and I run a risk of falling into a coma if my blood sugar level gets too low. This happens if I give myself an incorrect dose of insulin or if I do not eat the right amount of carbohydrate. I suppose missing my evening meal had upset the balance. Anyway, I managed to explain to the man that I am diabetic. He put me into a taxi and came with me to the casualty department of Queen Charlotte's Hospital Exbridge. By that time I had just about passed out. I cannot remember very much about my time in hospital but I imagine they put me onto a drip of glucose. When I was a bit better they called a taxi and I went home to bed.

Although I am rather vague about exactly where I went after I left the pub I am absolutely certain that I neither returned there, nor saw Brian Windsor again nor had anything to do with the theft of the car.

The next day I stayed in bed. I was still feeling a bit dazed. Then at about 4.00 p.m. there was a knock on the door. I ignored it because I was in bed and I assumed that one of my flat-mates would answer the door. They must have been out, because the knocking went on and the next thing I knew was that two policemen had burst into my flat. I protested but they said that I had stolen a car. They then arrested me and after I had put a few clothes on they drove me to the police station.

I was in the police station for about two hours when I was called out to take part in an identity parade. A woman picked me out. I do not know why. After that the police kept me in custody for a further period. Then they started to question me. They told me that Brian Windsor had said that I had taken a Porsche with him.

I told them I needed to get out to give myself an injection of insulin. They did not take any notice. I expect they thought it was some sort of illegal drug. I was offered food but I refused it because I thought that it might be dangerous to eat without my normal injection. I started to feel unwell. I was afraid that I would get into a coma again. I did not want to take that risk. That was partly because I had felt so terrible the night before and partly because I did not want my employers to find out that I am diabetic because I might lose my job. I was feeling very confused. I suppose that if I had been able to explain things properly to the police they would have let me get my injection kit. But I just could not handle the situation. In the end I just said that I had taken the car with Brian Windsor so that they would let me go home. They then charged me and released me on bail.

I had nothing to do with any theft. I only admitted it so that I could get out of the police station.

Personal details

I am 19 years old (date of birth 3rd March 1971).

I share a flat with two male friends. I work as a delivery man and take home about £120 a week. I will lose my job if I am disqualified from driving.

I have the following previous convictions:—

On 18th October 1986 I was sentenced by Exbridge Magistrates' Court to 3 months in a detention centre on various charges of criminal damage. This arose from an incident following a football match when I and several other youths smashed up a shop. I was drunk at the time.

[Note for candidates: the maximum sentence for criminal damage in this case is, on summary conviction, imprisonment for three months and/or a fine of £1,000 and, on indictment, imprisonment for 10 years and/or an unlimited fine.]

On 30th November 1988 I was convicted of driving without due care and attention by the Exbridge Magistrates' Court. I was fined £60 and my licence was endorsed (5 penalty points). I have paid this fine.

On 4th April 1989 I was placed on probation for a period of two years by the Exbridge Magistrates' Court on a charge of criminal damage. I had had an argument with a neighbour and kicked his car. I did not cause very much damage and paid for the car to be repaired.

COMMENTS ON THE PROSECUTION STATEMENTS (DOCUMENTS 2 TO 6)

Document 2

I do not possess a black hat. I was wearing jeans and a black leather jacket with silver studs on 29th June and also at the identity parade. But Brian Windsor and at least two other youths in the group we were drinking with were also wearing similar jackets. I am dark with a moustache but I cannot remember whether any of the other youths have moustaches.

Document 3

So far as I can remember, there were about 10 other men of about my age and height at the identity parade some of whom wore clothes fairly similar to mine. [**Note:** the colour photograph of the identity parade with the committal papers confirms that these recollections of the parade are correct.]

Document 4

The police account is substantially correct. I admit that I was alarmed to see the police in my flat unexpectedly, but that was not because I had a guilty conscience. I cannot remember saying "Christ I'm on probation."

Document 5

I do not agree with anything in Brian's statement. He is just making this up. He must have taken the Porsche after I had left the pub and then implicated me because he was still angry with me after our quarrel.

Document 6

I'm afraid that the summary of the interview is probably about right. I only admitted the theft because I was already feeling bad and was desperate to get home to give myself an injection before I passed out.

DOCUMENT 2

BLANKSHIRE POLICE

Name:	Rupert Morrison-Keys	Exbridge Station
Address:	Farnborough Court, Longwater, Exbridge	
Age/Date of Birth:	over 21	
Occupation:	Merchant banker	

Who states:—

This statement consisting of one page signed by me is true to the best of my knowledge and belief and I make it knowing that if it is tendered in evidence I shall be liable to prosecution if I have wilfully stated in it anything which I know to be false or do not believe to be true.

Dated 29th June 1990   (signed) R. Morrison-Keys

I am the registered owner of a Porsche motor car registration number 1 RMK. On Friday 29th June I took my girl friend, Melissa Hunterwell, for a meal at the White Horse public house, Exbridge. The restaurant is upstairs. We arrived at about 8.00 p.m. and parked the Porsche in the pub car park. At about 10.45 p.m. we returned to the car park and found that the car had been stolen. A woman told us that she had seen two youths driving the car away at about 10.00 p.m. She said one of the youths had a moustache and was wearing a black hat and a black leather jacket. I then reported the matter to the police.

No one had permission to drive my car away.

(signed) R. Morrison-Keys

Taken by D. Ferguson D.C. 30
Date: 29th June 1990 Time: 11.12 p.m.
(signed) D. Ferguson

DOCUMENT 3

BLANKSHIRE POLICE

Name:	Debbie Montgomery	Exbridge Station
Address:	Homeswood Farm, Wishford, Exbridge	
Age/Date of Birth:	over 21	
Occupation:	Secretary	

Who states:—

This statement consisting of one page signed by me is true to the best of my knowledge and belief and I make it knowing that if it is tendered in evidence I shall be liable to prosecution if I have wilfully stated in it anything which I know to be false or do not believe to be true.

Dated 30th June 1990   (signed) D. Montgomery

On Friday 29th June 1990 I went to the White Horse public house with a friend, Alex Gibson. We parked in the pub car park just after 10.00 p.m. As we were crossing the car park to the pub I saw two young men in a Porsche. They seemed to be having some difficulty in getting the car started. I remarked to Alex that they looked a bit young to be driving a Porsche and it looked rather fishy. I thought we had better report the incident to the police but Alex thought we did not have enough to go on. I noticed that the car had a personalised number plate with the number 1 and what looked like initials. But I cannot remember the letters. It was too dark to see the car's colour.

I did not see both of the young men. But I noticed that one of them was dark, had a moustache and was wearing jeans and a black leather jacket with silver studs on it.

I later heard a man in the pub telling the manager that his Porsche had been stolen. So I gave him my name and address.

I attended an identification parade held at Exbridge police station at 7.00 p.m. today. At this parade I picked out Geoffrey Harris as one of the two young men whom I saw in the Porsche motor car on Friday 29th June.

Dated 30th June 1990   (signed) D. Montgomery
Taken by D. Ferguson D.C. 30

Date: 30th June 1990 Time: 7.30 p.m.
(signed) D. Ferguson

DOCUMENT 4

BLANKSHIRE POLICE

Name: David Ferguson   Exbridge Station
Address: Exbridge Police Station
Age/Date of Birth: over 21
Occupation: Detective Constable

Who states:—

This statement consisting of one page signed by me is true to the best of my knowledge and belief and I make it knowing that if it is tendered in evidence I shall be liable to prosecution if I have wilfully stated in it anything which I know to be false or do not believe to be true.

Dated 30th June 1990   (signed) D. Ferguson

On Saturday 30th June at 11.40 a.m. I, with DC Young, visited Uxbridge Road in connection with an unrelated investigation. There we saw a young man whom I now know to be Brian Windsor emerging from a garage. When he saw us he tried to run away. We detained him and looked inside the garage. There we saw a red Porsche motor car registration number 1 RMK. It was evident that Windsor had been unscrewing the number plates with a view to replacing them with a spare set which was lying beside the vehicle. I arrested Windsor on suspicion of theft.

After making certain further enquiries I, with DC Young, went to 31A Gower Road, Exbridge at 4.10 p.m. intending to interview Geoffrey Harris. We knocked on the door several times without response. We formed the impression that someone was in. So we gained entry through a window. We searched the flat and discovered a young man, whom I now know to be Harris, in bed. Harris seemed very alarmed. We told Harris that we had reason to believe that he had been involved with the theft of a car. Harris said "Oh Christ, I'm on probation." We then cautioned him and told him that we were arresting him on suspicion of theft. After Harris had dressed we took him to the police station for questioning.

At 4.40 p.m. we arrived at the police station. Harris declined to say anything. At 5.30 p.m. I produced Harris to Police Sergeant Parker, the designated Custody Officer at the Police Station who authorised Harris to be kept in police custody pending the holding of an identity parade.

At 7.00 p.m. on Saturday 30th June an identification parade was held under the supervision of Inspector White. At the parade Miss Debbie Montgomery identified Geoffrey Harris as the person she had seen in a Porsche car in the car park at the White Horse public house on 29th June 1990.*

After the identification parade had been held Harris was taken to an interview room where I interviewed him at 7.40 p.m. by way of a tape

486

recorded interview. On Monday 2 June 1990 I prepared a balanced summary of the interview which I now produce (exhibit number D.F.1).

Following the interview the custody officer formally charged Harris with theft of a motor car jointly with Brian Windsor. Harris said "OK, OK, can I go now?" He was then released on police bail to appear at the Exbridge Magistrates' Court on 2nd July 1990.

(signed) D. Ferguson

* [Note: the record of the identification parade with a colour photograph (**neither of which are provided**) is included as an exhibit with the committal papers. The record of the arrest and interview of Windsor by Ferguson is also included (**but is not provided**).]

DOCUMENT 5

BLANKSHIRE POLICE

Name:	Brian Windsor	Exbridge Station
Address:	34 Uxbridge Road, Exbridge	
Age/Date of Birth:	December 9, 1970	
Occupation:	Salesman	

Who states:—

I, Brian Windsor, wish to make a statement. I want someone to write down what I say. I have been told that I need not say anything unless I wish to do so and whatever I say may be given in evidence.

Dated 30th June 1990   (signed) B. Windsor

On Friday 29th June 1990 I went to the White Horse public house. I met some other young men there. Among them was Geoffrey Harris. We had a few pints and started talking about cars. Geoffrey said that he could take any car. It was just a question of keeping cool and you could get away with it. He said he had taken a Ferrari once and sold it after changing the number plates. He knew a dealer who did not ask too many questions. I believed him because I know he is tough. He is always in and out of jail. The police know he does lots of jobs but he is generally too clever for them.

Anyway he dared me to come with him to take a car in the car park. He pointed to a really posh Porsche and said we ought to try that one. I had consumed about 8 pints of lager and I was feeling a bit light headed. So I agreed to come with him. We went to the car and he opened it. I drove it while he sat beside me. Then he started looking rather unwell and said he felt sick. I assumed he had drunk too much. So I dropped him off in the middle of town. I drove the car home and locked it in the garage. In the morning I did not know what to do. I noticed for the first time that the Porsche had personalised number plates. I thought it would be too conspicuous to keep those on so I started to unscrew them with a view to putting on different number plates. I was disturbed by a policeman.

I now realise how foolish I have been. I would never have taken any notice of Geoffrey if I had not drunk too much.

I have read the above statement and have been told that I may correct, add or alter anything that I wish. This statement is true. I have made it of my own free will.

(signed) B. Windsor

This statement was taken by me on 30th June 1990 at Exbridge police station commencing at 12.30 p.m. and finishing at 1.05 p.m.

(signed) D. Ferguson D.C. 30

DOCUMENT 6

BLANKSHIRE POLICE

BALANCED SUMMARY OF TAPE RECORDED INTERVIEW

Person interviewed: Geoffrey Harris
Place of interview: Exbridge police station
Date of interview: June 30, 1990
Time-commenced: 7.40 p.m.   concluded: 8.46 p.m.
Tape reference No: GH1
Interviewing officers: D. C. Ferguson
Officer preparing summary: D. C. Ferguson
Exhibit No: D.F.1

This record consisting of 2 pages is the exhibit referred to in the statement made and signed by me. (signed) D. Ferguson

---

Signature of officer preparing Record: D. Ferguson

TAPE TIMES SPEAKER

[Harris gave his name and address. He asked why he had been arrested.]

0m 20s   Ferguson   Now we explained all that. It's about the theft of a car which you and young Windsor took yesterday.

              Harris   Are you on about the Porsche at the White Horse?

0m 30s   Ferguson   So you know it happened at the White Horse then?

488

	Harris	Well I had nothing to do with it. I told Brian not to be silly. Did he take it then?
0m 40s	Ferguson	You know you both did. Brian's told us all about you and your suggestions.
	Harris	I don't believe you, you're just trying to frighten me.
	Ferguson	Well he's made a statement telling us all about it. Here it is if you don't believe me. And quite apart from that you've been picked out at an identity parade by a woman who says she saw you in the car. How do you explain that?
1m 20s	Harris	I don't understand it. Brian's lying that's all. Here I don't feel very well. I've got to have my injection. Can I go and answer the questions later.
	Ferguson	Is the lady who identified you lying as well?
	Harris	Look there must be some mistake. Can I see my solicitor. He'll explain that I need my injection.
2m 25s	Ferguson	You can see your solicitor when we've got some of these facts straight. Who's your solicitor now? The one that acted for you last time or the one that represented you when you got sent inside. I shouldn't think he'll be much use to you now. And I don't think either of them would advise you to take drugs, sunshine.
		[During further questioning Harris continued to deny stealing the car. He accused Windsor of lying. He asked again to be permitted to leave.]
1h 5m 40s	Ferguson	Come on let's get on with this. Tell the truth and you can go home.
	Harris	All right. I helped Brian to take the car. The others dared me. It was Brian's idea.
1h 5m 50s	Ferguson	Who were the others?
	Harris	I don't know. What does it matter? I feel terrible. Can't I go now?
		[The tape was then concluded after the standard form had been completed.]

DOCUMENT 7

4 Rosegate Street
Exbridge

4th September 1990

Dear Sir,

I understand that the Crown Prosecution Service deal with all prosecutions and I would be glad if this letter could be passed to the solicitor dealing with the case of the theft on 29th June 1990 of a Porsche motor car from the car park at the White Horse public house at Exbridge.

On that evening I was with Miss Debbie Montgomery. We had been to a film and went on to have a drink at the White Horse at about 10.00 p.m. We parked the car and walked through the car park. Debbie made some comments about a Porsche motor car. She likes Porsches. There were a couple of men in the car who were having some difficulty in starting it. It was a very thundery night and just as we arrived it had started to pour with rain. I certainly could not see the two men clearly and I doubt whether she did.

When we heard that a Porsche had been stolen from the car park Debbie said that she had thought there was something fishy about the two men. She gave her address and telephone number to the owner of the stolen car. The police later telephoned her and she arranged to go down to the police station to make a statement. I went with her. She initially told the police that she could not give a description of the two men because she had not seen them clearly enough. The police said that they would arrange an identification parade. We were sitting in the reception waiting for the parade when we saw the police taking a dark man with a moustache through to the cells. Debbie said "That must be the man I saw."

At the parade she picked out the man we had seen being taken to the cells. The police then took down her statement in which she said that the man she had seen in the car park was dark with a moustache.

I said nothing about it at the time because I did not want to let Debbie down in front of the police. But I now feel it would be wrong to remain silent. Debbie is rather suggestible and prone to dramatise things. I am sure that it never occurred to her that the Porsche might have been stolen until we spoke to the owner. I have remonstrated with her, but she seems determined to stick to her story whether it is true or not. I think she is looking forward to giving evidence. All she seems to be concerned about is what to wear in court.

I would be grateful if this letter could be kept confidential because she will be very upset if she finds out that I have written to you.

Yours faithfully

(signed) Alex Gibson

490

DOCUMENT 8

Queen Charlotte's Hospital
Exbridge

14th September 1990

Dear Sir

Geoffrey Harris

I am writing in response to your enquiry about your above mentioned client. I apologise for the delay which is due to my absence from the hospital on leave.

I am a Senior Registrar employed at Queen Charlotte's Hospital. I am part of a team of doctors specialising in cases of diabetes. On Friday 29th June 1990 I was called to the Casualty Department at the Hospital to examine a patient called Geoffrey Harris who was in a coma and was thought to be diabetic. My notes, taken shortly after the examination, indicate that I took some blood tests and found that his condition was indeed the result of a low level of glucose in his blood. After I had treated the condition he stayed in hospital under observation for some time. He recovered sufficiently to be discharged at 1.30 a.m. on Saturday morning.

My notes show that I examined Mr. Harris at 10.15 p.m. on 29th June. I have examined the records kept by the Casualty Department which show that Mr. Harris arrived at the Department in a semi-conscious state at 9.35 p.m. on 29th June. He was brought in by a man who told the Duty Nurse that he had found Mr. Harris lying on the pavement and that Harris had indicated to him that he was diabetic. Harris was initially examined by one of the housemen on duty that evening at 9.45 p.m. who called me in.

As you may know chronic diabetes is a condition caused by the patient not being able to produce sufficient insulin naturally. A chronic diabetic has to keep the correct amount of sugar in his blood by injecting insulin and consuming sufficient quantities of sugar or carbohydrates. If the appropriate balance is not maintained the patient feels ill and eventually goes into a coma. Mr. Harris' state could have been caused either by Harris failing to eat sufficient carbohydrates or by failing to inject himself with the correct amount of insulin.

In my opinion, Mr. Harris must have been in a deteriorating condition for at least an hour before he actually went into coma on 29th June. During that period he would have felt faint and confused and might well be unable to remember events precisely. So far as the events on 30th June are concerned, Mr. Harris would probably have suffered residual discomfort for 24 hours after being in a coma. In order for him to maintain ordinary health it is necessary for him to administer insulin injections regularly and to regulate his food intake very carefully. If he were kept without insulin for a period of hours he would begin to feel unwell and might lose the capacity to think logically.

I have asked both the duty nurse and the duty housemen whether they remember the case. I am afraid that they have no recollection of it. That is probably because that particular night was unusually busy for the Casualty

Department. Friday and Saturday nights are always busy. But on that particular evening there had been a pile-up on the motorway and there were several really urgent cases to attend to. In fact some of those injured had to be referred to another hospital.

I myself will not be available to attend court. My Department is grossly under-staffed and you will appreciate that my absence from hospital might well put my patients' health at risk. But I have no objection to this letter being produced in court, and would be happy to answer any further queries you may have.

Yours faithfully

(signed) Felicity Metcalfe (MD MRCP)

Summer 1990

LITIGATION

(CRIMINAL)

SUGGESTED ANSWER

1. (a) There are likely to be three matters dealt with at the first hearing. As the hearing is the very next day it is most unlikely that mode of trial can be dealt with because the prosecutor will not have had time to give the necessary information under the advance disclosure rules. The following will therefore be dealt with:—

   (i) Adjournment and remand. Since the case is to be defended then it will not go ahead on the first appearance because the prosecution will not have their witnesses there. The Crown Prosecutor will apply for an adjournment to which we are likely to consent since we are not ready to proceed either.

   (ii) The court will thus have to consider bail. Windsor appears to be in police custody at the moment although our client has police bail. If the magistrates adjourn the case they will remand the defendants. As our client is already on police bail it is unlikely that the prosecutor will oppose bail in this case but if he should do so, (perhaps because of some apparent change of circumstances) we will need to make a full bail application.

   (iii) The question of legal aid will have to be dealt with. A written application should be lodged at court before the hearing and this will be dealt with very swiftly. If not, an oral application should be made to the court at the start of the hearing and a written statement of means will need to be supplied.

(b) It would not be correct to represent Windsor. We already know from Harris's statement that Windsor has apparently incriminated Harris in the theft of the car, which Harris denies. There is therefore an obvious conflict of interest between them in relation to the substance of the case.

It would of course not necessarily follow that if we were instructed only to make an adjournment or bail application for Windsor that any conflict of interest would arise but in the course of obtaining the necessary information to complete a legal aid form and to apply for

493

bail for Windsor we would probably be given information which would then make it improper for us to continue acting for Harris. This will be because information obtained in confidence from Windsor could not be used on Harris's behalf later and this might handicap us since we might need to cross-examine Windsor during the trial as to his credit. In that situation we would have to decline to act for either of the accused. In all the circumstances it is much safer not to act for Windsor even in respect of bail and legal aid applications.

2. The legal aid form, duly completed, is at the end of this answer. It would have been necessary to give details in the spaces concerned having ticked the relevant boxes:—

   (i) There is a real danger of a custodial sentence because of the seriousness of the offence in view of the value of the property involved. Similarly because Harris has had a custodial sentence before and is presently on probation there is a risk of custody.

   (ii) There is a serious danger of loss of livelihood because Harris has a job which depends on his possession of a driving licence. His licence is already endorsed with five penalty points and he is liable to disqualification if convicted of theft of a motor car.

   (iii) In addition since this would be Harris's first offence of dishonesty it could be contended that this would affect his reputation although his present reputation is far from good.

   (iv) Although there are a number of important matters of evidence involved in the case we do not, strictly speaking, have full instructions in relation to these at the time of completing the legal aid form. Nonetheless it might be possible to refer to disputes concerning confessions under section 76 and section 78 of the 1984 Police and Criminal Evidence Act.

   (v) There may be a need to trace the witness, namely the man who picked Harris up from the street. However strictly speaking it is not clear that we know the importance of this witness at this stage.

   (vi) Diabetes is not a material disability in a case like this.

   (vii) Clearly expert cross-examination is likely to be needed in view of the identification parade; similarly if Windsor testifies for a prosecution you will need to attempt to discredit him by expert cross-examination.

   (viii) There is an issue of mistaken identity in the present case.

XYZ & CO
1 High St
Exbridge.

July 6, 1990

Dear Mr. Harris
I refer to your request to let you know the maximum penalties in case you were to be convicted of theft of the Porsche.
Theft is an offence which can be tried either in the Magistrates' Court or in the Crown Court. The penalties differ depending on the court which

tries the offence. If the offence is tried in the Magistrates' Court then the Magistrates' maximum sentencing power is 6 months detention in a Young Offender Institution and/or a fine up to a maximum of £2,000. If the offence were tried in the Crown Court then the maximum sentence is 10 years' detention in a Young Offender Institution and/or an unlimited fine. You should note however that even if the case is heard by the Magistrates they have the power if they find you guilty to commit you to the Crown Court for sentencing if, when they hear about your previous record, they conclude that their own sentencing powers are inadequate. In that case the Crown Court could give you up to the maximum of 10 years and an unlimited fine. I must stress that these sentences are the maxima and in reality there is no risk of your getting anything like the Crown Court maximum sentence.

Another point which you must bear in mind is that if you are committed you will be in breach of the probation order which was made over a year ago. The effect of being in breach of a probation order is that you may be sentenced again for the original offence of criminal damage and your probation order set aside. The maximum penalty for criminal damage is three months' detention in a Young Offenders Institution and/or a fine of up to £1,000 that may run consecutively to any custodial sentence you receive for the present offence. In other words the Magistrates could in principle send you to prison for a total of nine months in respect of this offence and breach of probation.

Another aspect which is particularly important in your case is your driving licence. The court can impose penalties of disqualification in addition to the custody and fine set out above. You could be disqualified for the theft of the motor car and there is no set maximum period for which they could disqualify you. Even if they decide not to disqualify you for that offence in itself they will still be obliged to endorse your licence with a further eight penalty points. Unfortunately as you already have five penalty points on your licence this will give you 13 in all and the rule is that where you have a total of more than 12 penalty points endorsed on your licence within a three-year period then in principle the court must disqualify you for at least six months under the penalty points rules. The court can if it sees fit decide not to disqualify you for the full six months, or even not to disqualify you at all if they decide that there are mitigating circumstances which might cause them to take a more lenient view.

Unfortunately in your case there do not seem to be any mitigating circumstances except the probable loss of your job. The law is that the court can only take account of hardship if it is "exceptional hardship." It is possible that we could argue in court that the loss of your job would amount to exceptional hardship but it is far from clear whether this would be accepted.

Perhaps you would like to make an appointment to call in to the office to discuss matters further.

Yours sincerely

4. (a) We would probably have advised full committal for the following reasons:—

    (i) Because identification is in issue and under the guidelines such cases are better dealt with by full committal.

495

(ii) Because we wish to make a submission of no case to answer which would come about after we had cross-examined the prosecution witnesses in an attempt to discredit them; in the present case we may also have called our own evidence.

At this stage as far as we know the evidence against Harris is weak. The crucial point is that Brian Windsor is not a competent witness against Harris at this stage as Windsor will not have pleaded either guilty or not guilty and therefore he is still technically a defendant and thus the prosecution cannot call him. That means that at this stage all there is against Harris is the identification evidence and his confession. At the committal we can attempt to get the confession excluded as being obtained in circumstances such as to render it unreliable. If we do succeed in getting the confession excluded a submission of no case to answer might well succeed. One other reason for asking for a full committal is that it may be desirable to ask for reporting restrictions to be lifted so that by publicising the incident perhaps in the local paper we may hope to find the man who took our client to hospital on June 29, 1990.

(b) The prosecution need to give sufficient evidence to show that there is a case on which to commit Harris by either calling witnesses who give evidence on oath or, if we consent, by tendering written statements in the form required by section 102 of the Magistrates' Courts Act 1980. We will only consent to such evidence if it is totally uncontroversial.

At the start of the proceedings we would request that reporting restrictions be lifted in order as indicated above to attempt to obtain publicity to trace the man who took our client to hospital. If the co-defendant Windsor objected then the court would have to decide whether restrictions should be lifted in the interests of justice generally.

The Law of Evidence applies at committal proceedings and thus we should approach the prosecution to ensure that parts of the statement which are inadmissible (e.g. hearsay or references to character) are removed from the statements. This is important in respect of the victim's evidence which contains hearsay and the Balanced Summary of the interview which refers to the fact that Harris is known to the police.

We would wish to cross-examine Miss Montgomery in order to probe her identification and attempt to discredit her; we would also wish to attack the evidence of D.C. Ferguson in connection with our attempt to have the confession excluded. The basis for asking the court to exclude it would be that it has been obtained in such circumstances as amounted either to oppression or which was such as to render the confession unreliable. If we are unsuccessful in getting the confession excluded then the Magistrates are very likely to commit our client for trial.

If on the other hand the confession is excluded then Miss Montgomery's evidence on its own would probably not suffice and the Magistrates would be likely to discharge the defendant. The court must have regard to the "Turnbull" guidelines and in particular since her evidence is of poor quality given the lighting conditions at that time of night the statement that she only had a short time in which to see them and that she cannot remember or did not see the colour of the car could be vital.

After the prosecution evidence has been given we could if we wished call Harris to give his evidence. There is no obligation to do so and indeed it is rare in practice to call defence evidence at committal but this is a case where it might be worthwhile in order to attempt to have the case dismissed at the committal.

At the end of the case the court will deal with witness orders. We will require full witness orders in respect of all the witnesses except perhaps Rupert Morrison-Keys. His evidence is actually uncontroversial if the hearsay reference is taken out of it and in that case we might accept a conditional witness order in respect of him.

At the end of the case the court clerk will give the usual alibi warning to us and the defendant requiring that particulars of any alibi be given either then and there or to the prosecution no later than seven days thereafter. Our client is rather vague as to his alibi at present. When we do obtain details subsequently they should be given to the prosecution. Even though at that time we will be technically late and the trial judge does have a discretion to refuse leave to put in the alibi evidence it is inconceivable that the court would refuse to admit it in the circumstances.

Harris will need to have his bail continued to the Crown Court proceedings and legal aid extended for the Crown Court about which there should be no difficulty as there has been no change in means.

5. (a) **Document 2. Rupert Morrison-Keys.**
   The inadmissible hearsay evidence should be taken out but nothing in this statement is otherwise disputed so there is no need to call the victim nor to challenge his evidence if the prosecution call him.

   (b) **Document 3. Miss Montgomery.**
   Miss Montgomery's evidence is evidence of identification and therefore the guidelines in *R.* v. *Turnbull* apply. Therefore in this case the judge will have to give the jury a strong warning in accordance with the guidelines to the effect that they should act with great caution before convicting in reliance on the correctness of identification evidence and, since the evidence appears to be of poor quality, the judge should go on to tell the jury that they should only convict if there is other evidence which they think supports the correctness of the identification. In particular the judge must mention the following matters:—
   (i) The judge should point out that the fact that the witness has no motive to lie does not mean she may not be mistaken. They should not conclude from the fact that they find her convincing that her evidence is necessarily correct.

   (ii) The judge should remind the jury carefully of all the relevant circumstances of the identification including time, lighting conditions, period of observation, and specifically remind them of any weaknesses which have appeared in the evidence.

   (iii) The judge should point out to them items in the case which are

497

capable of being supporting evidence. He must also indicate that if they disbelieve the alibi of Harris that that may not in itself necessarily indicate guilt. He should point out that people invent alibis out of panic or fear and they must therefore consider why Harris might have lied about his alibi.

(iv) The judge must also point out the importance of the identity parade and he may direct the jury that the confession (if it is not excluded) and the evidence of Brian Windsor if he testifies may support the identification.

At this stage we do not of course know fully about the irregularity in identification procedures.

(c) **Document 4. D. Ferguson.**
It is possible that the entry into the flat was illegal in all the circumstances but although under section 78 of the 1984 Police and Criminal Evidence Act there is a discretion in the court to exclude evidence having regard to circumstances in which it is obtained it is most unlikely that this will render anything subsequently obtained inadmissible. Harris disputes the contents of what it is claimed he said but in any event the words referring to his probation should not be left in this account because they would tell the jury that Harris has a previous conviction.

(d) **Document 5. B. Windsor.**
This statement in itself is not admissible as against Harris but of course if Windsor pleads guilty as we believe he is to do he will become competent and compellable for the prosecution. In principle he should be sentenced before he testifies though this is within the discretion of the judge and practice varies. Obviously the prosecution will only want to call him if it seems he will give evidence willingly.

There is no doubt that on his own version Windsor is an accomplice of Harris within the guidelines in *D.P.P.* v. *Davies* and therefore the judge will need to direct the jury carefully on the need for corroboration in such a case. In addition to the fact that he is an accomplice pure and simple there is further ground why the judge might consider that firm direction on corroboration is necessary and that is because of the grudge he may have against Harris following a quarrel.

Corroboration is other independent evidence which is admissible in itself and supports the evidence requiring to be corroborated in a material particular and implicates the accused. Thus the evidence of Miss Montgomery and confession might amount to corroboration.

If Windsor gives evidence along the lines of his statement the evidence is very damning. However the references to Harris's previous character must be deleted. The problem is that if we attack the credit of Windsor strongly and suggest that he is fabricating his story because of the past quarrel, then by section 1(*f*)(ii) of the Criminal Evidence Act 1898 our client, since we will have made imputations on the character of the prosecution witness, will be liable to cross-examination on his own criminal record if he testifies. In the circumstances of this case it is probably going to be necessary to call him to testify since we need to put forward a firm alibi defence.

When Harris's previous record is brought out by the prosecution in cross-examination the judge should give the jury a direction that their knowledge of his record is only relevant to Harris's credibility as a witness but inevitably the jury are likely to be prejudiced against him even though his previous convictions do not involve dishonesty. The judge has a power to exclude evidence of the previous convictions if he thinks it would be unfair to admit it but there is no reason for him to exercise that power here. Unfortunately therefore the price of attacking this prosecution witness will be that our client's record comes out. Where the record is likely to come out then a common ploy is for the defence themselves to volunteer the evidence before cross-examination takes place which may have the effect of giving the impression of candour to the jury.

(e) **The Confession—Document 6.**
All references within this confession which indicate previous involvement with the police should be edited out.

Under section 76 of the 1984 Police and Criminal Evidence Act a confession may not be put in evidence if it was or may have been obtained by oppression or a consequence of anything said or done which was likely in the circumstances existing at the time to render it unreliable. The prosecution must prove admissibility beyond reasonable doubt as a *voire dire* in the absence of the jury. We should make a submission that the confession should be excluded in the light of the following:—

 (i) By section 58 of the 1984 Act Harris is guaranteed the right to see a solicitor in private. There has been a refusal to permit him to see a solicitor here. Although there is a power to postpone an interview in the case of a serious arrestable offence that power can only be exercised by an officer of Superintendent or above and this does not appear to have been the case here. In any event the interrogation must be suspended whilst a solicitor is called and this has not happened either. In the light of some recent case law it is possible that this alone might lead to exclusion of the confession.

(ii) On the basis that the police did not know Harris was a diabetic their conduct in relation to that would not be *oppression* in all probability but nonetheless the confession may be unreliable. The words "tell the truth and you can go home" would appear to be an invitation to confess which is improper. Given all the surrounding circumstances and particularly the defendant's anxiety about insulin it would seem the confession ought to be excluded.

If the breaches are not sufficient to render the confession unreliable under section 76 the judge has a further discretion under section 78 of the Act to exclude any prosecution evidence if it appears to the court that its admission would have such an adverse effect on the

499

fairness of the proceedings that it ought to be excluded. The court can take into account the circumstances in which such evidence was obtained. Here the refusal of a solicitor might be grounds for having the confession excluded under section 78 even if the confession were found to be prima facie reliable.

6. (a) The Crown Prosecution have a general duty to act as a "minister of justice" and must not press for a conviction at all costs. They have a duty to bring relevant facts before the court or to supply them to the defence. In the present situation there is therefore a duty for them to pass on evidence such as this to the defence. The prosecution may direct that Gibson should be interviewed and a statement taken or alternatively the necessary details may simply be given to the defence and matters left to them as to how it should be dealt with.

   (b) We will need to interview Gibson in advance. We cannot simply put the letter in evidence because it is not in an appropriate form. If Gibson maintains what he says when we interview him then we will inevitably have to call him as a witness notwithstanding his reluctance. His evidence is necessary to weaken the identification by Miss Montgomery. A witness order should be obtained to ensure Gibson's presence at court.

The new evidence will help us to undermine Miss Montgomery's evidence because it shows her change of mind on seeing Harris at the police station. It should be possible either to cross-examine her about this before the jury or alternatively to ask the judge to send the jury out whilst we submit that all the evidence of Miss Montgomery should be excluded because the identity parade was fatally flawed since she should not have been able to see Harris at the police station. The judge may then be willing to exclude Miss Montgomery's evidence. Alternatively the judge may direct that the matter should be dealt with when the jury are present and then we will have to call Mr. Gibson as a witness to discredit Miss Montgomery if she persists in her assertion that she can identify our client.

7. (a) This record is hearsay but would be admissible under section 24 of the Criminal Justice Act 1988 because it amounts to a statement in a document as to a fact of which direct oral evidence would be admissible, and the document was created or received by a person in the course of his occupation and the person who supplied the information had personal knowledge of the relevant matter. We do not know how the records were compiled although it is obvious they were written up by a nurse or a doctor on duty from personal knowledge. Notwithstanding strict admissibility under section 24 of the Act the court must however go on to consider the discretions in section 25 of the Act. The Crown Court may direct that the statement should *not* be admitted if it is not in the interests of justice to admit it. The matters to which the court should have regard include the important matter of whether its admission or exclusion would result in unfairness to the accused and the source and authenticity of the document. In the present case since the document is clearly authentic and is in the accused's favour it should be admitted. The court ought also to

have regard to the extent to which the information supplied could not be obtained from any other source and since this would indeed appear to be the case here it is a further argument in favour of admitting the document. The document will need to be formally proved to the court and produced by someone who can show from where it originates and what it is.

(b) The evidence of Dr. Metcalfe is admissible:

   (i) she can positively identify Harris as being present and in a coma at 10.15 p.m. on June 29 in hospital. Since the prosecution's identification evidence would seem to indicate that the theft of the car took place after 10.00 p.m. this would seem to be a conclusive alibi. If Dr. Metcalfe made her notes contemporaneously with the event described she could use her notes to refresh her memory giving oral evidence. However the notes themselves would be admissible under section 24 of the Act subject to the same considerations as in Part (a) above which here would tend again to favour admissibility of the document.

  (ii) Dr. Metcalfe is an expert and therefore is allowed to give opinion evidence about matters within her expertise. Here her expertise would clearly include being able to give an opinion on Harris's state of health and this will be material in showing why he himself is unable to give a detailed account of his alibi. She could also indicate what she would have believed to be his state of health in the afternoon of June 30 and this would also be helpful in connection with the exclusion of the confession evidence. We might therefore wish to call Dr. Metcalfe at the *voire dire* stage of the proceedings.

(c) It is generally considered best to call oral evidence and this would particularly be so in the case of evidence which ought to be fairly conclusive like the present. She could therefore be made to attend by a witness order. However her evidence could be admitted under section 24 of the 1988 Act by production of her notes. Alternatively she could put all her conclusions in the form of an expert's report and this is admissible under section 30 of the Act. An expert's report may be admissible even if the maker does not attend to give oral evidence despite being available to do so. The expert evidence must be disclosed to the other side in advance under advance disclosure rules made in respect of Crown Court proceedings. In the present case it would be likely that the evidence would be admitted without Dr. Metcalfe being called. In any event if we were to disclose this to the prosecution it is possible that they would see that their case is hopeless and the prosecution would be terminated by them offering no evidence at trial.

CANDIDATES NUMBER

Reasons for wanting Legal Aid	*Note: if you plead NOT GUILTY neither the information in this form nor in your statement of means will be made available to the members of the court trying your case unless you are convicted or you otherwise consent. If you are acquitted, only the financial information you have given in your statement of means will be given to the court.*	
	Tick any boxes which apply and give brief details or reasons in the space provided.	
1. I am in real danger of a custodial sentence for the following reasons ☑ *(You should consider seeing a solicitor before answering this question)*	The offence involved is a serious one involving theft of valuable property; I have had a custodial sentence before; and I presently am on probation.	For court use only
2. I am subject to a: suspended or partly suspended prison sentence ☐ conditional discharge ☐ probation order ☑ supervision order ☐ deferment of sentence ☐ community service order ☐ care order ☐ *Give details as far as you are able including the nature of offence and when the order was made*	I am subject to a probation order from Exbridge Magistrates Court made on 4 April 1989 on a charge of criminal damage for a period of 2 years.	
3. I am in real danger of losing my job because: ☑	I am in danger of losing my job because I already have 5 penalty points on my driving licence. I may be disqualified under the penalty points system if convicted.	
4. I am in real danger of suffering serious damage to my reputation because: ☑	I have no previous offences of dishonesty.	

5. I have been advised by a solicitor that a substantial question of law is invoived *(You will need the help of a solicitor to answer this question)*	☑	There may be problems of admissibility of evidence particularly of an alleged confession and the applicability of ss.76 and 78 of the 1984 Police and Criminal Evidence Act.	
6. Witnesses have to be traced and interviewed on my behalf *(State circumstances)*	☑	(I need to trace a witness who gave me a lift on the day of the offence and who would be an alibi witness).	

Reasons (Cont) *Tick any boxes which apply and give brief details or reasons in space provided.*

7. I shall be unable to follow the court proceedings because: a) my understanding of English is inadequate b) I suffer from a disability *(Give full details)*	 ☐ ☐		For court use only
8. The case involves expert cross examination of a prosecution witness *(Give brief details)*	☑	An important prosecution witness may be Brian Windsor who is also charged with this offence and I believe will falsely implicate me. It will be necessary to cross-examine him and an alleged indentification witness.	
9. The case is a very complex one, for example, mistaken identity *(You may need the help of a solicitor to answer this question)*	☑	There is an issue of mistaken identity here. I was picked out at an identity parade by a woman who claimed to have seen me at the time and I contend she is mistaken.	
10. Any other reasons: *(Give full particulars)*	☐		

Reasons for Refusal

This section must be completed by the Justices' Clerk if the application is refused because:

(a) It does not appear desirable in the interests of justice, and

(b) The applicant is entitled to apply for legal aid to the area committee.

State briefly the reasons for that decision.

Signed .... Justices'Clerk

For court use only

Date ....

Litigation (Criminal)—Legal Aid Application Form.

Summer 1990

SOLICITORS' FINAL EXAMINATION QUESTIONS

FRIDAY, 6TH JULY (2.00 P.M. TO 4.00 P.M.)

Candidates should answer all questions.

LITIGATION

(CIVIL)

You are an assistant solicitor in the firm of Smythes, Solicitors, 5 High Street, Exbridge, Blankshire. In June 1990 you are instructed by Easyride Motors Ltd., a company dealing in second hand cars. The sales director, Raymond Lucas, tells you that in April 1990 he was approached by Jonathan Fowler one of the partners of Fowler and Co. a firm of agents and valuers. Mr. Fowler told him that he was looking for a four-wheel drive vehicle for the firm which would be suitable for driving round farms. He chose a Toyonda Ranger, a Japanese four-wheel drive truck, and agreed to purchase it for a price of £5,650 inclusive of VAT. A deposit of £2,000 was paid but the balance of £3,650 remains outstanding. Mr. Lucas instructs you to recover this debt. Mr. Lucas gives you the invoice (**Document 1**) and you take a statement from him (**Document 2**).

1. A letter before action produces no response. Mr. Lucas instructs you to commence proceedings. He asks you whether the action should be taken in the High Court or the County Court. Advise him. (Do not assume because proceedings are subsequently taken in the High Court that this is necessarily on your advice.) (*8 marks*)

2. Mr. Lucas instructs you to commence proceedings in the High Court. There are District Registries at both Southcliffe and Exbridge.

   (a) Fill in (as at 20th July 1990) the form of Writ provided with the question paper including the indorsement of claim. [Candidates are **not** expected to complete the figure for fixed costs. Please include the completed form with your answer paper and ensure that you have written your Examination Number on the form.] (*20 marks*)

505

    (b) You commence proceedings. What documents would you serve on the other side and in what way and/or ways could you effect service?

(6 marks)

3.   You learn that Robert Fowler, the senior partner of the firm of Fowler and Co. and the uncle of Jonathan Fowler, has an appointment to see one of the partners in Smythes (Mr. Clifford) who deals with conveyancing. Mr. Clifford tells you that he has acted for Mr. Robert Fowler before and that he understands that Mr. Fowler will be instructing him in a property transaction of which he does not yet know any details. Can Mr. Clifford act for Mr. Robert Fowler in that transaction? *(4 marks)*

4.   The form of acknowledgement of service is returned indicating that the proceedings are to be contested.

    (a) Would it be appropriate to apply for summary judgment under Order 14? Give full reasons for your answer.

    (b) Outline the procedural steps you will need to take if you are instructed to make an application under Order 14 (whether or not in accordance with your advice). [Do **not** prepare the documents.]

(10 marks)

5.   The application under Order 14 is to be heard on 4th September 1990. On 3rd September you receive a copy of a letter which has been sent to the court by Jonathan Fowler (**Document 3**). You telephone Mr. Lucas who tells you that this is the first time that he has had any details of Mr. Fowler's complaints about the vehicle. Mr. Lucas instructs you to proceed with the application on 4th September. Mr. Jonathan Fowler attends the hearing on 4th September.
What orders/directions could the court make on the application? What orders/directions do you consider it likely that the court will make?

(10 marks)

6.   Leave to defend is given. The other side serve a Defence and Counterclaim (**Document 4—extract only**).

    (a) Make brief notes of what Further and Better Particulars of the Defence and Counterclaim (considering only Document 4) you would request from the other side.

    (b) What action can you take if your request is refused?   *(12 marks)*

7.   The plaintiffs wish you to arrange for an independent engineer to inspect the vehicle. What steps can you take to carry out those wishes?

(4 marks)

8.   The other side send you a copy of a report from a consultant engineer (**Document 5**). You confer with Mr. Lucas who tells you that he has made enquiries and now has evidence that the Toyonda Ranger was damaged because it was driven on unleaded petrol by Jonathan Fowler. You take statements from two witnesses (**Documents 6 and 7**). You are able to have the vehicle inspected by James Russell of Russell Engineering Consultants, who send you a written report (**Document 8**).

   (a) Comment on the admissibility of Mr. Barker's statement (**Document 5**).

   (b) What evidence would you adduce to counteract the allegation that the vehicle was defective when sold? What procedures are necessary in order to adduce that evidence?

   (c) Will it be necessary for you to give the other side advance warning of James Russell's report (**Document 8**)?   (*26 marks*)

Total = *100 marks*

DOCUMENT 1

EASYRIDE MOTORS LTD.   59 Station Road
Motor Dealers   Southcliffe
Registered in England 231475001   Blankshire
Registered Office:
59, Station Road, Southcliffe, Blankshire.

Jonathan Fowler
Fowler and Co.
5 Martin's Lane
Exbridge
Blankshire

Invoice No. 4597

23 April 1990

Vehicle		**Price**	
Toyonda Ranger	£4913		
VAT at 15%	£737	£5,650	
	Less deposit	£2,000	
	Balance due		£3,650

DOCUMENT 2

Raymond Lucas of 14 Heather Drive, Southcliffe will say:—

I am the sales director of Easyride Motors Ltd. The company deals in second-hand vehicles from premises in 59 Station Road, Southcliffe, Blankshire. In April 1990 I was approached by Jonathan Fowler of Fowler and Co., agents and valuers, whose premises are at 5 Martin's Lane, Exbridge who was looking for a four-wheel drive vehicle to use in the business. I found him a five year old Toyonda Ranger (registration number B457 KNW). He test drove the vehicle and inspected it. It was agreed that he would purchase it at the price of £5,650. He drove the car away on 23rd April 1990 on payment of a deposit of £2,000. The balance of the price was to be paid by the end of May 1990. We do not normally give credit but we agreed to in this case because Jonathan Fowler explained that the firm's financial year ended at the end of April and that they would find it more advantageous from a tax point of view to settle the transaction in the new financial year. He sounded genuine. Fowler and Co. are an old-established firm with whom we have often done business in the past.

It is now 14th June and we have not received the balance due from Fowler and Co. I tried to telephone Jonathan Fowler on several occasions in the last two weeks but on each occasion I was either told that he was out of the office or at a meeting. I saw him by chance in Exbridge a few days ago and got the impression that he was trying to avoid me. Finally, a couple of days ago I lost my temper with his secretary and did get her to put me through to him. I said that I was surprised not to have received the balance due from him. He just said "You've got a nerve ringing me up to put pressure on me. The Toyonda has completely let us down. It's cost the firm hundreds of pounds in lost business." I then asked what exactly was the matter and he responded by swearing at me and putting the phone down on me.

I do not believe that there is anything wrong with the vehicle. It was thoroughly overhauled by our usual garage, Regent's Garage Ltd., just before we sold it, and it had been granted an MOT certificate.

I have, however, heard that Fowler and Co. are in financial difficulties because of the current slump in the property market. There are rumours that they owe considerable sums of money to the bank and may have to stop operating. I do not know what assets the firm has. Jonathan Fowler is a young man in his early twenties who only qualified as an agent recently. I doubt whether he has any assets worth speaking of. I understand that his uncle, who is the senior partner in the firm, is pretty comfortably off. I believe that there are other partners in the firm but I do not know who they are.

DOCUMENT 3

Fowler and Co.
Agents and Valuers
5 Martin's Lane
Exbridge

30th August 1990

Dear Sir,

I am writing about the application by Easyride which is due to be heard on 4th September.

I wish to make it clear that I shall be opposing this action very strenuously.

I am amazed that Easyride have the impertinence to claim that there is any money due to them. I bought the Toyonda Ranger in good faith, having been assured that it had just been serviced and that it would run satisfactorily for many years. On the day after I acquired the car I drove it up to Tolbin Farm in the village of Tolbin. As you may know, Tolbin is in a very remote rural area. I had intended to survey the farm for a client. The vehicle broke down on a farm track miles from anywhere. In consequence I had to spend the rest of the day arranging for the vehicle to be towed away by Fixit Garage for repairs and getting myself back to Exbridge. Not only was this very irritating in itself but it resulted in my client losing the opportunity to purchase the farm. He is now threatening to withdraw his custom.

When the garage mechanic inspected the vehicle he told me that the engine was worn out and was beyond economic repair. I have already told Easyride to take the Toyonda Ranger back because it is worthless.

In the circumstances I do not consider that there is any obligation to pay for the vehicle. I shall be asking the Court to grant me the return of the deposit of £2,000 and my expenses.

I am sending a copy of this letter to the plaintiffs.

Yours faithfully

Jonathan Fowler

DOCUMENT 4

EXTRACT FROM DEFENCE AND COUNTERCLAIM

[Formal Heading, etc.]

DEFENCE

1. It is admitted that the Plaintiffs sold to the Defendants the Toyonda Ranger Motor Vehicle for the sum of £5,650 on the date alleged and that a deposit of £2,000 was paid but it is denied that the Defendants are indebted to the Plaintiffs in the alleged or any sum.

2. It is admitted and alleged that the Plaintiffs sold the said motor vehicle in the course of their business and that it was an implied term of the contract that the said motor vehicle would be of merchantable quality. Further it was expressly warranted by the Plaintiffs that the said motor vehicle had been fully serviced prior to delivery and would run satisfactorily for many years.

3. In breach of the said condition the said motor vehicle was not of merchantable quality and was so defective that on 24th April 1990 it broke down and is beyond economic repair.

4. By reason of such breach of condition the Defendants are entitled to reject the said motor vehicle and gave notice of rejection to the Plaintiffs requiring them to collect it.

5. Further or alternatively the Plaintiffs are in breach of warranty and guilty of misrepresentation in consequence whereof the Defendants have suffered loss and damage.

6. In the premises the Defendants are entitled to set off such loss and damage in extinction or diminution of the Plaintiffs' claim.

COUNTERCLAIM

7. The Defendants repeat paragraphs 2, 3 and 4 hereof and are entitled to the return of their deposit as money paid for a consideration that has wholly failed.

8. Additionally the Defendants repeat paragraph 5 hereof and counterclaim damages to the extent that the same are not taken into account by the claim to set off in paragraph 6 hereof.

[PRAYER AND FORMAL PARTS]

DOCUMENT 5

Rigby Hardwick and Barker
Consulting Engineers
The Harrage
Exbridge

28th September 1990

Dear Mr. Fowler,
Report on Toyonda Ranger B457 KNW

1. At your request I examined the above vehicle at your premises on 27th September.

2. The vehicle was purchased from Easyride on 23rd April of this year for the price of £5,650. Easyride gave you a guarantee that the vehicle had been fully serviced immediately before sale, was suitable for driving over farm tracks in bad weather and would run satisfactorily for many years. On the 24th April, a mere day after sale, the vehicle broke down.

3. Following the breakdown the vehicle was towed back to Fixit Garage and was found to be beyond economic repair. Since that time it has been situated at your premises and, obviously, has been out of service.

4. My examination of the vehicle revealed that two of the valves in the engine are defective. Their failure caused the engine to cease to operate. It would not be possible to replace the valves themselves; the only option would be the purchase of a new engine. In view of the poor condition of the bodywork of the vehicle, I doubt whether fitting a new engine would make financial sense. I therefore share the view of Fixit Garage that the vehicle is beyond economic repair.

5. The two valves must have been defective when the car was sold to you the day before the car broke down. In my opinion the defect is caused by metal

fatigue, a problem which, in my experience, is unfortunately often encountered in Toyonda Rangers. The defect would have been obvious to a competent mechanic because the engine would have run with a grating noise for some time before finally failing altogether.

6. I therefore consider that you have a valid case against Easyride. I happen to know that the mechanic they usually employ either fails to service the vehicles concerned or else is completely incompetent. You may be interested to learn that I have been consulted about another case where Easyride sold a defective vehicle as serviced and it is quite plain that no such service had ever taken place.

(signed) Roy Barker M. Inst. C.E.

DOCUMENT 6

Phillip Underhill of 12 Endless Street, Southcliffe will say:—

I recently completed my training as a Chemical Engineer. I have obtained employment with an Engineering Company in Hamburg. That employment starts on 1st October 1990. In the meantime I am working temporarily in a petrol filling station on the main A421 road Fulchurch Blankshire. The filling station is about 7 miles from the village of Tolbin.

At about the end of April I was serving in the filling station when a man drove up in a Toyonda Ranger. The filling station is not self-service. The driver, a young man of about 25, rushed up to me and asked me to fill up the vehicle with petrol. I told him that we only had unleaded petrol, having run out of leaded petrol following the Easter holiday rush. We were waiting for a delivery of leaded petrol. In answer to his question I told him that the nearest garage was some miles away. He asked me whether using the wrong sort of petrol would damage the vehicle. I told him that I did not know but could check this for him. But he said that he was nearly out of petrol and as he was late for a very important appointment, he would have to run the car on unleaded petrol and hope for the best.

I remember the incident because some hours later he reappeared and said that the vehicle had broken down. I assume that this was because he had used unleaded petrol in the vehicle. I helped him to telephone a garage to tow the car away. In the course of this I learned that he is called Fowler and works for Fowler and Co. of Exbridge.

I understand that this information may be of some relevance in pending court proceedings. I would, in principle, be happy to help; but I am afraid that I shall be moving to Hamburg in Germany on 29th September in order to start my new job. My ten year old brother, Michael, was with me at the time.

(signed) Phillip Underhill

DOCUMENT 7

Michael Underhill of 12 Endless Street Southcliffe will say:—

I am 10 years old (date of birth 10th June 1980).

My brother, Phillip, has a temporary job working at a petrol filling station in Fulchurch. During my Easter holidays I sometimes went with Phillip to help him with his work there. On one occasion I remember that a man came into the filling station and asked Phillip to put unleaded petrol in his Toyonda Ranger because we had sold out of ordinary petrol. Later the man came back and said that the Ranger had broken down. We helped him. Phillip told me that the Ranger had broken down because the man used green petrol instead of ordinary petrol.

I know that the man must have come in some time between Bank Holiday Monday (16th April) and Wednesday 25th April when my school term started.

(signed) Michael Underhill

DOCUMENT 8

Russells
Consultant Engineers
Unit 41
Commercial Road
Exbridge

14th October 1990

Dear Sirs,

Toyonda Ranger B457 KNW

I examined the above vehicle on 12th October as requested by you; and I have read the report of Roy Barker dated 28th September.

I agree with Mr. Barker that the engine has ceased to function and that the cause of this is to be found in the two defective valves to which he refers. I could find no other defects. Indeed, in other respects, the vehicle appeared to be in good condition for its age.

In view of your suspicion that unleaded petrol might have been put into the vehicle, I examined the vehicle specifically to ascertain whether that was the case. I discovered traces of unleaded petrol in the engine, although the vehicle itself had evidently been drained of unleaded petrol and about a gallon or so of leaded petrol had been put into it.

In view of my findings I am in no doubt that the car was driven with unleaded petrol and that this caused the failure of the two valves, in turn leading to the failure of the engine. I do not think that the condition of the valves is consistent with metal fatigue as suggested by Mr. Barker. In fairness to Mr. Barker I should perhaps add that I would probably not have discovered the true reason for the breakdown had I not been alerted to the possibility that the vehicle might have been driven with unleaded petrol.

Incidentally, the vehicle shows clear signs of having been serviced recently.

James Russell MSc. M.Inst.C.E.

512

Summer 1990

LITIGATION

(CIVIL)

SUGGESTED ANSWER

1. There is no financial limit on the jurisdiction of the High Court. Nor is there any need for a geographical connection with the District Registry where the writ is issued. On the other hand the County Court has a jurisdictional limit of £5,000 in contract cases and there must be some local connection with either the place where the cause of action arose or the place of business of the defendant. Accordingly the action could be started in this instance in either the High Court or County Court. The following are relevant factors:—

    (a) By sections 19 and 20 of the County Courts Act 1984, if an action is commenced in the High Court but the plaintiff recovers less than £3,000 then unless the court considers that there was sufficient reason for commencing proceedings in the High Court the plaintiff will only recover costs on the appropriate County Court scale (*i.e.* scale 2). Thus there will be a shortfall between the amount recovered for costs *inter partes* and the solicitor and own client costs. In the present case the amount claimed is £3,650 so unless a lesser sum is awarded perhaps because of a reduction due to some defect in the vehicle there would seem not likely to be any penalty for starting in the High Court.*

    (b) It must also be borne in mind that even if the action is commenced in the High Court the case can be transferred to the County Court for trial either by the District Judge of his own motion or by the parties agreeing. In that case the jurisdiction of the County Court will be unlimited. The fact that the action will be transferred later is not necessarily a reason for starting in the County Court however.*

    (c) There are tactical advantages in respect of the High Court proceedings. In the first place the receipt of a High Court writ is psychologically of greater impact on the defendant's mind than receiving a County Court summons. Moreover a plaintiff has greater control over the stages of the early part of the action and judgment in default is usually obtainable more quickly in the High Court. Generally speaking enforcement procedures are more efficient in the High Court but that does not matter a great deal in the present case because County Court judgments of over £2,000 may be transferred to the High Court for enforcement. Moreover on transferral

513

the judgment will carry interest at 15 per cent. per annum whereas interest on the judgment is not currently available in the County Court itself. As we are suing for more than £2,000 however, these factors are not necessarily material.

2. (a) A copy of the writ is attached at the end of this answer. The following points should be noted:—

    (i) Clearly on the facts we are given here it would be better to commence the action against the partnership rather than Jonathan Fowler personally in order to give us wider rights of enforcement against the other partners' personal assets and partnership assets.

    (ii) The endorsement claims interest at 15 per cent. per annum since there appears to be no contractual provision relevant here. If one is willing to limit a claim to interest at that rate under section 35A of the Supreme Court Act 1981 a computation can be provided as indicated. This will be advantageous to the extent that it would allow us to sign judgment in default of notice of intention to defend without the need for a hearing to fix interest.

    (iii) The figures for fixed costs would of course have to be completed properly by reference to Order 62 Appendix III in a real writ but for examination purposes this would not be required.

(b) The defendant must be served with a sealed copy of the writ together with an acknowledgment of service form. A notice should strictly speaking be served of the capacity in which any individual is served with the documents stating that he is served as a partner or manager. The following methods of service are available:—

    (i) Personal service on any partner.

    (ii) Service on any partner by ordinary first class post at his usual or last known address (this will be effective on the seventh day after the date of posting).

    (iii) Insertion of the documents through the letter box of any partner's home address.

    (iv) Service by ordinary prepaid post to the principal place of business of the partnership in which case service is effective seven days after posting.

    (v) Personal service at the principal place of business of the partnership on the person having control or management of the business. The person served need not be a partner and could be, *e.g.* the office manager in which case service is effective immediately.

3. Once a partnership are made defendants in an action each and every partner is liable and may have his own assets taken in execution of the judgment. Robert Fowler is therefore in that position. Although normally when enforcing a judgment one would attempt first to enforce it against partnership assets rather than private assets it may be that there are insufficient partnership assets in which case one would naturally look to the personal property of the partners. At that time the fact that we know Robert Fowler's means and resources might well be

an important aspect. There could be a difficult conflict of interest and the fact that another one of the partners in our firm is acting for Robert Fowler would not make any difference because the knowledge acquired by Mr. Clifford would be deemed to be known to the whole firm. Accordingly it would probably be safer not to act for Robert Fowler because one would then be in danger of not being able to use information acquired confidentially in the best interests of Easyride Motors Ltd. our present clients.

4. (a) The statement of claim has been served endorsed on the writ in this case and the defendants have given notice of intention to defend. At that stage the plaintiff can apply for summary judgment and this is particularly appropriate in debt cases. The purpose of the application is to prevent the case going on to a full trial with consequent considerable delay and expense. When one wishes to make an application for summary judgment an affidavit needs to be prepared in which the plaintiff or its representatives swears that the defendants have no defence to the action. Apart from the telephone call referred to in our instructions there seems never to have been any indication that there is any arguable defence nor what the substance of such defence would be. There was no specific complaint about the nature of the problem in respect of the motor vehicle until the debt was chased up and this certainly gives some grounds for doubting the sincerity of the complaints. Similarly there was no response to our letter before action and accordingly it would seem appropriate to apply for summary judgment especially because our client believes the defendants are trying to buy time in view of their financial difficulties.

(b) Application is made by summons supported by affidavit. In the present case it would be better if the affidavit were sworn by Mr. Lucas; the affidavit must swear that the contents of the Statement of Claim are true and that Mr. Lucas believes there is no defence to the action; in addition the affidavit must contain a statement that Mr. Lucas is duly authorised by the plaintiff company to make the affidavit. The summons should be issued and affidavit lodged at court. A hearing date will be endorsed on the summons and a copy of the summons together with a copy of the affidavit to be used at the hearing must be served on the defendants not less than 10 clear days before the hearing date. The form of summons indicates to the defendants that if they wish to oppose it they must themselves swear a defence and provide a copy at least three days before the hearing.

5. As indicated above the defendant should file an affidavit in reply to an application for summary judgment. In the present case the defendants have not done so. We could therefore in principle ask for an adjournment but quite often it is in the plaintiff's best interests, given that he wishes to proceed with dispatch, to go ahead despite the fact that what Jonathan Fowler may say at the hearing will take us by surprise. Although oral evidence is not usual the rules do permit the District Judge to take into account other methods of putting evidence before

515

him and he would probably permit Jonathan Fowler to give oral evidence and argue despite the lack of affidavit. At the hearing the following orders are possible:—

(i) Judgment for the plaintiffs with costs. The onus at the hearing is upon the defendant to satisfy the District Judge that there is an issue or question which ought to be tried or that there ought to be a trial for some other reason. If the District Judge is not satisfied that there is an arguable defence he will give judgment for the whole of the claim together with interest and probably in the present case fix costs although he does have a discretion to award taxed costs.

(ii) The second possibility is that the District Judge will give unconditional leave to defend. If the defendants raise a triable issue or convince the District Judge that there is some other reason why there should be a trial then they will be given leave to defend. Costs in the cause will then be ordered.

(iii) The third possibility is conditional leave to defend. This arises where some arguable defence has been put forward but the District Judge doubts the bona fides of the defendant or believes the defence may well be a sham. He will give leave to defend subject to conditions and if these conditions are not fulfilled then the plaintiff will get judgment. The most common condition is the payment into court of all or part of the sum claimed and this occurs where the District Judge might suspect that the real reason for defending is inability to pay. In the present case an order would probably be for the defendants to pay into court the amount claimed before they are given leave to defend. Costs in the cause would also be ordered.

(iv) Finally the summons may be dismissed if there is something in the plaintiff's conduct which makes their application improper. In particular if the plaintiff knew that the defendants might be entitled to unconditional leave to defend the summons should be dismissed. The plaintiff will usually be ordered to pay costs of the summons.

If leave to defend is ordered then the District Judge should go on to give directions for trial. The point of this is to avoid the delay and expense of a further hearing of a later summons for direction. Provided that the parties know at this early stage what directions they are likely to require any further interlocutory hearings can often be avoided. In the present case the directions are likely to be that a defence should be served within 14 days; and that if there is going to be expert evidence in relation to this vehicle then an appropriate order allowing the obtaining and mutual exchange of experts' reports should be made; it may be necessary to order that the vehicle be preserved until expert examination can take place.

On the few facts we know here probably leave to defend will be given if Jonathan Fowler appears to give convincing evidence of the vehicle's shortcomings. It is possible also for the court to give summary judgment in respect of part of the claim and if Jonathan Fowler were to contend that the problems with the vehicle had cost him say several hundred pounds then there would seem to be no problem with giving judgment for the balance. Conditional leave to defend might appear to be the more likely possibility here given that the defendants did not make any prompt complaints about the problems with the vehicle.

6. (a) This defence is vague in a number of respects. The purpose of further and better particulars would be to cut down the scope for manoeuvre where the defence is brief or vague and the following would appear to be relevant points:—

   Paragraph 2. It would be necessary to find out if the alleged warranty was supposed to be oral or written. Since our own client is likely to have any documents if it is written (*i.e.* his terms of business) it is more likely that it will be oral. We will therefore want to know if the warranty is said to be oral, by whom it was given and on what occasion and what precisely the words used were.

   Paragraph 3. We need to have more details of lack of merchantable quality and a complete schedule of the defects relied on including the date and circumstances in which the vehicle broke down and what the cause of breakdown was said to be.

   Paragraph 4. We need to ask whether the notice of rejection which is supposed to have been given was oral or written since our client does not mention the matter. If it is said to have been in writing we need to know what the document was, what its terms were and when it was sent; if oral we need to know exactly what was said and by whom and to whom at the plaintiffs.

   Paragraph 5. We need full particulars of the alleged loss and damage in order to enable us to compute what if any sum ought to be allowed in deduction from our claim in respect of the set-off and counterclaim. If we do not have these figures we will be in difficulty in dealing with any payment into court and arguing our case fully at trial.

   (b) Our request for further and better particulars will be formally drafted like a pleading and served by letter on the defendants. If they decline to supply it voluntarily we will issue a summons asking for it. If there is to be a summons for directions because all directions were not in fact given at the summary judgment application then that will be an appropriate time. The order would probably be that we should have the costs in any event since clearly our request for further and better particulars would be reasonable.

7. A party should always have an opportunity of obtaining expert evidence in relation to the subject-matter of an action. We would therefore first write and ask for permission to be given for our expert to inspect the vehicle voluntarily. If agreement was refused to our request then at the Summons for Directions (or by separate summons if there is to be no Summons for Direction) we should apply for an order that the action be stayed unless the defendants permit the plaintiff to inspect the vehicle. Again we are likely to be awarded costs in any event since our request is clearly reasonable.

8. (a) This is the expert report from the defendant's expert. It would seem Mr. Barker is certainly qualified to be an expert and his report would be admissible so far as relevant and accepted by us. If it is not accepted by us then Mr. Barker will have to attend to testify. Even

517

though he is clearly an expert there are parts of his evidence which are inadmissible in particular the second and third paragraphs of his report which appear to be hearsay and/or based on hearsay from other persons. Moreover paragraph 4 contains inadmissible hearsay in the reference to Fixit Garage.

Paragraph 5 is admissible opinion evidence and evidence of findings in respect of similar cars is admissible even if Mr. Barker has no personal knowledge of this since it would be within the sphere of his knowledge as an expert.

Paragraph 6 on the other hand is quite inadmissible. References to the conduct of the mechanic in the past would only be acceptable if it were within the similar fact evidence principle which it clearly is not.

(b) (i) Mr. Lucas would be called to give evidence that to the best of his knowledge the vehicle was in good working order when it was sold.

(ii) Mr. Russell the mechanic would then be called in order to establish the contents of his expert evidence. He is entitled to give his opinion evidence based on matters within his expertise.

(iii) Phillip Underhill is a trained chemical engineer but his evidence is not really expert evidence but simply factual evidence about the use of unleaded petrol. If he is out of the country his statement could be served with a notice under section 2 of the Civil Evidence Act 1968 within 21 days of setting down for trial and a reason applicable under section 8 of the Act as to why he cannot be called could be claimed namely that he is beyond the seas. In that situation his evidence would be admissible as of right.
When the statement is admitted the court should have regard to section 6(3) of the 1968 Act in assessing how much weight to attach to his evidence and in particular the court should have regard to how contemporaneous the statement is with the events described and to any motive the maker may have had to conceal or misrepresent the facts. Neither of these factors ought to lead the court to reject the evidence in this case. Alternatively a notice to admit facts could be served on the defendant and if the defendant did not admit that unleaded petrol had been used the cost of proving those facts would be payable by the defendant. In the present case the service of a notice to admit facts might lead the other side to cease defending the matter since it would be conclusive.

It is of course best of all if Phillip Underhill will give oral evidence and if he returns from time to time to the country it may be possible to ensure that the trial date coincides with the return.

(iv) Michael Underhill could establish that a man put unleaded petrol in the vehicle and may be able to identify Jonathan Fowler. However he cannot give evidence about what his brother said which would be inadmissible hearsay. Before Michael can give evidence the court must be satisfied that he is competent to give evidence on oath. The test for competence is his ability to understand the nature of the oath and the importance of the occasion. In practice only if he were willing to come to court voluntarily would we use his evidence since a subpoena cannot be served on a minor.

(c) The report is of course privileged since it was obtained by us for the purpose of litigation. However if the evidence is to be given at trial under Order 38, rule 36 in principle the evidence will have to be disclosed to the other side unless both sides consent not to disclose their expert evidence or the court makes a direction to that effect. This would be extremely unusual in routine cases such as the present and therefore the position is almost certainly that each party will be required to disclose to the other side within a specified period of time the substance of any expert evidence on which that party proposes to rely in the form of a written statement. Accordingly we will have to disclose the substance of the report to the other side. There will probably have been directions about expert evidence at the summary judgment hearing in any event. In any case since the report is entirely favourable to our position and we have seen the other side's report there is no harm in disclosing it.

* NOTE TO READERS

A Question in the form of Q.1 would not now be set about such a modest amount. At the time of this paper the upper limit of the County Court jurisdiction was only £5,000 and there were certain costs penalties applicable in ss.19 and 20 of the County Courts Act 1984 (now repealed) for actions wrongly brought in the High Court. The answer to such a question would now almost certainly be to issue in the County Court.

COURT FEES ONLY

Writ indorsed
with Statement
of Claim
[Liquidated
Demand]
(O.6, r. 1)

IN THE HIGH COURT OF JUSTICE

19 90 .— E .—No.

Queen's Bench Division

[Exbridge   **District Registry]**

Between

Easyride Motors Ltd   Plaintiff

AND

Fowler and Co (a firm)

Defendant

(1) Insert name.   **To the Defendant (¹)**   Fowler and Co

(2) Insert address.   **of (²)**   5 Martins Lane Exbridge Blankshire

This Writ of Summons has been issued against you by the above-named Plaintiff in respect of the claim set out on the back.

Within 14 days after the service of this Writ on you, counting the day of service, you must either satisfy the claim or return to the Court Office mentioned below the accompanying **Acknowledgment of Service** stating therein whether you intend to contest these proceedings.

If you fail to satisfy the claim or to return the Acknowledgment within the time stated, or if you return the Acknowledgment without stating therein an intention to contest the proceedings, the Plaintiff   may proceed with the action and judgment may be entered against you forthwith without further notice.

(3) Complete
and delete as
necessary.   Issued from the (³) [Central Office] [Admiralty and Commercial Registry]
[Exbridge   District Registry] of the High Court
this   20th   day of   July   19 90.

NOTE:—This Writ may not be served later than 4 calendar months (or, if leave is required to effect service out of the jurisdiction, 6 months) beginning with that date unless renewed by order of the Court.

IMPORTANT

Directions for Acknowledgment of Service are given with the accompanying form.

Statement of Claim

The Plaintiff's claim is for the balance of the price of goods sold and
delivered by the Plaintiff to the Defendants on 23rd April 1990 and in
respect of which payment was due on 31st May 1990 and for interest
thereon pursuant to section 35A of the Supreme Court Act 1981 at the
rate of 15% per annum.

Particulars.

Purchase Price of Toyonda Ranger
registered number B457 KNW
sold on 23rd April 1990 and in respect
of which payment was due on May 31st 1990   5,650

less deposit·   2,000

Balance due   £3,650

And the Plaintiff claims:

(1) The said sum of £3,650

(2) Interest as aforesaid from 1st June 1990 to the date of issue
herein (50 days) equivalent to £75.

(3) Interest continuing at the daily rate of £1.50 until judgment
or earlier payment.

(Signed)

If, within the time for returning the Acknowledgment of Service, the Defendant
pay the amount claimed and £ X for costs and, if the Plaintiff
obtain an order for substituted service, the additional sum of £ Y
further proceedings will be stayed. The money must be paid to the Plaintiff s, their
Solicitor or Agent.

(1) If this Writ was
issued out of a
District Registry,
this indorsement
as to place where
the cause of action
arose should be
completed.

(2) Delete as
necessary.

(3) Insert name of
place.

(4) For
phraseology of this
indorsement where
the Plaintiff sues in
person, see
*Supreme Court
Practice*, vol. 2,
para 1.

(¹) (²) [The cause] [One of the causes] of action in respect of which the Plaintiff
claim relief in this action arose wholly or in part at (³)
in the district of the District Registry named overleaf.]

(⁴) **This Writ was issued by** Smythes
of 5 High Street Exbridge in the County of Blankshire

[Agent for xx
Of x
                                                                    ]

Solicitor s for the said Plaintiff whose address (⁴) [is] [are]
registered office is situated at 59 Station Road
Southcliffe, Blankshire.

Solicitor's Reference   **Tel. No:**

Index

ABSCONDING, 43.01. *See also* BAIL.
ABSOLUTE DISCHARGE, 47.22, 47.28
ACCOMPLICE,
  corroboration and, 28.06, 28.09–28.11,
    33.21
  evidence of, 23.04, 28.09–28.10. *See also*
    CO-ACCUSED.
  exam questions, 49.12
ACCUSED,
  character, evidence of. *See* CHARACTER.
  co-accused. *See* CO-ACCUSED.
  competence and compellability of,
    26.05–26.08
  evidence of, 26.05–26.08
  interrogation of. *See* POLICE QUESTIONING.
  right not to testify, without comment, 26.08
  silence, right of. *See* SILENCE.
  spouse, testimony of, 26.09–26.12
ACKNOWLEDGMENT OF SERVICE, 5.20–5.25
  return of, 5.25
  stay of execution. *See* STAY OF EXECUTION.
  transfer of proceedings. *See* TRANSFER.
ADMISSIBILITY OF EVIDENCE, 23.01–23.05
  judge's role, 23.01
  magistrates' court, in, 23.03–23
  procedure for determining, 30.23–30.26
ADMISSIONS, 25.03–25.08
  civil cases, in, 6.23, 25.03–25.07
    judgment on, 11.21
  civil hearsay and, 31.21–31.27
  confessions. *See* CONFESSIONS.
  county court, in, 17.22–17.24
  criminal cases, in, 25.08
  criminal hearsay, 30.01
  defence, in, 6.23
  directions and, 8.07
  formal, 25.03–25.08
  judgment on, 11.21
  not admitting, 6.24
  notice to admit facts, in response,
    25.05–25.07
  pleadings, in, 26.04
  summons for directions and, 8.07
ADMISSION, DEFENCE AND COUNTERCLAIM,
  County Court form of, 17.10, 17.20–17.30
ADVICE ON EVIDENCE, 10.06–10.12. *See also*
  COUNSEL.
AFFIDAVIT, 4.14–4.15
  discovery by, 7.07
  drafting questions, 49.06
  evidence, 31.34
  filing of, 4.15
  form of, 4.15
  pre-action discovery, in, 3.15

AFFIDAVIT—*cont.*
  service of writ, of, 5.17
  swearing of, 4.15
AFFIRMATION, 27.02. *See also* OATH.
ALIBI, 30.22
  warning at committal, 46.12, 46.18
AMENDMENT OF PLEADINGS. *See* PLEADINGS.
ANTECEDENTS, 47.03
  bail and, 43.11
APPEALS,
  against bail refusal, 43.23–43.24
  civil. *See* CIVIL APPEALS.
  criminal. *See* CRIMINAL APPEALS.
ARBITRATION,
  appeal from registrar, 21.03
  costs of, 17.56–17.57
  county court, referral for, 17.53–17.58
  personal injuries caused by untraced
    driver, 3.31
  solicitors not usually instructed, 17.57
ARREST, 41.02–41.05, 41.08
  arrestable offences, 41.03
  caution, 41.05
  constable, powers of, 41.04
  procedure, 41.05
  search after, 41.09–41.10
  statutory powers, 41.04
  with warrant, 41.02
  without warrant, 41.03–41.04
ASSOCIATE'S CERTIFICATE, 16.07
ATTACHMENT OF EARNINGS, 19.28–19.31,
  19.35
ATTENDANCE CENTRE ORDERS, 47.27
AUDIENCE,
  rights of, 4.25, 16.01

BAIL, 39.07, 40.02, 43.01 *et seq.*
  appeal against refusal, 43.23–43.24
  absconding, 43.01
  application procedure, 43.07 *et seq.*
  character, antecedents, etc., 43.11
  committal proceedings, 46.16, 46.18
  conditions, 43.14–43.21
    grounds for imposing, 43.15
    security, 43.17
    sureties, 43.16
    variation of, 43.19
  Crown Court, application to, 43.23
  custody officer and, 41.16
  evidence, strength of, 43.13
  exam questions, 49.10
  further applications for, 43.22–43.24
  High Court judge, application to, 43.24
  meeting objections to, 43.19

BAIL—*cont.*
  nature and seriousness of offence, 43.10
  pending appeal, 48.01
  previous bail record, 43.12
  prima facie right, 43.02–43.06
    imprisonment not possible, exceptions
      where, 43.03, 43.05
    imprisonment possible, exceptions
      where, 43.03–43.05
    relevant considerations in deciding,
      43.06, 44.10 *et seq.*
  relevant considerations, 43.06, 43.10–43.13
  remand in custody, 43.21
  security, 43.17
  social enquiry reports, 47.06. *See also*
    SOCIAL ENQUIRY REPORTS.
  sureties, 43.16
  variation, 43.19
BAILIFFS, 17.02, 17.16, 19.13
BANKRUPTCY,
  enforcement device, as, 19.36
BARRISTERS. *See also* COUNSEL.
  barrister's clerk, 4.31
BREACH OF CONTRACT. *See* CONTRACT
  CASES.
BRIEF. *See* COUNSEL.
BULLOCK ORDERS, 4.23–4.24, 14.15, 20.25.
  See further THIRD PARTY PROCEEDINGS.
BURDEN OF PROOF, 24.01 *et seq.*
  civil cases, in, 24.01
  criminal cases, in, 24.03–24.07
    defences, 24.07
    evidential, 24.07
    exceptions, etc., 24.05
    no case to answer, 24.06
  judge's summing up, 24.09

CAUSE OF ACTION,
  amendment of pleadings, 6.44
  joinder of, 4.21–4.24. *See further* JOINDER.
  place where arising, 5.04
  striking out, 6.34, 17.19
CAUTION, 30.16
  on arrest, 41.05
CHARACTER, EVIDENCE OF, 33.01 *et seq.*
  accused attempting to prove good
    character, 33.07 *et seq.*
  bail and, 43.11
  exam questions, 50.12
  giving evidence against co-accused,
    33.20–33.22
  imputations against prosecution witnesses,
    33.11–33.19
  relevant to credibility, 33.18–33.19, 33.22
  plea in mitigation, 47.55
  police photographs as, 41.31
  similar fact evidence, and, 33.03–33.05. *See*
    further SIMILAR FACT EVIDENCE.
  statutes allowing proof of convictions,
    33.06
CHARGE, 40.07, 41.16 *et seq.*, 41.21–41.23
  questioning after, 30.17, 41.21
  time of, 41.16, 41.21–41.23

CHARGING ORDERS, 19.24–19.27, 19.34
  High Court, in, 19.24–19.26, 19.34
  county court, in, 19.27, 19.34
CHILDREN. *See also* INFANTS.
  competence and compellability of, 26.04
  evidence of, 27.03
CHOICE OF COURT, 4.32, 17.14–17.15, 18.01
  et seq., 49.11
  control, 18.07
  county court, advantages of, 18.14–18.15
  criminal cases, in. *See* MODE OF TRIAL.
  enforcement, 18.09. *See further*
    ENFORCEMENT.
  general considerations, 18.01–18.05
  High Court, advantages of, 18.06–18.13
  interest, 17.14–18.13
  psychological advantages, 18.08, 18.11
  transfer, 18.12, 18.16
  venue, 17.15
CIVIL APPEALS, 21.01 *et seq.*
  arbitration, registrars', 21.03
  county court registrar, against, 21.02
  final orders,
    county court, in, 21.06
    High Court, in, 21.05
  interlocutory orders,
    county court, in, 21.01
    High Court, in, 21.04
CIVIL EVIDENCE. *See also* EVIDENCE.
  burden of proof, 24.01
  competence and compellability,
    26.01–26.02. *See further* COMPETENCE
    AND COMPELLABILITY.
  standard of proof, 24.02
CIVIL LITIGATION,
  financing of, 2.01 *et seq. See further* COSTS;
    FEES; LEGAL AID.
CIVIL PROCEEDINGS. *See* COUNTY COURT;
  HIGHT COURT PROCEDURE.
CO-ACCUSED,
  competence and compellability of,
    26.05–26.07
  confession implicating, 30.28
  conflict of interest, same solicitor,
    38.08–38.09
  corroboration, 28.12
  evidence against, 33.20–33.22
  evidence of, 26.05–26.07
  guilty plea by, 26.07
  separate trials, 26.06
CO-DEFENDANTS,
  costs and, 4.23–4.24, 20.25
CO-PLAINTIFFS, 4.18–4.19
COMMENCEMENT OF ACTION, 4.32, 5.01 *et*
  seq.
COMMENCING CRIMINAL PROCEEDINGS, 42.01
  et seq.
  arrest and charge, 42.07
  geographical restrictions, 42.03
  laying information, 42–04–42.07
  summons, 42.06–42.07
  time limits, 42.02
COMMITTAL FOR SENTENCING, 45.09

COMMITTAL PROCEEDINGS, 45.17, 46.01 *et seq.*
  alibi warning, 46.12, 46.18
  bail, 46.16, 46.18
  costs, 46.16
  Crown Court to which committed, 46.15
  defence evidence, 46.13–46.14, 46.25
  discharge not acquittal, 46.14
  evidence not called at, 46.28
  full, 46.05–46.16
  full or short, tactics, 46.19–46.28
    defence evidence, 46.25
    exploiting inconsistent evidence, 46.24
    inadmissible evidence, 46.22
    prosecution witnesses, 46.21
    rehearsing prosecution witnesses, 46.26
    speculative cross-examination, 46.23
  hearsay and written evidence at, 46.09, 46.17
  identification evidence, 46.19
  legal aid, 46.16, 46.18
  "natural" documents, use of, 29.14
  no case to answer, 46.10
  prosecution case and evidence, 46.08–46.09
  purpose of, 46.02–46.03
  reporting restrictions, 46.07, 46.18
  section 102 statements, 46.09, 46.17–46.18
  short form, 46.17–46.18
  witness orders, 46.09, 46.16, 46.18
COMMUNITY SERVICE ORDERS, 47.21, 47.28
COMPELLABILITY. *See* COMPETENCE AND COMPELLABILITY.
COMPENSATION ORDERS, 47.39
COMPETENCE AND COMPELLABILITY, 26.01 *et seq.*
  accused, 26.05–26.08
  accused's spouse, 26.09–26.12
  co-accused, 26.05–26.08
  children, 26.04
  civil cases, 26.02
  criminal cases, 26.03–26.12
COMPROMISE, 11.20, 16.01
  day of trial, on, 16.01
  persons under a disability, and, 15.02–15.09
COMPUTER RECORDS, 31.19
CONDITIONAL DISCHARGE, 47.18, 47.28
CONFERENCE. *See* COUNSEL.
CONFESSIONS, 23.03, 30.01 *et seq.*
  codes of practice and, 30.15
  document, as, 29.22
  editing of, 30.27
  identification of accused by part of, 30.19
  implicating others, 30.28
  improperly obtained evidence and, 34.01, 34.05
  interrogation of suspects, and, 30.11–30.19. *See also* POLICE QUESTIONING.
  judge's role, 30.24, 30.26
  jury's function, 30.26
  oppression, 30.04, 30.05, 30.21

CONFESSIONS—*cont.*
  present position, summary, 30.21
  statutory provision, 30.02, 30.03
  test for admissiblity, 30.04
  things found in consequence of, 30.08
  unfairness, 30.20, 30.21
  unreliability, 30.04, 30.06, 30.21
  "verbals," 30.12–30.13, 30.27
  voir dire, 30.23
    judge's function, 30.26
    Magistrates' Courts, in, 30.25
CONFISCATION ORDERS, 47.41
CONSTABLE, POWERS OF. *See* POLICE POWERS.
CONTEMPT OF COURT,
  non-disclosure of documents and, 7.08
CONTRACT CASES,
  damages for breach, 1.19
  enquiry agents and, 3.39
  enforcement, ability of, 3.38–3.39
  interim payments, 13.14
  letter before action, 3.40
  pre-action considerations, 3.37–3.41
  summary judgment and, 11.07–11.16. *See further* SUMMARY JUDGMENT.
CONTRACT OF EMPLOYMENT,
  damages and, 1.04
  obtaining details of, 3.12
CONTRIBUTION, 14.02. *See also* THIRD PARTY PROCEEDINGS.
CONVICTIONS,
  appeal against. *See* CRIMINAL APPEALS.
  civil proceedings, in, 31.28–31.33
    effect of pleading, 31.31
    procedure under s.11, 31.32–31.33
    relevance of, 31.29–31.30
    strict liability cases, 31.30
  offences committed under age of 14, 33.23
  previous, in criminal matters. *See* PREVIOUS CONVICTIONS.
  spent, 33.23
CORROBORATION, 24.04, 28.01 *et seq.*
  accomplice's evidence, of, 28.06, 28.09–28.11
    previous convictions and, 34.21
  co-accused, 28.12
  confessions implicating co-defendants, 30.28
  definition of, 28.02
  identification evidence, 28.13–18.15
  mutual, 28.11
  opinion evidence, 28.04
  prosecution evidence, 28.14
  warnings, 28.05 *et seq.*
COSTS, 2.03, 2.27, 16.06, 20.01 *et seq. See also* FEES; TAXATION OF COSTS.
  agreement as to, 20.26–20.32
    reasons for, 20.27–20.31
  amendment of pleadings, 6.46, 6.48
  assessed, 20.34
  Bullock Orders, 4.23–4.24, 14.15, 20.25
  choice of court and. *See* CHOICE OF COURT.
  co-defendants, 20.25

Costs—*cont.*
  committal proceedings, 46.16
  consequential amendments, 6.48
  convicted offender, 47.42
  counsel, restrictions on use of, 20.17
  counterclaim, on, 20.24
  county court arbitration, 17.56–17.57
  county court, in, 20.16
  discovery, non-party, 7.09
  draftsmen, 20.28
  fixed, 20.33
  fixed costs indorsement of writ, 5.03
  further and better particulars, 6.31
  interlocutory applications, 20.18–20.23
    in any event, 20.20
    in the cause, 20.19
    of the day, 20.22
    reserved, 20.23
    thrown away, 20.21
  legally aided client, 2.18, 20.03–20.04,
    20.12
    client's own, 2.23–2.24
    defendant, and, 2.23
    opponents' costs, 2.25–2.26
    statutory charge of legal aid fund,
      2.23–2.24
  meaning, 20.01
  notice to admit facts, 26.05–26.07
  oral examination, 19.08
  orders in criminal legal aid cases,
    39.24–39.25
  other countries, in, 20.05
  payment into court and, 12.02 *et seq.*
  Sanderson orders, 4.23–4.24, 20.25
  taxation of, 20.08 *et seq. See further*
    TAXATION OF COSTS.
  taxation between parties, 20.09–20.13
    court fee, 20.29
    hearing for, 20.32
    High Court, in, 20.09–20.15
    indemnity basis, 20.13
    solicitor and own client basis, 20.14
    standard basis, 20.09–20.12
  two or more defendants, 4.23–4.24, 20.25
  untraced drivers, Motor Insurance Bureau,
    and, 3.31
Counsel, 4.25 *et seq. See also* BARRISTER.
  advice by, 4.26, 4.27
    on damages, 1.27
    evidence, 10.06–10.12
  advocate as, 4.29–4.30
  audience, rights of, 4.25
  brief fees, 10.16
  briefing, 4.26, 10.16
  clerk, role of, 4.31
  client and, 4.27, 4.32
  conference with, 4.27
  conference with client, 10.13
  conference with experts, 10.14
  defence, drafting of, 5.28
  drafting pleadings, 4.28
  fees and refreshers, 10.16
  interlocutory applications, 4.30

Counsel—*cont.*
  open court, in, 4.29
  opinion, 4.26
  substituted, 4.31–4.32, 10.16
  taxation of costs, and, 20.17
Counterclaim, 6.05
  costs, 20.24
  county court, in, 17.27
County Court, 17.01 *et seq.*
  admission, defence and counterclaim, form
    of, 17.10, 17.20–17.30
  admissions in, 17.22–17.24
    part of claim, 17.23
    unliquidated sum, in action for, 17.24
    whole claim, of, 17.22
  advantages of trial in, 18.14–18.15. *See*
    further CHOICE OF COURT.
  amendment of pleadings, 17.33
  appeals. *See* CIVIL APPEALS.
  appeal against registrar, 21.02
  arbitration, 17.53–17.58
    costs, 17.56–17.57
    legal aid and, 17.58
  attachement of earnings, 19.28–19.31,
    19.35
  bailiffs, 17.02, 17.16
    service by, 17.16
  capacity of parties, 17.11
  charging orders in, 19.27, 19.34
  commencing proceeding, 17.07–17.12
  companies, and, 17.11
  constitution and personnel, 17.02
  costs in, 20.16
  costs, taxation of. *See* TAXATION OF COSTS.
  counterclaim, 17.27
  default summons, 17.06
  defence, 17.25
  directions in, 17.38–17.40
  discovery, 17.43–17.45
  enforcement of judgments, in High Court,
    19.14
  enforcement procedures. *See*
    ENFORCEMENT.
  execution, warrant of, 19.13, 19.33
  extensions of time, 17.32
  final orders, 21.06
  financial limits, 17.02
  fixed date summons, 17.05
  further and better particulars, 17.18
  garnishee proceedings, 19.23, 19.34
  High Court judgments enforced in, 19.37
  infants and, 17.11
  inspection of property, 17.46
  interest, 17.13–17.14
  interim payments, 17.47
  interlocutory applications, 17.31
  interlocutory orders, 21.01
  joinder in, 17.12
  judge, 17.02
  judgment at pre-trial review, 17.41
  judgment in default, 17.26
  originating application, 17.03
  particulars of claim, 17.09, 17.17

COUNTY COURT—*cont.*
  payments into court, 17.34–17.37
  plain note, 17.10
  preparation for trial, 17.51
  pre-trial review, 17.38–17.42
    arbitration referral, 17.53–17.58
    judgment at, 17.41
  registrar, 17.02
  service, 17.16
  striking out pleadings, 17.19
  summary judgment, 17.28–17.30
  summons, 17.04–17.06, 17.08. *See further*
    SUMMONS.
    request for, 17.08
  transfer from High Court, 18.12, 18.16
  third party proceedings, 17.48–17.50
  trial, 17.52
  venue for proceedings, 17.15
COURT ORDERS, 4.09
CRIMINAL APPEALS, 48.01 *et seq.*
  against conviction, 48.01
  against sentence, 48.01, 48.02
  bail, 48.01
  case stated, by way of, 48.04
  case stated, legal aid, 40.21
  Court of Appeal (Criminal Division), to,
    48.05
  Crown Court, from, 48.04, 48.05
  equivocal plea, 48.02
  House of Lords, to, 48.06
  legal aid, 48.05
  magistrates' court, from,
    Crown Court, 48.01–48.03
    Divisional Court of Queen's Bench
    Division, 48.04
CRIMINAL EVIDENCE. *See also* EVIDENCE.
  accused, evidence of, 26.05–26.08
  burden of proof, 24.03–24.07
    defences, 24.07
    evidential, 24.07
    exceptions, etc., 24.05
  children, evidence of. *See* CHILDREN.
  competence and compellability, 26.01,
    26.03–26.12. *See further* COMPETENCE
    AND COMPELLABILITY.
  evidential burden, 24.07
  no case to answer, 24.06
  standard of proof, 24.08–24.09
CRIMINAL LEGAL AID, 39.01 *et seq.*, 40.03
  acquittal, 39.22, 40.23
  appeals, 48.05
  appeals by way of case stated, 39.23
  application procedure, 39.17
  assistance by way of representation, 39.04
  civil proceedings distinguished, 39.08
  committal proceedings, 46.16, 46.18
  costs, orders for, 39.24, 39.25
  criteria, 39.09–39.16
    means, 39.10
    interests in justice, 39.11–39.16
  Duty Solicitor schemes, 39.03, 39–05–39.07
  Green Form Scheme, 39.02
  matters covered by, 39.19, 39.20

CRIMINAL LEGAL AID—*cont.*
  not retrospective, 39.20
  payment of fees, 39.21
  police station, advice at, 39.03
  refusal and appeal, 39.18
CRIMINAL PROCEEDINGS,
  advice as to plea, 40.09
  assistance from prosecution, 40.08
  bail. *See* BAIL.
  charge, 41.16 *et seq. See further* CHARGE.
  classification of offences, 45.01 *et seq.*
  client admitting guilty, 38.04
  commencement of, 42.01 *et seq. See further*
    COMMENCING CRIMINAL
    PROCEEDINGS.
  defence solicitor, duties of, 38.02–38.09
    client admitting guilt, 38.04
    confidentiality, 38.03
    conflicts of interest, 38.08–38.09
    inconsistent instructions, 38.06
    previous convictions, 38.05
    prosecution witnesses, interviewing,
      38.07
  guilty plea, 40.07. *See* GUILTY PLEA; PLEA.
  legal aid. *See* CRIMINAL LEGAL AID.
  method of trial. *See* MODE OF TRIAL.
  outline of, 37.01 *et seq.*
  personal injury litigations and, 3.09
  preliminary considerations, 40.01 *et seq.*
    accused's account of case, 40.06
    assistance from prosecution, 40.08
    calling witnesses, 40.10–40.11
    charges, 40.05
    first interview, 40.04–40.07
    guilty plea. *See* GUILTY PLEA; PLEA.
    re-interviewing, 40.09
  prosecutor, duties of, 38.01. *See also*
    PROSECUTION.
  summary trial, 44.01 *et seq. See further*
    SUMMARY TRIAL.
CRIMINAL TRIAL, 44.01 *et seq. See also*
  SUMMARY TRIAL.
  commencing proceedings, 42.01 *et seq. See*
    further COMMENCING CRIMINAL
    PROCEEDINGS.
  joint, 44.02–44.02
  publicity, 45.22
  separate trials for co-accused, 26.06
CROSS-EXAMINATION, 27.20–27.27
  bias, 27.25
  credit, as to, 27.21–27.27
  issues in the case, on, 27.20–27.21, 27.23
  leading questions, 27.05
  speculative, at full committal, 46.23
  witness's previous convictions, 27.27
  witness's previous inconsistent statements,
    27.26. *See further* WITNESS.
CROWN COURT,
  acquittal rate, magistrates' court
    compared, 45.14
  advantages of trail in, 45.14–45.18
  appeals from, 48.05

CROWN COURT—*cont.*
appeal from magistrates' court,
48.01–48.03
bail application, 43.23
committal for sentencing, 45.09
committal proceedings. *See* COMMITTAL
PROCEEDINGS.
costs, 45.24
disclosure of prosecution evidence in, 45.16
jury, 45.14
sentencing, 47.10
CROWN PRIVILEGE, 35–02–35.04
CUSTODY OFFICER, 41.15–41.17
bail and, 41.16
custody records, 41.15, 41.22
interrogation and, 41.22

DAMAGES, 1.01 *et seq.*
clothes and property damaged in accident,
1.09
contract cases, 1.19
counsel's advice on, 1.27
interest, 1.20–1.25. *See further* INTEREST.
statement of claim, 6.14
loss of earnings, 1.03–1.07
preliminary steps, 3.12
medical expenses, 1.11, 1.18
personal injury cases, in, 1.01–1.18
categorisation, 1.01 *et seq.*
general damages, 1.01, 1.13–1.18. *See
further* GENERAL DAMAGES.
loss of earnings, 1.03–1.07
pleading damages, 1.01
provisional damages, 1.26
special damages, 1.02–1.12. *See further*
SPECIAL DAMAGES.
pleading interest, 1.25
provisional, 1.26
vehicle repairs, 1.08
visiting expenses, 1.12
DEBT. *See* CONTRACT CASES; JUDGMENT
DEBT.
DEFENCE, 5.27, 6.04, 6.22–6.25
admissions in, 6.23
county court, in, 17.25
denials, 6.25
extension of time limits, 5.28
judgment in default, 11.18–11.19
not admitting, 6.24
pleading matters of law, 6.15
DEFERRED SENTENCE, 47.58
DELAYS, 8.01, 11.22–11.24
defendant, by, 11.06. *See also* JUDGMENT IN
DEFAULT; LIMITATION.
DIRECTIONS, 8.01 *et seq.*
admissions, 8.07
agreed, 8.07
agreements and admissions, 8.07
"automatic," 4.06, 8.09, 8.10–8.11
discovery, 8.12
expert evidence and, 8.05, 8.13, 9.02,
9.04
photographs, sketch plans, 8.14

DIRECTIONS—*cont.*
"automatic"—*cont.*
police accident reports, etc., 8.14
setting down for trial, 8.15
defendant and, 8.03
discovery and inspection, 8.12
interim payment proceedings, 13.03
split trials, order for, 8.16
summary judgment proceedings, 11.15
summons for, 8.02
agreements and admissions, 8.07
county court, transfer to, 8.06
defendant's notice under, 8.03
expert evidence, limiting, 8.05
hearing of, 8.04–8.09
witness statements, order for exchange,
8.08
third party proceedings, and, 14.09–14.14.
See further THIRD PARTY
PROCEEDINGS.
timing of, 8.01
DISABLEMENT BENEFITS, 1.06
DISABILITY, PERSONS UNDER, 15.01 *et seq.*
See also INFANTS.
compromise and, 15.02–15.09
defendants, as, 15.10
guardian ad litem, 15.10
investment of compromise money, 15.08
next friend, 15.01–15.09
plaintiffs, as, 15.01–15.09
DISBURSEMENTS. *See* FEES.
DISCOVERY, 7.01 *et seq.*
affidavit, by, 7.07
application to court, 7.06
automatic, 4.06, 7.03–7.05, 8.12
county court, in, 17.43–17.45
format, 7.03–7.04
general, 7.06
incomplete, 7.07
non-compliance with, 7.08
non-party, against, 3.18, 7.09
costs of, 7.09
orders for, 7.06
particular, 7.06, 7.07
personal injury arising out of accident on
land, 7.06
photocopying and, 7.04
pre-action, in personal injuries cases,
3.15–3.16
private privilege, 7.05
privileged documents, 7.02, 7.05
refusal, 7.07
summons for, 7.06
third party proceedings, 14.09
not automatic, 7.06
time for, 7.03
witness statements, privileged, 7.02
DISMISSAL FOR WANT OF PROSECUTION,
11.22–11.24
DISQUALIFICATION FROM DRIVING,
47.29–47.38
application for lifting of, 47.33
combination with other penalties, 47.38

DISQUALIFICATION FROM DRIVING—*cont.*
concurrent, not consecutive, 47.34
discretionary, 47.30
endorsement,
obligatory, 47.30
two or more offences, 47.32, 47.34
exceptional hardship, 47.37
general mitigation, 47.35
in outline, 47.29
mandatory, 47.30
period of, 47.33–47.34
points system, 47.31–47.32, 47.34 *et seq.*
exceptional hardship, 47.37
presence of offender required, 47.34
special reasons, 47.35
"totting up," 47.31–47.32, 47.34
exceptional hardship, 47.37
DIVISIONAL COURT,
appeal from magistrates' court, 48.04
DOCUMENTARY EVIDENCE, 36.02–36.04
agreed, 10.10, 36.02
"ancient," 36.03
disputed, notice, 10.11
hearsay, as. *See* HEARSAY.
originals and copies, 10.12, 36.03
public documents, 36.04
secondary evidence of contents, 36.03
tape-recordings, etc., 36.03
witness (section 102) statements,
46.17–46.18
DUTY SOLICITOR, 39.03, 39.05–39.07

EARNINGS, ATTACHEMENT OF. *See*
ENFORCEMENT.
EARNINGS, LOSS OF, 1.03–1.07. *See further*
DAMAGES.
ENDORSEMENTS. *See* DISQUALIFICATION.
ENFORCEMENT, 19.01 *et seq.*
attachment of earnings, 19.28–19.31, 19.35
bankruptcy, 19.36
charging orders, 19.24–19.27, 19.34
choice of methods of, 19.32–19.37
exam questions, 49.08
execution, 19.10–19.16, 19.33
county court, in, 19.13–19.14
High Court, in, 19.10–19.12,
19–14–19.16
stay of. *See* STAY.
fieri facias, 19.10–19.16
garnishee proceedings, 19.17–19.23, 19.34.
See further GARNISHEE.
judgment debtor's means, obtaining
information, 19.02–19.09
oral examination, 19.04–19.09
application procedure, 19.05
costs, 19.08
county court, in, 19.09
High Court, in, 19.05–19.08
procedure, 19.06
unco-operative debtor, 19.07
status report, 19.03
ENQUIRY AGENTS, 3.39
ENTRY, SEARCH AND SEIZURE, 41.07–41.08

EVIDENCE,
advice on, 10.06–10.12
affidavit, by, 31.34
agreed, 10.10
burden of proof. *See* BURDEN OF PROOF.
character, of. *See* CHARACTER.
civil cases, in. *See* CIVIL EVIDENCE.
civil and criminal distinguished,
22.01–22.02
corroboration. *See* CORROBORATION.
criminal cases, in. *See* CRIMINAL
EVIDENCE.
cross-examination. *See* CROSS-
EXAMINATION.
documentary. *See* DOCUMENTARY
EVIDENCE.
examn questions, 49.07, 49.12
examination in chief, 27.04–27.19. *See
further* EXAMINATION IN CHIEF.
expert. *See* EXPERT EVIDENCE.
function of, 23.01–23.05
hearsay. *See* HEARSAY EVIDENCE.
identification, of. *See* IDENTIFICATION
EVIDENCE.
improperly obtained, 34.01 *et seq.*
introductory, 22.01–22.02
leading questions, 27.05
medical. *See* MEDICAL EVIDENCE.
notice to admit facts, 10.08
opinion, of, 32.01 *et seq. See further*
EXPERT EVIDENCE; OPINION
EVIDENCE.
pleadings and, 6.16–6.19
real, 36.01
re-examination. *See* RE-EXAMINATION.
witnesses. *See* WITNESSES.
written, under Civil Evidence Act 1968,
10.07
EXAMINATION IN CHIEF, 27.04–27.19
hostile witnesses, 27.15, 27.17–27.19
leading questions, 27.05
previous consistent statements,
27.11–27.14
refreshing memory, 27.06–27.10
in court, 27.06–27.10
out of court, 27.06
unfavourable witnesses, 27.15–27.16
EXAMINATION TECHNIQUE, 49.01 *et seq.*
drafting documents, 49.06
EXHIBITS,
interlocutory applications and, 4.16
EXPERT EVIDENCE, 9.01 *et seq.*, 32.03 *et seq.*
ambit of, 32.04–32.05
automatic directions in personal injuries
cases, 8.10, 8.13, 9.02, 9.04
criminal cases, admission as document in,
29.24
disclosure, order for, 9.04–9.14
expert witness, 4.27
conference with, 10.14
defined, 32.03
subpoenas and, 10.09
jury, matters for decision by, and, 32.04

EXPERT EVIDENCE—*cont.*
  medical evidence, 3.11, 9.06–9.11
    client's own doctor, 3.11
    counsel and, 4.27
    defendant's own, 9.07, 9.08
    updating, 9.13
  medical reports, 9.06–9.11
    exchange of reports, procedure on, 9.11
    filing reports with court, 10.03
    lodging, 9.14
    voluntary exchange, 9.10
  medical and psychiatric reports in criminal
    cases, 47.07–47.08
  meetings of experts, order for, 9.12
  non-personal injury cases, 9.06
  opinion, of, 32.03 *et seq.*
  personal injury cases, in, 9.06–9.11
  privilege, 9.03
  procedure for admitting, 32.06–32.07
  voluntary disclosure, 9.10

FEES, 2.01 *et seq. See also* COSTS; TAXATION
    OF COSTS.
  advance payments on account, 2.01–2.03
  cash-flow and, 2.01–2.03
  client's misconceptions relating to, 2.01
  disbursements, 2.02, 2.03
    legal aid cases, in, 2.05
  legally aided client, 2.05, 2.06 *et seq. See
    also* CRIMINAL LEGAL AID; LEGAL
    AID.
  insurance company client, 2.04
  privately paying client and, 2.01–2.03
  time recording, 20.02
  trade union clients, 2.04
  unsuccessful clients and, 2.02
FIERI FACIAS, WRIT OF, 19.10–19.14. *See also*
    ENFORCEMENT.
  walking possession, 19.12
FINES, 47.18–47.19, 47.28
FINGERPRINTS, 41.11
FORFEITURE ORDERS, 47.40
FORMAL ADMISSIONS. *See* ADMISSIONS.
FURTHER AND BETTER PARTICULARS,
    6.26–6.32
  answering, 6.29
  costs and, 6.31
  county court, in, 17.18
  drafting questions, 50.06
  format of, 6.26
  procedure, 6.27–6.28
  request for, 6.32
  running of time, 6.30

GARNISHEE PROCEEDINGS, 19.17–19.23,
    19.34
  county court practice, 19.23, 19.34
  High Court, in, 19.18–19.22, 19.34
GENERAL DAMAGES, 1.10, 1.13–1.18
  assessment of, 1.15, 1.16
  future earnings, 1.16
  future expenses, 1.18
  labour market, loss on, 1.17

GENERAL DAMAGES—*cont.*
  loss of amenity, 1.15
  loss of earning capacity, 1.17
  meaning, 1.10
  pain and suffering, 1.14
GREEN FORM SCHEME, 2.07 *et seq. See also*
    CRIMINAL LEGAL AID; LEGAL AID.
  assistance by way of representation, 2.08
  claiming from Legal Aid Board, 2.12
  client contribution, 2.09
  criminal cases, 39.02. *See further* CRIMINAL
    LEGAL AID.
  eligibility, 2.09
  maximum level, 2.09, 2.10
  scope of, 2.07
GUARDIAN AD LITEM, 15.10
  county court and, 17.11
GUILTY PLEA, 40.07, 45.19. *See also* PLEA.
  as mitigating factor, 47.53
  co-accused, 26.07
  equivocal, 48.02
  plea in mitigation, 47.53
  postal, 44.06

HEARSAY EVIDENCE, 29.01 *et seq.*
  civil proceedings, 31.01 *et seq. See*
    HEARSAY IN CIVIL PROCEEDINGS.
    summary, 31.23–31.27
  criminal proceedings, in. *See* HEARSAY IN
    CRIMINAL PROCEEDINGS.
  defined, 29.01–29.02
  first hand, 31.02 *et seq.*, 31.24
  second hand, 31.02 *et seq.*, 31.12–31.17,
    31.25
HEARSAY IN CIVIL PROCEEDINGS, 31.01 *et
    seq.*
  agreement, by, 31.01
  as of right, 31.08–31.09
  attacking credibility of absent witness,
    31.11, 31.16
  computer records, 31.19
  counter notices, 31.06–31.07, 31.09,
    31.24–31.25
  document as part of a record, etc.,
    31.12–31.17, 31.25
  first hand, 31.02 *et seq.*, 31.24
  inclusionary discretion, 31.02
  informal admissions, 31.21–31.27
  previous consistent statements,
    31.04–31.07, 31.09
  previous inconsistent statements, 31.20,
    31.26
  second-hand, 31.02 *et seq.*, 31–12–31.17,
    31.25
  section 2 of 1968 Act, 31.03–31.10,
    31.17–31.18, 31.24
    counter-notice, 31.06–31.07, 31.09,
      31.24
    notices, 31.04–31.09, 31.24
    relationship with section 4, 31.17–31.18
    value of statements admitted, 31.10,
      31.24
  section 4 of 1968 Act, 31.12–31.17, 31.25

HEARSAY IN CIVIL PROCEEDINGS—*cont.*
section 4 of 1968 Act—*cont.*
notice and counter-notice, 31.14–31.15, 31.25
summary of Civil Evidence Act provisions, 31.23–31.27
weight, 31.10, 31.16, 31.20, 31.24–31.26
witness called, 31.04–31.05
witness not called, 31.06–31.09
HEARSAY IN CRIMINAL PROCEEDINGS, 29.01 *et seq.*
admissions, 30.01. *See also* ADMISSIONS; CONFESSIONS.
basic rule, 29.01
committal proceedings, at, 46.09, 46.17
confessions, 30.01 *et seq. See further* CONFESSIONS.
depositions in magistrates' court proceedings, 29.26–29.28
documentary evidence, 29.08–29.24
business documents, 29.10
confessions, 29.22
criminal investigations or proceedings, created for, 29.1–29.17
Criminal Justice Act 1988, background to, 29.09
discretion of court, 29.15
discretions, 29.23
expert evidence, 29.24
first-hand, 29.11, 29.12
"natural" documents, 29.14
production of document, 29.21
second-hand, 29.13–29.16
statements prepared for court proceedings, 29.16
unavailability, reasons for, 29.12
use to discredit witness, 29.20
usefulness of, 29.08
weight, 29.17
dying declarations, 29.29
exceptions to rule, 29.02 *et seq.*
public documents, 29.25
res gestae, 29.29
signed written statements, 29.03–29.07
HIGH COURT PROCEDURE, 4.01 *et seq.*
acknowledgment of service. *See* ACKNOWLEDGMENT OF SERVICE.
advantages over county court, 18.06–18.13. *See further* CHOICE OF COURT.
categories of case, 8.15
charging orders, 19.24–19.27, 19.34
choice of court. *See* CHOICE OF COURT.
commencement of action. *See* COMMENCEMENT OF ACTION; WRIT.
county court,
enforcement of judgment in, 19.37
transfer to, 18.12, 18.16
defence. *See* DEFENCE.
directions. *See* DIRECTIONS.
discovery. *See* DISCOVERY.
District Registrars, 4.03
district registry practice, 4.09
Divisions of High Court, 4.01

HIGH COURT PROCEDURE—*cont.*
drawing up orders, 4.09
enforcement. *See* ENFORCEMENT.
expert evidence. *See* EXPERT EVIDENCE.
fieri facias. See ENFORCEMENT.
final orders, 21.05
garnishee proceedings. *See* GARNISHEE.
inspection. *See* INSPECTION.
interim payments and. *See* INTERIM PAYMENTS.
interlocutory applications. *See* INTERLOCUTORY APPLICATIONS.
interlocutory orders, 21.04. *See further* INTERLOCUTORY APPLICATIONS.
joinder. *See* JOINDER.
judge in chambers, 4.04
judges, 4.04
Masters, role of, 4.02
notice to admit facts, 10.08
oral examination as to means, 19.04–19.08
originating summons, 3.15, 4.10
parties. *See* JOINDER.
payment into court. *See* PAYMENT INTO COURT.
pleadings. *See* PLEADINGS.
Rules of Supreme Court, 4.05–4.08
extension of time limits, 4.07
failure to comply, 4.06
service of writ. *See* WRIT.
statement of claim. *See* STATEMENT OF CLAIM.
stay of execution. *See* STAY OF EXECUTION.
striking out pleadings, 6.33–6.37
summary judgment (O. 14). *See* SUMMARY JUDGMENT.
termination without trial. *See* TERMINATION OF ACTION.
transfer of proceedings. *See* TRANSFER.
trial. *See* TRIAL.
writ. *See* WRIT.
HOSTILE WITNESSES, 27.15, 27.17–27.19
HOUSE OF LORDS,
criminal appeals to, 48.06

IDENTIFICATION, EVIDENCE OF, 28–13–28–15, 41.25 *et seq.*
committal proceedings, and, 48.19
corroboration and, 28.13–28.15
dock identification, 41.25
full committal proceedings, and, 46.19
parades, 41.25–41.31. *See further* IDENTIFICATION PARADES.
IDENTIFICATION PARADES, 41.25–41.31
conduct of, 41.26–41.30
photographs and, 41.27–41.29
refusal, 41.25
IMPRISONMENT, 47.14–47.17, 47.26
IMPROPERLY OBTAINED EVIDENCE, 34.01 *et seq.*
misuse of police powers, effect of, 41.13–41.14
INDEMNITY, 14.03–14.04

INFANTS. *See also* CHILDREN; PERSONS
   UNDER DISABILITY.
  compromise of claim, 15.02–15.09
  defendants, as, 15.10
  investment of compromise money, 15.08
  next friend, appointment of, 15.01–17.11
  payments into court, 12.11, 15.09
  plaintiff, as, 15.01–19.09
INFERENCES OF FACT, 25.11
INFORMATION, LAYING OF, 42.04–42.07
INQUEST,
  personal injury litigation and, 3.09
INSPECTION, 7.01 *et seq. See also* DISCOVERY.
  non-party, against, 3.18, 7.09
  pre-action, 3.17–3.18
  property, of, 7.10
  usual arrangements for, 7.04
INSURANCE, 1.06
  motor, 3.19–3.31. *See further* MOTOR
    INSURANCE.
  subrogation, 3.24
INSURANCE COMPANIES,
  adding defendants, 6.41
  Sanderson orders and, 4.23–4.24, 14.15,
    20.25
  service of writ and, 5.18
  solicitors and, 3.20
INTEREST, 1.20–1.25
  computation at trial, 16.04
  contract cases, 1.22–1.24
    as of right, 1.23
    at court's discretion, 1.24
    judgment debts, 1.24
  damages, 1.20–1.25, 6.14
    in county court, 17.13
  debt, contract providing for, 6.11
  judgment debts, 1.24, 17.14, 18.13
    in county court, 17.14
  judgment in default of notice of intention to
    defend, 11.04
  liquidated sum, no provision for, 6.12
  payment into court, on, 12.04, 12.07
  personal injuries, 1.21
  pleading, 1.25, 6.10–6.14
  statement of claim and, 6.10–6.14
  unliquidated sum, 6.14
INTERIM PAYMENTS, 13.01 *et seq.*
  affidavit, 13.04
  application, method of, 13.03–13.07
  contract cases, 13.14
  county court, in, 17.47
  directions, 13.12
  grounds for, 13.03
  hardship, 13.05
  hearing, 13.07
  meaning, 13.01
  payment into court, 13.12
  payment to plaintiff, 13.12
  personal injury cases, 13.01–13.13
  refusal of, grounds for, 13.08–13.11
  summary judgment, and, 13.12
  time for application, 13.13

INTERLOCUTORY APPLICATIONS, 4.02–4.04,
  4.11–4.16
  affidavits, 4.14–4.15. *See also* AFFIDAVIT.
  evidence, by, 31.34
  appeal to judge in chambers, 4.04
  costs, 20.18–20.23
  counsel and, 4.30
  county court, in, 17.31
  District Registrars, 4.03
  ex parte, 4.12
  exhibits, 4.16
  High Court judges, 4.04
  Masters and, 4.02
  summons, by, 4.13
  "return day," 4.13
INTERLOCUTORY ORDERS,
  appeals, county court registrar, from, 21.01
  appeals, High Court judge from, 21.04

JOINDER. *See also* THIRD PARTY
  PROCEEDINGS.
  causes of action,
    counterclaims, as, 4.22
    plaintiff, by, 4.21
    defendant, by, 4.22
  county court, in, 17.12
  meaning, 4.17
  parties, of,
    defendant, by, 4.20
    leave of court, with, 4.19
    plaintiff, by, 4.18
  reasonableness, costs and, 4.24
  third party as co-defendant, 14.15–14.16
JUDGE,
  admissibility of evidence and, 23.01
  confessions, role regarding, 30.24, 30.26
  payments into court kept secret from, 12.02
  previous convictions, discretion regarding,
    33.17
  summing up, 23.02, 24.09
  voir dire and, 30.26
JUDGMENT,
  enforcement of. *See* ENFORCEMENT.
  in default. *See* JUDGMENT IN DEFAULT.
  summary. *See* SUMMARY JUDGMENT.
JUDGMENT ON ADMISSION, 11.21
JUDGMENT DEBTS, 1.24
  interest on, 1.24, 17.14, 18.13
JUDGMENT IN DEFAULT,
  county court, in, 17.26
  defence of (O. 19), 11.18–11.19
  final, 11.02
  interest and, 11.04
  interlocutory, 11.03
  notice of intention to defend, of,
    11.01–11.05, 11.19
    final, 11.02
    interlocutory, 11.03
    procedure, 11.01
    setting aside, 11.05
JUDICIAL NOTICE, 25.02
JURY, 45.14

KNOCK FOR KNOCK. *See* MOTOR INSURANCE.

LEADING QUESTIONS, 27.05
LEGAL AID, 2.05, 2.06 *et seq.*
adding defendants, 6.42
application for, procedure, 2.14–2.17
assessed costs and, 20.34
certificate,
grant of, 2.16
amendment of, 2.19
conditional or unconditional, 2.18
discharge of, 2.21
revocation of, 2.20
chances of success worsening, 2.22
client's own costs, 2.18, 2.23–2.24
costs and, 2.27, 20.03–20.04, 20.12, 20.34
county court arbitration, and, 17.58
criminal cases, in. *See* CRIMINAL LEGAL
AID.
disbursements, 2.05
exam questions, 49.05
financial eligibility, 2.15
Green Form Scheme, 2.07–2.12. *See
further* GREEN FORM SCHEME.
hardship to successful non-legally aided
defendant, 2.26
nature of, 2.13
opponents' costs, 2.25–2.26
payments into court and, 12.10
refusal of, 2.17
solicitor/client relationship and, 2.22
statutory charge, 2.23–2.24
system for provision of, 2.–06
unreasonable client, 2.22
LEGAL PROFESSIONAL PRIVILEGE. *See*
PRIVILEGE.
LETTER BEFORE ACTION, 3.40–3.41
LIMITATION,
issue of writs and, 5.07
pleadings, 6.15
time limits in criminal cases, 42.02
LIMITED COMPANY,
service of writ on, 5.15, 17.11
LOSS OF EARNINGS. *See* DAMAGES.

MAGISTRATES' COURT,
acquittal rate compared with Crown Court,
45.14
admissibility of evidence and, 23.03–23.05
appeal to Crown Court, 48.01–48.03
appeal to Divisional Court, 48.04
"case hardening" of, 45.14
costs, 45.24
disclosure of prosecution case in advance,
45.16
jurisdiction of,
geographical, 42.03
mode of trial. *See* MODE OF TRIAL.
legal and evidential matters before, 45.15
mode of trial hearing, 45.05–45.12. *See
further* MODE OF TRIAL.
publicity at, 45.22
sentencing, 47.11, 47.13, 47.17–47.19
suspended sentences, 47.17
speed of, 45.20

MAGISTRATES' COURT—*cont.*
summary trial by, 44.01 *et seq. See further*
SUMMARY TRIAL.
MEDICAL EVIDENCE. *See* EXPERT EVIDENCE.
MEDICAL EXPENSES,
damages and, 1.11
future, 1.18
MEDICAL REPORTS. *See* EXPERT EVIDENCE.
MITIGATION,
plea in. *See* PLEA IN MITIGATION.
MODE OF TRIAL, 37.01–37.04, 45.01 *et seq.*
accused's option, 45.10
categorisation of offences, 45.02–45.04
changing, 45.11
Crown Court, advantages of, 45.14–45.18
co-defendants election, 45.12
exam questions, 50.11
hearing, 45.05–45.12
magistrates, advantages of, 45.19–45.24
stress factor, 45.21
tactics in representations to magistrates,
45.10
MOTOR INSURANCE, 3.19–3.31
comprehensive, 3.23
disclosure by insured, 3.28
excess, 3.26
knock for knock agreement, 3.27
Motor Insurers' Bureau, 3.29 *et seq.*
no claim bonus, 3.25
opponent's policy, 3.28
repudiation of policy, 3.28
Road Traffic Act, 3.21
subrogation, 3.24
third party, fire and theft, 3.22
types of, 3.21–3.23
uninsured drivers, 3.30
untraced drivers, 3.31
MULTIPLICAND, 1.16
MULTIPLIER, 1.16

NEGLIGENCE,
personal injuries. *See* PERSONAL INJURIES
CASES.
res ipsa loquitur, 25.10
NEGOTIATION,
compromise, termination of action by,
11.20
ethics of, 7.02. *See also* PROFESSIONAL
ETHICS.
payment into court, 12.01 *et seq.*
personal injury cases, with insurance
company, 3.32–3.36
scope of authority, 3.34
without prejudice, 3.36
NEXT FRIEND, 15.01
county court, 17.11

OATHS, 27.01
children and. *See* CHILDREN.
OFFENCES, 45.01 *et seq.*
indictment only, 45.03
purely summary, 45.02
taken into consideration, 48.04

533

OFFENCES—*cont.*
triable either way, 45.04 *et seq.*
OPINION EVIDENCE, 32.01 *et seq.*
civil proceedings, in, 32.02
experts, by, 32.03 *et seq. See further*
EXPERT EVIDENCE.
fact and speculation distinguished, 32.01
ORIGINATING SUMMONS, 3.15, 4.10

PAROLE, 47.14, 47.26
PARTIES,
amendment of pleadings, 6.39–6.43
defendant, adding, 6.39, 6.41
procedure, 6.40
exam questions, 49.04
joinder of, 4.17–4.20, 4.23–4.24. *See
further* JOINDER.
PARTNERSHIP,
service of writ on, 5.16
PAYMENT INTO COURT, 2.24, 12.01 *et seq.*,
16.05
acceptance of, 12.05–12.06
amount of, tactics, 12.03
consequences, 12.02
costs, likely orders, 12.02
county court, in, 17.34–17.37
court's management of money paid in,
12.12
increasing amount of, 12.03, 12.07
infants and, 12.11, 15.09
interest on, 12.04, 12.07
interim payment and, 13.12
legal aid cases, 12.10
procedure, 12.01
refusal of, 12.09
secrecy from judge of, 12.02, 12.13
time for, tactics, 12.08
PERSONAL INJURIES CASES,
applications to court, 3.14–3.18
attending criminal proceedings, 3.09
automatic directions, 8.06–8.08
damages. *See* DAMAGES.
defendant's insurers, notice to, 3.28
defendant's own medical report, 9.08
discovery,
automatic directions, 8.12
pre-action, 3.15–3.16
employers, contact with, 3.12
examining damages vehicle, 3.08
first meeting with client, 3.03–3.04
general damages, 1.01, 1.13–1.18. *See
further* GENERAL DAMAGES.
Inland Revenue, writing to, 3.13
inquests, 3.09
Inspecting scene of accident, 3.07
inspection, pre-action, 3.17–3.18
insurance, 1.06, 2.04. *See further*
INSURANCE; MOTOR INSURANCE.
interim payments, 13.01 *et seq. See further*
INTERIM PAYMENTS.
interviewing witnesses, 3.06
letter before action, 3.41
medical evidence. *See* EXPERT EVIDENCE.

PERSONAL INJURIES CASES—*cont.*
motor insurance, 3.19 *et seq. See further*
MOTOR INSURANCE.
negotiations with insurance company,
3.32–3.36
medical examination, 3.35
service of writ and, 3.32
scope of authority, 3.34
without prejudice, 3.36
police accident report, 3.05, 8.10
pre-action considerations, 3.01 *et seq.*
discovery, 3.15–3.16
inspection, 3.17–3.18
provisional damages, 1.26
quantum,
counsel's advice on, 1.27
information relevant to, 3.10 *et seq.*
special damages, 1.02–1.12. *See further*
SPECIAL DAMAGES.
split trials, 1.26
statement of claim. *See* STATEMENT OF
CLAIM.
summary judgment and, 11.07, 11.17
uninsured drivers, 3.31
untraced drivers, 3.31
PHOTOGRAPHS IN CRIMINAL CASES, 41.12
identification parades, and, 41.27–41.29
no evidence of allowed, 41.31
photographing arrested persons, 41.12
PLAINT NOTE, 17.10
PLAINTIFF,
co-plaintiffs, 4.18–4.19
PLEA, 44.06, 44.08. *See also* GUILTY PLEA.
advice on, 40.09
equivocal, 48.02
PLEA IN MITIGATION, 47.08, 47.14,
47.43–47.58
capacity for reform, 47.54
character witnesses, 47.55
circumstances at time, 47.47
conduct inr relation to police and court,
47.51–47.53
contrition, 47.54
deferred sentence, 47.58
effect on others, 47.48
guilty plea, 47.53
offence, circumstances of, 47.44
offender, 47.45–47.50
other penalties, 47.49
previous convictions, 47.46
recommendation by advocate of sentence
type, 47.57
social enquiry report, use of, 47.08, 47.45,
47.56
time in custody, 47.50
PLEADINGS, 6.01 *et seq.*
abuse of process, as, 6.37
amendment of, 6.38 *et seq.*
cause of action, 6.44
county court, in, 17.33
consequential, 6.48
costs and, 6.46, 6.48
facts, 6.45

PLEADINGS—*cont.*
  amendment of—*cont.*
    leave of court, 6.45
    legal aid implications, 6.42
    method of, 6.47
    parties, 6.39–6.43
    policy of court on, 6.46
  close of, 6.07
  content of, 6.08 *et seq.*
  counsel and, 4.28
  counterclaim. *See* COUNTERCLAIM.
  defence. *See* DEFENCE.
  documents, contents of, 6.19
  drafting questions, 49.06
  "embarrassing," 6.36
  evidence and, 6.16–6.19
  frivolous, scandalous and vexatious, 6.35
  further and better particulars. *See*
      FURTHER AND BETTER PARTICULARS.
  heading of, 6.08
  interest, 6.10–6.14
  law, 6.15
  no reasonable cause of action or defence,
      6.34
  previous convictions in civil cases,
      6.16–6.19, 31.28–31.33
  reply, 6.06
  special damages. *See* SPECIAL DAMAGES.
  statement of claim. *See* STATEMENT OF
      CLAIM.
  striking out, 6.33–6.37
    county court, in, 17.19
  types of, 6.02–6.06
POLICE ACCIDENT REPORT, 3.05, 8.10
POLICE BAIL. *See* BAIL.
POLICE DETENTION, 41.15–41.24
  charge, time for, 41.16, 41.21–41.23
  Codes of Practice, right to read, 41.20
  custody officer, 41.15–41.17
  custody records, 41.15, 41.22
  interrogation in, 41.20–41.24
    further questioning, 31.17, 41.21
    provisions of Code of Practice,
        41.21–41.23
  interviews, tape recording, 41.24
  plea in mitigation, and time spent in, 47.50
  right to consult solicitor, 41.20
  right to inform other person, 41.20
POLICE INFORMERS, 35.04
POLICE POWERS, 41.01 *et seq.*
  arrest, 41.02–41.05, 41.09–41.10. *See
      further* ARREST.
  detention, 41.15–41.24. *See further* POLICE
      DETENTION.
  entry, search and seizure, 41.07–41.08
  fingerprints, 41.11
  identification parades, 41.25–41.31. *See
      further* IDENTIFICATION PARADES.
  misconduct in, effect of, 41.13–41.14. *See
      also* IMPROPERLY OBTAINED
      EVIDENCE.
  photographing, 41.12
  search after arrest, 41.09–41.10

POLICE POWERS—*cont.*
  stop and search, 41.06
POLICE QUESTIONING, 30.11–30.19
  after charge, 30.17, 42.21
  caution, 30.16
  Codes of Practice, 30.14–30.19
  present position, summary, 30.21
  showing statements made by others, 30.18
  unfairness, 30.20–30.21
  "verbals" and, 30.12–30.13
  written records, 30.19
PRE-ACTION CONSIDERATIONS IN CIVIL
      CASES,
  choice of court. *See* CHOICE OF COURT.
  contract cases, 3.37–3.41
  personal injuries cases, 3.01–3.36
PRE-TRIAL REVIEW, 17.38–17.42
PRESUMPTIONS, 25.09–25.10
  res ipsa loquitur, 25.10
PREVIOUS CONVICTIONS, 33.02 *et seq.*, 38.05
  accused bringing in character evidence,
      33.07 *et seq.*
  civil cases, in, 6.16–6.19, 31.28–31.33
  credibility, going to, 33.22
  effect of character evidence, 33.18–33.19
  evidence given against co-accused,
      33.20–33.22
  imputations against prosecution witnesses,
      33.11–33.19
  judge's discretion, 33.17
  knowledge by solicitor, 33.05
  magistrates' court, in, 45.15
  offences committed under age of 14, 33.23
  plea in mitigation, 47.46
  pleadings and, 6.16–6.19
  sentencing and, 47.03
  similar fact evidence, and, 33.03–33.05
  spent, 33.23
  statutes allowing proof of, 33.06
  witnesses, of, 27.27
    cross-examining on, 27.27
PRIVILEGE, 35.01 *et seq.*
  Crown or public, 35.02–35.04
  discovery and inspection and, 7.02, 7.05
  entry, search and seizure, 41.08
  expert evidence and, 9.03
  private, 7.05, 35.05–35.09
    legal professional privilege, 35.06–35.07
    self-incrimination, 35.08
    without prejudice, 35.05
  proof of privileged matters by other means,
      35.09
PROBATION, 47.13, 47.16, 47.28
PROFESSIONAL ETHICS,
  client admitting guilt, 38.04
  co-accused, same solicitor, 38.08–38.09
  confidentiality, 38.03
  conflict of interest, 38.08–38.09
  criminal prosecutions and, 38.01 *et seq.*
  defence solicitor in criminal matters,
      38.02–38.09
  exam questions, 49.03
  inconsistent instructions, 38.06

PROFESSIONAL ETHICS—*cont.*
  interviewing prosecution witnesses, 38.07
  legal aid, confidentiality and, 2.22
  negotiation. *See* NEGOTIATION.
  previous convictions, knowledge of, 38.05
PROOF, 25.01 *et seq.*
  burden. *See* BURDEN.
  common knowledge, matters of, 25.02
  formal admissions. *See* ADMISSIONS.
  inferences of fact, 25.11
  judicial notice, 25.02
  law, procedure and custom, 25.02
  political and administrative matters, 25.02
  presumptions, 25.09–25.10
  standard. *See* STANDARD.
PROSECUTION,
  assistance for defence, 40.08
  role of, 40.08
PUBLIC INTEREST IMMUNITY, 35.02–35.04

QUANTUM OF DAMAGES. *See* DAMAGES.

REAL EVIDENCE, 36.01
REDUNDANCY PAYMENTS, 1.06
RE-EXAMINATION, 27.28
  previous consistent statements, 27.13
REGISTRAR,
  appeal from, 21.02, 21.03
REPLY, 6.06
REPORTING RESTRICTIONS, 46.07, 46.18
RES IPSA LOQUITUR, 25.10
REVISION TECHNIQUES, 50.01 *et seq.*
ROAD TRAFFIC,
  disqualification. *See* DISQUALIFICATION.
  endorsements. *See* DISQUALIFICATION.

SANDERSON ORDERS, 4.23–4.24, 14.15,
    20.25. *See further* THIRD PARTY
    PROCEEDINGS.
  insurance companies, 4.23
SEARCH,
  arrest, after, 41.09–41.10
    at police station, 41.10
    away from police station, 41.09
  entry and search premisers, 41.07–41.08
  stop and search of premises, 41.07–41.08
  stop and search, 41.06
  warrant, 41.08
SELF INCRIMINATION, 35.08
SENTENCING, 47.01 *et seq.*
  absolute discharge, 47.22, 47.28
  adjournments, 47.01
  advocate recommending sentence, 47.57
  aims of, 47.09
  antecedents, 47.03
  appeal against. *See* CRIMINAL APPEALS.
  attendance centre orders, 47.27
  bail pending, 47.01
  committal for, 45.09
  community service orders, 47.21, 47.28
  compensation orders, 47.39
  conditional discharge, 47.18, 47.28
  confiscation orders, 47.41

SENTENCING—*cont.*
  consecutive or concurrent, 47.10
  costs, 47.42
  Crown Court, by, 47.10
  dealing with, powers of court, 47.13
  deferred sentence, 47.58
  discharges, 47.18, 47.28
  disqualification from driving, 47.29–47.38.
      See further DISQUALIFICATION.
  exam questions, 49.13
  facts of case, disputes as to, 47.02
  fines, 47.18–47.19, 47.28
    combined with other sentences, 47.19
  forfeiture orders, 47.40
  imprisoment, 47.14–47.17, 47.26
  legal aid, 47.14
  magistrates' court, 47.11, 47.12
  medical and psychiatric reports, 47.07
  mitigation, plea in. *See* PLEA IN
      MITIGATION.
  mode of trial, tactics, 45.23
  offences taken into consideration, 47.04
  offenders,
    between 17 and 20, 47.23–47.28
    over 21, 47.14,–47.22
  parole and, 47.14, 47.26
  part-suspended sentences, 47.16, 47.26
  probation, 47.13, 47.16, 47.28
  remission, 47.14
  reports, 47.05–47.08
    defence's own, 47.08
  social enquiry reports, 47.06, 47.08, 47.25
  suspended sentences, 47.13, 47.15–47.16
    magistrates' court's powers, 47.17
    part-suspended, 47.16, 47.26
  "tariff" or "individualised, 47.09
  young offender,
    custodial, 47.23–47.27
    non-custodial, 47.28
SERVICE,
  acknowledgment. *See* ACKNOWLEDGMENT
      OF SERVICE.
  documents other than writs, 5.19
  writ, of, 5.08–5.18. *See further* WRIT.
SICKNESS BENEFIT, 1.06
SILENCE, RIGHT OF, 30.32
  alibi evidence, as to, 30.22
  in court, 30.22
SIMILAR FACT EVIDENCE, 33.03–33.05
  civil cases, in, 33.05
  criminal cases, in, 33.03–33.04
SOCIAL ENQUIRY REPORTS, 47.06, 47.08
  plea in mitigation and, 47.08, 47.45, 47.56
SOCIAL SECURITY BENEFIT,
  damages and, 1.06–1.07
  preliminary steps, 3.13
SOLICITOR,
  client admitting guilt, 38.04
  confidentiality, 38.03
  criminal trials, duties in, 38.02 *et seq.*
  fees of. *See* FEES.
  legal aid and relationship with client, 2.22.
      See further LEGAL AID.

SOLICITOR—*cont.*
  legal professional privilege, 35.06–35.07.
    See further PRIVILEGE.
  payment in advance, 2.02
  professional ethics and. *See* PROFESSIONAL
    ETHICS.
  right of accused to consult, 41.20
SPECIAL DAMAGES, 1.02–1.12
  amended computation served immediately
    before trial, 6.09
  amendment of statement of claim and, 6.09
  benefits received, 1.06–1.07
  clothes and property damaged in accident,
    1.09
  collections, 1.06
  Compensation Recovery Unit, 1.06
  contract of employment and, 1.04
  full particulars served, 10.15
  gifts, 1.06
  loss of earnings, 1.03–1.07
  maintenance at public expense, 1.07
  medical expenses, 1.11. *See also* MEDICAL
    EXPENSES.
  other earnings, 1.06
  other expenses, 1.10
  pleadings, 1.01, 6.09
  private insurance, and, 1.06
  redundancy payments, and, 1.06
  tax rebates and, 1.05
  vehicle repairs, 1.8
  visiting expenses, 1.12
SPENT CONVICTIONS, 33.23
SPLIT TRIALS,
  orders for, 8.16
STANDARD OF PROOF, 24.01 *et seq.*
  balance of probabilities, 24.02
  beyond reasonable doubt, 24.08
  civil cases, in, 24.02
  criminal cases, in, 24.08–24.09
STATEMENT OF CLAIM, 5.26, 6.03. *See also*
    generally PLEADINGS.
  amendment of, 6.09
  cause of action, amendment of, 6.44
  contents of, 6.20–6.21
    debt, 6.20
    personal injury, 6.21
  county court, in, 17.17
  damages, interest on, 6.14
  debt, 5.26, 5.27, 6.20
  interest and, 6.10–6.14
    debt, contract providing for, 6.11
    no provision for, 6.12
  law, 6.15
  liquidated demand, 5.26, 5.27
  negotiations continuing, 5.28
  particulars of injury, 6.21
  personal injury, contents of, 6.21
  prayer, 6.20, 6.21
  previous convictions, 6.16–6.19
  special damages, 6.09. *See also* SPECIAL
    DAMAGES.
  unliquidated damages, 5.26, 5.28
STATUTORY SICK PAY, 1.06

STAY OF ACTION, 11.25
STAY OF EXECUTION, 5.23, 16.09, 19.16
STOP AND SEARCH, 41.06
STUDY METHODS, 49.01 *et seq.*
  study group system, 49.01
SUBPOENA, 10.09, 40.11
SUBROGATION,
  motor insurance, in, 3.24
SUMMARY JUDGMENT, 11.06–11.17, 11.19
  affidavit, 11.10
  cases where applicable, 11.07
  conditional leave to defend, 11.15
  contract cases and, 11.08–11.16
  county court, in, 17.28–17.30
  directions, 11.15
  dismissal of summons, 11.16
  hearing of summons, 11.12–11.16
  interim payment, and, 13.12
  judgment for plaintiff, 11.13
  method of application, 11.10–11.11
  negligence cases, 11.07, 11.17
  time for application, 11.09
  unconditional leave to defend, 11.14
SUMMARY TRIAL, 44.01 *et seq.*
  absence of defendant, 44.05–44.06
  defect in process, 44.04
  defence case, 44.12
  guilty plea by post, 44.06
  joint trials, 44.02–44.03
  no case to answer, 44.11
  non-appearance of prosecution, 44.07
  plea, 44.06, 44.08
  procedure,
    on guilty plea, 44.06, 44.13
    on not guilty plea, 44.08–44.12
  prosecution case, 44.08–44.10
  rebuttal evidence, 44.12
  verdict, 44.12
SUMMONS,
  County Court, in, 17.04–17.06, 17.08
    default, 17.06
    fixed date, 17.05
    request form, 17.08
    service of, 17.16
    where issued, 17.15
  interlocutory application, 4.13
SUPREME COURT, RULES OF, 4.05–4.08
  extension of time limits, 4.07
  failure to comply, 4.06
  Supreme Court Practice, 4.05
SUSPENDED SENTENCES, 47.13, 47.15–47.16,
    47.26
SURETIES, 43.16. *See further* BAIL.

TAPE RECORDING,
  interviews, 41.24
TAX REBATES,
  damages and, 1.05
TAXATION OF COSTS, 4.03, 20.08 *et seq. See*
    also COSTS; FEES.
  between parties, 20.09–20.13
  county court scales, 20.16
  court fee, 20.29

TAXATION OF COSTS—*cont.*
  hearing, 20.32
  High Court, in, 20.09–20.15
  indemnity basis, 20.13
  solicitor and own client basis, 20.14
  standard basis, 20.09–20.12
TERMINATION OF ACTION, 11.01 *et seq.*
  compromise, by, 11.20. *See also*
    COMPROMISE.
  dismissal,
    delay, for, 11.23
    intentional and contumelious, 11.24
    want of prosecution, for, 11.22–11.24
  judgment in default,
    defence, of, 11.18, 11.19
    notice of intention to defend, of,
      11.01–11.05
  judgment on admission (O. 27), 11.21
  stay of action, 11.25
  summary judgment. *See* SUMMARY
    JUDGMENT.
THIRD PARTY PROCEEDINGS, 4.20, 4.24, 6.43,
    14.01 *et seq.*
  adding third party as defendant,
    14.15–14.16
  acknowledgment of service, 14.08
  between defendants, 14.17
  Bullock Order, 4.23–4.24, 14.15, 20.25
  commencement of, 14.05–14.08
  connected issues in, 14.04
  contribution, 14.02
  county courts, in, 17.48–17.50
  course of, 14.09–14.14
  directions, summons for, 14.09–14.14
  discovery, 14.09
    not automatic, 7.06
  ex parte application, 14.06
  indemnity, 14.03–14.04
  notice, 14.05
  plaintiff's actions, 14.15–14.16
  Sanderson Order, 4.23–4.24, 14.15, 20.25
  service of notice, 14.07
  third party, role at trial, 16.02
TRANSFER OF PROCEEDINGS, 5.24–5.25
  indorsement on writ and, 5.04
TRIAL, 16.01 *et seq.*
  associate's certificate, 16.07
  audience, rights of, 16.01
  compromise, 16.01. *See further*
    COMPROMISE.
  county court. *See* COUNTY COURT.
  criminal cases, in. *See* CRIMINAL TRIAL;
    SUMMARY TRIAL.
  estimated length of, 8.10
  fixed dates for hearings, 10.04–10.05
  interest, 16.04. *See also* INTEREST.
  judgment, 16.03
    drawing up, 16.08
  preliminary warned list, 10.05
  preparations for, 10.01 *et seq.*
  scheduling of, 10.05
  setting down for, 10.01–10.03
    automatic directions, 8.11, 10.2

TRIAL—*cont.*
  setting down for—*cont.*
    experts' reports filed with court, 10.23
    necessary documents, 10.01
  statement as to readiness, 10.01
  stay of execution. *See* STAY OF EXECUTION.
  termination, without, 11.01 *et seq. See*
    further TERMINATION OF ACTION.
  third party, role at, 16.02. *See further*
    THIRD PARTY PROCEEDINGS.

UNEMPLOYMENT BENEFIT, 1.06

"VERBALS," 30.12–30.13
VOIR DIRE, 30.23–30.26

WANT OF PROSECUTION, DISMISSAL FOR,
    11.22–11.24
WARRANT,
  arrest with or without, 41.02–41.05
    search and, 41.09
  search, 41.08
WITNESSES,
  character, in plea of mitigation, 47.55
  competence and compellability, 26.01 *et*
    seq. See further COMPETENCE AND
    COMPELLABILITY.
  convictions of, 27.27
  criminal cases, in, 40.10–40.11
    orders, 40.11, 47.15, 47.17
    summons or subpoena, 40.11
  cross-examination. *See* CROSS-
    EXAMINATION.
  depositions by, 29.26–29.28
    dangerous ill, 29.27
  examination. *See* EXAMINATION.
  expert. *See* EXPERT EVIDENCE.
  hostile, 27.15, 27.17–27.19
  identification parades, 41.30
  imputations against, 33.11–33.19
  interviewing, personal injury cases, in, 3.06
  orders, 40.11, 46.16, 46.18
  previous convictions of, 27.27
  previous consistent statements by,
    27.11–27.14
    hearsay and, 31.04–31.05, 31.26
  previous inconsistent statements by, 27.06,
    27.17–27.19, 27.26
    civil cases, in, 31.21, 31.26
  re-examination, 27.13, 27.28
  refreshing memory, 27.06–27.10
  section 102 statements, 46.09, 46.17–46.18
  showing photographs to, 41.27–41.29
  signed written statements, 29.03–29.07
  subpoena, 10.09, 40.11
  unfavourable, 27.15–27.16
  witness orders, 40.11, 46.16, 46.18
WITNESS STATEMENTS, 29.03–29.07
WRIT, 4.10
  acknowledgment of service. *See*
    ACKNOWLEDGMENT OF SERVICE.
  address for service, 5.05
  affidavit of service of, 5.17

WRIT—*cont.*
amendment of, 6.38 *et seq.*
commencement of action by, 5.01 *et seq.*
contents of, 5.01–5.02
court seal on, 5.07
indorsements,
address for service, 5.05
fixed costs, 5.03
general, 5.02
place where course of action arose, 5.04
special, 5.02
issue of, 5.06, 5.07
timing of, 3.01
lapse of, 5.07

WRIT—*cont.*
negotiations continuing by agreement, 3.32
service of, 4.08, 5.08–5.18
individuals, on, 5.09–5.14
insurance companies and, 5.18
limited company, on, 5.15
nominated solicitor, on, 5.12, 5.18
partnership, on, 5.16
personal, 5.09, 5.11
postal, 5.10, 5.15. 5.16
proof of, 5.17–5.18
refusal of, 5.09
substituted service, 5.13